LEARNING AND MEMORY

LEARNING

AND

MEMORY

BARRY SCHWARTZ

SWARTHMORE COLLEGE

DANIEL REISBERG

REED COLLEGE

W·W·NORTON AND COMPANY · *New York London*

Printed in the United States of America.

The text of this book is composed in Baskerville, with the display set in Modum # 216 Medium. Composition and manufacturing by The Haddon Craftsmen, Inc.
Book design by Jacques Chazaud.

Cover illustration: Louise Nevelson, *Black Cord*, 1964. Painted wood; 104 ½ × 117 ¾ × 12 ¼ inches. Collection of Whitney Museum of American Art. Gift of Anne and Joel Ehrenkrantz 91.1.

Library of Congress Cataloging-in-Publication Data

Schwartz, Barry, 1946–
    Learning and memory/by Barry Schwartz and Daniel Reisberg.
      p. cm.
    1. Learning, Psychology of. 2. Memory. 3. Reisberg, Daniel.
  I. Title.
  BF318.S38 1991
  153.1—dc20   90-45226

ISBN 0-393-95911-2

W.W. Norton & Company, Inc., 500 Fifth Avenue, New York, N.Y. 10110
W.W. Norton & Company, Ltd., 10 Coptic Street, London WCIA IPU

  4 5 6 7 8 9 0

To Our Children

To Our Children

Contents

Preface

There is an obvious path to take in designing a textbook about learning and memory. One begins with so-called learning theory, and examines how organisms (usually laboratory rats and pigeons) learn to make associations among various environmental events, or associations behaviors and environmental events. One then turns to the studies of memory that grew out of this associationist base. That is, one turns to studies of memory in the "verbal learning" tradition, in which human subjects learn to associate verbal stimuli and verbal responses.

This path offers the advantage of providing clear continuity between studies of animal learning and studies of human memory. In both cases, the emphasis is on the learning of relatively simple associations. There is also considerable resemblance between the experimental methods employed in these two research traditions.

However, the study of animal learning and research on human memory have both progressed enormously in recent years, and this progress has carried both of these fields far from their associationist roots. Instead, a more "cognitive" approach now permeates both the human and the animal work, with a corresponding change both in theory and in experimental method. As a result, an emphasis on the historical communalities of these fields—their shared associationist base and their shared methods—carries the risk of not representing the contemporary scene in either field.

For many, this is an argument for divorcing the study of animal learning from the study of human memory, and for covering these broad topics in different courses, with different textbooks. Such a divorce allows an emphasis on contemporary work, and a corresponding deemphasis of the issues and the history shared by these fields. But this approach also carries a risk—namely, that we fail to integrate these two fields, fail to detect the areas in which work in animal learning and work in human memory truly can enrich each other. And when areas of convergence and integration are missed, what is missed along with them is an account of why the divergences that do occur are necessary. Examining these areas of study together helps one to see when and why different research methods and theories are called for.

In this text, we have tried an approach that is neither a traditional marriage nor a divorce. We have brought the two fields together with a strong emphasis not on history, but on contemporary work. We have not showcased the shared historical roots, or the shared methods of these fields (although these are still covered in the present text). Instead, we have sought to build more modern bridges between the animal and human work—for example, with an emphasis on the cognitive underpinnings of animal learning, or with a discussion of the sophisticated descendants of associationism currently under scrutiny in the field of human memory. In the process, we have tried to convey a full and sophisticated view of the state-of-the-art in both fields. We hope we have made plain the commonalities and also the contrasts between the human and animal work, since both of these need to be examined and understood.

The first chapter provides both a historical and a philosophical context for the chapters to follow, seeking to locate the roots of contemporary work both in animal learning and in human memory, and to describe, in general terms, the research methods that characterize them. Chapters 2 through 6 then cover the key topics in animal learning. In two chapters on Pavlovian conditioning (Chapters 2 and 3), students move from a discussion of the conditioning process as conceived by Pavlov, in which contiguity between events is the crucial variable, to a modern view that emphasizes contingency analysis, cognitive representation, and rehearsal. Similar developments, from contiguity to contingency, are traced for the domain of operant conditioning in Chapter 4, which discusses basic conditioning phenomena, avoidance learning, and conditioned reinforcement. Chapter 5 discusses intermittent reinforcement and choice, with an emphasis on new developments that relate learning theory to areas of behavioral biology and microeconomics. Chapter 6, on the stimulus control of operant behavior, discusses the processes of discrimination and generalization, as well as concept learning and memory. This discussion identifies central problems that are engaging researchers now, in addition to enumerating principles that have already been developed. Research in these domains has indicated that neither the phenomena that learning theorists study nor the organisms in which they study them are as simple as had once been supposed. Cognitive processes involving representation of, organization of, and memory for past experiences contribute importantly to what organisms learn and do, and these processes must be studied and understood. This chapter thus provides a clear bridge to the remainder of the book, which focuses on memory.

In Chapter 7, we turn to an examination of human memory. Chapter 7 itself covers major developments of the 1960s and 1970s, with an emphasis on the "information processing" that was hypothesized as being central to the acquisition of new knowledge. Chapters 8 and 9 then consider how this early picture was enriched (and complicated) by further research. In Chapter 8, we examine the close interrelations between forms of learning and forms of test. We consider the possibility that there may be no such thing as "good learning in general," but only "good learning for this sort of test" or "good learning for that sort of test." In this context, we consider work contrasting "implicit" and "explicit" forms of remembering. Chapter 9 picks up a related theme: the interdependence between the learning process and what one already knows. We consider how prior knowledge can promote both learning and retrieval from memory, but also how prior knowledge can distort what is learned or what is remembered.

Chapters 10 and 11 confront directly the nature of prior knowledge. How is knowledge represented in memory? How does one locate knowledge within the vast storehouse that is memory? Chapter 10 surveys theories of conceptual knowledge, such as one's knowledge of what a "birthday party" is, or one's understanding of words like "dancing" or "running," and so on. What is it that is stored in memory to represent these mundane bits of knowing? Then, in Chapter 11, we ask how these memories are interconnected, both to allow representation of more complex knowledge and to allow one to locate sought-for information within the vast network of what one knows. Chapter 11 also discusses an important new theoretical development, "connectionism" (or "parallel distributed processing"), as an account of how knowledge is acquired, stored, and used.

In Chapter 12, we consider the varieties of information that we all seem to remember—memories for words, and sights, and sounds, and smells. Is all of this information stored in one general memory? Or are there several memories, each specialized to hold a certain type of information? Here contemporary work on imagery is covered, and we ask whether a single memory theory is possible, or if separate theories (and, indeed, separate memories) will be required for explaining memories of verbal materials and then memories of visual materials. At the same time, we consider the broader methodological problem of how one determines if multiple memories are demanded by the evidence, or whether a single type of memory, holding diverse types of information, will suffice.

Chapter 13 concerns the problem of forgetting, and looks at both why and what we forget. Evidence for and against "decay" theory and "interference" theory is presented. Discussion then turns to Freud's repression theory of forgetting, and also to current work on how emotion shapes remembering.

Finally, Chapter 14 places memory research in a somewhat broader context, asking how we make judgments or reach decisions based on remembered evidence. Here we review evidence that principles of decision-making and judgment flow naturally from research on memory. In a nutshell, the argument is that humans are quite skilled in making decisions, but often do so based on biased or partial information, thanks to the ordinary workings (and the ordinary failings) of memory. Hence memory's strengths and weaknesses are reflected in the judgments that we make. We discuss how often this may lead us to make fallacious (or at least unwarranted) judgments. We consider the evidence from laboratory studies and from real-world examples; we consider evidence pertinent to how we make mundane decisions, and also enormously important ones.

Having finished what has truly been an enjoyable and untroubled collaboration, we wish to thank several people for their contributions to this book in particular and to our intellectual development more generally. Barry Schwartz owes a profound intellectual debt to his two principal teachers, Charles Catania and David Williams. Catania inspired his interest in learning theory and taught him to appreciate the power of language. Williams helped Schwartz to see that the empirical foundations on which learning theory rested were a good deal less secure than one might have guessed from a look at the edifice that had been erected above them.

For advice and guidance on the manuscript itself, Schwartz wishes to thank Hugh Lacey, whose collaboration on a briefer text on learning, *Behaviorism, Science, and Human Nature* (Norton, 1982), helped sharpen his thinking in many ways that are reflected in this one. Also, Peter Holland of Duke University, Nancy Innis of the University of Western Ontario, Lucie Johnson of Bethel College, Charles Locurto of Holy Cross College, and Fred Valle of the University of British Columbia offered detailed and helpful comments that helped improve another text that was the parent of this one, *The Psychology of Learning and Behavior,* Third Edition (Norton, 1990). Bill Beckwith of the University of North Dakota, Julie Felender of San Diego State University, and William F. McDaniel of Georgia College read early drafts of several of the chapters of this book and helped to shape its final form. Paul Rozin of the University of Pennsylvania and Norton editor Don Fusting read and evaluated the entire manuscript to make sure that both authors were taking their critics' advice. Finally, Rebecca Schwartz took time out from a very busy schedule to help with proofreading.

Daniel Reisberg also has several people to thank. Many people have played a role in shaping the thinking that led to his contribution to this book. He wishes to single out, however, the earliest and then the most recent of these. His first psychology instructor was clearly the person who led him into the field. He was also principal author of Reisberg's first publication in psychology. Now, many years later, he is co-author of this text. Although Reisberg and Schwartz have worked at different ends of the field for many years, Schwartz's influence can still be detected in Reisberg's thoughts about psychology, and about psychology teaching.

In recent years, though, there is no question about who has most marked Reisberg's thinking. Many of his ideas have grown directly out of conversations with Friderike Heuer; indeed, he often cannot say for certain that they are his ideas, rather than hers. Friderike has been his visible partner in research, but has also been a hidden partner, an unacknowledged co-author, on virtually everything he has written over the last years. She has caught his inconsistencies, detected his unclarities, unmasked covert assumptions, and, over and over, led him to better arguments, not to mention better prose. She has been the best possible critical audience, and also a continuous source of suggestions about research, about theory, about teaching. She has made psychology richer for Reisberg, and more challenging, and more fun. She has done the same for his life.

Robert Crowder of Yale University, John Jonides of the University of Michigan, Eugene R. Long of the University of North Carolina, and Michael McCloskey of Johns Hopkins University all read earlier versions of Chapters 7–14, and provided many helpful comments. They have clearly made this a better book, and we hope they forgive us for the few suggestions not followed. Chad Dodson's assistance, in gathering bibliographic materials, was far better than superb, and the book would have been less accurate, less complete, and less timely without him. Wynona Karbo also provided great help in the finishing stages of the volume.

LEARNING AND MEMORY

1 Conceptual and Historical Foundations

This is a book about learning, but what exactly is learning? Consider these cases:

A. The students wished to learn all the equations in the textbook.

B. The researchers hoped to learn the cause of the disease.

C. Jacob's parents hope that he will learn to use better table manners.

D. Monica is learning how to play tennis.

E. Henry wants to learn new study habits.

F. Years after graduating, Noah finally realized how much he had learned in college.

In some of these cases, learning involves the acquisition of new knowledge. In Case A, the knowledge is already available in the textbook; the goal of learning, therefore, is simply to place this knowledge in students' memories. Case B is different; here, the learning involves the *discovery* of previously unknown information. Other cases of learning, such as Case C, seem not to involve new knowledge at all; instead, the goal of learning is a change in behavior patterns. In still other cases, such as D, the learning may involve both new behaviors and new knowledge. In E, learning involves new behavior patterns that may lead to the acquisition of new knowledge. Finally, as an added complexity, there is Case F, which seems to indicate that sometimes one learns without even realizing one is learning.

It seems clear from these examples that there is much diversity in what we call "learning." It is probably not surprising, therefore, that psychologists have studied learning using a variety of approaches, and have tried to explain learning with a variety of different accounts. On the modern scene, these different approaches can be roughly organized into two broad categories, each with its own complexities and with its own emphases and methods. One of these is generally termed **learning theory**, or **behavior theory**. Learning theory has to a large extent been committed to the view that a few general principles can be found that describe virtually all learning. It has focused on the role played by environmental events in learning processes, and has taken changes in *behavior* to be the primary evidence that learning has occurred. Indeed, it has sometimes been guided by the view that learning simply *is* changes in behavior. Research within this tradition has primarily been done with laboratory animals like rats, pigeons, dogs, or monkeys.

The other approach to learning is generally called the **cognitive** approach. Rather than focusing on environmental events, the cognitive approach emphasizes events that take place inside the learner. That is, cognitive research seeks to describe the role of the person's own mental activity in learning and remembering. Thus cognitive psychologists are concerned with people's expectations and strategies, and also with the knowledge that each person brings to the learning situation. Rather than focusing on behavioral change, this approach has centered on learning as the acquisition of new *knowledge*, and its research is generally done with humans.

These two approaches to learning are often regarded as quite separate from each other, as if they were concerned with entirely different problems, entirely different topics. It is a premise of this book, however, that this is a mistake. As we will see throughout this text, there are numerous points of contact between current research in the learning theory tradition and current research in the cognitive tradition. Many results from learning theory laboratories seem to demand cognitive explanations. Many findings in cognitive laboratories are better understood when we put them in the context of studies of animal learning.

We are not suggesting that these two approaches to learning are interchangeable; there are real and substantial differences between their methods of investigation and they sometimes offer competing explanations for similar learning phenomena. Nevertheless, we believe that they are not as distinct from each other as it sometimes appears. And given the range and variety of learning phenomena that exist, it is probably an asset that we can draw on these different methods of investigation and different patterns of explanation. It is virtually certain that our ultimate understanding of learning will be enriched by both the learning theory and cognitive approaches.

In this chapter, we present a sketch of the conceptual and historical foundations of these two approaches to learning and memory. In the next five chapters, we examine the learning theory approach in more detail. In Chapter 7, we turn to the cognitive approach; the remainder of the book then focuses on this approach to learning.

The Roots of Learning Theory

PHILOSOPHICAL BACKGROUND

When we attempt to understand and explain our own behavior, or the behavior of other people, we usually appeal to the commonsense notion that people act freely, in accord with their intentions or purposes, to achieve certain goals. People have reasons for their actions and these reasons explain the actions. Because people are free to act, and have reasons for acting, we hold them responsible for what they do.

We do not normally use the same commonsense ideas to explain the behavior of inanimate things like golf balls or airplanes, or even the behavior of animate things (cockroaches, birds, fish) other than people. Instead, we explain the behavior of golf balls and cockroaches in more mechanistic terms: in terms of gravitational forces, innate mechanisms, and so forth. However, prior to the sixteenth century, an account of behavior in terms of intentions and goals was not restricted to humans, or even to living things. Explanations of the movements of inanimate physical objects employed concepts that were similar to the ones used to explain human behavior. The movement of the planets, for example, was often understood in terms of the purposes or goals of their existence. Then, owing largely to the Italian astronomer Galileo (1564–1642), the dominant conception of the physical world began to change. Physical bodies were seen to move in lawlike and predictable ways. Such machine-like regularity was attributed not to forces within the body, like goals or purposes, but to forces outside the body. These outside forces completely determined physical motion. Thus planets moved, in this view, because of external, gravitational forces that acted on them. When such forces were understood, we would have a complete account of physical motion that left nothing either to chance or to the goals and desires of the moving body.

DESCARTES AND HOBBES: MAN AS MACHINE AND AS REASONER

In Galileo's thinking, physical forces were the key to understanding the motion of inanimate objects. It was inevitable, though, that this mechanical view would eventually be applied to the behavior of living things, including people. The move in this direction began with the French philosopher René Descartes (1596–1650). Descartes divided behavior into two classes: voluntary and involuntary. Voluntary behavior was governed by reason—by the mind. Its source was thus nonmechanical and nonphysical. In contrast, involuntary behavior was purely mechanical, just as the motion of inanimate objects was mechanical. When a child touched a hot flame with a finger, the fire set in motion a nerve in the finger. The motion was transmitted up to the brain where "animal spirits" were released. These spirits traveled back down the nerve, swelling the muscles in the fingers and causing them to be pulled back. Descartes's own analogy was to the mechanism by which one caused a bell at one end of a rope to ring by tugging on the other end of the rope.

The "machine" by which Descartes accounted for involuntary action has come to be known as the **reflex arc**. A **stimulus** (the fire) is transmitted from the finger to the brain by a nerve impulse. This stimulus starts the machine, which has as its output a motor **response** (finger withdrawal). Somewhere in the brain, stimulus input and response output are **associated** by means of nervous connections. Though the specific understanding of how reflexes work has undergone many revisions through the years, the broad outline of the reflex arc has basically remained intact. There are countless reflexes in virtually all organisms. Among the most familiar in people are the knee jerk and the eyeblink.

For Descartes, the reflex arc accounted for all the behavior of nonhuman animals, and also the involuntary behavior of humans. The other domain of human action—voluntary action—was unique to humans. The mind was aware of reflex actions, though it could not control these actions. In contrast, the mind had complete control over nonreflex actions. And the actions of the mind were not subject to physical laws. They were governed by reason.

This claim, that mechanism explains only involuntary behaviors, was challenged by a British philosopher, Thomas Hobbes (1588–1679). Hobbes, like Descartes, viewed voluntary action as the province of the mind. However, in a departure from Descartes's view, Hobbes proposed that the activities of the mind could themselves be explained by mechanical laws. Observable actions originated in incipient motions in the mind that Hobbes called "endeavours." While "endeavours" were unobservable, they were physical and, as such, they behaved in the same lawlike way that reflexes did. "Endeavours" occurred in the service of a set of human

Descartes's illustration of the reflex arc, by means of which stimulation of the foot (B) by fire (A) is transmitted to the brain (D-E-F). (Reprinted from Descartes, "De Homine," in *Philosophical Works*, Cambridge University Press, 1911.)

motives concerned with the pursuit of pleasure and the avoidance of pain. Philosophers before Hobbes had argued about whether pursuit of pleasure and avoidance of pain *ought* to be good reasons for action. For Hobbes, this was a false issue: Whether these reasons were good or bad, they were simply and unalterably human nature. Thus Hobbes extended the mechanical views of Descartes to all human action.

ASSOCIATIONISM

Hobbes argued that the mind worked in accordance with natural laws like the ones that explained the motion of inanimate objects. What were the laws of mental activity? A philosophical tradition known as **British empiricism** or **associationism** took as its task the discovery of the laws of the mind. The leading figures in this tradition were John Locke (1632–1704) and David Hume (1711–1776).

For the associationists, the source of all knowledge was sensory experience. People are born knowing nothing and gradually build up knowledge of the world by accumulating bits of sensory information. The young child looks at a closed book and sees not a book but a small rectangular patch of color. The older child looks at the book and sees the same patch of color, but also knows other things about this rectangle. He knows that it is called a book and that inside the book are many other rectangles—thin white ones with even rows of black marks on them. He knows the black marks are words and the words are strung together to form sentences. He knows the book will not stand up and walk away or turn its own pages. The older child knows all this without directly experiencing any of it through his senses. How does the child come to possess this knowledge? The associationist answer is that in the past the child has directly experienced the pages of the book, the print on the pages, and so on. These experiences have occurred closely together in time and have occurred repeatedly. These two features of experience, **temporal contiguity** and **repetition**, allow the child to associate the sight of a closed book with its contents. With enough repetition, the sight of the book calls forth a large set of past sensations, or ideas, that are now bound together as a single unit. In this way the full, detailed idea of a book is compounded out of a history of individual sensory impressions. Moreover, from these associations of ideas arise more complex notions, like that of causation. Hume said, "We have no other notion of cause and effect but that of certain objects which have been always conjoined together" (Hume, 1739, Book 1, Part 3, Section 2).

What determined when and how associations were formed, and how powerful they would be? The basic principle of association was **contiguity**: Two experiences that occurred closely together in time were likely to be associated. But there were other factors that influenced the formation of associations. The philosopher Thomas Brown (1778–1820) identified some of them:

1. The intensity of the sensations.

2. The similarity of the sensations.

3. The recency of their pairing.

4. The frequency of their pairing.

5. The number of other associations of which the sensations to be associated were also a part.

6. The similarity of the association to be formed to other, past associations.

In the mind of another English philosopher, John Stuart Mill (1806–1873), sensations were like chemical elements. They combined to form compound ideas in the same way that hydrogen and oxygen combined to form water. Just as the science of chemistry was developing laws of combination for the physical elements, so also the science of the mind could develop laws of combination for mental elements—a mental chemistry of ideas.

This progress in philosophical speculation about human thinking and action laid a foundation for the study of human nature as a scientific endeavor in search of natural laws. Descartes argued that some human action was lawlike and mechanical. Hobbes argued that all human action was lawlike and mechanical. The associationists began to develop the laws. In addition, associationism argued that the mind was not preformed but was shaped by experience, and that through this experience simple elements of knowledge were built, brick upon brick, into complex ideas. These two aspects of associationism have dominated the study of learning for much of its history.

BIOLOGICAL BACKGROUND: DARWIN AND EVOLUTION

The idea that the behavior of people was governed by natural laws, like the behavior of other animals and the behavior of falling stones, flew in the face of prevailing philosophical and religious views. According to these more traditional views, people, possessed as they were of reason and a soul, were unique among living things. People acted with intelligence and foresight, and in accord with moral principles. Surely, neither stones nor chickens displayed intelligence or moral sense.

The intellectual development that most undercut these traditional views was Charles Darwin's theory of evolution by natural selection. Darwin (1809–1882) spent many years as a careful observer of nature. In 1859 he published *The Origin of Species* in which he proposed a theory of how species changed and how they were related. Darwin began with the view that life in the natural world was a battle among organisms for limited resources. Those individuals that won the battle and obtained the necessary resources would survive and reproduce. Those organisms that lost the battle would die off. The critical insight for Darwin was that members of a species were not identical. Individuals differed in subtle but important ways, and these individual variations gave some members of a species a competitive advantage over others. The successful species members passed on their advantageous qualities to their offspring. The offspring thus also enjoyed a competitive advantage over other species members. In each generation the organisms that possessed these superior qualities lived longer and had more offspring than organisms that lacked these qualities. Over the course of many generations, more and more of the surviving members of the species shared the qualities that had initially given a handful of individuals an advantage. Ultimately these qualities became a universal characteristic of the species: All members of the species had them. Thus the old species, which did not in general have these qualities, would have evolved into a new one that did. And the process of evolution was a continuing one; it was the way nature worked and would continue to work.

Darwin's theory thus contained three crucial elements. First, there was variation among members of a species. Second, there was some mechanism of transmission of important characteristics from parents to offspring. And third, there was a process of natural selection that served gradually to increase the number of members of a species with these advantageous characteristics.

What was responsible for the variation among members of a species? Darwin did not know. Indeed, the origin of modern genetics was almost half a century in the future. However, Darwin argued that variation was not purposeful and intelligent; it was random. There was no grand design that ensured that an individual species member would develop characteristics that increased its chances for survival. Many of the variations that occurred might even be harmful to the organism. However, natural selection ensured that, over generations, only the useful individual variations would come to characterize the species. Thus neither nature nor the individual needed to act with purpose. Random variation was quite unreasoning—a process of blind trial and error on a truly grand scale. Natural selection was nature's exercise of intelligence, by ensuring that only "intelligent" (that is, advantageous) variations endured.

Darwin's theory had a major influence on all aspects of the intellectual world. With respect to the views then developing about human nature, the theory of natural selection suggested that there was continuity among species, that the prevailing dichotomy between "man and beast" was inappropriate. That new species very slowly evolved out of old ones suggested that species that were close together in evolutionary time had many characteristics in common. The notion of species continuity made it easier to argue against the prevailing wisdom that people were, in all important respects, unique. If people had reason, they were not necessarily the only living things that did. Perhaps what is more significant, one could argue that "reason" was something of a myth. Natural selection produced "intelligent" species changes by unintelligent means. "Intelligent" behavior by individual organisms might be the product of a similar, unintelligent mechanism.

Darwin did not offer this last speculation; Herbert Spencer (1820–1903), a contemporary of his, did (Spencer, 1880). Spencer suggested that organisms engaged in essentially random activity and that some of that activity resulted in pleasurable consequences. These pleasurable consequences worked to select the activities that preceded them; that is, pleasurable consequences made the activities that led to them more likely to recur. In this way, the organism would eventually come to produce mostly activities that had produced pleasure (or eliminated pain) in the past. If one makes the plausible assumption that the things that give pleasure are the very things that promote survival, one has an application of Darwin's theory to the lives of individual organisms. Some unknown mechanism produces random variation in behavior. The particular activities that promote survival by producing pleasurable consequences are selected. Ultimately the behavioral repertoire comes to consist exclusively of activities that promote survival. Is behavior intelligent, planned, and goal-directed? For Spencer the answer was no. It is not the intelligence of the actor (that is, the organism that is acting in response to stimuli from the environment) that is responsible for action. It is selection by the environment that determines future action on the basis of the consequences of past actions.

THE EMERGENCE OF A SCIENCE OF LEARNING

Against this background of developing argument from philosophy and biology, it is not surprising that a move to study human nature scientifically would emerge. All obstacles to the scientific study of humans were removed. Descartes had argued that only some human action stemmed from material and mechanical sources. Hobbes argued that all human action could be understood in terms of mechanical principles. And Darwin's theory added credibility to the views of Hobbes. Meanwhile the associationists were searching for accounts of the growth of knowledge (complex ideas from simple ones) along the lines being developed by the science of chemistry. In addition, Spencer was applying Darwin's views to behavior, with the idea that the development of a behavioral repertoire in an individual was analogous to the evolution of behavioral repertoires in different species.

With these ideas in place, it is easy to imagine a swell of enthusiasm for a science of human nature. Indeed, one can even see the specific lines along which such a science might develop. One might begin a scientific investigation of human nature with the expectation that an explanation of human action and learning would look something like this:

1. The newborn infant is born with a collection of simple reflexes. Simple stimuli are registered in the brain and trigger simple responses.

2. As the infant gains experience, different simple stimuli get associated with each other. The taste and smell of milk, originally two independent sense experiences, become connected through contiguity. Subsequently, the taste of milk suggests its smell and, conversely, the smell of milk suggests its taste.

3. Since different stimuli are now associated with each other, they begin to trigger each other's reflexes. The smell of milk or the sight of a nipple may trigger sucking. The taste of milk may trigger sniffing.

4. As development continues, more and more stimuli get associated with each other and more and more reflexes get connected. Thus complex sensory experiences, like the perception and understanding of a flag, get built from the association of simple experiences, in this example from associating red, white, blue, star, and stripe. Similarly, reflexes become chains, with the response of one reflex serving as the stimulus for the next.

5. Of all the reflexes that occasionally occur, only some will produce consequences that have survival value (are pleasurable). It is these reflexes alone that will remain in the repertoire of the developing organism.

6. Thus the normal adult may be viewed as someone who has learned to recognize complex stimuli by building up associations of simple ones, and who has learned to engage in complex sequences of behavior by chaining together simple reflexes.

PAVLOV AND CONDITIONED REFLEXES

The beginning of the modern, scientific study of learning may be found in the work of Ivan P. Pavlov (1849–1936). Pavlov was a Nobel Prize-winning Russian physiologist. At around the turn of the century he shifted his attention from physiology to what he called "psychic reflexes." Pavlov knew that dogs reliably salivated when food was placed in their mouths, and he was studying the role of the "salivary reflex" in digestion. His research took a permanent detour when he discovered that the dogs also salivated in response to stimuli that reliably appeared just prior to the delivery of food (for example, the laboratory coats of the researchers). What could be producing salivation to stimuli that preceded food delivery? Presumably, salivation to the food itself was a built-in characteristic of dogs. But a connection between the sight of a laboratory assistant and salivation could hardly be built in. It had to be that the dogs' experience in the laboratory was somehow responsible for the salivation that occurred to objects other than food. The reflex connection between a lab coat and salivation had to be learned, or conditioned. Having observed these psychic or conditioned reflexes, Pavlov devoted the rest of his life to a study of the laws of their formation (Pavlov, 1927). This kind of learning has come to be called **Pavlovian** or **classical conditioning**.

Ivan Petrovich Pavlov. (Courtesy of Sovfoto.)

Why was Pavlov so excited about his discovery? He saw it immediately as a window to the laws of the mind. It was clear to Pavlov that while inborn reflexes formed a significant part of organisms' behavior, a great deal of behavior could not be inborn. That people respond to a flame applied to a finger is almost surely inborn. But that people also respond to a shout of "Fire!" is not. The word "fire" must somehow be associated with actual flames so that either the flames or the word will produce the appropriate reflex. Salivation to a lab coat had to be an instance of the association of inborn responses with new stimuli.

Thus, for Pavlov, the study of conditioned reflexes was the study of the laws of association of ideas. Organisms began with a set of simple reflexes, and experience in the world both broadened the range of events that would produce the reflex and combined simple reflexes into complex reflex sequences. All of knowledge and action could be understood in terms of the elaboration through experience of simple, inborn reflexes. But unlike the "ideas" of the associationists, reflexes could be seen and measured. Thus Pavlov's discoveries opened the way for an objective science of learning.

THORNDIKE AND THE LAW OF EFFECT

When the reflex arc concept was applied to moderately complex situations in which the experimenter did not provide the triggering stimuli, it ran into problems. These can best be discussed with an example, one extensively studied by American psychologist E. L. Thorndike (1874–

1949). Imagine a cat in a cage, the door of which is held fast by a simple latch. Just outside the cage is a piece of fish in a dish. The cat moves around in the cage, sniffing its corners. Suddenly it sees the fish, moves to the part of the cage closest to it, and begins extending its paws through the bars toward the fish, which it cannot reach. The cat reaches more and more vigorously and begins scratching at the bars. After a while this activity stops and the cat starts moving actively about the cage. A few minutes later it bangs against the latch inadvertently and frees it. The door opens and the cat scampers out and eats the fish. The cat is replaced in the cage and a new piece of fish is placed in the dish. The cat goes through the same sequence of activities as before and eventually opens the latch, again inadvertently. This is repeated again and again. Gradually the cat stops extending its paws through the bars and spends more and more of its time near the latch. Next the cat begins directing its activity almost exclusively at the latch, now no longer inadvertently. Ultimately the cat develops a quick and efficient pattern of movements that enables it to open the latch and free itself almost immediately.

This situation, while much simpler than the natural environment, is considerably more complicated than one in which only reflexes are studied. How can the reflex arc be used to explain the behavior of the cat? To answer this, we could start by enumerating the relevant reflexes. There might be a sniffing reflex, a looking reflex, a reaching reflex, a jumping reflex, a running reflex, and so on, but could there be a latch-

Edward L. Thorndike. (Courtesy of the Granger Collection, New York.)

opening reflex? No, but perhaps latch opening reflects a complex combination of reflexes. The next task is to identify the stimuli that trigger the reflexes. This is more difficult. What are the odors that trigger sniffing? What triggers agitation? The fish presumably triggers reaching, but, if so, why does the cat stop reaching? The latch might trigger some set of paw movements, but, if so, why didn't these movements occur when the cat was first in the cage? And doesn't the fish have something to do with the latch-opening response?

It is clear that much work would be required for the reflex arc to provide a satisfactory account of the actions of the cat. It seems more plausible that we should seek some theoretical framework that establishes an alternative to the notion of simple reflexes. It is this latter route that Thorndike took. To explain this seemingly goal-directed feature of behavior, Thorndike proposed a mechanism called the **law of effect** (Thorndike, 1898, 1911), a law closely related to the Darwinian principles we have already discussed. According to Thorndike, behavior occurs in a kind of random, trial-and-error fashion, varying in form from moment to moment. The law of effect tells us that if some of these variations happen to be followed closely in time by pleasurable consequences or rewards (for example, getting fish), they are strengthened or stamped in and become more likely in the future. Other variations may not be followed by pleasurable consequences, or may even be followed by noxious or unpleasant consequences or punishers. If they are, they get weakened and become less likely in the future. In this way only those activities that produce rewards get selected from an organism's full range of activity and continue to occur in the future.

Thorndike's discovery of the law of effect identified a process, apart from Pavlovian conditioning, that had to be understood for the laws of learning to be fully formulated. Moreover, since so much of human behavior seemed nonreflexive and goal-directed, it seemed clear at the outset that any explanation of human behavior would depend heavily on the process Thorndike had discovered. As a result, much of the research done on learning over the years has focused on the law of effect. The changes in behavior produced by the law of effect are typically referred to as **instrumental** or **operant conditioning**. The term "operant" is used because the behavior *operates on,* or has an effect on, the environment.

A Cognitive Approach to Learning

The approach we have just described is built on a set of assumptions about learning, about behavior, and, indeed, about human nature. The learning theory approach, as we have seen, draws primarily on two paradigms, Pavlovian conditioning and operant conditioning. This makes sense if we assume that the laws of learning revealed in these paradigms are widely applicable, that is, if a few general principles account for a broad range of learning. Likewise, the learning theory approach allows us to examine carefully how learning is influenced by various environmental events. Built into this is the assumption that much of learning can be understood in these terms—that is, we do not need to examine the internal processes, those taking place inside of the organism, that mediate between environmental stimuli and behavior.

It seems likely that much learning can be understood in these terms, that much can be explained by a few broad principles that focus on environmental events. However, in recent years learning theorists have come to realize that in many cases of learning, the internal processes involved are too complex and too important to be ignored. This has led to increased interaction between the learning theory approach and the cognitive approach, to which we now turn.

THE ROLE OF COGNITION WITHIN LEARNING

Consider a simple episode of learning, say, a Pavlovian procedure in which a tone is paired with food. On Trial 1 the tone is sounded and two seconds later food is delivered. For this trial to have any effect at all, the animal must perceive both the tone and the food. Thus one of the mediating processes that is absolutely essential for conditioning is *perception*. Moreover, if the animal is to form an association between the tone and the food, then when the food appears the animal must remember that it was preceded by a tone. Thus a second necessary mediating process is *memory*.

Now consider the second trial. The tone sounds. As with the first trial the animal must perceive the tone. But it must do more as well. It must recognize that this tone is, in important respects, like the tone on Trial 1. Thus it must put its perceptual experiences into appropriate *categories*. To do this, it must remember the tone from Trial 1. Similar processes are required when the food comes. Thus, at the very least, the phenomena of conditioning depend on the processes of perception, memory, and categorization to mediate between the occurrence of environmental events and behavior.

The processes of perception, memory, and categorization come even more clearly into play when we consider other, more complex forms of learning. Consider what you are doing right now. To put it generally, you are seeking to learn the material in this chapter. This involves your reading and understanding the chapter, and somehow storing it in memory. Some *representation* of the chapter's contents is being placed in your memory, and, if your memory is tested later on, you must retrieve this representation from memory.

THE PROMISE AND PROBLEMS OF INTROSPECTION

How should we study these various processes? One very obvious possibility is to ask the learner. After all, the processes are taking place inside the learner, and one might reasonably argue that only she is able to observe what is going on. Thus our method might be one of collecting self-report data, that is, records of subjects' introspections, or "looking within."

Many early psychologists proposed exactly this method—namely, introspection—as our best, and perhaps only, way to study the mind. In the late nineteenth century, for example, Wilhelm Wundt (1832–1920) and his student Edward Bradford Titchener (1867–1927) developed careful introspective techniques that were designed to make the introspector as careful and objective as possible. However, psychology soon became disenchanted with this way of doing research, and it is not hard to see why. For one thing, one might worry that the mere fact of translating an internal experience into a verbal report may distort, or not do justice to, the original experience. It also turns out that different researchers, supposedly introspecting about the same phenomenon, often report different results. What should we conclude from this? Perhaps each researcher is correct, and they are simply having different experiences. Or perhaps the researchers are having similar experiences but describing the experience in different terms. This is a particularly thorny problem, for how could we ever resolve the issue? To see the concern, consider the problem of determining whether what you call "severe pain" is equivalent to what someone else calls "moderate pain." Think about just how difficult this would be to find out.

Last, but not least, one might worry that people are simply unaware of a great many mental events; in this case, introspection could not possibly be used to study these events. For example, what is your phone number? Now, how did you find this out? One might expect that you used some system or strategy for "looking up" this information in memory, and then bringing this information into awareness. We will see in later chapters that a complex series of events is required, even for this simple bit of remembering. None of these events, however, is part of your conscious experience. Instead, the telephone number simply "comes to you," without effort, without any noticeable steps or strategies on your part. If we relied on introspection as our means of studying mental events, then we would have no way of examining these processes.

For these and other reasons, psychology soon turned away from introspection as a method. In fact, psychology moved as far away as possible from introspection. In the early twentieth century, many psychologists argued that the mind, and subjective experience, could be understood only via introspection. However, because introspection was worthless as a scientific tool, a scientific psychology would have to avoid discussion of these "invisible" internal processes or events. Instead, psychology would have to focus on observable entities—events in an organism's environment and the organism's behavior in that environment. This led to an approach to psychology known as **behaviorism**, an approach that dominated the field for much of the early twentieth century.

THE ROOTS OF COGNITIVE PSYCHOLOGY

Since 1960 psychology has moved away from behaviorism and has welcomed a new branch of study, called **cognitive psychology**. In fact, cognitive psychology's entry into the field has been dramatic enough to cause many to speak of the "cognitive revolution." Cognitive psychology has been concerned primarily with processes of learning, memory, and thinking, but has also explored many other domains as well. Cognitive psychology is characterized not by a particular theory or set of principles, but by a willingness to explain observable behaviors by means of complicated but hidden processes.

To understand the roots of cognitive psychology, we must return to the seventeenth-century philosopher René Descartes. As we mentioned earlier, Descartes divided behavior into two classes: voluntary behavior governed by reason, and involuntary behavior governed by what has come to be called a reflex arc. Some of Descartes's successors, like Hobbes, sought to explain both classes of behavior by mechanical laws. As we have seen, it is this approach that eventually grew into the contemporary learning theory perspective.

Other philosophers, however, sought to preserve and develop Descartes's claim that the mind, and our powers of reason in particular, could not be explained by mechanical laws; instead, these entities demanded a different kind of account, and a different approach. One prominent figure adopting this view was Immanuel Kant (1724–1804), and it is his method that, in many ways, led to the principal research strategy of cognitive psychology.

KANT'S "TRANSCENDENTAL" METHOD

In Kant's **transcendental** method, one begins with the observable facts. For Kant, these included the fact that humans can and do reason about spatial and temporal relations, and also the fact that we can and do reason about cause and effect. Kant's research strategy was then, in essence, to work backwards from these observations. Given these "effects," what can we figure out about the "causes"? What must the mental world be like in order to make these observations possible? In essence Kant asked, "How could the observed state of affairs have come about?" (See Flanagan, 1984, for further discussion of this method.)

Employing this method, Kant was able to discover a great deal about the mind. In particular, Kant came to the conclusion that humans were not passive recipients of experience, as the associationists' view implied. Learning was not stamped in by environmental events. Instead, Kant argued, the learner must begin with certain concepts, certain categories, and these are then actively used to organize one's experience.

For example, consider our understanding of spatial relations, including concepts like "next to" or "far from" or "in between." We know that humans understand these concepts, and can reason and converse about them coherently and competently. That is the observation with which we begin. Now, what makes this understanding possible? How does the young infant learn about these concepts and acquire this competence?

Kant argued that concepts like these could be acquired only if the organism *started out* with some understanding of spatial relations. That is, one could not simply learn these concepts from experience. Why not? Why couldn't one learn, for example, from the experience of perceiving, say, that Susan is standing *next to* Johanna? Kant would argue that a description of one's experience in these terms presumes that one *already has* the concept in question. After all, what is actually experienced is closer to this: Susan is currently before your eyes. You flex your eye muscles in a certain way. Now Johanna is before your eyes. If you understand this as "Susan is next to Johanna," you are describing the experience in a certain way. The experience is understood in this fashion only by virtue of being placed in a certain category or scheme. Hence the category must be around prior to the experience, since it is the category that makes the experience, understood as it is, possible. Therefore, the category cannot be derived from experience. Kant called categories like this a priori categories of experience, and these included those categories we use to understand spatial and temporal relations as well as cause and effect.

Kant therefore took two major steps in the direction that was to become modern cognitive psychology. First, his theory emphasized the role of the perceiver in making experience possible, thanks to the categories and concepts that a perceiver brings to bear on a stimulus. This theme will be very much echoed in the chapters to come. Second, Kant proposed a research strategy for how we might learn about entities and events that cannot be directly observed: We observe the organism's actions and reason backwards from these to uncover the processes and capabilities that makes the actions possible. As we will see later on in this chapter, Kant's application of this strategy differs in many ways from the research of modern cognitive psychologists. Nonetheless, the logic of the method remains essentially the same.

THE COMPUTER AS METAPHOR

In the years after Kant, philosophers continued their efforts toward an understanding of memory, knowledge, and the mind. Scientific research on these questions, however, did not get under way in earnest until the 1950s. There are, to be sure, exceptions to this claim, and in later chapters we will discuss the ideas of one of the giant figures in the history of psychology, William James (1842–1910), as well as important work by Frederick Bartlett (b. 1932) and George Katona (b. 1940). Nonetheless, for the two centuries after Kant, the associationists' approach dominated the study of the mind.

There are two reasons for this. For one, we have mentioned the introspective method advocated by Wundt and his followers. This method and Wundt's approach in general were enormously influential in the late nineteenth century. When psychology became disenchanted with this method, for the reasons already discussed, it led many to set aside the study of mental phenomena altogether.

A second reason, though, is probably more critical. In using Kant's method, one seeks to reconstruct the unseen processes or capacities that led to the observed data. But where does one begin? How does one generate hypotheses about invisible entities? Should we frame our explanations in terms of magnetic fields, or biochemistry, or divine intervention? Which of these factors (or some other) will illuminate the workings of learning, memory, and other psychological phenomena?

In the 1950s a new approach to psychological explanation became available, and turned out to be immensely fruitful. This new approach was suggested by the rapid developments in electronic information processing, including developments in communications technology and, of course, in computers. It quickly became clear that computers were capable of immensely efficient information storage and retrieval and of performance that seemed to involve decision-making and problem-solving. Psychologists began to explore the possibility that the mind employed processes and procedures similar to those used in computers. Psychological data were soon being explained in terms of "buffers" and "gates" and "central processors," all terms borrowed from computer technology. (See, for example, Broadbent, 1958; Miller, Galanter, & Pribram, 1960.)

The computer metaphor provided a new language for describing psychological processes and explaining psychological data. Given a particular performance, say, on a memory task, one could hypothesize a series of **information-processing** events that made the performance possible. As we will see, hypotheses framed in these terms led psychologists to predict a host of new observations, and thus served both to organize the available information and to lead to many new discoveries.

The influence of the computer metaphor led to a blossoming of psychological research in the 1960s and 1970s and provided a major impetus for the development of modern cognitive psychology. It is worth noting that the use of this metaphor does not commit us to claiming that "the mind is just like a computer" or "the mind is nothing more than a complex computer." These strong claims may or may not turn out to be true; for now, these claims remain highly controversial. (For discussion, see Charniak & McDermott, 1985; Churchland, 1984; Dreyfus, 1979; Haugeland, 1981, 1986; Pylyshyn, 1984; Winston, 1984.) In any event, these claims are far stronger than we need. For our purposes, it is sufficient to argue that the mind is *enough* like a computer that we can profitably explain much about the mind by using the language of computer processing, and that the use of such language leads to the discovery of new facts about intellectual performance.

EXPLANATIONS AT THE LEVEL OF "SOFTWARE"

What does it mean to adopt the language of computer processing? What is this language? We can understand a computer's internal processes at two different levels. Physically, we can think of the computer's **hardware**; that is, we can think of the computer as an electronic device that consists of many, many switches. Switches can be either on or off, and the computer's behavior is completely governed by the on/off patterns of the switches. Inputs are initially encoded into a set of electrical signals that turns various switches on and off; outputs are produced by the appropriate decoding of the various switches. We can think of this level of the computer's activity as analogous to the nervous system of living organisms.

For a great many purposes, however, we do not need to worry about *how* the computer physically accomplishes what it does; we can instead focus on what it is the computer accomplishes. That is, we can examine the computer's *function* rather than how this function is physically realized or implemented. In these terms, we will understand the computer's performance in terms of its **software**, that is, the program that governs the running of the computer. The software consists of a set of instructions, or program, that specifies step by step what the computer should do. The program is written in a language that the computer decodes into its own language of switch settings. The program is implemented, in other words, by means of the action of many electronic switches. The program is written, however, in symbolic form, often a form rather different from the switch settings through which the program will run.

Many people who work with computers deal only with the software, and remain ignorant about how the software instructions are actually implemented. A programmer telling a computer to "PRINT X," for example, must make certain that this instruction is compatible with the rules of the programming language, but need not be concerned with how the computer actually carries out this instruction. The programmer may be entirely ignorant of, or entirely indifferent to, how electricity flows through this or that circuit in order to make the printing happen; all the programmer needs to know is that the instruction has the desired effect. In fact, many programming languages are designed to run on different kinds of computers, and so the instruction may be implemented via one specific procedure on one machine but via a different procedure on another machine. The programmer, however, can ignore these complications, knowing only that the instruction is legitimate and will somehow be carried out.

There are many advantages to understanding the computer at the level of software and, by extension, many advantages to framing our hypotheses about the mind in the same terms. To name just one advantage, we have already noted that it is possible to describe the software even when one is ignorant about how the software is implemented. This is, in actuality, immensely useful to psychology, since we still have much to learn about the biological bases for most learning and memory phenomena. If we insisted on a hardware (that is, nervous-system) description of these phenomena, then our progress would be considerably delayed. If, however, a software description turns out to be both possible and useful, then we can press forward despite our ignorance about how the software is implemented. We know, in the domain of computers, that software descriptions are possible and useful; it seems worth exploring whether the same is true with psychological explanations.

Most research in cognitive psychology therefore proceeds at the level of "software." That is, research seeks to describe the mind in functional terms, rather than describing exactly how these functions are physically realized. In this book, for example, we will speak of "information" being "stored" and "retrieved." We will have relatively little to say about how these functions are biologically realized. This does not mean we will be vague or imprecise; it is possible to characterize these functions in considerable detail. But these characterizations will remain largely at the level of function, and not how the function is actually implemented.

One might wonder if this is a reasonable and productive way to explain psychological phenomena. The answer to this concern lies in the progress cognitive psychology has made in the last three decades. This approach—theorizing at the level of software, borrowing many specific concepts from computer processing—has been enormously fruitful, making it clear that it is indeed useful.

Let us sum up where we are. In Kant's transcendental method, we begin with observable facts and ask, roughly, what made these facts possible. Kant himself was concerned largely with the capacities that were required to make possible general classes of performance—for example, the kinds of mental categories one would need in order to reason about spatial relations. For most cognitive psychologists, in contrast, this logic is used to ask about the specific processes or events that make a particular performance possible, for example, remembering a particular type of fact or solving a particular type of problem and so on.

When cognitive psychologists seek to reconstruct the processes that led to a specific accomplishment, their accounts are framed in terms of functionally defined processes (the software), rather than biological mechanisms (the hardware). In addition, many of the specific processes hypothesized are processes known to be important in computer processing.

The Experimental Paradigms of Modern Learning Theory

In the previous sections we discussed the historical and philosophical backgrounds for both the learning theory and cognitive approaches. It should be emphasized, though, that both of these approaches share a strong commitment to research and a strong hope of generating theories that are well grounded in data. In this section, we take a closer look at the methods employed within each of these traditions, first for learning theory and second for the cognitive perspective.

PAVLOVIAN CONDITIONING

Since the initial findings of Pavlov and Thorndike, the methods used to investigate the kinds of learning they identified have changed. Only rarely do modern researchers study salivating dogs or cats trapped in boxes. Modern methods retain the essence of the work of Pavlov and Thorndike while permitting greater degrees of experimental precision and control.

We begin with Pavlovian conditioning. Pavlov's discovery was that environmental events that initially had no relation to a given reflex could come, through experience, to trigger the reflex. Prior to experience, organisms possessed a number of reflexes that were built into the nervous system. Because these reflexes were built in (that is, not conditional upon experience), Pavlov called them **unconditioned reflexes**. An unconditioned reflex has two components. There is first the environmental event, or stimulus, that triggers it, as food in the mouth triggers salivation. This environmental trigger is called the **unconditioned stimulus**, or **US**. Second, there is the reflex response itself—for example, salivation. This is called the **unconditioned response**, or **UR**. The relation between the US and the UR is typically schematized in this way:

US (Food) → UR (Salivation).

Pavlov thought that conditioning occurred when some other stimulus, the **conditioned stimulus**, or **CS**, produced the reflex response. The response produced by the CS was called the **conditioned response**, or **CR**. The CS (tone) is presented and followed closely in time by presentation of the US (food in the mouth); each of these pairings is a "trial." After a number of pairings of the tone and food (CS and US), the dog begins salivating reliably when the tone comes on, in anticipation of the food. This anticipatory salivation is the conditioned response (CR). The procedure typically employed to produce Pavlovian conditioning is depicted in Figure 1–1.

As Pavlov conceived it, the crucial aspect of the conditioning procedure was the pairing, in close temporal contiguity, of CS and US. This pairing eventually led to a change in the structure of the nervous system such that the occurrence of the CS would excite the part of the brain that usually was excited by the US. In this way conditioned excitation developed.

Since Pavlov's time, the essential elements of Pavlovian conditioning procedures have been retained, but the range of different CSs, USs, and organisms studied has expanded enormously. We will see some of the

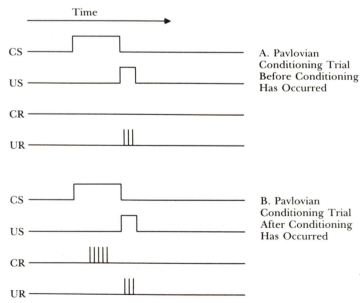

FIGURE 1–1.   *The Pavlovian Conditioning Paradigm.* In *A*, early trials are depicted. The CS is presented and followed by the US. URs (vertical lines) occur to the US but there are no CRs. In *B*, after conditioning has occurred, CRs (vertical lines) occur to the CS and before the US. The organism has now been conditioned.

methodological variety that characterizes modern research in Pavlovian conditioning in the next two chapters.

OPERANT CONDITIONING

Thorndike went on to other types of problems after his discovery of the law of effect, and the transformation of his demonstration into a program of research was largely left to others. One of Thorndike's most notable followers was B. F. Skinner (1904–1990). Skinner took up the study of rewards and punishments in the 1930s and developed a set of methods and terminology that have characterized much of the study of learning ever since. To begin with, Skinner made a clear distinction between operant conditioning and Pavlovian conditioning. These are compared diagrammatically in Figure 1–2.

In this figure, the various components of the two types of conditioning are presented in the order in which they occur. Thus in the case of Pavlovian conditioning, the CS is followed by a CR, which is followed by a US and a UR. The lab coat (CS) triggers salivation (CR) in anticipation of food (US), which also triggers salivation (UR). In the case of operant conditioning, the response (R) is followed by the US, which is presumably

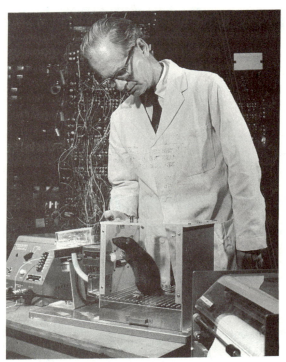

B. F. Skinner. (Photo by Nina Lean, *Life* magazine, © Time, Inc.)

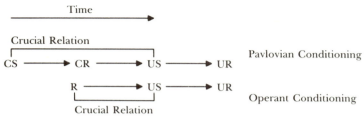

FIGURE 1–2. *Comparison of Pavlovian and Operant Conditioning Procedures.* In both procedures the sequence of events is the same. However, the crucial components of the sequence for each procedure are different. In Pavlovian conditioning it is the relation between CS and US that is responsible for the CR. After conditioning, the CS causes the CR. In operant conditioning it is the relation between the response (R) and the US that is crucial.

followed by a UR. The cat opens the latch (R), producing fish (US), which produces salivation (UR).

When these two conditioning paradigms are placed next to each other in this way they appear remarkably similar. But there is a critical difference. In Pavlovian conditioning it is the relation between the CS and the US that is crucial for conditioning. The consequence of the CR, if there is one, is unimportant. To continue our example, the dog gets the food whether it salivates or not. In contrast, in operant conditioning it is the relation between the response and the US that is crucial. If latch opening did not produce fish, the cat would not come to open the latch reliably.

THE UNCONDITIONED STIMULUS (US) OR REINFORCER

Let us now consider the US as it is used in the two types of conditioning paradigms. In the examples discussed thus far the US was the same—food. In general, stimuli that are USs in Pavlovian conditioning experiments can be (and have been) USs in operant conditioning experiments. Typically, USs are biologically important, that is, they produce strong unconditioned responses. The set of USs that is commonly used is rather small. Food, water, and electric shock are the most common USs.

Though Pavlovian USs and operant USs may be the same, they are usually referred to by different technical terms. Operant USs are generally called rewards or, more technically, **reinforcers**. This is a useful term, because the presentation of a US like food may be thought of as strengthening or reinforcing the behavior that preceded it. This is really all that the law of effect says. Thus when food is presented in an operant conditioning experiment it is called a reinforcer; when it is presented in a Pavlovian conditioning experiment it is called a US.

Reinforcers belong to one of two general classes—positive and negative. The positive reinforcers are USs like food or water that increase the likelihood of the behavior that precedes them. Negative reinforcers are reinforcers in a different way: They tend to be noxious USs, such as electric shock. These reinforcers increase the likelihood of behavior that *eliminates* them—for example, behaviors that cause the termination of the shock. When such stimuli are *presented* rather than eliminated after a response, they are usually called **punishers**.

MEASURING THE OPERANT RESPONSE

Once Thorndike had provided the groundwork for research on operant conditioning, investigators could have continued the study of reinforcement and punishment using his methods. There were, however, several details that made his methods less than optimal. The most serious one was the response that was being measured. Latch opening is a complicated and time-consuming response, and it requires the constant intervention of the experimenter. In trying to evaluate the effects of reward on latch opening, it is not clear which characteristics of the response we should measure. Should we measure how much time it takes the cat to open the latch from the time it is placed in the cage? Should we measure how long it takes once latch opening begins? Should we measure the smoothness of its execution or the force exerted on the latch by the cat?

Skinner suggested that perhaps the best measure of operant conditioning would be one that allowed an estimate of the likelihood of occurrence of the response (its probability) at any moment. There are difficulties in judging the probability of a response directly, but some idea of its probability can be inferred from its frequency. It is often true that the more frequently one does something in general, the more likely one is to do it at any particular time. Thus Skinner argued that operant conditioning experiments should measure the frequency or rate of occurrence of the response (Skinner, 1950). With this aim, it would be desirable to measure a response that can be made rapidly and with little effort. Furthermore, the experimental situation should allow the animal to make the response repeatedly, without intervention. In this way one could develop very fine measurements of conditioning as it occurred. The response would perhaps initially occur only occasionally in an hour as the organism explored its environment. As the response was followed by reinforcement, its frequency would increase, ultimately to perhaps 75 or 100 times per minute. If such a response could be found, one could measure the strength of conditioning (in responses per minute) with ease and simplicity.

THE CONDITIONING CHAMBER

Having developed this strategy, Skinner set out to develop the experimental situation in which to execute it. The product was an appa-

ratus like the one shown in Figure 1–3. The control panel and the rat
are enclosed in a soundproof, opaque chamber, usually with a little
peephole to permit observation from outside. The lever, feeder,
lights, and tone are electrically connected to automated equipment
outside the chamber. The response to be measured is the lever press.
Each time the rat presses the lever, a switch is closed. This switch closure may be arranged to produce food and at the same time automatically count the responses.

For Skinner, the lever press is an ideal response. It can be made rapidly and repeatedly with minimal expenditure of effort. It is not as
ideal for the rat. Left alone, rats will rarely press a lever. If they do, it
is often inadvertent. They may brush their tails across it, or bump into
it. This creates a minor problem. In order for the law of effect to
work—for behavior to be strengthened by satisfying consequences—

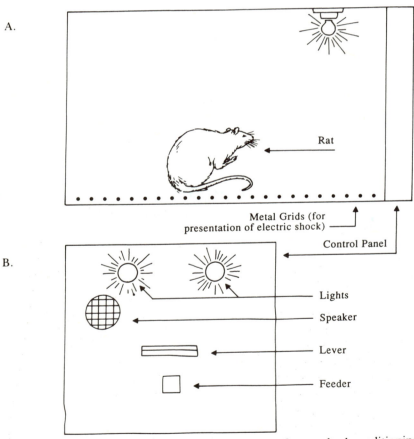

FIGURE 1–3. *The Rat Conditioning Chamber.* Diagram of a standard conditioning
chamber for rats *(A)*, and a rat's-eye view of the control panel housed in the
chamber *(B)*.

the behavior must occur at least once so that the satisfying consequence may be produced. The way to solve this problem is to help the
rat along a bit by means of a procedure called **shaping by successive
approximation**. The experimenter observes the rat, and rather than
waiting for a lever press to occur, the experimenter waits for any movement toward the lever, then delivers food. This makes movements toward
the lever a bit more likely. The experimenter now waits until the rat
moves closer to the lever before presenting food. Each food delivery
requires a response that is closer to a lever press than the one before it.
Within a rather short time the lever-press response may be firmly established using this technique.

Shaping of behavior by successive approximation is so commonplace
in the natural environment that we hardly notice it. When we teach
children to swim, to dress themselves, or to write the alphabet, we start
with simple, easily executed components and gradually develop the desired response. If we waited for the desired response to occur full-blown
before we reinforced it, few children would ever swim or write.

The second very commonly used apparatus is shown in Figure 1–4. The

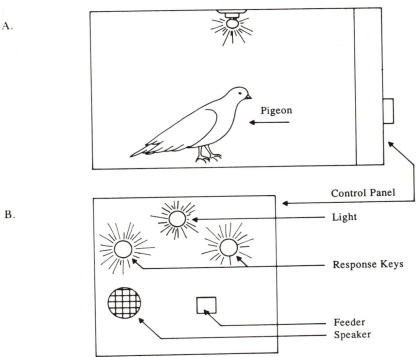

A.

B.

Control Panel

Light

Response Keys

Feeder
Speaker

Pigeon

FIGURE 1–4.   *The Pigeon Conditioning Chamber.* Diagram of a standard conditioning
chamber for pigeons *(A),* and a bird's-eye view of the control panel housed in the
chamber *(B).*

components of this chamber are essentially equivalent to those in the rat chamber, but it accommodates a different animal—the pigeon. There is only one major difference between this apparatus and the previous one. Rather than pressing a lever, the pigeons are required to peck at one of the round disks or keys mounted above the feeder. Thus rats press a lever for food and pigeons peck a key for food. The keys themselves are usually translucent and different colored lights can be used to illuminate them from behind.

Thus the major functional difference between the rat chamber and the pigeon chamber is the response one measures. However, from the experimenter's point of view, this difference is more apparent than real: The responses are, in both cases, the closure of a switch that sends an electric signal each time the key is pecked or the lever is pressed. The way in which the switch is closed is of little interest. The rat may "peck" the lever (press it with its nose) and the pigeon may "press" the key (hit it with its wings) and it will still be treated as the same response. Indeed, rats and pigeons may make the response in a different way each time. As long as (and only when) the switch is closed, it is a lever press (or key peck). This research strategy indicates something very important about operant conditioning. What is conditioned in operant conditioning experiments is not a single response but a whole class of responses. The operant is actually a *response class.*

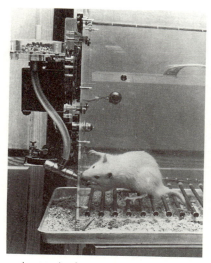 

A rat trained to press a lever for food reinforcement (courtesy of Pfizer Inc.) *and a pigeon pecking a lit key for food reinforcement* (photo by W. Rapport, courtesy of B. F. Skinner).

And the individual members of this class need have only one thing in common—that they close the switch.

Constraints on Learning

We have already noted that the learning theory approach seeks to uncover principles of broad generality, the so-called "laws of learning." It is consistent with this goal to study learning by using a small number of paradigms, and to extrapolate what we learn to different and often more complex cases. This means generalizing from one situation to another, and often generalizing from one species to another. But is this a sensible strategy? Species certainly *seem* to differ in what they learn: Pigeons learn to fly, rats do not; warblers learn to sing, snakes do not. For that matter, (some) humans learn calculus, while other species do not. Even within a single species, what is learned in one situation may be quite different from what is learned in other situations: For example, much of what a pigeon learns to do while feeding is quite different from what a pigeon learns to do while fleeing from a predator, and so on.

In response to this question, then, the learning theorist would agree that it is plain that the *content* of what is learned changes from situation to situation, and from species to species. But this does not mean that the *processes* of learning are different. One could argue, for example, that the law of effect is equally relevant to pigeons learning to fly and rats learning to run and snakes learning to slither. In each case, the behavior must first occur before there can be the possibility for the behavior's being reinforced. Once the reinforcement has occurred, this increases the probability of the behavior being repeated. In this way, *what* is learned will vary from case to case, but *how* the learning occurs will be uniform. It is this view that allows the learning theorist to regard the rat's lever press and the pigeon's key peck as essentially equivalent. Indeed, it is this view that gives the learning theorist some confidence that by studying rats and pigeons we can find out about people.

LEARNING ABOUT HUMANS BY STUDYING ANIMALS

Almost from its inception, research within the learning theory tradition has focused on the study of animals. That animals have been the subjects of study reflects some of the assumptions that have guided this research. Central among these assumptions is the view that complex behavior can be understood in terms of simple principles—principles that will show their influence even in the barest of environments, even with the simplest of organisms. Though rats, dogs, and pigeons display little of the richness and complexity of humans, their behavior can be understood in terms of the same principles that underlie our behavior, principles like the law of effect. The supposition is that once the law of effect has been fully understood as it applies to the behavior of nonhumans, it can then be applied to complex, human behavior. Hand in hand with this, many learning theorists would argue that the differences in complexity between humans and nonhumans are largely quantitative, not qualitative. This is not to say that all differences between species can be understood in these terms. The claim is merely that different species have much in common, that there is "continuity" among species. Therefore we can sensibly study a small number of species (such as rats and pigeons), and then extrapolate what we learn to many other species, including humans. Our discussions of Darwin and of associationism tell us how learning theorists can feel justified in this assumption.

Moreover, there is much to be gained by studying animals. Using animal subjects allows one to maximize experimental control. One can construct very simple environments in which animal behavior may be studied. One can control the past experience of animal subjects and expose them, if necessary, to conditions of stress and deprivation. The same obviously cannot be done with humans. In short, an experimenter can create a wholly artificial world in which animals are born, raised, and studied. Potentially significant environmental conditions can be created, singly or in combination. With human subjects one can only approximate this degree of experimental control. While conditions can be controlled for a few hours by the experimenter, the human subject comes into the laboratory with a rich history of previous experience that the experimenter cannot control. To what extent do these uncontrollable natural experiences influence the effects of the laboratory experience? There is no way to know. Thus there is much to be gained by studying animals other than humans.

However, while learning theory has adopted a general assumption of species continuity and has used it to seek principles of broad generality, it has also been mindful of the fact that species do differ in many ways. Part of what the pigeon does may reflect general principles of behavior, but other parts of pigeon behavior may reflect systems of action that are specific to that species and its close relatives. Likewise, while some of the pigeon's behaviors will carry over from one situation to another, other behaviors will be situation-specific. This claim is often framed in terms of what are called **constraints** on learning. Even though much of an organism's behavior is governed by the operation of general laws, such as the law of effect, the operation of these laws is influenced by biological constraints on what can be learned, when it can be learned, and how it is learned. With this said, the difficult problem facing the researcher is to separate the species- or situation-specific behavioral characteristics from the general ones.

UNBIASED ENVIRONMENTS

If behavior is governed both by universal principles and by more specific ones, how can we uncover the universal principles? Learning theorists proposed that the best thing to do is to bring the pigeon or rat into an artificial, laboratory environment. This environment, by virtue of being totally new to the species, renders species-specific and situation-specific behaviors largely irrelevant, and so it prevents species- and situation-specific behavior patterns from exerting their influence. In a sense, this resembles what the physicist does to investigate the force of gravitation. To remove the influences of other factors (friction, air resistance), the physicist constructs an artificial, laboratory situation within which the action of nongravitational forces is prevented. In this way, the artificial environment brings the forces under study into full view.

To put this more specifically, the theories of evolution and natural selection teach us that what shapes a species is selection pressure from the environment. Organisms that are poorly suited to their environments do not survive, and so do not pass on their genes to subsequent generations. Organisms that are well suited to their environments do reproduce and do pass on their genes. Thus pressure from the environment ultimately yields organisms whose central characteristics are well attuned to their surroundings, organisms that are specialized for dealing with the stimuli and the tasks of a particular habitat. Therefore if one studies the behavior of organisms in the natural environment, one is likely to observe a great many genetically determined behavior patterns that are specifically adapted to precisely that environment.

What we want, though, is the inverse of this. If one's interest is in general principles of behavior, rather than principles unique to the pigeon or the rat, one does not want to study these organisms in their natural environments. Instead, one wants to study these animals in an environment in which genetically determined patterns are irrelevant, in which the biological specializations cannot be applied. In short, to maximize the chances of obtaining principles of behavior that are true for all organisms, one should study behavior in an artificial and unbiased experimental environment. In this kind of environment, the organism cannot fall back on specially adapted, genetically determined patterns of behavior. As a result, we can expect to observe the impact of more general—not specialized—rules of behavior and learning.

What does it mean to say that an experimental environment is artificial and unbiased? In general, we may be confident that our experimental environment is unbiased if we are able to substitute one CS for another, or one operant for another, without having a major effect on the results of our experiment. Said differently, if we are truly uncovering general laws of learning, it should not matter which stimulus or which response we examine. Hence, we should be able to substitute different stimuli and responses without changing the pattern of data we obtain. This seemingly simple idea requires some elaboration, so let us make the notions of **unbiased environment** and **substitutability** more concrete and systematic.

Substitutability does not mean that the set of effective stimuli, operants, and rewards must be the same for all organisms. If this had to be the case in order for our principles to be general, there would be no hope of uncovering general principles. Different species possess different sensory systems. They receive and interpret different aspects of the physical world. As a consequence, the set of possible effective stimuli will differ from one species to another. The same is obviously true of operants. Pigeons fly and peck, and rats never will. Finally, reinforcers are also likely to differ from species to species. Food and water will presumably act as reinforcers for any species, but other stimuli, like running in an exercise wheel, may serve as reinforcers for rats but not for pigeons.

If substitutability does not require stimulus equivalence and operant equivalence, what does it require? The answer to this question comes from focusing not on the three classes of events—stimuli, operants, and reinforcers—but on the *relations* between the classes.

The difference between situations involving substitutable elements and those involving nonsubstitutable ones is depicted graphically in Figure 1–5. This figure presents two hypothetical outcomes of a Pavlovian and an operant conditioning experiment. Suppose, in the Pavlovian experiment, we use two CSs and two USs. CS_1 is a tone and CS_2 is a light, while US_1 is a shock and US_2 is food. A different group of pigeons experiences each CS–US combination. Consider first the results in Panel A1 of Figure 1–5. Each point corresponds to one of the four groups. What does Panel A1 tell us? First, US_2 (food) is more potent than US_1 (shock) since the points on the right of the graph are higher than the ones on the left. Second, CS_2 (light) is more effective than CS_1 (tone) since the CS_2 points are higher than the CS_1 points. However, there is no interaction between CSs and USs. CS_2 is more effective than CS_1 with either US (the two lines are parallel). That is, we can substitute one CS for another; if the US is more potent for one CS, it will be more potent for all. Likewise, we can substitute different USs; if a CS is more effective for one, it should be more effective for all. Thus we would conclude that the situation involves substitutable elements.

Compare these results to those in Panel A2. Now the lines are not parallel; they cross. CS_2 is more effective than CS_1 in combination with US_1, but the reverse is true in combination with US_2. Results like these would indicate nonsubstitutable elements.

Panels B1 and B2 make the same point for operant conditioning. Suppose Reinforcer 1 is food, Reinforcer 2 is escape from shock, Operant 1 is wing flapping, and Operant 2 is key pecking. Results like those in Panel B1 would suggest that escape from shock is a more potent reinforcer than food, and that key pecking is more easily trained than wing flapping.

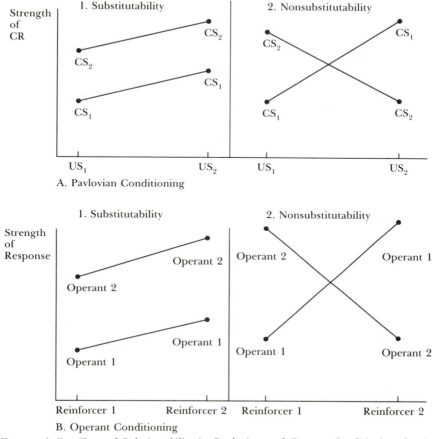

FIGURE 1-5. *Tests of Substitutability in Pavlovian and Operant Conditioning.* In *A*, animals experience different combinations of two CSs and two USs; in *B*, they experience different combinations of required operants and reinforcers. Results like those in Panels A1 and B1 would indicate substitutability, while the results in Panels A2 and B2 would indicate nonsubstitutability.

Results like those in Panel B2 would indicate that pecking is more easily trained than wing flapping for food, but that the reverse is true to escape shock. As in Panel A2, such a result would indicate nonsubstitutability of elements.

We have now made clear both why an unbiased experimental situation is important and what a demonstration of unbiasedness requires. But in performing an experiment, which pattern of data is obtained: Panel A1 or A2, B1 or B2? Research in learning was conducted for years before this question was asked; that is, before any program of experiments like the one depicted in Figure 1-5 was carried out. That is because learning theorists essentially assumed that if such experiments were done, they would produce results indicating that CSs and USs (and operants and reinforcers) were substitutable (as in A1 and B1). They assumed that their experimental situations were unbiased, so that the principles they discovered were general. But as we will see, recent evidence has suggested that this assumption is sometimes unwarranted. As a result, learning theorists are now careful to determine whether the findings they obtain in experiments pass tests of substitutability or fail them.

Research Methods within Cognitive Psychology

In contrast to learning theory, the cognitive approach has placed far less emphasis on the discovery of broadly applicable principles and, hand in hand with that, has elected not to focus on a small set of research paradigms. What characterizes cognitive research, therefore, is not a particular group of experimental procedures. Instead, the research is characterized in part by the logic of the methods used, as well as by the types of data that are typically collected. We will discuss these now by means of an example. (We will return to this example in Chapter 7, where we will place it in a richer theoretical context; for now, our focus is on the method, rather than the theory itself.)

RESEARCH IN COGNITION: AN EXAMPLE

We begin with an observation: As a test of subjects' memories, we read them a list of, say, 30 words. Immediately after the presentation, we ask subjects to write down as many words from the list as they can. In this sort of task, subjects are likely to remember anywhere from 10 to 20 words, but in a particular pattern: Subjects are extremely likely to remember the first word on the list, slightly less likely to remember the second, slightly less likely to remember the third, and so on. Subjects are also extremely likely to remember the *last* word on the list, slightly less likely to remember the next-to-last, and so forth. The pattern of subjects' recall is sketched in the curve in Figure 1–6. The figure shows the U-shaped relationship between a word's position within the series, or **serial position**, and the likelihood of recalling that word. The memory advantage for the words at the list's beginning is referred to as a **primacy effect**; the advantage for words at the list's end is referred to as a **recency effect**. As we will see in a moment, it will also be convenient to talk about all of the list *except* the list's end; we will refer to this as the **pre-recency** portion of the curve.

What lies behind this pattern? What is going on in subjects' minds to produce the primacy and recency advantages, with poorer performance

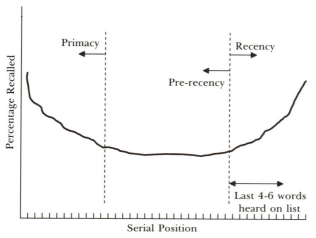

Serial Position

(i.e., position within the *presentation* sequence)

FIGURE 1–6.   *The Relation between Serial Position and Recall.* Subjects are quite likely to recall the first few words presented to them on a list (the so-called primacy effect) and also the last few words presented (the recency effect).

for the words in the list's middle? One hypothesis draws on the conception shown in Figure 1–7, a conception that we will examine in detail in later chapters. From Figure 1–7, it has been hypothesized that information that has just been heard or just been seen is placed initially in **primary memory** (described in some texts as **short-term memory**). Primary memory is limited in size, and so as new information arrives it will displace the previous contents of primary memory. These previous con-

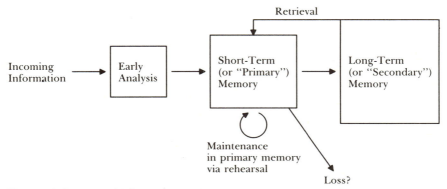

FIGURE 1–7.   *An Initial Conception of Memory's Architecture.* On this view, information gathered from the environment is initially held in primary memory. The information can be maintained here, or transferred to the larger, more enduring secondary memory. If placed in secondary memory, the information can be retrieved for later use.

tents will be lost *unless* they have been transferred to a much larger storage system, namely, **secondary memory** (often labeled **long-term memory**). Secondary memory is assumed to be vast in size, but entry into this storehouse is not trivial. That is, the learner must spend some time and effort to transfer information from primary memory to secondary memory.

This sketch leaves much unsaid, but it is enough to support an account of the primacy and recency effects. As subjects listen to the word list, words are initially placed in primary memory and are then displaced as new words are heard. At the end of the list's presentation, therefore, primary memory will contain the last few words in the list, since no additional words arrived to displace these. If we assume that subjects have easy access to the half-dozen words contained in primary memory, then we have an account of the recency advantage: At the list's end, the last few words on the list are still in primary memory, and are easily reported from this memory.

What about primacy? Think about this task from the subjects' point of view. When the first word is presented, subjects have that word, and only that word, to think about. No other word on the list has this privilege. Therefore much attention is lavished on that word, making it quite likely that the word will be entered into secondary memory. When the second word arrives, subjects have only two words to think about, the first and the second. Therefore, the second word also receives much attention, although less than the first did, and also has a high likelihood of entry into secondary memory. This continues in like manner for the third and fourth words, with each having to share the subjects' attention with a larger and larger number of other words.

By the time seven or eight words have been presented, subjects are probably dividing their attention as finely as they can. Therefore, as more and more words arrive, subjects' only option is to abandon thinking about the very early words and just think about the most recently heard six or seven or eight words. Words in the middle of the list, therefore, never get more than a one-eighth share of the subjects' attention and efforts. As a consequence, the very early words are quite likely to be stored in secondary memory, while words in the middle of the list are not. When the time comes to report the words, the early words will be remembered, producing the primacy effect, and the middle words may not be.

This is a lot of theory to explain our initial result, including assumptions about memory's structure and about the subjects' strategies and capacities. Moreover, there is nothing inevitable about this account: The account is compatible with the observed results, and so could be what lies behind the results. However, other accounts can also be constructed to explain the observed data. Therefore we cannot simply assume the correctness of this conception.

How could we find out if this account is correct? The proposal is that the "recency" items are being retrieved from primary memory and that the "primacy" items—and, in fact, all the "pre-recency" items—are being retrieved from secondary memory. If we could find a way to disrupt primary memory, therefore, it should disrupt recall only of the recency items. This is easy to do: Immediately after the list's end, we can require subjects to do something else for, say, 60 seconds, and only at the end of this other task report the words from the list. We could, for example, ask subjects to count backwards by threes from 500 for 60 seconds, as an **interpolated task** between the list presentation and the recall. This interpolated task will presumably require primary memory—for example, to remember where one is in the counting. This should displace whatever was in primary memory, which, using this theory, is the list's last few words. Our account predicts, therefore, that the interpolated task should disrupt the recency effect. The activity should have no impact on the pre-recency performance, since everything but recency is coming from secondary memory. This prediction turns out to be correct.

We can also do the converse—manipulate the pre-recency recall without touching recency. One way to do this is to vary the *rate* at which the list is presented. If we slow down the rate of presentation, this will allow subjects to devote more time and attention to all of the list's contents, making it easier for all items to be placed in secondary memory. Since the pre-recency words depend on secondary memory, this should improve memory performance for these words. Since the recency words are not coming from secondary memory, this manipulation should have no impact on subjects' recall of the end of the list. This prediction also turns out to be correct.

A third prediction involves the specific errors that subjects make. For reasons we will not detail here, it is believed that the organization of secondary memory relies heavily on associations among words' *meanings*. Primary memory, on the other hand, seems to rely heavily on a representation involving words' *sound*. If subjects make mistakes, therefore, we might predict that, in primary memory, they will confuse "sound-alike" words—reporting "rattle" when they actually heard "cattle," and so forth. In secondary memory, subjects may become confused among "similar-meaning" words—reporting "cows" when they heard "cattle," etc. Thus we predict sound-alike errors for the last few words on the list, that is, in the recency portion of the curve, and meaning-based errors for the remainder of the list. Again, this prediction turns out to be true.

In sum, these results—and, we should say, many other findings as well—fit with the conception we have offered. However, several things should be noted about this account, and this evidence. First, no one has ever seen a "primary memory" or a "secondary memory." Instead, we propose that these exist because they play a key role in a well-supported account of the data. That is, we infer the existence of these memories because they seem to be required if we are to explain the evidence. In this sense, we *reconstruct* what the unobserved structures and processes must be.

Second, notice that, in supporting our account, we have several forms of data available to us. We can manipulate subjects' activities, as we did with the interpolated task, and look at how this changes the quality of performance—in our case, the number of words remembered. We can also manipulate the stimuli themselves, as we did with rate, and look at how this changes performance. We can likewise look in detail at the performance, asking not just about the overall quality of performance, but also about the specific errors. In addition, we sometimes wish to ask about the speed of subjects' performance, although we have not used that method in this example. The assumption here is that mental processes are very quick, but nonetheless do take a measurable amount of time. By timing how quickly subjects answer various questions, we can ask what factors speed up mental processes and what factors slow them down. We will see this method in use at various points in our discussion in later chapters.

Third, one sort of evidence has *not* been considered—namely, the subjects' own reports about what is going on, about what strategies they are using. As we discussed earlier, introspection is a research tool of uncertain value. It is entirely possible that subjects do not know what is going on in the performance of this (or any) memory task. If subjects claim to know what is going on, there is reason to believe they may be mistaken (e.g., Nisbett & Wilson, 1977); hence we cannot simply take subjects' testimony at face value.

Finally, it is worth noting that we have built our argument with several lines of evidence: Our account had to be compatible with the initial observations, namely the primacy and recency effects. But our account also led us to predict other observations, predictions that, as it turns out, were all correct. This pattern is a common one in research: We start with data, construct an account of those data, then seek further results to confirm, or disconfirm, our account. In addition, it is important that no one line of data is by itself decisive. As we mentioned, if the primacy and recency effects were all we had to go on, there would be other ways to explain them. Likewise, if the other individual results we have mentioned were also considered in isolation, we could find different ways to explain them. The key comes in finding an account that will fit all of the available data. When we have done our work well, there will be just one such account, and this will be our assurance that we have correctly reconstructed what is going on, invisibly and never directly observed, in the mind.

This method of **backward inference**, inferring invisible processes to explain visible results, is essential for modern cognitive psychology. But it is by no means unique to cognitive psychology. The same method shows up in other disciplines as well. Physicists, for example, do not observe electrons directly, but instead infer electron activity from the "tracks" electrons leave in orbitals, from momentary fluctuations in magnetic fields, and so on. From these *effects* of particles, physicists figure out what the *causes* must be like. In this fashion, physicists also "do science on the invisible," making important discoveries about particles that no one has ever seen and reaching firm conclusions about events that have never been observed. So cognitive psychologists are in good company.

Summary

The psychology of learning and memory represents an attempt to extend the methods of science to the understanding of learning and action. It is characterized by two general approaches. The learning theory approach focuses on the environmental determinants of learning, emphasizes learning as a change in behavior, and does most of its research with nonhuman subjects in a small number of experimental settings. The cognitive approach focuses on determinants of learning and memory that are internal to the learner, emphasizes learning as the acquisition of knowledge, and does most of its research with human subjects in a wide variety of experimental settings.

Modern learning theory has its roots in philosophy, biology, and early experimental psychology. From philosophy, learning theory was influenced by Descartes's conception of the reflex arc, and by Hobbes's extension of the reflex to the whole range of human activity as well as his suggestion that all action is in the service of producing pleasure and avoiding pain. Learning theory was also influenced by the doctrine of associationism, offered by Locke, Hume, and Mill, which saw all knowledge as deriving from experience, with complex ideas being the result of associations among simple ones. From biology, learning theory was influenced by Darwin's theory of evolution, which suggested that there were significant similarities among species. These influences, together with Pavlov's discovery of the conditioned reflex and Thorndike's discovery of the law of effect, sowed the seeds for learning theory as we know it today.

Modern learning researchers use methods that are far more rigorous than those of Pavlov and Thorndike to develop principles of Pavlovian and operant conditioning. They study nonhuman subjects in highly artificial, simplified, experimental settings. From these studies they expect to derive general laws that characterize the learning of all species in all situations. This expectation gains justification from the learning theorists' beliefs (1) that learning involves simple associations between stimuli or between responses and stimuli, (2) that complex behavior can be understood as the combination of simple elements, (3) that learning is largely determined by external, environmental influences, and (4) that principles of learning transcend species and situational boundaries.

Empirical and theoretical developments in recent years have required modification of this central core. Learning theorists have come to realize that there are many species- and situation-specific principles of learning that must be recognized and understood so that they may take their place alongside the general principles (and be differentiated from them). They have also realized that the cognitive processes of organisms—processes including perception, representation, and memory—are too important to an account of learning to be ignored.

Cognitive psychology has, of course, focused on these cognitive processes from its very beginnings. In its early years, psychology sought to understand memory and mental representations by having subjects use introspection to talk about events taking place in their minds. However, the method of introspection was soon set aside. In its place, psychologists sought to explain processes like perception and memory by reconstruction: Given the observable data, one reconstructs what must have occurred in the mind in order to have brought about the observable data. One typically then seeks further data to test the correctness of these hypothesized processes or events.

The data used by cognitive psychologists come in many forms: We can examine subjects' degree of performance on a task (such as how many words from a list are correctly remembered); we can examine how performance is changed when we manipulate subjects' strategies or when we change the stimulus materials themselves; and we can also examine the specific errors that subjects make. Each of these is used in a converging pattern of evidence to confirm (or disconfirm) the correctness of our hypotheses about mental events that cannot be directly observed.

In generating hypotheses about mental events, cognitive psychologists frame their accounts in functional terms, rather than in biological terms. Many of the specific processes hypothesized are borrowed from our understanding of computer processing, and the computer has served as a powerful metaphor for explaining how the mind acquires, represents, and uses information.

PART 1
BASIC PROCESSES
OF LEARNING

2 Pavlovian Conditioning: Basic Principles

A man hears a song on the radio that was popular years ago, when he and his wife first fell in love. The long-absent feelings of new love come rushing back.

A woman leaves the hospital after recovering from a serious automobile accident. As she is about to enter the taxi that will take her home, she is overwhelmed with terror.

In both of these examples, a stimulus that was once of no particular emotional significance comes to produce a powerful emotional response. And there is nothing unusual about these examples. We are all accustomed to having our emotions manipulated by seemingly innocuous stimuli. Successful novels, plays, films, and television shows are successful in part because they move us to experience strong emotions. But they move us even though we do not directly experience any significant (unconditioned) stimuli. How do these initially insignificant stimuli get their power over us?

It is extremely likely that the Pavlovian conditioning process makes a contribution. Through Pavlovian conditioning, the range of environmental stimuli that can trigger emotional reactions is expanded, as we shall see. Indeed, for most of us the occurrence of unconditioned stimuli that produce strong emotional reactions is relatively rare. Most of our emotions are produced by stimuli whose significance has been acquired. Understanding Pavlovian conditioning can tell us about that process of acquisition. Thus the significance of Pavlovian conditioning processes goes far beyond Pavlov's salivating dogs.

This chapter and the next will explore principles of Pavlovian conditioning. We will discuss the different kinds of phenomena that have been observed in studies of Pavlovian conditioning, and ask what it is that organisms actually learn when they are subjected to Pavlovian procedures. We will also attempt to determine what aspects of the conditioning situation are actually crucial to producing learning.

The Classic Conditioning Experiment

As you will recall from Chapter 1, Pavlov's pioneering research on conditioned reflexes, begun around the turn of this century, involved the study of salivation in dogs. In a typical experiment, the dog is brought into a soundproof room and strapped into a harness. A salivary gland, which has been moved to the outside of the cheek by minor surgery, is connected to recording equipment that measures salivation in drops. At the start of the experiment bits of food, which serve as the unconditioned stimulus (US), are placed in the dog's mouth, and the number of drops of saliva produced is recorded. Then the stimulus to be used as the conditioned stimulus (CS) is occasionally presented for brief periods. Typically the CS does not produce any drops of saliva. It is important to be sure of this before conditioning is attempted, for if the CS produces salivation in its own right, then when it is paired with the US and salivation occurs it is difficult to know whether this salivation is the result of the conditioning experience or is directly produced by the CS.

The CS is, let us say, a ticking metronome. The US is meat powder placed in the mouth. Every few minutes the CS is presented, and 15 seconds later, while the CS is still on, meat powder is placed in the mouth. Each of these pairings of CS and US is a trial. For the first few trials there is no noticeable response during the CS and copious salivation during the US. After a dozen trials or so (this varies from animal to animal) the dog begins to salivate during the CS and before the US. This anticipatory salivation is the conditioned response. If we recorded salivation in each trial, the data might look like those in Figure 2–1.

In the first few trials salivation occurs only to the US. In the 10th trial the first drops of anticipatory salivation appear. By the 20th trial salivation to the CS is at its maximum. Although salivation is what is measured with care in these experiments, other responses appear to be conditioned

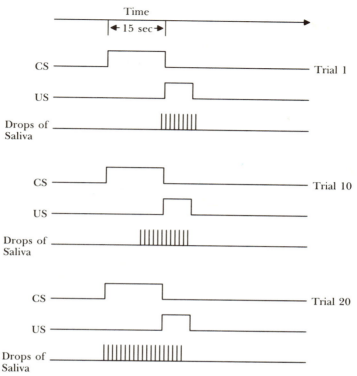

FIGURE 2–1. *Development of a Conditioned Reflex.* In Trial 1, the dog salivates (vertical lines) only after food is presented. In Trial 10, a few drops of saliva come before the delivery of food. By Trial 20, salivation begins at the onset of the CS and continues throughout the trial.

as well. The dog shows signs of general excitement or agitation when the CS is on, and if sufficient movement is possible, the dog may even sniff at or lick the CS (see Zener, 1937, for an early example). However, the form of these additional activities and, indeed, whether or not they even occur will differ from one animal to the next. What virtually all animals do have in common is that they salivate when the CS is present.

Acquisition and Extinction

When an organism is exposed to a Pavlovian conditioning procedure, conditioned responses do not typically start occurring at full strength all of a sudden. Instead what tends to happen is that, over trials, the occurrence of a CR gradually becomes more likely. In addition the CR grows steadily stronger when it occurs. A hypothetical curve depicting the acquisition of the CR is depicted in Figure 2–2A.

Figure 2–2 presents the probability of a CR over trials of CS–US pairing. What happens is that the probability increases gradually until a leveling-off point, or **asymptote**, is reached. How quickly that asymptote is reached, and how high it is, will depend on a number of factors, some of which are discussed later in this chapter.

What would happen if, after the CR reached an asymptote, we continued presenting the CS but now without the US? Would the CR become a permanent fixture? The answer is no. As depicted in Figure 2–2B, CRs would gradually decrease, and would ultimately stop occurring altogether. This phenomenon is known as **extinction**.

The Scope of Pavlovian Conditioning

The scope of Pavlovian conditioning extends well beyond the basic demonstration of conditioned salivation in dogs. Indeed, virtually all modern research is carried out with animals other than dogs and with responses other than salivation. The extension of Pavlovian research to new situations is partly an attempt to assess the generality of the phenomena that Pavlov observed. Obviously, Pavlovian conditioning would be neither

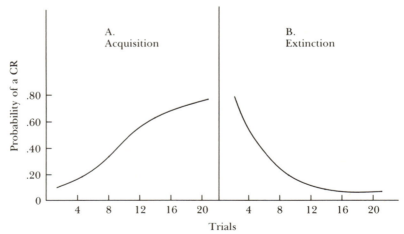

FIGURE 2–2. *Acquisition and Extinction of a CR.* Depicted in *A* is the gradual increase in the probability of a CR as CS–US pairings occur. *B* shows the gradual decrease in probability as CS presentations continue, but without the US.

very interesting nor very important if it were found only in dogs salivating to clicking metronomes. That is not the case. The phenomena of Pavlovian conditioning have proven to be quite general and robust.

To illustrate the scope of Pavlovian conditioning phenomena, we will briefly describe four of the most common settings that are currently employed for Pavlovian conditioning experimentation. They involve the study of conditioned eyeblinks in rabbits; conditioned fear (or conditioned emotional responses) in rats; conditioned pecking, or autoshaping, in pigeons; and taste aversion learning in rats. Later, we will consider the role of Pavlovian conditioning in human behavior.

EYEBLINK CONDITIONING

In eyeblink conditioning experiments, rabbits are restrained and a small electrical device for measuring eyeblinks is attached to one eyelid. The US is typically a brief puff of air delivered to the eye. The CS can be almost anything—a light, a tone, a tactile vibration. The CR of interest is an eyeblink to the CS, in anticipation of the US.

Data from a representative experiment are presented in Figure 2–3. The figure presents the proportion of trials in each block of 82 trials in which an eyeblink to the CS occurred. As the data make clear, development of reliable CRs was a gradual matter, and even after 600 trials CRs

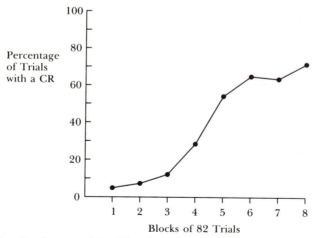

FIGURE 2–3. *Development of Conditioned Eyeblink in the Rabbit.* Each point represents the proportion of trials out of 82 in which an eyeblink occurred to the CS. Very little responding occurred in the first three blocks. In the fourth block, the rabbit responded in 28% of the trials. By the sixth block, responding occurred in 65% of the trials. (After Schneiderman, Fuentes, & Gormezano, 1962.)

were not produced on every trial. Nevertheless, it is clear that conditioning occurred, since at the beginning of training the CS produced virtually
no eyeblinks (Schneiderman, Fuentes, & Gormezano, 1962; see also
Schneiderman, 1973).

CONDITIONED FEAR

If the US in a Pavlovian conditioning experiment is a brief, moderately painful electric shock (usually delivered to the feet through bars in
the floor of the chamber), the conditioned response produced is often
identified as conditioned fear. As an innocuous CS like a tone or a light
is repeatedly followed by the shock, the animal becomes afraid when
the tone or light appears, in anticipation of the shock. Conditioned responses taken to indicate fear may be measured in a variety of ways:
Changes in heart rate or blood pressure, tensing of relevant skeletal
muscles, excessive urination or defecation, and the like are all reliable
indices of what experimenters call fear. However, the conditioned fear
response that is most commonly measured is something else, something known as **conditioned emotional response (CER)**, or **conditioned
suppression**.

Suppose we place a hungry rat in an operant conditioning chamber and
train it to press a lever to produce food. Though not every lever press
produces food, they do so reliably enough that the rat comes to press the
lever at a steady, high rate—say 50 times per minute. Now, with lever
pressing well established, we introduce Pavlovian conditioning trials.
Periodically a tone (CS) is sounded for 30 seconds, after which a brief
electric shock (US) is delivered to the rat's feet. These Pavlovian conditioning trials are completely independent of lever pressing and food; that
is, lever presses continue to produce food, and have no effect at all on
either the tone or the shock.

As the presentations of tone and shock proceed, something very interesting happens. The rat stops pressing the lever while the tone is on.
The appearance of the tone, signaling shock, results in the suppression
of lever pressing for food. Thus we have the designation "conditioned
suppression" (Estes & Skinner, 1941). Why does the rat stop pressing
the lever? It does not seem to make sense. The rat is going to get
shocked anyway, whether or not it presses the lever. It might as well
make the best of a bad situation and get some food as well. While the
answer to this question is complex, and not altogether clear, it seems as
though the rat stops pressing the lever because the tone, through pairing with shock, produces fear, and when the animal is afraid it loses
interest in food. Thus, it stops pressing the lever (see Rescorla & Solomon, 1967).

The degree of conditioning that occurs in a situation like this is measured with a statistical technique known as a **suppression ratio**, which is

$$\frac{\text{Rate of response during the CS } (A)}{\text{Rate during the CS } (A) + \text{Rate with the CS absent } (B)}$$

or

$$\frac{A}{A + B}.$$

When there is no suppression, this ratio will be 0.50, because A will equal B. When suppression is total, the ratio will be zero because A will be zero. Thus, we can measure the strength of conditioning by determining how close the suppression ratio is to zero.

Some illustrative data are presented in Figure 2–4, from an experiment with rats in which a noise was the CS and a moderate (1-milliamp) shock was the US. As can be seen in the figure, conditioning is much more rapid than in the case of conditioned eyeblinks, with suppression almost complete after five noise–shock trials (Kamin, 1969).

The phenomenon of conditioned suppression is important for two reasons. First, it is a convenient and powerful technique for studying Pavlovian conditioning. Second, and perhaps more significant, it shows that Pavlovian conditioning can have profound effects on voluntary, goal-directed, seemingly intelligent activity. So it is that a person who suffers from claustrophobia, a fear of being in closed-in spaces, may find it impossible to concentrate on the details of an important business deal being negotiated in a modern, windowless conference room. Indeed, this person may find it impossible even to get into the elevator that will take

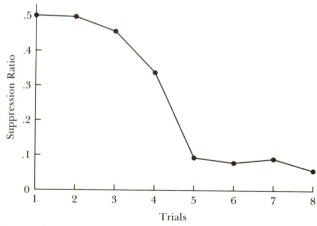

FIGURE 2–4. *Conditioned Suppression of Lever Pressing in the Rat.* Each point represents the ratio of response rate during the CS to overall response rate over the course of 8 noise–shock trials. The lower the suppression ratio, the greater the magnitude of conditioned fear. (Adapted from Kamin, 1969, Figure 3.)

him to the conference room. What this means is that Pavlovian conditioning effects are not restricted to the domain of reflexes like salivation or eye blinking. Pavlovian conditioning can influence the full range of an organism's activity. This makes the significance of Pavlovian conditioning processes very great indeed.

AUTOSHAPING

We saw in the last chapter that one of the standard methods for studying operant conditioning involves training pigeons to peck lit keys for food. Well it was discovered 20 years ago that very similar methods could also be used to study Pavlovian conditioning (Brown & Jenkins, 1968). Suppose a pigeon that has already been trained to eat from the feeder is placed in the conditioning chamber with the response key dark. Every minute or so, the key lights up for 6 seconds, after which the feeder operates and the pigeon has access to grain for 4 seconds. The grain comes whether or not the pigeon pecks at the key; in other words, nothing on the pigeon's part is required to produce food. Nevertheless, pigeons come quite reliably to peck at the key. Some typical results (Schwartz, unpublished) are presented in Figure 2–5, which plots the proportion of trials, in successive blocks of 10 trials, in which a key peck occurred.

When first discovered, this phenomenon was given the name **auto-shaping**. The reason for this is that, Pavlovian conditioning aside, it represented a technique for the automatic shaping of key pecking. The

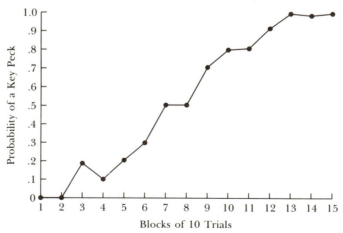

FIGURE 2–5. *Autoshaping in the Pigeon.* Each point represents the proportion of trials in a 10-trial block in which a key peck occurred in a procedure in which brief illuminations of the key light were followed by food delivery. (From Schwartz, unpublished data.)

experimenter did not have to sit quietly and patiently watching the pigeon, and shape the pigeon's key peck using the method of shaping by successive approximation. Instead the shaping process could be automated by just having a timer that turned on the key for brief periods prior to each food delivery. No matter what the pigeon might be doing when food came early in its training, eventually its behavior would be drawn to the lit key. Thus, at first, autoshaping was viewed as a modest, technological advance. Very quickly, however, it came to be seen as an interesting example of Pavlovian conditioning, worthy of detailed investigation. Nevertheless, its initial name has stuck, though it is sometimes also called sign tracking (see Hearst & Jenkins, 1974; Locurto, Terrace, & Gibbon, 1981; Schwartz & Gamzu, 1977).

TASTE AVERSION LEARNING

Our final example of a common Pavlovian conditioning procedure is called **taste aversion learning**. In a taste aversion experiment thirsty organisms (typically rats) are given an opportunity to drink water that has been distinctively flavored, often with a taste that is highly preferred to ordinary tap water. After drinking for a while, the rats are either exposed to X rays or injected with one of a number of different drugs. Whether by X ray or by drug, the rats are made sick to their stomachs. After being given a day or so in which to recover from their gastrointestinal distress, the rats are offered a choice between the flavored water that had preceded their illness and tap water. Often after only a single such experience, rats will avoid the flavored water, apparently having come to associate it with their gastrointestinal distress. Thus, it seems we have another instance of Pavlovian conditioning in which a CS (taste) that is followed by a US (illness) comes very rapidly to be associated with that US (Domjan, 1981; Domjan & Wilson, 1972; Garcia & Koelling, 1966; Revusky & Garcia, 1970; Rozin & Kalat, 1971).

What these four examples indicate is that in addition to affecting reflexes like salivation and eye blinking, Pavlovian conditioning procedures can influence whether and what organisms consume, and whether they will engage in goal-directed instrumental activity for reinforcement. The broad range of Pavlovian conditioning phenomena makes clear how important it is to understand the conditioning process.

The Pavlovian Conditioned Response (CR)

When a CS and a US are repeatedly presented together, the CS eventually comes to trigger responses that it did not trigger previously. This is how we know that conditioning has occurred. If we are interested in assessing the strength of conditioning, there are a number of different features of the conditioned response that we can measure. We can measure the **latency** of the CR, which is the time between the onset of the CS and the beginning of the CR. The presumption is that as conditioning gets stronger, the latency to make a CR will get shorter. We can measure the **magnitude** of the CR; for example, we can count the number of drops of saliva produced by a metronome paired with food, or the amount of suppression of lever pressing to a noise that has been paired with shock, as in Figure 2–4. Our expectation here is that as conditioning gets stronger, CR magnitude will increase. Finally, we can measure the **probability** of a CR, the likelihood that a CR will occur on any given CS presentation. As conditioning gets stronger, the probability of a CR should increase, as in Figures 2–3 and 2–5.

The question, however, is for which CRs we should be measuring latency, magnitude, or probability. What determines the kind of CR that pairings of CS and US will produce? Pavlov believed that the CR mimicked the UR. Thus if food produced salivation, a CS would produce anticipatory salivation. And if shock produced an increase in heart rate, a CS would produce an increase in heart rate. Recent research has made it clear, however, that the matter of CR determination is not as simple as this. While CRs sometimes mimic URs, frequently they do not. And the form they take can be influenced by a number of factors (see, for example, Holland, 1977, 1980).

In the last decade, a great deal of research has been done on the nature of the CR, and researchers have discovered many extremely exciting phenomena. What these phenomena point to is the conclusion that CRs will almost always take a form that serves the organisms' needs in some way. In other words, CRs typically help organisms adapt to whatever challenge the environmental US is posing. Sometimes it is adaptive for CRs to mimic URs. But most of the time it is more adaptive for CRs to be different from URs. Indeed, often it is adaptive for CRs to be exactly the opposite of URs.

THE ADAPTIVE FUNCTION OF THE CONDITIONED RESPONSE

If you were an engineer designing a new model car and you came up with some radical engine modifications, one of the first questions your supervisors would ask is "Why?" What do the modifications do? What is their function? How do they improve the car or make it more attractive to potential buyers? Before embarking on major design changes, one wants to have a good reason.

Similarly, if you were an engineer designing organisms, and you came up with Pavlovian conditioning as a feature of a new, experimental model, we would want to know why. What would it accomplish? What function would it serve? Of course, there are no "designers" of organisms. That work is done by natural selection, and not every characteristic of organisms serves a useful function. So it is possible that Pavlovian conditioning is just an irrelevant decoration, like tailfins once were on cars. But still, it is reasonable to wonder whether the capacity for learning by Pavlovian conditioning would have evolved and been selected if it didn't make some important contribution to the organism's well-being.

What might that contribution be? Clearly, the potential virtue of Pavlovian conditioning is that it allows organisms to anticipate the occurrence of important events like food or physical danger. But whether anticipating such events actually helps will depend on what the organism does when the Pavlovian CSs occur. If an organism learns that a tone reliably precedes shock, but does nothing useful with that information, then Pavlovian conditioning is a mere decoration.

By and large, organisms not only learn Pavlovian CS–US relations, but they develop CRs that do them some good. Take Pavlov's classic case of conditioned salivation. Saliva begins the digestive process. Ordinarily, food in the mouth triggers salivation, but digestion is facilitated if saliva is already present before the food is ingested. Conditioned salivation produces this result. Indeed, there are other conditioned responses to food in the mouth that also aid digestion. For example, insulin plays a critical role in the metabolism of sugars. It is released by the pancreas in response to the presence of sugar in the digestive tract. It is also released as a CR to sweet tastes in the mouth (Deutsch, 1974).

Another indication that Pavlovian CRs are adaptive comes from recent experiments on conditioning of sexual arousal. Male rats were given access to sexually receptive females. In some cases access was reliably preceded by a set of distinct environmental stimuli (CSs). In other cases, it was not. The presence of CSs greatly facilitated sexual performance by shortening the males' latency to begin copulation and decreasing the time to ejaculation once copulation had begun (Zamble, Haddad, Mitchell, & Cutmore, 1985). One appreciates the adaptiveness of speeding up the reproductive process when one realizes how vulnerable and defenseless to predation rats are while in the midst of this essential activity.

Another recently discovered Pavlovian CR that has clear adaptive value involves the release of brain chemicals known as **endorphins**. Endorphins are morphine-like substances that, among other things, work like morphine to reduce sensitivity to pain. When animals are exposed to Pavlovian conditioning with shock as the US, sensitivity to shock comes to diminish in the presence of the CS, evidence that the CS is triggering endorphin release (Fanselow & Baackes, 1982; MacLennan, Jackson, & Maier, 1980; see Hollis, 1984, for another example, and Hollis, 1982, for a general discussion of the functional value of CRs).

CRs THAT OPPOSE URs

Some of the most striking evidence for the adaptiveness of Pavlovian CRs comes from studies in which the CR is actually the opposite of the UR. For example, a typical unconditioned response to shock is an increase in heart rate. This response is useful in that it is part of a general arousal that mobilizes the animal to respond to danger. However, in well-trained animals the CR to a Pavlovian signal for shock is a *decrease* in heart rate (Obrist, Sutterer, & Howard, 1972). This antagonistic CR may serve the animal by reducing the physiological wear and tear that long periods of high cardiovascular output produce.

Particularly dramatic examples of CR–UR antagonism come from studies in which drugs of various kinds are used as USs. A series of experiments has been performed using morphine as a US. Among morphine's many effects is that it produces analgesia—it reduces pain sensitivity. One can measure this effect by placing a rat's paw on a hotplate and seeing how long it takes for the rat to withdraw its paw. Under the influence of morphine analgesia, paw withdrawal should be, and is, slower, presumably because the morphine makes the heat less painful. If the injection is a CS and morphine is the US, what is the conditioned response to the injection itself? We find out by giving the rat an injection of neutral salt water and placing its paw on the hotplate. What we observe is that the rat removes its paw even faster than a rat without morphine experience. The heat seems to hurt *more* as a result of the injection. Thus the conditioned response to injection is an *increase* in pain sensitivity while the unconditioned response to morphine is a decrease in pain sensitivity (Siegel, 1975, 1977, 1978; Siegel, Hinson, & Krank, 1978; see Siegel, 1979, 1983, for reviews). This conditioning of pain sensitivity can also be produced with CSs like lights and tones; it is not restricted to the injection procedure itself (Siegel, Hinson, & Krank, 1978).

Findings like these are of interest to students of conditioning, but they have a broader significance as well. With many drugs, people's responses to them change systematically as they continue to use them. Specifically, a given dose of a drug becomes progressively less effective as a person's experience with it continues. We say that the person has developed a **tolerance** to the drug. To produce an effect of a given magnitude, larger and larger doses of the drug must be administered. Tolerance has traditionally been viewed as the result of a physiological process of adaptation. While this may partly account for tolerance, the conditioning studies just described suggest that tolerance may also be the result of Pavlovian conditioning.

To see this, consider Figure 2–6. The figure plots pain sensitivity in arbitrary units. An animal receives 6 water injections, during which its pain sensitivity stays constant at 15 units. Then the animal starts receiving morphine. In the figure, each morphine injection reduces pain sensitivity

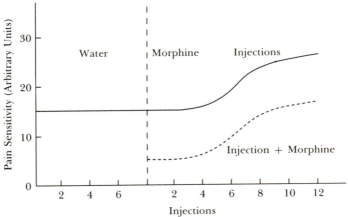

FIGURE 2–6. *A Conditioning Model of Morphine Tolerance.* The figure presents hypothetical changes in pain sensitivity as a function of experience with morphine. First, the animal receives six injections of water and its pain sensitivity remains constant. Then it starts getting morphine injections. In the figure, morphine always reduces pain sensitivity by 10 units (solid curve minus dashed curve). Thus there is no tolerance to morphine itself. However, as a result of injection–morphine pairings, pain sensitivity starts increasing to the injection. By the twelfth injection the morphine makes the animal no less pain sensitive than it was before morphine injections began.

by 10 units; that is, morphine has a constant analgesic effect. However, Pavlovian conditioning develops such that the injection itself starts producing CRs of increased pain sensitivity. The net result is that morphine stops being effective—not because the effect of morphine per se has changed, but because the ambient level of pain sensitivity it must counteract has increased steadily. Thus the widespread phenomenon of drug tolerance may be understood as reflecting, at least in part, the effects of Pavlovian conditioning.

Let us consider one very important consequence of the possibility that drug tolerance might be the result of antagonistic Pavlovian CRs. Imagine an animal that continues to get morphine injections in the presence of the same environmental cues. These cues come to produce CRs that antagonize the effects of morphine so that to produce a constant net effect, ever larger doses of the drug must be used. Now the animal is placed in a novel environment and given its current (large) effective dose of morphine. What should happen? In the absence of the environmental cues that trigger antagonistic CRs, this dose of morphine should act unopposed and produce a whopping effect. Indeed, the same dose that produces the expected analgesic effect in the familiar, conditioning environment produces overdose and in some cases death in the novel environment (Siegel, Hinson, Krank, & McCully, 1982). It is an open question how often death by drug overdose among human drug addicts comes not from taking more than the usual amount of the drug, but from taking the usual amount in an unusual (unconditioned) environment (see Poulos, Hinson, & Siegel, 1981, for a general discussion of the application of Pavlovian conditioning principles to drug addiction).

OPPONENT PROCESS THEORY

These examples of conditioned responses that are the opposite of unconditioned responses are consistent with a recent theory of motivation that is quite broad in scope and has been extremely influential. It is known as the **opponent process theory**, and has been developed principally by Richard L. Solomon (Solomon & Corbit, 1974; Solomon, 1980; Schull, 1979). Let us consider the general theory first and then see how it can be applied to Pavlovian conditioning.

The opponent process theory rests on a few simple ideas:

1. Any stimulus that produces an immediate hedonic or emotional effect also produces a later effect that is opposite in direction to the initial effect. The initial hedonic effect is called the a-process and the later effect is called the b-process.

2. The magnitude and duration of the a-process are fixed, determined by the particular stimulus being experienced. However, the b-process is dynamic. With repeated exposure to the stimulus, the b-process begins earlier, has greater magnitude, and lasts longer. These changes in the b-process reverse themselves as time passes without exposure to the stimulus.

3. Whether the b-process grows with repeated stimulation depends critically on the time interval between stimulations. If the stimulations are widely spaced, there is no change in b-process.

4. The actual hedonic or emotional state experienced by an organism is determined by the difference in magnitude between a- and b-processes at any given moment $(a - b)$. If $a > b$, the result is an A-state, while if $a < b$, the result is a B-state.

These ideas are depicted in the first two panels of Figure 2–7. Panel A of the figure displays the a- and b-processes that occur during the first few exposures to a stimulus. The b-process begins and ends slightly after the a-process, which begins with the onset of the stimulus and ends with

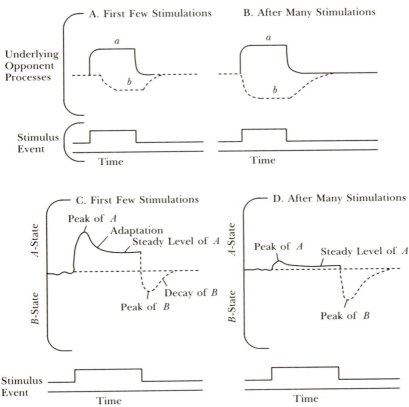

FIGURE 2–7. *Opponent Process Theory.* Panels A and B depict *a*- and *b*-processes. The *a*-process begins with the onset of the stimulus and ends with its offset. The *b*-process begins some time after the stimulus begins and ends some time after it ends. More important, the *b*-process becomes increasingly pronounced with repeated stimulus presentations, as can be seen by comparing Panels A and B. Panels C and D present *A*- and *B*-states that result from the interaction of *a*- and *b*-processes. Comparison of Panels C and D shows that as repeated stimulation increases the *b*-process, this results in a substantial decrease in the *A*-state. (After Solomon, 1980.)

its offset. Panel B depicts the *a*- and *b*-processes after many stimulations. The *a*-process is unchanged, but the *b*-process now begins earlier, lasts longer, and is stronger than it was before. The net result of these two underlying processes ($a - b$) is shown in the second two panels of Figure 2–7, early in exposure in Panel C and after substantial exposure in Panel D. Each point on these curves is obtained by subtracting *b*-process from *a*-process in Figures 2–7A and B. In Figure 2–7C, the *A*-state has a peak at the onset of the stimulus, because the *b*-process is delayed. The beginning of *b*-process reduces the *A*-state (labeled *adaptation* in the figure).

When the stimulus goes off, only b-process remains, with the result that the organism is now in a B-state. Repeated stimulation changes the b-process, with the result displayed in Panel D. Now the organism experiences virtually no A-state and a prolonged, substantial B-state.

Let us consider a concrete example of the opponent process theory in action. Suppose the stimulus being presented repeatedly is shock, and the response being measured is heart-rate change. We would expect that with the first few stimulations there would be an immediate increase in heart rate (A-state) which lasted until the shock went off. This would be followed by a brief decrease in heart rate, below base level (B-state), after which heart rate would return to normal. Now consider what heart rate would look like after many shocks. As Figure 2–7D indicates, there would be a very small A-state, because of the growth of the b-process. What this means is that we would detect only a small increase in heart rate to the shock. This would be followed by a substantial decrease in heart rate (B-state) when the shock ended. This is precisely the pattern of heart-rate change to shock that has been observed experimentally (see Solomon, 1980).

The opponent process theory fits well with our discussion of conditioned responses to morphine injection. An unconditioned response to morphine is analgesia (decreased pain sensitivity). The conditioned response to the injection itself is hyperalgesia (increased pain sensitivity). According to opponent process theory, analgesia is a-process and hyperalgesia is b-process. The b-process grows with repeated morphine injections. When water is injected during a test trial, the a-process does not occur because it is dependent on the administration of morphine. But the b-process does, because it is conditioned to the injection itself. The occurrence of b-process without a-process results in B-state—hyperalgesia (see Eikelboom & Stewart, 1982, and Baker & Tiffany, 1985, for critical discussions of opponent process theory, especially as applied to conditioning).

HABITUATION AND CONDITIONED OPPONENT RESPONSES

Opponent process theory can help us understand another conditioning phenomenon that is pervasive and important. It can be illustrated with this example. When one of us first moved into a house less than two blocks from a commuter rail line, he thought he would never again have a good night's sleep as the chugging and whistling of the train jolted him awake every hour or so. Within a week or two, the train's noises went virtually unnoticed. This getting used to regular and repeated stimulation so that one stops responding to it is known as **habituation**.

Habituation is a process that is so commonplace we hardly notice it. As we drive the same route to work every day, we stop noticing irrelevant (and sometimes even relevant) sights and sounds along the route. When we play peekaboo games with young infants, our first few efforts trigger screams of delight (or fear), but after a while, the infants stop responding. At first our pet dog sits up alertly, cocks its ears, and perhaps barks at the sounds of the mail carrier coming up the walk, but soon these sounds become familiar and our dog shows no interest. Familiarity breeds not contempt, but indifference. As stimuli become familiar, they continue to register in the relevant sensory systems, but organisms seem to stop paying attention to them and responding to them.

The phenomenon of habituation has long been recognized by students of learning, and research on the neural mechanisms involved in habituation may well provide crucial insights into how the nervous system functions, and especially how it is changed by experience (Baker & Tiffany, 1985; Groves & Thompson, 1970; Kandel, 1976, 1979; Peeke & Petrinovich, 1984; Thompson & Spencer, 1966). However, until recently, despite its importance, habituation has been relegated to a rather dusty and neglected corner of the discipline. The reason for this is that it was not regarded as "real" learning. First, it wasn't quite real learning because it wasn't permanent. If your dog, or the infant, or you experience some period of time without exposure to the stimuli in question, the habituation is undone. After a few weeks' vacation, for example, the commuter train noises become disruptive again for a while. Second, it wasn't quite real learning because it was thought that learning involves the putting together, or association, of different stimuli and events, CSs and USs or responses and reinforcers. Habituation seems to involve only repeated experience with a single stimulus, and not association between it and something else.

This is no longer true. It is now understood that habituation can sometimes be extremely long lasting, and that it is often associative in nature (Hinson, 1982; Randich, 1981; Randich & LoLordo, 1979; Wagner, 1976, 1979, 1981; Wagner & Larew, 1985; Whitlow & Wagner, 1984). The development of opponent process theory and the finding that CRs are often the opposite of the URs they accompany have contributed to this new attention to habituation as a learning process.

Think about how opponent process theory relates to habituation. We have already discussed drug tolerance as an opponent process phenomenon. Drug tolerance is just an example of habituation, with repeated presentations of a constant stimulus (a drug) having ever smaller effects. According to opponent process theory, tolerance, and habituation generally, are the result of the buildup of an opponent, b-process that cancels out more and more of the a-process that goes along with it. Now add to this account the evidence that the opponent response is often conditioned to particular environmental stimuli that precede the US and you have a conditioning account of habituation. Habituation occurs because conditioned responses develop that oppose and cancel out the unconditioned ones.

An experimental example that confirms this associative account of habituation concerns a phenomenon known as the **US preexposure effect**. This effect is as follows: Suppose you are doing an experiment in which a tone is going to be followed by shock. Before exposing the animal to pairings of tone and shock, you expose it to several presentations (US preexposures) of the shock by itself. Now, you do the tone–shock presentations. The result of these preexposures to shock is that they *reduce* the amount of conditioning that develops to the tone. Why? Well, you might imagine that a weak US will produce less conditioning than a strong one (which is generally true). Preexposure to the shock produces habituation, and thus effectively weakens it. Preexposure therefore produces less conditioning because it is essentially equivalent to using less intense shock during conditioning trials (see Randich & LoLordo, 1979).

Now where does association come in? What is the CS with which the preexposed shock is associated? The answer is that the preexposed shock becomes associated with the experimental environment or **context**. If shock preexposure occurs in one type of environment, and tone–shock conditioning occurs in a different environment, the US preexposure effect does not occur. Habituating opponent responses are conditioned to the environment in which US preexposure occurred. Therefore, they do not occur in the tone–shock conditioning environment, and the shock that occurs in that environment is effectively just as strong as if the animal had never experienced it before (Hinson, 1982).

It is most unlikely that all examples of habituation involve conditioned opponent responses, and a great deal of attention is currently being directed at determining what the different types of habituation may be and which types occur under which circumstances. However, it is clear that associative learning plays a significant role in at least some habituation phenomena, and this insight has probably gotten habituation out of its dusty, neglected corner for the foreseeable future.

ASSOCIATION: THE PROCESS UNIFYING DIVERSE CRS

We have seen that the form that conditioned responding takes can vary from one situation to the next, and is influenced by a wide range of factors. Does this mean that the business of Pavlovian conditioning research should be a cataloging of which CSs and USs produce which CRs under which circumstances? The answer is no. For the most part, researchers on conditioning are not interested in mapping the diversity of Pavlovian CRs. They are interested instead in discovering common principles that underlie all these varied examples. What are these common principles? What is it that all particular manifestations of Pavlovian conditioning have in common? The answer to this question is that every instance of Pavlovian conditioning, no matter what the form of the CR, reflects the development of an **association** between the CS and some aspect of the US. And it is the discovery of the laws that describe the development of these associations, no matter how they may be manifested in behavior, that is the real concern of researchers in Pavlovian conditioning. If the principles of association are the same from one situation to the next, Pavlovian laws will be powerful and general, even if these associations are reflected in different ways across different situations. Another way of stating this point is that the rules by which organisms learn the relations between CSs and USs may be general, even if the rules governing performance of CRs reflect that learning may be situation-specific.

What Is Learned in Conditioning

When an animal experiences Pavlovian conditioning trials, what does it learn? How is it changed? We can identify a number of possibilities—two of which are diagrammed in Figure 2–8. In Figure 2–8A, a broken line (representing learning) connects the CS with the UR. According to this view, the conditioning subject learns to associate the CS with the response, that is, the tone with salivation. Figure 2–8B depicts a learned association between the CS and the US, that is, between the tone and food. The question, in short, is whether the subject learns a stimulus–response (S–R) association as in 2–8A, or a stimulus–stimulus (S–S) association as in 2–8B.

Researchers have attempted to answer this question for years with equivocal results (see Mackintosh, 1974, pp. 85–97; Rescorla, 1980a). One can find evidence supporting both S–R and S–S views of the conditioning process. Thus we cannot resolve the issue. What we can do is present some of the evidence that has accumulated in support of each view.

Consider the following experiment. A dog receives a large number of trials in which a buzzer is paired with a light. No USs are presented. After this initial training the light is paired with food, which produces salivation. After a number of trials the light comes to elicit anticipatory salivation. Now the buzzer is sounded. Does the buzzer alone elicit salivation? What might we expect on the basis of the two hypothetical learning

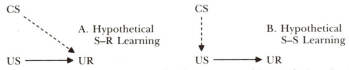

FIGURE 2–8. *Two Theoretical Models of What Is Learned in Pavlovian Conditioning Experiments.* The broken lines indicate hypothetical learned associations between CS and UR in A, and between CS and US in B.

processes depicted in Figure 2–8? If conditioning involves S–R association (Figure 2–8A), then the buzzer should not produce salivation. When the buzzer was being paired with the light, salivation was not occurring. If, on the other hand, conditioning involves S–S association, the buzzer might well elicit salivation, for the S–S association between buzzer and light could have been formed before food was introduced into the experiment. The results of the experiment are clear. The buzzer does elicit salivation (Brogden, 1939; Prewitt, 1967; Rescorla, 1980b; Rizley & Rescorla, 1972). This phenomenon is known as **sensory preconditioning** to highlight the fact that sensory conditioning (between two CSs like buzzer and light) occurs prior to any conditioning of either CS with a US. The sensory preconditioning procedure is diagrammed in Figure 2–9A.

This result might seem to resolve the issue of what the animal learns in a conditioning experiment. The matter is complicated, however, by results of experiments employing procedures like the one depicted in Figure 2–9B. This is a diagram of a **second-order conditioning** proce-

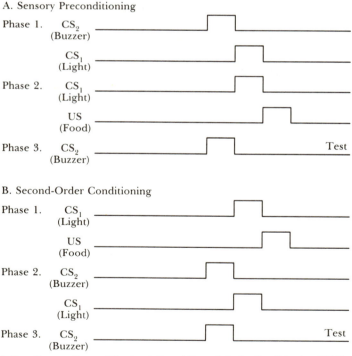

FIGURE 2–9. *Sensory Preconditioning (A) and Second-Order Conditioning (B) Procedures.* The procedures differ only in that the order of Phases 1 and 2 is reversed. That is, in sensory preconditioning pairing of CS_2 and CS_1 precedes pairing of CS_1 and US, while in second-order conditioning pairing of CS_2 and CS_1 follows pairing of CS_1 and US.

dure. A CS (CS_1) is paired with a US. Then a new CS (CS_2) is paired with CS_1 and we look for conditioned responses to CS_2. Sensory preconditioning and second-order conditioning procedures are nearly identical. They differ only in that in sensory preconditioning pairing of CS_2 and CS_1 precedes pairing of CS_1 and US, while in second-order conditioning pairing of CS_2 and CS_1 follows pairing of CS_1 and US.

Suppose one did a second-order conditioning experiment pairing CS_1 with food until CS_1 produced anticipatory salivation and then pairing CS_2 with CS_1 until CS_2 also produced salivation. Then suppose one paired CS_1 with shock until CS_1 elicited leg withdrawal. Now when CS_2 was presented alone, would the animal salivate or withdraw its leg? Let us go back to Figure 2–8 and see what the two models of conditioning we outlined would lead us to expect. The S–R model (Figure 2–8A) suggests the view that when CS_2 and CS_1 are paired, the animal learns an association between CS_2 and salivation, not between CS_2 and CS_1. Thus when CS_2 is presented, the animal should salivate. On the other hand, the S–S model (Figure 2–8B) suggests that CS_2 is associated with CS_1. If CS_1 is now associated with shock and not food, the animal should withdraw its leg when CS_2 is presented. What the animal does is salivate (Konorski, 1948). An outline of the experimental procedure and the results one would expect on the basis of the two models in Figure 2–8 are presented in Figure 2–10.

These results might lead one to conclude that sensory preconditioning results in S–S associations while second-order conditioning results in S–R associations, but this is not the case. There are now a number of demonstrations that second-order conditioning can produce S–S associations. We will discuss just one.

Pigeons were initially exposed to trials in which a response key was lit briefly and followed by the delivery of food. As diagrammed in Figure 2–11, sometimes the key was red and sometimes it was yellow. The pigeons came to make conditioned responses to both key colors. The CRs were pecks at the lit keys (see Figure 2–5, p. 50). Then second-order conditioning was begun. One group of pigeons had two kinds of second-order conditioning trials: key illumination with a vertical line (CS_2) followed by red (CS_1), or key illumination with a horizontal line (CS_2) followed by yellow (CS_1). The second group of pigeons received four types of second-order conditioning trials: vertical followed by red, vertical followed by yellow, horizontal followed by red, and horizontal followed by yellow.

Would we expect the groups to differ in the rate at which they learned to peck the second-order CSs? That depends on what we think they are learning. Suppose they are learning S–S associations. Then Group 1, with consistent pairings, should learn faster than Group 2. Group 1 must make only two associations while Group 2 must make four. But suppose, on the other hand, they are learning S–R associations. Now we might expect no difference between the groups. Since red and yellow both produce peck-

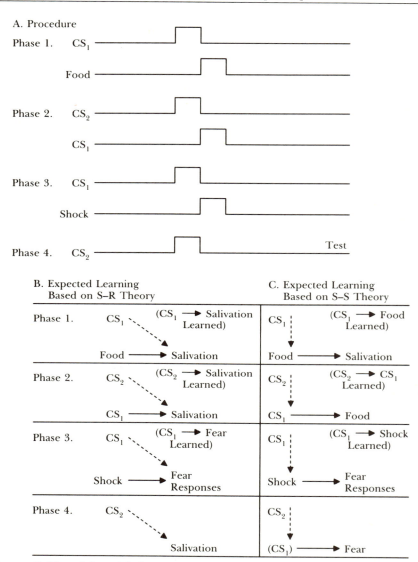

FIGURE 2–10. *A Second-Order Conditioning Experiment and Expected Results Based on S–R and S–S Theories.* Part A depicts a second-order conditioning procedure. Part B depicts the learning that an S–R theory of conditioning would predict the procedure should produce. The subject learns a CS_2–salivation association so that changing the stimulus (US) paired with CS_1 does not change the response produced by CS_2. Part C depicts the learning that an S–S theory of conditioning would predict the procedure should produce. The subject learns a CS_2–CS_1 association so that changing the US from food to shock (Phase 1 vs. Phase 3 of Part A) will change the response produced by CS_2 from salivation to fear.

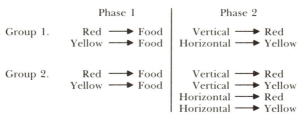

	Phase 1	Phase 2
Group 1.	Red ⟶ Food	Vertical ⟶ Red
	Yellow ⟶ Food	Horizontal ⟶ Yellow
Group 2.	Red ⟶ Food	Vertical ⟶ Red
	Yellow ⟶ Food	Vertical ⟶ Yellow
		Horizontal ⟶ Red
		Horizontal ⟶ Yellow

FIGURE 2–11. *A Second-Order Conditioning Test of What Is Learned in Conditioning.* Group 1 received consistent CS_2–CS_1 pairings while Group 2 received inconsistent pairings. Group 1 learned faster than Group 2, suggesting that both groups had made S–S associations. (After Rescorla, 1979a.)

ing, whether horizontal and vertical are paired with red or yellow will not matter; in either case they will be paired with pecking. In fact, Group 1 learned faster than Group 2, suggesting that they had learned S–S associations (Rescorla, 1979a).

MANIPULATING REPRESENTATIONS

There is another line of research that supports the view that Pavlovian conditioning often involves the formation of associations between CSs and USs. Actually, to be more precise, what this research suggests is that associations are formed between CSs and **internal representations** of USs. It has now been shown that representations of CS–US associations are formed even in the absence of any overt behavior that reflects the associations. Further, it is possible to alter already established CRs with procedures that change the animal's representations of the US without affecting the CR itself directly.

As an example of the first type of finding, if pigeons experience tone–food pairings, they show little or no evidence of conditioning to the tone. They do not approach and peck at the sound source the way they peck at a key light CS in autoshaping experiments (see Figure 2–5). If one observed pigeons receiving tone–food pairings, one would probably conclude that no association had been formed, because one would observe no changes in the pigeons' behavior over trials while the tone was on. Yet if we take pigeons that have had tone–food pairings and expose them to second-order conditioning trials of key light followed by tone, they start pecking the key. That is, the tone can be used as a US to produce Pavlovian key pecking (see Rescorla, 1980a). What this result indicates is that during tone–food pairings pigeons do indeed form an association, so that the tone evokes a representation of food. When the key light is then paired with the tone, it is paired with the representation of food evoked by the tone. Conditioned key pecking is the result, even though key light and food have never themselves been paired.

As an example of the second type of finding, animals might first be given pairings of a CS and food or of a CS and an aversive loud noise, until clear evidence of conditioning is obtained. Next, with the CS absent, an attempt is made to **devalue** the US. In the case of the loud noise it might be presented repeatedly until the animal habituates to it. In the case of food it might be presented while the animal is satiated. After these attempts to devalue the US, the CS is again presented in a test trial. The finding is that as a result of US devaluation, the CS produces much less responding (Bouton, 1984; Holland & Rescorla, 1975; Holland & Straub, 1979; Rescorla, 1973, 1974; Rescorla & Holland, 1977).

We can explain this finding in the following way: Conditioning involves an association of representations of the CS and the US. Initially the US is represented as powerful and potent, so that strong conditioned responding occurs. Then the US is devalued, and a new representation of a less potent US is formed. When the CS is now presented, it activates this less potent representation. The result is less conditioned responding.

It is difficult to see how we could make sense of either of the above types of results without appealing to representational processes that mediate between environmental inputs and behavior. Moreover, these results also tell us about what kind of representation is most likely being formed. It is a representation that tells the animal what goes with what (a stimulus–stimulus representation), and not one that tells it what to do (a stimulus–response representation).

What does all this evidence tell us about the question with which we began this section? Does Pavlovian conditioning involve S–S or S–R associations? The best answer at present seems to be that organisms may learn both types of associations. The processes of association formation of which organisms are capable are a good deal more varied and flexible than Pavlov might have imagined.

Variables Affecting Pavlovian Conditioning

We have now discussed how Pavlovian conditioning is measured and the nature of the conditioned response, and we have explored research on what is learned in Pavlovian conditioning. We turn next to considering some of the variables that influence the course of conditioning.

THE CS AND THE US

The CSs and USs one chooses to use in an experiment have a major impact on conditioning. We have already seen that both of them influence the form that the CR takes. But they have other influences as well.

Some USs produce faster conditioning than others. For example, one might achieve asymptotic levels of conditioning with a shock to the feet as a US in 10 or so trials, while with a puff of air to the eye it might take 100 trials or more to reach an asymptote. In addition, different USs will produce different asymptotic levels of conditioning. Using conditioned suppression as a measure of conditioning, a strong shock might produce an asymptotic suppression ratio of close to zero while a weaker shock might produce an asymptote at 0.20.

Conditioned stimuli also affect the rate of conditioning. The more salient or noticeable a CS is, the faster the animal learns the CS–US association. Salience is itself influenced by a variety of factors. First, if we compare stimuli of the same general type, more intense stimuli are more salient than less intense ones; a loud tone is more noticeable than a soft one. Second, if we compare between types, organisms will be more attentive to stimuli affecting certain sense modalities rather than others. People, for example, tend to notice visual stimuli more than auditory ones. The same is true of pigeons, while the reverse is true of rats.

These two influences on CS salience suggest that for any given species we could establish a hierarchy of salience that would be constant no matter what context we studied the CSs in, and no matter what past experiences the organism has had with them. However, both of these suggestions are false. As it turns out, the salience of any given CS is affected by what kind of US it is being paired with. In addition, the salience of a stimulus may grow or diminish as a function of an organism's experience with it. We discuss these influences on CS salience elsewhere in this chapter, and in the next.

While it is easy to determine that the CS and US one uses affect the course of conditioning, it is not as easy to determine what the nature of the effect is. To see the complication, let us break the conditioning process down into two logically distinct components:

1. CS–US pairing ——— Formation of association

2. Association formation ——— Triggering of CRs

We assume that in Pavlovian conditioning CS–US pairings lead to the formation of an association between them, or between the CS and the UR, which in turn leads to the occurrence of CRs. In actual experiments it is the occurrence of CRs that tells us that an association has been formed. We take measures of the CR as a straightforward reflection of properties of the association that underlies its occurrence. But this may be a mistake. Suppose there are two different sets of rules involved in determining the occurrence of Pavlovian CRs. One set of rules governs association formation while the other governs performance of responses. CS and US choice could affect conditioning by affecting either or both of these sets of rules. For example, we know that different USs produce different CRs. Suppose that whether we use shock or food as a US has no bearing at all on the formation of a CS–US association. Its effect is on the association–CR relation. With shock we begin to see CRs as soon as the CS–US association begins to form, while with food we do not see CRs until the CS–US association is relatively strong. These assumptions are depicted in Figure 2–12. If we simply did a comparison of CS–shock and CS–food procedures by measuring conditioned responses, we would get the impression that shock produces faster learning than food. But in fact, as shown in Figure 2–12, the growth of association would be the same in both cases; the real difference would be in the relation between association formation and the occurrence of the CR.

The distinction we are making is sometimes referred to as a learning–performance distinction. Association formation represents learning and CR occurrence represents performance. It might more accurately be described as an *association learning/response learning* distinction. The critical point is that however we characterize the difference, it is clear that there is one, at least in principle. And when we see differences in rate of CR development, we cannot be sure whether such differences reflect differences in association or differences in CR learning, or both (see Wasserman, 1981).

This problem we have raised is present in all conditioning experiments. We can never see associations directly; we can only see the behavior presumed to reflect them. We make inferences about associations based

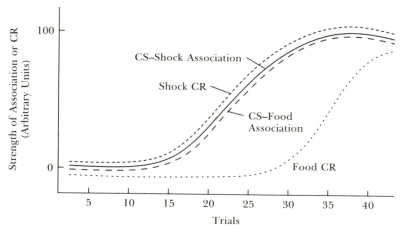

FIGURE 2–12. *Growth of Association vs. Growth of CR.* The separate hypothetical curves showing the growth of CS–shock and CS–food associations over trials and the growth of shock and food CRS over trials are shown. The pattern of data in this figure would mean that association formation is identical whether food or shock is the US, but the association–CR relation is different in the two cases. Thus by Trial 25 CS–shock and CS–food associations are equally strong, but shock CRs are occurring reliably while food CRs are not.

on the behavior. But determining the appropriate inference to make will always be problematic. We could largely solve the problem if all CSs and USs produced the same CRs. Then we could be confident that the differences in behavior we saw in various experiments reflected differences in underlying associations, since the association–CR relation would be constant across experiments. But as we have seen, CRs vary widely depending on the CS and the US being used, so that the uncertainty depicted in Figure 2–12 is always with us.

TEMPORAL RELATIONS BETWEEN CS AND US

Standard Pairing A variable that has a profound influence on the course of conditioning involves not the CS or the US independently, but the temporal relation between them. Indeed, in the beginnings of research on conditioning Pavlov focused much of his attention on how the arrangement of the CS and US in time affected the course of conditioning. No doubt he was influenced by the associationist philosophers, who gave temporal contiguity special prominence in their discussions of the association of ideas. Let us investigate, then, how conditioning is affected by the temporal relations between CS and US.

Figure 2–13 depicts a variety of common arrangements of CS and US. The upward deflections of the lines indicate the times when the CS or US is present. The type of procedure we have essentially assumed in our discussion thus far is diagrammed in Figure 2–13A. It is labeled **standard pairing**, and it is characterized by a fairly short interval between the CS (which comes first) and the US. In the diagram the CS–US interval (which is measured from the onset of the CS to the onset of the US) is 2 seconds.

Delay Conditioning What happens if the CS–US interval is quite long? This type of procedure is depicted in Figure 2–13B. The procedure is called **delay conditioning**. Conditioned responses can be produced with the delay procedure just as with the standard-pairing procedure. What is interesting about the delay procedure is the temporal pattern of conditioned responses. Early in training, when CRs first begin to occur, they tend to start at the beginning of the CS and continue right through the onset of the US. However, late in training, when the animal is experienced, the temporal pattern of CRs changes. Now when the CS comes on, there are no CRs. Conditioned responses begin to occur about midway through the CS, and from that point increase in frequency until the end of the trial. It seems as though the CS has become two CSs—CS(early) and CS(late). The animal seems to learn that the US is not going to come when the CS first comes on, with the absence of CRs a result of this learning.

Simultaneous Conditioning Figure 2–13C represents a procedure that is not commonly used in Pavlovian conditioning experiments—simultaneous conditioning. Here, both onset and offset of CS and US are coinci-

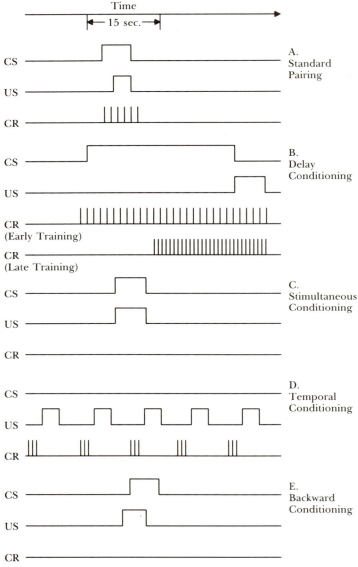

FIGURE 2–13. *Schematic Drawing of Some Pavlovian Conditioning Procedures.* The bottom line of each drawing indicates the pattern of conditioned responding typically observed with the procedures.

dent. The reason this procedure is not often studied is that it typically does not produce conditioning. This seems a bit peculiar. Here, the temporal contiguity of CS and US is perfect, and since temporal contiguity seems an important determinant of conditioning, this procedure ought to succeed. Why doesn't it? The answer is a phenomenon known as **overshadowing**. Overshadowing refers to the fact that if two stimuli are presented together as a compound CS, one may completely dominate or overshadow the other even though both would be perfectly effective if presented separately. For example, suppose we present a tone and a light followed by food for many trials, until the compound is reliably producing CRs. If we then present the tone and the light separately on test trials, it may turn out that only one of them produces CRs.

Overshadowing occurs because one stimulus is more salient than another, and thus dominates it. Even though both stimuli are present, the organism pays attention to only one of them. The phenomenon of overshadowing may explain the failure of simultaneous conditioning in that if CS and US, say, light and shock, are presented together, the shock may so dominate or overshadow the light that the light is not even noticed. By presenting the light even a fraction of a second before the shock, one can ensure that it will be noticed and that conditioning will occur.

Consistent with this idea, there is now good evidence that simultaneous conditioning *does* occur in sensory preconditioning and second-order conditioning experiments. Indeed, in sensory preconditioning, simultaneous presentation of two stimuli seems more likely to produce an association than successive presentation. What sensory preconditioning and second-order conditioning have in common is that the two stimuli that become associated are neutral stimuli, like lights and tones, not USs like shock. Thus overshadowing is less likely to occur (Rescorla, 1980b, 1982).

Temporal Conditioning Figure 2–13D presents a conditioning procedure in which there are no CSs. Instead the US is presented repeatedly, with a constant time interval between US presentations. After a while animals come to make CRs just before each occurrence of the US. As in the case of delay conditioning, animals seem able to discriminate the passage of time. And it is the passage of a fixed amount of time after the last US that serves as a CS for the next US. This type of procedure is appropriately referred to as **temporal conditioning**.

Backward Conditioning Finally, Figure 2–13E depicts a procedure that is just like the standard-pairing procedure, with one important exception— the CS comes *after* the US. The procedure is appropriately called **backward conditioning**. Like simultaneous conditioning procedures, backward conditioning procedures typically fail to produce conditioned responses. If a tone is sounded after food is delivered to a dog's mouth, the tone will not produce salivation. Again, this seems to pose a problem for the simple view that temporal contiguity is all that is needed for conditioning to occur. The temporal contiguity between CS and US is the same in Figures 2–13A and 2–13E. Yet one procedure is optimal and the other is a failure. Thus it seems that temporal contiguity is not enough—the CS must precede the US (but see Burkhardt & Ayres, 1978, and Shurtleff & Ayres, 1981, for some cases in which backward conditioning procedures *do* produce conditioning).

If we think for a moment about these various temporal relations between CS and US and their effects on conditioning, we can see that it makes good sense for conditioning to be sensitive to temporal variables. Imagine driving on a country road that twists and turns around a mountain. Many of these twists and turns require you to reduce your driving speed substantially. Various road signs saying DANGEROUS CURVE are situated to warn you of these impending curves. Think of the curves as analogous to USs, the signs as analogous to CSs, and stepping on the brake as analogous to a CR. Now consider what you would do if the relations between the signs and the curves were like those depicted in Figure 2–13. A situation analogous to Figure 2–13A would have signs posted, say, 0.1 mile before curves. You would learn to apply the brakes as soon as you saw the sign. But suppose the signs appeared 2 miles before the curves. This would be analogous to Figure 2–13B, and you would quickly learn not to brake until you had traveled a substantial distance past the sign. If there were no signs, but curves appeared at regular intervals (Figure 2–13D), you would learn to apply the brake in anticipation of each curve. But now suppose the sign appeared at the curve (Figure 2–13C), or just beyond it (Figure 2–13E). If under these conditions you lived long enough to learn anything at all, it would surely be that you cannot count on signs. Whether or not you applied the brakes would not be controlled by the appearance of these signs.

What this analogy points out is the adaptive significance of Pavlovian conditioning. By associating CSs with USs, organisms come to identify warnings for impending significant events. Responding to these warnings allows them to prepare in some way for the US to come. If the CS does not allow them to prepare because of its temporal relation to the US, as in simultaneous and backward conditioning, conditioning usually does not occur.

QUALITATIVE RELATIONS BETWEEN CS AND US

While associationist philosophers focused on temporal contiguity as a key determinant of association, they did not ignore others. One of these others was the qualitative relation between the ideas to be associated. The more similar two ideas were, for example, the more easily they became associated. For many years the experimental study of association via Pavlovian conditioning virtually ignored qualitative relations between CS and US. But all of this changed as a result of a landmark experiment published in 1966. This experiment, by Garcia and Koelling, was an early and dramatic demonstration of constraints on learning of the sort mentioned in Chapter 1 (p. 29). It involved the phenomenon of taste aversion learning.

Rats were exposed to a procedure in which whenever they licked at a tube containing a flavored solution, the lick produced both a click and a light flash. Thus at the same instant the rats experienced a taste, a light, and a noise. Some of the rats were subsequently poisoned; other rats received shock to the feet. After a number of such trials, the drinking of the rats was evaluated with a procedure in which the light and noise were separated from the taste. On one day licks at a tube produced the flavored solution, but no light or noise, while on the next day licks at a tube produced light and noise, but tap water instead of the flavored solution.

The results of this experiment are presented in Figure 2–14. The number of licks at the tube per minute is presented for both pretests with audiovisual and taste cues separated and posttests (after conditioning) with audiovisual and taste cues separated. The top part of Figure 2–14

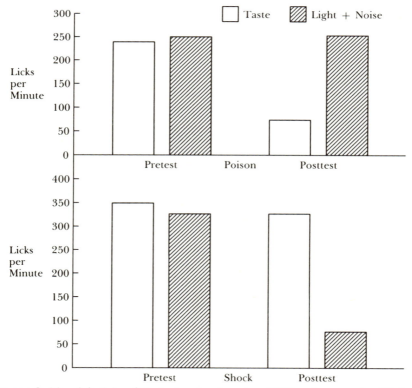

FIGURE 2–14. *Selectivity of Taste Aversion Learning.* With poison as the US (top part), rats associate the poison with taste and not with light or noise. With shock as the US (bottom part), the reverse is true. (After Garcia & Koelling, 1966.)

presents data from rats that experienced poison as a US; the bottom part presents data from rats that experienced shock. It is clear that with poison as a US, taste dominated noise and light as a CS. The rats showed no change in drinking from the "bright, noisy" water between pre- and posttests and a substantial decrease in drinking from the flavored water. On the other hand, with shock as the US exactly the reverse was true. There was no decrease at all in drinking the flavored water and a substantial decrease in drinking the "bright, noisy" water (Garcia & Koelling, 1966; see also Domjan & Wilson, 1972, and Wilcoxin, Dragoin, & Kral, 1971). We must conclude that taste aversion learning reflects neither the power of taste as a CS nor the power of poison as a US, but the power of the two in combination. When the combination is broken (as when shock is the US), we find little conditioning to the taste. Thus the phenomenon of taste aversion learning seems to depend on a special relation that exists between tastes and illness. They seem to "belong" together.

The phenomenon of taste aversion learning is special. Taste and poison seem to go together. Taste and pain to the feet do not, nor for that matter do audiovisual stimuli and stomach illness. This should strike an intuitive chord. If after eating a fine dinner out, you go home and get sick to your stomach, it is likely that you will associate the illness with something you ate. You will not associate illness with the color of the wallpaper in the restaurant, with the music played by the violinist, with the floral pattern on the china you ate from, with the people who accompanied you, or with the ride home. Each of these other stimuli bears the same temporal relation to your illness as does the food. Yet surely it will be the food, and not any of the other cues, that you will subsequently avoid. Indeed, studies of taste aversion learning with humans have obtained the same evidence of selectivity of association as have studies with rats (see Bernstein, 1978; Bernstein & Webster, 1980; Cannon, Best, Batson, & Feldman, 1983; Garb & Stunkard, 1974; Lamon, Wilson, & Leaf, 1977; Logue, 1985; Logue, Ophir, & Strauss, 1981; Pelchat & Rozin, 1982; Seawright, Kaiser, Dame, & Lofgren, 1978). As it turns out, what the rat learns from the taste aversion experiment is similar to what you might learn from the restaurant. The rat seems biased to behave as if "it must have been something I ate" (but see Best, Best, & Henggeler, 1977, and Krane & Wagner, 1975, for some counterexamples).

That taste aversion learning exemplifies selectivity of association between CS and US, or what is sometimes called **associative bias**, is not the only thing that makes it unusual. It is also unusual in that powerful taste–illness associations can be formed in a single trial. Furthermore, associations can be formed even if the interval between the CS and the US is as long as 24 hours. This is rather a far cry from the temporal relations depicted in Figure 2–13. Finally, the selectivity of associability between taste and illness is not the result of organisms' past experiences with the consequences of their meals. It has been shown in newborn rats that have had no feeding experience at all (Gemberling & Domjan, 1982;

for extensive discussion of taste aversion see Baker, Best, & Domjan, 1977; Domjan, 1981, 1983; Logue, 1979; Revusky & Garcia, 1970; Rozin, 1976; Rozin & Kalat, 1971).

While taste aversion learning has generated an enormous amount of research interest, it is not the only instance of conditioning in which qualitative relations between CS and US are important. The phenomenon of taste aversion has given rise to several attempts to locate other, similar examples, and many other examples have indeed been located. In one such investigation the CS was a light and the US was an aversive blast of air. For different groups the exact nature of the CS and US was varied, in location and in temporal character. Thus the light and the air blast came either from the floor of the conditioning chamber or from the ceiling. Also, either they came on and stayed on for a fixed period of time or they pulsed on and off. For two groups the CS and US were the same in both location and temporal character. They were either both on the floor and constant or both on the ceiling and pulsed. These two groups learned faster than other groups, for which the CS and US differed in either location or temporal character or both. In all groups the temporal relation between CS and US was the same. Thus differences in conditioning had to do with differences in CS–US similarity rather than with differences in temporal contiguity (Testa, 1975).

Subsequent investigations of the importance of qualitative relations of CS and US have taken advantage of the second-order conditioning phenomenon. Recall that second-order conditioning involves first pairing CS_1 with a US, then pairing CS_2 with CS_1. Since CS_1 and CS_2 can be any stimuli at all, using this technique frees researchers from the constraints on investigations of similarity that having to use a US imposes. One can investigate various aspects of similarity by varying the properties of CS_2 and CS_1. Strong evidence that similarity hastens second-order conditioning has been obtained in experiments of this type. For example, associations between two colors or two line orientations are learned faster than color–line orientation associations. Stimuli that appear in the same spatial location are associated faster than stimuli in different spatial locations. Stimuli that impinge on the same sense are associated faster than stimuli that impinge on different senses. In sum, it seems that no matter what aspect or feature of stimuli one assesses to evaluate their similarity, the more alike they are in that feature the faster an association is formed (see Rescorla, 1980a; Rescorla & Furrow, 1977; Rescorla & Gillan, 1980; Testa, 1974, 1975). Stimulus similarity has a potent influence on Pavlovian conditioning.

And physical similarity is not the only qualitative relation between CS and US that makes a difference. As in the case of taste aversion learning, it seems to be common for certain types of CSs and USs to belong together even if they are not physically similar to each other.

In one Pavlovian conditioning study, pigeons received a CS of a red light and a tone. For some of the pigeons the US was food and for others it was electric shock. After the pigeons in each group had come to make reliable CRs to the compound CS, the red light and the tone were occasionally presented separately. The pigeons that were receiving food as the US responded much more to the light than to the tone. The reverse was true for the pigeons receiving shock as the US. Thus which element of the tone–light compound dominated the association depended on the nature of the US (LoLordo, 1979; see also Foree & LoLordo, 1975; Jacobs & LoLordo, 1980; Shapiro, Jacobs, & LoLordo, 1980; Shapiro & LoLordo, 1982; Shettleworth, 1972b).

We can make sense of these results if we think about the types of stimuli that usually signal food or danger to birds in nature. Birds typically identify food by its visual properties. Often the presence of a predator is accompanied by alarm calls from conspecifics. Thus the bias to associate visual cues with food and auditory ones with danger in the laboratory corresponds nicely to the types of cues these animals typically rely on outside the laboratory (see Rozin & Kalat, 1971; Schwartz, 1974; Seligman, 1970; Seligman & Hager, 1972; Shettleworth, 1972a).

Why should this be so? Does it do any good to be sensitive to qualitative relations between CSs and USs in forming associations? Does this sensitivity somehow allow an organism to function more effectively in its environment? It has been suggested that there is functional value in being attuned to qualitative relations like stimulus similarity. Suppose we think of Pavlovian conditioning not as the formation of associations, but as the discovery of causes and effects. Causes precede effects as CSs precede USs, but causes have more to do with their effects than just temporal proximity. It would be extremely useful if organisms were somehow able to pick out cause–effect temporal relations from other, merely accidental temporal relations. And this sensitivity to similarity makes the detection of cause–effect relations easier. While it is not infallible, causes will often be similar to effects in spatial location, time course, sense modality, and so on. The rat that associates taste with poison or light and click with shock seems to be performing a causal analysis. Things we ingest make us sick and things from outside inflict pain to our feet. While both the idea that Pavlovian conditioning involves learning cause–effect relations and the idea that sensitivity to similarity facilitates the discovery of cause–effect relations are controversial, they are not implausible. They also suggest a conception of Pavlovian conditioning that makes it an even more significant contributor to learning in general than we had previously indicated.

Pavlovian Conditioning and Inhibition

Pair a tone with food and an animal will eventually salivate to the tone. Pair a light with shock and the animal will display fear to the light. Pair a click with a puff of air to the eye and the animal will blink when the click sounds. These are three very different Pavlovian conditioning phenomena. Yet they are all instances of the same general phenomenon—Pavlovian **excitatory conditioning**. Through pairing of CS and US, the CS comes to excite a CR. But what happens if, after excitatory conditioning has occurred, the subject receives presentations of the CS without the US, so that, for example, a tone that has been paired with food and elicited salivation is presented repeatedly to a dog without being followed by food? Behaviorally, it is easy to tell what happens; the dog stops salivating to the tone. This phenomenon of extinction is depicted in Figure 2–2. The question is: What does the animal learn during extinction? Does extinction involve the erasure of the conditioned reflex so that the animal that has undergone conditioning and extinction is more or less the same as an untrained animal, or does it involve something different? Pavlov thought that extinction involved the development of active **inhibition** of the conditioned response rather than simply the erasure of a CS–US connection.

What is inhibition? This seems like such an obvious question that one wonders why it needs to be asked. We use the word frequently in everyday language to describe a force within us that keeps us from doing certain things. Thus there are sexual inhibitions, inhibitions about performing in front of strangers, inhibitions about speaking one's mind, and so on. As a descriptive term in common use, "inhibition" seems straightforward enough. However, what could inhibition possibly mean as a property of a reflex? Recall our simple model of the reflex arc discussed in Chapter 1. A stimulus triggers a neural impulse that goes to some part of the brain. There it *excites* another neural impulse that in turn triggers the reflex. In short, a US excites a UR. Food excites salivation. How could a US inhibit a UR? If there is no connection between the US and the UR, the UR will not occur, but is that what we mean by inhibition? Do we wish to say that a puff of air to the eye inhibits salivation because salivation does not occur? Clearly not. Air puffs neither excite salivation nor inhibit it. They are simply independent of it. Inhibition refers to the active suppression of some behavior that would, under other circumstances, be expected to occur.

Using this model, Pavlov found that there existed both excitatory and inhibitory reflexes and that Pavlovian conditioning could produce both excitatory and inhibitory *conditioned* reflexes (see also Konorski, 1948, 1967). So let us turn to the study of inhibition in Pavlovian conditioning.

CONDITIONED INHIBITION OF BEHAVIOR

The study of conditioned inhibition poses methodological problems that are not present in the study of conditioned excitation. A sign of conditioned excitation is the presence of some response that was not present before conditioning. However, a sign of conditioned inhibition is the absence of a response we might otherwise expect to occur. But the mere absence of that response does not guarantee that conditioned inhibition is present. The response could be absent for a host of other reasons. A nonlaboratory example will help clarify this problem.

Imagine being at a large, boisterous, friendly party. Everyone seems to be having a good time. There is just one man sitting off by himself in a corner looking blank. How are we to account for the man's behavior? Two possibilities immediately present themselves. Perhaps the man is shy and lacks confidence. Although he is eager to meet some of the people at the party, he is too inhibited to get up and introduce himself. Therefore he sits alone, actively suppressing the urge to mingle. The second possibility is that he is bored—utterly uninterested. He is not suppressing anything because there is nothing to suppress. This, in capsule form, is the problem in ascertaining the presence of inhibition. Are we to explain the man's behavior in terms of inhibition or in terms of lack of excitation? Both accounts are consistent with his sitting by himself, and both accounts are consistent with the absence of salivation, fear, eyeblink, or any other CR when a CS is presented. How can we separate inhibition from lack of excitation?

DETECTING INHIBITION

There are a number of ways to detect inhibition, many of which were initially identified by Pavlov. All the procedural devices used in studying inhibition assume that excitation and inhibition interact. Thus the general strategy for detecting inhibition involves, first, establishing some excitation and, second, presenting the supposedly inhibitory stimulus. If the stimulus really is inhibitory, then its presence should reduce the amount of excitation one observes (see LoLordo & Fairless, 1985; Miller & Spear, 1985; Rescorla, 1969).

External Inhibition and Disinhibition Suppose a dog has been exposed to a procedure in which a light is paired with food. After a number of trials, the dog reliably salivates to the light. Now on one trial the light is presented and the dog begins to salivate. In the middle of the trial a tone, which has never been presented before, is sounded. Salivation stops. Pavlov called this phenomenon **external inhibition**. He interpreted it as an indication that a novel external stimulus can inhibit whatever neural processes are taking place in the cortex. If excitation of fear is taking place, the novel stimulus will inhibit fear.

But what if *inhibition* is taking place? Now, according to Pavlov, presentation of a novel stimulus will inhibit inhibition. But what does this mean? Well, suppose that salivation to a CS has been extinguished and that extinction produces inhibition. The CS is presented and the dog does not salivate. If a novel stimulus is now presented along with the CS, the dog will start to salivate. This inhibition of inhibition is called **disinhibition**. Pavlov saw it as a way to differentiate inhibition from a lack of excitation. If a dog is inhibiting salivation, then a novel stimulus will produce it. If, on the other hand, a dog is not salivating simply through lack of excitation, then a novel stimulus will have no effect on salivation (see Brimer, 1970, for a demonstration of disinhibition).

Stimulus Compound Tests Consider another example. Two dogs are exposed to a procedure in which a light is paired with shock until conditioned fear responses have been established. Prior to this conditioning one of the dogs has had experience with a tone. The tone was presented repeatedly until it was no longer novel, that is, no longer an external inhibitor. The other dog has also experienced the tone, but in a procedure designed to make it an inhibitor of fear. The task is to find out whether it actually is an inhibitor of fear. To do so, periodically, in the midst of their experience with light–shock pairings, we present the dogs with a compound of light and tone. If the tone has become a conditioned inhibitor of fear, then we would expect the second dog to show less sign of conditioned fear than the first dog to the light–tone compound. This test for conditioned inhibition is known as a **summation test**.

A variant of this compounding procedure involves taking two dogs and giving them the same experience with tones as before. For one dog it is a neutral stimulus and for the other it is (supposedly) a conditioned inhibitor. Now the dogs are exposed to *training* with light + tone paired with shock. If the tone has become a conditioned inhibitor, one would expect the second dog to take longer than the first to develop conditioned fear responses. This technique for detecting conditioned inhibition is known as a **resistance to reinforcement test**.

Direct Measures of Inhibition Though most of the time detecting inhibition requires looking for either a reduction in or a retarded development of excitation, there are a few situations in which evidence of inhibition is more direct. For example, in the autoshaping situation, in which a lit key precedes food and pigeons come to peck the key (see Figure 2–5), when a key light has been made inhibitory pigeons respond to its appearance by withdrawing from it. Thus, an excitatory key light produces approach while an inhibitory one produces withdrawal (Bottjer, 1982; Hearst & Franklin, 1977). Similarly, in the taste aversion learning procedure, in which tastes paired with poison are avoided, a taste that has been made inhibitory is actively approached and consumed (Batson & Best, 1981; Best, 1975).

Conditions Producing Inhibition

EXTINCTION

A dog has been exposed to pairings of tone and food until a strong CR to the tone has developed. How can the conditioned reflex be eliminated?

If the dog is simply removed from the experiment and not exposed to tone–food pairings for a year or so, and then placed back in the experimental situation, it will salivate profusely on the very first tone presentation. Thus conditioned reflexes are not easily forgotten. However, if the dog is simply exposed to presentations of the tone without food, conditioned salivation will gradually extinguish (see Figure 2–2). Just as CRs can be established by pairing CS and US, so they can be eliminated by presenting CS alone. The phenomenon of extinction is obviously a very important and useful feature of conditioning. It shows that organisms are responsive to changing environmental conditions. If this were not true, organisms would forever be at the mercy of whatever stimulus relations happened to be present in the environment during their early lives.

What happens during an extinction procedure? At the end of the procedure we are left with a subject that looks just like a naive subject. The CS is presented and no CR occurs. It is possible that extinction literally amounts to the unlearning or erasure of the previously conditioned response, and that a naive subject and one that has undergone conditioning followed by extinction will be undifferentiable.

Pavlov had a different view. He thought that extinction was not unlearning, but new learning. He thought that in extinction procedures the previously excitatory CS became inhibitory. By using one of the devices for detecting inhibition outlined above, one could presumably show that the naive subject and the one whose reflex had been extinguished were quite different.

Surprisingly, the evidence available makes it difficult to decide this issue. Experiments involving the compounding technique described above have found that the extinguished CS does not appear to have inhibitory properties (LoLordo & Rescorla, 1966). It seems to work like a neutral stimulus. On the other hand, Pavlov showed that if an extinguished CS, which previously elicited salivation, is presented along with a novel stimulus (external inhibition), disinhibition is the result and salivation reappears. The problem may be that extinction procedures do produce inhibition, but just enough to cancel out the previous excitation. The result of such a cancellation would be that an extinguished CS had neither residual excitation nor residual inhibition associated with it when it was used in a compounding experiment. Thus it would work just like a neutral stimulus in such experiments.

The plausibility of this account comes from another type of experiment. Suppose we pair a tone with shock, making the tone an excitor of fear. Then we extinguish the tone by presenting it without shock. Along with the tone we also present a light—a neutral stimulus. Now suppose that each tone presentation produces inhibition that is associated with both the tone and the light. Since the tone was excitatory, we may not be able to detect its inhibitory properties since they just cancel out its excitatory ones. But what about the light? Since it started out neutral, its inhibitory properties have nothing to cancel out. Thus it should clearly be inhibitory in stimulus-compounding tests. This procedure is diagrammed in Figure 2–15A. It contrasts with the procedure in Figure 2–15B in that the procedure in B does not permit tone–light associations to be formed because the two stimuli are never presented together. Results of experiments of this type do indicate that the light becomes inhibitory for Group A but not for Group B. Thus extinction does indeed involve the buildup of an inhibitory association (see Rescorla, 1979b).

INHIBITION OF DELAY

By referring back to Figure 2–13B one will be reminded of the delay conditioning procedure. A long presentation of a CS is followed by a US. After extended training, subjects tend to make CRs only in the latter part of the CS. The question to focus on here is what is going on early in the CS? Is the early part of the CS simply nonexcitatory or could it actually be inhibitory? Pavlov thought the latter was true, and his evidence came from the use of external inhibition as a research tool. When a novel stimulus was presented in the latter part of a CS in a delay conditioning procedure, it inhibited the salivary CR. If, on the other hand, the novel stimulus was presented early in the CS when no salivation was occurring, it produced salivation. Pavlov interpreted this as an instance of disinhibition; the external inhibitor inhibited the process currently in force, which was itself inhibition. The net result was excitation. Similar results have been obtained with delay conditioning procedures using very different methods (Rescorla, 1967b, 1968).

DISCRIMINATION AND GENERALIZATION

Imagine a dog exposed to the following procedure: On some trials a tone is paired with food; on other trials a light is presented and not

A	B
Phase 1. Tone − Shock	Phase 1. Tone − Shock
Phase 2. Tone + Light − 0	Phase 2. Tone − 0
Phase 3. Test Light	Light − 0
	Phase 3. Test Light

FIGURE 2–15. *Procedure to Test Whether Extinction Produces Inhibition.* Groups A and B experience tone–shock pairings in Phase 1. In Phase 2, Group A receives tones without shock, to extinguish fear to the tone. A light is presented along with the tone in extinction. Group B receives separate presentations of tone and light, both without shock. Then in Phase 3 the inhibitory power of the light is tested for both groups. Only for Group A is the light inhibitory, since only for that group are light and tone associated. Thus extinction must make the tone inhibitory also.

followed by food. If we plotted the development of conditioned salivation over the course of conditioning trials, it would look something like the curves in Figure 2–16. Early in the procedure conditioned salivation occurs to both the tone and the light. This phenomenon is called **stimulus generalization**. Conditioning experience with one stimulus (in this case, the tone) is generalized to other stimuli (in this case, the light). After a while, however, while conditioned salivation to the tone continues to grow, conditioned salivation to the light begins to wane. The two curves continue to diverge until salivation occurs to the tone on nearly every trial and salivation never occurs to the light. We describe this result as the development of a **discrimination** between the tone (CS$^+$), which is paired with food, and the light (CS$^-$), which is not.

The question that concerns us is whether, in the course of discrimination training, the CS$^-$ remains a neutral stimulus or becomes an inhibitory one, and the evidence is clear and compelling. Virtually all the techniques for uncovering inhibition already discussed have been used in assessing the status of a CS$^-$ and all have provided evidence that the CS$^-$ is a powerful conditioned inhibitor (see Rescorla, 1969). In addition, there is another source of evidence for inhibition that has not yet been discussed. It comes from the study of generalization gradients.

Excitatory and Inhibitory Generalization Gradients Let us return for a moment to the hypothetical dog that has been exposed to Pavlovian discrimination training and produced the data in Figure 2–16. Let us suppose that

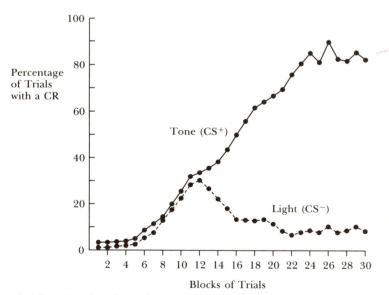

FIGURE 2–16. *Hypothetical Development of a Pavlovian Discrimination.* Initially the animal responds to both the CS$^+$ and the CS$^-$. After some training, responding to the CS$^-$ drops off while responding to the CS$^+$ continues to increase.

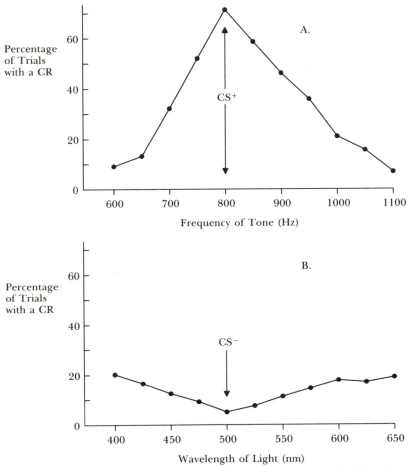

FIGURE 2–17. *Hypothetical Generalization Gradients of Excitation (A) with a Tone as CS⁺, and Inhibition (B) with a Light as CS⁻.* In A, maximum responding occurs to the CS⁺ and drops off systematically as the tones presented are more and more different from the CS⁺. In B, minimum responding occurs to the CS⁻ and responding increases as lights are more and more different from the CS⁻. The inhibitory gradient (B) is less sharp than the excitatory one, a typical research finding.

the tone CS⁺ was a pure tone of frequency 800 Hz (tonal frequency corresponds to what we call pitch). Let us further suppose that the light CS⁻ was of wavelength 500 nm (wavelength of light corresponds to what we call color). Now suppose that in addition to presentations of the CS⁺ and CS⁻, the dog also received occasional presentations of tones that differed in frequency from the CS⁺ and lights that differed in wavelength from the CS⁻. None of these stimuli was followed by the US. If the experimenter recorded the percentage of trials in which the various tones elicited a CR, she would observe a pattern of responding like that in Figure 2–17A. This pattern is called an **excitatory generalization gradient**.

The CS $^+$ produces the most responding and, as other tones are more and more different from the CS $^+$, the amount of responding they produce decreases.

What about the different lights, though? The CS $^-$ produces no salivation, as we know. If this is due merely to the absence of excitation, then we would also expect other colors to yield no salivation. On the other hand, if the CS $^-$ is inhibitory, then we might expect other colors to be somewhat less inhibitory (just as other tones are somewhat less excitatory than the CS $^+$). If this is so, we would expect salivation to increase as the light presented is more and more different from the CS $^-$ in wavelength. This is in fact what is observed, as can be seen in Figure 2–17B (see Moore, 1972).

BACKWARD CONDITIONING

There is one other condition under which inhibition is produced— backward conditioning. Recall that if a US *precedes* a CS (backward conditioning), conditioning does not occur (Figure 2–13E). This assertion can now be modified. Conditioning does occur, but not excitatory conditioning. Rather, the CS becomes a conditioned inhibitor. Consider what a sequence of trials in a backward conditioning experiment would look like. The most obvious characteristic of this procedure is the temporal contiguity of CS and US, with US coming first. Despite this contiguity, excitatory conditioning does not occur. But what does the CS tell the animal? The CS tells it that the US is over. Said another way, the CS is paired with the *termination* of the US. This may be sufficient to make the CS inhibitory. Indeed, there is ample evidence, from experiments like some we have already described, that a CS that is paired with the termination of a US becomes an inhibitory stimulus (see LoLordo & Fairless, 1985; Rescorla, 1969).

Conditioned Inhibition: What Is Learned?

We have reviewed some of the techniques that are available for examining conditioned inhibition, and some of the procedures that produce it. It is time now to turn to a question that has generated a great deal of research attention in the last few years: When organisms develop conditioned inhibition, what is it exactly that they are learning? The issues involved here are similar to issues we already encountered in discussing conditioned excitation, but the possibilities are somewhat more complex.

In discussing excitation, we saw that the possible forms that learning could take were S–S and S–R associations. In the case of inhibition, matters are not this simple. The reason for this is that inhibitory learning, whatever its form, cannot stand by itself. It is parasitic on excitation (Fowler, Kleiman, & Lysle, 1985). If we put a dog in a box and just keep presenting tones periodically, the tones will not come to inhibit salivation, or fear, or anything. We might say that unless something in the animal's experience has led it to expect a US of some kind to appear, its failure to appear will not lead to inhibition.

The fact that inhibition is parasitic on excitation creates complications when we are trying to ascertain what is learned in inhibition-producing procedures because it implies that inhibitory learning must bear some relation to already established excitation. Thus, inhibition must interact with and modify excitatory associations that have previously been established. And the question is, what are the locus and the form of that modification?

There are several possibilities, outlined in an important paper by Rescorla and Holland (1977; see also Holland, 1985) that set the tone for much research that followed it. One is that the inhibitor works directly on the CR, reducing its magnitude. This is analogous to the S–R position discussed earlier. A second is that the inhibitor works on the internal representation of the US, reducing *its* magnitude. It is as if an animal used to experiencing a strong shock as a US thinks to itself that shock is mild when the inhibitor appears. As a result, responding is reduced. Finally, it is possible that the inhibitor works not on the representation of the US by itself, but on the connection between the US and the excitatory CS it has been associated with.

To make this last possibility concrete, imagine a procedure in which an organism gets two types of trials. On one type, CS_1 is followed by a US. On the other type, CS_2 and CS_1 occur together, with no US. On a procedure like this, an organism will come to make CRs to CS_1 alone, and not to the CS_2–CS_1 combination. In addition, CS_2 will become inhibitory. Now what it means to say that an inhibitory stimulus works on the excitatory CS–US connection is that when CS_2 appears along with CS_1 it tells the animal that despite the strong connection it has established between CS_1 and the US, this time the US will not be coming. In effect, the organism is learning a kind of conditional rule. It is learning something like "CS_1 means US but only if CS_2 is not around." In this sense, CS_2 is working to modulate the relation between CS_1 and the US.

Experimental efforts to determine which of these three different possibilities for inhibition actually holds have met with mixed results. There is very little evidence to suggest that an inhibitory CS directly reduces the CR. However, there is substantial evidence for both of the other possibilities. Whether the inhibitory stimulus works on internal representations of the US or on the CS–US relation seems to depend upon various details of procedure (see Holland, 1985).

The idea that an inhibitory stimulus affects the CS–US relation is especially intriguing, and warrants further discussion. Researchers have suggested that when stimuli become inhibitory in this fashion, they don't actually become associated with either the excitatory CS or the US. Instead, they have been described as **occasion setters**. They tell the organism that "on this occasion, when the CS that has reliably been followed by the US occurs, it will not be followed by the US." Because they tell the organism this, CRs to the excitatory CS do not occur on those occasions when the inhibitory CS is also present (Holland, 1985, 1986; Jenkins, 1985; Rescorla, 1985, 1987; Ross & Holland, 1981, 1982; Ross & LoLordo, 1986, 1987).

To illustrate the difference between "occasion setting" and association, consider the following experiment. On some trials, CS_1 is followed by the US. On other trials, CS_2 and CS_1 are followed by no US. As we saw, CS_2 becomes inhibitory, and when it is presented with CS_1, no CRs occur. Now, another type of trial is added. On this type of trial, CS_2 is followed by the US. Before long, it becomes excitatory, just as CS_1 is. That is, CS_2 produces CRs. Finally, the critical test occurs; another trial is presented in which CS_2 and CS_1 occur together. What should happen? Before, CS_2 had told the organism that on this occasion, there would be no US to follow CS_1. And that message hasn't changed. However, in the meanwhile, CS_2 has itself become directly associated with the US. With both CS_2 and CS_1 associated with the US, the organism ought to make conditioned responses. But it does not. Despite the direct association that has been established between CS_2 and the US, its occasion-setting role has not been altered. The organism has no evidence that the old message that CS_2 conveyed about the relation between CS_1 and the US has changed. In effect, the organism might be saying to itself something like "I know that by itself, CS_2 means US. But when it is with CS_1, it means no US. I guess, then, that no US is coming" (Jenkins, 1985).

The notion that an inhibitory CS, instead of entering directly into an association with other CSs or USs, sets conditions that modify the effects of those other associations takes us a long way from Pavlov and the origins of conditioning. No longer are CSs just stimuli that trigger reflexes. They may have their effects without triggering anything. And this is true of excitatory as well as inhibitory conditioning, as there are now some demonstrations of occasion setting in the excitatory domain (Rescorla, 1987). The image we may have of Pavlovian conditioning involving drooling dogs or blinking rabbits needs to be replaced. An alternative image—one that is broad enough to incorporate both the traditional literature on conditioning and the more modern literature—is one that views conditioning as one of the means by which organisms perform a causal analysis of events in their world. It is a way to figure out what goes with what, or what follows what, or what signals what, or what predicts what, and, most important, to figure out the precise conditions under which these relations between environmental events hold. While dogs may sometimes drool, or rabbits blink their eyes, or pigeons peck at lit keys, these features of conditioning are only incidental to the core of the phenomenon, which involves finding regularities in and extracting information from the environment. As we will see in the next chapter, most modern developments in our understanding of Pavlovian conditioning compel this kind of cognitive view of the process (see Bolles, 1985).

Summary

The chapter began with a review of Pavlov's initial investigations of conditioning, and then considered some of the issues that concern modern researchers and some of the methods used to study those issues. The major points made in the chapter are these:

1. Pairing of a CS and a US produces gradual acquisition of a CS–US association, after which presentation of the CS alone extinguishes that association.

2. These Pavlovian phenomena have been demonstrated in an enormously wide variety of organisms, with a wide range of CSs and USs.

3. The CR may sometimes mimic the UR, may sometimes be different from the UR, and may sometimes actually be antagonistic to the UR. However, its form will generally allow it to serve important adaptive functions.

4. This diversity of CRs necessitates a diversity of techniques for measuring conditioning. However, researchers assume that although the form of the CR may vary from one situation to the next, the process of association that underlies the occurrence of CRs does not.

5. The Pavlovian conditioning process has been extended in scope to include the phenomenon of habituation, partly through its relation to the opponent process theory of motivation.

6. The phenomena of sensory preconditioning and second-order conditioning have been used to answer one of the central theoretical questions in Pavlovian conditioning:

What kind of association is learned? Evidence suggests that both CS–US and CS–CR associations may be formed, depending on the circumstances.

7. The course of Pavlovian conditioning is affected by a wide range of variables, including (a) the nature of the CS, (b) the nature of the US, (c) temporal relations between the CS and US, and (d) qualitative relations between the CS and US.

8. Pavlovian conditioning procedures can produce inhibition as well as excitation. Techniques for detecting inhibition, including disinhibition and stimulus compounding, have indicated that extinction, discrimination, delay conditioning, and backward conditioning all produce Pavlovian inhibition.

3 Explanations of Pavlovian Conditioning

Pavlov conceived of the conditioning process as one that proceeded inexorably and mechanically as the conditioned stimulus (CS) and the unconditioned stimulus (US) were repeatedly paired. Organisms did not decide whether to associate CS and US. They did not ask themselves whether it did them any good to form particular associations. In short, they were not especially selective about the associations they formed; as long as CS and US were paired, the end result was an association.

We said little in the last chapter to challenge this conception, but there were a few hints that might provide another way of thinking about the conditioning process. Recall our discussion of the temporal relation between road signs and dangerous curves. As we illustrated the various possible temporal relations, it was obvious that some would be considerably more useful than others. And our inclination to use the signs as guides to stepping on the brake would reflect their differential usefulness. Thus in cases of simultaneous or backward pairing we would not depend on road signs to tell us when to step on the brake. Is it possible that organisms are selective about the associations they form, and that this selectivity is somehow a reflection of the relative usefulness of the CS–US relation?

What would make one kind of CS–US relation more useful than another? Again, thinking about the road signs is helpful. Useful road signs are signs that *predict* or *provide information* about driving conditions ahead. Being forewarned gives us the opportunity to prepare for or do something in anticipation of these driving conditions. It would be adaptively beneficial to organisms if Pavlovian associations were formed only when CSs predicted or provided information about impending USs.

Indeed, if we think of Pavlovian conditioning as a kind of predictive or causal analysis, we can even see virtue in the fact that it usually takes numerous CS–US pairings before an association is formed. Suppose we learned after a single pairing of CS and US. If we did, then any stimulus that happened, accidentally, to precede, say, a shock would produce conditioned fear. Since there is surely always some stimulus around when a shock (or some natural aversive event) occurs, we might end up walking around in fear of almost everything. But if conditioning requires multiple pairings, this possibility is largely eliminated. A tone might precede a shock once, or even twice, by accident. But if the tone precedes the shock 20 or 30 times, it can no longer be an accident. Thus gradual association formation actually enhances our chances of responding only to CSs that are reliable predictors of USs. Of course, there may be some circumstances, as when the US is extremely dangerous, when a rapidly formed, even if erroneous, association is more adaptive than a slowly formed, though accurate one. The taste aversion phenomenon may be an instance in which the high stakes involved promote speed of association over accuracy.

Even repeated pairing is not enough to get us to respond selectively to CSs that are predictors of the US. Consider the relation between the presence of a crowd at the train station and the appearance of a train. Frequently they are paired; the crowd forms in close temporal contiguity with the train's appearance. Yet despite this consistent pairing, we know that the crowd is not the best predictor of when the train will come. For trains sometimes come without crowds (for example, late at night), and crowds sometimes form without trains (for example, when trains are delayed, or when another train that connects with our train has arrived at the station and discharged passengers). Correctly identifying CSs that are good predictors of USs requires more than just sensitivity to CS–US pairings.

What both of these examples suggest is that it would be extremely useful to organisms to form CS–US associations only when the CS provided information about the occurrence of the US that was reliable, and not available from other sources. We will see that such selectivity is indeed characteristic of Pavlovian conditioning. This chapter is devoted to a discussion of the mechanisms of Pavlovian conditioning that make such selectivity possible.

Necessary Conditions for Pavlovian Conditioning

For Pavlov, conditioning involved the simple, mechanical association of two events that occurred closely together in time. Special moments of contiguity between CS and US stamped in a connection between them. But in 1967 Robert Rescorla suggested that contiguity of CS and US, while perhaps necessary for conditioning to occur, was not sufficient. What was necessary in addition was that there be a differential **contingency** between CS and US (Rescorla, 1967a). What is the difference between contiguity and contingency?

CONTINGENCY

Let us consider a commonplace example. Imagine a person who habitually listens to the forecast of the next day's weather. Sometimes the weather report predicts rain and the next day it rains. Sometimes the weather report predicts warmth and sunshine and the next day it is warm and sunny. There are therefore numerous instances in which the forecast is paired with the actual weather, that is, the forecast is accurate. One might expect that the forecast would influence this person's behavior. If the weather report were always this accurate, we could describe it mathematically in the notation of probability theory in this way:

$$p(\text{rain/rain forecast}) = 1.0 \tag{1}$$

$$p(\text{no rain/no rain forecast}) = 1.0 \tag{2}$$

$$p(\text{rain/no rain forecast}) = 0.0 \tag{3}$$

$$p(\text{no rain/rain forecast}) = 0.0 \tag{4}$$

These probability statements may be read as follows:

1. The probability that it will rain given that the forecast was rain is 1.0; that is, every time the forecast is rain, it will rain.

2. The probability that it will not rain given that the forecast was no rain is 1.0; that is, every time the forecast is no rain, it will not rain.

Statements (3) and (4) follow necessarily from (1) and (2) and may be translated in the same way. In describing the relation between weather forecasts and the weather, we would say that a differential contingency existed between forecast and weather such that the forecast provided information about the weather. If weather forecasting were this good, one could choose clothing each night with complete assurance that it would be appropriate for the next day's weather.

But let us be more realistic. Suppose that it rained every time the weather forecast said it would, but that it also rained about once in every 10 times that the forecast said it would not. Now our probability statements would look like this:

$$p(\text{rain/rain forecast}) = 1.0 \tag{5}$$

$$p(\text{rain/no rain forecast}) = 0.1 \tag{6}$$

$$p(\text{no rain/no rain forecast}) = 0.9 \tag{7}$$

$$p(\text{no rain/rain forecast}) = 0.0 \tag{8}$$

The weather reports are still quite helpful. Whenever they say rain, it will rain, though occasionally it will rain when they say it won't. It still is sensible to pay attention to the weather report.

But now let us suppose that the probability statements looked like this:

$$p(\text{rain/rain forecast}) = p(\text{rain/no rain forecast}) = 0.2 \tag{9}$$

$$p(\text{no rain/rain forecast}) = p(\text{no rain/no rain forecast}) = 0.8 \tag{10}$$

What do these expressions convey? What (9) says is that rain is just as likely to come when the forecast is no rain as when the forecast is rain. The probability of rain is 0.2, which means that one day in five, on the average, it will rain, and listening to the forecast will provide absolutely no information about the next day's weather. Whether it rains and whether the forecast predicts rain are independent of each other.

If this were the state of accuracy in meteorology, it would make no sense to listen to weather forecasts. Notice, however, that there are still occasions in which the forecast of rain (or no rain) is paired with the outcome rain (or no rain). Thus this last situation represents a case in which contiguity continues to exist between CS and US but a differential contingency between CS and US is absent.

Let us return now to the Pavlovian conditioning experiment. Imagine a standard procedure in which a tone is paired with shock (see Figure 3–1A).

In the language of probability, the procedure could be described as follows:

$$p(\text{shock/tone}) = p(\text{no shock/no tone}) = 1.0 \tag{11}$$

$$p(\text{shock/no tone}) = p(\text{no shock/tone}) = 0.0 \tag{12}$$

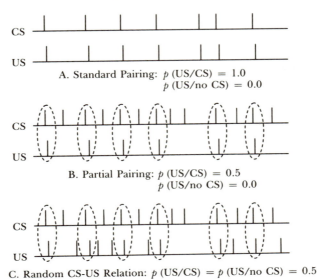

A. Standard Pairing: p (US/CS) = 1.0
p (US/no CS) = 0.0

B. Partial Pairing: p (US/CS) = 0.5
p (US/no CS) = 0.0

C. Random CS-US Relation: p (US/CS) = p (US/no CS) = 0.5

FIGURE 3–1. *Diagram of Informative and Noninformative CS–US Relations.* In A, every CS is followed by a US. In B, seven additional CSs are added to the CS–US pairings. Now the CS is no longer a perfect predictor of the US, though it is still a good predictor. In C, seven additional US presentations are also added. Now the occurrence of the CS is no longer a good predictor of the US.

Now suppose we added some extra tones so that only half the tones were followed by shocks:

$$p(\text{shock/tone}) = 0.5 \qquad (13)$$

$$p(\text{shock/no tone}) = 0.0 \qquad (14)$$

The tone is not as informative as it was before (there are frequent false alarms), but it still provides valuable information: Shock will never come unless a tone has come first (see Figure 3–1B).

But now suppose we added some extra shocks as well—shocks that occurred during the intertrial interval (see Figure 3–1C). Indeed, suppose we added enough shocks so that shock was just as likely to come in the absence of the tone as in its presence. In probability terms,

$$p(\text{shock/tone}) = p(\text{shock/no tone}) \qquad (15)$$

As in the case of the weather report, here the tone provides no useful information about the shock. Tone and shock continue to be paired as they were at the start of the experiment; they are sometimes contiguous. However, the extra tones and extra shocks have eliminated the differential contingency between tone and shock that was present at the start of the experiment.

What Rescorla proposed was that if a subject were exposed to this last procedure, conditioning would not occur despite the presence of CS–US pairings. To confirm this he exposed dogs to a variety of Pavlovian fear conditioning procedures. One group of dogs (A) received standard CS–US pairings. A second group (B) received the same number of CSs and USs but they were always unpaired. What would we expect the effect of this procedure on Group B to be? From Pavlov's contiguity view of conditioning, we would expect that this procedure would produce no conditioning. From the contingency view, we would expect something different:

$$p(\text{shock/no tone}) > p(\text{shock/tone}) \tag{16}$$

The *absence* of the tone predicts shock, while the presence of the tone predicts safety. Thus we might expect the CS to *inhibit* fear as a result of this procedure.

A third group (C) also received the same number of CSs and USs, but they were neither paired nor unpaired: They were independent. The occurrence of the CS provided no information about the occurrence of the US, though pairings occasionally occurred by chance (as in Equation 15). Here, the contingency view would predict no conditioning to the CS. Finally, a fourth group (D) also received independent presentation of CS and US with one important exception: If the US was scheduled to be delivered more than 30 seconds after the most recent CS, the US was automatically canceled. Thus while the number of accidental CS–US pairings for these last two groups would be the same, the groups would differ in that, for the last group, the probability of shock following the tone would be greater than the probability of shock in the absence of the tone. That is,

$$p(\text{shock/tone}) > p(\text{shock/no tone}) \tag{17}$$

since some shocks scheduled in the absence of the tone would not actually be delivered. Thus the contingency view would predict conditioned fear in this last group. These four procedures and the expected results are depicted in Figure 3–2.

The results of the experiment confirmed Rescorla's analysis. For the first (standard pairing) and last (positive contingency) groups, the tone produced conditioned fear; for the third group (pairing but no contingency) it had no effect, and for the second group (no pairing but a negative or inhibitory contingency) it became an inhibitor of fear.

It therefore seems clear that our understanding of Pavlovian conditioning requires a change. Up until 1967 it was believed that presentation of CS and US contiguous in time would result in conditioning. However,

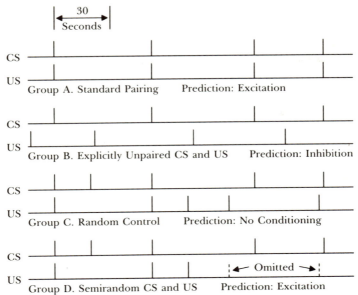

FIGURE 3–2. *Diagram of Procedures Used to Test the Contingency Theory of Conditioning.* Group A receives only pairings of CS and US. The expectation is that this "standard" pairing procedure will produce excitatory conditioning. Group B receives only unpaired presentations of CS and US. The contingency theory of conditioning predicts inhibitory conditioning in this group. Contiguity theory would predict no conditioning, either excitatory or inhibitory. Groups C and D receive the same number of CS–US pairings. They differ only in that, for Group D, USs scheduled to come more than 30 seconds after the last CS are omitted (broken lines). According to contiguity theory, the groups should not differ. However, according to contingency theory, the CS should be informative for Group D and not for Group C so that only Group D should show excitatory conditioning.

Rescorla's experiments demonstrated that the organism is sensitive to the degree to which one stimulus provides information about the other. In some way the organism computes probabilities—of US/CS and of US/no CS—and the outcome of this computation determines whether a potential CS will actually be an effective CS.

THE SIGNIFICANCE OF CONTINGENCY: FEAR AND ANXIETY

The presence of CSs that predict or provide information about USs can have significant practical consequences. In the literature of clinical psychology, a distinction has long been maintained between fear and anxiety. Fear is said to be objective: It is focused on particular objects or situations. It is at the heart of a type of psychopathology known as **phobia** (for example, fear of heights, fear of closed-in spaces, fear of crowds). Anxiety, on the other hand, is subjective: It is unfocused or diffuse. It is difficult or impossible to specify the source of the anxiety, and thus difficult or impossible to prevent it from occurring. Anxiety, rather than fear, is thought to be the main component of many types of psychopathology in which people find themselves emotionally paralyzed without being able to identify the source of the paralysis. This leaves them withdrawn, unable to act, and miserable.

As we have seen, there is much evidence that fear can be established by Pavlovian conditioning. Procedures using shocks as USs and tones or lights as CSs reliably produce fear to the light or tone. What about anxiety? Is there something to be said about anxiety from a Pavlovian point of view? In recent years research in Pavlovian conditioning has produced some important insights into the nature and origins of anxiety. To discuss these insights, it is best to return to an earlier example.

Suppose a rat has been pressing a lever for food. Lever pressing occurs at a high and steady rate. Now a tone is occasionally sounded, and followed by a painful electric shock. These tone–shock pairings produce Pavlovian conditioned fear that is indicated by a change in the rate at which the rat presses the lever. During the tone, lever pressing is substantially, sometimes entirely, suppressed. This phenomenon, as we saw earlier, is called **conditioned suppression** or **conditioned emotional response (CER)**. From what we know about Pavlovian conditioning, what should we expect to happen if, instead of being paired, tone and shock are explicitly unpaired? Shocks occur during the session, but never just after a tone. Such a procedure ought to make the tone a conditioned inhibitor of fear. We might expect to observe suppression of lever pressing in the absence of the tone and frequent lever pressing in the presence of the tone. This indeed is what happens. Now suppose the tone and shock are neither paired nor unpaired: The occurrence of tone provides no information about the occurrence of shock—or in the notation of probability:

$$p(\text{shock/tone}) = p(\text{shock/no tone})$$

Since we now know that Pavlovian conditioning depends on an informative relation between CS and US, we would expect that this procedure would not produce conditioning. But what does that mean with respect to lever pressing? Does it mean that lever pressing will continue at the same steady rate as before the shock was introduced?

Indeed, such a procedure does not produce conditioned fear to the tone. Rats behave no differently in the presence of the tone than in its absence. What they do is suppress lever pressing at all times. Although lever pressing has nothing to do with shock, and although failure to press costs the rats food, they stop pressing the lever altogether. In addition, the rats do not simply stop pressing the lever: They also huddle in a corner of the chamber, frozen with terror. Even more dramatic is the fact that when these rats are examined after the experiment, they are found to have a substantial number of stomach ulcers—ulcers not produced by the shock itself (since animals exposed to the tone–shock pairings fail to develop ulcers) but produced by the unpredictability of the shock (Seligman, 1968, 1969, 1975; Weiss, 1970, 1977).

In the situation in which tone is paired with shock the animal becomes afraid of the tone, but when the tone is gone the animal is safe—it can relax. The fear is objective and while it is certainly debilitating, it ends when the objective stimulus ends. On the other hand, in the situation in which shock is unpredictable, there is no stimulus that might prepare the animal for the shock. Shock may come at any time, without warning. Hence the animal cannot in any way mitigate its effect. The result is akin to what clinicians call **anxiety**: an emotional state that is generally and profoundly debilitating and that completely suppresses effective action. It may be that exposure to unpredictable aversive events is what produces anxiety—in humans as well as in rats.

Imagine a child in a doctor's office. The doctor's style with children is honesty. When something is going to hurt, he says so; when there is no likelihood of pain, he also says so. The behavior that results bears an interesting resemblance to the behavior of rats that receive tone–shock pairings. Children are deathly afraid when the doctor warns them about impending pain, but otherwise are relaxed and cooperative. Now imagine a different doctor. This one, in order to avoid having to deal with wrought-up children, always tells her patients that her procedures will involve no pain. Then, before they can resist, she catches them by surprise with the injection or whatever else must be done. At first this second doctor will have less trouble than the first. Ultimately, however, her patients will become generally frightened and resistant to treatment of any kind. While there are no danger signals to produce crying and tensing, there are also no safety signals to produce relaxation (see Seligman & Binik, 1977). We have come to the other side of the coin of the importance of contingency to Pavlovian conditioning. Stimuli that predict significant future events are important not only because of what they predict, but also because of what their absence predicts. Pavlovian conditioning is important not only because CSs signal USs and produce adaptive conditioned responses, but because the absence of these CSs provides important information that allows relaxation. Conditioned fear implies conditioned relaxation. Anxiety, on this view, is simply fear of *everything*, because there are no signals for safety. Both conditioned fear and conditioned relaxation are probably critical to the emotional well-being of organisms.

LOCATING THE US IN TIME

Now we know that simple pairing of CS and US is not enough to ensure conditioning; unless the CS is a differential predictor of the US, condi-

tioning does not occur. It is only under these conditions that a CS provides information about a US. But is a contingency between CS and US
enough to ensure conditioning? Is the idea of informativeness fully captured by our measure of predictiveness, or are there other aspects of
informativeness in addition to contingency?

Research in recent years has pointed to other ways in which CSs may
provide more or less information about USs that are not reflected in
measures of contingency. Consider, as an example, the relation between
cold winter temperature and snowfall. Winter cold is certainly a predictor
of snow; p (snow/cold) $> p$(snow/no cold). Yet it is not an especially
good predictor. The reason is that in winter it is cold enough to snow for
months at a time, yet it only snows occasionally during these months.
Thus while we can be absolutely certain that when it is cold it will snow
and when it is warm it will not, the fact that it is cold does not allow us
to predict the timing of snowfalls.

Now consider a conditioning experiment. A lit response key is paired
with food delivery with pigeons as subjects. The CR to be measured is
pecking at the lit key. For all subjects, p(food/key) $= 1.0$ and p(food/no
key) $= 0.0$. Thus at some point while the key is lit, and only while the
key is lit, food will come. Obviously we would expect pigeons to learn
quickly to peck the lit key. But while all subjects are the same in the
key–food relation they experience, they differ in another respect. For
some pigeons trials (key illuminations) last 5 seconds, for others 10
seconds, for others 20 seconds, for others 30 seconds, and so on. The
time between key illuminations is 30 seconds for all pigeons.

Notice what effect this manipulation of trial duration has. It does not
affect the predictiveness of the CS. What it does affect is the extent to
which the CS localizes food delivery in time. As the CS grows longer and
longer, uncertainty about exactly when food will come increases. If the
trial duration gets long enough, its relation to food will become like the
relation of winter to snow. And it turns out that manipulating trial duration has a profound effect on conditioning: The longer the trial, the
slower the conditioning (see Gibbon, Locurto, & Terrace, 1975; Terrace,
Gibbon, Farrell, & Baldock, 1975). Thus in addition to being sensitive to
the contingency between CS and US, organisms are sensitive to the
information the CS provides about when in time the US is coming.

As it turns out, it is not the absolute duration of a trial that is critical
to conditioning. Rather, it is the ratio of the trial duration to the duration
of the intertrial period. Thus if in the experiment just described every
time we increased the trial duration we increased the intertrial period
proportionately (for example, if 5-second trials were separated by 30
seconds, then 10-second trials would be separated by 60, 20-second trials
by 120, and so on), trial duration would have no effect (Gibbon, Baldock,
Locurto, Gold, & Terrace, 1977; Gibbon & Balsam, 1981). What this
means is that it is the ability of a CS to localize the US relative to the other
cues that is critical to conditioning.

To see this, think of yourself as the pigeon. Just by being put in the conditioning chamber you know you will be getting food. Suppose your experimental session lasts 30 seconds and the key is lit for 15 of them. While it is true that the key enables you to localize food to a 15-second period, you could localize it to a 30-second period even without the key. But now suppose the session lasts 30 minutes, and during that time the key is lit once, for 15 seconds. The key permits no better temporal localization in this case than in the last, but just being in the box provides much *worse* temporal localization in this case than in the last. Thus the difference between the key and the box as temporal localizers of food has grown. And this is what seems to be critical to conditioning. If we just increase trial duration without increasing intertrial period, we decrease the difference between the key and the box as temporal localizers of food. But if we increase intertrial periods in proportion to trials, we maintain the difference between the key and the box. As trials and intertrial periods keep getting longer, both the key and the box become worse and worse at localizing food in time. However, the advantage of the key over the box is preserved. As a result, conditioning is unaffected (see Gibbon, 1977, 1981, for a theoretical account of these results).

INFORMATIVENESS, REDUNDANCY, AND BLOCKING

Our discussion of the effect of trial duration in the last section raised an important issue. We saw that trial duration effects depended on the CS's ability to localize the US, not absolutely, but relative to other cues like the experimental chamber itself. This implies something significant about the selectivity of association. It implies that organisms may be sensitive not only to whether a given CS is predictive of a US, but to whether it is *more* predictive than other CSs. In other words, conditioning may involve the selective association of a US with the most predictive CS. Is there additional evidence that this kind of selection of the best predictor occurs?

In a sense, the mere fact that conditioning occurs to a CS is evidence for selective association. When we take an animal out of its home cage and put it in the conditioning chamber, we are providing it with a CS. USs like shock or food occur in the chamber, but not outside it. The chamber is a pretty good predictor of the US. Why doesn't conditioning occur to the chamber? We will see, later in this chapter, that under some conditions it does. The reason it does not under most conditions is that although the chamber is a good predictor, the CS is a better one. It is better because it localizes the US better in time, and because $p(US/CS) > p(US/chamber)$. Thus the fact that conditioning occurs to CSs rather than to experimental chambers demonstrates that association is selective.

But there is still more dramatic evidence for selectivity. In the last chapter we discussed the phenomenon of **overshadowing** (p. 71). Recall that if a CS is a compound of two stimuli and one of them is more salient or noticeable than the other, nearly all the conditioning that occurs will occur to the more salient stimulus: The less salient one may be completely overshadowed. Whether overshadowing will occur is typically a function of the intrinsic properties of the CSs. But there is one set of conditions in which overshadowing can occur even if both stimuli are quite salient. This kind of overshadowing results from an animal's past experience with the stimuli. It is further evidence for selective association based on the informativeness of the stimuli.

Evidence for overshadowing based on prior experience comes from an important series of experiments by Kamin (1969). The basic experiment involved the following procedure: Rats were exposed to 16 trials in which tone was followed by electric shock. Then they were given 8 trials in which a compound stimulus of the tone and a light was followed by shock. Finally, they were given a presentation of the light alone to see whether it produced any conditioned responses. What might we expect the result of such an experiment to be? The tone alone provides information that shock is coming, and the rats presumably learn this in the first 16 trials. Then light and tone together are followed by shock. What does the light tell the animal? As far as one can tell, everything to be known in this situation can be learned from the tone. The light is a redundant, noninformative addition to the situation. Thus, despite pairing of light and shock, and despite the fact that the light is a differential predictor of shock [that is, p(shock/light) $>$ p(shock/no light)], we might expect no conditioning to the light because it adds nothing that the animal has not already learned from the tone. And we get virtually no conditioning. That this effect is due to the experience the rats have with the tone alone is clear from another procedure Kamin tried. If light and tone are presented as a compound from the beginning, and then light is tested by itself, it produces strong conditioned responses. This overshadowing of control by one stimulus as a result of experience with a second stimulus has been called the **blocking effect**.

Since Kamin's original experiments, variants have been designed to elucidate the mechanism that underlies the blocking effect. Suppose rats receive 16 trials of tone–shock followed by 8 trials where light and tone are given together. On these last 8 trials, however, there is no shock. Is the light still redundant? In this case, because the light is telling the animal that shock is *not* coming, the light is not redundant. On the contrary, the light becomes an extinction stimulus. After 8 of these trials the tone is again presented alone. Although 8 extinction trials would usually be sufficient to reduce substantially the amount of conditioned responding obtained, one discovers that on this procedure the tone has undergone virtually no extinction. It is the light that has been associated with no shock while the tone has been blocked or protected from extinction. Consider what this phenomenon requires the animal to do. The animal first notices the light, a new stimulus. Then the animal fails to receive a shock, a new event. If there had been no new stimulus, extinction to the tone would have begun. Instead the animal seems to associate the change in the US with the change in the CS.

In a similar experiment, tone–shock pairings were followed by tone + light–shock pairings. With the compound, however, the shock was more intense. When the light was tested alone, a substantial amount of conditioning was revealed. Here again, the introduction of the light was correlated with an important change in the US. As a result the light was not a redundant stimulus. The four procedures just described are diagrammed in Figure 3–3, along with the result each procedure produces.

The essential thing to realize about the phenomenon of blocking is that the selectivity of association occurs even though the two stimuli are equally predictive of the US. The animal seems to know what the tone tells it—to know, as it were, what it knows—and somehow to decide not to bother about the light because it adds nothing. Thus association involves not just selecting the most predictive stimulus. It seems also to involve evaluating each new stimulus as it appears and comparing what it tells us with what we already know. If that comparison tells us that the new stimulus is no more predictive than the old one, even if it is no less predictive, we do not form an association.

The Rescorla–Wagner Theory

The research of Rescorla and Kamin, among others, seems to demand a change in our conception of the conditioning process. Animals do not evaluate pairings of CS and US in a vacuum. These pairings are evaluated against a background that may include other presentations of CS and US unpaired, or include presentations of other CSs that are also reliable predictors of the US. Conditioning occurs only when an evaluation of the entire context reveals that a particular CS is a good (perhaps the best available) predictor of the US. This new conception of Pavlovian conditioning makes the conditioning process seem a lot more complex than it used to seem. It also raises an immediate and insistent question. How do animals do it? By what mechanism are they able to keep track of CSs and USs, estimate probabilities, compute probability differences, and ultimately make CRs to the CS? The requirements of the task seem sufficiently demanding to tax human intellectual capacity. Yet it is claimed that something of the sort is accomplished routinely by nonhumans. It seems clear that probability calculations of this type are automatic, in just the way that calculations of the trajectory of a thrown ball, which allow one to catch the ball, are automatic. However, we still need an account of the mechanism by which this automatic calculation might occur.

A possible account of how animals might discover the informativeness

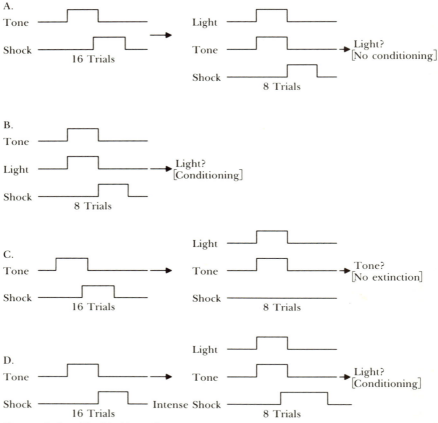

FIGURE 3–3.   *The Blocking Effect.* Parts A–D depict procedures in which the redundancy of the light as a CS is varied. In A the light is redundant (the animal has already learned all there is to be learned from the tone) and no conditioning occurs. In B, C, and D the light is not redundant, and it has measurable effects on the animal's behavior. In B, since the animal has not learned anything yet, about either the tone or the light, neither is redundant and thus neither is blocked. In C the light signals no shock, and thus blocks the tone from extinction. Finally, in D the light is correlated with an increase in shock intensity. Thus the light is not redundant and is not blocked.

or predictiveness of potential CSs was proposed by Robert Rescorla and Allan Wagner (Rescorla & Wagner, 1972; Wagner & Rescorla, 1972). Their theory explains complex contingency analysis in terms of simple associations of the sort Pavlov had in mind. It can account for most of the old familiar phenomena of conditioning as well as for the new dramatic ones. Finally, it has the virtue of precision. The theory is specified in such clear detail that one can derive from it predictions about the behavior of a subject in untried experimental situations. Consider the idealized representation of a standard conditioning curve shown in Figure 3–4. Curves

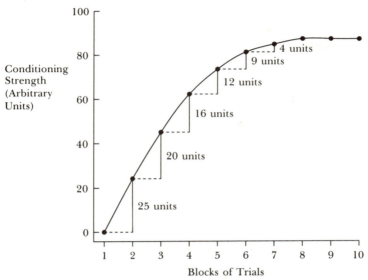

FIGURE 3–4.   *Idealized Learning Curve.* The curve is negatively accelerated, which means that the amount of change in conditioning strength (in arbitrary units) gets smaller and smaller with repeated trials.

of this form are called *negatively accelerated.* The changes in the value of conditioning strength (y-axis) with conditioning trials (x-axis) are very substantial early in training. However, as training proceeds and the leveling-off point, or asymptote, is approached, changes in strength of conditioning with each trial get smaller and smaller. The intuition captured by a negatively accelerated curve like this is that the experimental subject does not profit equally from each trial. How much one profits depends on how much one already knows. When one knows nothing, profits are substantial. When one knows a great deal, profits from further trials are small. Rather than learning a fixed amount with each trial, one seems to learn a fixed proportion of the difference between one's present level of learning and the maximum. As that difference gets smaller (as one learns more), the amount of new learning produced by further trials gets smaller.

The Rescorla–Wagner theory begins with the fact that the typical learning curve for Pavlovian conditioning has this negatively accelerated form. With this as a starting point, the theory attempts to characterize the learning curve mathematically. The theory describes the growth of associative strength (*V*) with repeated conditioning trials. The change (symbolized as Δ) in associative strength on any trial, $n(\Delta V_n)$, is expressed as follows:

$$\Delta V_n = K(\lambda - V_{n-1}) \qquad (18)$$

What do these various symbols represent? V, associative strength, is the measure of learning. It is a theoretical quantity that is not equivalent to the magnitude or probability of any particular CR, but is assumed to be closely related to these measures of conditioned responding (see Figure 2–12, p. 68, for an illustration of possible differences between associative strength and conditioned responses).

The symbol K is a reflection of the salience of the CS and the US used in a particular experiment; K can vary between 0 and 1 ($0 \leq K \leq 1$). We saw in the last chapter that the particular CS and US used in an experiment can affect the rate of conditioning, and K reflects this fact. The bigger K is, the bigger will be the change in V on any given trial. Thus salient stimuli mean large Ks which mean large ΔVs, which mean large changes in association from trial to trial.

Finally, the symbol λ is a reflection of the fact that different USs support different maximum levels of conditioning. The asymptote of conditioning will vary with the US chosen, and different asymptotes are reflected as different λs. For example, the more intense the US, the higher the asymptote of conditioning, and the higher the λ. The quantity λ is always greater than or equal to 0 ($\lambda \geq 0$).

What Equation 18 expresses is simply that the change in associative strength on trial n (ΔV_n) will be proportional to the difference between λ (the asymptote) and the previous associative strength, V_{n-1}. Since V will grow from trial to trial, the quantity ($\lambda - V_{n-1}$) will get smaller and smaller, so that ΔV_n will also get smaller and smaller. This is simply a description of the negatively accelerated learning curve. Eventually V will equal λ, so that ($\lambda - V_{n-1}$) will be 0, and conditioning will be complete (the asymptote will be reached).

Let us work through an example. Suppose $V = 0$, $K = 0.3$, and $\lambda = 90$ in Trial 1 of a conditioning experiment. If we apply Equation 18 to repeated trials, we get:

Trial 1: $\Delta V_1 = 0.3(90 - 0) = 27.0$

Trial 2: $\Delta V_2 = 0.3(90 - 27) = 18.9$

Trial 3: $\Delta V_3 = 0.3(90 - 45.9) = 13.2$

Trial 4: $\Delta V_4 = 0.3(90 - 59.1) = 9.3$

Trial 5: $\Delta v_5 = 0.3(90 - 68.4) = 6.5$

Total associative strength after five trials $= 74.9$

Associative strength grows 27 units on Trial 1, 18.9 on Trial 2, 13.2 on Trial 3, 9.3 on Trial 4, and only 6.5 on Trial 5. Clearly, the change in associative strength on any trial gets smaller and smaller as conditioning proceeds, which is what the negatively accelerated learning curve requires. To examine the effect of the value of K on learning rate, you might work through the above example with $K = 0.5$. Under these conditions, after five trials associative strength will be about 87 units.

Let us now examine how this simple, elegant theory can be applied to the phenomenon of blocking.

RESCORLA–WAGNER THEORY AND COMPOUND STIMULI

What does the Rescorla–Wagner theory say about conditioning involving compound stimuli? Let us call CS_1 "A" and CS_2 "X." According to the theory,

$$V_{AX} = V_A + V_X \qquad (19)$$

In short, the associative strength of a compound stimulus is equal to the sum of the associative strengths of its parts. If we did an experiment in which tone and light were presented as a compound CS right from the start, the growth of associative strength would look like this:

$$\Delta V_{A \text{ (tone)}} = K(\lambda - V_{AX}) \qquad (20)$$

$$\Delta V_{X \text{(light)}} = M(\lambda - V_{AX}) \qquad (21)$$

The only difference between Equations 20 and 21 is in the constants K and M. Recall that part of what determines the value of that constant is the salience of the CS. If tone and light were equally salient, then $K = M$ and Equation 20 = Equation 21. If so, we would expect the associative strength of both tone and light to grow in equal steps. If, after presenting them together for 50 trials or so, we tested each of them alone, we would expect each of the stimuli to yield exactly half of the associative strength of the compound.

Now let us consider blocking. Recall that in Kamin's experiments on blocking, one CS (a tone) is paired with shock for a number of trials, and then a second CS (a light) is added, so that trials contain tone + light followed by shock. Under these conditions the light does not acquire any associative strength. Suppose a tone is paired with shock for 6 trials with $\lambda = 90$ and $K = 0.7$. After 6 trials (the reader can work it out) the associative strength of the tone is about 89 units. Now the tone and light are presented together, followed by shock. Assuming that the tone and light are equally salient (that is, $K = M = 0.7$), this is what the theory predicts:

$$\Delta V_A = K(\lambda - V_{AX}) \qquad\qquad \Delta V_X = M(\lambda - V_{AX})$$
$$\text{Trial 1: } \Delta V_A = 0.7(90 - 89) = 0.7 \qquad \Delta V_X = 0.7(90 - 89) = 0.7$$

It is apparent from this trial that the theory predicts that virtually no conditioning will occur to the light. Since V_{AX} is already so close to the asymptote, further trials will result in only the most minimal increases in associative strength. Thus prior conditioning with the tone (A) "blocks" subsequent conditioning to the light.

But suppose that when we introduce the light we double the intensity of the shock. As we have seen, according to the theory, changing the intensity of the US will change the asymptote, or λ. Suppose our new λ, with the higher shock intensity, is 150. Now let us examine what just the first trial of tone + light followed by greater shock should produce:

$$\Delta V_A = K(\lambda - V_{AX}) \qquad\qquad \Delta V_X = M(\lambda - V_{AX})$$
$$\text{Trial 1: } \Delta V_A = 0.7(150 - 89) = 42.7 \quad \Delta V_X = 0.7(150 - 89) = 42.7$$

It is clear that the theory predicts that if introduction of the light as a CS along with the tone is accompanied by an increase in US intensity, the light will not be blocked from conditioning. And as we saw in describing Kamin's experimental results earlier, the light is not blocked under these conditions.

RESCORLA–WAGNER THEORY AND INHIBITION

Now consider another variation on the blocking experiment in which, when the light is added, the US intensity is *decreased* rather than increased. Suppose λ with our lower shock intensity is 50. Again, let us examine what just the first trial of tone + light followed by lower shock should produce.

$$\Delta V_A = K(\lambda - V_{AX}) \qquad\qquad \Delta V_X = M(\lambda - V_{AX})$$
$$\text{Trial 1: } \Delta V_A = 0.7(50 - 89) = -27.3 \quad \Delta V_X = 0.7(50 - 89) = -27.3$$

Notice that the change in V, associative strength, will be negative. The associative strength of the tone will drop from 89 to 61.7 as a result of the trial with diminished shock. What about the light? Since its associative strength prior to this trial was 0, its associative strength after the trial will be negative, -27.3 to be exact. But what can a negative associative strength possibly mean? The answer is *inhibition* (Mackintosh & Cotton, 1985).

In the last chapter we indicated that conditioning can be either excitatory or inhibitory, and we devoted substantial attention to conditioned inhibition. Now we see how the Rescorla–Wagner theory captures the fact that conditioning can be inhibitory. Inhibition occurs whenever V is negative, that is, less than zero.

At first glance, it is not obvious that the Rescorla–Wagner theory can handle inhibition. Inhibition requires a V that is less than zero, but neither of the variables in their equation, K or λ, can ever be less than zero. A very weak CS would have a salience (K) of about 0, and the weakest possible US, namely no US at all, would have a λ equal to 0. How can we produce a negative V when none of the terms contributing to V can be negative?

The answer to this question reveals something important about inhibition. On any given trial, the change in V will be negative only when the expression $(\lambda - V_n)$ is negative. Since λ itself can never be negative, the expression will be negative only when V_n is greater than λ. And V_n will be greater than λ only when some excitation has already been established. Indeed, for V to be greater than λ, it must be greater than zero, which means that some excitation has already been established. What all of this boils down to is something we already saw in the last chapter: Inhibition is parasitic on excitation. Inhibition will not develop to a CS that signals the absence of a US unless there is something else in the situation (V greater than zero) to signal the presence of the US. Inhibition will develop to a stimulus that signals the absence of an otherwise expected US, or to a stimulus that signals a weaker than otherwise expected US, or to a stimulus that signals a less probable than otherwise expected US (LoLordo & Fairless, 1985; Mackintosh & Cotton, 1985; Wagner & Rescorla, 1972).

A Surprising Prediction Aside from accounting for the various phenomena of conditioning we have already discussed, the Rescorla–Wagner theory can make predictions about the outcomes of experiments that had not been done prior to the formulation of the theory. Sometimes these predictions can be surprising. To be able to derive such a surprising prediction, and then to confirm it experimentally, would be strong support for the theory.

Let us consider just one example. Suppose we give an animal two types of trials: Either a tone is followed by shock or a click is followed by shock of the same intensity. We present these two types of trials until conditioning to both stimuli is asymptotic. Suppose $\lambda = 100$ and $K_{tone} = K_{click} = 0.2$. Now suppose we present a new type of trial. The tone, the click, and a new stimulus, a light ($K_{light} = 0.2$), are all presented together, followed by the same shock. What should happen? From the blocking experiments we discussed, we might expect that the light will be blocked; since it is redundant, no conditioning to it should occur. But what does the Rescorla–Wagner theory say?

Since V_{tone} and V_{click} are asymptotic, they each equal 100. But now they are being presented together, and recall that $V_{AX} = V_A + V_X$. So $V_{tone} + V_{click} = 200$. And we are assuming that $K_{light} = K_{tone} = K_{click} = 0.2$. Thus

$$\Delta V_{click} = 0.2(100 - 200) = -20$$

$$\Delta V_{tone} = 0.2(100 - 200) = -20$$

$$\Delta V_{light} = 0.2(100 - 200) = -20$$

One trial of tone + click + light followed by shock should reduce the associative strength of each stimulus by 20 units. In the case of the tone and the click, this means reduction in V from 100 to 80. But what about the light? Since it began with $V = 0$, this trial (and succeeding ones) should make the light inhibitory. Thus even though the light is paired with shock, and predicts it, the theory says it should become a conditioned inhibitory stimulus. And it does (Kremer, 1978).

Thus the Rescorla–Wagner theory has proved to be an extremely powerful device for understanding Pavlovian conditioning phenomena. It provides a way of describing seemingly complex processes, involving the evaluation of probabilities and the selection of best predictors, in a mechanical, trial-by-trial fashion. The organism does not need to be able to consider its various experiences with CSs and USs over time, and combine them in some complex fashion, to be able to respond as though it were making these considerations. The Rescorla–Wagner theory gives us an idea how the animal can find a simple solution to the complex problem of forming selective, informative associations. We will see in Chapter 8, in discussing what is called **implicit memory**, that people are often affected by past experiences without their being able to identify, or reflect upon, these effects. In many ways, the Rescorla–Wagner theory reflects this as a feature of the conditioning process. We will also see, in Chapter 11, that formulations very much like the Rescorla–Wagner theory have been developed to account for many rather complex aspects of human memory and cognition.

Conditioning and Changes in CS Effectiveness

The Rescorla–Wagner theory is remarkably successful at accounting for a wide range of phenomena with a relatively simple and elegant mechanism. It tells us much about the processes that govern the growth of association. At the same time, there are aspects of conditioning that the Rescorla–Wagner theory does not address and that subsequent theoretical proposals have tried to capture. As it stands, the Rescorla–Wagner theory is incomplete.

The incompleteness lies in the theory's treatment of the CS and its effectiveness. Recall that in the Rescorla–Wagner equation, CS effectiveness is captured by K, an indication of salience. In the theory, K, and thus salience, does not change. The salience of a CS may be influenced by many factors, including its intensity, the sensory modality it affects, the type of organism being studied, and the type of US being used. But whatever these factors are, the salience of the CS at the start of the experiment is its salience throughout the experiment. Over the course of conditioning, V is the only thing that changes.

In recent years, several lines of evidence have converged to make it clear that salience is not a fixed property of CSs. Salience changes in important ways as a result of an organism's experience with both the stimuli themselves and what they predict. Let us turn, then, to a discussion of how experience changes the effectiveness of CSs and how these changes affect conditioning.

LATENT INHIBITION

Suppose one group of rats is given a few experimental sessions in which a tone is periodically sounded. Nothing else occurs during the session. Then that group and another, inexperienced group are exposed to sessions in which the tone is paired with food. Should the two groups differ in any way in the rate at which they learn the tone–food association?

The Rescorla–Wagner theory gives us no reason to expect a difference. Since the CS and the US are the same for both groups, K and λ should be the same. Since neither group has experienced any tone–food pairings, V should be 0 for both. The two groups should condition at the same rate.

They do not. The reliable finding in experiments of this type is that preexposure to the CS (as in the first group) significantly slows conditioning. This phenomenon has come to be called **latent inhibition** (Reiss & Wagner, 1972). The idea is that presenting the CS without the US endows it with inhibitory properties even before any excitation has been developed for the inhibition to counteract. Thus the inhibition is latent. Once CS–US pairings begin and excitation starts to develop, this "latent" inhibition starts to show itself by canceling out some of the excitation. This is why animals preexposed to the CS learn more slowly than inexperienced animals. They have to overcome this latent inhibition.

What does the Rescorla–Wagner theory say about this? What happens to V during tone presentations? The theory tells us that the λ associated with no US is 0. Associative strength, V, to the tone at the start of the experiment is also 0. Thus each time the tone is presented, the change in V will be:

$$\Delta V = K(0 - 0) = 0$$

The theory tells us that no inhibition will develop to the tone. Indeed, as a general point, the theory tells us that the development of inhibition is impossible unless something in a situation is already producing excitation (Wagner & Rescorla, 1972). Then what is going on?

First, let us ask if the tone actually becomes an inhibitor with preexposure. Suppose we took the two groups of rats, one preexposed to the tone and one inexperienced, as before, and subjected them to this procedure: On some trials a light is paired with a US; on other trials the light together with the tone are paired with no US. On this procedure we would expect animals to learn a discrimination, eventually showing excitation to the light and inhibition to the tone. Now if preexposure to the tone has already made it an inhibitor, the preexposed group should learn the discrimination faster than the inexperienced one because in this case latent inhibition to the tone does not have to be overcome. The latent inhibition actually contributes to the inhibition that will be the end result of the discrimination.

The predictions one would make for these two experiments on the assumption that preexposure makes the tone a latent inhibitor are depicted in Figure 3–5. The results of such experiments are clear: Whether Procedure A or Procedure B is used, preexposure slows conditioning (Reiss & Wagner, 1972). Thus preexposure does not make a CS an inhibitor. But if preexposure does not make a CS an inhibitor, why does it slow conditioning? A glance at the Rescorla–Wagner equation gives us the key. The rate of conditioning is influenced by K, a reflection of the salience of the CS. Perhaps, then, what preexposure to the CS does is reduce its salience. Perhaps animals learn to ignore it. Such a process would require an addition to the Rescorla–Wagner theory—a set of rules that specify how K can be changed by experience.

LEARNED IRRELEVANCE

Latent inhibition is not the only phenomenon that suggests a mechanism by which CS salience changes. A related phenomenon occurs when the organism experiences both the CS and the US, presented uncorrelated with each other. Conditioning is slowed when the stimuli are later correlated. This phenomenon has come to be called **learned irrelevance**, to capture the possibility that during uncorrelated preexposure organisms learn that the CS is unpredictive and thus irrelevant. As a result of this learning, the salience of the CS is reduced so that later, when the

	Phase 1	Phase 2	Prediction	Result
A. Group 1.	Tone	Tone ⟶ Shock		
			2 faster than 1	2 faster than 1
Group 2.	Nothing	Tone ⟶ Shock		
B. Group 1.	Tone	Light ⟶ Shock		
		Tone + Light ⟶ Nothing		
			1 faster than 2	2 faster than 1
Group 2.	Nothing	Light ⟶ Shock		
		Tone + Light ⟶ Nothing		

FIGURE 3–5. *Test of Latent Inhibition.* If preexposure to a CS makes it an inhibitor, it should slow learning down later if excitatory conditioning occurs (A). However, it should speed up learning later if inhibitory conditioning occurs (B).

stimulus is relevant, organisms learn about it slowly because they are largely ignoring it (see Baker & Mackintosh, 1977, 1979; Tomie, 1976; and see Tomie, 1976; and Balsam & Tomie, 1985, for a slightly different account of learned irrelevance).

ANOTHER LOOK AT BLOCKING

There is other evidence that also suggests that animals learn to ignore stimuli—that K can change with experience. It comes from experiments on blocking. Recall that in a typical blocking experiment animals may first experience tone–shock pairings. Then they experience compounds of, say, the tone and a light, paired with shock. We indicated before that no conditioning occurs to the light. It is blocked from association with shock by the already conditioned tone.

This description of blocking is actually not quite accurate. In fact some conditioning does occur to the light—on the first trial in which it is presented. No more learning occurs on subsequent trials, but on the first trial animals do form some light–shock association. If your measure of conditioning is sensitive enough, you can actually detect the effects of this single trial (Kamin, 1969; Mackintosh, 1975; Mackintosh, Bygrave, & Picton, 1977).

How can we understand this peculiar effect? The answer has been suggested by Mackintosh (1973, 1975). His argument is that blocking occurs because animals learn that the light is redundant. As a result of this learning, the salience of the light decreases. On the first blocking trial, tone + light are paired with shock. This has two different effects. First, some association between light and shock is formed, because the light is salient. But second, the salience of the light is reduced, because it is redundant. As a result of this reduced salience, further pairings of tone + light and shock will not add to the associative strength of the light. Thus, in Mackintosh's account, blocking, like latent inhibition, involves learning to ignore irrelevant or redundant stimuli.

SURPRISE AND CS SALIENCE

There is now some evidence that CSs will decrease in salience even when they are not redundant. Imagine this situation: The bell signaling the end of class period is reliably preceded by the shuffling of books and papers by your fellow students. Paper shuffling might be thought of as a CS with the bell as the US, and since the former is a reliable predictor of the latter, an association between them should form. Once the association has formed, what happens? Probably, you will make CRs to the CS, joining the paper shufflers. But how much attention will you pay to the CS? After conditioning is asymptotic, you will probably respond to both the CS and the US as if you were on automatic pilot. What this means is that even though the CS is neither irrelevant nor redundant, your attention to it will diminish. Indeed, your attention will diminish precisely because conditioning is asymptotic. Part of what it means for conditioning to be asymptotic is that there are no surprises left in the situation for you, and if there are no surprises left in the situation, your attention to various aspects of it will decrease.

What this analysis implies is that as an inevitable consequence of conditioning, the salience of CSs—even predictive ones—will diminish. For attention to a stimulus to stay high, some aspects of the situation must remain surprising. Is there any experimental evidence to support this analysis? In one particularly clear example, rats were exposed to pairings of a CS with a mild shock, until conditioned responses developed. Now, the same CS was paired with a stronger shock and the learning of these rats was compared to the learning of rats that had not experienced the first phase of training. It would seem straightforward that the rats with prior training should learn faster than the inexperienced ones. After all, they had already developed a CS–shock association. But in fact, the reverse was true; they learned more slowly. This indicates that along with learning the CS–shock association, these experienced rats were learning to ignore the CS. The resulting drop in CS salience slowed subsequent conditioning (Hall & Pearce, 1979; Pearce & Hall, 1980).

PSYCHOLOGICAL STATUS OF THE RESCORLA–WAGNER THEORY

The Rescorla–Wagner equation, appropriately modified to allow for possible changes in CS salience, does an excellent job of describing what goes on in a conditioning experiment. Armed with the equation and suitable estimates of K and λ, we can accurately predict the results of a wide range of conditioning experiments. But the predictive power of the Rescorla–Wagner theory raises questions. What are the psychological processes that yield results consistent with the Rescorla–Wagner theory? Do organisms actually use the equation (unconsciously) to determine whether or not to associate a CS with a US? Or does conditioning involve quite different psychological processes that happen to produce results that conform to the Rescorla–Wagner equation? Researchers can agree on the predictive accuracy of the Rescorla–Wagner equation, but then go on to give that equation a variety of different psychological interpretations. We can explore one of these interpretations in the context of a specific question: Why does the strength of association ever reach an asymptote? In other words, why does Pavlovian conditioning ever stop?

We will consider an answer to this question that focuses on the role of rehearsal in conditioning.

Rehearsal and Conditioning

We have taken it for granted that though CS–US pairings might continue forever, a point is reached at which they no longer have an effect. This point, or asymptote, tells us that the association is as strong as it will ever be. Is this a useful feature of the conditioning process? Let us think about the growth of association as the growth of certainty. The stronger our association of CS and US, the more certain we are that when the CS comes, the US will follow. How might we change our orientation to CS–US pairings once certainty is reached?

One way of thinking about the process is this: As conditioning proceeds, before the asymptote is reached, when CSs or USs occur we pay attention to them. We think about them, rehearse them in the way we might repeat a new friend's telephone number over and over to ourselves, mull them over. They are the focus of our mental resources. One might say that we are seeking to understand or make sense of them. But as the association grows stronger, we are making more and more sense of them, understanding them better and better. As a result we pay less and less attention to them. When we understand them fully—or when the asymptote is reached—we do not focus on them at all. And because we have stopped focusing on them, we stop learning about them.

Using this kind of language to describe conditioning can lead to some misunderstanding, so a few points of clarification must be made. First, that we stop focusing on a CS and US does not mean that we stop responding to them. We continue to make both CRs and URs. It is just that we make them kind of automatically, like the way we tie our shoes or start our car (Pearce & Hall, 1980). Second, the idea of focusing or paying attention should not be equated with being consciously aware of. We might be aware that we are tying our shoes without really thinking about it. Similarly, we might be aware of tone and shock without thinking about them either.

Now why should we stop paying attention to well-understood CSs and USs? The idea here is that we cannot pay attention to everything. The CS and the US are not the only things going on in our lives. We want to be sure that we can pay attention to things we do not yet understand. As a device for uncluttering our attentional resources, the conditioning process works so that the less attention a given CS–US relation needs, the less it gets. The virtue of this process is not apparent in the laboratory. So little is going on in the experimental chamber that the organism really has no need to unclutter its attentional resources. But a mechanism like this, if it exists, was designed for real life, not the laboratory. And in real life there is always a great deal going on.

This line of argument can be summarized as involving three steps:

1. We only learn about things to the extent that we process them.

2. We only process things to the extent that they are surprising, that is, to the extent that we do not yet fully expect them.

3. As conditioning proceeds, CS and US become less surprising. As a result they get processed less. And therefore we learn less about them.

This approach to the conditioning process has been developed most fully by A. R. Wagner (1976, 1978, 1979, 1981). With it, we can understand many of the phenomena we have already discussed. According to Wagner, when conditioning begins and the CS comes, we rehearse it. We do the same when the US comes, and this process continues even after the trial has ended. The development of association depends not just on the pairing of CS and US, but on our active, simultaneous processing of them. In other words, an association between CS and US will be formed only to the extent that they are rehearsed together. Once the association is formed, presentation of the CS alone will trigger a memory of the US. This memory in turn will trigger the CR.

But stimuli will not always be rehearsed when they are presented, even if they are significant. If a representation of the stimulus has already been activated, a new presentation of that stimulus will not produce rehearsal. Activation of a representation can be accomplished in one of two ways: by the presentation of the stimulus itself, or by the presentation of another stimulus that is associated with the first stimulus. Thus as an association grows, CS presentation activates our memory of the US so that the actual presentation of the US induces very little rehearsal and therefore results in very little change in the strength of association. This is why we learn less and less on each new trial. Eventually, when presentation of the CS fully activates memory of the US, learning is complete. Association has reached an asymptote.

Let us consider how this framework explains some conditioning phenomena that have by now become familiar.

BLOCKING

Many CS–US pairings, in establishing an association, make the US fully predicted by the CS. As a result, presentation of the CS activates our representation of the US so that we do not rehearse the US when it occurs. Because of this, no further CS–US association is formed (asymptote is reached). Now, a new CS is presented along with the old one. Because the old CS activates the US representation, when the US is itself presented, it is not rehearsed. Because of this, simultaneous rehearsal of the new CS and the US is prevented. The result is no association between them—blocking.

LATENT INHIBITION

When we present a CS by itself numerous times, before presenting CS–US pairings, conditioning is retarded as a result of the CS preexposure. This phenomenon, called latent inhibition, seems to indicate that organisms learn to ignore irrelevant CSs. But we can also explain this finding in terms of rehearsal. Suppose that when CSs are preexposed, organisms learn to associate them with the context in which they occur. When the context–CS association is formed, the CS is fully predicted and stops being rehearsed. Now when CS–US pairings occur, association formation is slowed because the CS gets less of the organism's attention than it otherwise would.

With this account we can make a testable prediction. If CS preexposure occurs in context A, while CS–US pairings occur in context B, no retardation should occur. Since the CS is not fully predicted in context B, it should be rehearsed in that context. This prediction has been confirmed experimentally (Anderson, O'Farrell, Formica, & Caponegri, 1969; Peeke & Vino, 1973; Wagner, 1976).

HABITUATION

In our detailed discussion of Pavlovian conditioning in the previous chapter, we mentioned a phenomenon known as **habituation, a decrease in response to a stimulus with repeated presentation**. Effectively, habituation refers to the fact that organisms get used to stimuli as they become increasingly familiar.

The phenomenon of habituation is absolutely pervasive. Virtually all organisms habituate to all kinds of different stimuli—from tones and lights to shocks and air puffs. Traditionally habituation has been viewed as a kind of learning that is even more fundamental than Pavlovian conditioning. It is a change in response to a stimulus, as a result of exposure to that stimulus, that is nonassociative in nature. But as we saw in Chapter 2 (p. 59), while there is little doubt that some aspects of habituation reflect nonassociative learning, it has become clear in the last few years that habituation is also associative—that it is another example of Pavlovian conditioning.

Let us consider an example of habituation and think about how we might explain it in Pavlovian terms. Suppose we present shocks repeatedly to an organism without a CS. Then we introduce CS–shock pairings. It turns out that the preexposures to the shock substantially impair the formation of a CS–shock association (see Randich & LoLordo, 1979). In terms of habituation, we might say that shock preexposure results in the animal's getting used to the shock, so that by the time it is used in Pavlovian trials it is a much less effective US. Preexposure has effectively made the shock a weaker US than it would otherwise have been.

If we were going to explain habituation in associative terms, we would say that repeated presentations of the shock make it less and less surprising, so that it is rehearsed less and less, and thus becomes less effective. This decrease in surprisingness, and thus in rehearsal, would be the result of the development of an association between the shock and some environmental stimulus that predicted it. It is because the shock was predicted that it became unsurprising and thus unrehearsed. But what could that predictive environmental stimulus be in a situation in which no CSs are actually being presented?

The answer is that the predictive environmental stimulus is the experimental environment itself. Just being in the conditioning chamber predicts shock. Perhaps the chamber is the CS. If this is true, then habituation to the US should be specific to the experimental context in which it occurs. If we were to present it in a novel context, it would not be predicted by the context. It would therefore be surprising, get rehearsed, and be fully effective. Thus we can test our associative account of habituation by seeing whether habituation transfers to an environment that is different from the one in which it occurred.

The evidence from experiments of this type provides a clear indication that habituation results at least in part from a context–US association (Baker & Mackintosh, 1977, 1979; Hinson, 1982; Randich & LoLordo, 1979; Tomie, 1976). One recent series of experiments of this type provides a vivid demonstration that the context is indeed a CS (Hinson, 1982). In one experiment it was first demonstrated that US preexposure only interfered with conditioning if preexposure and conditioning occurred in the same context. Thus the context was a CS. But if the context is a CS, it should be like other CSs. For example, one should be able to extinguish the context–US association. This was demonstrated in a second experiment. Two groups of subjects received US preexposures in a particular context. One group was then exposed to that context, without USs, for a period of time (extinction). The second group was simply left alone in a different context for an equivalent period of time. Then both groups were exposed to CS–US pairings in the original context. The second group showed impaired CS–US association as a result of habituation to the US, showing that the simple passage of time did not undo habituation. In contrast, the first group showed no impairment. Thus, just as a context–US association could be formed, it could also be extinguished.

Let us summarize this section. We began by asking why it is that conditioning ever stops. The answer we have sketched is one that argues that conditioning depends on the active processing of CS and US, and that this processing will occur only so long as the CS and US remain surprising. Once they are fully predicted, processing, and hence conditioning, has reached an asymptote. With this account, phenomena like blocking, latent inhibition, and habituation can be understood.

What it means for animals to process stimuli actively, or to rehearse them, is not entirely clear. Each of us, no doubt, has intuitions about what it means for human beings to rehearse or to engage in active processing, but whether these intuitions can be applied to the learning of nonhumans is unclear. Furthermore, we will see in our discussion of human memory that notions of "active processing" and "rehearsal" are complex and many-faceted in the human case. Which, if any, of these many facets fit the animal exposed to Pavlovian conditioning procedures is for now an open question.

Summary

We began this chapter by suggesting that Pavlovian conditioning would be much more useful to organisms if the formation of associations was selective. More specifically, if we were designing a Pavlovian conditioning device, we would want it to be sensitive to whether the CS provided information about, or predicted, the US. We then proceeded to show that Pavlovian conditioning does seem to be selective in precisely this way. Phenomena pointing to that selectivity include:

1. The fact that CS–US pairing is not enough to produce conditioning. For conditioning to occur, there must be a contingency between CS and US. In the absence of contingency, organisms may develop debilitating states of anxiety.

2. That conditioning depends on how well the CS localizes the occurrence of the US in time.

3. The demonstration that predictive CSs will be blocked from conditioning if they are redundant; that is, if they provide no information that is not already available to the organism from some other source.

These demonstrations of selectivity led us to inquire about how animals might actually accomplish this substantial intellectual feat. The Rescorla–Wagner theory provided us with a mechanism that yields selective association by means of a relatively simple, mechanical process. We saw how the Rescorla–Wagner theory could explain acquisition, blocking, and inhibition.

But there are some phenomena that seem to be outside the scope of the Rescorla–Wagner theory. The theory cannot explain latent inhibition, and it has difficulty with the fact that blocking does not occur until after the animal has learned that the added, redundant CS is in fact redundant. These findings led us to consider the possibility that organisms learn to ignore uninformative stimuli and to pay attention to informative ones.

We turned next to asking why it is that conditioning ever stops, why associative strength reaches an asymptote. We considered an answer based on the idea that animals learn to associate events only if they process them actively, or rehearse them. They rehearse them only if these events are surprising. As association grows, events become less surprising and rehearsal diminishes. As a result, so does learning. The view can accommodate phenomena like blocking and latent inhibition. It can also explain the phenomenon of habituation.

4 Operant Conditioning

Our discussion of Pavlovian conditioning should have made it clear that we will never be able to understand behavior fully without understanding Pavlovian conditioning processes. However, no matter how well we come to understand Pavlovian conditioning, it will not tell us all we need to know. As we saw in Chapter 1, much of our behavior seems to be governed by its anticipated consequences, to be voluntary and goal-directed. And Pavlovian CRs typically are neither. Indeed, the consequence of a Pavlovian CR has little to do with whether or not it occurs. Suppose you routinely salivated and went to the dining room for dinner when your grandfather clock chimed 6 P.M. The clock's chimes had become a CS for salivation. If on a particular day someone offered you a sizable reward for not salivating when the clock chimed six, you could not help yourself. Salivate you would, despite your goal of obtaining the reward (see Sheffield, 1965). In contrast, you would have no trouble refraining from entering the dining room for the reward.

Most of the behavior of many organisms, including humans, is more like walking to the dining room than like salivation. Our behavior is voluntary and goal-directed, and it is controlled by its consequences. Any reasonably comprehensive theory of behavior must be able to tell us about the determinants of this type of activity.

In this chapter, we will investigate the determinants of voluntary, goal-directed activity. We will examine the various kinds of relations that may hold between behavior and its consequences, and what effects those various relations have on behavior. We will ask what is necessary for the conditioning of voluntary behavior to occur, and compare answers based upon *contiguity* between response and consequence with answers based upon *contingency,* as we did in the case of Pavlovian conditioning. Finally, we will explore what kinds of consequences actually control behavior. The principle that has formed the cornerstone of virtually all conceptual and empirical work on the control of behavior by its consequences is the law of effect. Thus, we start our discussion with it.

The Law of Effect

We saw in Chapter 1 that it was Thorndike's explicit aim to explain goal-directed activity. His explanation was formulated as the law of effect. According to Thorndike, organisms engaged in a wide range of behaviors, essentially at random. Some of these behaviors were followed by positive events—rewards or reinforcers. The result was that these behaviors became more likely in the future. Some of these behaviors were followed by negative events—punishers. The result was that these behaviors became less likely in the future. The end result of the combined action of rewards and punishers was the creation of a repertoire of behaviors that produced positive consequences. All other activities dropped out, or stopped occurring.

The operation of the law of effect reflects a conditioning process the hallmark of which is that behavior is sensitive to, or governed by, its consequences. This conditioning process is referred to as instrumental or operant conditioning. Both names are descriptive. Behavior is *instrumental* in obtaining rewards. It *operates on,* or has an effect on, the environment. While Pavlovian CRs may have environmental effects, that is not what is distinctive about them. That is not what controls them. Operant responses, in contrast, can be understood only by understanding the consequences they produce.

Perhaps the most significant aspect of the law of effect is its relation to our everyday descriptions of our voluntary actions. We typically explain our actions by pointing to the future, to anticipated *goals.* We explain our actions by giving *reasons,* by saying what we *expected* the result of the actions to be. The law of effect is an attempt to explain these actions not by appeal to some future events—to goals or expectations—but by appeal to the past. We do something in the present because when we did it in the past, it was followed by a reward. The law of effect bears the same relation to voluntary behavior that the theory of natural selection bears to evolution. Species do not evolve because of what they anticipate the consequences of their evolution to be. They simply evolve. Some of the changes in species that occur in reproduction will result in decreased fitness. Members that have undergone these changes will not survive to reproduce. Other changes will result in increased fitness. Species members that undergo these changes will flourish.

Evolution works by the environmental selection of just those random species changes that promote survival. The seemingly intelligent process of evolution is actually accomplished by a mechanism that is quite unintelligent. Some theorists suggest that the law of effect works in precisely the same fashion. It selects from a pool of behavioral variation just those behaviors that are followed by positive consequences. According to these theorists, the seemingly goal-oriented, intelligent behavior of organisms is actually the product of the mechanical action of the law of effect.

The Behavior–Consequence Relation

The major focus of research on the law of effect is on the relation between behavior and its consequences, between responses and outcomes. We can identify four general types of behavior–consequence relations. First, behavior can produce positive consequences. You might study hard for an examination and do well when you take it. This relation is known as **positive reinforcement**. According to the law of effect, the positive outcome should increase the likelihood that you engage in the behavior (studying) in the future. Second, behavior can produce negative consequences. You drive too fast and get a speeding ticket. This relation is known as **punishment**. The negative outcome should decrease the future likelihood of the behavior (speeding). Third, behavior can result in the elimination or removal of negative or unpleasant stimuli that are already present. Thus you might turn off a boring television show. This relation is known as **negative reinforcement** or **escape**, and it should also increase the future likelihood of the behavior. The elimination of a negative stimulus should be a positive consequence just as the production of a positive stimulus should be. Finally, your behavior might result in the elimination, prevention, or removal of positive stimuli. Thus if you and your friends become rowdy at a party, the host might turn off the music. This relation is known as **omission**, and it should decrease behavior.

These possible relations between behavior and consequences are summarized in Figure 4–1. The law of effect tells us which of these relations should make the response more likely in the future (upward arrows in Figure 4–1), and which should make it less likely (downward arrows). The study of operant conditioning is essentially the study of response–consequence relations like those in Figure 4–1. Do these relations in fact alter the future likelihood of behavior as the law of effect says they should, and if they do, what kinds of variables influence their effectiveness in controlling behavior? Our focus in this chapter will be on studies of positive

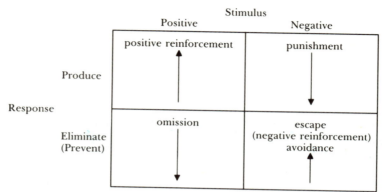

FIGURE 4–1.   *Possible Response–Consequence Relations.* Stimuli may be either positive or negative and responses may either produce or eliminate (prevent) them. According to the law of effect, some of these response–consequence relations will increase the future likelihood of the response (upward arrows) and some will decrease the future likelihood of the response (downward arrows).

reinforcement, though the principles we discuss may be applied to the other types of response–outcome relations depicted in Figure 4–1 as well. We will also discuss another relation between behavior and consequences that is represented in Figure 4–1. That relation, known as **avoidance**, refers to responses that *prevent* negative stimuli rather than eliminating them. We will see that avoidance learning poses special problems for accounts of operant conditioning, and thus has an especially important place in the theoretical development of learning theory.

Conditioning and Extinction

Imagine setting out to do an operant conditioning experiment with a rat. The operant to be trained is a lever press. The reinforcer is food. The rat has been deprived of food. How do we proceed? We might first get the rat accustomed to eating from the feeder. Then we could arrange our equipment so that when the rat presses the lever, closing a switch, the feeder operates automatically, delivering a pellet of food. Then we could just sit back, watch, and wait. Eventually, as the rat moved about in the experimental chamber, it would press the lever by accident. Food would come and conditioning would be on its way. According to the law of effect, the food delivery would make lever pressing more likely. The rat would eventually press again and produce food again. Lever pressing would become still more likely. In this way the probability of a lever press would keep increasing. As a result the frequency with which the rat presses the lever would keep increasing. If we were to plot the frequency of lever pressing over time, we would observe a curve like that depicted in the left part of Figure 4–2. We might say that by the end of 10 minutes the lever-press response has been fully learned, or **conditioned**.

Now suppose that somewhat later we disconnect the feeder. Lever presses no longer produce food. We would then observe the gradual decrease and eventual cessation of lever pressing, as in the right part of Figure 4–2. This phenomenon, known as **extinction**, parallels extinction in Pavlovian conditioning when previously established CSs are no longer followed by USs.

If we did our experiment in this way, the rat would eventually learn to lever-press. But we might have to wait a long time before it pressed the lever for the first time, by accident. And until that first press was made, no conditioning could possibly occur. To eliminate these potentially long and uneventful waiting periods, experimenters usually help the rat along. As we saw in Chapter 1, the experimenter trains the rat to press the lever using a technique known as **shaping by successive approximation**. Initially, food is delivered if the rat just moves close to the lever. Once the rat is spending most of its time by the lever, an actual paw movement toward the lever might be required. Then the rat might be required to touch the lever. Only once it is touching the lever would the experimenter demand an actual lever press. Each food delivery depends on a closer approximation to the final product, the lever press, than the one preceding it. By means of shaping, we can substantially shorten the initial acquisition period.

Creating Behavioral Units

Let us consider the early conditioning experience of our rat in somewhat more detail. Prior to any experimental treatment the rat lives in its laboratory cage. While in its cage the rat engages in a variety of different

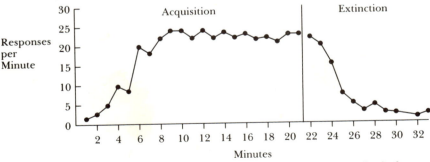

FIGURE 4–2. *Acquisition and Extinction of Lever Pressing.* This hypothetical curve depicts the growth in the frequency of lever pressing over time, followed by its extinction when reinforcement is discontinued.

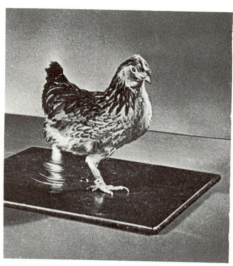

A chicken trained to "dance" after pulling on a string that turns on the music. (Courtesy of Animal Behavior Enterprises.)

activities: It eats, licks from a water spout, grooms, sniffs about the cage, pokes its nose through the openings in the cage, rears on its hind legs, and so on. It never does anything like lever pressing. Then the rat is placed in the experimental chamber. After an initial fear reaction to being handled, and to being in a novel environment, the rat begins to do the same kinds of things it does in its cage: It sniffs, rears, explores, and grooms. The feeder operates and the rat approaches it hesitantly, picks up the food pellet, and chews it. The feeder operates a few more times until the rat shows no hesitancy in approaching it and ingesting the food. Now the rat spends most of its time around the feeder—sniffing at it, poking its nose at it, rearing on its hind legs, and so on.

The experimenter next introduces a contingency between food delivery and an aspect of the rat's behavior. Whereas previously, food came no matter what the rat did, now to produce food the rat must press the lever that is located a few inches away from the feeder. The rat eventually leaves the area of the feeder and continues exploring—sniffing, rearing, and poking its nose at different areas of the experimental chamber. At last it rears right near the lever, and when it comes down its front paws brush against the lever and depress it. The feeder operates and the rat scurries over to get the food pellet. It returns to the area around the lever and sniffs around. This time while sniffing at the lever, the rat's nose inadvertently depresses it. Again the feeder operates. Now the rat returns to the lever and begins exploring it with its paws. Again the lever is depressed and again the feeder operates. At this point the rat's behavior is extremely inefficient. Most of its activity around the lever—its pawing and sniffing

The pig that went to market. The picture shows a pig trained with operant techniques to push a market cart. (Courtesy of Animal Behavior Enterprises.)

and rearing—does not depress the lever and close the switch. But occasionally the switch is closed and the feeder operates. The rat comes to spend all of its time around the lever. It has clearly learned something. But what has it learned?

Careful observation would reveal that the rat has not learned to do anything new and different. It has learned to do the same things it has been doing for months in its cage, but to do them in a particular place. With continued experience, the rat's behavior changes. It learns that rearing is unnecessary to produce food; only landing on the lever is necessary. It learns that sniffing at the corners of the lever is unnecessary to produce food; only depressing the lever with the nose is necessary. The rat seems to identify the single feature that each of its different activities with respect to the lever share, and that is the downward deflection of the lever. Once this information is acquired, the efficiency of the rat's behavior increases dramatically. The rat may end up lying down with its mouth poised at the feeder, reaching one paw over to the lever to depress it smoothly and economically.

One could tell a similar story about pigeons learning to peck keys. Adult pigeons do not have to learn to peck. What they have to learn is to peck at a particular place. Early in training the pigeon's behavior is erratic; it bobs up and down, stretches its neck, pecks around the lit key, and so on. Later in training the pigeon has eliminated virtually all the unnecessary behavior and it stands by the key, striking it efficiently and accurately, again and again.

What these examples are intended to suggest is that an operant contingency creates a new unit of behavior. Before training, lever pressing and key pecking do not exist as integral units of activity in the animal's repertoire. If we drew up an exhaustive list of the rat's activities in the experimental chamber after the first few reinforcements, it might include eating, grooming, sniffing, rearing, and pawing. Most of these activities would be directed at the lever. By the end of training, a new category of activity—lever pressing—has been created, and added to the others. The rat continues to rear, sniff, groom, and paw as before. But when it is around the lever, it lever-presses.

THE FORM OF THE BEHAVIORAL UNIT

What determines the form that this new unit of activity takes? Largely it is the requirement for reinforcement specified by the experimenter. The lever press is defined not by the way the rat moves the lever, but by the way the lever must be moved in order to close the switch. The contingency relating lever movement to feeder operation is what defines the response class. Thus if the contingency required not merely switch closure but switch closure that lasted for 5 seconds, the rat would develop a different behavioral unit. Instead of making brief, discrete lever presses, the rat would hold the lever down. The particular muscle movements in this lever-holding situation might look very different from the movements that occurred in lever-pressing situations. Alternatively, the rat might be required to exert a substantial force on the lever, so that reinforcement depended on lever presses of at least 100 grams of force (customarily, 10 or 15 grams of force is required). Again, the resulting behavioral unit would look very different from what one would observe with a more straightforward lever-pressing requirement. The rat might have to throw its whole body into each response.

Thus an operant contingency results in the development of new behavioral units. But what is meant by "new" and by "unit"? Clearly, the muscle movements of the rat are not new. Each of them has occurred countless times before as part of one activity or another. What is new is the sequence of old and familiar muscle movements. What is new is the organization of those old movements. It is much like the practiced pianist learning a new piece. The particular movements involved in playing the piano are old and familiar. Yet when the pianist learns a new piece, he is learning something new. It is a new combination of old and well-practiced movements. Once the piece is well learned, the pianist will play it not as a sequence of individual movements but as a single, well-integrated act. This is what is meant by a "unit." Once the sequence of movements, be it a lever press or a sonata, is well established, it is a permanent part of the behavioral repertoire. The rat will stop pressing the lever if lever presses stop producing food. However, if a few months later the rat is returned to the experimental chamber, it will press the lever—not as a by-product of rearing or sniffing, but in its smooth and efficient form (see Herrick, 1964; Notterman & Mintz, 1965; Schwartz, 1980, 1981, 1982; Vogel & Annau, 1973).

Contingency Learning

We have now seen that reinforcement has two effects on responses that produce it. First, it increases their frequency. Second, it actually establishes stereotyped, organized behavioral units. Thus when food follows lever pressing, the rat's lever press is transformed from an improbable, often accidental, inefficient activity into a highly probable and extremely efficient one.

The question we turn to now is this: What is it about the response–reinforcer relation that produces conditioning? In Thorndike's formulation of the law of effect, the suggestion was that the critical feature of the response–reinforcer relation was temporal contiguity. If the response was followed closely in time by the reinforcer, it increased in frequency. This view parallels Pavlov's view about what produced Pavlovian conditioning. For Pavlov, CS and US had to occur closely together in time. But we saw in the previous chapter that CS–US contiguity is not enough to ensure Pavlovian conditioning. What is also required is a differential contingency between CS and US, such that the probability of the US given the CS is greater than the probability of the US given no CS, or $p(US/CS) > p(US/no\ CS)$. Is the same true of operant conditioning? Is a response–reinforcer contingency required, or is simple contiguity enough?

Attempts to assess contingency learning in operant conditioning parallel studies we have already reviewed in the domain of Pavlovian conditioning. And what these studies generally indicate is that organisms can indeed distinguish dependence between response and reinforcer from independence. They can distinguish contingency from contiguity.

One demonstration involved rats lever-pressing for food (Hammond, 1980). The experimental session was divided by the experimenter into 1-second periods. In each period the rat could either press the lever or not. If the rat pressed the lever, food would come with a given probability, say, $p = 0.05$. That is, on the average, 1 out of every 20 times that the rat pressed the lever, food would come. In those seconds in which the rat did not press the lever, food never came. Thus in this procedure:

$$p(\text{food/lever press}) = 0.05$$

$$p(\text{food/no lever press}) = 0.00$$

Under these conditions there was a contingency between lever pressing and food, and all rats learned to press the lever. Next the probability of food without a lever press was made equal to its probability with a lever press. That is, in each second

$$p(\text{food/lever press}) = p(\text{food/no lever press}) = 0.05$$

Under these new conditions the contingency was absent: There was no longer any reason for the rats to press the lever. Food came every 20 seconds or so no matter what they did. On the other hand, occurrences of close temporal contiguity between lever pressing and food were preserved. If temporal contiguity was critical, lever pressing should have persisted. If a contingency between response and reinforcer was critical, lever pressing should have stopped. And it did stop. Moreover, rats exposed from the beginning of training to this lack of contingency never developed lever pressing in the first place. Thus this experiment provides direct evidence that contiguity of response and reinforcer without contingency is not sufficient to produce conditioning (see Baker, 1976, and Killeen, 1978, for supporting evidence).

CONTINGENCY LEARNING IN INFANTS

There is other experimental evidence that organisms can distinguish response-dependent from response-independent reinforcement. In this case the experimental subjects in question are 3-month-old infants.

Consider an infant subject lying in its crib with its head resting on a pillow. Under the pillow is a switch that operates whenever the infant turns its head. Mounted on the opposite side of the crib is a mobile. For one group of infants, whenever they turn their heads on the pillow and close the switch, the mobile moves for a few seconds. These infants quickly learn to turn their heads to move the mobile. When the mobile moves, they smile and coo and seem delighted. For a second group of infants, movement of the mobile is out of their control. The mobile is made to move roughly as often for these infants as the infants who control the mobile's movement make it move. Not surprisingly, the infants in this group do not increase the frequency with which they turn their heads on the pillow. What is surprising is the infants' response to the mobile. Early, they smile and coo just as the infants who control the mobile do. However, after a few appearances of the mobile, the smiling and cooing stop. Apparently the reinforcing character of the mobile depends on the infants' power to make it move, or on the synchrony between the infants' behavior and the mobile's movement. It is only in the relation between behavior and consequence that the experiences of the two groups of infants differ. Yet the responses of these two groups to the mobile are dramatically different. It thus appears that even young infants distinguish reinforcement that depends on their responses from reinforcement that is independent of them (see Watson, 1967, 1971).

LEARNED HELPLESSNESS

Consider the following experiment. Two dogs are to be trained to make a response to avoid an electric shock. The required response will be jumping over a barrier from one side of a box to another. Before that training occurs, they are placed in a very different type of situation. They are brought into separate rooms so they cannot see or hear each other, and are strapped into harnesses so that movement is restricted. Near their noses is a small metal panel. If they touch the panel with their noses, the movement of the panel operates a switch (just as the rat's lever press does). Both of these dogs occasionally receive shocks. One dog, called the "control" dog, can turn off the shock by pushing the panel. The second dog, called the "yoked" dog, cannot exercise any control over the shock. Whenever the control dog is shocked, the yoked dog is shocked. Whenever the control dog turns off the shock by pushing the panel, the yoked dog's shock is also terminated. Thus the two dogs receive an identical number and temporal pattern of shocks. Not surprisingly, the control dog learns to push the panel and eventually escapes shock on nearly every trial.

Now the two dogs are placed in the apparatus in which they must jump a hurdle to avoid shock. The control dog quickly learns to make this response and in a short time is receiving virtually no shocks. Similarly, an untrained dog that has not been exposed to the shock in the harness learns quickly to avoid shock by jumping over the hurdle. For the yoked dog, however, it is a different story. When the dog receives a shock, it whines and yelps and seems distressed. In addition it makes no movement across the hurdle. As trial after trial goes by, this dog continues to whine but grows more and more passive. Ultimately the dog simply lies down, hardly moving, with its muscles almost completely flaccid, and makes no effort at all to escape or avoid the painful shock. The dog has becomes completely helpless. This phenomenon has been identified in the literature as **learned helplessness** (Maier & Seligman, 1976; Seligman, 1975).

What could be responsible for this complete failure to learn by the yoked dog? It must have been something that happened to the dog in the harness, for both control and untrained dogs learned to jump the hurdle with great ease. But what could the helpless dog have learned in the harness? There are two clear alternatives. One possibility is that while it is in the harness, whatever the animal is doing when shock comes is punished, through temporal contiguity of the response and shock. As a result most of the dog's behavior is punished. This may result in the "passivity" that is subsequently observed in the hurdle-jumping situation. A variant of the account is that some posture that the dog accidentally adopts reduces the amount of current that actually passes through the dog when shock is delivered. If so, this posture might be reinforced and might be generalized to the hurdle-jumping situation. Then it might compete with the development of hurdle jumping, for if the dog continues to adopt that posture during shock, the actual intensity of the shock will continue to be reduced. Thus the adoption of that posture will continue to be reinforced.

The second alternative is that what the dog learns in the harness is that important events (shocks) are independent of its behavior. It learns that nothing it does makes a difference. In the language of probability, the dog learns that $p(\text{shock/Response A}) = p(\text{shock/Response B}) = p(\text{shock/Response C}) = \ldots = p(\text{shock/no response})$. When subsequently placed in the hurdle-jumping situation, this dog's previous learning about the independence of behavior and consequence interferes with its learning that now its behavior does matter.

Consider the implications of this second alternative. First, it is directly opposed to the idea that temporal contiguity of response and consequence is all that is necessary to produce conditioning. It says that organisms are able to distinguish situations in which reward is response dependent (control dogs) from situations in which reward is independent of responding (yoked dogs). This is a distinction that the contiguity interpretation of conditioning explicitly denies. Second, this alternative account says that when response and consequence are independent, the organism learns that important environmental events are not subject to its control and this learning may produce a profound inability to learn in situations in which important events are controllable.

How is one to decide between the two views? Is there an empirical phenomenon that is consistent with one account but not the other? Suppose helplessness results from the development of passivity because each of the dog's active responses while in the harness has been punished. If so, then actually training an animal to be passive should result in even more dramatic helplessness. If, on the other hand, helplessness results from learning that behavior and consequence are independent, then training an animal to be passive (a case where consequence does depend on behavior) will not result in helplessness.

To decide the issue, groups of control and yoked dogs were established as before. The difference was that in order to escape electric shock, the control dog had to remain still for a period of time. The dogs learned this task, and after considerable training in which control and yoked dogs received an identical number and pattern of shocks, all dogs were tested in the hurdle-jumping situation. If the learning of passivity produced helplessness, we would expect the control dogs to be more helpless than the yoked dogs. If the learning of independence between behavior and consequence produced helplessness, we would expect only the yoked dogs to be helpless. This in fact is what was observed. Control dogs rapidly learned to jump the hurdle while yoked dogs sat, whined, and took the shock. It seems, therefore, that the phenomenon of helplessness provides a clear indication that organisms can discriminate response-dependent from response-independent environmental events (Maier, 1970; see also Alloy & Seligman, 1979; Jackson, Alexander, & Maier, 1980; Minor, Jackson, & Maier, 1984; Rosselini, DeCola, & Shapiro, 1982).

LEARNED HELPLESSNESS AND DEPRESSION

The phenomenon of learned helplessness has played a major role in influencing learning theorists to revise their understanding of the most fundamental aspects of the conditioning process. But beyond this theoretical significance, helplessness has also had a profound effect on our understanding of the causes, treatment, and possible prevention of human depression. The pioneering work in this area has been done by Martin Seligman (for example, 1975; see also Abramson, Seligman, & Teasdale, 1978; Peterson & Seligman, 1984). It is the learning of independence between behavior and consequence—the learning of helplessness—that, according to Seligman, is at the root of many cases of depression. There are many parallels between the symptoms of depressive patients and the symptoms of helpless animals. Both are passive; both have difficulty learning in situations in which responses are effective; both fail to display aggression in situations that usually call it forth. Both lose weight, appetite, and interest in social interaction. Moreover, if patients classified as depressive are exposed to learning tasks, they behave in the same way as nondepressive people who have just been exposed to lack of control.

Still more impressive is that therapy that seems to alleviate depression also seems to alleviate laboratory-induced helplessness, and vice versa. Electroconvulsive shock and the administration of certain psychoactive drugs have been used effectively to mitigate depression for some time. When they are administered to animals that have been exposed to helplessness-inducing lack of control, the helplessness syndrome is broken. Similarly, "therapy" that has effectively eliminated helplessness in dogs seems to break up depression in people. If dogs that have been made helpless are dragged back and forth over a hurdle that nonhelpless dogs hop over to avoid electric shock, after a good deal of dragging the helpless dogs learn to make the responses themselves (Seligman, Maier, & Geer, 1968). They are cured of helplessness. Likewise, if depressive patients, who assert that they are unable to do anything effectively, are forced to engage in simple tasks at which they cannot fail, the difficulty of the tasks can gradually be increased until they are performing normally. The depressive person must be forced to experience success; it is necessary to demonstrate that her behavior can control environmental events. Once made, the demonstration seems to break up the depressive syndrome.

Finally, Seligman suggests that the laboratory phenomenon of helplessness can also teach us how to prevent depression. If dogs are exposed to uncontrollable electric shocks after they have had experience controlling shock, helplessness does not develop. The possible parallel to depression is clear. If people, in the course of development, are exposed to many situations in which their behavior is effective, then subsequent exposures to lack of control (some of which, after all, are inevitable) ought not to produce depression. We have already seen that even young infants can distinguish response-dependent from response-independent environmental events. What that suggests is that the potential for development of helplessness, or of immunization from it, is present at a very young age.

In addition to its likely relation to clinical depression, learned helplessness, or, more accurately, lack of control over significant environmental events, has recently been shown to have other pathological effects that may prove to be of even greater scope and importance than its effects on depression. There is now evidence with rats that a lack of control over aversive stimuli can suppress activity in the body's immune system, and increase susceptibility to cancer (Laudenslager, Ryan, Drugan, Hyson, & Maier, 1983; Visintainer, Volpicelli, & Seligman, 1982). Given the extraordinary importance of the immune system to resisting and controlling disease processes of all kinds, these findings seem to provide significant preliminary indications of how physical well-being depends upon a certain kind of psychological well-being.

The relation between learned helplessness and depression (and, perhaps, other forms of psychopathology) is more complex than we have indicated here. Various psychological steps mediate between the actual experience of a lack of control and the development of depression (see, for example, Abramson, Seligman, & Teasdale, 1978). People must first *perceive* their lack of control. They must then *explain* it to themselves in a way that suggests that it will persist into the future. Only then is depression the likely result of helplessness. But even with these added complications, there is no doubt of the importance of learned helplessness in starting the unfortunate ball rolling.

Contingency Learning in General

The collective evidence strongly points to the view that operant conditioning depends on a contingency between response and reinforcer. In the absence of such a contingency, conditioning does not occur. Indeed, when a response–reinforcer contingency is absent, organisms may learn precisely that, and become helpless. We can depict all possible contingency relations between response and consequence with a diagram like that in Figure 4–3.

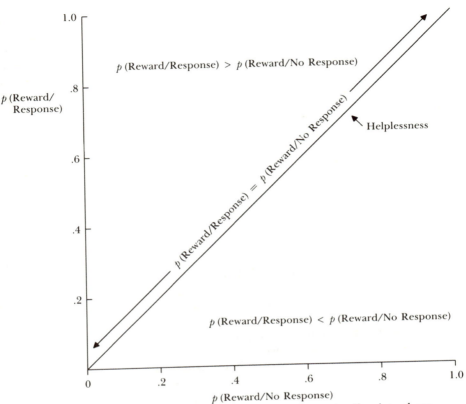

FIGURE 4–3. *Diagram of the General Operant Contingency Space.* At all points above the diagonal line, reward is more likely given the response than given no response. Under these conditions the response should increase in frequency. At all points below the diagonal line, reward is less likely given the response than given no response, and the response should decrease in frequency. Note that if the situation involves a punishing stimulus like shock instead of a reward, conditions above the diagonal should produce a response decrease while conditions below the diagonal should produce an increase. The diagonal itself represents independence of response and consequence. These are the conditions that produce learned helplessness.

Figure 4–3 plots p (reward/response) on the y-axis, and p (reward/no response) on the x-axis. The diagonal line represents conditions in which the two probabilities are equal and there is no contingency. As one moves from the lower left to the upper right on this diagonal, the overall probability of reward increases, but at all points it is no more likely if a response occurs than if it does not. All points above the diagonal represent situations in which p (reward/response) > p (reward/no response). Any such situation should result in conditioning of the response. All points below the diagonal represent situations in which p(reward/response) $< p$(reward/no response). Any such situation should result in an animal's learning not to make the response. We can also generalize this diagram to situations involving punishment instead of reward. Now points above the diagonal should result in decreased responding while points below it should result in increased responding. To suggest that animals are sensitive to response–outcome relations as depicted in this diagram is to suggest that conditioning results from contingency rather than contiguity.

Reaching this conclusion about operant conditioning parallels the conclusions we reached in the previous chapter about Pavlovian conditioning. We can divide possible relations between CS and US in Pavlovian conditioning, or between response (Resp) and reward or reinforcement (Rft) in operant conditioning, into three classes:

1. p(US/CS) $> p$(US/no CS) p(Rft/Resp) $> p$(Rft/no Resp)
2. p(US/CS) $= p$(US/no CS) p(Rft/Resp) $= p$(Rft/no Resp)
3. p(US/CS) $< p$(US/no CS) p(Rft/Resp) $< p$(Rft/no Resp)

The first pair of statements indicates a positive contingency between either US and CS or reinforcer and response. Under these conditions, Pavlovian and operant conditioned responses develop. The second pair of statements indicates conditions in which there is no contingency between CS and US or response and reinforcer. The effect of these procedures can be profound. If the situation is traumatic, then independence between CS and US produces a generalized debilitation that we called anxiety in Chapter 3. Similarly, independence of response and reinforcer under some circumstances produces a general debilitation that we have called helplessness. Whether generally debilitating or not, however, it is clear that independence of CS and US or of response and reinforcer yields effects that are quite different from the effects of a positive contingency. Finally, the third pair of statements describes conditions in which there is a negative contingency between CS and US or response and reinforcer. We saw in the previous chapter that such a contingency produces Pavlovian conditioned inhibition. We have not discussed the effects of operant procedures of this type. It is clear that such negative contingencies eliminate the particular activity under study. If reinforcement depends on not responding, then organisms already trained to respond will stop (Hammond, 1980; Reynolds, 1961).

IS CONTINGENCY DETECTION ACCURATE?

We have now reviewed the evidence that organisms can distinguish response-contingent from noncontingent environmental events. But does the fact that they can make this distinction under some circumstances mean that they do make this distinction in general? Said another way, is response–reinforcer contingency detection accurate?

To think about this issue, let us consider what an organism must do to determine whether or not a response–reinforcer contingency is present. Figure 4–4A presents a table depicting all possible combinations of response and reinforcer that could occur in an operant conditioning experiment. For purposes of comparison, Figure 4–4B depicts similar combinations of a CS and a US in a Pavlovian conditioning experiment. Thus response and reinforcer, or CS and US, may occur in combination (a and e); a response may occur without the reinforcer or the CS without the US (b and f); the reinforcer may occur without the response or the US without the CS (c and g); or finally, neither response nor reinforcer, CS nor US, may occur (d and h).

Consider the Pavlovian conditioning case first. We have seen that conditioning occurs if $p(US/CS) \neq p(US/no\ CS)$. How does one compute that information? First, $p(US/CS)$ is $e/(e + f)$. Second, $p(US/no\ CS)$ is $g/(g + h)$. Thus to compute a Pavlovian contingency requires computing $[e/(e + f)] - [g/(g + h)]$. In short, one needs to pay attention to all four possible CS–US combinations.

To see this concretely, consider Figure 4–5, which diagrams four possible sets of combinations. In each set, there are 100 CS and US events. Let us compute the degree of contingency present in each.

Contingency $= p(US/CS) - p(US/no\ CS) = [e/(e + f)] - [g/(g + h)]$

A. $[60/(60 + 20)] - [15/(15 + 5)] = 0.75 - 0.75 = 0$

B. $[20/(20 + 60)] - [5/(5 + 15)] = 0.25 - 0.25 = 0$

C. $[60/(60 + 20)] - [5/(5 + 15)] = 0.75 - 0.25 = 0.50$

D. $[15/(15 + 5)] - [20/(20 + 60)] = 0.75 - 0.25 = 0.50$

A. Operant Conditioning		
	Reinforcer	No Reinforcer
Response	a	b
No Response	c	d

B. Pavlovian Conditioning		
	US	No US
CS	e	f
No CS	g	h

FIGURE 4–4. *Possible Response–Reinforcer and CS–US Relations in Conditioning Experiments.* Table A depicts the possible event pairs in an operant conditioning experiment. A response could either produce a reinforcer (a) or not (b); a reinforcer could come without a response (c); or neither response nor reinforcer could occur (d). Table B depicts similar combinations in a Pavlovian conditioning experiment. A US could follow a CS (e) or not (f); a US could come without a CS (g); or neither a US nor a CS could occur (h).

A

	US	No US
CS	60 _e_	20 _f_
No CS	15 _g_	5 _h_

B

	US	No US
CS	20 _e_	60 _f_
No CS	5 _g_	15 _h_

C

	US	No US
CS	60 _e_	20 _f_
No CS	5 _g_	15 _h_

D

	US	No US
CS	15 _e_	5 _f_
No CS	20 _g_	60 _h_

FIGURE 4–5. *Examples of Possible CS–US Combinations.* In A and B there is no CS–US contingency: $p(\text{US/CS}) = p(\text{US/no CS})$. In A that probability is 0.75, while in B it is 0.25. In C and D there is a contingency: $p(\text{US/CS}) = 0.75$, while $p(\text{US/no CS}) = 0.25$. Examples C and D differ in the frequency of CS–US pairings.

Thus only in C and D are contingencies between CS and US present. In both A and B there is no contingency. The difference between them is simply that the US is more likely in A than in B. In C and D there is the same degree of contingency, though again the US is much more likely in C than in D.

Let us look at what would happen if an organism failed to evaluate all four cells of each table. Suppose an organism evaluated only _e_ and _f_, only the occasions on which the CS occurred. Such an evaluation might suggest the presence of a contingency in A but not B, since $e/(e+f)$ is 0.75 in A, but only 0.25 in B. Thus the organism would erroneously interpret A as involving a CS–US contingency. Now suppose the organism evaluated only _e_ and _g_, occasions in which the US occurred. Such an organism might detect a contingency in A and B (where there is none) and in C, but detect no contingency in D (where one is actually present). Thus accurate contingency detection requires examination of all possible combinations.

Pavlovian conditioning experiments ensure that this evaluation is possible. The experimenter controls presentation of both the CS and the US, and can thus ensure that CS–US, CS–no US, no CS–US, and no CS–no US combinations will all occur. There is no guarantee that an organism will actually evaluate all these combinations properly, but at least the organism will experience them. The fact that conditioning does not occur when $p(\text{US/CS}) = p(\text{US/no CS})$ suggests that proper evaluation does indeed occur. However, it turns out that for such an accurate evaluation to develop, organisms need protracted experience. If exposure to a conditioning procedure is brief, organisms will act as if there is a CS–US contingency even when there is none (Benedict & Ayres, 1972; Kremer & Kamin, 1971; Quinsey, 1971; Rescorla & Wagner, 1972). It seems as though a few chance occurrences of CS and US together have a big effect that requires substantial experience with the other possible combinations to dissipate.

But now let us consider an operant conditioning experiment. The crucial difference between an operant and a Pavlovian experiment is that the experimenter cannot control occurrences of the operant response. As a result, experiments cannot guarantee that subjects will experience all the cells of the tables depicted in Figures 4–4 and 4–5. And as a result of this, organisms may indeed behave as if there is a response–reinforcer contingency even when there really isn't one, or indeed behave as if there isn't one even when there is.

Think again for a moment about learned helplessness. After experiencing uncontrollable shocks, dogs do nothing to control shocks in a new situation in which shocks are controllable. This is what it means for them to be helpless. But the very fact of helplessness implies a failure of accurate contingency detection. In the second phase of a helplessness experiment, p(reinforcement/response) > p(reinforcement/no response), yet the dogs act as if this is not so. Why? One reason is that since they do not initiate responses, they get no information about Cells a and b in Figure 4–4A. Thus they cannot possibly detect the contingency that is present.

Now consider the opposite case of an organism that comes to an experiment biased to evaluate environmental events as under its control. It makes a response and the reinforcer occurs. It makes the response again and the reinforcer occurs again. It keeps making responses and keeps obtaining reinforcers. It is sampling only Cells a and b in Figure 4–4A. Little does it know, nor will it ever find out, that the reinforcer will come even if it does not make the response. If reinforcers are frequent but noncontingent, as in an operant situation equivalent to Figure 4–5A, this organism may never discover the noncontingency because it is always responding. There is substantial evidence that this kind of bias does indeed operate routinely in people (Allan & Jenkins, 1980; Alloy & Abramson, 1979; Alloy & Tabachnik, 1984; Arkes & Harkness, 1985; Crocker, 1981; Einhorn & Hogarth, 1978; Jenkins & Ward, 1965; E. A. Skinner, 1985; Ward & Jenkins, 1965).

Because one cannot ensure that subjects will sample all possibilities in operant conditioning studies, one cannot be sure that they will detect contingencies accurately. The subject who samples only Cells a and b is likely to behave as if a contingency is present when in fact there is none.

What does this imply about contingency detection in operant conditioning? It seems to imply that contingency is not necessary for conditioning to occur. If one somehow forced an organism to experience all possible response–reinforcer combinations, it would presumably eventually correctly detect the presence or absence of a contingency. Thus contingency learning certainly can occur. But if, for whatever reason, the organism enters the experiment biased to sample the different cells selectively, as in the second part of a helplessness experiment, contingency learning will not occur.

Operant Conditioning: What Is Learned?

In our discussion of Pavlovian conditioning, we saw that over the years considerable attention has been devoted to determining whether conditioning involves the formation of S–S associations or S–R associations. Similar issues arise in the case of operant conditioning. Superficially, it would seem that operant conditioning involves learning the relation between response and consequence, an R–S association (with "S" referring to the stimulus that is the reinforcer or punisher). However, an account like this raises some conceptual difficulties. It is obvious that, in general, causes must precede effects. But in the case of operant, response–reinforcer relations, the "cause" of the response, the reinforcer, *follows* it rather than preceding it. As a result, something other than the reinforcer that the response will be producing must be present before the response occurs to cause it. The question is, what is that something?

Among the various answers to this question that have been suggested over the years, one in particular has been especially prominent and influential. It has been suggested that what actually causes the operant response is some stimulus in the situation that has become associated, through Pavlovian conditioning, with the reinforcer. Thus, for example, the sight of the lever might become associated with food, and subsequently come to trigger lever pressing. On this account, operant conditioning is actually a result of S–R association rather than R–S association (see Hull, 1943, and Spence, 1956, for the most influential theories of this type).

Until recently, though this matter was much debated, it was not subjected to experimental analysis. In the last few years, however, techniques used to study the issue in the Pavlovian domain have been adapted to the operant domain. The results of this research make it quite clear that operant conditioning involves the formation of associations between response and consequence (see Colwill & Rescorla, 1985a, 1986; Rescorla, 1987).

Let us examine a few examples. If rats are trained to press a lever for one type of food, and to pull on a chain for another type of food, they learn to make both responses. If one of the foods is then devalued, by associating it with an injection that produces stomach illness, the rats will stop making the response that produces that food, though they continue making the other one. Since the association of the food with stomach illness does not change any of the stimulus aspects of the situation that might hypothetically be responsible for the response, one is forced to conclude that the response occurs not because it is associated with any aspects of the experimental chamber, but because it is associated with the reinforcer. When the value of the reinforcer is eliminated, so is the source of the response (Colwill & Rescorla, 1985a).

In a second example, rats were again trained to make two responses for two different reinforcers. After they learned, the contingency between one of the responses and its reinforcer was reduced. It was reduced by giving the animals additional reinforcers independently of their responses. We have just reviewed the evidence that when a response–reinforcer contingency is reduced or eliminated, responding is reduced or eliminated. What happened in this study was that only the response that had been producing the now freely given reinforcer was substantially diminished. The other response continued to occur largely as before. Again, since the stimulus aspects of the experimental chamber were unchanged by the addition of response–independent reinforcers, the implication is that what was being changed was the association between response and reinforcer (Colwill & Rescorla, 1986).

What this new evidence tells us is that our superficial hypothesis that operant conditioning involves learning the relation between response and outcome is probably correct. A somewhat less technical way to say this is that operant conditioning involves learning to expect that responses produce reinforcement. For many years, explanations of behavior that appealed to things like "expectations" were carefully avoided by learning theorists. In contrast, not only are modern learning theorists willing to appeal to expectations, they can actually find ways to manipulate and measure them.

Avoidance Behavior

Traditional efforts to explain operant behavior without appealing to expectations meet their greatest challenge in the phenomenon of **avoidance behavior**. Avoidance behavior is a pervasive feature of everyday life. Much of our daily activity serves the function of avoiding negative or aversive stimuli that would occur if we did not behave appropriately. We hand in assignments on time to avoid reprimands from the teacher, pay our bills to avoid paying interest, fill the gas tank to avoid running out on a deserted stretch of highway, steer the car to avoid going off the road, refrigerate our food to avoid spoilage, and so on. It is probably true that each of us makes dozens of avoidance responses every day.

Though avoidance behavior is so pervasive, it is often not obvious. We can see why if we think about what the consequences of habitually successful avoidance responding is. As a consequence of making avoidance responses, we don't run out of gas, don't go off the road, don't pay interest, and don't spoil our food. In short, we make the response and nothing happens. The reinforcer for avoidance is a nonevent, the absence of something bad. While the absence of a significantly aversive event would certainly be noticeable in a context in which such events were routinely occurring, it would not be especially noticeable if we made avoidance responses so reliably that the aversive event virtually never occurred. Then it would only be when we failed to make the avoidance response, and the aversive stimulus occurred, that we experienced anything noticeable.

It is for just this reason that the phenomenon of avoidance has produced a great deal of experimentation and theorizing in learning theory. What sustains avoidance responding? How can a nonevent be a reinforcer? If a nonevent like not running out of gas is a reinforcer, why doesn't it reinforce all kinds of activities, like shopping for food, paying bills, and studying? These activities also have the result that we don't run out of gas. Most of the research on avoidance learning has been concerned primarily with answering these questions. We will first describe the phenomena of avoidance learning as they are studied in the laboratory and then turn to various theoretical efforts to explain avoidance.

DISCRETE-TRIAL SIGNALED AVOIDANCE

There are two standard procedures for studying avoidance, and many variants on each of them. In one type of avoidance procedure, animals are exposed to discrete trials. Periodically a stimulus (say, a tone) is presented. If the animal makes the required response while the tone is on, it prevents shock from occurring at the end of the tone. If the animal does not make the required response, when the tone goes off it is followed by prolonged electric shock. If the animal now makes the required response, it turns off, that is, escapes, the shock. Thus avoidance procedures of this type are actually escape–avoidance procedures. Figure 4–6 presents a schematic diagram of the standard escape–avoidance procedure.

In one of the more common types of avoidance experiment, animals are placed in a chamber that is divided in half by a barrier. The animal is placed on one side of the chamber, or **shuttle box**, and is required to jump over the barrier to the other side of the box to escape or avoid shock. Dogs exposed to such a procedure will learn to avoid shock in 20 trials or so (Solomon & Wynne, 1953). Rats exposed to the same procedure will learn to avoid shock in 40 or 50 trials (Kamin, 1956).

The development of avoidance responses often follows a reliable

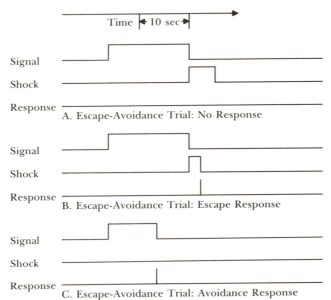

FIGURE 4–6.   *Schematic Diagram of the Standard Escape–Avoidance Procedure.* Depicted are a trial in which no response occurs (A), a trial in which an escape response occurs (B), and a trial in which an avoidance response occurs (C). A response is indicated by a vertical line.

pattern. Early in training, animals do not avoid shock at all; when the shock comes on, they suffer through it for a while, jumping about in the box, and eventually jump over the hurdle. In other words, they escape the shock but do not avoid it. As trials proceed, animals continue to escape and not avoid; however, the latency of their escape responses grows shorter and shorter (but see Bolles, Moot, & Nelson, 1976, for some contradictory evidence). There comes a point at which they escape the shock virtually at the moment it begins. When finally they begin to avoid, the avoidance response comes at the onset of the stimulus that signals shock; the animals do not wait until just before the shock is due to arrive.

SHOCK POSTPONEMENT

The second standard type of avoidance procedure, which we will call a shock-postponement procedure, includes neither discrete trials nor signals. The animal is placed in the chamber and the session begins. A timer is set, let us say, to time a 5-second interval. When the timer has timed 5 seconds, a brief, inescapable electric shock is delivered; then the timer begins again. Each 5 seconds another brief shock will occur. If the animal makes a response (lever press or hurdle jump), the first timer is deactivated and another timer begins to operate. It is set, let us say, to time 30-second intervals. After 30 seconds, the same brief shock will occur. Timer 2 will be deactivated and Timer 1 will be reactivated. However, if the animal makes another response before 30 seconds has elapsed, Timer 2 will reset to the beginning, and start timing 30 seconds all over again. Every time the animal responds, Timer 2 will reset and start again. If ever the animal fails to respond within 30 seconds and a shock occurs, Timer 1 will become active and stay active, delivering shocks every 5 seconds until the animal responds again.

This **shock-postponement procedure** (also known as **free-operant avoidance** or **Sidman avoidance**, after the researcher who developed it) has two important variables: the two time intervals (see Hineline, 1977; Sidman, 1953, 1966). Timer 1 in the example above times the interval between two shocks, or the *shock–shock (S–S) interval.* Timer 2 times the interval between response and shock or the *response–shock (R–S) interval.* In the example, the S–S interval is 5 seconds and the R–S interval is 30 seconds. If the animal could tell time, it could respond exactly once every 30 seconds and never receive a shock. Though animals are not this efficient, a well-trained dog may respond only five or six times a minute and virtually never receive a shock. Rats respond more frequently than dogs and typically receive some shocks no matter how well trained they are, but at the peak of their performance rats may receive only a few shocks an hour instead of the 720 shocks an hour they would receive by not responding.

By varying the R–S and S–S intervals, one can influence the rate at which an animal responds. If the R–S interval is short, say, 5 seconds, response rate is high; if the R–S interval is long, say, 60 seconds, response rate is low. Similarly, if the S–S interval is 5 seconds, response rate will be high; if it is 60 seconds, response rate will be low. In all cases the responding of animals on this type of procedure moves in the direction of maximum efficiency without ever reaching it as the R–S and S–S intervals are varied. The significance of this second avoidance procedure, in contrast with the first, is that the procedure contains no explicit signal warning the organism of impending shock. That animals can learn to avoid in such circumstances has important implications for explanations of avoidance, as we shall soon see.

These, then, are the two most common avoidance procedures: *discrete-trial, signaled avoidance,* in which a stimulus periodically signals an impending shock and a response during the signal avoids the shock; and *free-operant, unsignaled avoidance,* in which shocks are arranged to occur repeatedly and an animal must respond steadily to prevent or postpone them. Organisms learn to avoid shock effectively when exposed to either procedure. What is the nature of this learning process? What part of the avoidance procedure is crucial for learning to occur? Let us turn to a discussion of several different accounts of avoidance.

Theories of Avoidance

If one were to describe the phenomenon of avoidance to an individual who knew nothing about learning theory, that individual would probably have no trouble providing an explanation. It seems obvious and intuitive that if an animal knows that the only way to avoid pain is by making a response, it will surely learn to make it.

Let us attempt to make this intuitive explanation a bit more rigorous. What it means to "know" about avoidance contingencies is that a response leads to no shock and no response leads to shock. Despite the simplicity of this intuitive explanation of avoidance, learning theorists have found it unsatisfactory, because our intuitive account appeals to what animals expect the consequence of their behavior to be. It is forward looking, or *teleological*. And much of learning theory can be seen as an attempt to replace this teleology with other kinds of explanations. Indeed, the law of effect is precisely such an attempt: Behavior that is apparently forward looking and teleological is explained in terms of its past reinforcing consequences. So the task of learning theory is to find the reinforcing consequence of avoidance responding. But it is not easy to identify the reinforcer.

What event maintains avoidance? Our intuitive account suggests that the absence of shock is the crucial event. But how can the absence of something be an event? When does it start? How long does it last? An organism that has never received a shock will not press a lever to avoid shock. Can we say that the absence of shock reinforces your reading of this chapter? What most of the different theories of avoidance have in common is the search for an event, other than the absence of shock, that can be said to maintain responding.

We will discuss three different theories that have attempted to explain avoidance. Efforts have been made to account for avoidance (1) in terms of joint action of Pavlovian and operant conditioning *(two-factor theory)*, (2) in cognitive terms, that is, based on what an organism expects to happen in such procedures *(cognitive theory)*, and (3) in biological terms, that is, based on built-in responses to danger that characterize different species *(biological theory)*. We will take up each of these theories in turn and discuss the problems they encounter.

TWO-FACTOR THEORY

Perhaps the most influential theory of avoidance views it as the product of both Pavlovian and operant influences. It is therefore usually called **two-factor theory**. It was initially formulated by Mowrer, and subsequently elaborated upon by Solomon and his collaborators (Miller, 1948; Mowrer, 1947; Rescorla & Solomon, 1967; see also Dinsmoor, 1977, for a related account).

Consider a discrete-trial, escape–avoidance procedure. A tone is presented and followed by shock. First, the animal learns to escape the shock. The reinforcer for escape responding is shock termination. While escape is occurring, however, Pavlovian conditioning is also occurring; on each trial, tone (CS) is paired with shock (US). After a number of trials, the tone should elicit fear just as the shock does. The animal may now make the escape response to escape from the fear-provoking CS. But *escape* from the CS is *avoidance* of the US. Thus the two-factor theory of avoidance suggests that avoidance is not really avoidance at all. It is escape from a stimulus that, through pairing with shock, has become fear provoking. The tone becomes a conditioned aversive stimulus. And two-factor theory tells us that animals will respond to eliminate a conditioned aversive stimulus.

Notice how elegantly two-factor theory solves the problem mentioned earlier of having a nonevent (the absence of shock) maintain avoidance; it is not the absence of shock at all but the elimination of the CS that maintains avoidance. Similarly, since escape is crucial to successful avoidance behavior, the theory maintains that both Pavlovian and operant factors influence and maintain avoidance.

Two-factor theory seems a sensible and straightforward account of discrete-trial avoidance learning. But what of the shock-postponement procedure mentioned earlier? Recall that in this procedure there is no stimulus that signals shock. What can the CS be under these conditions? It turns out that Pavlovian conditioning can occur when there is no CS other than the passage of time. If the US occurs at regular intervals, then the passage of a certain amount of time can become a CS and elicit responses. This temporal conditioning may well be occurring in shock-postponement procedures. Time between a response and shock is constant, and one could easily imagine that fear could be conditioned to a period of time after the last response. When the organism made a response, fear would be low or nonexistent. As time passed without a response, fear would grow. When it became sufficiently intense, the response would occur, escaping the fear and as a by-product avoiding the shock. There is ample evidence that animals that learn to avoid shocks on shock-postponement procedures do not distribute their responses randomly in time; rather, the likelihood of a response increases as the time since the last response increases (Anger, 1963). This seems to provide support for a two-factor interpretation of avoidance learning in shock-postponement procedures.

What evidence is required to support the two-factor theory of avoidance? To begin with, it is clear that when avoidance is being learned the signal should be fear evoking. There is no doubt that it is. There are a number of experiments that are variants on the following procedure:

Animals are first trained to escape and avoid shock in a standard discrete-trial procedure. After they have learned to avoid shock, they are put in a new situation, in the presence of the signal for shock. Now if they learn to make a response that is completely different from the previous avoidance response, they can escape the signal. Shock never occurs in this new situation. Animals reliably learn to make the response that escapes the signal (J.S. Brown & Jacobs, 1949; McAllister & McAllister, 1962; Miller, 1948; see also Kamin, Brimer, & Black, 1963). What could possibly be maintaining the response if the signal is not fear evoking?

There is other evidence in support of two-factor theory. This evidence shows that if a CS that has been made to elicit fear through a standard Pavlovian conditioning procedure is presented to an animal while it is responding to avoid shock, the CS will increase the animal's rate of responding. Consider, as a concrete example, a dog that has been trained to jump over a hurdle to avoid shock on a shock-postponement procedure. After it has learned to avoid reliably, it is placed in a new situation and exposed to pairings of tone and shock. These Pavlovian conditioning trials presumably make the CS a conditioned elicitor of fear. Now the animal is returned to the avoidance procedure. It responds, say, six times a minute. Occasionally the tone is presented. It turns out that presentations of the tone reliably produce increases in the rate at which the animal makes avoidance responses—sometimes to double the rate without the tone (Rescorla, 1967b). Moreover, if the animal is exposed to a Pavlovian conditioning procedure that includes a CS$^-$ or safety signal (an inhibitor of fear), and that stimulus is then occasionally presented while the animal is making avoidance responses, the rate of avoidance responding decreases significantly, often to half the rate that occurs in the absence of the CS$^-$ (Rescorla & LoLordo, 1965).

What these experiments show is that stimuli known to produce or inhibit fear can alter the rate of avoidance responding. By itself this fact does not necessarily support two-factor theory. Support comes from the inference that since Pavlovian conditioned fear can affect the rate of avoidance responding, it is therefore a necessary component of all avoidance responding. In an ordinary avoidance experiment, escape and avoidance develop at the same time that conditioned fear is presumed to develop. As a result, one cannot isolate conditioned fear from the operant consequences of responses and attribute a significant causal role to fear itself. The virtue of the experiments described above is that conditioned fear is produced in one situation and the operant consequences of responses occur in a different situation. When the CS is then presented and it influences responding, this effect can be attributed to fear alone. The drawback of these experiments is that it can never be proven that because a CS for fear *can* influence avoidance, it *does* influence avoidance in an ordinary discrete-trial procedure. Nevertheless, these experiments certainly suggest that the two-factor account of avoidance may be accurate.

There is another side to the story, however. Just because two-factor theory has been so influential and successful in generating further research, a great many facts have been revealed that point persuasively to its inadequacy as an account of avoidance. We will review some of these facts and the problems they pose below.

Locating the Conditioned Stimulus (CS) We have seen that it is easy to identify the CS in discrete-trial procedures and difficult, but not impossible, in shock-postponement procedures. There is another type of avoidance procedure in which the difficulty in specifying the CS grows substantially. In this procedure, shocks are programmed to be delivered so many times per hour, but unlike the shock-postponement procedure, they are distributed randomly in time. One shock may follow another by a few seconds or by many minutes; there is no fixed time between shocks that might serve as a temporal CS. Rats will learn to press a lever on this procedure if the consequence of lever pressing is a reduction (not necessarily to zero) in the overall frequency of shocks (Herrnstein & Hineline, 1966; see also Herrnstein, 1969).

Locating the Conditioned Response (CR) Pavlovian fear conditioning presumably produces conditioned fear responses. A wide variety of different responses have been used at different times as indices of conditioned fear. If conditioned fear is a crucial component of avoidance responding, we should expect to observe conditioned fear responses in avoidance procedures. Moreover, we should expect fear CRs to terminate abruptly when the avoidance response occurs. The evidence on this matter points clearly to the conclusion that fear CRs are not reliably observed in avoidance experiments (see Rescorla & Solomon, 1967). Sometimes they are observed; sometimes they are not. Sometimes when they are observed they occur at the wrong time. There is no set of fear responses of which it can be said that at least one was observed each time an investigator looked for it.

There is additional evidence that fear does not reliably occur in avoidance situations, especially not when avoidance responding has been well maintained for some time. When dogs are used as subjects, one can observe signs of fear manifested in their facial expressions and in their posture and gait. Pet owners have little difficulty in determining whether their dogs are afraid. If one watches dogs that have been successfully avoiding for some time, one sees no external sign of fear at all. On the contrary, the dogs appear quite nonchalant and relaxed as they make their avoidance responses (Solomon & Wynne, 1954).

Finally, perhaps the clearest evidence against the idea that the avoidance CS is fear provoking comes from experiments that attempt to measure fear of the CS in situations other than the avoidance situation. We discussed in Chapter 2 the phenomenon of conditioned suppression. When animals are responding for food and a Pavlovian CS for shock is presented, responding for food is suppressed. This conditioned suppression is often used as a measure of Pavlovian fear conditioning. If the CS in an avoidance experiment is fear provoking, its presentation should suppress lever pressing for food.

When one does experiments of this type, one finds evidence against two-factor theory. In one very well-known experiment, rats were exposed to an escape–avoidance procedure for varying numbers of trials. Then the avoidance CS was presented while the animals were responding for food. For animals with only modest amounts of avoidance training, two-factor theory was confirmed; the more training they had, the more the CS suppressed responding for food. However, for animals with extensive training, the CS produced almost no suppression at all (Kamin, Brimer, & Black, 1963). Thus just as dogs with extensive avoidance experience do not look afraid, rats with extensive training do not show fear (suppression) to the CS. Indeed, it is fair to say that there is little relation to be found between the effectiveness of avoidance responding after extended training and conditioned suppression to the avoidance CS (Mineka, 1979, 1985; Mineka & Gino, 1979, 1980; Starr & Mineka, 1977).

In summary, there are a number of different lines of evidence to suggest that fear is not present in avoidance situations, at least not after avoidance responding has been fully learned and is being sustained. It is difficult to maintain that escape from fear is what sustains avoidance responding in light of this evidence.

Extinction of Avoidance   Let us examine closely what happens during an avoidance trial in which the animal successfully avoids shock. The CS occurs and is followed by a response. As a result the US does not occur. Thus each successful avoidance trial is a Pavlovian extinction trial: CS followed by no US. From what we have already seen in Chapter 2, extinction of Pavlovian conditioning should be relatively rapid: Probably within 50 trials, and certainly within a few hundred trials, the CS should stop eliciting fear. Thus the two-factor theory of avoidance might lead one to expect the course of avoidance learning to look something like the following:

1. Trials 1–30: Escape but no avoidance; acquisition of conditioned fear.

2. Trials 31–100: Reliable avoidance and concomitant extinction of conditioned fear. As a result of extinction of fear, extinction of avoidance.

3. Trials 101–130: Return to escape but no avoidance. As each trial occurs, the CS is again paired with shock and conditioned fear is reestablished.

4. Trials 131–200: Reliable avoidance returns. This of course carries with it extinction of fear and extinction of avoidance.

5. Trials 201–230: Escape but no avoidance. Etc.

The cycling of periods of escape with periods of avoidance ought to continue indefinitely as fear alternately undergoes extinction and reconditioning. If one disconnects the shocker so that shock never occurs, avoidance responding should continue until fear is extinguished; then it should cease entirely.

Thus two-factor theory implies an interesting and detailed set of predictions both about trial-by-trial avoidance behavior and about the course of extinction. None of these predictions is confirmed by available evidence. First of all, once avoidance responding is acquired, it typically occurs reliably. The predicted cycling of escape and avoidance over blocks of trials does not occur. More significantly, when the shocker is disconnected, animals often continue to make avoidance responses for hundreds and hundreds of trials. Typically the experimenter's patience wears out before the animal's responses do. Whereas complete extinction of fear in a conditioned suppression procedure may occur within 12 trials if the shock is mild, and within 50 if the shock is extremely intense, no sign of extinction of avoidance responding may be seen even after 200 trials (Annau & Kamin, 1961; Solomon, Kamin, & Wynne, 1953; Solomon & Wynne, 1954; for a few exceptions to this pattern see Denny, 1971; McAllister & McAllister, 1971).

It might be argued that avoidance situations are sufficiently traumatic that once responding develops it can never be extinguished; responses once learned are irreversible. As it turns out, there are at least two methods one can use to produce very rapid extinction. The first method is simply to have the shock occur whether or not the avoidance response occurs. When shock is delivered whether or not the animal jumps over the hurdle or presses the lever, extinction is rapid (Davenport & Olson, 1968).

The second method for producing rapid extinction is known as **flooding** or **response blocking**. To take a typical example, an animal that has been trained to jump across a barrier from one side of a box to the other to avoid shock is placed on the side in which the trials begin as normally. The CS is presented. When the animal attempts to make the avoidance response, it encounters a floor-to-ceiling obstruction that makes it impossible to get to the other side of the box. The animal is thus forced to remain in the presence of the CS. Shock is not delivered. When the avoidance response is blocked in this way, avoidance responding is rapidly extinguished. Moreover, the speed of extinction is directly related to the amount of time animals are forced to experience the CS (Baum, 1969, 1970; Schiff, Smith, & Prochaska, 1972).

Thus avoidance responding can be extinguished, but not simply by performing the operations that one would expect to produce extinction of conditioned fear. All the data taken together show that while fear, when present, may influence avoidance responding, fear is not necessary for the occurrence of avoidance and its elimination does not result in the cessation of avoidance. It seems clear that an alternative to two-factor theory must be found.

COGNITIVE THEORY

We have seen that two-factor theory's attempt to circumvent the problems inherent in an intuitive account of avoidance has met with problems of its own. Let us then return to the intuitive account. Perhaps if the intuitive account, based on what an organism knows, expects, and desires, can be made more rigorous, the problems connected with it will disappear. Seligman and Johnston have attempted to provide such a rigorous cognitive theory (Seligman & Johnston, 1973; see also Hilgard & Marquis, 1940; Richie, 1951).

The postulates of the cognitive theory are simple and direct. These are:

1. An animal prefers no shock to shock.

2. An animal expects that if it responds, no shock, rather than shock, will occur.

3. An animal expects that if it does not respond, shock will occur.

4. Expectancies are strengthened when they are confirmed and weakened when they are disconfirmed. The expectancy that a response leads to no shock is confirmed whenever a response occurs and is not followed by shock. It is disconfirmed whenever a response occurs and is followed by shock. Similarly, the expectancy that no response leads to shock is confirmed whenever shock occurs in the absence of a response and is disconfirmed whenever shock does not occur in the absence of a response.

5. Finally, the probability of an avoidance response increases as the degree of confirmation of the two expectancies (2 and 3 above) increases.

In addition to these cognitive characteristics of the theory, there is also an emotional component. It contains just two principles:

1. Fear is conditioned to a CS paired with shock.

2. Fear is extinguished when a CS is not paired with shock.

It is important to note that these principles merely state that ordinary Pavlovian conditioning and extinction may occur in avoidance procedures. We will see that according to the theory, while Pavlovian conditioned fear may play an important role in the initial occurrence of avoidance responses, it has no role at all in the maintenance of avoidance responses.

Let us now apply the theory to what is known about avoidance. First, how are avoidance responses initially acquired? An inspection of the cognitive part of the theory reveals that expectancies can play no role in response acquisition. How is the animal to develop the expectancy that responding leads to no shock if it does not already make the response? It is the emotional, Pavlovian component of the theory that explains the initial occurrence of responses. The theory contends that responses elicited by either shock or the CS provide the basis for early avoidance responding. If the response required by the experimenter closely resembles responses elicited by shock or the CS, learning of expectancies will begin rapidly; if, on the other hand, the response required by the experimenter does not closely resemble elicited responses, the learning of expectancies will be slow—indeed, they may not be learned at all (see Bolles, 1970, and Masterson & Crawford, 1982, for support).

Once avoidance responses begin to occur and expectancies begin to develop, the cognitive component of the theory takes over. Let us see how it accounts for a number of avoidance phenomena that have posed problems for two-factor theory. First, consider the major stumbling block, extinction. Why is extinction by disconnecting the shocker slow, while extinction by response blocking and by presenting shock whether or not the response occurs is fast? Each time the animal makes the response and shock does not occur, the expectancy that responding leads to no shock is confirmed and, according to the theory, strengthened, with the result that the probability of the response increases. Thus extinction by turning off the shocker does nothing to alter one of the critical expectancies. The other expectancy, that no responding leads to shock, would be disconfirmed if the animal did not respond; however, the extinction procedure usually does not begin until the probability of a response is so high that the animal responds on virtually every trial. Thus there is no effective opportunity for disconfirmation of this expectancy. Here is where response blocking comes in. When the animal is not allowed to make the response, it is forced to experience disconfirmations of the expectancy that not responding leads to shock. Ultimately it develops the expectancy that not responding leads to no shock and stops responding. Thus even though the other expectancy, that responding leads to no shock, is never disconfirmed, response blocking can produce extinction. This account makes sense of the fact we mentioned earlier that prevention of the avoidance response makes a major contribution to the effectiveness of response blocking over and above the extinction of fear to the CS. If the avoidance response was not prevented, the new expectancy that not responding leads to no shock could never develop.

Note that extinction of the avoidance response in this way does not imply anything about the status of conditioned fear. It is logically possible for fear to be present even after the avoidance response has been extinguished. The determinants of fear are different from the determinants of avoidance. There is in fact evidence that fear is often present in very dramatic form during response-blocking procedures, and that it may persist even after avoidance responding has stopped (Baum, 1970; Mineka & Gino, 1979).

Now what of extinction by presentation of shock whether or not the response occurs? With this procedure, the expectancy that not responding leads to shock is unaltered. However, the expectancy that responding leads to no shock is disconfirmed. Disconfirmation reduces the strength of the expectancy and the probability of the response. Thus the two effective extinction procedures are effective for different reasons; each operates on and weakens a different expectancy.

The theory does an impressive job of explaining much of what we know about aversive control. It cannot, however, explain everything. There are still some aspects of aversive control that resist explanation by the cognitive theory:

For example, why does a Pavlovian CS for fear that is taken from a different situation and imposed on an avoidance procedure increase responding even in animals whose behavior has been maintained on the avoidance procedure for many, many sessions? Presumably in these animals the relevant expectancies are as strong as they can be. Moreover, consider what expectancies might have developed to the CS during Pavlovian fear conditioning. Here, shock occurred whether or not the animal responded. Thus the CS might well evoke the expectancies that responding and not responding lead to shock. If these expectancies had any effect, it would be to decrease the likelihood of a response rather than to increase it.

Thus there is still work to be done before a complete account of avoidance is available. The cognitive theory does manage to account for much of what is known about avoidance, but not all.

BIOLOGICAL THEORY

The biological approach to avoidance learning is not really incompatible with the earlier ones; indeed, the ideas of this approach are an important part of the cognitive theory. What distinguishes this approach from the others is primarily emphasis.

Imagine an animal living its life in a relatively hostile natural environment. Among the most important things it must learn is a set of responses that protects it from danger; it must learn to avoid its predators. On the basis of any of the theories we have discussed so far, we might expect avoidance of a predator to develop after a substantial number of trials in which the animal first escapes from the predator, or learns what stimuli (CSs) reliably signal the arrival of a predator so that these stimuli can be escaped and the predator avoided. Animals that learn to avoid in this way in the wild are likely to wind up inside another animal before they learn to avoid it. It seems clear that if animals are to survive in the natural environment, they must learn to escape danger quickly.

Robert Bolles pointed this out and went on from there to outline an approach to avoidance learning that focused on the repertoire of defensive responses with which members of different species are endowed and the relation between those responses and the ones required in the laboratory (Bolles, 1970; see Masterson & Crawford, 1982, for a related account). Bolles contended that each species has a set of built-in defensive responses—called **species-specific defense reactions** or **SSDRs**. Common SSDRs include freezing, attack, and flight. When a danger situation develops, an organism will make one of its SSDRs. If this response eliminates the danger, all is well; if not, the animal will make another SSDR; and another, and another, until one of them succeeds. Only when all of the animal's defensive repertoire has been sampled and proven ineffective will non-SSDRs occur. The order in which SSDRs are tried may be random or, more likely, SSDRs may be arranged on a hierarchical scale, with some being reliably tried before others.

What are the implications of this account of avoidance in nature for our understanding of avoidance in the laboratory? It follows from this account that the single most important determinant of avoidance will not be whether a CS is present, whether a response turns off the CS, whether a response can escape shock, or any of the other variables we have considered. Rather, what will largely determine the rapidity of acquisition of avoidance responses is the response the animal is required to make. If the response resembles an SSDR, the animal will learn quickly; if the response does not resemble an SSDR, the animal will learn slowly or not at all. It is Bolles's contention that while other variables may influence the rate at which avoidance is learned, their influence is insignificant in comparison to the influence exerted by the relation between the required response and the animal's SSDR repertoire.

Consider the relation between the biological theory and the cognitive theory. The cognitive account of avoidance explicitly acknowledges the importance of responses elicited by the aversive stimulus. The cognitive theory also acknowledges (1) that expectancies cannot develop until the avoidance response is occurring and (2) that it is likely that the avoidance response will arise from those responses elicited by the aversive stimulus. Cognitive theory then focuses on what happens after the response is occurring. The biological theory focuses instead on what determines the early occurrences of the responses; what happens later is of lesser importance. Thus the difference between the biological view of avoidance and the cognitive view is a difference in emphasis rather than a confrontation between logically incompatible formulations.

What is the evidence for the biological theory? Is there reason to believe that the response one requires in an avoidance experiment has a major influence on avoidance learning? The answer is unequivocally yes (Masterson & Crawford, 1982). In the case of the rat, some avoidance responses may be learned in one or two trials; an example is jumping out of a box. Other avoidance responses may require many hundreds of trials for acquisition; an example is the familiar lever press. Bolles suggests that the reason lever-press avoidance is learned at all is that the animal may accidentally make an SSDR (such as freezing or attacking) on the lever. If this does not happen, the rat may never learn to lever-press, and indeed some rats do not learn.

It is important to this theory that a response that is difficult to acquire as an avoidance response is easily learned under other circumstances. Otherwise it would be neither interesting nor surprising that organisms learn some responses only with great difficulty. It would surprise no one if 10,000 trials were required to train a rat to stand on its head in any situation. One could argue that lever pressing was similarly difficult to learn if it were not for the fact that it is easily learned under conditions of appetitive reinforcement.

The same pattern of data characterizes the pigeon. Pigeons learn to lift their heads, flap their wings, hop on a foot switch, and fly very rapidly in avoidance situations. However, they learn to peck a key to avoid aversive stimuli only with the greatest difficulty. It may take up to 20 hours of painstaking training to develop key-peck avoidance responding. Obviously the key peck is acquired with great ease under conditions of food reinforcement (see Bedford & Anger, 1968; Hineline & Rachlin, 1969; Schwartz, 1973).

These two examples are sufficient to make a case that the response one chooses to require has a major effect on the results of one's experiment. This is because some responses (non-SSDRs) will not occur in danger situations. Ideally, with the biological theory in hand, one can study the behavior of a particular species in nature, catalog the defense reactions of that species, and then make detailed predictions about which avoidance responses will be rapidly learned in the laboratory and which will be slowly learned (see Grossen & Kelley, 1972, for an example).

Conditioned Reinforcement

The two-factor theory of avoidance depends upon the idea that through conditioning, a neutral stimulus—a CS—can become aversive, and there is no doubt that it can. What about the other side of the coin? Can a neutral stimulus, through conditioning, become positive? The answer to this question is yes. Neutral stimuli can become positive, and when they do, their presentation can reinforce behavior. We call such stimuli **conditioned reinforcers**. They are extremely important to an understanding of human behavior, and thus have been the subject of a great deal of research.

Certainly, the kinds of stimuli, like food or water, that reinforce the behavior of animals in experiments can also reinforce human behavior. But what, for example, makes money a reinforcer? What makes an "A" grade on an examination a reinforcer? People engage in extraordinary amounts of operant behavior for reinforcers like these. Let us consider what makes money as a reinforcer different from food. That food is a reinforcer does not depend on an organism's having had experience with it. It is simply a biological fact about organisms that they will do things to get food. Food is a significant event, an unconditioned stimulus (US). Money is not. We are not born ready to work for money. The power of money (or good grades) as a reinforcer derives from our experience with it. We learn that money is a reinforcer. And according to behavior theory, we learn that such stimuli as money or good grades are reinforcers through conditioning—thus their designation as conditioned reinforcers.

Consider an example. We expose a rat to numerous pairings of a click and food. Then we attempt to train the rat to press a lever. Lever presses produce not food, but just the click. The rat learns to press the lever for the click (B.F. Skinner, 1938). Or consider a second example. Rats are trained to press a lever, with lever presses producing both a click and food. Then lever pressing is extinguished; it no longer produces food. For some rats it produces nothing; for others, however, it produces the click. The second group takes longer to stop responding than the first (Bugelski, 1938). Extinction is slowed down because the click is reinforcing.

ESTABLISHING A CONDITIONED REINFORCER—PREDICTIVENESS

These two examples of conditioned reinforcement look just like Pavlovian conditioning. A neutral stimulus (click) reliably precedes an unconditioned stimulus (food). Instead of evaluating conditioning by determining whether the neutral stimulus produces salivation or some other CR, we evaluate its power to reinforce operant behavior. Thus, it is not surprising that the variables that are important to Pavlovian conditioning are important to conditioned reinforcement. Recall that for Pavlovian conditioning to occur, the CS must be predictive or informative; mere temporal contiguity between CS and US is not enough. Well, the same seems to be true of conditioned reinforcement.

Consider the following experiment. Rats already trained to press a lever for food experienced trials with the lever absent in which food presentation was preceded by two stimuli, S_1 and S_2, as depicted in Figure 4–7A. For one group of rats (Group B), S_1 was also occasionally presented alone, without S_2 or food, as in Figure 4–7B. After this training, the rats were placed in an extinction situation in which lever presses produced only S_1 for some animals and only S_2 for others. Based on our discussion of predictiveness in Chapter 3, what would we expect the results of such an experiment to be? Let us consider first the rats (Group

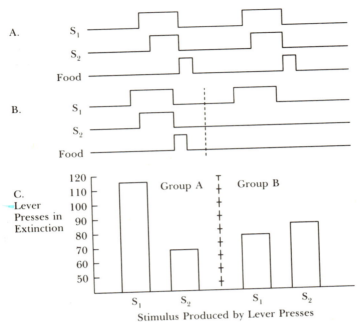

FIGURE 4–7.   *Effects of the Informative Value of Stimuli on Their Effectiveness as Conditioned Reinforcers.* Part A depicts the S_1–S_2–food sequence received by Group A. Part B depicts the two types of sequences received by Group B. Part C depicts responses in extinction for both groups when lever presses produced either S_1 or S_2. (After Egger & Miller, 1962.)

A) that experienced only the stimulus sequences depicted in Figure 4–7A. S_1 and S_2 both reliably preceded food. However, since S_1 appeared a half second before S_2, the appearance of S_2 was *redundant;* all the information available regarding food was carried by S_1. If the predictiveness of a stimulus is essential to its conditioned reinforcing power, we would expect these rats to have responded more when responses produced S_1 than when responses produced S_2.

Now consider the second group of rats (Group B). When S_1 and S_2 and food occurred in sequence, S_2 was again redundant. However, some of the time only S_1 occurred. As a result of these extra trials, S_1 no longer made S_2 redundant; sometimes S_1 was followed by food but sometimes it was not. Now S_2 was the best predictor of food. On the basis of informativeness, we would expect these rats to have responded more in extinction for S_2 than for S_1.

As can be seen in Figure 4–7C, the predictions based on informativeness were confirmed experimentally. Rats in Group A pressed more for S_1 than for S_2 in extinction. Rats in Group B pressed more for S_2 than for S_1 (Egger & Miller, 1962; see also Egger & Miller, 1963, and Seligman, 1966, for similar results). Note that while this experiment can't be taken to show that informativeness is *necessary* for a stimulus to become a conditioned reinforcer, it does show that the more informative a stimulus is, the more effective it is.

Having found that the predictiveness of a stimulus contributes to its conditioned reinforcing power, we are left with a difficult and subtle question: What is it about the predictiveness of a stimulus that makes the stimulus reinforcing?

OBSERVING RESPONSES

Imagine a pigeon trained to key-peck for food. Not every peck produces food. Instead, food is available only at certain times. Sometimes it is available for a peck every 10 seconds and sometimes it is available for a peck every 40 seconds. But the pigeon has no way of telling which of these two conditions is in effect at any given moment. The pigeon can obtain food, when it is available, by pecking either of two keys. As far as getting food is concerned, it makes no difference which key the pigeon pecks.

But in another respect it does make a difference. If the pigeon pecks one of the keys, it can obtain information. The key will turn red if the 10-second interfood period is in effect and green if the 40-second interfood period is in effect. In contrast, if the pigeon pecks the other key, it obtains no information; that key will turn yellow no matter which interfood period is in effect.

In a procedure like this, despite the fact that pecks on either key serve equally well to produce food, pigeons show a dramatic preference for the key that provides information (Bower, McLean, & Meachem, 1966; see also Hendry, 1969a,b; Wyckoff, 1952). The argument is that red and green are reinforcing precisely because they provide information about the availability of food. The pigeon pecks this key to "observe" what contingencies are currently operative in the experiment. For this reason, responses like these are sometimes called **observing responses**.

There are many demonstrations in the literature that animals will make observing responses, responses the sole consequence of which is to provide information. This has led to the view that it is just this informativeness that gives conditioned reinforcers their reinforcing power. What influences the effectiveness of a conditioned reinforcer is how much news it provides, not whether the news is good or bad. An alternative view is that a stimulus will be a conditioned reinforcer if it provides news, but only so long as the news is good.

To clarify the difference between these positions, think about the kinds of observing responses people make, like reading newspapers, listening to weather reports, and so on. Suppose that weather reports in two cities are extremely reliable. They provide equally good information about the next day's weather. In one of the cities, however, the weather reports are usually bad news. It rains a lot in that city. In the other city the weather reports are usually good news. Will that difference between the two cities influence how likely we are to listen to weather reports? If our eagerness to listen to weather reports is affected by their content, it implies that there is more to observing than just news. Stimuli that provide information may be reinforcing both because of their informativeness and because of their association with the events they predict. If the events they predict are bad, these stimuli will not be reinforcing, no matter how much information they provide.

Experimental evidence suggests that animals will make observing responses for informative stimuli only if the information they provide is good news. In one experiment, pigeons pecked a key for food, which was available at irregular intervals. Some of the time their pecks also produced electric shocks. The pigeons were given the opportunity to peck another, observing key, which gave them information about whether they were in a shock period or a shock-free period for pecks at the food-producing key. When pecks at the observing key produced signals for *both* shock-free periods and shock periods, high rates of observing responding occurred. However, when observing key pecks produced signals only for shock periods (that is, during shock-free periods observing key pecks produced no signal), observing responses were not sustained (Dinsmoor, Flint, Smith, & Veimeister, 1969; see also, Auge, 1974; Dinsmoor, 1983; Dinsmoor, Browne, & Lawrence, 1972; Fantino, 1977; Fantino & Abarca, 1985; Fantino & Moore, 1980). Note that a procedure that signals only shock periods provides just as much information as a procedure that signals both shock and shock-free periods. The absence of a signal for shock when an observing response occurs is itself a signal for no shock. Nevertheless, observing responses were not maintained under these conditions.

But there is another side to this story. Think again about listening to weather reports. Let us compare three imaginary cities. In City A it rains 90% of the time, in City B it rains 10% of the time, and in City C it rains 50% of the time. In all three cities weather reports are always accurate. How might our tendency to listen to weather reports differ in the three cities? In terms of the quality of the news we get, we will get good news most often in City B and least often in City A, with City C in the middle. Thus, based on the experiment just described, we might listen to the weather most often in City B and least often in City A. But what about the *quantity* of the news we get? Now the rankings are different. In Cities A and B we are pretty certain about the weather without listening to the weather report. After all, in both of these cities the weather is the same 90% of the time. In contrast, in City C we are maximally uncertain about the weather. We have the most information to gain by listening to the weather report. If our observing responses are influenced by how much information they provide, we should listen to the weather more often in City C than in A or B.

Experiments like this have been done with animals. The typical procedure is one in which either of two different experimental conditions may be in effect at any given moment, and observing responses tell the animal which one is actually in effect. What is varied is the probability of the two conditions. When they are equally probable, the situation is like the weather in City C. When one is much more probable than the other, the situation is like Cities A and B. A typical finding in such experiments is that animals are most likely to make observing responses when they are most uncertain about what experimental condition is in effect, that is, when the two conditions are equiprobable (Green & Rachlin, 1977; for a review, see Fantino, 1977). Thus it does appear that the magnitude of reinforcement provided by the occurrence of a conditioned reinforcer is related not just to the quality of the event it signals, but to the quantity of information it provides.

In addition to this evidence for the importance of the quantity of information provided by observing responses, one experiment suggests that there may be species differences in observing responses. We saw that pigeons will not make observing responses if the only news they can get is bad. What about people? Human subjects were exposed to a procedure in which observing responses told them either whether reinforcement was currently available or not or whether high or low effort was required to produce reinforcement. Two different observing responses were possible. One of them produced only good news. When reinforcement was available or low effort was required, a signal appeared; otherwise it did not. The second observing response produced both good and bad news—one signal for reinforcement or low effort and a second signal for no reinforcement or high effort. This second source of information was vastly preferred to the first (Perone & Baron, 1980; but see Fantino & Case, 1983, for conflicting data). Thus, for people, observing responses may be under purely informational control even if for pigeons they are not.

TOKEN REINFORCERS

In introducing our discussion of conditioned reinforcement we asked about the kinds of reinforcers that are commonplace in human life. Among the most obvious of them is money. Is money a conditioned reinforcer? If it is, is it reinforcing because of the information it provides about other reinforcers?

We cannot provide a definitive account of how money comes to be a reinforcer, either in the life history of an individual or in the development of a culture. But whether or not conditioning experience makes money a reinforcer, it is clear that its reinforcing power does not derive from the information it provides. Money enables us to obtain other reinforcers, and its power as a reinforcer surely derives from this property. In addition, if money is a conditioned reinforcer, it is different in important ways from a light that signals food. First, unlike the light, we must actually do something with the money before we can obtain the unconditioned reinforcer. Second, money is associated with a wide range of different unconditioned reinforcers—food, shelter, clothing, entertainment, and so on. We might describe it as a **generalized conditioned reinforcer,** by virtue of its relation to multiple unconditioned reinforcers. It might be that it is this generalized character of money as a reinforcer that gives it its extraordinary power. Does learning theory have anything to tell us about reinforcers like money?

Within the domain of research on conditioned reinforcement there is a body of experimentation with reinforcers very much like money. These reinforcers are referred to as **token reinforcers.** Some of the earliest investigations of conditioned reinforcement involved procedures in which chimpanzees responded for tokens (poker chips) that could subsequently be exchanged for food (Figure 4–8). It was assumed that if responding was maintained by token reinforcement, this would be evidence that tokens acquire reinforcing value by virtue of their association with food. Among the interesting findings that came out of these studies were the following:

1. Some chimpanzees worked as hard for tokens (exchangeable for grapes) as they did for grapes.

2. Chimpanzees would work for tokens even if a delay of 1 hour was imposed between obtaining the token and exchanging it for food, provided they could hold on to the tokens during the delay period.

3. Chimps would learn a new response for token reinforcement, even if a delay was imposed between obtaining the token and exchanging it. With no delay, the chimps learned as rapidly with token reinforcement as with food reinforcement.

4. When chimps housed in pairs were simply given tokens, struggles for dominance, begging, and even stealing of tokens were observed (Cowles, 1937; Wolfe, 1936).

Other research with token reinforcement has indicated that by using tokens one can get animals to produce substantial amounts of operant responding for very infrequent food rewards. In one such study chimps had to trade in 50 tokens for each delivery of food. To obtain a single token a chimp had to make 125 operant responses. Thus this procedure had the chimps making 6250 responses for each food delivery (Kelleher, 1958).

Results of this sort lend some plausibility to the claim that conditioned

FIGURE 4–8. *Token Reinforcement.* A chimp has been trained to deposit tokens to produce food reinforcement. (Courtesy of Yerkes Regional Primate Research Center, Emory University.)

reinforcement, at least in the form of tokens, controls behavior in the same way that money does. What makes this claim even more plausible, however, is the use of token reinforcement in applications. Token reinforcement provides an effective means of controlling behavior in settings as diverse as mental hospitals and schools. In these settings, tokens do indeed have the status of money. They are exchangeable for a variety of unconditioned reinforcers, and some of these "cost" more than others, so that tokens must be accumulated, budgeted, and so on (Atthowe & Krasner, 1968; Ayllon & Azrin, 1968; O'Leary, 1978; O'Leary & Drabman, 1971). While there are some suggestions that tokens derive their effectiveness from characteristics that the notion "conditioned reinforcer" does not completely capture, at the very least it seems reasonable to conclude that the associative processes that make stimuli conditioned reinforcers contribute to the effectiveness of token reinforcement (see Schwartz & Lacey, 1988, for discussion).

THE FUNCTIONS OF CONDITIONED REINFORCERS

We have treated the stimuli produced by observing responses as conditioned reinforcers and we have treated tokens as conditioned reinforcers. They have in common an association with unconditioned reinforcers. But there is also much to distinguish them. Stimuli produced by observing responses provide information, but do nothing to move the animal closer to reinforcement. Tokens, in contrast, are an essential step in the path to reinforcement. Without first earning tokens, the chimp could never get food. What these differences between different types of conditioned reinforcers reveal is that conditioned reinforcers can serve a variety of different functions, and thus can have a variety of different properties. We will identify some of them here.

First, conditioned reinforcers provide feedback. They tell the organism that it has done the right thing. The chimp earns tokens only for appropriate responses. The student earns an "A" only for appropriate responses.

Second, conditioned reinforcers tell the organism what to do next. The chimp presses a lever 100 times and gets a token. The presence of the token tells the chimp that it is time to stop pressing the lever and start exchanging the token.

Third, conditioned reinforcers serve to bridge long periods between unconditioned reinforcers. The chimp might make 6250 responses for each food delivery if it earns tokens along the way, but not if it does not.

Finally, conditioned reinforcers may have hedonic functions. It may feel good to obtain them in the way it feels good to obtain food. When the instructor says "Good backswing!" to his tennis pupil, the "good" provides feedback about having performed correctly. It also tells the pupil that it is time to move on to another aspect of the game. But it may also make the pupil feel good (see Martin & Levey, 1978).

We can illustrate these multiple effects of conditioned reinforcers with an example. Consider the "treasure hunts" that young children find so entertaining. They go off in search of a secret destination, where they find a message giving them a clue to another destination. The search continues from destination to destination, each one bringing them closer to the treasure. What are the functions of the messages they find? First, they provide feedback, letting the children know that they are on the right track. Second, they provide information, telling the children what to do next. Finally, they provide excitement and exhilaration, with the excitement growing as the children draw closer to the end. Thus these treasure hunt messages combine all the effects of conditioned reinforcers that we identified separately.

Though it is not easy to isolate these various characteristics of conditioned reinforcers empirically, we can separate them logically (but see Cohen, Callisto, & Lentz, 1979, for an attempt at empirical separation of the different properties of conditioned reinforcers). And from one situation to another, conditioned reinforcers may be effective by serving one or more of these different functions.

Summary

In addition to being influenced by Pavlovian contingencies, behavior is affected by its consequences. The study of operant conditioning is the study of how contingencies of reward and punishment influence the future likelihood of the behavior that produces them. The law of effect tells us that responses that produce positive consequences (reinforcement), or eliminate (escape) or prevent (avoidance) negative consequences, will increase in frequency. Responses that produce negative consequences (punishment), or prevent positive ones (omission), will decrease in frequency.

When operant responses produce reinforcement they become more frequent or probable in the future. When reinforcement is discontinued (extinction), the frequency of operant responses decreases. In addition, reinforcement affects the form of the operant. While early in training responses will be extremely variable and contain many extraneous components, as training proceeds responses become highly stereotyped and efficient. The animal must discover which properties of its responses are critical to producing reinforcement. Once this discovery is made, efficient responses that possess this property emerge.

As in the study of Pavlovian conditioning, ideas about what is necessary for conditioning to occur initially focused on temporal contiguity of response and reinforcer. However, recent research has suggested that response–reinforcer contiguity is not enough. Organisms can distinguish response-dependent from response-independent reinforcement. Indeed, one of the consequences of response–outcome independence can be learned helplessness, which in humans can lead to clinical depression. Findings like these have suggested that organisms can distinguish contingency from contiguity, and that the former is necessary for conditioning. Nevertheless, though the evidence is clear that organisms *can* distinguish contingency from contiguity, there is also evidence that they do not always do so. Various biases can influence both which response–outcome combinations organisms will experience and what they will learn from these experiences.

In the study of avoidance learning the central issue has been to identify the reinforcer. How can a nonevent (the absence of the aversive stimulus) be the reinforcer? A number of different theories have attempted to explain this puzzle of avoidance. Two-factor theory suggests that avoidance is actually escape from the fear-provoking CS. It can explain much that is known about avoidance, but it is faced with insurmountable problems. It is not possible to find the fear-provoking CS in certain types of avoidance experiments. There is good evidence that well-trained animals continue to avoid even though they are no longer afraid of the CS. Avoidance responding does not stop even though many successful responses should result in the extinction of fear of the CS.

A more successful theory is cognitive theory, which essentially formalizes our intuitive account of avoidance learning. Cognitive theory can explain most of what is known about avoidance learning, but not everything. It cannot tell us how avoidance responding originates. To explain this we can appeal to the final theory, biological theory. The biological theory of avoidance suggests that the major influence on avoidance learning will be the response one chooses to train as an avoidance response. If it matches one of the organism's built-in responses to danger, learning will be rapid; if not, learning will be very slow.

Reinforcement is central to operant conditioning. While some stimuli, like food, are reinforcing independent of the organism's experience, reinforcers can also be created by conditioning. Reinforcers established in this way are called conditioned reinforcers. Conditioned reinforcers are established by Pavlovian conditioning, and once established, their presentation can train and sustain operant behavior. Critical to establishing a conditioned reinforcer is that it provide information about the unconditioned reinforcer. Indeed, organisms will reliably make observing responses, responses that produce these informative conditioned reinforcers, even though observing responses have no direct effect on obtaining the unconditioned reinforcer. And how likely they are to make observing responses depends on how uncertain they are about reinforcement without the conditioned reinforcers. Yet informativeness is not enough. If observing responses produce only bad news, they are not sustained. To be a conditioned reinforcer not only must a stimulus provide information, but it must provide good information; that is, it must be associated with a positive unconditioned reinforcer.

Sometimes conditioned reinforcers involve more than either information or association with unconditioned reinforcers. Sometimes they are links in a chain leading to the unconditioned reinforcer. Examples of such conditioned reinforcers are token reinforcers. Organisms respond to produce tokens, and the tokens are later traded in for such items as food. Token reinforcement is the laboratory analog of money as a reinforcer. And token reinforcement procedures have been used extensively in attempts to apply principles of learning theory in a variety of settings.

PART 2

COMPLEX

LEARNING

PROCESSES:

CHOICE AND

STIMULUS

CONTROL

5 The Maintenance of Behavior: Intermittent Reinforcement, Choice, and Economics

Our discussion of operant conditioning in Chapter 4 was concerned primarily with specifying the different kinds of contingencies that can hold between operant behavior and environmental events, and with indicating the effects on behavior of those different contingencies. The emphasis there was on learning—on the modification of operant behavior by its consequences, and particularly on the acquisition of new classes of operant behavior. Certainly any serious attempt to explain human behavior will have to offer some account of how behavior is modified.

But there is another aspect of behavior that also requires attention. By the time most people have reached adulthood, most of the different kinds of activities they will engage in for the rest of their lives have already been acquired. People know how to speak and read, they know as much mathematics as they ever will, they know whatever is needed to perform their jobs, they know how to drive, they know how to play certain kinds of games, how to cook, and so on. Once a relatively complete repertoire of behavior has been established, what sustains it? What keeps already-acquired behavior occurring? In short, what environmental conditions are responsible for *maintaining* behavior once it has been established?

Not surprisingly, learning theorists have sought to explain the maintenance of behavior in terms of the same behavior–outcome relations used to explain its acquisition. The claim is that behavior is maintained by just those contingencies of reward, punishment, escape, and avoidance that originally established it.

At first blush this may seem implausible. Any of us, after a casual inspection of just the last few days of our lives, can produce a long list of activities we engaged in without reinforcement of any sort. Doing our jobs does not result in reinforcement hour after hour and day after day. Neither does studying. Even recreational activities are not always reinforced. Why then do we continue to engage in these activities?

A possible answer is that even if a behavior is not reinforced each time it occurs, it may still be true that the behavior is maintained by reinforcement. It is possible that reinforcement that is only occasional or intermittent can still effectively control behavior. When we are acquiring an operant, it may be reinforced on virtually every occurrence. But once it is acquired, such regular reinforcement may not be required to sustain it.

If intermittent reinforcement can maintain behavior, is it plausible that our daily activities can be understood solely in terms of their reinforcing environmental consequences? Consider a rat in a conditioning chamber, pressing a lever for food. Only some of its lever presses are reinforced. The rat presses the lever steadily, perhaps as often as 60 times per minute. This kind of situation captures the intermittency of reinforcement in the natural environment, but clearly something is still missing. The rat must simply "decide" whether or not to press the lever at any given moment. The conditioning chamber really offers little else to do and no reinforcement other than food. It is not surprising that under these circumstances a rat (or a person) will produce the operant repeatedly. But our lives are not that simple. A ubiquitous feature of human life is choice. The issue for us is not whether or not to engage in some activity for intermittent reinforcement. Rather we must decide which activity and which reinforcement. Should we study, and obtain presumed reinforcements like knowledge and good grades, or should we pass the evening chatting with friends? Should we order strawberry shortcake for dessert, and be reinforced by the pleasant taste, or grapefruit, and be reinforced by our slender shape? Should we practice law or practice plumbing? Should we go north for Christmas to ski or south to lie on the beach? Virtually every kind of human activity is the result of a choice among possible behaviors and possible reinforcers. For learning theory to have a claim on explaining our daily existence, it must be able to tell us not only about intermittent reinforcement, but also about choice.

While it is true that even the rat pressing the lever has choice available (between pressing and not), this is surely a degenerate form of choice. It is degenerate largely because it is hard to imagine what could possibly induce the rat not to press the lever in the typical, impoverished experimental setting. Thus to study choice one must give organisms real choices. One must establish situations in which different kinds of activities produce different kinds of outcomes, and find out what influences an organism's decision to allocate time and energy to one activity rather than another.

For choices to be significant ones, it must be the case that choosing between A and B means you can't have both. You can't be both a lawyer and a plumber; you can't ski and soak up the sun; you can't both study and socialize. If we could do all the things among which we are choosing, then choice would largely involve deciding what to do first. Sometimes choice is like this. But often, choosing one alternative precludes others. One way of looking at choices of this type is that people have limited resources of time, energy, and money, and choosing involves making decisions about how these limited resources should be allocated. Viewed in this light, the study of choice overlaps with the discipline of **economics**. Economics is primarily concerned with specifying the factors that influence the allocation of limited resources, both at the level of individual people and at the level of entire societies or economic systems. Thus learning theory and economics share common concerns. Both disciplines view organisms as making choices about the allocation of their resources. For economics the coin of the realm is money, while for learning theory it is operant behavior. But these differences in currency are not necessarily an obstacle to using the principles from one domain to explain the phenomena observed in the other. And we will see that learning theory has come in recent years to depend on central economic concepts to explain the determinants of choice behavior in animals. Thus in this chapter, on the maintenance of behavior, we will focus on three major issues. What are the effects on behavior of intermittent reinforcement? How do organisms make choices among alternative operants and outcomes? And how can concepts from economics be used to help us understand choice behavior?

Schedules of Intermittent Reinforcement

We know from the law of effect that when a response (lever press or key peck) regularly produces reinforcement, the response increases in probability. But we also know that human experience does not characteristically include reinforcement each time a given response occurs. What happens to behavior when it is reinforced intermittently, as most human behavior presumably is? The answer is that how behavior is affected by intermittent reinforcement depends on exactly how that intermittent reinforcement is arranged. The study of the effects of intermittent reinforcement on behavior is usually referred to as the study of **schedules of reinforcement**. A reinforcement schedule is simply a rule that specifies how often, and under what conditions, a particular response will be reinforced.

Basic Schedules of Reinforcement

All schedules of reinforcement have one thing in common: Reinforcement depends on the occurrence of a response. With schedules in which each response is reinforced, called **continuous reinforcement (CRF)** schedules, a single response is all that is required for reinforcement. With other schedules, reinforcement may depend on something in addition to a particular response, either the passage of a certain amount of time (**interval schedules**) or the occurrence of a certain number of previous responses (**ratio schedules**). Each of these types of schedules can be subdivided. The intervals required for reinforcement may be fixed (each interval is the same) or variable. Similarly, ratios may be fixed (each reinforcement depends on the same number of responses) or variable. These four types of schedules—**fixed interval, variable interval, fixed ratio**, and **variable ratio**—are the most basic types of reinforcement schedules (Ferster & Skinner, 1957).

FIXED-INTERVAL (FI) SCHEDULES

When reinforcement is arranged on an FI schedule, a single response after the passage of a fixed amount of time produces reinforcement. If the value of the interval is 1 minute (FI 1-min), then one lever press or key peck, a minute or more after the interval has begun, produces reinforcement. Responses *during the interval* do nothing. The passage of the interval by itself does nothing. Reinforcement depends on both the passage of time and a single response. If the experimental subject could tell time, then it could simply relax until a minute was up and then make a single response, thereby producing a maximum amount of reinforcement with a minimum amount of effort. While organisms do not perform quite this efficiently on FI schedules, they do learn to predict the length of the interval.

VARIABLE-INTERVAL (VI) SCHEDULES

On variable-interval schedules, reinforcement also depends on the passage of time and a single response. However, unlike FI schedules, the time between reinforcements on VI schedules varies from one reinforcement to the next. The value of the VI schedule is the average time between reinforcements. Thus, for example, a VI 2-min schedule might make the first reinforcement available after 1 minute, the next 2 minutes later, the next 4 minutes later, the next 30 seconds later, and so on.

Although it is possible to obtain reinforcement for each response on a VI schedule simply by waiting for the interreinforcement interval to elapse, there is no way for the subject to predict the length of a particular interreinforcement interval. This difference between VI and FI schedules results in a striking difference in the pattern of responding maintained by the two types of schedules.

FIXED-RATIO (FR) SCHEDULES

On a fixed-ratio schedule, reinforcement depends on the completion of a certain number of responses; time is irrelevant. If the value of the ratio is 50 (FR 50), every 50th response is reinforced. If the subject responds rapidly, reinforcements may be only seconds apart, and if the subject responds slowly, reinforcements may be many minutes apart. The passage of time does not make reinforcement any more likely.

VARIABLE-RATIO (VR) SCHEDULES

On a variable-ratio schedule, the number of responses required for reinforcement varies from one reinforcement to the next. On a VR 50 schedule, the animal might first have to make 60 responses, then 30, then 85, then 50, then 15, then 70, then 40, and so on. The value of the VR schedule specifies the average number of responses required for reinforcement.

Having defined the different basic schedules of reinforcement, we must examine their effects on behavior. Doing this involves first determining that behavior in fact continues to occur when it is reinforced in accord with one of these schedules. If these schedules can maintain behavior, the next issue to address is whether their effects on behavior are different.

Can Schedules of Reinforcement Maintain Behavior?

Imagine a rat that has just been trained to press a lever for food. After it has obtained 50 reinforcements on a CRF schedule, we decide to expose it to an intermittent reinforcement schedule. We choose an FR 200 schedule; that is, every 200th lever press will produce food. What will be the effect of this schedule? If you examine Figure 4–2 (p. 123), you might predict that the FR 200 schedule will not maintain responding. Instead the rat will probably have stopped pressing the lever long before it has made 200 responses and earned even a single FR reinforcement. This phenomenon, as we have seen, is called extinction. It would also occur if we were to shift a rat from a CRF schedule to, say, an FI 10-min schedule. Thus it might appear that the power of reinforcement schedules to maintain responding is severely limited. Contrary to appearances, however, it is quite possible to sustain responding on schedules that require many hundreds of responses for a single reinforcement, or many minutes to elapse between reinforcements. The trick is to bring the animal to the target schedule gradually. Thus, rather than shifting from CRF to FR 200, one might shift from CRF to FR 3, then to FR 10, then to FR 20, then FR 50, and so on. One would wait before making each shift until the animal was responding on the current ratio fairly reliably, without frequent pauses.

Why should it be that an abrupt transition from CRF to FR 200 cannot maintain behavior while a gradual transition can? The answer to this question lies in a phenomenon known as the **partial reinforcement effect**. It is now well established that if reinforcement is discontinued (extinction), it will take longer for an animal to stop responding if its responses had previously been intermittently reinforced than if they had been regularly reinforced (see Amsel, 1962, 1967; Mackintosh, 1974). This effect probably results, at least in part, from the fact that when extinction follows regular reinforcement, one can quickly learn that conditions have changed. Indeed, a single unreinforced response is enough to tell you that things are not as they were. In contrast, when extinction follows partial reinforcement, it is more difficult to tell that conditions have changed. After all, in the past many responses have occurred without reinforcement despite the fact that reinforcement is still occasionally forthcoming. Imagine using sweets as a reinforcer to induce a child to do its homework. Every night the child obtains candy or ice cream when its homework is done. After a while you decide that the child should be doing its homework without the promise of a reinforcer, so you end the contingency. It will take the child only one night to discover that the rules of the game have changed. In contrast, if the child had been getting reinforcement every four or five nights, discovery that reinforcement had been discontinued would take much longer.

Let us see how the partial reinforcement effect can explain why gradual transitions to schedules that deliver reinforcement infrequently can maintain behavior while abrupt transitions cannot. Suppose we shift a rat from CRF to an FR 3. It presses the lever and no food comes. Extinction has begun, but it will press the lever a few more times before it gives up. Once it does persist for a few more presses, it will satisfy the FR requirement and obtain another reinforcement. After a while it will become accustomed to this schedule and press away with no hesitation. Now you change the ratio to an FR 10. Again, extinction will begin. But this time the rat, already accustomed to intermittent reinforcement, will take longer to discover that conditions have changed. It will make at least 10 lever presses before it quits. And since the 10th press will produce food, lever pressing will continue. We can see that as we increase the ratio, more and more responses are required before an animal can distinguish extinction from the previous ratio. This means that cessation of responding will take longer and longer to be complete. And this means that the animal will persist long enough to obtain food on the new ratio. Through this process, reinforcement can be made increasingly infrequent and still maintain responding. While there are limits to how many responses an organism will make for a single reinforcer, the limits are very large indeed.

Patterns of Behavior Maintained by Reinforcement Schedules

Now that we know that schedules of reinforcement do indeed maintain operant behavior, we can ask about how they do so. Are the patterns of behavior maintained by different schedules different and, if so, in what way? Typical patterns of responding maintained on the four basic reinforcement schedules are depicted in Figure 5–1. In Figure 5–1, the passage of time is represented on the x-axis and cumulative responses are represented on the y-axis. The downward marks indicate occurrences of reinforcement. Graphs like these are known as **cumulative records**. It is clear from Figure 5–1 that the different schedules produce strikingly

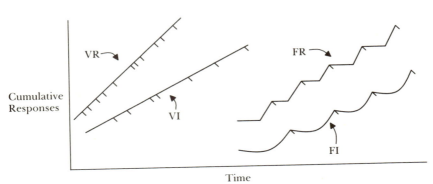

FIGURE 5–1. *Typical Patterns of Responding Generated by the Four Basic Reinforcement Schedules.* The downward strokes indicate reinforcements and the rate of responding at any point in time is represented by the slope of the curve at that point. Note that variable-ratio (VR) and variable-interval (VI) schedules maintain steady rates of responding, with VR response rate higher than VI response rate. Fixed-ratio (FR) and fixed-interval (FI) schedules maintain patterns of responding characterized by a pause after each reinforcement.

different patterns of responding. Variable-ratio and variable-interval schedules are similar in that they produce relatively constant patterns of responding in time. They differ in that variable-ratio schedules maintain higher rates of responding than variable-interval schedules. Similarly, fixed-ratio schedules generate higher rates of responding than fixed-interval schedules—when the organism is responding at all. The most noticeable characteristic of both FR and FI schedules is that for some time after each reinforcement there is no responding.

It should not be thought that the different schedules produce response patterns like those in Figure 5–1 independent of their values. The value of the schedule (that is, VI 1-min versus VI 10-min, or FR 10 versus FR 200) also influences the pattern of responding. However, the effects of variations in the value of the schedule depend on the nature of the schedule itself.

On VI and VR schedules, increases in the value of the schedule (decreases in the frequency of reinforcement) do not change the shape of the cumulative record; as long as reinforcement is frequent enough to maintain responding at all, responses occur at a uniform rate. Changes in the frequency of reinforcement change the *slope* of the curves (that is, the rate of responding). Within limits, the more frequent reinforcement is, the steeper the slope of the curve is.

On FR and FI schedules, the effect of the schedule value is different. Changes in schedule value primarily affect the length of the pause after reinforcement. Once responding occurs, it tends to occur at a high, steady rate whatever the schedule value may be. Small fixed ratios, like FR 10 or FR 20, may result in no postreinforcement pause at all. The response pattern for an FR like that would look like the graph for the VR in Figure 5–1. Very large fixed ratios, like FR 200, may produce long postreinforcement pauses, followed by a burst of responses, then another long pause, then another burst, and so on until the ratio is completed. These pauses after responding has begun are taken as signs of what is called **ratio strain**. That is, the value of the ratio is almost too large to maintain responding. Within these limits, fixed-ratio schedules produce patterns of responding like that in Figure 5–1: There is a pause after reinforcement, whose duration varies with the size of the ratio, followed by a uniform, high rate of responding until the ratio is completed.

On FI schedules, the schedule value primarily influences the postreinforcement pause. Well-trained animals may not emit their first response until two-thirds of the interval has elapsed. Once responding starts, one sometimes observes response patterns like those on FR schedules—responding begins at a high rate and stays at that rate until reinforcement. More often, when responding starts, it starts slowly and builds up gradually to the high rate that characterizes the end of the interval. Thus one observes gentle, elbowlike curves in records of performance on FI schedules. The pattern is referred to as an **FI scallop**.

The Study of Choice: Concurrent Schedules of Reinforcement

At the beginning of this chapter we suggested that a central element of human behavior that is not adequately captured in simple operant conditioning experiments is choice. Our actions almost always represent choices among alternatives. Learning theorists have been cognizant of the significance of choice in human activity, and have attempted to study choice behavior experimentally. What characterizes the study of operant choice behavior is the focus on how the likelihood of a given class of operant behavior is affected not just by *its* reinforcement history, but by the reinforcement history associated with *other* possible classes of operant behavior. In a typical choice experiment, a pigeon might be confronted with two lit response keys, say, one yellow and one blue. Pecks at the two keys might produce food according to two independent VI schedules of reinforcement. A well-trained pigeon in such a situation will peck a few times on one key, then switch to the other, then switch back to the first, and so on, obtaining reinforcement for pecks on both keys. Procedures of this type are referred to as **concurrent schedules**, which are more generally defined as two or more schedules that operate simultaneously and independently, each for a different response. By studying the behavior of animals exposed to concurrent schedules of reinforcement, we can begin to evaluate how the availability of an alternative source of reinforcement influences a given operant behavior.

Suppose, for example, we expose a pigeon to a single VI 3-min schedule of food reinforcement for pecking. It comes gradually to peck the key at a steady, moderate rate of perhaps 40 pecks per minute. Now we introduce a second key, this one associated with a VI 1-min schedule. The pigeon will begin pecking this key, and gradually, over time, it will peck less and less at the first key. What this simple demonstration shows is that the frequency of operant behavior can be altered even if the schedule of reinforcement that is maintaining it is not altered. What affects the frequency of the operant in this case is the frequency of reinforcement available for another operant.

THE MATCHING LAW

The behavior of animals exposed to concurrent VI schedules of this type is remarkably reliable. It turns out that responses are emitted to the two keys (or levers) in direct proportion to the frequency of reinforcement obtained for those responses. If we call the response keys *A* and *B,* then

$$\frac{\text{Resp on } A}{\text{Resp on } A + \text{Resp on } B} = \frac{\text{Rft on } A}{\text{Rft on } A + \text{Rft on } B}$$

or

$$\frac{R_A}{R_A + R_B} = \frac{r_A}{r_A + r_B} \tag{1}$$

The relative frequency of responding on an alternative matches the relative frequency of reinforcement for responses on that alternative. This relation is called the **matching law** (see Herrnstein, 1970; de Villiers, 1977).

This matching law provides a roughly accurate description of the behavior of a wide variety of organisms in a wide variety of choice situations. It is as true of lever-pressing rats as of key-pecking pigeons; it is as true of situations involving aversive stimuli as of situations involving food (Baum, 1975; de Villiers, 1974). Also, the matching law applies not just to reinforcement frequency, but to other aspects of reinforcement as well. If one varies the magnitude of reinforcement available for responses on each of two keys or levers, relative frequency of responding matches relative magnitude of reinforcement. That is,

$$\frac{R_A}{R_A + R_B} = \frac{M_A}{M_A + M_B} \tag{2}$$

where M = magnitude of reinforcement. Thus if one schedule provides 8 seconds of food availability for each reinforcement while the other provides 4 seconds, and both schedules provide reinforcements with the same frequency, an animal will prefer the first to the second by a ratio of about 2:1 (Catania, 1963). And if one varies the delay of reinforcement between two alternatives, relative frequency of responding matches the reciprocals of the delays. That is,

$$\frac{R_A}{R_A + R_B} = \frac{\dfrac{1}{D_A}}{\dfrac{1}{D_A} + \dfrac{1}{D_B}} \tag{3}$$

where D = delay in reinforcement. Thus, if one schedule provides reinforcement with a 2-second delay while the other provides it with a 4-second delay, the animal will prefer the first to the second by the same 2:1 ratio (Chung & Herrnstein, 1967).

THE MATCHING LAW IN OPERATION

The matching law tells us how factors such as frequency, magnitude, and delay of reinforcement independently affect choices. It also provides a framework for studying these variables in combination. For example, it might be the case that if frequency, magnitude, and delay of reinforcement were manipulated simultaneously, the equation

$$\frac{R_A}{R_A + R_B} = \frac{r_A \times M_A \times D_A}{(r_A \times M_A \times D_A) + (r_B \times M_B \times D_B)} \tag{4}$$

would describe the result. A particularly impressive example of the study of these variables in combination investigated the joint effects of reinforcement magnitude and reinforcement delay on choice (Rachlin & Green, 1972). Consider pigeons faced with the following choice: If they peck a green key, they obtain 4 seconds of access to food, but they must wait 4 seconds to get it. If they peck a red key, they get 2 seconds of access food, but they get it immediately. Which of these alternatives should pigeons prefer? We can answer this question by using the matching law. To do so, we must assume that even immediate reinforcement involves some delay, since it takes the pigeon time to get its beak to the feeder. So let us assume that the pigeon's choice is between 4 seconds of food delayed 4 seconds and 2 seconds of food delayed 0.1 second. According to the matching law:

$$\frac{\text{Resp-red}}{\text{Resp-red} + \text{Resp-green}} = \frac{\dfrac{\text{Rft time-red}}{\text{Delay-red}}}{\dfrac{\text{Rft time-red}}{\text{Delay-red}} + \dfrac{\text{Rft time-green}}{\text{Delay-green}}}$$

or

$$\frac{R_{\text{red}}}{R_{\text{red}} + R_{\text{green}}} = \frac{\dfrac{T_{\text{red}}}{D_{\text{red}}}}{\dfrac{T_{\text{red}}}{D_{\text{red}}} + \dfrac{T_{\text{green}}}{D_{\text{green}}}}$$

By substituting the values of T and D used in the experiment, we get:

$$\frac{R_{\text{red}}}{R_{\text{red}} + R_{\text{green}}} = \frac{\dfrac{2}{0.1}}{\dfrac{2}{0.1} + \dfrac{4}{4}} = 0.95$$

Thus the matching law predicts that pigeons will overwhelmingly prefer the smaller immediate reward to the larger delayed one, which indeed they do.

But now suppose that this choice between red and green is only a part of a larger procedure, one depicted in Figure 5–2. Here, a trial begins with pigeons faced with two white keys. If they peck the right key 15 times, all the lights in the box go out for 10 seconds (10-second delay). Then the two keys come on again, one red and one green. A peck on the red key immediately produces 2 seconds of access to food while a peck on the green key produces 4 seconds of access to food, after a delay of 4 seconds (the direct choice between red and green that we just worked through). If they peck 15 times on the left white key, all the lights also go off for 10 seconds. But now when the lights come back on, only the left key is lit, with a green light. A peck on the green key produces 4 seconds of food after a 4-second delay.

What might we expect the pigeons to do on this procedure? We already

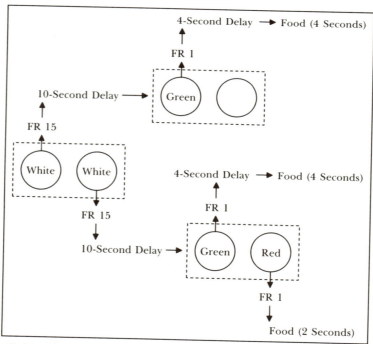

FIGURE 5–2.   *Diagram of a Procedure to Study Effects of Magnitude and Delay of Reinforcement on Choice.* Animals are initially confronted with a choice between two white keys. Fifteen pecks on the left key commits them, 10 seconds later, to the availability of 4 seconds of food with a 4-second delay. Fifteen pecks on the right key gives animals a choice, 10 seconds later, between 4 seconds of food with a 4-second delay and 2 seconds of food immediately.

know that if given the choice between red and green (bottom right of Figure 5–2), pigeons vastly prefer small immediate reinforcement to large delayed reinforcement. Thus when the keys are white, pecks at the left key will force the pigeons into a relatively unpreferred state of affairs (large delayed reward), while pecks at the right key will give them the opportunity to choose a more preferred state of affairs (small immediate reward). Thus we might think pigeons will prefer the right white key because only pecks at it give them access to the red key. What does the matching law have to say?

We know that the relevant equation is this:

$$\frac{R_{left}}{R_{left} + R_{right}} = \frac{\dfrac{T_{left}}{D_{left}}}{\dfrac{T_{left}}{D_{left}} + \dfrac{T_{right}}{D_{right}}}$$

What are the values of T and D to be plugged into the equation? The values of T are the same as before, 4 and 2 seconds. But the values of D have changed; after the pigeon has pecked at the white keys, there is going to be a 10-second delay before the keys turn red or green no matter which key the pigeon chooses. Thus we must add 10 seconds to both values of D we used before. That gives us:

$$\frac{R_{left}}{R_{left} + R_{right}} = \frac{\dfrac{4}{10+4}}{\dfrac{4}{10+4} + \dfrac{2}{10+0.1}} = 0.60 \tag{6}$$

Thus the matching law predicts that pigeons will choose the left white key about 60% of the time even though left-key choices will not give them access to the reinforcement conditions they prefer (small immediate reward).

The matching law seems to have made an unlikely pair of predictions. It is telling us that a pigeon will prefer the left white key to the right one even though pecks on the left key put it in a situation in which 4 seconds of food with a 4-second delay is the only possible outcome. When given an immediate choice between that outcome and another one (immediate 2 seconds of food) the pigeon prefers the other one. Thus even though the pigeon should prefer immediate small reinforcement to delayed large reinforcement (red to green), if we make it commit itself far enough in advance (left white key versus right white key) it will choose a delayed large reinforcement over an immediate small one.

The results of the experiment confirmed these unintuitive predictions based on the matching law. When choosing between red and green, pigeons pecked red virtually all the time. But when choosing between left and right white keys, they pecked left 65% of the time.

To make these results more intuitive, consider this example. When faced with a choice between $10 now and $12 next week, which would you choose? We suspect that many would choose the immediate $10. But what if you were faced with a choice between $10 a year from now and $12 a year and a week from now? Under these conditions, everyone would choose the $12. The addition of a year to the delay of both outcomes makes the difference in delay between them insignificant—for pigeons as well as people.

This last example should alert you to the variable that will determine which white key the pigeon prefers (everything else held constant); it is the time interval between the left–right choice and the red–green choice. There should be some duration between these choices at which pigeons will be indifferent between left and right. We can guess at this duration by turning again to the matching law:

$$\frac{R_{\text{left}}}{R_{\text{left}} + R_{\text{right}}} = 0.50 = \frac{\dfrac{4}{x+4}}{\dfrac{4}{x+4} + \dfrac{2}{x+0.1}} \tag{7}$$

By solving for x in this equation, we find that the value of x at which pigeons should peck left and right white keys with equal frequency is 4 seconds. When the experimenters systematically varied the time between the initial choice of left or right and the later choice of red or green, they obtained the results presented in Figure 5–3. The prediction, based on the matching law, that with a delay of 4 seconds between the initial choice and the final response pigeons should be indifferent between left and right keys was exactly confirmed.

This particular instance of the matching law has potential practical application. We could characterize the behavior of the pigeon when it is confronted with choice between red and green as a choice of less useful outcome (2 seconds of food) over a more useful outcome (4 seconds of food) because the former is immediate. We get the pigeon to choose the more useful alternative when the commitment occurs so far in advance that both outcomes are substantially delayed. Then the relative immediacy of one outcome over another becomes unimportant. One can imagine many human choices between immediate small reinforcement and delayed large reinforcement. Consider, for example, the choice between going to the movies and studying on a particular evening. We could imagine that going to the movies involves a small but immediate reinforcement (an evening's entertainment) while studying involves a large delayed reinforcement (a good exam grade). Given the choice, at 7:45 P.M., between studying and an 8 P.M. movie, the student, like the

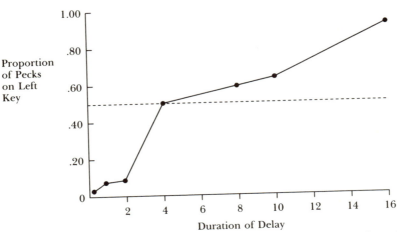

FIGURE 5–3. *A Test of the Matching Law.* The figure depicts the proportion of left-key choices as a function of the delay imposed between early choice and later reinforcement. The point of indifference between left and right keys falls just where the matching law predicts—at 4 seconds delay. (After Rachlin & Green, 1972.)

pigeon, might choose the small immediate reinforcement. But if the choice were required at 9 A.M., so that now both reinforcers were going to be delayed, the student might choose to study. If we arranged contingencies so that people had to commit themselves to one or the other outcome well in advance, the chances of commitment to studying rather than going to the movies might increase.

Almost everyone can recognize numerous instances in daily life that demand "self-control" or "self-discipline." We must resist the temptations of modest, short-term pleasures in the service of substantial, long-term benefits. The dieter must fight off the impulse to eat dessert. The reformed smoker must fight off the impulse to "bum" a cigarette from a friend. We keep ourselves from making small purchases now, so that we can save our money toward some large purchase later. We restrain ourselves from showing anger at a friend immediately after some hurtful act so that we can preserve a valued, long-term friendship. In all of these cases, we know what is in our long-term interests, and we have little difficulty acting in ways that serve these interests so long as short-term temptations are remote. But when they become immediately available, self-control becomes difficult.

There are differences among species and among individuals in ability to resist short-term temptations. Pigeons are more impulsive than people; and children are more impulsive than adults (Ainslie, 1975; Millar & Navarick, 1984; Mischel, 1966, 1974). But organisms can be trained to control their impulsiveness, and situations can be arranged that make self-control easier. For example, it is easier to resist temptation if the desired items (or stimuli that are associated with them) are not actually visible. Out of sight, out of mind. And it is easier to resist temptation if organisms have something to do while they are waiting for the better, but delayed item to become available. And above all, it is easier to resist temptation if circumstances can be arranged that allow for early commitment, so that the actual choice is made when neither item is immediately available (see Ainslie & Herrnstein, 1981; Grosch & Neuringer, 1981; Mischel, 1966, 1974; Rachlin, 1974).

MATCHING AND MAXIMIZING

We have seen that the matching law provides a powerful description of how animals allocate responses among alternatives. The distribution of responses matches the distribution of reinforcement. But in recent years controversy has arisen as to whether the matching law provides a description of the process of choice or only a description of the end result. The distinction here is subtle, and we can perhaps make it clear by analogy. In discussing Pavlovian conditioning, we saw that animals form associations selectively, on the basis of the informativeness of various CSs. The question that arose was how they do it. One possible answer was that animals actually compute informativeness in some way. In this view the process matches the product. But the Rescorla–Wagner theory provided a different answer. Selective association is the result of trial-by-trial increases and decreases in associative strength. In this view the process does not match the product. Holders of these two views do not dispute that selective association is the final product of conditioning; the dispute centers on identifying the underlying process. With respect to operant choice behavior, the dispute is between those who hold that matching as the product results from matching as the process and those who hold that matching as the product results from a different process. The different process is known as **maximizing**. Some who hold the maximizing view suggest that at any given moment animals will choose the alternative response that maximizes the likelihood of a reinforcement at that moment. Others suggest that while maximizing does not govern moment-by-moment response allocation, it does govern overall response allocation. Animals choose so as to maximize the overall likelihood of reinforcement.

There have been several attempts to design procedures in which matching and maximizing views yield clearly different predictions about behavior. We will describe one of them to help illustrate the difference between the two views (Mazur, 1981).

Pigeons were given a choice between two pecking keys, each of which was associated with VI food reinforcement. A single timer determined the availability of reinforcement at random intervals, and each reinforcer was allocated to the left or right key randomly with an equal probability. When a reinforcer was allocated to the left key, a peck on that key was required to produce it, and pecks on the right key had no effect. Moreover, and critically, until that left-key reinforcer was actually collected, the timer was stopped, so that no progress toward the next reinforcer could be made until the currently available one was actually earned. Thus, for example, if the next reinforcer was allocated to the left key, and for some reason the pigeon spent 20 minutes pecking at the right key, it would earn no reinforcer during that period, nor would it get any closer to earning a reinforcer. Only after a left-key peck produced the reinforcer that was currently available would the timer that determined reinforcer availability start working again.

A pigeon that was maximizing its reinforcement rate on a procedure like this would peck the two keys with equal frequency. Unfortunately, though, since equal frequencies of reinforcement would be available on the two keys, such a maximization strategy would also be a matching strategy. Suppose, however, the procedure was changed so that, while reinforcement periods were still assigned with equal probability to left and right keys, for left-key pecks only one in ten reinforcement periods actually contained food. The other nine just involved a brief period of dead time in which no food was available and no pecks could occur. What should the maximizing organism do in such a procedure? The answer is that it should continue to peck the two keys with equal frequency. It may not "like" the consequences of left-key pecks as much as it "likes" the consequences of right-key pecks. But it can't get access to the next right-key reinforcement period until it gets through the current left-key one. In other words, there is nothing the pigeon can do about the fact that half of its reinforcement periods will be associated with the left key. By confining itself largely to the right key a pigeon will introduce substantial delays between the time that a reinforcement period sets up on the left key and the time that it is earned, and as a result, it will reduce the overall frequency of reinforcement obtained. On the other hand, under these new conditions, right-key pecks will be reinforced ten times as frequently as left-key pecks, and if pigeons obey the matching law, they should start pecking the right key almost exclusively, and in the process, cost themselves reinforcement.

What did the pigeons actually do? In this condition, and several other conditions like this, by and large, pigeons moved in the direction of matching. In the particular condition just described, pigeons switched from pecking the two keys about equally to making about 85% of their pecks on the right key. As a result, they obtained about a third less reinforcement than they would have had they continued to distribute their responses equally. Thus, this experiment supports the view that the matching *result* reflects a matching *process*.

It would be nice if our story could end here. Unfortunately, there are other experiments that suggest the opposite conclusion—that organisms do in fact engage in a process of maximization. The final story on this issue has yet to unfold (see Baum, 1981; Herrnstein & Heyman, 1979; Herrnstein & Vaughan, 1980; Prelec, 1982; Rachlin, Battalio, Kagel, & Green, 1981; Rachlin, Green, Kagel, & Battalio, 1976; Shimp, 1966, 1969; Silberberg, Hamilton, Ziriax, & Casey, 1978; Staddon, 1983; Staddon, Hinson, & Kram, 1981; Staddon & Motherall, 1978; Timberlake, 1980).

CHOICE AND FORAGING

At this point in the discussion, we could be both impressed by and skeptical of the power of the analysis of choice we have developed. What, after all, does an account of pigeons choosing which of two keys to peck for food tell us about choice in general? This is certainly a reasonable concern. As it happens, recent developments in behavioral biology have produced results that converge with the results of behavior theory experiments, and suggest that the principles we have been discussing may actually be quite general.

Behavioral biologists have been concerned with understanding the foraging patterns (food-seeking behavior) of various species of animals in their natural environments: what governs which foods an animal selects, where it looks for food, how long it stays in one feeding place before leaving, and so on. Are there some general principles that can describe foraging patterns across diverse types of organisms living in diverse types of environments? The answer seems to be yes, and the set of general principles that has developed has come to be called **optimal foraging theory** (see Allison, 1983; Charnov, 1976; Collier, 1983; Fantino & Abarca, 1985; Kamil & Roitblat, 1985; Krebs, 1978; Krebs & Davies, 1978; Krebs & McCleery, 1984; Pyke, Pulliam, & Charnov, 1977; Shettleworth & Krebs, 1982; Staddon, 1980a,b; Stephens & Krebs, 1986; Timberlake, Gawley, & Lucas, 1987).

Optimal foraging theory says that feeding behavior is sensitive to the relation between the amount of energy that is expended in finding, securing, and consuming food and the amount of energy or nutrition that the food provides. Patterns of foraging optimize the relation between energy gain and energy expenditure. For example, what size prey should a predator be interested in? One might think that the answer to this question is simple: The bigger the better. Actually, many factors enter into the decision. Suppose large prey are scarce. Then a predator will spend a great deal of energy in fruitless searches for large prey. Or suppose it takes a great deal of work to subdue large prey. Then the net return in energy may be greater for smaller and more easily managed prey. Finally, preference for prey size should be influenced by the relative abundance of prey of all sizes in the environment. If food is scarce, perhaps a predator will take anything. If food is abundant, the predator may be more selective.

Or consider organisms that find their food in clumps or patches. They roam around in search of a patch of food. When they locate it, do they stay and eat or leave and seek out another? This might depend on how abundant the food in this patch is in comparison with the abundance of food patches in general. And having found a patch and started searching for food within it, when should an animal leave that patch to seek out a more bountiful one? We might expect that the animal should stay until it has eaten everything in the patch. But this simple view ignores the energy cost involved in searching for food within the patch. If the food gets sufficiently depleted, it may take more energy to find a bit of remaining food than the animal will derive from eating it. At this point it is time to move on. But decisions about moving on should depend not only on likely energy cost/gain relations in that patch, but on what they are likely to be in other patches. Thus if food in the general environment is plentiful, an animal should move on sooner than if it is scarce.

Optimal foraging theory can make precise predictions about how such variables as prey size and quality, food density within a patch, and food availability in the environment as a whole will influence foraging behavior. When these predictions are tested either in the natural environment or in laboratory simulations of natural environmental conditions, they prove to be extremely accurate. The foraging behavior of organisms as diverse as sunfish, great tits, owls, crabs, bees, and various rodents seems to be well accounted for by optimal foraging theory.

For our purposes, the important point about optimal foraging theory is that it has much in common with the accounts of choice behavior offered by learning theory. The issue of prey choice can be studied in the learning theorist's laboratory with concurrent schedules in which the type and magnitude of reinforcement are varied. The issue of when animals will leave one patch for another can be studied with concurrent schedules in which the schedule types are varied. Indeed, there have been a number of recent attempts to introduce precisely the variables that concern optimal foraging theory within the learning theorist's laboratory, with results that are generally consistent with both the principles of optimal foraging theory and the principles of choice reviewed in this chapter (for some examples, see Collier, 1983; Fantino & Abarca, 1985; Hamm & Shettleworth, 1987; Lea, 1979; Mellgren, 1982; Shettleworth, 1985; Shettleworth & Krebs, 1982; Timberlake, Gawley, & Lucas, 1987). This convergence suggests that studies of choice among concurrent schedules really do tell us something important about choice in nature.

Operant Behavior and Economics

Whether choice is best described as reflecting matching, maximizing, or some combination of both, it is clear that organisms distribute their responses among alternatives in an orderly way. We can use the matching law to predict how organisms will allocate their behavior when confronted with a variety of alternatives offering different combinations of frequency, magnitude, and delay of reinforcement. The matching law brings us much closer to an account of human behavior in the everyday environment than simply observing how different reinforcement schedules maintain responding. It does so by explicitly acknowledging, and building into experimental settings, the fact that the occurrence of any given behavior represents a choice among alternatives. It tells us that even choice is orderly and predictable. Choice can be understood with principles derived from the learning theorist's laboratory.

Viewed through the lens of the matching law, questions about choice become questions about how organisms allocate their limited resources. When those organisms are pigeons or rats, the resources in question are behaviors. When those organisms are people, the limited resources may be behaviors as well. But people have another type of limited resource available. That resource, of course, is money. And issues relating to how people allocate their limited resources, both in behavior and in money, have traditionally been the province of the discipline of economics. It is therefore not surprising that in recent years learning theorists have begun to apply concepts developed in economics to their own domain. The matching law is coming to be viewed as a special case of the operation of economic principles that are far more general. We will sketch some of these recent applications of economic principles to operant behavior with an emphasis on two issues. We will be looking at the implications of these new developments for the matching law, and we will be looking at how the economic analysis brings learning theory still closer to an account of human behavior in the natural environment (see Allison, 1983; Collier, Johnson, Hill, & Kaufman, 1986; Green & Kagel, 1987; Green, Kagel, & Battalio, 1987; Hursh, 1980, 1984; Hursh & Bauman, 1987; Lea, 1978; Rachlin, 1980; Rachlin, Battalio, Kagel, & Green, 1981; Rachlin, Green, Kagel, & Battalio, 1976; Staddon, 1983; Timberlake, 1980; Timberlake & Peden, 1987).

THE CONCEPT OF DEMAND

One of the central concepts in economics is the concept of **demand**. Informally, the demand for a given commodity is the amount of that commodity that will be purchased, or consumed, at a given price. In economics, one is typically interested in how demand for a commodity is affected by changes in the price of that commodity. Thus, for example, suppose a typical family purchases 2.5 pounds of bread per week when bread costs 50¢ a pound. What will happen to that family's consumption as the price of bread rises to $1, $2, or even $3 a pound? We could plot bread purchasing as a function of the cost of a pound of bread. Such a plot, like the one in Figure 5–4, is called a **demand curve**.

The striking thing about this curve is how little consumption is affected

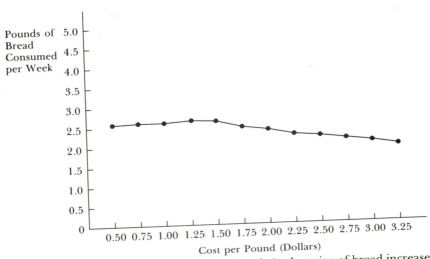

FIGURE 5–4. *Hypothetical Demand Curve for Bread.* As the price of bread increases from 50¢ per pound to $3 per pound, the amount of bread consumed decreases slightly. Because consumption of bread is relatively unaffected by price, demand for bread is said to be inelastic.

by price. Even though the cost of bread increases by a factor of 6, consumption of bread decreases only a little, and the amount of money spent on bread each week rises steadily. When consumption of a commodity is relatively unaffected by its price, demand for this commodity is said to be **inelastic**. Most of the commodities we view as necessities of life are characterized by inelastic demand curves like the one in Figure 5–4.

In contrast, consider the demand curve in Figure 5–5, this time for movies. Plotted in Figure 5–5 is a hypothetical relation between the price of a movie and the number of movies seen per week. When movies cost $5, the average person sees one movie per week. As the price of movies increases, the number of movies seen drops precipitously. By the time the price of movies has increased to $10, the person has virtually stopped seeing them. A demand curve like the one in Figure 5–5, in which consumption is dramatically affected by price, is said to reveal demand that is **elastic**. Most of the commodities we tend to view as luxuries might fall on demand curves like the one in Figure 5–5.

What have demand curves to do with operant conditioning and, more specifically, with the matter of choice? To answer this question, we must first decide what is the equivalent of the price of a commodity in typical choice experiments. Pigeons and rats do not have money. What they do have is responses. Key pecks and lever presses are their coin of the realm. Thus the behavioral equivalent of price might be the schedule of reinforcement—the number of responses, or amount of time, that must be "spent" to purchase a reinforcer.

In typical choice experiments the reinforcer used is food, a commodity

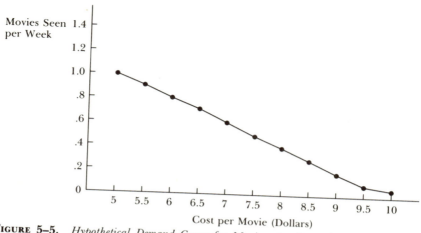

FIGURE 5–5. *Hypothetical Demand Curve for Movies.* As the price of movies increases from $5 per movie to $10 per movie, the number of movies seen per week drops. Because consumption of movies is markedly affected by price, demand for movies is said to be elastic.

for which demand is relatively inelastic. Moreover, the reinforcer is typically the same for both alternative operants. The two alternatives may differ in the frequency, magnitude, or delay of food they offer, but they both offer food. Under these circumstances we can expect that demand will be insignificant in determining choice, since whatever the demand curve may be, it will be the same for both alternatives.

But such a circumstance is a highly artificial one. Human choices are rarely between two schedules that offer the same reinforcer. More commonly, people must choose between different reinforcers. The matching law might provide a device for finding out the relative value of two different reinforcers by measuring an organism's choice responses for them. Thus if a rat were indifferent between an alternative that offered one pellet of dry food every minute and one that offered a piece of chocolate chip cookie every 5 minutes, we might be tempted to suggest that a piece of chocolate chip cookie was five times as valuable to the rat as a dry food pellet.

It is when the matching law is extended to account for choices among different types of reinforcers that the concept of demand becomes relevant. To see this, consider the following experiment. Rats were given the opportunity to press two levers. Presses on one lever produced food pellets. Presses on the other lever produced a burst of electrical stimulation of the rat's brain in an area sometimes called a "pleasure center." It is called a pleasure center because rats, and other animals, will engage in high rates of operant behavior to produce such stimulation. When lever presses produced either food or brain stimulation on FR 2 schedules, the rats vastly preferred the brain stimulation to food. They produced nine brain stimulations for each food pellet. This fact, according to the matching law, would suggest that brain stimulation is much more valuable than food. But this is not the case. When the FR was increased to 8 for both reinforcers, the amount of food the rats produced was unchanged. In contrast, the amount of brain stimulation produced dropped precipitously, to a point where the rats were producing more food than brain stimulation. If one had only the data from the FR 8 to examine, one would assume that food was more valuable to the rat than brain stimulation (Hursh & Bauman, 1987; Hursh & Natelson, 1981).

In truth, it makes no sense to say that one of the reinforcers was more valuable than the other. What distinguished the two reinforcers was their elasticity. Food is inelastic; it is a necessity. Brain stimulation is elastic; it is a luxury. When both are cheap (FR 2), demand for brain stimulation exceeds demand for food. But as they grow more expensive, the demand curve for brain stimulation drops precipitously (see Figure 5–5), eventually falling below the curve for food. Thus the concept of demand, elastic and inelastic, is essential for us to understand the pattern of the rat's choices between these reinforcers as the price of both of them changes. It follows that, in general, when choices are between different commodities, making sense of an organism's pattern of preference will depend on knowing what the demand curves for those commodities look like. Understood in this way, the matching law holds only when the demand curves for both reinforcers are the same, or similar, in form.

DEMAND AND INCOME

In discussing demand elasticity we said that when demand for a commodity is elastic, the amount consumed will decrease as price increases. Strictly speaking, this is not quite accurate. Suppose the price of movies increases from $5 to $10, as in Figure 5–5. But suppose as well that your income increases from $200 per week to $400 per week. Under these conditions the cost of movies, as a proportion of your total income, has remained the same. Not surprisingly, demand for luxuries (commodities with elastic demand) only decreases dramatically when the price *as a proportion of income* increases. The absolute price of a commodity is less important than its relative price—its price relative to your income.

How is the concept of "income" embodied in the operant conditioning experiment? Remember, the rat's or pigeon's "money" is its operant responses. Thus its income would be the number of responses it has available. In most operant conditioning experiments this quantity is not fixed. An experimental session might last a fixed amount of time or until a fixed number of reinforcers has been earned. But the number of responses that occur within the session is left free to vary. Thus if the cost (schedule) of a reinforcer were to go up, an animal could always adjust to this change by increasing its rate of responding. In essence, in the typical operant conditioning experiment the amount of income available to the animal is under its control.

Conditions like this will minimize the effects of demand on choice, because increases in absolute price need not imply increases in relative price. To create a situation that is more closely analogous to the typical human one, one would have to establish a procedure in which animals had only a fixed number of responses (income) available per session. Now changes in price (schedule) of reinforcers might have dramatic effects on choice, as a function of the elasticity of the demand for the reinforcers. A few experiments of this type have been done (Elsmore, 1979; Rachlin, Green, Kagel, & Battalio, 1976). In one such experiment, baboons were given a choice between food and heroin infusion. Under experimental conditions that were typical in that there was no constraint on the number of responses that could occur in a session, neither food nor heroin demand seemed terribly elastic. That is, neither food choices nor heroin choices were very dramatically affected by price (FR requirement). Then the procedure was changed. The baboons were given a fixed income of responses per day that could be allocated either for the purchase of heroin or for the purchase of food. Now the differential demand for the two reinforcers made its presence felt. When both reinforcers were cheap, the baboons chose each of them roughly equally. As the cost (schedule) increased, demand for heroin dropped while demand for food stayed constant. Food demand was inelastic while heroin demand was elastic, a difference that could be revealed only when the animals' income was kept controlled by the experimenter.

This example shows again how the matching law is relatively uninfluenced by demand in typical experimental settings. The lack of influence results from the lack of constraint on income (responses). When income is constrained, a circumstance much more like everyday circumstances than the typical operant experiment, demand becomes critically important.

SUBSTITUTABILITY OF COMMODITIES

There is another central economic concept that has much to do with choice behavior, but until recently has been neglected by learning theory. The matching law and the typical experimental situations used to study it acknowledge that how well a reinforcer will maintain an organism's behavior depends on what else is available in a situation. Thus a VI 3-min schedule of food reinforcement may maintain a great deal of responding in isolation, but very little responding if a VI 10-sec schedule of reinforcement is also available. The matching law offers a precise specification of how alternative sources of a given reinforcer will affect the power of a particular source of that reinforcer to sustain responding.

But consider for a moment whether it makes sense that the effect of an alternative reinforcer will be the same no matter what the relation is between the alternative reinforcer and the original one. Suppose we are interested in determining what kinds of manipulations will reduce people's use of gasoline in commuting to work. We could increase the price of gasoline, but the demand for gasoline is relatively inelastic since people must get to work. We could offer people a choice between gasoline and gasohol (a mixture of gasoline and alcohol). Under these conditions we might expect that as the price of gasoline increased relative to the price of gasohol, people would allocate increasing resources to gasohol. These two substances, gasoline and gasohol, **substitute** very well for each other. Alternatively, we might improve the availability of reliable, inexpensive, public transportation. Again, public transport and private transport substitute well for each other. But suppose, instead, that we increased the availability of cheap, convenient, downtown parking. What effect would this have on the use of gasoline? Presumably it would increase the use of gasoline, because using gasoline and having convenient parking available are **complements**; the more you have of one, the more you want of the other. Finally, suppose we offered people a host of amusements—movies, theaters, restaurants, etc.—as alternatives to gasoline on which to spend their money. These reinforcers are neither substitutes nor complements to gasoline use; they are relatively independent of it.

The point is that to determine the effect of introducing an alternative reinforcer on behavior maintained by a reinforcer that is already present, we must know something about the relation between the reinforcers. When they are substitutes, interaction between the alternatives will be great, and the more attractive we make one of them, the less the other will be chosen. If they are complements, interaction will again be great, but now the more attractive we make one, the *more* of the other will be chosen. Finally, if they are neither substitutes nor complements, interaction will be minimal.

Now let us consider the typical operant choice experiment. The reinforcers for the two alternatives are the same—food pellets. They are maximally substitutable. Thus it follows (as the matching law tells us) that the more attractive we make one alternative (in terms, say, of price or reinforcement schedule), the more it will be chosen over the other. But what the principles of substitutes and complements tell us is that this typical experimental outcome is just a special case—one that holds only for substitutable reinforcers. If we give animals a choice between food and water, we obtain a quite different pattern of results. What we find is that the more attractive we make one alternative, the more an animal consumes of *both* alternatives. This is because food and water complement each other. A thirsty animal will eat less and a hungry one will drink less. As we alleviate one or the other of these needs, an animal's consumption of the complementary commodity will go up. Thus the matching law cannot be generalized to cases involving complementary reinforcers.

OPEN AND CLOSED ECONOMIC SYSTEMS

Our discussion of the application of economic concepts to operant behavior has shown us that the matching law, which seemed to be an extremely general formulation, is actually a somewhat restricted one. The matching law holds most clearly when the alternative reinforcers are substitutable, when demand for the reinforcers is inelastic (or if elastic, similar), and when income is not fixed by the experimental procedure. By allowing us to see the matching law as restricted in these ways, these economic concepts cast the typical methods of operant conditioning experiments in a new light. They suggest the importance of variables like substitutability, elasticity, and income that have previously been neglected. We can illustrate the way in which these economic concepts make us aware of previously ignored issues by introducing one further concept to the analysis of operant conditioning experiments: an **open** or **closed economic system**.

Imagine being in a department store trying to decide whether to spend your money on some new clothes or some record albums. Your income is fixed, and we might expect to be able to say something about how the price of these items, together with their respective demand curves, will influence your purchasing decision. If the demand for both is relatively elastic, we might expect that as the price of one increases, your demand for it will decrease, resulting in your choice of the other item. But suppose that your uncle is in the record business, so that if you are willing to wait a little while, he will give you any record you want for free. Under these conditions we might expect that knowing all there is to know about income, demand, and price would not be much help in predicting what you will purchase. The reason is that because of your uncle, record albums are not really a part of this system of economic concepts. You have an alternative source of this commodity to which economic considerations do not apply. A circumstance like this is described as an open economic system. It is to be contrasted with a closed economic system, in which access to commodities occurs only through the expenditure of income. The interplay we have described between income, demand, and price is only expected to occur in a predictable fashion if the economic system is a closed one.

Why bother with making this distinction when in the lives of most people the economic system is distinctly closed? Few of us have uncles who actually give us free access to commodities we really want. The reason for making the distinction is that in typical operant conditioning experiments it is an extremely important one. When one does experiments with animals as subjects and food as the reinforcer, one first deprives the animals of food, often until their body weight has been reduced to some fixed proportion of normal weight. Once this is done, the animals are given experimental sessions every day. They are weighed after the sessions and if they have not obtained enough food to maintain their body weight at the desired level, they are given a food supplement between sessions. This feature of experimental procedures is so standard that it is almost never mentioned in articles that report experimental methods and results. Everyone does experiments this way.

Our economic analysis tells us that this feature of standard conditioning experiments is not just incidental. Rather, it is very significant. It turns what would otherwise be a closed economy, during experimental sessions, into an open one. For like you and your decision to purchase clothes rather than records, the pigeon or rat has an "uncle" (the experimenter) in the food business. If it is willing to wait a little while, it can have all the food it needs for free, without expending its income (its responses). In short, economic analysis tells us that what goes on during an experimental session should be significantly affected by whether food supplements are available afterward.

And does it make a difference that food is made available between sessions? The answer is yes, at least under some circumstances. Suppose we are interested in determining how rate of responding is affected by the value of the schedule of reinforcement. We might expose animals to a series of FR schedules and a series of VI schedules and see how response rate changes as the schedule changes. If we did this, we might observe data like those plotted in the top of Figure 5–6 (Felton & Lyon, 1966; Catania & Reynolds, 1968; Collier, Hirsch, & Hamlin, 1972; Hursh, 1978).

Panel A shows that as the FR increases in size, response rate first increases, then decreases. Panel B shows that with VIs there is a steady decrease in responding as the VI increases. Since as the schedule value increases an animal must increase its rate of response to obtain the same quantity of food in a session, these curves indicate that animals will obtain less food as the cost of food goes up. The demand for food seems to be elastic.

But both of these curves were taken from standard procedures, in which supplemental feeding occurs between sessions. If instead we eliminate these feedings, closing the economic system, there is a very dramatic change in the animal's behavior. As Panels C and D indicate, when the system is closed, rate of responding continues to increase as the schedule value increases, whether the schedule is a VI or an FR. Thus the demand for food is inelastic, at least when the economic system is a closed one.

It is important to emphasize that the manipulation that produced the data in Panels C and D, in contrast to A and B, was a trivial one. What was manipulated was a feature of procedure that had become so standard that researchers had not even really considered it as a potential variable.

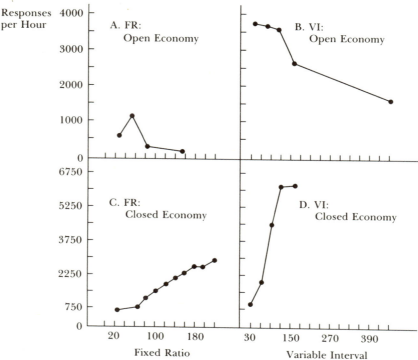

FIGURE 5–6.   *The Effect on Response Rate of an Open or a Closed Economy.* In Panels A and B the economy is open, and response rate tends to decrease as the schedule value increases. In Panels C and D the economy is closed, and response rate increases as schedule value increases. (Data in Panel A are from Felton & Lyon, 1966; Data in Panel B are from Catania & Reynolds, 1968; Data in Panel C are from Collier, Hirsch, & Hamlin, 1972; and data in Panel D are from Hursh, 1978.)

As we can see, it is not merely a potential variable, but often a potent one. However, there is some uncertainty about whether the open or closed nature of the "experimental economy" is always a significant variable. For example, there is evidence that feedings that occur after a session affect behavior that occurs during the session only if such supplemental feedings are provided rather soon after the session is over (Timberlake, Gawley, & Lucas, 1987). In effect, supplemental feedings have to be treated by the animal as related in some way to what goes on in the session in order to affect what the animal does during the session. And if the feedings are provided several hours after the session has ended, they don't seem to count. How large the time interval is over which organisms will integrate their activities no doubt varies from species to species, but it does seem to impose a qualification on the effects that extraexperimental events have on intraexperimental ones (see Collier, Johnson, Hill, & Kaufman, 1986; Hursh, 1978, 1984; Hursh & Bauman, 1987; Timberlake & Peden, 1987).

INDIFFERENCE AND BUDGET CONSTRAINTS

In real life, people obtain a fixed income (at least over brief periods of time) and have to decide how to spend it. If you take home $400 a week, you must decide how much of that to spend on housing, food, clothing, entertainment, and so on. We could think of this situation as involving choices among different bundles of commodities, with the bundles differing in how much of each commodity they contain.

We can exemplify this type of choice by imagining going to a bakery to buy bread and cake. We can use the money to purchase rolls, or pastries, or some combination of both. If each roll or pastry cost 50¢, we could purchase a wide range of "bundles" for a given amount of money. What kinds of bundles would we prefer?

Three possible answers are depicted in Figure 5–7. Each of curves *A*, *B*, and *C* is called an **indifference contour**, because each represents different combinations of rolls and pastries about which a hypothetical person is indifferent. Any combination along a curve is as good as any other. In curve *A*, 20 rolls and no pastries, 20 pastries and no rolls, 10 of each, and various other combinations are all equally good. For a person with this indifference contour, rolls and pastries are completely

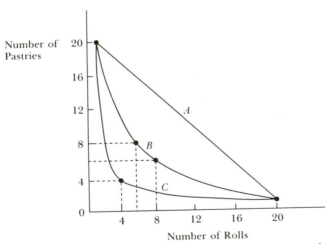

FIGURE 5–7. *Indifference Contours and Substitutability.* The three curves depict hypothetical points of equal value for different combinations of rolls and pastries. A person will be indifferent among all combinations depicted by each curve. Curve *A* is a straight line, indicating complete substitutability of rolls and pastries. Any combination of each totaling 20 is as good as any other combination. Curve *B* depicts imperfect substitutability: 8 pastries and 6 rolls, or the reverse, are just as good as 20 of either. A person with indifference curve *B* would value variety. Curve *C* reflects still less substitutability. Here 4 rolls and 4 pastries are as good as 20 of either.

interchangeable, or substitutable. This is not the case for curve B. A person with this indifference contour wants variety: 8 rolls and 6 pastries, or the reverse, are as good as 20 of either. Thus this person is willing to sacrifice the absolute number of baked goods she receives to get some variety. For a person with indifference contour B, rolls and pastries are less substitutable. This lack of substitutability is even more pronounced in curve C. Now, 4 pastries and 4 rolls are as valued as 20 of either.

Now consider the set of indifference contours depicted in Figure 5–8. Each of them has the same shape, so that each represents equal substitutability of commodities. They differ in the number of rolls and pastries that can be combined. According to economic theory, the farther up and to the right an indifference contour is on a graph of this sort, the more it is preferred (for example, P. Newman, 1965). Thus all points on curve 5 are preferred to any points on curve 4, all points on curve 4 are preferred to any on curve 3, and so on. What determines which indifference contour will be operative in a given situation is the combination of the price of the commodities and the income available for the purchase. Available income and price impose constraints on what can be purchased. Such constraints are represented by the dashed line in Figure 5–8, called

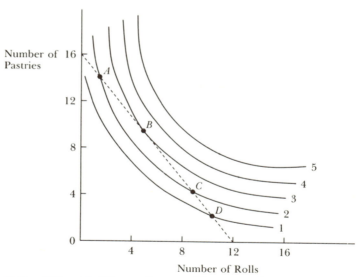

FIGURE 5–8. *Different Indifference Contours.* The curves have the same shape, indicating equal substitutability. Economic theory tells us that a given indifference contour is preferred to any below it and to its left. The dashed line indicates a budget constraint, such as would be present if a person had only a limited amount of money to spend in the bakery. According to economic theory, people will prefer that bundle of commodities within the budget constraint that lies on the highest indifference curve. In this case, bundle B on curve 3 would be preferred to bundles A, C, and D on curves 1 and 2.

a **budget line**. A budget line simply reflects the amount of income one has available to spend on whatever bundles of commodities are under consideration. In the case of a pigeon pecking a key for food, the budget line would represent the time it had available to respond or the number of responses it was permitted to make in an experimental session. We can predict that, given the constraint of the budget line, a person will choose that bundle of commodities that falls within the budget and lies on the highest indifference contour. In Figure 5–8 this is point *B*, 10 pastries and 5 rolls.

A number of experiments of this sort have been done with laboratory animals, choosing between bundles of food and water or two types of soft drink. The budget line, or constraint on choice, is determined by the schedule of reinforcement, by the cost (in responses) of a unit of reinforcement. The consistent finding is that the animals choose in accordance with what one would predict from Figure 5–8. They produce bundles of commodities that lie on the highest indifference contour (Rachlin, Battalio, Kagel, & Green, 1981; Rachlin, Green, Kagel, & Battalio, 1976).

This type of analysis can be applied most generally if the commodities involved are income and leisure. Income can of course be used to purchase all kinds of combinations of commodities. Figure 5–9 depicts a graph of income–leisure combinations. Organisms might ideally prefer a case in which income and leisure are both high, like point *A* in Figure 5–9. However, most of us must work for income. As a result, gains in income involve costs in leisure, and decisions about working are choices of particular leisure–income bundles. Figure 5–9 presents a series of indifference contours representing different leisure–income combinations.

In the laboratory, a schedule of reinforcement imposes a budget constraint—a rule that specifies how much leisure must be given up for units of income. A simple constraint is a ratio schedule, depicted as line *BC* in Figure 5–9. On a ratio schedule, the more an animal works (responds), the more income it earns. However, the more it works, the more leisure it loses. According to this type of analysis, there is some combination of work and leisure that will be optimal under a given budget constraint or schedule. That is the combination that falls on the highest indifference contour, point *D* in Figure 5–9. Experimental evidence indicates that income–leisure choices can be predicted from this economic analysis (Green, Kagel, & Battalio, 1987; Rachlin, Battalio, Kagel, & Green, 1981). Thus even on a simple schedule of reinforcement, how much an animal responds may reflect the choice of the particular income–leisure bundle that lies on its highest indifference contour.

We have discussed a few examples of the application of economic principles to operant choice behavior. Thus far the evidence suggests that the behavior of animals in conditioning experiments conforms to what economic theory says people will do when confronted with similar choices. What this implies is that operant behavior constitutes a kind of economic decision-making. Animals decide how to allocate their scarce

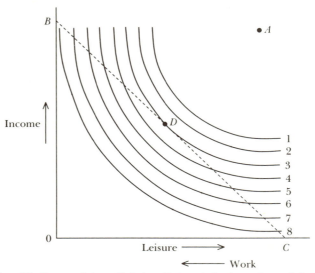

FIGURE 5-9.   *The Income–Leisure Relation.* Point *A* depicts what might be an ideal state of affairs for an organism: substantial income with little work. However, since income requires work, actual choices represent a trade-off of leisure for income. Indifference contours 1–8 depict different families of trade-offs, in decreasing order of preference. A schedule of reinforcement imposes a constraint, or budget line, which specifies how much work is required for a given amount of income. Line *BC* represents a ratio schedule in which income is directly related to work. Point *D* on line *BC* represents the income–leisure combination that falls on the highest indifference contour, and thus should be preferred to all other combinations.

behavioral resources, and the rules by which they make their decisions seem to be the same rules that people use. To the extent that economic theory provides us with a framework for understanding human choice, learning theory may also, since it seems to embody, in the laboratory, so many of the factors that are central to economic analysis.

Summary

This chapter, on the maintenance of operant behavior, was an attempt to bring learning theory a few steps closer to conditions that exist in the natural environment. Behavior in the natural environment is not always reinforced and usually involves choices among alternatives. As we have seen, learning theorists have studied the effects of partial reinforcement and the determinants of choice. Some of the principles that have emerged from this study are these:

1. Behavior can be maintained by intermittent reinforcement. There are different types of intermittent reinforcement, called schedules of reinforcement, and each of them maintains behavior in characteristic patterns.

2. Different schedules maintain different patterns of behavior. Fixed schedules are characterized by pauses after reinforcement, while variable ones are characterized by steady response rates. Ratio schedules maintain higher response rates than do interval schedules.

3. The determinants of choice can be summarized for a variety of circumstances by the matching law. The matching law tells us that the allocation of responses among alternatives will match the relative frequency, magnitude, and delay of reinforcement offered by the alternatives. Whether the matching one observes is the result of a matching process or a maximizing process that influences an organism's choice remains in dispute.

4. Behavior analogous to that observed in choice experiments in the laboratory has been observed in the foraging of a wide variety of different species in their natural environments.

5. However, recent efforts to bring concepts from economics into the laboratory have revealed that the matching law is just a special case of the operation of far more general economic principles. These principles involve the interplay of demand elasticity, income, price, and commodity substitutability, in open and closed economic systems. They view the organism as making choices that are all on its highest indifference contour that lies within the budget constraint imposed by the operative reinforcement schedule. These principles capture all the phenomena explained by the matching law, as well as a wide range of others that the matching law cannot explain. They also bring the phenomena of animal choice in the laboratory much closer to the phenomena of human choice in the natural environment.

6 Stimulus Control of Operant Behavior

The law of effect tells us that operant behavior is controlled by its consequences: Reinforcing consequences make behavior more likely while punishing consequences make it less likely. We can understand much of what organisms do by appealing to this one simple principle. It tells us how a series of interactions with the environment can result in a repertoire of effective, adaptive behaviors.

However, the law of effect cannot tell us everything. Consider an example. A pigeon is first exposed to a procedure in which a response key is alternately red and green, and pecking is reinforced no matter what the color of the key. The pigeon comes to peck the key at the same rate whether it is red or green. Then the procedure is changed; pecks in red no longer produce food. The pigeon is responsive to this change, and eventually stops pecking the key when it is red; however, the pigeon continues to peck the key when it is green. Can we explain this change in the pigeon's behavior solely by appeal to the law of effect, by appeal to the relation between response and reinforcer?

The answer is that we cannot. The relation between pecking and food has not changed from the first to the second part of our experiment. It is still true that the pigeon must peck the key for food, and that food follows key pecking. What has changed is that another element of control over the pigeon's behavior has been introduced. The pigeon has learned that the peck–food relation is operative only when the key is green. The color of the key, in addition to the reinforcement, comes to control pecking. Green on the key *sets the occasion* on which pecking is reinforced (see Chapter 2, p. 86; Holland, 1985, 1986; Rescorla, 1985; Ross & Holland, 1981, 1982; Ross & LoLordo, 1986, 1987). The pigeon has learned that the consequences of pecking red are different from the consequences of pecking green. It has come to discriminate pecking red from pecking green. It has developed an **operant discrimination**, a phenomenon in which environmental stimuli in addition to the reinforcer come to control operant behavior. The study of this type of phenomenon is known as the study of **discrimination learning**, or of **stimulus control**.

Any theory of behavior that aspires to comprehensiveness must be able to account for stimulus control. It is hard to think of a single example of operant behavior that is reinforced all the time—under all circumstances. The law of effect may tell us how organisms learn *what* to do, that is, what behavior is effective. But just as important as knowing what to do is knowing *when* to do it. It is easy to teach all the skills required for driving a car—how to accelerate, to slow down, to steer left and right, and so on. What is more difficult, but essential, is teaching what the appropriate conditions are for doing each of these things. Similarly, we teach children the basic arithmetic operations so that they execute addition, subtraction, multiplication, and division quickly and accurately. Armed with these skills alone, their knowledge of arithmetic will be of no use whatever in solving problems—either in their math class or in daily life. To solve problems, one must know not only the basic operations, but also which circumstances call for which operation. This process of discrimination learning, or stimulus control, is the main concern of this chapter.

Discrimination and Generalization

The study of stimulus control of operant behavior has two faces, both of which can be seen in Figure 6–1. Figure 6–1 presents hypothetical data one might obtain from a pigeon exposed to a procedure in which the response key is alternately red and green. Pecks when the key is red produce food, while pecks when the key is green do not. We call red the S^+ and green the S^-. By the end of an hour the pigeon is pecking about 60 times per minute when the key is red. When the key is green it is hardly pecking at all. This is one of the faces of stimulus control. The pigeon has learned a **discrimination**. It has learned to discriminate the consequences of pecking in red from the consequences of pecking in green, and it adjusts its behavior accordingly.

But look at what the pigeon does early in its training. In the beginning

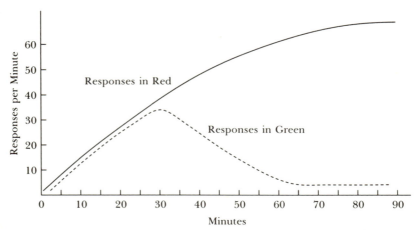

FIGURE 6-1.   *Development of a Discrimination.* A pigeon's pecks are reinforced when a key is red, but not when it is green. Initially, response rate increases in red and green; the pigeon generalizes its experience in red to the green key. Eventually, however, though response rate in red continues to increase, response rate in green decreases; the pigeon learns to discriminate the consequences of pecking red from the consequences of pecking green.

it responds as much in green as it does in red. Even though pecking in green has never been reinforced, the pigeon generalizes from its experience in red to green. This phenomenon of **generalization** is the other face of stimulus control. When we study discrimination, we study how organisms come to respond differently in the presence of different stimuli. When we study generalization, we study how organisms come to respond similarly in the presence of different stimuli. Understanding stimulus control involves understanding the processes of discrimination and generalization.

One reason an organism might respond similarly to different stimuli is that it cannot tell that they are different. The untutored wine drinker may respond identically to all red wines because he can't tell them apart. For this person, learning a discrimination would mean learning to identify the differences between, say, a Bordeaux and a Burgundy. And one can use discrimination learning experiments as a way to determine the kinds of perceptual distinctions of which an animal is capable. One can find out about such things as color sensitivity, shape sensitivity, smell sensitivity, and the like by asking whether animals can learn to respond differently to stimuli of different color, shape, or odor. Studies like this have revealed some surprising perceptual sensitivities in animals. For example, rats and monkeys can distinguish different tunes. And pigeons can distinguish Stravinsky from Bach (D'Amato & Salmon, 1982; Porter & Neuringer, 1984).

Though findings like these are interesting and important, for the most part they are not what research on discrimination is about. When a pigeon is taught a red–green discrimination, as in Figure 6–1, red and green are chosen precisely because we know the pigeon can tell them apart. The pigeon's task in such an experiment is not learning to distinguish red and green, but learning that pecking in red and pecking in green have different consequences. If the pigeon were unable to discriminate red from green at the start of the experiment (if, for example, it was completely without color vision), it could never possibly learn to peck red but not green. But knowing that red and green are different, while necessary for an operant discrimination, is not sufficient. The pigeon must also learn that this difference makes a difference—that pecking red is reinforced while pecking green is not. This is the learning depicted in Figure 6–1; the pigeon knows the difference between red and green just as well at the beginning of the procedure as at the end. The data in Figure 6–1 reflect the development of differential control over pecking by red and green rather than the development of a perceptual distinction between them. That is why the study of operant discrimination and generalization is also known as the study of stimulus control.

Procedures for Studying Stimulus Control

There are a variety of different procedures used in studying operant discrimination and generalization. In one type of discrimination learning procedure, called a **successive discrimination**, stimuli are presented successively, one at a time, and the animal must learn to respond when one stimulus is present and not when the other is present, or to make one response in the presence of one stimulus and a different one in the presence of the other stimulus. The example in Figure 6–1, of the pigeon trained to peck red but not green, is an example of a successive discrimination.

The second common type of discrimination is called a **simultaneous discrimination**. Here, two stimuli are presented together and the organism must choose between the alternatives. Thus the pigeon might face two keys—one red and one green—and learn to peck the one correlated with reinforcement. Or the rat might be confronted with a T-maze, like the one in Figure 6–2. It would run from the start box to the choice point, and have to learn whether to choose the left or right arm. A somewhat more complex example of a simultaneous discrimination is presented in Figure 6–3. Here, the rat must learn to jump at whichever card is different from the other two.

There are also procedures for studying the phenomenon of generalization. When we discussed generalization in Pavlovian conditioning in Chapter 2 (pp. 81–84), we saw that even though an organism might

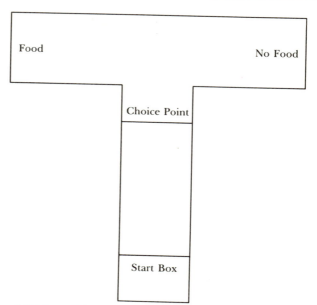

FIGURE 6–2. *A T-Maze.* This device is often used to study simultaneous discrimination in rats. The rat runs from the start box to the choice point, and then must choose to turn left or right.

generalize from the stimuli with which it was trained to other stimuli, such generalization is rarely complete.

We can explore the extent of an organism's generalization by presenting it with stimuli that differ in varying degrees from the training stimuli. In Chapter 2 we discussed a hypothetical example of Pavlovian discrimination in which a tone of a particular pitch is a CS$^+$ and a light of a particular color is a CS$^-$. Such training should make the tone excitatory and the light inhibitory. To see how much this excitation and inhibition generalize to other tones and lights, we conduct a generalization test during which other tones and lights are presented and conditioned responses to them are recorded. If we did such a test, we might obtain results like those in Figure 6–4.

Figure 6–4 presents two **generalization gradients**, a gradient of excitation (Part A) and a gradient of inhibition (Part B). The animal responds most to the training tone (CS$^+$), and less and less to tones that are increasingly different from it. The animal responds least to the training light (CS$^-$), and more and more to lights that are increasingly different from it.

When animals are exposed to generalization tests after operant conditioning, the results are similar to those in Figure 6–4. Figure 6–5 presents an excitatory generalization gradient for tones of differing pitch after training in which a 1000-Hertz (Hz) tone was S$^+$, and Figure 6–6 presents an inhibitory generalization gradient for lights of different color after

FIGURE 6–3. *A Rat Performing a Complex Simultaneous Discrimination.* Reinforcement is delivered only if the rat jumps at the "odd" card, the one that differs from the others. (Photo by Frank Lotz Miller from Black Star.)

training in which a 570-nanometer (nm) light was S⁻ (Jenkins & Harrison, 1960; Terrace, 1971; see Honig & Urcuioli, 1981, for a review).

The similarity between the phenomena of stimulus control observed in operant conditioning procedures and those observed in Pavlovian conditioning procedures certainly suggests that a single account might explain them both. It is not surprising therefore that efforts to explain discriminative control of operant behavior have employed concepts that we have already encountered in discussing Pavlovian conditioning. Let us turn, then, to an exploration of the mechanisms that seem to underlie operant discrimination and generalization.

The Process of Discrimination

Before we can begin to specify the conditions that produce discriminative control, we need a device or procedure with which to measure it. There

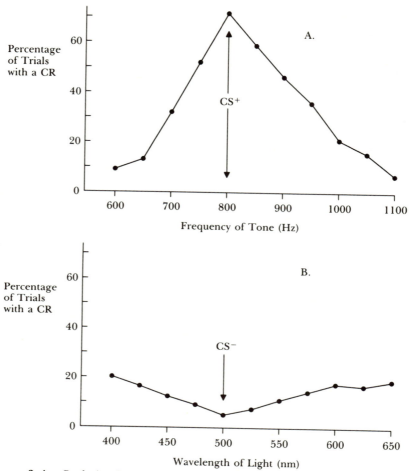

FIGURE 6–4. *Pavlovian Generalization Gradients of Excitation (A) with a Tone as CS⁺ and Inhibition (B) with a Light as CS⁻.* In Part A, maximum responding occurs to the CS⁺ and drops off systematically as the tones presented are more and more different from the CS⁺. In Part B, minimum responding occurs to the CS⁻ and responding increases as lights are more and more different from the CS⁻.

are several possibilities. To see if a stimulus is controlling behavior, we could simply remove it from the situation and assess whether behavior changes. Alternatively, we could introduce the supposedly controlling stimulus into a new situation and see if the behavior we think it controls transfers along with it. There are many studies of these types in the literature on discriminative control (see Mackintosh, 1977). However, we are going to focus on studies employing a different type of test of discriminative control—the **generalization test.** As Figure 6–5 shows, an animal trained with a particular stimulus as S⁺ responds to other, similar

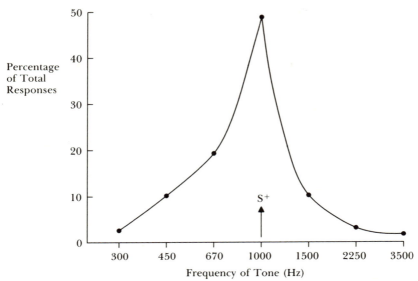

FIGURE 6–5. *Excitatory Generalization Gradient for Tone Frequency in a Pigeon.* The S[+] had been a 1000-Hz tone. The points represent the percentage of all responses made during the generalization test that were made to each particular stimulus. (After Jenkins & Harrison, 1960.)

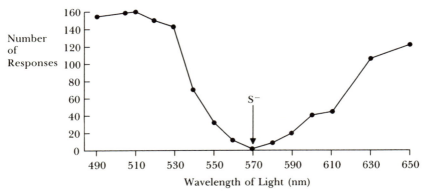

FIGURE 6–6. *Inhibitory Generalization Gradient for Wavelength in a Pigeon.* The S[−] had been a 570-nm light. Responses increased as the distance between the test stimulus and S[−] increased. (After Terrace, 1971.)

stimuli. However, it responds less and less to those stimuli as they become less and less similar to S[+]; that is, the generalization gradient has a peak at S[+]. The fact that responding changes as the stimulus changes implies that the stimulus is controlling the response. Suppose one administered a generalization test for color to a pigeon that had been trained to peck a green key for food, and one obtained a gradient like that in Figure 6–7A. The gradient is completely horizontal, or flat. Apparently the pigeon generalizes completely from green to all colors. When flat

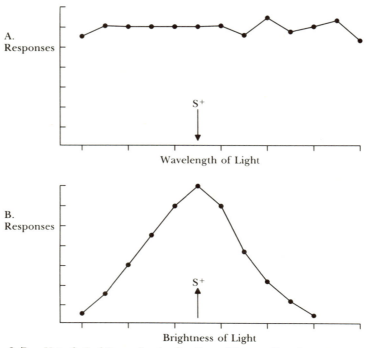

FIGURE 6–7.   *Hypothetical Generalization Gradients.* The gradient in Part A is flat and indicates lack of control over responding by wavelength of light. The peaked gradient in Part B indicates control of responding by intensity or brightness of light.

generalization gradients such as these are observed, we infer that the stimulus dimension being varied (in Figure 6–7A, key color) is not controlling the pigeon's behavior. Why might this be? What can account for the failure of a stimulus to control operant responding?

PREDICTIVENESS AND REDUNDANCY

To answer this question, let us review some conclusions we reached in Chapter 3 on Pavlovian conditioning. We concluded that in order for conditioning to occur, a differential (predictive) contingency must exist between the CS and the US; if the US is no more likely in the presence of the CS than in its absence, there is no conditioning. If more than one predictive CS is present, then conditioning will occur to the CS that is most predictive. If a number of equally predictive CSs are present, then conditioning might occur to all of them. Alternatively, the presence of one especially salient CS might *overshadow* conditioning to any of the others.

How do these facts relate to the case of the pigeon pecking the green key? Suppose that, by analogy with Pavlovian conditioning, in order for a stimulus to control operant responding it must be a differential predictor of reinforcer availability. Does the green key meet this criterion? Considered in contrast to stimuli outside the chamber, it does. Reinforcement is available in the chamber, but not outside it. Therefore green is a differential predictor of reinforcer availability. However, green is not the *best* predictor of reinforcer availability. The green key shares its predictive relation to reinforcer availability with the houselight, the wire mesh floor, the sound of the exhaust fan, and a host of other stimuli that are present in the chamber and absent outside it. Any one or more of these stimuli might overshadow the green light and effectively control pecking. Suppose, for example, the pigeon's responding were controlled by the brightness of the key and not by its color. If this were true, then a generalization test in which stimuli were different colors but the same brightness would be presenting the same effective stimuli to the pigeon again and again. Though the objective stimulus would be changing as color changed, that aspect of the stimulus that was exercising control would remain constant. Control of key pecking by brightness could be revealed in a second generalization test, one in which the color of the key remained green but its brightness was varied. Such a test might yield the gradient in Figure 6–7B. If so, one could conclude that the stimulus controlling pecking was the brightness of the light on the key and not its color.

When there are a number of redundant (equally predictive) signals for reinforcer availability, which of them will control responding is influenced by two factors. First of all, one stimulus may be inherently more salient than the others, and overshadow them. For example, in one study pigeons were trained to peck a lit key for food in the presence of a tone. Both the tone and the key light were always present as redundant signals for food. After this training, generalization tests for tone frequency yielded flat gradients like the one in Figure 6–7A. In contrast, a second group of pigeons was trained to peck a key in the presence of the tone, but in total darkness. For this group, generalization tests for tonal frequency yielded gradients like the one in Figure 6–7B (Rudolph & Van Houten, 1977). Clearly, for the first group of pigeons the key light overshadowed the tone in controlling pecking.

The relative salience of a stimulus may also be influenced by an animal's past experience. Suppose a pigeon has had previous experience in which a tone was a signal for reinforcer availability. The pigeon is then exposed to a procedure in which a tone and a light are redundant signals. It is likely that the tone will control responding. Without the prior experience with the tone, the light might well control responding. In a confirming experiment, two groups of pigeons were trained to peck a lit key for food in the presence of a 1000-Hz tone. Key light and tone were redundant signals. Prior to the experiment, one of the groups had received prolonged experience in which the delivery of the daily ration of food to the pigeons in their home cages was signaled by the 1000-Hz tone. When, after training, both groups were given generalization tests for tonal frequency, the group with no preexperimental experience with the tone produced a flat gradient, as in Figure 6–7A, while the group with preexperimental experience produced a peaked gradient, as in Figure 6–7B (D.R. Thomas, Mariner, & Sherry, 1969; see also Lawrence, 1950). Thus prior experience in which a stimulus is a nonredundant signal seems to ensure control by that stimulus in situations in which it competes with other equally predictive stimuli.

In many everyday situations we face the problem of determining which of a set of stimuli is actually predictive of reinforcement. Some teachers welcome informality and others expect us to be formal. When we encounter a new teacher, how do we decide how to behave? What is the cue that tells us what pattern of behavior will be reinforced? There are many possible cues we might depend on: the age of the teacher, the teacher's dress or classroom style. Which of these cues we choose may be influenced by our past experience in interaction with young or old, casually or formally dressed teachers.

Or when given a first written assignment in a class, how do we decide what to do? Should we be speculative or careful, comprehensive or cursory? We might attempt to solve this problem by relating this assignment to assignments we have done in the past, in other classes. But what past assignments make appropriate comparisons? Should we think about past classes in the same subject, at the same level of sophistication, of the same size? Making this decision is essentially deciding which stimulus (subject, class size, level) is predictive of reinforcement for a given type of written work.

On the other hand, if we are in the role of teacher rather than student, we must appreciate that students face this very problem. A large component of successful teaching is precisely the identification of which stimuli should control behavior. The way to do this is to eliminate redundancy, to set up contingencies so that only the stimulus that the teacher wants to control behavior is actually predictive of reinforcement.

In summary, we have seen that in situations in which a number of different stimuli bear an equally predictive relation to the availability of food, the particular stimulus that will effectively control responding is largely beyond experimental control. The inherent salience of different stimuli and the relevant past experience of the experimental subject will combine to determine what the effective stimulus will be. The experimenter is not helpless, however. The way to ensure control of responding by a particular stimulus is to make that stimulus the best predictor of reinforcer availability. And the way to do this is by discrimination training.

DISCRIMINATION TRAINING AS A STIMULUS SELECTOR

Consider the following experiment. One group of pigeons was trained to peck a green key with a vertical white line superimposed on it. After some training, the pigeons were given a generalization test with lines that differed from the vertical in 22.5-degree steps. The resulting flat gradient of generalization is presented in Figure 6–8A. A second group of pigeons was given discrimination training. The vertical line on a green background was the S$^+$; key pecks in its presence produced food. The green key by itself was the S$^-$; pecks in its presence did not produce food. After the pigeons had learned to peck the S$^+$ and not the S$^-$, a generalization test for line orientation was administered. The resulting sharply peaked gradient is depicted in Figure 6–8B.

Finally, a third group of pigeons was given discrimination training in which green + vertical was the S$^+$ and red without a line was the S$^-$. The subsequent generalization test for line orientation produced the flat gradient depicted in Figure 6–8C (F.L. Newman & Baron, 1965; see also Wagner, Logan, Haberlandt, & Price, 1968).

Let us attempt to explain these data. The flat gradient in Figure 6–8A suggests that some stimulus other than the line was controlling pecking. Since the line and the green key color and a host of other stimuli were all equally predictive of reinforcer availability, control of responding by the line could have been overshadowed by many different things.

This possibility was eliminated for the pigeons whose data are in Figure 6–8B. For this group, pecks were reinforced only when the line was present. Green was also present at this time, as were other aspects of the situation like the houselight and the exhaust fan. However, green was also present during periods when pecks were not reinforced. Thus discrimination training established the vertical line as the *best predictor* of reinforcement, with the result that the line controlled pecking, as witnessed by the peaked generalization gradient.

The discrimination training received by the group whose data are in Figure 6–8C also established the vertical line as a better predictor of reinforcement than most other aspects of the situation. Environmental stimuli such as the houselight and exhaust fan noise were present during S$^-$ periods as well as S$^+$ periods. Thus these stimuli should have been eliminated from competition with the line for control of responding. Notice, however, that the line was not the best predictor of reinforcement; the green key was equally good (S$^-$ was both the absence of the line and the presence of red on the key). The resulting flat generalization gradient suggests that green overshadowed the line and controlled pecking when the two stimuli were equally predictive of reinforcement.

We see, therefore, that discrimination training can be used to ensure control of responding by a particular stimulus. It accomplishes this by establishing that stimulus as the best predictor of reinforcement. All

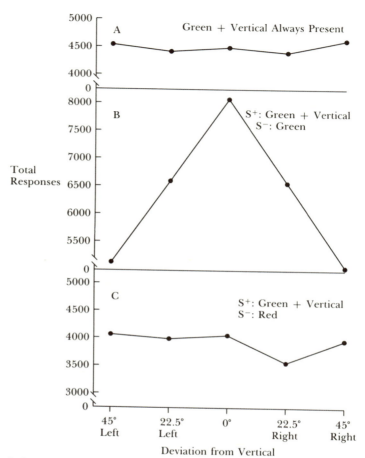

FIGURE 6-8. *Effect of Discrimination Training on Stimulus Selection.* Each part of the figure presents a generalization gradient for line orientation for a different group of pigeons. Group A was simply trained to peck a green key with a white vertical line for food. Group B had green + vertical as an S⁺ and green without vertical as an S⁻. Group C had green + vertical as S⁺ and red without vertical as S⁻. (After F. L. Newman & Baron, 1965.)

other aspects of the environment that might potentially control responding are present all the time, both when reinforcement is available and when it is not. The S⁺ is present only when reinforcement is available.

DISCRIMINATION TRAINING AND INCIDENTAL STIMULI

The effects of discrimination training need not always be so dramatic, shifting control of responding entirely from one aspect of the situation to another (as suggested by the data in Figure 6–8). It is also possible that in the absence of discrimination training, numerous background or **incidental stimuli** share control of responding so that each of a variety of generalization tests will yield moderately peaked gradients, and that discrimination training eliminates control by all stimuli but the S $^+$, with the result that the generalization gradient about the S $^+$ is sharpened.

In a test of this proposition, two groups of pigeons were trained to peck a colored key for food. Generalization tests with other colors yielded a moderately peaked gradient. One of the groups was then given additional training pecking the colored key but now with a white vertical line superimposed on it, and a second generalization test for color. The second gradient was no more peaked than the first one. The other group was given discrimination training: The same color on the key as before was S $^+$ and a white vertical line on a dark key was S $^-$. A generalization test for color after this discrimination training produced a much sharper gradient than before (Switalski, Lyons, & Thomas, 1966).

We can speculate that in the absence of discrimination training, key pecking was controlled by the color of the key in addition to, perhaps, the brightness of the key and a number of aspects of the situation completely unrelated to the key, like the houselight, the noise of the fan, the wire mesh screen underfoot, and so on. If we consider the controlling stimulus to be a compound, including key color and also a host of background or incidental stimuli, then it is not surprising that the pigeons pecked so much at colors other than the training stimulus. When these other colors were presented, other elements of the compound were still present. Thus when the pigeon pecked at the colored key, it was a peck under the control of color + brightness + fan + houselight, etc. Changing the color of the key represents a rather small change in the total stimulus compound, so that the relatively small change in responding is not surprising.

When we expose the pigeon to a discrimination between the color and the vertical line, the former signaling reinforcer availability and the latter signaling its absence, we establish key color as the best predictor of reinforcer availability. By doing this, discrimination training effectively eliminates control of responding by incidental stimuli. No longer is the controlling stimulus a compound that includes color; now the controlling stimulus is effectively color alone. The colors presented during generalization testing are a lot less similar to the training stimulus under these conditions (when incidental stimuli are irrelevant) than under the previous, nondiscriminative conditions (see Hull, 1952; Mackintosh, 1974, 1977).

Another set of experiments makes this same point about incidental stimuli more graphically (Jenkins & Harrison, 1960, 1962; see also Hanson, 1961). Some pigeons were trained to peck a key for food in the continual presence of a 1000-Hz tone. A generalization test with other tonal frequencies produced the gradient depicted in Figure 6–9A. Other pigeons learned a discrimination: The 1000-Hz tone signaled reinforcer

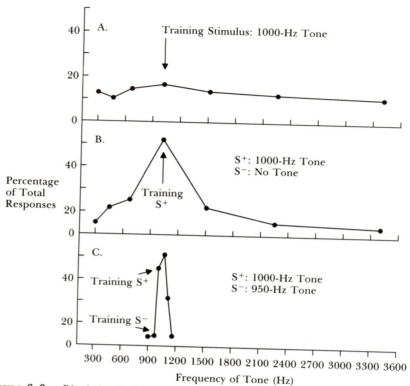

FIGURE 6–9. *Discrimination Training as a Sharpener of Generalization Gradients.* The figure presents the percentage of all responses made during generalization testing that were made in the presence of each different tone. The gradient in Part A, after nondiscrimination training, is flat. The gradient in Part B, after discrimination training with a 1000-Hz tone as S⁺ and no tone as S⁻, is peaked. The gradient in Part C, after discrimination training between 1000 Hz (S⁺) and 950 Hz (S⁻), is even more peaked. (After Jenkins & Harrison, 1960, 1962.)

availability (S⁺), and no tone signaled nonreinforcement (S⁻). This group produced the generalization gradient depicted in Figure 6–9B. A final set of pigeons also learned a discrimination: The 1000-Hz tone was S⁺ and a 950-Hz tone was S⁻. This group produced the generalization gradient in Figure 6–9C.

Based on the preceding discussion, we would conclude that the flat gradient in Figure 6–9A is the result of the overshadowing of the tone by other, equally predictive but more salient "incidental" stimuli. Discrimination training makes the tone a better predictor of reinforcement than any other stimulus, and the result is the peaked gradient in Figure 6–9B indicating control of responding by the tone. But what aspect of the tone is exercising control? Is it pitch, or loudness, or loudness and pitch in combination? For the group of pigeons whose data are in Figure 6–9C, even this source of competition among potential controlling stimuli is eliminated. The only difference between S$^+$ and S$^-$ is pitch (1000 Hz versus 950 Hz). Not only is the tone a better predictor of reinforcement than incidental stimuli, but the frequency or pitch of the tone is a better predictor of reinforcement than any of its other characteristics. As a result the generalization gradient for tonal frequency produced by this group is even more peaked than the one in Figure 6–9B.

Let us summarize the data in Figure 6–9 as a way of summarizing the entire section. When there is no best predictor of reinforcement, almost any aspect of the experimental situation might control responding (Figure 6–9A). When the presence of a tone is established as the best predictor of reinforcement, then one or more aspects of the tone will control responding, and control by incidental stimuli will be eliminated (Figure 6–9B). When the frequency of the tone is the best predictor of reinforcement, then that *specific* aspect of the tone will control responding and control by other aspects of the tone will be eliminated (Figure 6–9C). In general, the way to assure control of responding by any particular aspect of a situation is to make that aspect the best predictor of reinforcement.

If we were to describe the results in Figure 6–9 less formally, we would be inclined to say that discrimination training teaches animals to *pay attention*. It teaches them on which parts of the environment to focus and which parts to ignore. When a tone is S$^+$ and no tone is S$^-$, then the animal learns to pay attention to the tone. When a 1000-Hz tone is S$^+$ and a 950-Hz tone is S$^-$, then the animal learns, more specifically, to pay attention to the frequency of the tone. There is a long history of attempts to investigate attention as a critical part of the process of discrimination learning, and we turn now to a discussion of some of the issues involved in the study of attention.

ATTENTION

What does it mean to say that an animal is "paying attention" to a stimulus aside from the fact that the animal's responding is controlled by that stimulus? This question has been confronted by numerous investigators over the years. A number of different answers have been proposed, but many have the same general character. Discrimination learning is conceived as a two-part process: One learns what stimuli are relevant— what one must pay attention to; and one also learns to do specific things in the presence of specific stimuli. As an example, consider a young child learning to cross city streets. What the child might learn first is that traffic lights and vehicles are the relevant stimuli. Then the child would learn to walk when the light is one color but to wait when the light is a different color, and to walk when the vehicles are stopped or far away but to wait when the vehicles are moving and close by.

Transfer of Training Attempts to show that paying attention is a separable part of discrimination learning have often involved experiments on **transfer of training**. Animals trained on one kind of discrimination problem are then given a different kind, and the measure of interest is the extent to which training on the first problem affects, or transfers to, learning the second one.

In one kind of transfer-of-training experiment, two groups of subjects first experience different discrimination problems. For example, both groups might receive circles or squares that are red or green. For Group 1, red stimuli are S$^+$ and green stimuli are S$^-$ regardless of shape. For Group 2, squares are S$^+$ and circles are S$^-$, regardless of color. As the animals master the discrimination, we might imagine the learning process as involving the following steps:

1. For Group 1, color is relevant and shape is irrelevant. That is, color is predictive of reinforcement availability while shape is not. For Group 2, shape is relevant (predictive of reinforcement) and color is not.

2. For Group 1, specifically, red predicts reinforcement and green predicts its absence. Therefore responses should occur only when red is present. For Group 2, squares predict reinforcement and circles its absence. Therefore responses should occur only when squares are present.

Alternatively, the discrimination process might involve only a single step—learning specifically about S$^+$ and S$^-$ and not first about the dimensions (color or shape) of which they are a part.

This phase of the experiment and a second, test phase are depicted in Figure 6–10. What might we expect the effects of Phase 1 to be when the groups are exposed to Phase 2, in which blue is the S$^+$, yellow is the S$^-$, and diamonds and triangles are irrelevant? Note first that the specific stimuli being employed are all different in Phase 2 from those in Phase 1. However, the relevant dimension in Phase 2 is color—the same dimension that was relevant in Phase 1 for Group 1, but a different dimension from what was relevant in Phase 1 for Group 2. If learning a discrimination involves first learning to attend to the relevant dimension and then learning which specific stimulus is S$^+$, Group 1, having already learned to attend to color, should learn faster in Phase 2 than Group 2. On the other hand, if discrimination learning involves simply learning to respond to S$^+$ and not S$^-$, neither group should be helped more than the other by past experience, since the specific S$^+$ and S$^-$ (blue and yellow) were not a part of the previous training.

These experiments are described as pitting **intradimensional shift** (different values on the same dimension: blue and yellow instead of red and green, as in Group 1) against **extradimensional shift** (different relevant dimensions: colors as S$^+$ and S$^-$ instead of shapes, as in Group 2). The reliable observation in rats, pigeons, monkeys, human children, and human adults is that the intradimensional shift is learned faster than the

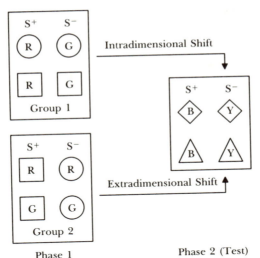

FIGURE 6–10. *The Intradimensional Shift versus the Extradimensional Shift.* Groups 1 and 2 must learn to respond to blue (S $^+$) and not yellow (S $^-$) in Phase 2, after prior training. Group 1 has previously learned to respond to red (S $^+$) and not green (S $^-$). For this group, the new problem represents an intradimensional shift. S $^+$ and S $^-$ are different in Phase 2 compared to Phase 1, but they are on the same dimension (color). Group 2 has previously learned to respond to squares but not circles. For this group, the new problem represents an extradimensional shift. Both the specific S $^+$s and the dimension on which they fall are different in Phase 2 compared to Phase 1.

extradimensional shift, providing support for the view that discrimination learning involves learning to pay attention to relevant (predictive) stimulus dimensions (Mackintosh & Little, 1969; Shepp & Eimas, 1964; Shepp & Schrier, 1969; for related findings, see Kendler & D'Amato, 1955; Kendler & Kendler, 1962; Sutherland & Mackintosh, 1971). In fact, to be more accurate, the evidence seems clear that discrimination learning involves both learning to pay attention to relevant dimensions and learning to ignore irrelevant dimensions. Animals like those in Group 1 in Figure 6–10 seem to learn in Phase 1 not only that color is relevant, but that shape is irrelevant (see Kemler & Shepp, 1971; Mackintosh, 1973, 1975).

We have encountered before the idea that organisms learn which stimuli to pay attention to and which ones to ignore, in our discussion of how the effectiveness of the CS may change in the course of Pavlovian conditioning (Chapter 3, pp. 108–112). The more salient a stimulus is, the more the animal pays attention to it, and the faster the conditioning. And according to one account of the conditioning process, a stimulus stays salient only if it is the best available predictor of the US. Otherwise its salience decreases: Animals learn to ignore it (Mackintosh, 1975).

The present account of discrimination learning as involving learning to pay attention is similar, but not identical, to our discussion of the Pavlovian conditioning case. For rather than learning to pay attention to a particular stimulus (for example, red), what we are suggesting is that animals learn to pay attention to an entire dimension (for example, color). The extradimensional shift/intradimensional shift studies we just discussed make this plausible, since in those studies, positive transfer occurs in intradimensional shift animals even though all the particular stimuli used in Phase 2 are different from the ones used in Phase 1.

THE PROCESS OF DISCRIMINATION: CONCLUSIONS

In learning a discrimination, animals learn to pay attention and to respond to the best predictor of reinforcement. When there are multiple, equally good predictors, they may each control responding or some may be overshadowed by others. Overshadowing seems to depend on both past experience with various stimuli and nonexperiential predispositions to perceive some stimuli as more salient than others. Explicit discrimination training establishes one stimulus (the S$^+$) as a better predictor of reinforcement than any other. As a result, control of responding by that stimulus is enhanced and control of responding by other, incidental stimuli is eliminated. Indeed, animals seem to learn that these other stimuli are irrelevant.

Is this all there is to the matter of discriminative control? The answer is no. Why, in generalization testing, is there a *gradient* of responding? We know that the pigeon has little difficulty distinguishing among different colors. The reason it pecks a red key after having been trained to peck a green one is not that it cannot distinguish red from green. Such a discrimination is readily learned when the relation between each of the stimuli and reinforcement availability is different. Nor does it peck the red key because its responding is not controlled by color; the fact that the generalization gradient has a peak at S$^+$ clearly indicates that key color is controlling responding. It is possible that key color is not the *only* stimulus controlling responding—that is, stimuli such as the houselight and the fan noise may also exert control. If this were so, then during generalization testing for color these other, incidental stimuli would be present no matter what color was on the key, and might be responsible for the responding that occurred to the different colors. While this account might explain why some responding occurs to colors other than the S$^+$, it cannot explain why different amounts of responding occur to different colors as a function of how different they are from the S$^+$. Thus there must be more to the phenomena of stimulus control of operant behavior. While the predictiveness of the relation between S$^+$ and reinforcement availability may account for the discriminative control of responding, something else is required to account for the generalization of responding.

The Process of Generalization: Excitation and Inhibition

You will recall that we discussed discrimination and generalization in Pavlovian conditioning in terms of the concepts of conditioned excitation and inhibition. Excitation builds up as a CS$^+$ is followed by food in trial after trial, and inhibition builds up as a CS$^-$ is presented without food. When excitation and inhibition have developed sufficiently, they reliably produce or inhibit the CR. In discussing generalization, Pavlov made clear his view that excitation and inhibition, though conditioned to particular CSs, were not confined to those stimuli. Rather, they were also produced by other stimuli that were similar to the CSs. Similarity could be judged on a variety of dimensions: color, pitch, loudness, brightness, size, location, and so on. The appropriate dimension in any particular situation depended both on the nature of the CS and on which aspect of the stimulus controlled the subject's responding. One could judge whether the dimension chosen for study was appropriate by determining whether, in generalization testing, one obtained orderly, peaked gradients like the ones depicted in this chapter.

An account of stimulus generalization in operant conditioning that parallels Pavlov's has had a long and prominent history, owing principally to the writings of Kenneth W. Spence (1936, 1937; see also Hull, 1943, 1952). Spence's theory of discrimination and generalization states that when a stimulus is associated with reinforcement, a gradient of excitation develops around that stimulus. Peak excitation is produced by the training stimulus, with orderly decreases in excitation as stimuli are further and further removed from it. In short, the theoretical excitatory gradient looks like the one depicted in Figure 6–5. Similarly, when a stimulus is associated with nonreinforcement, a gradient of inhibition, like the one depicted in Figure 6–6, develops about it.

THE PEAK SHIFT

What is the relation between the excitatory gradient and the inhibitory one? If the S$^+$ and the S$^-$ are chosen from independent stimulus dimensions, like the color of light as S$^+$ and the pitch of tone as S$^-$, there is no relation between the gradients. However, if both S$^+$ and S$^-$ are taken from the same stimulus dimension, for example, red light versus green light, the gradients interact.

In particular, according to the Spence theory, the gradients add together algebraically. To determine the net excitatory value of any stimulus, one simply subtracts its inhibitory value (taken from the inhibitory gradient) from its excitatory value (taken from the excitatory gradient). In this way a resultant gradient, derived by subtracting inhibitory value from excitatory value for every stimulus, may be obtained.

Let us consider an example. Suppose a pigeon is trained with a 500-nm stimulus as S^+ and a 540-nm stimulus as S^-. The theoretical excitatory and inhibitory gradients are depicted in Figure 6–11A. These curves depict theoretical quantities of excitatory and inhibitory strength. It is assumed that they translate fairly directly into responses. If the values of the inhibitory gradient are subtracted from the values of the excitatory gradient, the resulting gradient is what appears in Figure 6–11B. There are two important features of this gradient. First, it is not symmetrical. The points on the side of S^+ near S^- are much lower than the corresponding points on the side of S^+ away from S^-. Second, the peak of the gradient is not at S^+; rather, it is shifted away from S^-. The peak in Figure 6–11B is at 480 nm instead of 500. Indeed, Figure 6–11B would lead one to expect more responding to the 460-nm stimulus than to the S^+. Thus the Spence theory makes the remarkable prediction that animals trained with S^+ and S^- on the same dimension will respond more, in generalization testing, to a novel stimulus than to the one with which they were trained.

This phenomenon, known as **peak shift**, reliably occurs in generalization tests that follow discrimination training. Some typical data from an early observation of peak shift are presented in Figure 6–12. One group of pigeons was trained to peck a 550-nm stimulus and there was no S^-. A second group was also trained to peck the 550-nm stimulus and S^- was a 590-nm stimulus. The generalization gradient for that second group displays both the asymmetry and the peak shift that the Spence theory predicts (Hanson, 1959; see Hearst, 1968, for another example, and Honig & Urcuioli, 1981, and Rilling, 1977, for general discussions).

TRANSPOSITION AND THE NATURE OF PERCEPTUAL JUDGMENT

The phenomenon of peak shift provides impressive support for the Spence theory of discrimination learning. However, it is possible to suggest an alternative account of peak shift that has nothing to do with the interaction of excitation and inhibition. This account derives from another phenomenon, known as **transposition**, initially studied some 50 years ago by the Gestalt psychologist Wolfgang Köhler (Köhler, 1939).

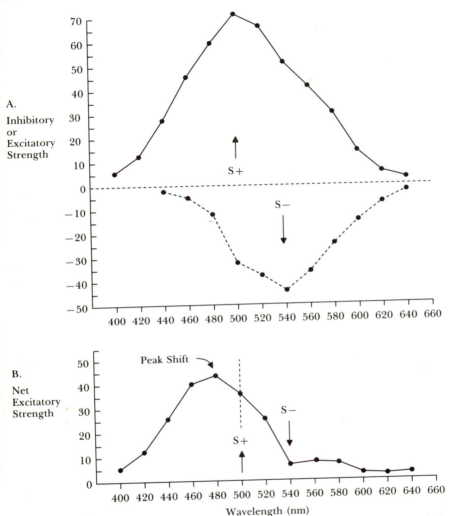

FIGURE 6–11. *Spence's Theory of Discrimination and Generalization.* Hypothetical gradients of excitation about S⁺ and inhibition about S⁻ are depicted in Part A. The resultant gradient when excitatory and inhibitory gradients are combined is depicted in Part B. Note that the peak of the resultant gradient is shifted away from S⁻.

In addition to providing an alternative to the Spence account of peak shift, transposition puts the more general issue of identifying the effective stimulus in any discrimination learning situation in a new perspective.

Köhler argued that stimuli are judged not in absolute terms, but relative to one another. Throughout this chapter we have been treating stimuli as if they were absolute, independent entities. We label the bright-

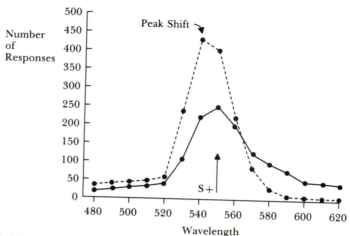

FIGURE 6–12.   *The Phenomenon of Peak Shift.* Results of generalization tests for two groups of pigeons trained to peck a key illuminated with 550-nm light. For one group (solid line) there was no S⁻. The peak of the gradient is at S⁺. For the second group (broken line), S⁻ was 590 nm. The peak of the gradient is shifted away from S⁻. (After Hanson, 1959.)

ness of the key or the intensity of a tone as a stimulus, without regard to the other lights and noises present in the chamber. This approach, while convenient and simple, does not square well with what is known about perception. Stimuli do not exist as absolute entities in a vacuum; they are a part of situations, and they are perceived as part of situations. If one looks at a burning candle at midnight, one perceives the candle to be very bright indeed. However, if the same candle is lit at noon on a sunny day, it appears dim. The brightness of the candle is evaluated against a background of illumination. When we describe the candlelight as bright, what we really mean is that it is bright relative to its background. If the background changes, the brightness of the candle will also change.

The relative nature of perceptual judgment bears upon discriminative control in the following way: A pigeon may be exposed to a discrimination procedure in which S⁺ is a key illuminated with a 20-watt bulb and S⁻ is a key illuminated with a 10-watt bulb. When the pigeon learns the discrimination, what has it actually learned? Has it learned that the 20-watt stimulus signals food, as we have been assuming throughout this chapter, or has it learned that the brighter stimulus signals food, as the facts of perception suggest? If it learns the latter, consider how it will respond to the stimuli presented during a generalization test. If a 40-watt stimulus is presented, it will be even brighter than the S⁺. Having learned to respond to the brighter of two stimuli, the pigeon may make more responses to the 40-watt stimulus than it does to the 20-watt stimulus. But this is precisely the phenomenon we have labeled as peak shift above. In short, it may be that peak shift has nothing to do with the interaction between excitatory and inhibitory gradients, but rather that it is a reflection of the fact that animals evaluate stimuli in terms of their relation to one another.

In studies of chickens and chimpanzees, Köhler observed that when they were trained with the brighter of two stimuli as S $^+$, then were tested with the S $^+$ along with a still brighter stimulus, they would reliably choose the new, brighter stimulus. Köhler called this phenomenon **transposition**, by analogy to the fact that the notes that comprise musical melodies do not change their relation to each other when the melodies are transposed to a different key.

Tests of transposition typically involve, first, the training of a discrimination between two stimuli and, second, presenting test trials in which a choice is offered between new stimuli that are on the same dimension as the training stimuli. A transposition or relational choice is one in which the stimulus chosen has the same relation to the other stimulus as the S $^+$ does to the S $^-$. A nontranspositional, or absolute, choice is one in which the stimulus chosen is the one that is closer or more similar to the S $^+$. A typical transposition test is diagrammed in Figure 6–13. In the most impressive demonstrations of transposition, a new stimulus is presented along with the S $^+$ and the new stimulus is chosen because it bears the same relation to the S $^+$ as the S $^+$ did to the S $^-$.

Is there a way to distinguish empirically these two accounts of peak shift? The answer is yes. What effect, if any, should the degree of difference between the test and training stimuli have on transposition/peak shift? The relational account would certainly suggest that it should make no difference. If S $^+$ is a square of 100 cm^2 area, and S $^-$ is a square of 60 cm^2 area, the animal learns to choose the larger square. If then confronted with 150- and 250-cm^2 squares, or 250- and 500-cm^2 squares, or 500- and 1000-cm^2 squares, the animal should in all cases choose the larger square.

The Spence account makes a different prediction. As is clear from

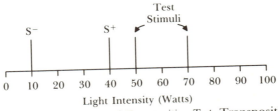

FIGURE 6–13. *Schematic of a Typical Transposition Test.* Transposition Test, Phase 1:10 watts, S $^-$; 40 watts, S $^+$. Animals learn to choose the S $^+$. Phase 2: 50 and 70 watts presented. Animal's choice is a test of transposition. Possible outcomes: (1) Choice of 50 watts is an *absolute* choice, a choice of the stimulus closest to S $^+$. (2) Choice of 70 watts is a *relational* choice, a choice of the brighter stimulus.

Figure 6–11, there comes a point on the stimulus continuum where the inhibitory gradient contributes little to the overall generalization gradient. At this point the excitation will be greater for a stimulus closer to S⁺ than one farther from it even though the closer stimulus is smaller than the far one. The Spence theory would predict that at this point transposition will not be observed. Thus the two theories differ clearly in their predictions about the effect of the distance between test and training stimuli in transposition tests: The relational theory predicts no effect and the Spence theory predicts a switch from transposition to choice of the stimulus nearest S⁺ as the distance increases.

The experimental evidence supports neither theory. As the distance between test and training stimuli increases, the likelihood of transposition decreases, a finding that supports Spence's theory. However, choices do not really reverse; rather, animals seem to respond randomly to the test stimuli, not consistently choosing one or the other (see Riley, 1968). On the other hand, in generalization tests, rather than choice tests between two stimuli, the reversal predicted by Spence's theory is the rule. In Figure 6–12, the fact that more responses occur to the 540-nm stimulus than to the 550-nm stimulus (the phenomenon of peak shift) supports the relational theory as well as the Spence theory. However, the fact that there is less responding to the 530-nm stimulus than to the 540-nm stimulus supports only Spence.

This evidence would seem decisive. However, there is evidence from a different type of discrimination study, known as the **intermediate size problem**, that provides strong support for relational theory. Suppose animals are trained with a 150-cm² square as S⁺, and 100- and 200-cm² squares as S⁻, as diagrammed in Figure 6–14A. Since gradients of inhibition will develop symmetrically on both sides of the S⁺, the Spence theory would predict no peak shift or transposition. The likely effect of this procedure in a generalization test is that the generalization gradient will be narrowed, as depicted in Figure 6–14C. Indeed, generalization tests after training of this type have produced extremely narrow gradients: An example is in Figure 6–15. One group of pigeons, labeled "control," was trained to peck a 550-nm key for food. A second group, labeled "experimental," had the 550-nm key as S⁺, but also had 540- and 560-nm keys as S⁻. Thus this was a kind of "intermediate color" problem. When both groups were then given generalization tests, the experimental group's generalization was much narrower than the control group's (Hanson, 1961). The important thing to note about this gradient is that there was no peak shift; responding decreased symmetrically on either side of S⁺.

According to the relational theory, animals exposed to this type of intermediate size problem learn to choose the stimulus of intermediate size. If given three new stimuli, transposition will occur and the intermediate stimulus will be chosen, though it is further from S⁺ than one of the outside stimuli. This is what occurs in such experiments (Gonzalez,

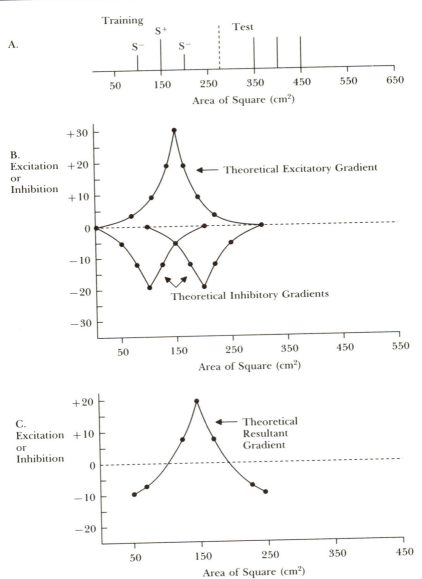

FIGURE 6–14. *The Intermediate Size Problem.* The procedure is depicted in Part A; an S⁺ is sandwiched between two S⁻s. Theoretical gradients of excitation and inhibition consistent with Spence's theory are depicted in Part B and the resultant gradient is depicted in Part C. The expected gradient in Part C is not shifted at all. It remains symmetrical with a peak at S⁺. Thus Spence's theory would predict a choice of the stimulus closest to S⁺ in any test with three new stimuli.

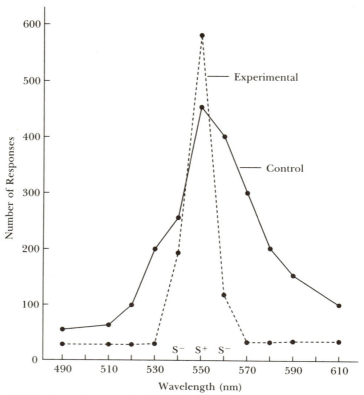

FIGURE 6–15. *Generalization after "Intermediate Color" Training.* The experimental group was trained with 550 nm as S$^+$, and 540 and 560 nm as S$^-$. The control group just had 550 nm as S$^+$. Then both groups had generalization tests. The gradient for the experimental group was narrow, but symmetrical about the S$^+$. (After Hanson, 1961.)

Gentry, & Bitterman, 1954). On the other hand, tests of generalization after training of this type produce gradients like those predicted by Spence's theory, as we see in Figure 6–15.

Another experimental test of the relational theory is the following: Rats were exposed to cards that were divided in half. The bottom halves of the cards were an intermediate shade of gray. The top halves of the cards were either one of three lighter shades or one of three darker shades. The animals had to learn to make a left turn when the top of the card was darker than the bottom and a right turn when the top of the card was lighter than the bottom. The procedure is diagrammed in Figure 6–16. After they learned, they experienced a number of test trials. On these trials the bottom of the card was no longer an intermediate gray, but one of the other six shades. Sometimes, for example, two of the darker stimuli were arranged with the lighter of the two on top. The animals had learned to make a left turn in the presence of each of these stimuli. However, they

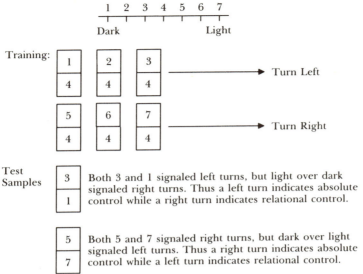

FIGURE 6–16. *A Test of Control of Responding by Stimulus Relations.* A procedure studied by Lawrence and DeRivera (1954) that provided support for the relational view of discrimination learning is diagrammed schematically.

had learned to make a right turn when confronted with the pattern light above dark. Which response did they make? One response would indicate that their responding was controlled by absolute stimulus properties and the other would indicate that their responding was controlled by relations among stimuli. In the overwhelming majority of such test trials the animals' responses were appropriate to the relation between the stimuli and not their absolute characteristics (Lawrence & DeRivera, 1954).

What is one to make of all this evidence? Tests for transposition itself tend to confirm the relational view. Studies of generalization gradients tend to confirm the Spence view. Perhaps both views are correct some of the time. In transposition tests, animals are given a *choice* between stimuli. It is perhaps not surprising that under these conditions they respond to the relation between them, since they are both available for direct comparison. In generalization tests, animals are presented with one stimulus at a time. It is not surprising that relational control is less likely under these conditions. Thus transposition and the peak shift may actually be different phenomena, the first being the product of the perception of stimulus relations and the second being the product of the interaction between gradients of excitation and gradients of inhibition. It is even possible that animals respond to relational properties of stimuli in general, and that discrimination training produces gradients of excitation and inhibition.

For example, it might be that an animal in a discrimination experiment learns that the S^+ is the "brighter" stimulus and not that it is the "40-watt" stimulus. At the same time, reinforcement might produce a gradient of excitation about relatively bright stimuli and a gradient of inhibition about relatively dim ones. The controversy we have discussed between the theories of Spence and of Köhler may actually be a reflection of the different kinds of questions researchers ask about stimuli and behavior. Köhler and others who have argued for the relational view seem primarily concerned with discovering what the effective stimulus is. Spence and his followers seem primarily concerned with discovering how the stimulus, whatever it is, controls operant behavior (see Zeiler, 1963, for a theoretical framework that attempts to incorporate the research findings that support each of the two views).

Concepts

Our focus in discussing discrimination and generalization has been on how stimuli control the occurrence of operant behavior. We have largely ignored the issue of specifying what the stimulus is. But in our discussion of transposition and relational learning this issue came to the fore. The dispute between relational and absolute views is not a dispute about how stimuli control behavior so much as it is a dispute about what the effective stimuli are.

Let us examine what it means to say that the controlling stimulus in an experiment is a relation, say, "brighter than." Saying that an organism's responding is controlled by the relative brightness of a stimulus does not mean that it is incapable of detecting absolute brightness. All it means is that for some reason the organism has fixed on relational rather than absolute properties in defining the S^+. Similarly, when the organism is given a new pair of stimuli in a generalization test and it again responds to the brighter one, this does not mean that it cannot distinguish this new stimulus from the training stimulus. What it may mean is that the organism is treating all stimuli that stand in the "brighter than" relation to other stimuli as functionally equivalent. The organism is forming a class containing members that, though distinguishable from one another, have one property in common—"brighter than"—that is used to define the class. Once the class is formed, the organism sometimes may not make distinctions among its members when it responds.

These kinds of classes of objects or stimuli that are united by some common property are often what we mean when we talk about **concepts**. Our concept of a square, for example, might be defined by the properties that it is (1) a closed figure (2) with four sides (3) of equal length and (4) forming equal angles. Anything that has these properties is treated as an instance of the concept, and other properties that might distinguish one square from another (size, color, and so on) are disregarded. If, on the other hand, we make distinctions between the concepts "large square" and "small square," then size gets added to our list of defining properties. Or if we are interested in the concept "rectangle," then "sides of equal length" gets dropped from the list.

The number of different ways we can classify into concepts the stimuli of everyday life is limitless. And there is probably no aspect of life more central or important than this classifying activity. If we treated all stimuli as unique, intelligent activity would be impossible. There would be no point in learning. Having learned how to hammer a small nail into a block of wood would not help us at hammering large nails, or tacks. If each act of hammering was in all respects unique, then we would have no reason to generalize our experience with some hammering experiences we have already encountered to new ones. We would have to learn how to hammer in each new situation from scratch. Unless we generalized from past experience to future situations, learning would have no point. And unless we grouped stimuli into classes that were in some way equivalent, there would be no possibility of generalization. One very central way in which we come to put distinct objects or events into equivalence classes is by forming concepts that unite them. Thus the forming and using of concepts is at the heart of all learning—of all intelligence.

Though we have not talked about concepts earlier in the book, a number of the phenomena we have discussed can be understood as reflecting the formation of a concept. Let us consider just one example, the training of a rat to press a lever. When we discussed the development of a lever-press operant in Chapter 4, we indicated that early in training lever presses are extremely variable in form and contain much extraneous activity. As training proceeds, the extraneous activity drops out and an efficient, stereotyped lever press emerges. It is possible that one of the things the rat is learning early in its training is the concept "lever press," that it is learning which aspects of its behavior define the lever press and which aspects are incidental to it. Learning to lever-press may involve the development of a concept by the rat that matches the concept of the experimenter.

If the number of different concepts we can form is limitless in principle, it is certainly not limitless in fact. What determines the way organisms will come to classify stimuli? What properties will be used to define our concepts? These are extremely complicated issues that have occupied philosophers and psychologists for many years. We cannot address them in general form here, though we will take them up in greater detail in Chapter 10. For now we can ask whether the phenomena of discrimination and generalization have anything to tell us about the formation of concepts (for interesting discussions, see Fodor, 1975; Rosch & Lloyd, 1978; E.E. Smith & Medin, 1981).

Think for a moment about the process of discrimination. When faced with discriminative stimuli, the organism must determine which of their many properties to pay attention to and which to ignore. Having learned this, the organism may treat any stimuli that have the critical property as equivalent; that is, it may generalize equally to all stimuli that possess the central property. Thus having been trained with a 4-cm, white square as S^+ and a circle as S^-, a pigeon might respond equally to 2-, 8-, and 16-cm squares and to red, green, and blue ones. We might be tempted to say that the pigeon "had" the concept of "square." Of course, it is possible that the pigeon comes to treat various squares as equivalent without really "having" the concept (closed figure, four sides of equal length, etc.). But it is possible that discrimination training may contribute to determining which of the many possible concepts become actual concepts by singling out particular properties of stimuli as predictive of reinforcement, making them worthy of attention and definitional of a concept.

For many years the study of human concept learning was based on an approach very much like our account of discrimination learning (Hull, 1920; see Bruner, Goodnow, & Austin, 1956, for a classic series of experiments based on this approach). To study concept learning, people would be presented with stimuli like the ones in Figure 6–17. These stimuli vary on four different dimensions, and can take one of three values on each dimension. The experimenter would arbitrarily identify some combination of values of dimensions as defining the positive set. For example, gray circles might define the positive set. Then the subject would be presented with stimuli and have to guess whether each stimulus was positive or not. The experimenter would indicate whether the subject was correct. Eventually, the subject would discover which values of which dimensions were critical and which were irrelevant.

We can think of this task as involving the creation and discovery of an artificial concept. The concept "gray circle," like the concept "square," has a number of critical features that define it. The subject's job is to identify these critical features.

What must the subject learn to solve this problem? There is no difficulty in discriminating the individual stimuli. There is no difficulty in discriminating the feedback for correct and incorrect choices ("right" and "wrong" are analogous to reinforcement and no reinforcement in animal experiments). The problem is in determining which features of the stimuli are relevant and which are irrelevant. Indeed, this task is essentially a complex version of the one used in extradimensional shift/intradimensional shift experiments, described above (pp. 216–17). Thus the subject must learn that size and number are irrelevant, and that shape and brightness are relevant. Having learned this, the subject must also learn which particular values of shape and brightness (circle and gray) are positive. Solving the discrimination problem may be thought of as involving the same processes that are involved in forming the concept "gray circle." This, at least, was the view that guided the investigators doing the research. They assumed that all concepts were characterized by having

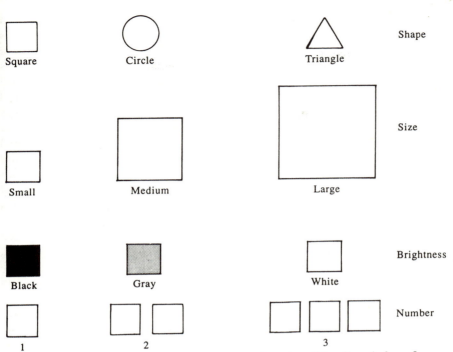

FIGURE 6–17. *Stimuli Used in Studies of Concept Learning.* Stimuli varied on four dimensions (shape, size, brightness, and number), with three values on each dimension. All combinations of values of dimensions were presented, and the subject had to figure out which stimuli were positive. Thus in a given experiment, if "gray circles" defined the positive set, then stimuli containing 1, 2, or 3 small, medium, or large gray circles were positive, and all other stimuli were negative.

clear-cut, defining attributes, and that by studying the different strategies people used in learning these artificial concepts they would come to know about concept learning in general (see Chapter 10 for further discussion).

ABSTRACT CONCEPTS

While many concepts are defined by the presence of certain properties (like square, mammal, lever press, and so on), there are also concepts for which the defining properties are not obvious. Consider, for example, the concepts "same" and "different." The particular attributes that will determine to which of these concepts a given pair of stimuli belong will depend on the particular stimuli being investigated. Concepts like "same" and "different" may be said to be **abstract**, in that we can use the concepts to classify stimuli without having any specific stimulus features to use as concept identifiers. In other words, what stimulus features we use to classify stimuli as "same" or "different" will vary with the nature of the particular stimuli we are classifying.

There has been a great deal of research, with organisms of various species, on the learning of concepts like "same" and "different." Two commonly used procedures for exploring this issue involve what are called **matching-to-sample** and **oddity** discriminations. Typical procedures are diagrammed in Figure 6–18. In these procedures, the center key first lights up red or green. A peck on this key illuminates the side keys—one red and one green. Reinforcement depends on pecking the side key that is the same color as (matching) or a different color than (oddity) the center key.

There are many variants on this procedure. Sometimes the center key stays lit when the side keys come on. Sometimes there are delays imposed between sample presentation and the opportunity for choice. In general, whatever the procedure, pigeons, and members of other species often studied in learning theory experiments, perform quite accurately (see Carter & Werner, 1978, for a review).

Matching-to-sample and oddity discriminations can be solved by appeal to the concepts of "same" and "different." But of course they can also be solved in other ways. For example, an animal on a matching task could learn: "If red, peck red; if green, peck green." The same alternative possibility is true of other procedures used to study same–different learning. For example, pigeons have been trained so that when the sample stimuli match, pecks at the left key produce food, while when they don't match, pecks at the right key produce food (Honig, 1965; Malott &

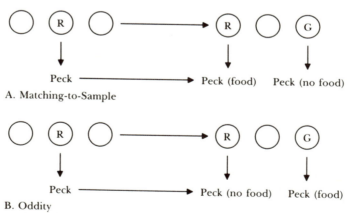

A. Matching-to-Sample

B. Oddity

FIGURE 6–18. *Matching-to-Sample and Oddity Procedures.* In the first part of a trial the center key lights up red or green. A peck produces the second part of a trial, in which one side key is red and the other is green. If the pigeon is required to match, it must peck the side key that is the same color the center key was. If the pigeon is required to perform oddity, it must peck the side key that is a different color from what the center key was.

Malott, 1970; Zentall & Hogan, 1974, 1976, 1978). In this case the pigeons could be relying on their concepts of "same" and "different." But they could also be learning:

a. If red–red, peck left.

b. If green–green, peck left.

c. If red–green, peck right.

d. If green–red, peck right.

A way to determine what the pigeon is learning is to conduct a transfer test. After it has learned any of these tasks with red and green, switch to blue and yellow. Or to see just how general the concept is, switch to circle and square. Experiments of this type, which look for transfer from one set of stimuli to another, have found only partial support for the notion that pigeons learn the abstract concepts of "same" and "different." There is often some positive transfer from training to test stimuli, but the transfer is far from complete. In addition, how much transfer there is depends on how different the training and transfer stimuli are. Thus pigeons might show substantial transfer from red–green to blue–yellow, but not to circle–square (see Honig, 1965; Malott & Malott, 1970; Urcuioli, 1977; Urcuioli & Nevin, 1975; and Zentall & Hogan, 1974, 1976, 1978, for suggestions of positive evidence, and see Carter & Werner, 1978; and Premack, 1978, for critical discussion of the evidence). With people and chimpanzees there is clear, positive evidence for such abstract concepts as "same" and "different," but for all other species the evidence is problematic (Premack, 1976; Woodruff, Premack, & Kennel, 1978).

NATURAL CONCEPTS

Even if some abstract concepts cannot be identified by a set of defining attributes the way "square" is, the idea that concrete concepts have this organization dominated thought in psychology for many years. That is one of the justifications for using experiments like the one outlined in Figure 6–17 as simulations of the process of concept learning. But if we think a little about many of our everyday concepts, it quickly becomes apparent that they often do not possess defining features. Think about concepts like "dog," "game," and "tool." Is there even a single property that all the things we call games, tools, or dogs share? The answer is no. For any feature we might choose, we could quickly generate counterexamples: objects that clearly belonged in the concept that did not have that feature. Concepts like these are often called **natural concepts** (see Wittgenstein, 1953; Rosch, 1975, 1978; E. E. Smith & Medin, 1981). Though natural concepts have definitions, it is not clear that these definitions can specify properties or features of objects that are both *necessary* and *sufficient* to make the objects fit as instances of the concept. We will have more to say about the nature and organization of natural concepts in Chapter 10. For now, let us ask whether there is any evidence that animals possess natural concepts.

A series of experiments has explored this question with pigeons as subjects. The general method used involves presenting the pigeon with a series of slides. Some of the slides include instances of the natural concept (S$^+$); other slides do not (S$^-$). Pecks at a key when an S$^+$ slide is on produce food while pecks at a key when an S$^-$ slide is on do not. The question of interest is whether pigeons learn to peck the key only when an S$^+$ slide is present. Concepts explored using this method have included vehicles, trees, water, human-made objects, fish, and a particular person (Herrnstein, 1979; Herrnstein & de Villiers, 1980; Herrnstein & Loveland, 1964; Herrnstein, Loveland, & Cable, 1976; Lea, 1984; Lea & Ryan, 1983; Lubow, 1974). Sample stimuli typical of the ones used in these experiments are presented in Figure 6–19.

Stimuli A and B are positive and negative instances used in training with "water" as S$^+$; C and D are positive and negative instances used with "trees" as S$^+$; and E and F are positive and negative instances used with a particular person as S$^+$. In general the stimuli are just ordinary scenes that may or may not happen to contain the S$^+$. The S$^+$ is often not the focus of the stimulus, as in Figure 6–19C.

In one such experiment that used the stimuli in Figure 6–19, pigeons were given daily sessions that included brief exposure to each of 80 slides. Half of the slides were S$^+$ and half were S$^-$, and they were presented in random order from day to day. Pecks while an S$^+$ was on were reinforced, whereas pecks while an S$^-$ was on were not reinforced. For some pigeons the S$^+$ was water, for some it was trees, and for some it was a young woman. In each case the pigeons mastered the discrimination to a very high degree of accuracy. Moreover, they did so extremely rapidly (Herrnstein, Loveland, & Cable, 1976). Does this mean that the pigeons had learned these three concepts in a way that roughly matches our own concept learning? There is another possibility. Perhaps the pigeons learned no concept at all and simply memorized all 80 slides. There are two ways to test this possibility. First, one could take the same 80 slides and divide them randomly into two groups of 40, with half of them arbitrarily S$^+$ and the other half S$^-$. If pigeons are simply memorizing the slides, this kind of task should be no more difficult than one involving a real concept. Remarkably, when this is done, pigeons do learn the discrimination. Thus they seem capable of memorizing 80 slides. However, learning this "pseudoconcept" takes much, much longer than learning a real one (Herrnstein & de Villiers, 1980; see also Vaughan & Greene, 1984).

A second test is a transfer test. Once the concept has been learned with 80 training slides, one can present the pigeons with new examples of S$^+$

A

B

C

D

E

F

FIGURE 6-19.   *Discrimination of Natural Objects by Pigeons.* Pigeons were presented with slides of ordinary street scenes and were required to discriminate them by the presence or absence of either water, trees, or a particular person. This figure presents examples of some typical stimuli presented. A positive example of water is in A and a negative is in B. A positive example of a tree is in C and a negative is in D. A positive example of the particular person is in E and a negative is in F. In all cases the majority of pigeons responded correctly to these stimuli. (From Herrnstein, Loveland, & Cable, 1976. Photographs by Richard Herrnstein, copyright © 1976.)

and S⁻ and see how long it takes them to learn with these new instances. When these kinds of tests are done, transfer is almost complete. Pigeons respond differentially to new S⁺s and S⁻s on first presentation almost as much as they do to the training stimuli (Herrnstein, 1979; Herrnstein & de Villiers, 1980; Herrnstein, Loveland, & Cable, 1976). Thus it seems possible that pigeons are able to learn natural concepts of the sort that at least resembles human natural concepts.

Indeed, the evidence from these experiments leads to a more remarkable conclusion than that pigeons are capable of learning these concepts. It seems that they learn these natural concepts faster and with greater accuracy than they learn the kinds of concepts that have clear-cut defining properties, with stimuli like those in Figure 6–17. How might we account for this seemingly paradoxical fact that complex, ill-defined concepts are more easily acquired than simple, well-defined ones?

One way to make sense of the ease with which natural concepts are acquired is to realize that instances of these concepts are characterized by a host of different stimulus features. It is true that none of these features is definitional and a part of all instances. However, all of these features are relevant. Thus the pigeon can derive useful information by paying attention to many of the different features of a stimulus. Though some features are more informative than others, and thus more profitably attended to, there is something to be learned from even modestly informative features. Informativeness is not an all-or-none affair. In contrast, with simpler, precisely defined concepts, the number of relevant features is sharply reduced; only definitional features are relevant and all other features are irrelevant. By paying attention to the wrong aspect of a stimulus, the pigeon will learn nothing useful at all. Thus non-natural, well-defined concepts pose a much greater attentional challenge to the pigeon than do natural, ill-defined concepts.

The central domain of non-natural concepts is in science, where enormous importance is given to precision of definition. We want organisms to be either vertebrates or invertebrates. We don't want pseudovertebrates or semivertebrates. We don't want any geometric shapes that are "squarish." Our own experience can show us how difficult it is to master such precise concepts. We must be sure our definitions include all the features used to define these concepts. Otherwise we will make significant mistakes in classifying objects. While such precisely defined concepts are of great benefit in organizing our knowledge of the world, they are not easy for us, or for pigeons, to learn.

Learning Theory and Memory

In introducing our discussion of concepts, we indicated that unless organisms grouped individual stimuli or events into classes, they would never be able to profit from the past. Learning requires generalizing from the past to the present or the future, and generalization in turn requires some kind of categorization. But, of course, learning requires more than just generalizing from the past to the present. It also requires remembering what happened in the past. Throughout our discussions of Pavlovian and operant conditioning, the process of remembering has just been taken for granted. Now it is time to turn our attention to remembering. What are memory processes like, and what role do they play in the phenomena of learning?

Most of the rest of this book is devoted to exploring these questions. Modern cognitive psychology is largely concerned with human memory processes, and there is a lot to be said about the character of human memory. However, as we will see, a great many of the characteristics of human memory are intimately related to our ability to reflect on what we experience, our ability to develop and to use complex strategies when we attempt to remember things, and our ability to use language. Thus it is difficult simply to extrapolate from research on human memory to understand the role of memory processes in the phenomena that have concerned us in the first part of this book. Instead what we will do in the remainder of this chapter, before turning explicitly to the study of human memory, is examine research on memory processes in the same experimental situations, with the same organisms, that have yielded most other principles we have discussed so far. As we will see, there are certainly points of overlap between studies of animal memory in conditioning settings and studies of human memory in verbal ones. But to eliminate the potential complications posed by characteristics and abilities that may be distinctively human, we will restrict our discussion here to the animal conditioning domain.

REMEMBERING AND KNOWING

All learning involves memory. All knowledge involves memory. When we say that we know something, we imply that we have experienced it or thought about it before and that we remember our experience. When we say that we know the rules of a card game like bridge, we mean that we once learned them and now remember them. But when we say that it takes a good memory to be a good bridge player, we are not referring to memory for the rules of the game. Instead we are referring to memory for the bids that have been made and the cards that have been played in a given hand. Similarly, when we are trying to memorize a new phone number we can take advantage of aspects of phone numbers in general that we already know or remember. We know that phone numbers in the United States contain a three-digit Area Code, a three-digit exchange, and a four-digit specific number. We may take advantage of this background knowledge when we try to remember the new number. But when we talk about remembering phone numbers, we don't have this background information in mind as part of what we remember.

Studies of memory are not generally studies of the background knowledge that makes an essential contribution in all memory tasks. That is because asking how this background knowledge gets formed is essentially the same as asking how learning occurs. Thus all studies of learning are essentially studies of the development of background knowledge, and there is no need to distinguish one from the other.

There is another aspect of memory that can be distinguished from learning. Playing bridge well requires that we remember events that have occurred in a given hand—previous bids and plays. This demand on our memory occurs in hand after hand, no matter how well we have learned the rules of bridge, bridge bidding systems, strategies for playing the cards, and whatever other skills we need to play bridge well. No matter how perfect our knowledge of this background information may be, how well we perform in a given hand will depend on how well we remember events from that hand. And when that hand is over we can forget it completely, though we should not forget our background knowledge (and indeed, we may even want to incorporate aspects of the hand *into* our background knowledge). The memory processes that researchers on animal memory typically study are analogous to the processes that allow us to remember the cards that are being played in a particular bridge hand (see Honig, 1978; Roitblat, Bever, & Terrace, 1984; Spear & Miller, 1981). What do we know about this aspect of memory?

DELAYED MATCHING-TO-SAMPLE

Let us discuss memory concretely by referring to the experimental context in which it is most often studied, known as **delayed matching-to-sample**. A typical trial from a delayed matching-to-sample procedure with pigeons is shown in Figure 6–20. A trial begins with one of three keys lit with red light. The key stays lit for, say, 5 seconds, then goes out. After a waiting period known as the **retention interval** or **delay interval** (10 seconds in Figure 6–20), two keys are lit—one red and one green. The pigeon must peck the red key—the key whose color matches the sample—to obtain reinforcement.

Let us put ourselves in the pigeon's place and analyze the task before us in a matching-to-sample situation. A trial like the one in Figure 6–20 begins and our knowledge of the situation tells us:

1. I have to peck the correct key later to get food.

2. Which key is correct depends on the color I see now. Therefore I will have to peck red later.

3. There is going to be a retention interval, so I had better work on remembering red.

Thus, we (and probably the pigeon) know the "rules of the game" just as the bridge player does. Nevertheless, unless we can effectively remem-

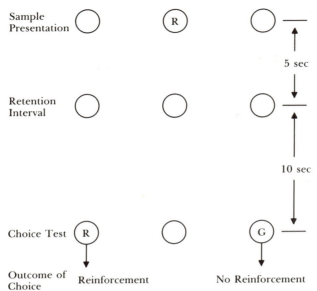

FIGURE 6–20.   *The Delayed Matching-to-Sample Procedure.* The pigeon observes the sample (red) for 5 seconds, after which it experiences a 10-second retention interval with all keys dark. During the retention interval it must somehow remember the sample. When the retention interval ends, it is given a choice between red and green. To obtain food it must peck red, thus matching the sample. On other trials, green would be presented as the sample and therefore choice of green would produce food.

ber what the sample is on a given trial, we will not make the correct response and will not get food. Questions about how the pigeon remembers the sample, and what kinds of manipulations can facilitate or interfere with that memory, are the kinds of questions researchers ask about how memory operates.

One of the major determinants of performance in delayed matching-to-sample is the duration of the retention interval. The longer the animal has to remember the sample, the worse it performs. The relation between retention interval length and accuracy is depicted in Figure 6–21 (Grant, 1976; see also Nelson & Wasserman, 1978).

These data are from pigeons, one of the two types of organisms studied extensively on this procedure. When monkeys (the other commonly used organisms) are studied, they are similarly affected by the length of the retention interval, though they are better able to manage long retention intervals than pigeons (see D'Amato, 1973; Grant, 1981a).

Why does matching performance deteriorate as the retention interval increases? We can understand this effect by thinking about what happens as we try to remember a new person's name. Suppose that during a party you are in the midst of a conversation with a friend. During the conversa-

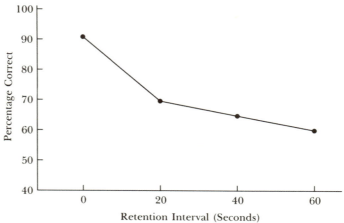

FIGURE 6–21. *Matching Accuracy as a Function of Retention Interval in Pigeons.* As the time between the removal of the sample and the choice point increases, the pigeon's accuracy decreases. Since with no memory at all animals would be correct by chance 50% of the time, these data show that when the retention interval gets to be 1 minute long, the animals might do almost as well without having bothered to look at the sample. (After Grant, 1976.)

tion your friend points out an unfamiliar person in the room, and mentions the person's name. If you wanted to remember the name you might rehearse it—repeat it to yourself again and again. But since you are in the middle of a conversation, you can't rehearse it. If this unfamiliar person should come over to you and your friend shortly after you have heard her name, you may still remember it. But if she comes by five minutes later, there is a good chance you will have forgotten. It is almost as if when you hear the name, some kind of image or trace is created, and as time passes without rehearsal, the trace decays. Indeed, precisely this kind of account has been offered to explain performance on matching-to-sample tasks (Roberts & Grant, 1976; see J. Brown, 1956, 1958, and Peterson & Peterson, 1959, for examples with humans).

If this account is true, we might expect that the longer the stimulus presentation is, the stronger the trace will be, and the longer it will last. Thus if your friend said to you, "Her name is *Joanna Jones, Joanna Jones, Joanna Jones,*" you might still remember 10 minutes later, even without rehearsal. Supporting evidence for this view comes from studies in which the sample presentation time is manipulated. Indeed, the data in Figure 6–21 come from such a study. The data in that figure were obtained when samples were presented for 4 seconds. In other conditions, sample duration was 1, 8, or 14 seconds. The complete results of that study are presented in Figure 6–22.

The figure shows that for any given retention interval, the longer the

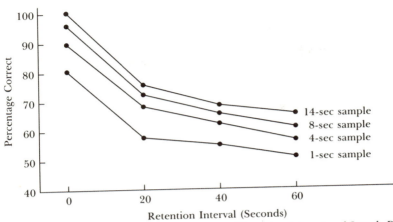

FIGURE 6–22. *Matching Accuracy as a Function of Retention Interval and Sample Duration.* Each curve shows that matching accuracy decreases as retention interval increases. However, the longer the sample duration, the more accurate the matching at all retention intervals. As in Figure 6–21, 50% accuracy represents chance performance. (After Grant, 1976.)

sample is presented the better the performance. Thus the notion that inputs produce images or traces that decay over time and whose strength is a function of the duration of the inputs has some empirical support.

WORKING MEMORY AS ACTIVE

These data make memory look like a rather passive process. Inputs produce faithful traces that decay over time. Organisms do nothing to keep the traces strong. They do not rehearse, for if they did they could manage to survive the retention interval with the memory intact (just as you could remember the name by repeating it to yourself). Is there evidence from studies of matching to indicate that memory is a more active process than this?

Indeed, there is good reason to believe that the notion of memory as a fading trace cannot explain much that is known about memory. It may not even be the correct explanation of the data in Figure 6–22. Think again about trying to remember someone's name at the party. Suppose that you do try to rehearse it. You will be much better able to rehearse if you are not carrying on a conversation than if you are. Features of the conversation may *interfere* with your rehearsal. Is it possible that pigeons are rehearsing the color of the sample but that their rehearsal is being interfered with?

The answer is yes. During the retention interval the pigeon is looking around in the experimental chamber. It sees a variety of different objects of a variety of different colors. Any or all of these inputs can interfere with rehearsal. We could reduce interference simply by turning out the lights in the box during the retention interval. When one does this, matching accuracy increases dramatically (for example, Grant & Roberts, 1976; Roberts & Grant, 1978; but see Tranberg & Rilling, 1980, for data suggesting a different interpretation of these experiments).

Thus memory processes are susceptible to interference. The particular type of interference we have been discussing is called **retroactive interference** because the interfering stimulus comes after the stimulus to be remembered. It is also possible to produce **proactive interference** (see Chapter 13 for further discussion of memory interference effects). For example, suppose that prior to some red sample trials we illuminate the key with green light for a few seconds. Then we present the sample, followed by the retention interval and the choice. The initial exposure to the green light reduces matching accuracy, and how much it is reduced depends on how much time there is between the interfering stimulus and the sample. The closer together they are, the greater the interference (Grant, 1975; Grant & Roberts, 1973; Jarvik, Goldfarb, & Corley, 1969).

We might interpret these retroactive and proactive interference effects in a way that is consistent with a simple trace-decay account of memory. We could imagine that the image formed of the interfering stimulus simply obscures the image of the sample stimulus. Thus, rather than making rehearsal difficult, interfering stimuli make the trace fainter. However, there are other aspects of memory that cannot be explained by appeal to this kind of fading-trace theory.

First, there is evidence that an animal's ability to perform matching tasks can be greatly improved with practice. In one dramatic example with a monkey, its accuracy was barely above 50% at a retention interval of 20 seconds even after many hundreds of training trials. But training continued and the monkey was eventually able to perform at 80% accuracy at a 2-minute retention interval (D'Amato, 1973). What could the monkey have been doing so that it improved with practice? One possibility is that it was learning more effective strategies for rehearsing the sample so that its memory could survive the long retention interval. It is not clear how a fading-trace account of matching performance can explain why practice improves accuracy.

Second, suppose animals are solving the matching problem in the following way: The sample comes and goes, leaving them with a fading trace; then choice stimuli appear and the animal chooses the stimulus that matches the trace. How could this type of process meet the challenge posed by the procedure in Figure 6–23? This procedure is known as a **symbolic matching** procedure. The sample is either red or green. The choice stimuli are horizontal and vertical lines. The pigeon must learn the arbitrary rule that "if the sample was red, choose vertical; and if the

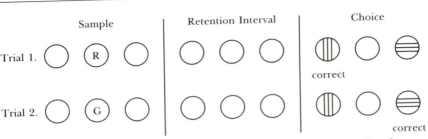

FIGURE 6–23.   *The Symbolic Matching Procedure.* Sample stimuli are red and green and choice stimuli are horizontal and vertical lines. The organism must learn an arbitrary rule that red means choose vertical and green means choose horizontal.

sample was green, choose horizontal." With a procedure like this, the pigeon cannot choose the choice stimulus that matches its fading trace of the sample, because neither one does. Nevertheless, pigeons are able to perform such tasks at high levels of accuracy (see Carter & Werner, 1978, for a review). Indeed, they are essentially as accurate in symbolic matching as they are in regular matching. This demonstration of symbolic matching eliminates the possibility that successful matching performance is the result of a literal match between sample and choice stimuli (see Maki, Gillund, Hauge, & Siders, 1977; Roitblat, 1980, 1982).

There is another line of evidence that suggests that rehearsal processes can be turned on and off, and thus that memory is an active process. It comes from a simple variant of delayed matching studies, called **directed forgetting**, in which an additional stimulus is presented on every trial. When the sample goes off, it is followed by a "remember" stimulus or a "forget" stimulus. What the "remember" stimulus actually indicates is that a choice phase will be coming. The "forget" stimulus indicates that a choice phase will not be coming. To examine the effects of these "remember" and "forget" cues, an occasional choice trial is presented following a "forget" cue. Accuracy is much lower on these "forget" probe trials than it is on "remember" trials, indicating that the "forget" cue is telling the animal not to bother to rehearse. Interestingly, just how much worse accuracy is depends on when in the retention interval the "forget" cue occurs. If it occurs near the end of the interval, accuracy is high, while if it occurs near the beginning, accuracy is low. It seems as though an animal will rehearse the sample until or unless it receives a "forget" cue. If the cue does not come until late in the retention interval, so that substantial rehearsal has occurred, or the animal does not have to remember for very long until the test comes, the animal is able to remember the sample (Grant, 1981b, 1984, 1986; Kendrick, Rilling, & Stonebraker, 1981; Maki & Hegvik, 1980; Rilling, Kendrick, & Stonebraker, 1984).

In sum, it seems clear from the growing body of research on memory in matching-to-sample situations that memory is an active process that mediates between environmental inputs and behavior.

Spatial Memory and Cognitive Maps

Matching-to-sample tasks are not the only settings used to study memory processes. In recent years, a great deal of attention has been devoted to the study of what is called **spatial memory**, or memory for places. One of the primary reasons for this attention is that rats, and other animals, have demonstrated a quite prodigious ability to learn and remember things about the places they have been. It seems as though animals construct highly detailed and accurate maps—**cognitive maps**—of their environments.

Consider the maze diagrammed in Figure 6–24. It consists of a central platform and eight identical arms radiating out from the center. Typically in T-maze experiments only one of the arms has food, and the rat must learn to return to the correct arm. But suppose we reversed the task, putting food at the end of each of the eight arms of the radial maze. Now what the rat has to learn is a way of visiting each of the eight arms and obtaining the food, without returning to any already-visited arm. In the T-maze experiment the rat must learn a "win–stay" strategy. In the radial-arm maze the rat must learn a "win–shift" strategy.

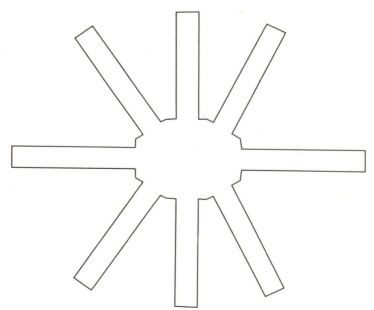

FIGURE 6–24. *An Eight-Arm Radial Maze.* In experiments using this maze all eight arms had food at the end; the rat's task was to learn to visit each of the arms without repeating any. (After Olton & Samuelson, 1976.)

How do rats perform on this task? The answer is: remarkably well. Within 20 exposures to the maze rats learn virtually never to reenter an arm they have already visited. Indeed, they seem to learn this task with less difficulty than they learn a simple T-maze (Olton, 1978, 1979; Olton & Samuelson, 1976).

Let us think about what the task requires. First, the rat must learn the rules of the game—what the maze is like, that it should not return to already-visited arms, and so on. But second, the rat must also depend on memory for where it has already been on any given day. On each trial it must keep track of where it has already been in order not to repeat a visit. Once it has successfully ended a session by visiting all eight arms, it can erase this particular memory while keeping the reference background knowledge intact for the next session.

There are a number of different ways that rats might meet these task requirements. First, they could develop a rigid pattern of responses, always choosing arms in the same order. This would ease memory requirements since the responses could simply be run off automatically, each one triggering the next. But there is good evidence that such a rigid behavior pattern does not develop. Rats do not visit the same arms in the same order every day. Indeed, the pattern of arm visits is almost random (Olton, 1978, 1979). Second, it is possible that they can smell the food at the end of arms, or smell their own odors in arms they have already visited. If so, again memory would be spared. They could simply learn either "go to the smell of food" or "don't go to the smell of rat" and perform accurately. But this possibility has also been ruled out. Dousing the maze with after-shave lotion to obscure other odors does not impair performance. Also, if after the rat has made a number of choices the arms it has chosen are rebaited with food, it does not return to those arms. Instead it visits arms not yet visited, though food odors are emanating from all arms (Olton, 1978, 1979). Finally, if instead of trying to obscure odor cues, one rotates the maze so that spatial cues no longer provide accurate information about where the rat has and has not been, the rat's performance deteriorates. Even though odor cues are present to tell the rat what to do, it makes mistakes by visiting locations that used to contain unvisited arms, but now, after rotation, contain arms that were already visited (Olton, Collison, & Werz, 1977; Olton & Samuelson, 1976). Thus it seems as though the rat masters the task by learning the maze (that is, building a cognitive map), and then using its memory to keep track of where it has already been.

And unlike memory processes we discussed in delayed-matching experiments, the rat's memory for the maze is highly resistant to disruption. One can start a session and after the rat's first four choices, impose a delay of up to 4 hours. When the rat is then returned to the maze, it goes to the unvisited arms just as unerringly as if there had been no delay at all. Thus there is little or no decay of memory over a 4-hour retention interval (Beatty & Shavalia, 1980).

This kind of spatial learning and memory ability is not restricted to rats in mazes. A series of experiments has been done with chimpanzees in the outdoor compound in which they live. The compound is roughly an acre in size, with many trees, bushes, and variations in terrain. In one experiment chimps were carried through the compound along a semirandom route full of twists and turns and backtracking. They watched as food was hidden in each of 18 different locations. Then they were returned to the center of the compound and released to find the food. Not only were they able to find most of it, but they did so efficiently, in extremely systematic fashion. They visited various hiding places in a pattern that minimized the distance they had to travel from place to place and that bore no relation to the path that had been used by the experimenter to hide the food in the first place. In a second, similar experiment, food was hidden in 18 places, but in 9 of those places it was fruit and in the other 9, vegetables. Chimps prefer fruit to vegetables, and they reflected this preference in their search patterns. When set free to search, almost all of their first 9 visits were to locations containing fruit (Menzel, 1978; see Olson & Maki, 1983, and Shettleworth, 1983, for evidence of similar abilities in birds).

It is difficult to understand this behavior in any way other than to assume that the chimps have a cognitive map of the compound. As they are carried around, they store information about food locations not on the basis of the path they are traveling, but on the basis of their cognitive map. They then work with this cognitive representation to determine the most efficient route to travel in gathering the food, just as a traveling salesperson might consult an actual map so that sales stops could be arranged to minimize traveling time. This kind of task solution depends on cognitive mediation between inputs and behavior that transforms and organizes the inputs significantly. An attempt to explain the chimps' behavior without appeal to these mediating processes would provide an extremely impoverished view of what the chimp can do.

Summary

The law of effect tells us about how the consequences of behavior affect its future likelihood of occurrence. But there are few behavior–consequence relations that are operative in all situations. How organisms come to produce operants in just those situations in which they are reinforced is the province addressed by research on stimulus control of operant behavior. The two sides of stimulus control—discrimination and generalization—are pervasive aspects of daily life, and understanding them is critical for a complete theory of behavior.

There are a variety of procedures used for studying discrimination and generalization. One can require organisms to make successive or simultaneous discriminations. And one typically studies generalization by presenting organisms with stimuli that differ in varying amounts from the training stimuli, and obtaining generalization gradients.

Our current understanding of the process of discrimination learning involves issues we have already encountered in our study of Pavlovian conditioning. Central principles of discrimination learning are these:

1. In any situation there are a large number of stimuli that may control responding, many of which are only incidental to the specific experimental task.

2. When a number of stimuli are equally predictive of reinforcer availability, they may share control over the operant. Alternatively, one stimulus may be more salient than the others and overshadow them in controlling responding.

3. In any situation, that stimulus that is the best predictor of reinforcer availability can be expected to control responding. Explicit discrimination training allows the experimenter to determine which stimulus will control responding by ensuring that the most informative relation is between that stimulus and reinforcement.

4. Discrimination learning involves learning to pay attention to relevant (predictive) aspects of the situation and learning to ignore irrelevant (unpredictive) aspects of the situation.

5. Discrimination learning involves the development of excitation to the S^+ and of inhibition to the S^-, as indicated in part by the observation of peaked generalization gradients of excitation and of inhibition.

The study of stimulus control is not generally concerned with determining how organisms perceive stimuli, but with how stimuli, once perceived, come to control behavior. Nevertheless, some aspects of research on stimulus control do address questions of perception. For example, transposition and related phenomena indicate that animals do not evaluate stimuli absolutely, independent of context. Rather, at least under some circumstances, a stimulus is evaluated in relation to other available stimuli. Lights are not "bright" or "dim" but "brighter" or "dimmer."

In addition, since discrimination learning often involves learning which of the many aspects of a stimulus are relevant and which others should be ignored, the study of discrimination has been a model for the understanding of the formation of concepts. Learning many concepts involves learning what their defining properties are. This means learning to focus on the respects in which instances of the concept are similar and to ignore the respects in which they are different. Many learning phenomena, including even the acquisition of a simple lever press, can be understood as involving concept learning of this kind.

But many of our concepts do not have defining properties. So-called natural concepts like "game" and "tool" seem to be characterized by a whole set of properties, some of which are possessed by many instances, but none of which is possessed by all. Recent research has indicated that pigeons are able to learn such complex natural concepts—indeed, that they learn them more easily than simple, well-defined ones. This suggests that seemingly simple, laboratory discrimination task may actually pose the quite difficult problem of identifying the single property or dimension on which S$^+$ and S$^-$ differ, and paying attention to that property. With natural concepts, though no single dimension is critical, many dimensions are relevant, making the problem of what to pay attention to less acute.

Finally, some research on stimulus control has centered on the characteristics of memory. Research both on delayed matching-to-sample and on spatial learning has indicated that memory is an active process, involving both rehearsal and organization of environmental inputs.

PART 3

COGNITION AND

MEMORY

7 The Route into Memory

I n Chapter 1, we described two basic approaches to learning: the learning theory approach and the cognitive approach. In Chapters 2 through 6, we concentrated on the learning theory approach: Our main emphasis was on learning as a process of behavior change; we studied that process with a small number of paradigms (mostly Pavlovian and operant conditioning paradigms) in the hope that these would yield truly general principles of learning, principles that could then be applied to a wide range of other paradigms and procedures.

In Part 3 of the book we now turn our attention to the cognitive approach to learning and, more precisely, to contemporary research on memory. In these chapters (and for the rest of this book) our emphasis will be on learning as a process of knowledge acquisition. Our focus will largely be on processes and strategies inside the mind, rather than on events and stimuli taking place in the environment. We will consider results from a wide range of procedures, almost all involving humans, as we attempt to specify the function of these invisible events.

Before we turn to these issues, we should reiterate a point already made in Chapter 1: The distinction between the learning theory and cognitive approaches is anything but clear cut. In considering results of the learning laboratory, we were led to discussion of representations and expectations on the part of the organism doing the learning; we had to consider what the organism was paying attention to, and what concepts the organism had. These themes came up several times in our discussion, but most forcefully in Chapter 6. In this regard, the learning theory approach has been much enriched by theorizing and methods borrowed from the cognitive approach to learning. Likewise, in the chapters to come, we will many times refer back to earlier materials, and will have several things to say about how human memory relates to memory in other species. In these ways, the cognitive approach can be enriched by the results of the learning laboratory.

The Beginnings: Acquisition, Storage, and Retrieval

There is an obvious way to organize our inquiry into memory. Before there can be a memory, some learning must occur; that is, new information must be acquired. Therefore, **acquisition** should be our first topic for discussion. (For example: What promotes acquisition? Is there a maximally efficient way to learn?) Then, once information has been acquired, it must be held in memory until it is needed. We might refer to this as the **storage** phase, and this will be our second topic. (For example: How is material stored—as images and "sensory" impressions, or in some more descriptive form? How fragile is the storage—why, and when, do we lose information from storage?) Finally, we *use* the information that is in memory; that is, we remember! Information is somehow stored in the vast warehouse that is memory, and must be "retrieved" from this warehouse and brought into active use. Therefore, **retrieval** will be our final topic for discussion.

This organization probably strikes you as being intuitively sensible; it is, for example, the way that most "electronic memories" (that is, computers) work. Information ("input") is provided to the computer, analogous to the acquisition phase. The information then resides in some dormant form, perhaps in the computer's memory, or perhaps on magnetic disk or magnetic tape. This would be the storage phase. Finally, the information can be brought back from this dormant form, often via a search process that hunts through the memory or the disk; this is the retrieval phase.

We will begin our inquiry in this chapter within this frame, examining acquisition, storage, and retrieval processes. In the next chapter, however, we will see that it is difficult to separate the acquisition and retrieval phases from each other. In discussing acquisition, for example, we might wish to ask: What is good learning? What guarantees that material is firmly recorded in memory? We shall discover that what is good learning in preparation for one kind of test may not be good learning in preparation for a different kind of test. Our ideas about how information is acquired must be interwoven with ideas about how that information will be retrieved.

In the same spirit, we cannot separate claims about acquisition and retrieval from claims about storage. To put it simply, how you learn and how well you learn depend heavily on what you already know. That fact needs to be explored and explained, and will be our focus in Chapter 9.

The Route into Memory: The Modal Model

Starting in the late 1950s, much theorizing in cognitive psychology was guided by a new way of thinking about mental events, a perspective known as "information processing." This perspective borrowed heavily from developments in electronic information processing, including developments in computers, as we mentioned in Chapter 1. Leaving the details aside, the notion was that complex mental events such as learning, remembering, and deciding could be understood as being built up out of a large number of discrete steps. These steps occurred one by one, each with its own characteristics and its own job to do, and with each providing, as its "output," the input to the next step in the sequence. Within this framework, theories about memory could often be illustrated with charts such as the one in Figure 7–1. In this diagram, each box represents a separate event, process, or storage space, and the arrows represent the flow of information from one process to the next. The research goal, within this framework, was to make the charts more and more complete by breaking down each box into still smaller boxes and continuing until the complex process under scrutiny could be described in terms of "elementary components."

A great deal of information-processing theory focused on the processes by which information from one's environment was detected, recognized,

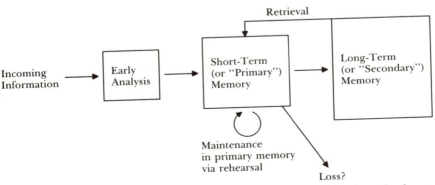

FIGURE 7–1. *An Information-Processing View of Memory.* In this view, the boxes represent separate events, processes, or storage spaces; arrows represent the flow of information from one process to another.

categorized, and entered into some sort of memory storage—that is, information acquisition. While there was considerable disagreement about details of this pathway of acquisition, there was reasonable consensus on the bold outline of events. One model, therefore, came to exemplify this consensus view. The early version of this consensus model was described by Waugh and Norman (1965); later details were added by Atkinson and Shiffrin (1968). The consensus model quickly came to be known as the "modal model."

According to the modal model, our general conception of information processing includes three separate kinds of memory storage: sensory memory, short-term memory, and long-term memory. When information first reaches our eyes or ears, it takes us a moment to discover what this new input is—a picture of a carrot, or the letter "H," or the word "outrageous," or whatever. To provide time for this discovery to happen, one must somehow hold on to the input in its "raw" form, as if a photograph or a tape recording were kept of the passing events in our world. The form of this information in this momentary record must be raw, that is, unanalyzed, since the point of this initial storage is to allow the analysis to take place. Such memories must therefore contain information similar to the sensory input itself, and so the memories are dubbed **sensory memories**. In the case of vision, the sensory memory is usually called **iconic memory**; for hearing, the sensory memory is called **echoic memory**.

Sensory memories are in several ways primitive: They hold only unanalyzed material, and they last, as we'll see, for only a very brief time. The hypothesis of the modal model is that sensory memories are quickly analyzed and the results of this analysis are then transferred to a somewhat more flexible, more useful storage: **short-term memory** (STM). Short-term memory provides a small storage repository in which information can be held while you are actively thinking about it, much as your desk contains the papers or books with which you are currently working. For example, as you read this sentence, how you interpret the early words will depend on what comes later; therefore, you will need to store the early words for a second or two, until you have read the entire sentence. Those early words, presumably, would be stored in STM. Or, if you are asked to multiply 23 by 12, you are likely to multiply 23 by 2, hang on to the result, then multiply 23 by 10, and finally add this result to the earlier one. The first result (46, the partial product) must be retained for a second or so, and this also draws on short-term memory.

You can easily see why short-term memory is sometimes referred to as **active memory** or **working memory**—it is where you store information while you are working on it. Just like your desk, short-term memory is supposed to make the information that is currently in use immediately available, to facilitate your mental work. But again, just like your desk, short-term memory is limited in how much it can hold. Hence, the modal model needs one more component, namely, a place to store the vast quantity of information that you do remember but do not currently need. This is **long-term memory** (or **LTM**).

At last, we meet a form of memory that seems close to what we ordinarily mean by memory. Long-term memory is supposed to be the storage place in which you retain memories for what you did yesterday, how you spent your childhood, a vast number of facts about your favorite topic, the names and faces of a hundred friends and acquaintances, and so on. The modal model therefore supposes long-term memory to be a storage place of great size, containing information that is not immediately active, so that this information must be dredged up when the time comes to utilize it.

We met a version of this model in Chapter 6, in considering the role of memory within animal learning. For animals and for humans, this model seems a sensible way to design memory. But sensibility of design cannot by itself persuade us that this model is accurate. There are many other "designs" we might consider that could serve just as well. Hence we will explore the evidence that supports the modal model, considering first sensory memories, then the reasons why short-term memory and long-term memory are viewed as separate entities, and finally how exactly short-term and long-term memories are characterized. After this presentation of the modal model's strengths, we will consider its weaknesses, and how it has evolved in response to various experimental challenges.

SENSORY MEMORIES

Sensory memories are perhaps too fleeting even to be given the label "memory," but, nonetheless, they serve an important memory function—they allow us to hold on to information that is no longer in the immediate environment. While the mental events involved in recognizing sights and sounds are extremely quick, they do require some time. Hence one needs access to the raw material of the input long enough for the recognition processes to occur. This would be no problem if it were not for the fact that the sights and sounds we experience are constantly changing. This is obvious for sounds, which are clearly spread out in time, but the same is true for vision because our eyes are constantly in motion, changing the point of focus (or "visual fixation") four or five times each second. Therefore the material actually in front of our eyes at any given moment is there only briefly, soon replaced by whatever is in front of our eyes when our visual fixation changes.

To keep up with this constant influx of information, it seems sensible to suppose, in keeping with the modal model, that the sensory input is momentarily stored in sensory memories. Fortunately, we also have direct evidence that this is correct, with much of the evidence stemming from a classic series of experiments on sensory memory by George Sperling (1960, 1963). Sperling reasoned as follows: Suppose that we show subjects in an experiment a matrix of letters, such as:

F C H D
J R P O
D N B A

We can present these letters very quickly using a device known as a **tachistoscope**, which shows stimuli for very brief and precisely measured periods of time, down to fractions of a second. We present the matrix for 50 milliseconds (abbreviated "msec"; 50 msec is 0.05 second) and then ask subjects to report as many of the letters as they can. At this speed, subjects are able to report only 4 or 5 of the 12 letters.

Why do subjects report so few letters? We know that the visual input itself (the tachistoscopic display) is extremely short-lived (50 msec). Sperling proposed that this visual input creates a sensory memory—a record, in essence, of exactly what the display looked like. This memory, he hypothesized, is true to the input (in essence it records a copy of the input) and so of course contains all 12 of the letters. But this memory, this **icon**, is highly transient, and fades within a second or so.

If, therefore, subjects are to report on the display, they must transfer the to-be-remembered information out of this transient form into some more enduring form. Subjects must **recode** this information (that is, the identities of the letters) from the short-lived visual representation (a visual "code") into some other, longer-lived form, or code. This recoding cannot be done instantaneously. That is, the mere reading of letters takes a certain amount of time. Subjects have access to the visual input only for the duration of the tachistoscopic display plus the duration of their sensory memory, and this time is sufficient only for the reading of 4 or 5 letters. The incompleteness in subjects' reports, in sum, is not a reflection of what was originally visible; instead, the incompleteness is merely a reflection of how much subjects could "rescue" from this fast-fading image before it completely faded from view.

How could we test this? The hypothesis is that the sensory memory briefly contains the entire display, but subjects have time to read off only a portion of the display—essentially just one row. Let us suppose that subjects can select which row this will be. Given our normal reading habits (left to right, top to bottom), this is likely to be the top row, but this doesn't have to be the case. Imagine that, just before presenting the matrix of letters, we give subjects a cue indicating that we're really interested only in the letters in the middle row, or perhaps the bottom one. Subjects in that case should be able to perform quite well—accurately reporting the requested row.

Three assertions are critical here: that this rescue operation starts out with a complete image (that is, all of the rows), that subjects have time to rescue (recode) only one row, and that subjects can control which row this will be. If we request the top row, subjects will recode this row from the icon, and should be able to report its contents a moment later; if we request the middle row, subjects will recode this row, and should be able to report it; and the same goes for the bottom row. In each case the recoding is possible because the entire display is assumed to be available at least initially. The display will fade in the time it takes to recode 4 or 5 letters, but, since we are requesting only 4 letters, fading is irrelevant to our task.

What if we provide a cue telling subjects which row we want, but the cue arrives simultaneously with the end of the display (that is, at the *end* of the 50-msec exposure)? Our hypothesis is that, at this moment, subjects still have a rather complete icon available to them, an icon that lasts (as it turns out) about a quarter of a second (that is, 250 msec). Even though we have turned off the actual, physical input, the icon preserves the display in a complete form. That means subjects still have access to a record of the *entire display,* and so they can use that quarter of a second to rescue any row they choose. To see the point, consider a contrasting case: What if we show subjects this 50-msec display and then, an hour later, tell them which row we really care about. By then, the display is long gone, and the icon is long faded. The only information that will remain, therefore, is whatever subjects recoded into a more enduring form, and that, we know, is limited to 4 or 5 letters. If those letters happen to be from the row we ultimately request, then subjects will correctly report the row. If the letters recoded by the subject happen to be from a row we don't ask about, subjects should do rather poorly. With a 3-row display, subjects have a one-third chance of having recoded letters from the correct row.

The key is this: In order for subjects to be helped by a cue telling them which row we want, the cue must arrive in time. If the cue arrives while the entire stimulus is still available (during the display itself, or before the sensory memory has faded), then subjects can direct their attention to the target row and read it. If subjects have sufficient time to read a single row, we would expect nearly 100% performance in this case. If the cue arrives too late, subjects will have already committed themselves to attending to just a few letters; the rest of the icon will have faded from view. Subjects will have a one-third chance of having chosen letters from the correct row. (That is, they will have chosen letters from the right row one-third of the time, and so, on that trial, get 100% right; they will have chosen letters from the wrong row the rest of them time, and so get 0% right. On average, they'll get 33 1/3% correct. We are assuming, of course, that subjects have no way to predict which row we'll ask about.)

We can, finally, turn to the data. We know that if there is no cue (if we simply tell subjects to report as much as they can), they'll report 4 or 5 of the 12 letters. This is called the **whole-report procedure**. If, on the other hand, we provide a cue about which row we want, and if the cue arrives in time, subjects should perform quite well (**partial report**). In Sperling's study, the cue was a tone, with a high pitch signaling the top row, a medium pitch the middle row, and a low pitch the bottom row. If the cue arrives too late, after the icon has faded, then the cue will not be helpful. Therefore, by looking at when the cue ceases to help, we will know how long the sensory memory lasts.

Figure 7–2 shows some of Sperling's early data. As we can see, subjects are still gaining considerably from the cue 300 msec after the stimulus has been physically removed; if the cue arrives as late as 1 second after the stimulus, the cue provides little help. That is, if the cue is delayed 1 second, partial-report performance is no better than whole-report performance (see also Averbach & Coriell, 1961).

We have dwelled on this experiment in part because it documents an important, though subtle, aspect of memory. Sperling's research on sensory memory also provides a model for how psychology proceeds in "doing science on the invisible." Neither Sperling nor anyone else has ever "seen" a sensory memory; no such memory is displayed in Figure 7–2. Instead, the figure shows some of the effects or consequences of sensory memory's presence, and by carefully considering these effects, we can discover the nature of the cause. As we discussed in Chapter 1, this kind of inference about *causes* by studying the *effects* is a familiar one in science: Physicists, for example, do not observe electrons directly, but instead infer electron activity from the "tracks" electrons leave in orbitals, from momentary fluctuations in magnetic fields, and so on. From

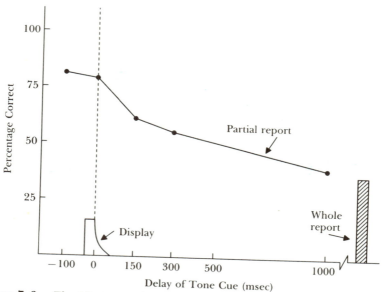

FIGURE 7–2. *The Advantages of Partial-Report Cues at Various Delays.* With "whole report" (no cue), subjects report only 4 or 5 of the display's 12 letters. With "partial report," subjects perform well if the cue arrives 100 msec before the display, or simultaneous with the display. Even if the cue arrives 300 msec after the display, subjects still benefit from the cue. (After Sperling, 1960.)

these effects of particles, the physicist makes discoveries about particles. Those who study memory and other brain functions often use the same technique.

Other researchers have extended Sperling's work to sensory modalities beyond vision, with the main research emphasis being on hearing (Darwin, Turvey, & Crowder, 1972; Moray, Bates, & Barnett, 1965). Experiments designed to parallel Sperling's studies have indicated that a sensory memory preserves an "echo" of auditory stimuli (the "echoic memory") for some seconds after the stimulus ends. As in vision, echoic memory depends on the appropriate stimulus parameters (loudness, contrast level, and so on). We will not take the time here to detail this auditory work, but it is worth mentioning a common experience that (at least informally) reveals the function of echoic memory: You have probably had the experience of concentrating on something (a book you are reading, or a letter you are writing) when someone walks into the room and asks a question. Thinking that you did not hear what was said, you say, "What?" At just that moment, though, you realize that you do know what was said, and that your request for a repetition was quite unnecessary. What has happened here? Because your attention was focused on something else, and not on the spoken input, you failed to process it—it reached your sensory (echoic) memory, but was never lifted beyond this momentary and unanalyzed form. You detected this lack of comprehension, and so requested more information. Nonetheless, the spoken words were maintained in your echoic memory and you could still retrieve the sounds from this sensory storage as soon as your attention was freed from the prior task.

In this situation, you were able to recall the sounds, so apparently they were stored somewhere in memory (specifically, in echoic memory). But for a brief moment, you had no idea what the sounds meant, what the words spoken actually were. That is because the information you recalled was only the "raw," unanalyzed sounds themselves, exactly what we would expect from a sensory memory. (If you had analyzed the sounds at that point—that is, figured out what was said—you would have had no reason to ask what was said!) Your "what?" was correctly initiated by the fact that you heard but did not understand the message at the time it occurred. Your "what?" was premature, though, as you still had access to the uninterpreted echo of the message and got, so to speak, a second shot at interpreting the message.

SHORT TERM AND LONG TERM: ONE MEMORY OR TWO?

The modal model talks about three different kinds of memories, and we want to make sure that this is right. Sensory memories are clearly special in several respects. They are very brief in duration, and they are closely tied to the sensory experience. These features of sensory memory are evident in Sperling's data, and these features suggest that sensory memory provides a distinct form of memory storage, different from what the model supposes STM to be, or from what the model claims about LTM.

However, do we really need to differentiate between STM and LTM? The issue here is this: Ultimately, we want our conceptions and theories of memory to be as simple as possible. The elegance and power of scientific explanation come from explaining diverse phenomena with a few laws. Pragmatically, if we can explain and predict psychological events with a simple model, we really do not care if a more complex model might have done just as well.

How many different memories are there? We will return to this question in Chapter 12, when we ask whether LTM itself needs to be subdivided into different memories for different types of material (visual memories versus verbal memories, memories for episodes versus memories for more general information, and so on). The question before us now is a specific version of this, namely, whether we need to identify STM and LTM as different storage systems. We can obviously remember things for both the short term (seconds or minutes) and the long term (years or decades), but we can also remember for a medium term (weeks), a long medium term (months), and so on. Are these differences in duration enough to justify speaking of a new type of memory for each length of storage? Do we have a memory specialized to hold on to information for an hour, a different memory specialized to hold on to information for a day, and so on? Surely, it would be simpler to argue for just a single memory, which could vary in how well and how long it held various contents. That is, perhaps some memories last only a short while in this memory, while others last for a longer period. This would still leave us asking what determines how long a memory lasts, and similar questions, but it would also leave us with a simpler, more elegant architecture. Given this possibility, why does the modal model make a distinction between short-term and long-term memory?

Much of the evidence for the STM—LTM distinction comes from the exploration of a single task, a task we first met in Chapter 1. Subjects are brought into the laboratory and read a series of words, like "bicycle, artichoke, radio, chair. . . ." The length of the list can vary, and so can the rate at which the words are presented. Experiments usually use lists between 15 and 30 words long, and present these words at a rate of about one word per second. Immediately after the last word is read, subjects are asked to repeat back as many words as they can. Subjects are free to report the words in any order they choose, which is why this is referred to as a **free-recall procedure**.

As described in Chapter 1, subjects usually remember 12 to 15 words in such a test, in a consistent pattern: Subjects are extremely likely to remember the first few words on the list, something known as the **primacy effect, and are also likely to remember the last 5 or 6 words on the list, a recency effect. Results of such a study are depicted in Figure 7–3, with a U-shaped curve showing the relation between position within the series (or serial position) and percentage of words recalled (Baddeley & Hitch, 1977; Deese & Kaufman, 1957; Glanzer & Cunitz, 1966; Murdock, 1962; Postman & Phillips, 1965).

This serial-position curve is easily explained by the modal model. According to the modal model, short-term memory is filled with whatever one is currently focusing on. In the list presentation, short-term memory will be filled with the few items that arrived most recently. At the end of the list, this will be the last few items heard, namely, the last few items on the list. Remembering our desk analogy, these items have just arrived on one's desk, and have not been pushed off by new materials. They will therefore be readily available, and will very likely be remembered. This is the source of the recency effect.

The primacy effect, on the other hand, comes from a different source: When subjects are presented with the list, they do their best to be good memorizers. When they hear the first word, they repeat it over and over to themselves ("bicycle, bicycle, bicycle . . ."). When the second word arrives, they repeat it, too ("bicycle, artichoke, bicycle, artichoke . . ."). Likewise for the third ("bicycle, artichoke, radio, bicycle, artichoke, radio . . ."), and so on through the list. Note that the first few items on

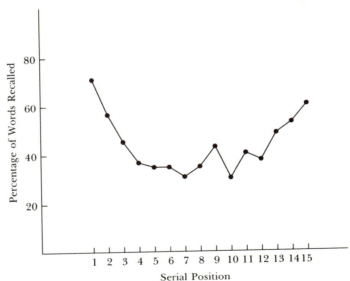

FIGURE 7–3. *The U-Shaped Serial-Position Curve.* Subjects are read a list of words, and then, immediately after this presentation, they must recall as many of the words as they can. Subjects are most likely to remember the first few words presented to them, and also the last few words. (After Glanzer & Cunitz, 1966.)

the list are privileged: For a brief moment, "bicycle" had all of the subject's attention lavished on it; no other word received this privilege. For a brief moment, "artichoke" had half of the subject's attention, more attention than any word except the first. When "radio" arrived, it received only one-third of the subject's attention. And so on through the list. Subjects tend to rehearse at most 5 or 6 words at a time (we learn this by asking subjects to rehearse out loud; see Rundus, 1971). Thus, when the 8th word arrives, the subject is probably rehearsing it together with the 5 prior words; likewise for the 10th word, and so forth. That is, words beyond the first few always share attention with several other words, receiving only a small fraction of the subject's efforts.

If we suppose that extra attention and time mean extra likelihood of transfer to LTM, then the early items on the list are the items most likely to reach this permanent storage, and thus are the items most likely to be remembered after some delay. This is the hypothesized source of the primacy effect.

On this conception, the symmetrical U-shaped curve receives a highly asymmetrical explanation. The last half dozen or so items from the list are recalled only from short-term memory. All other items, if recalled at all, are recalled from long-term memory. The first few items, thanks to the extra attention they received, are the items most likely to have reached LTM, and so are the most likely to be remembered.

This account of the serial-position curve leads to many predictions, and the success of these predictions has led psychologists to take this account seriously. We mentioned some of these predictions in Chapter 1; we will review those here, and consider some others as well. First, the modal model claims that short-term memory will be occupied by whatever has entered it most recently, and that the recency portion of the curve is coming from short-term memory. We therefore should easily be able to eliminate the recency effect by changing the procedure slightly: Rather than allowing subjects to recite what they remember immediately after the list's end, we can delay their recall by asking them to perform some other task for 30 seconds—for example, asking them to count backwards by threes from 201 for 30 seconds. This activity will itself draw on short-term memory (to keep track of where one is in the sequence and so on), and so will displace the recency items from short-term memory. This activity should have no effect except on recency, since everything but recency items is coming from long-term memory and thus is not dependent on current activity. Figure 7–4 shows that this prediction is exactly right: An activity interpolated between the list and recall eliminates the recency effect, but has no influence elsewhere in the list (Baddeley & Hitch, 1977; Glanzer & Cunitz, 1966; Postman & Phillips, 1965; other influential data were reported early on by Brown, 1958; Peterson & Peterson, 1959). Note that merely delaying the recall (with no interpolated activity) has no impact; in this case, presumably, subjects can continue maintaining the list's last few items in STM. However, when

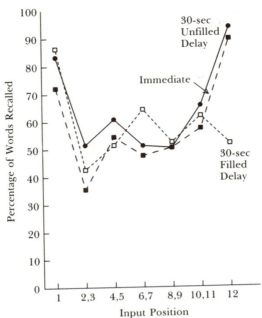

FIGURE 7–4.   *The Impact of Interpolated Activity on the Recency Effect.* With immediate recall, or if recall is delayed by 30 seconds with no activity during this delay, a strong recency effect is detected. If between hearing the list and the memory test subjects spend 30 seconds on some other activity, the recency effect is eliminated. This interpolated activity has no impact on the pre-recency portion of the curve. (After Baddeley & Hitch, 1977.)

subjects must do another task for 30 seconds, in between acquisition and test, the recency effect is essentially eliminated.

Conversely, the modal model predicts that we should be able to influence all performance except for recency by manipulating some factor relevant to long-term memory. For example, what happens if we slow down the presentation of the list? Now, subjects will have time to lavish more attention on all the items, increasing the likelihood of transfer into more permanent storage. Short-term memory, though, is limited by its size, not by ease of entry or ease of access, and so having more time to work on entry or access should have no influence. As predicted, Figure 7–5 shows that slowing list presentation improves retention of all the pre-recency items, but does not improve the recency effect (Glanzer & Cunitz, 1966). Other variables that influence entry into long-term memory have comparable effects. Using more familiar, more common words, for example, would be expected to ease entry into long-term memory, and does improve pre-recency retention, but has no effect on recency (e.g., Sumby, 1963).

The fact that the recency and pre-recency portions of the curve are

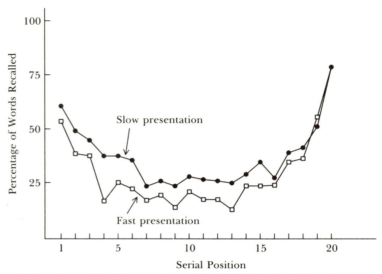

FIGURE 7–5. *Rate of List Presentation and the Serial-Position Effect.* Presenting the to-be-remembered materials at a slower rate improves pre-recency performance, but has no effect on recency. The slow rate in this case was 9 seconds per item; the fast rate was 3 seconds per item. (After Glanzer & Cunitz, 1966.)

open to separate sets of influences strongly indicates that these portions of the curve are the result of different memory mechanisms. As we have indicated, we will need to add some complexities to these studies. For now, though, note that the pattern of evidence—interpolated activity diminishes recency; amount of time and attention spent matter for everything but recency—fits with what one would expect based on the modal model. All of this gives us reason to argue that short-term and long-term memories are indeed different: They respond to different influences and are subject to different factors. This blocks us from trying to argue for a single, all-containing memory. Therefore, the time has come to look at the modal model in slightly more detail.

THE SIZE OF SHORT-TERM MEMORY

Let us start by filling in some details about short-term memory. STM is claimed to be of fixed size (approximately 7 ± 2 items). There are many pieces of evidence leading to this estimate (Chi, 1976; Dempster, 1981; Miller, 1956; Watkins, 1977). For one, the number of words in the recency portion of the free-recall curve, words presumably being reported from STM, tends to be 5 to 7. Second, we can test STM's capacity directly via a **digit-span task.** In this task, subjects are read a series of digits (such as "8, 3, 4") and must immediately repeat them back. If subjects do this successfully, they are given a slightly longer list (such as "9, 2, 4, 0"), and so forth. The list is gradually increased until subjects start to make errors. This task, it would appear, draws directly on STM; the errors should appear when we put more on the list than STM can hold. As it turns out, with 7 or 8 items on the list, subjects perform quite well. With 8 or 9 items, subjects will make errors. With lists longer than this, many errors will occur, primarily in the middle of the list—that is, we will get a primacy effect and a recency effect.

If STM has a capacity of 7 ± 2 slots, or items, we still need to ask what an "item" is, or what a "slot" holds. Can we remember 7 sentences as easily as 7 words, 7 letters as easily as 7 equations? Miller (1956) in fact proposed that STM holds 7 ± 2 **chunks**. The term "chunk" is a deliberately unscientific-sounding term, in order to remind us that STM does not hold a fixed quantity of information. Instead, Miller proposed, STM holds 7 ± 2 packages, and what those packages contain is largely up to the subject.

We have already mentioned the digit-span procedure, in which we simply read subjects a list of items and ask subjects to echo them back. Performance in this task actually turns out to depend enormously on how the subjects think about or organize the items. The subject might, for example, hear the list "H, O, P, T, R, A, E, G," etc., and think of this list as syllables, putting each pair of letters together: "ho, pit, rah, egg. . . ." In this case, the subject will remember approximately 7 syllables, or 14 letters! If the subject happens to form 3-letter syllables ("hop, tra . . ."), the subject may remember close to 21 letters, and so on (Postman, 1975; Simon, 1974).

This chunking process, however, does have a cost attached to it. STM seems able to hold 7 ± 2 digits or letters, but slightly fewer syllables, and slightly fewer words, and even fewer sentences. There are several reasons for this (see, for example, Chapter 12), but here is one: All we need to assume is that one's attention is required to "repackage" the to-be-remembered materials (assembling the letters into syllables, or the syllables into words), and so less attention is available for maintaining these items in STM. (Simon, 1974, offers a slightly different explanation of this finding.) This is, of course, consistent with our earlier claim that STM is closely associated with whatever one happens to be thinking about, whatever one happens to be attending to.

At the same time, though, we should not understate the flexibility of the chunking strategy and, consequently, the flexibility of what STM can hold. Consider a subject studied by Chase and Ericsson (1978, 1979; see also Ericsson, Chase, & Faloon, 1980; Chase & Ericsson, 1982). This subject happens to be a fan of track events, and when he heard the experimental numbers he thought of them as being finishing times for races ("3, 4, 9, 2," for example, became "3 minutes and 49 point 2 seconds, near world-record mile time"). He also associated numbers with people's ages and with historical dates. This subject then grouped these chunks into larger chunks, and then these into even larger chunks. The researchers studied this subject over several months of practice in a digit memory task. By the end of practice, the subject had increased his apparent memory span from 7 to 79 digits! However, there is good reason to believe that what was changed through practice was merely chunking strategy, and not the size of short-term memory itself. For example, after three months of practice, the subject was tested with sequences of letters, rather than digits. With the letters, the subject's memory span dropped back to a normal 6 consonants. Thus the 7-chunk limit is still in place, although, given the great flexibility of grouping, it seems odd to call this a "limit" for this remarkable subject.

SHORT-TERM MEMORY AND LONG-TERM MEMORY: HOW DO THEY DIFFER?

We have mentioned several claims about short- and long-term memory, according to the modal model. STM is, first of all, small in size, as we have just been discussing. In addition, STM is relatively easy to enter—all one has to do is attend to an item; the last 7 or so things attended to are automatically active in STM—but correspondingly fragile: Any subsequent items displace early items from storage. Items in STM are assumed to be easily accessible—there, so to speak, at one's fingertips. Just as there are many sources of information to which one might attend, there are many entrance paths into STM. STM may contain the last 7 items noticed in the environment, or it may contain items dredged up from one's past. (Think of the names of 7 good friends; the claim is that these are being activated from long-term storage and placed in short-term storage.) Short-term memory can also be filled by recycling items already in STM—this is presumably what happens when one repeats items over and over ("rehearses" them) as a memory strategy. The various arrows in Figure 7–1 illustrate these pathways into STM. Long-term memory, in contrast, is vast in size, as this is the repository in which we carry around all the things that we know. We mentioned some of the items on this vast list before—friends' names and phone numbers, lyrics to a dozen or so songs, countless events of our lifetimes, things we learned last semester, and so forth, not to mention the vast number of commonsense facts we all carry with us. One knows, for example, that water is wet, that night follows day, etc. All of this knowledge, both specific events and mundane commonsense items, must be stored somewhere; long-term memory is presumably the enormous warehouse for this storage.

In contrast to STM, however, it is not trivial to enter information in LTM, nor is it effortless to find information in this warehouse. We have already seen that items must be attended to and contemplated for some time before they can be entered into long-term memory; this plays a key role in our account of the primacy effect. One often-cited study makes this point nicely. Rundus (1971) ran subjects through a procedure similar to the list-learning studies we have already mentioned, but with one change: Subjects were asked to "think out loud" during the experiment, so that, as subjects repeated the list items to themselves, these repetitions could be tape-recorded and then later counted. Figure 7–6 shows the relation between how many times each item was repeated, on the one hand, and how likely it was that the item was remembered, on the other. As you can see, the relation is essentially perfect for all except the recency portion of the list. This is again confirmation of the modal model (since the recency items, coming from STM, should not depend on rehearsal) and clearly points to the degree to which time and effort pay off in later memorability.

To sum up, then, we now have an account of both the apparatus of memory and the entrance route into memory. This route can be defined either with emphasis on structures (items first reside momentarily in sensory storage, then are recoded into STM, then into LTM) or in terms

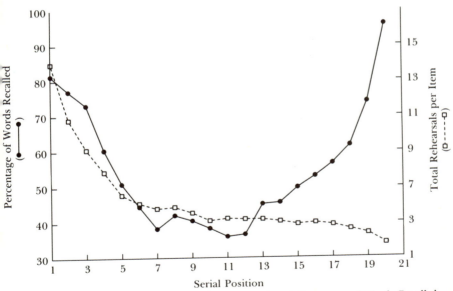

FIGURE 7–6. *Relation between Number of Rehearsals and Percentage of Words Recalled.* The solid line shows the number of words recalled (and should be read against the left vertical axis); the dashed line shows the number of times each word was rehearsed aloud (read against the right axis). The relationship between recall and number of rehearsals is virtually perfect for the pre-recency portion of the curve; the relationship vanishes for the recency portion of the curve. (After Rundus, 1971.)

of the processes themselves (through mechanisms we have not yet specified, attention helps move items along through this chain). In addition,
while much of the evidence we have mentioned comes from human studies, there is no reason to believe that this description is unique to humans.
Other species might need to hold on to sensory information long enough
to do early analyses; other species might need to keep some information
activated and immediately available, while leaving other information in
storage, not currently needed and so not currently activated.

Given this, it is no surprise that several of the procedures we have
described yield parallel results in other species. In Chapter 6 (pp. 241–
243), for example, we saw that active rehearsal is needed to maintain
information in pigeons' working memories. In Chapter 3 (pp. 113–117, we
discussed the role of rehearsal in Pavlovian conditioning and, in particular, the claim that rehearsal is needed to place information into long-term
memory. In addition, research indicates that pigeons show approximately
the same primacy and recency effects as humans do, if asked to learn about
series of stimuli (Olton, 1978; Roberts, 1981).

LONG-TERM RECENCY EFFECTS?

It should be clear that the recency effect (and the various factors that
influence it) plays an important part in supporting the STM–LTM distinction. The recency advantage in free recall, to reiterate, is hypothesized
to come from the fact that the last few items heard are still "on your
mind," still in STM, and so are easy to recall. Note the key assumption:
The recency items are in STM just prior to the test (because you just
heard them), and that's why they are well remembered.

For contrast, however, consider the following tasks: Take a blank piece
of paper and write down as many U.S. presidents as you can. Or list every
vacation you've ever taken together with your parents. In a sense, these
tasks are analogous to the list-learning task we've been discussing: What
you are trying to remember is material that you learned in some sequence; that is, the to-be-remembered material is ordered in a temporal
series. Your recall, though, is free, in the sense that you can write down
your memories in any sequence that you choose. And, oddly enough, the
results from tests like these are also analogous to those we've been
discussing. Figure 7–7 (from Roediger & Crowder, 1976) shows the data
from a study in which subjects were asked to recall the presidents, and
notice that the curve looks much like the U-shaped curves we've been
considering: Subjects were most likely to remember the early presidents
(Washington, Adams, Jefferson, etc.), just as in a primacy effect, and the
most recent ones (Kennedy, Johnson, Nixon, and Ford at the time of the
study), just as in recency. Subjects were less likely to remember the
presidents in the middle of the series (with the clear exception of Abra-
ham Lincoln!)

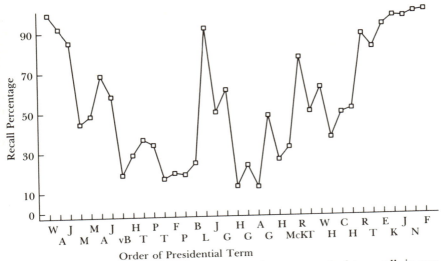

FIGURE 7-7. *The Long-Term Recency Effect.* Subjects were asked to recall, in any order (a free-recall criterion), the American presidents. The results yield a roughly U-shaped curve, with best memory for Washington, Adams, and Jefferson (a "primacy" effect) and also for Kennedy, Johnson, Nixon, and Ford (a "recency" effect). The exception to this pattern comes from the presidents whose names are associated with the Civil War. (After Roediger & Crowder, 1976.)

Similar results have been obtained with a variety of other ordered material—for example, rugby players recalling the teams they've played against that season (Baddeley, 1963; Baddeley & Hitch, 1977; Bjork & Whitten, 1974). For convenience, let's generate some terminology: Let's call the recency effect that results from list-learning experiments (that is, the recency effect we had been discussing prior to this section) the **standard recency** effect. In standard recency, one is recalling material learned just moments ago. For contrast, let's call these new effects, in which one is recalling material learned some time ago, **long-term recency** effects.

Both the task and the results for "long-term recency" seem similar to those for the "standard recency" effect. One would therefore think that we should find a single explanation that encompasses both the standard list-learning experiments and these other cases of primacy and recency effects.

On the other hand, though, the account we have so far for primacy and recency (namely, the account that goes with the modal model) is inapplicable to these long-term cases. According to the modal model, recency comes from the fact that anything in STM is easily remembered, and the last few items on the list are still in STM. This is because (1) these items were recently heard and (2) no new information has come along subsequently to push these items out of STM. However, for long-term recency, neither Point 1 nor Point 2 seems to be true: If, with no warning, I ask you to name the American presidents, your STM should contain whatever it was you were thinking about just before my asking, and that's probably not the American presidents. Presidents' names were not recently heard, and you did learn other material since the last time you heard presidents' names. Therefore, all the presidents' names are presumably being retrieved from long-term memory, and that shouldn't, on our account so far, lead to a recency effect.

This leaves us with two choices. We could continue to hunt for a unified explanation for standard recency and long-term recency, but that explanation won't be the modal model. The modal model, we just argued, applies to standard recency, but not to long-term recency. This would seriously undermine our efforts so far: We've been supporting the modal model by pointing to what a great job it does in explaining (among other things) recency. If we now explain recency in some other terms, this will dissolve an important line of support for the modal model.

A second choice would be this: Long-term recency and standard recency do look alike, but perhaps these effects come from rather different sources. Maybe the standard recency effect is produced as the modal model suggests, and long-term recency is produced in some other fashion. This isn't elegant, but maybe it's correct nonetheless.

We would, in fact, argue for this second option, and so preserve the modal model's account of standard recency. While long-term recency does superficially resemble standard recency, there are many important differences between these effects. For example, we have already seen that interpolated activity diminishes standard recency; it does not diminish long-term recency. (In fact, this is an identifying mark of long-term recency: Presumably there has been an enormous amount of mental activity interpolated between your learning of the American presidents and the recall test.)

Related to this, standard recency is produced only when subjects recall the to-be-remembered material in a certain order. That is, subjects' recall is free in the sense that they are allowed to recall in any order they choose. However, recall tends to follow a highly predictable sequence: In the list-learning experiments we've described so far, subjects have a strong tendency to start their recall with the last-heard words. And, in fact, this recency effect is markedly diminished if we force subjects to recall the words in the order in which they heard them (e.g., Tulving & Arbuckle, 1963). Both of these observations make sense within the modal model. If, at the end of hearing a long list of words, subjects must recall the first words on the list, what happens? At the list's end, the list's last half-dozen words are still in STM. If we force subjects to think about the list's beginning, that will bring the early words out of LTM and place them in STM, pushing out of STM the list's ending. With the list's ending out of STM, and with STM the alleged source of recency, this should (and does) diminish recency. No wonder subjects, if left to their own sequence, report the list's ending first, avoiding precisely this problem.

None of this is true in the long-term recency effect. This effect appears even if subjects' recall order is controlled—that is, if subjects have to report the presidents in historical order, the long-term recency effect still occurs (Roediger & Crowder, 1976). This is further evidence that the modal model account just does not apply to this case. In addition, though, it says that the data pattern itself for long-term recency differs from that for standard recency. This certainly fits with the claim that the resemblance between these two cases is merely superficial.

Relatively few studies have tried systematically to compare long-term and standard recency, but we would expect that other factors that do influence standard recency will not influence long-term recency, and vice versa. Again (and this does need to be put to the test), this would be an argument that the profile of long-term recency really is different from that for standard recency. That, in turn, would be a good argument for explaining these two cases with rather different mechanisms. And that, finally, would allow us to maintain the modal model as our theory of standard recency, even knowing that this explanation does not work for long-term recency. (This still leaves us to ask why long-term recency occurs, and we will have more to say about this in Chapter 11, when we talk about retrieval from LTM.)

AMNESIA

One last line of supporting evidence for the modal model should be mentioned. Ironically, this is a line of evidence that was, historically, a powerful argument in favor of the model, but, as our understanding has progressed, it has become one of the central considerations leading to the revision of the modal model. We will turn to the complications in a few pages; for now we focus on the classical picture.

A variety of circumstances or illnesses can lead to a loss of memory, or amnesia. Some forms of amnesia are retrograde; that is, they disrupt memory for things learned prior to the event which initiated the amnesia. Other forms of amnesia have the reverse effect, causing disruption of memory for experiences *after* the onset of amnesia; these are cases of anterograde amnesia. (Most cases of amnesia have both retrograde and anterograde memory loss.) One very famous case of an anterograde amnesia is found in a patient identified by his initials, H.M. (For a review of H.M.'s case, see Milner, 1970.) H.M. suffered from profound epilepsy, and a variety of attempts at cure had all failed. As a last resort, doctors sought to contain H.M.'s disease by serious brain surgery, specifically, by removing portions of the brain that seemed to be the source of the seizures (the hippocampus). The surgery did seem to improve the epilepsy, but at an incredible cost: H.M. seems unable to learn anything new. H.M. remembers with no problem events from before his surgery, and even now can hold a coherent and consistent conversation. Indeed, you can talk to H.M. for some time and believe there is no problem with his memory. However, the problem becomes clear if the conversation is interrupted: If you leave the room, for example, and come back 3 or 4 minutes later, H.M. seems to have totally forgotten the conversation. Quite simply, thoughts currently in mind can be kept there by H.M.; thoughts out of mind seem to be lost forever (Milner, 1966, 1970; Marslen-Wilson & Teuber, 1975).

H.M.'s specific surgical situation is extremely rare. (H.M.'s amnesia came as a horrible surprise to the surgeons. This particular surgery is no longer used, in part because of its consequences on memory.) Unfortunately, though, amnesias like H.M.'s are not so rare. A similar sort of amnesia can be found in patients who have been longtime alcoholics. The problem is not the alcohol itself; the problem instead is that alcoholics tend to have inadequate diets. Alcoholic beverages have a high caloric content, and so one can survive for a while on a diet of nothing but alcohol. However, alcoholic beverages are missing many of the basic nutrients, including vitamin B_1, thiamine. As a result, longtime alcoholics are vulnerable to a number of problems caused essentially by malnutrition. In particular, thanks to their thiamine-poor diet, long-term alcoholics can develop a syndrome called **Korsakoff's syndrome** (Rao, Larkin, & Derr, 1986; Ritchie, 1985).

A Korsakoff's patient seems in many ways similar to H.M. Memories from before the onset of alcoholism are easily remembered. Current topics can be maintained in mind as long as there is no interruption. New information, though, if displaced from mind, is seemingly lost forever. Korsakoff's patients who have been in the hospital for decades will casually mention that they arrived only a week ago; if asked the name of the current president, or about events in the news, they unhesitatingly give answers appropriate for two or three decades back, whenever the disease began (Marslen-Wilson & Teuber, 1975; Seltzer & Benson, 1974).

We will have more to say below about these tragic cases. (To the best of anyone's knowledge, these amnesias are irreversible.) For now, though, note that the clinical picture as we've sketched it so far fits well in the modal model. One could argue that these amnesiacs have intact long-term memories; that is why they remember events from before the amnesia's start. Likewise, the amnesiac patients seem to have an intact short-term memory; that is how they remember events as they think about them—information can be recycled and therefore maintained in STM indefinitely, just as in a normal individual. (It is worth mentioning that amnesiacs can often have a normal digit span, a task that we introduced above as measuring STM.) What seems to be wrong, though, is that the path from STM to LTM is disrupted, so that no new information can enter permanent storage. Hence if something is displaced from STM, it vanishes without a trace.

We emphasize that this picture must be complicated somewhat, when we consider further and more recent research, but, with the information so far, the amnesiacs seem to be striking confirmation of the claims about memory outlined in the modal model.

An Alternative Approach to Memory: Levels of Processing

Our survey of memory research has so far brought us from the late 1950s to the mid-1970s. In that decade and a half, the modal model was immensely successful, generating a great deal of research activity and making a long series of successful predictions (including those that led to the research we have described). Nonetheless, the model turned out not to be the final word, thanks in large part to a team of researchers in Toronto who challenged some of the model's basic assumptions and who also offered an inviting alternative. As we will see, this alternative preserves some of the main features of the modal model, but differs on key points.

PROBLEMS WITH THE MODAL MODEL

One assertion of the modal model was its claim that the likelihood of memory can be predicted by considering the amount of time and attention a subject spent thinking about an item, or the number of repetitions of the item in the subject's rehearsal. This latter point was the key to the Rundus experiment. However, Craik and Watkins reported experimental results in 1973 to challenge this claim (Craik & Watkins, 1973). The notion behind the Craik and Watkins procedure was that the modal model paid inadequate attention to the strategies and activities of the subject. While psychology had focused on the mental equipment of the subject, not enough emphasis had been given to what the subject was actually doing.

As a first step toward establishing this view, Craik and Watkins noted a difference between what they called **maintenance rehearsal** and **elaborative rehearsal**. The latter activity involves active steps that serve to establish items in long-term memory. As we will see, elaborative rehearsal involves thinking about what the to-be-remembered items mean, and how the items are related to each other, or to other things in the surroundings. Maintenance rehearsal, in contrast, accomplishes nothing beyond what its name implies: mere maintenance. In the modal model's terms, it merely keeps items in short-term memory by recycling them. You can think of maintenance rehearsal as a more or less mechanical process, just repeating the items over and over, presumably with no thought about what the items mean. A good example of maintenance rehearsal might be what happens after looking up a telephone number. One maintains the number in STM by rote repetitions. This holds the number in memory long enough to make the call, but it is forgotten soon thereafter.

The Craik and Watkins (1973) procedure attempted to show how important this distinction is by demonstrating the non-effects of maintenance rehearsal. Subjects were told to listen to a series of lists of words, and were told to monitor the sequence within each list for words beginning with the letter "B." Subjects were told that, at the end of each list, their task was to report the most recent word on the list that began with a "B." Thus, if the subject heard "basket, spoon, telephone, cub, lamp, fish, hair, plant, lake, book, chair, foot, baby, hill, tree," the subject was to report "baby." Things proceeded in this fashion until the end of the session, when, to the subjects' surprise, they were told that they now had to write down as many of the "B" words as they could. Up until that moment, subjects had no idea their memories were being tested, and no idea that they had any reason to remember "B" words other than the most recent one.

The stimuli in this experiment were actually devised with a scheme in mind. Sometimes the "B" words were positioned very closely together on the list (like "book, chair, foot, baby" in the example above); other words (like "basket" in the example) were followed by several words not beginning with "B." How should this matter for memory? If we extrapolate from the Rundus experiment, then words like "book" which are followed quickly by another "B" word reside in STM only a short time, and are rehearsed only a few times. They should therefore not be very well remembered. Words like "basket" are in STM for a longer time, and are therefore presumably rehearsed many times. Therefore, these words should be more likely to be remembered.

Craik and Watkins, however, had a different prediction, and they turned out to be right (see Figure 7–8). Since subjects have no expectation of the memory test, they have no reason to do elaborative rehearsal. This will lead subjects to do only maintenance rehearsal, especially since maintenance rehearsal, it is supposed, requires less effort. (We will see further support for this last assumption in a moment.) If subjects are doing only maintenance rehearsal, and if maintenance rehearsal has no long-term consequences, we expect that subjects' memories in this procedure will be very poor. More important, doing more of this ineffective rehearsal should not matter, and so we expect similar results if a "B" word was quickly followed by another (and so rehearsed only briefly) or if a "B" word was followed by another only after a long interval. All of this, in contrast to Rundus, is what the data show. It certainly looks like mere maintenance has no benefits for longer-term remembering, and is therefore clearly distinct from elaborative processing. (As we will see in Chapter 8, this conclusion will have to be tempered somewhat. Later

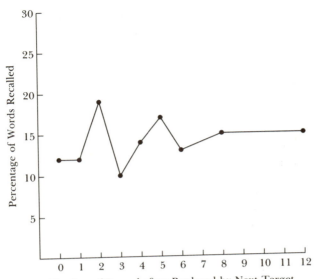

FIGURE 7–8.   *"Maintenance" Rehearsal Does Not Lead to Better Recall.* When subjects do not expect a memory test, there is no relation between the amount of rehearsal and likelihood of recall. (Compare this to Figure 7–6, showing what happens when a memory test *was* expected.) The number of rehearsals was manipulated in this study by varying the position of target words within the presentation list. Targets that were soon "replaced" by another target were presumably rehearsed only a few times; targets that were followed by another target only after many intervening items were presumably rehearsed many times. (After Craik & Watkins, 1973.)

evidence has shown that maintenance rehearsal does have some long-term memory benefits, provided that memory is tested in the right way. However, this leaves intact the central point, namely that we must make a distinction between maintenance and elaborative processing.)

A second study, by Watkins and Watkins (1974), made an even stronger point. Watkins and Watkins suppose that maintenance rehearsal also plays a role in the list-learning experiments we have been describing. Early in the list, subjects know that many words will intervene before the moment for recall comes; hence they will seek (via elaborative rehearsal) to enter these words into long-term memory. Later in the list, subjects know that they will need to retain words for only a brief moment before they can make their responses, so they shift to the less-effortful maintenance rehearsal. Let us further suppose that maintenance rehearsal does a great job in the short run; it makes the to-be-remembered items very easily available. This will then provide a modified account of the (standard) recency effect: Recency items are very well recalled because they have received the short-term benefits of maintenance rehearsal. They

have received no long-term benefits (because that is the nature of maintenance rehearsal), but this is irrelevant to the task at hand.

Watkins and Watkins reasoned that the shift to a strategy of maintenance rehearsal requires that the subjects know when they can afford this
helps-in-the-short-term-only strategy. That is, they must know when the
end of the list is near. This fact leads to their experiment: One group of
subjects was given lists to learn, but the lists varied randomly in length.
Sometimes the list was 8 words long, sometimes 20, sometimes 12, and
so on. Hence subjects had no idea as they progressed through the list
when they were 2 words from the end, when 12 words from the end. A
second group of subjects was run through the exact same procedure, with
the lists again varying in length. But this group was told, for each list, how
many words there would be. In addition, to help them keep track of where
they were in the list, these subjects were given a check-off sheet, with one
space for each word on the list, so they could check off the words as they
progressed and thus see at a glance how close they were to the list's end.
As predicted, subjects in this latter group showed a normal primacy and
recency pattern. Knowing when the list would arrive, they shifted to the
"cheaper" short-run strategy.

The first group, though, had a reduced recency effect, as can be seen
in Figure 7–9. The reduction is not large, but is quite consistent. Without
the knowledge of when to shift to a short-run strategy, these subjects
presumably were likely to take the cautious route, and not shift strategy.
Hence the words at the end of the list did not receive the brief boost that
comes from maintenance rehearsal, and so showed a somewhat weakened
recency effect.

The Watkins and Watkins procedure also included one additional step:
During the procedure, subjects were presented with a total of 7 lists, with
a recall test after each. After the 7th list had been presented, and after
its recall test had been run, subjects were unexpectedly given one last
test: They were asked to recall as much as they could from all of the
presented lists. What should we predict in this final test? Consider first
the "informed" group, namely, those who knew in advance the length of
each list. These subjects had done only maintenance processing on each
list's last few words, giving these words a short-run boost, but with no
long-lasting benefit. Therefore, these words are less likely to be remembered in the final test. In contrast, for the uninformed group, words at
the end of each list received the same elaborative rehearsal as all other
items on the list. Therefore, these words are likely to be remembered in
the long run. As Figure 7–9 shows, this is just what we see in the data:
In the immediate test, informed subjects show better retention of the last
few items than do the uninformed subjects. But, in the delayed test,
informed subjects show the reverse pattern: worse retention of the last
few items than do the uninformed subjects. Both of these effects (the
advantage with immediate testing, the disadvantage in delayed testing)
presumably come from the same source, namely, the informed subjects'

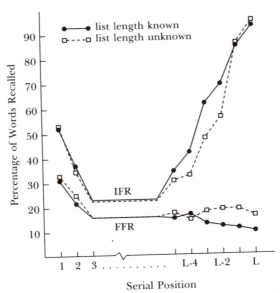

FIGURE 7–9. *The Role of Strategy Shifts in Free Recall.* When subjects know the length of a to-be-remembered list, they shift strategy from elaborative rehearsal to maintenance rehearsal as they approach the end of the list. Maintenance rehearsal of the last few items on the list helps memory performance in the short run, but provides little benefit for longer-term testing. Therefore the "list length known" group, because of this strategy shift, shows better memory for the list's end in the immediate free-recall test (IFR), but worse performance in the final, unanticipated free-recall test (FFR). The "L" on the x-axis means "end of list"; thus "L—4" means 4th word from the end of the list. (After Watkins & Watkins, 1974.)

shift to maintenance rehearsal. This pattern is, of course, exactly what we would expect if maintenance rehearsal and elaborative rehearsal have different effects, and if the choice between these two depends on subjects' strategies.

Apparently, therefore, subjects have at least two different options for how they rehearse material, and these options have different consequences for what will and will not be remembered later on. It is worth noting, though, that we did not consider this distinction in Chapter 6, when we discussed the role of rehearsal in animal learning. This is because the animal learning literature has not distinguished among types of rehearsal. This may turn out to be appropriate—perhaps humans have options available to them that are not available to other species. That is, perhaps humans have two ways to rehearse, and other species have only one. There is little evidence on this point, however, and so it remains to be seen whether other species also have the option of either maintaining or elaborating the to-be-remembered materials.

Returning to the human research, we need to take a closer look at these two rehearsal strategies, to ask more precisely how each works. Before we turn to this, though, we emphasize a theme that will come more and more to dominate the scene as we progress: We are not abandoning the modal model; we are instead emphasizing that the model simply does not say nearly enough about a key factor—the contribution of the subject (a contribution in terms of strategy, and, as we will see soon, a contribution in other regards as well).

LEVELS OF PROCESSING

What exactly is elaborative rehearsal? In the mid-1970s, Craik and Lockhart published a series of experiments in which they proposed a specific way to think about elaborative processing (Craik & Lockhart, 1972; Lockhart, Craik, & Jacoby, 1976). They proposed that we each have some degree of control over how we think about information from our environment, about how "deeply" we choose to think about it. At the most superficial, we can do what they called **shallow processing**. In the case of printed words, for example, we can look only at the appearance of the words: whether they are printed in red or green, in uppercase letters or lowercase, and so on. At the other extreme, we can do **deep processing**—we can think about what the words mean, what connotations they call up. In between are moderate levels of processing, if, for example, we think about the sounds the words make.

Craik and Lockhart suggested that it is deeper processing that leads to good memory, and only deeper processing that has this effect. Repetitions per se have no effect, as we have already seen in the previous section. More surprisingly, the intention to memorize has no direct effects. To see what this means, and to see why we might take this position seriously, consider the following experiment. (Actually, the experiment we will describe represents a composite of many procedures, all of which converge on the same pattern of evidence. See, for example, Bobrow & Bower, 1969; Craik & Lockhart, 1972; Hyde & Jenkins, 1969, 1973; Jacoby, 1978; Lockhart, Craik, & Jacoby, 1976; Parkin, 1984; Slamecka & Graf, 1978.)

We bring five groups of subjects into the laboratory. The first three groups are given no indication that this is a memory experiment. We tell the first group simply that we are studying how quickly people can make judgments about letters. They sit down in front of a computer screen and are shown a series of word pairs. For each pair, they decide as quickly as possible whether the two words are typed in the same case (both capitalized or both not) or typed in different cases. In Craik and Lockhart's terms, these subjects will be doing shallow processing. At the end of this sequence, the subjects are surprised to learn that their memories are being tested, and they are asked to write down as many of the words they have seen as they can remember.

The second group is told much the same thing, except they are instructed that we are studying how quickly people can make judgments about rhyme. If the two words on the screen rhyme, they press one button; if they do not, they press another; these subjects are doing medium processing. Again, a surprise memory test follows this presentation.

The third group is told that we are studying how quickly people judge meaning. They press one button if the words on the screen are synonymous, another button if they are not; these subjects are doing deep processing.

The fourth group is told directly that we are studying memory, and the subjects are asked to memorize the items. Here we are not certain what level of processing subjects are doing, but these subjects will have the intent to memorize. The fifth and final group is told the same, but with an additional instruction: This group is urged to think about the meaning of the items, and is told that this is an effective way to memorize (deep processing, plus the intention to memorize).

The results, given in Figure 7–10, can be briefly summarized: Group 3 (deep processing) remembers the items well. Group 2 (medium processing) remembers less well. Group 1 (shallow processing) does rather

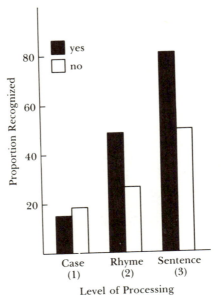

FIGURE 7–10.   *Deep Processing Improves Memory Performance.* In this study, subjects were asked questions about each of the to-be-remembered items. The "sentence" questions required deep processing, the "rhyme" questions required medium processing, and the "case" questions required only shallow processing. Half of the questions received "yes" answers, and half "no" answers. The results show that deep processing led to better memory than shallow processing, and "yes" answers led to better memory than "no" answers. (After Craik & Tulving, 1975.)

poorly. Group 5 (deep processing + intent to memorize) performs equivalently with Group 3 (for whom there was no intention to memorize); that is, there is no difference between "intentional" and "incidental" learning, provided that we have matched the level at which the intentional and incidental learners are processing the information. Intentional learning is what subjects are doing when they intend to learn, that is, when they know their memories will be tested. Incidental learning is what happens when subjects are merely exposed to the material with no expectation of a memory test. As the data turn out, the intention to learn seems to add nothing by itself.

Group 4 yields an interesting result. The other groups produce predictable performance, unchanging from experiment to experiment, from one group of subjects to another. Group 4, however, is not so consistent. Sometimes this group performs equivalently with Group 3 (deep processing) or Group 5 (deep processing + intention); sometimes this group performs at a slightly lower level. This reflects the fact that subjects bring to the experiment their own strategies for memorizing. Some subjects, for example, might believe that thinking about meaning is an optimal strategy, and so, if simply asked to memorize, they might spontaneously draw on deep processing. These subjects would then be indistinguishable from subjects in Group 5. Other subjects might believe that the best way to memorize is by listening to the sound of the word over and over. This less than optimal strategy would lead them to perform at a level slightly lower than Groups 3 and 5. (For studies of subjects' spontaneous strategies, see Anderson & Bower, 1972; Brown, 1979; Hyde & Jenkins, 1969; Nelson, 1976; Postman, 1964.)

One striking example of subjects' misconceptions about memory strategies is reported by a psychologist working in the field of memory, John Anderson (1985, pp. 112–113). Anderson reports that he himself served as a subject in a class memory experiment during his sophomore year of college. He was determined to perform well, and therefore applied his personal theory of memorizing: that the best strategy was to say the to-be-remembered items out loud, over and over, preferably as loudly and as quickly as possible. Needless to say, this "loud-and-fast" theory stands in contrast to the true means of improving memory, and, to Anderson's considerable embarrassment, his performance was the worst in his class.

Three lessons sum up this overall pattern: First, deep processing seems to lead to good memory: It pays to think about meaning. Second, the intention to memorize matters only by virtue of the fact that the intention calls up one strategy or another. The intention to memorize by itself contributes nothing. Material thought about deeply with no intention of learning produces just as much learning as material thought about in preparation for the examination next week. Third, subjects often bring a mixed bag of strategies and beliefs with them into the laboratory. If simply told to memorize, subjects will draw on this diverse set of strategies, and will benefit to the extent that their beliefs happen to be correct.

Results such as these led psychologists to considerable enthusiasm about the levels-of-processing perspective, and for the next half-dozen years a great deal of memory research was guided by this view. For example, it is an often-observed fact that aging causes a gradual deterioration of memory (although it is worth mentioning that this deterioration shows up on some measures of memory but not others). One hypothesis to be explored is that 60- and 70- and 80-year-olds are increasingly less likely to do deep processing, preferring instead the less effortful maintenance rehearsal, or perhaps just shallow (or moderate) processing. If only the aged could somehow be led to do deep processing, their memories would improve.

These various hypotheses met with mixed success (see Craik, 1977, Eysenck, 1974, and Till & Walsh, 1980, for overviews of this research). There is at least some evidence that the aged often do shallower processing, and there is some evidence that their remembering can be improved somewhat by encouraging deeper processing. However, it is clear for various reasons that this is not the entire account of this memory deficit.

Nevertheless, in research with normal subjects (neurologically intact, reasonably motivated, nondepressed college students), study after study has produced results that fit the general scheme we have just sketched: Deeper processing promotes memory (e.g., Elias & Perfetti, 1973; Jacoby & Craik, 1979; Till & Jenkins, 1973). Even if depth of processing turns out not to be our entire story of acquisition (see Chapters 8 and 9), it is an important part of the story. The idea of levels of processing therefore seems a clear step forward, fleshing out questions of processing that were largely untouched in the modal model, and simultaneously drawing our attention to the importance of subjects' activities.

The levels approach does preserve the central insights of the modal model. Craik and Lockhart distinguished between **primary memory** and **secondary memory**, a distinction parallel to that between STM and LTM. In this way, the hypothesized architecture of memory remains broadly the same, and, crucially, we still have a means of accounting for all the data we have described before. The shift in terminology seems appropriate for several reasons. Chief among them, one could claim that the labels "short-term" and "long-term" memory are misleading. What distinguishes these two storage places is not, strictly speaking, their duration. If one continues to think about something for a long period, thus maintaining it in STM, one can hold on to it in this storage for a very long time. Conversely, information might be in LTM (stored in this large-capacity warehouse, not dependent on continuing maintenance, and so not eroded by interpolated activity, etc.) but remain there only briefly. Short-term memories don't have to be short; long-term memories don't have to be long. Moreover, these terms invite confusion over whether "medium-term" memories form a distinct category, and so on. In brief, using these labels simply draws our attention to a less than informative feature of memory.

What we have preserved about the modal model, therefore, is the architecture of sensory memories, primary memory, and secondary memory. (Most modern psychologists prefer this terminology, although some prefer to speak of sensory memories, *working* memory, and secondary memory.) Primary memory is limited in its size (as in the modal model), and so new incoming information will displace this memory's current contents. The intimate connection between primary memory and ongoing mental activity still implies that entry into primary memory is a trivial affair, and that access to items in primary memory is quick and easy. Secondary memory is still conceived as being vast in size, and not dependent on ongoing activity (and so activity interpolated between learning and test will not interfere with secondary memory).

THE TROUBLE WITH LEVELS OF PROCESSING

The levels-of-processing approach was attractive to psychologists both because of its simplicity and for the support it received from laboratory data. At the same time, though, it soon became clear that this formulation, while useful in many ways, left several things to be desired.

The first of these concerns will be mentioned briefly, since we will discuss it more fully in the next chapter: A variety of data indicate that deep processing is the best way to establish a memory, *all other things being equal*. However, there are circumstances in which alternative modes of study can be just as good as (or even better than) deep processing. This will be true with certain types of memory tests, or certain types of memory hints. Thus deep processing looks like it will be a central principle for us, but needs to be placed in the context of a more complete theory.

Second, and clearly related to this, Craik and his collaborators quickly came to argue that at least one more principle must be added to our accounts of good memory. Consider the following task: Subjects are shown a word, then are shown a sentence with one word left out and must decide whether the previous word fits into the gap. For example, some subjects might see the word "chicken," then the sentence "She cooked the _____." Other subjects might see the word "chicken," then the sentence "The great bird swooped down and carried off the struggling _____." (The subjects' answer would be "yes" in both cases, since the word does fit in these sentences.)

In an experiment by Craik and Tulving (1975), subjects saw a series of pairs such as these—one word, one sentence. At the end of the series, there was a surprise memory test, with subjects asked to remember all the words they had seen. Subjects were more likely to remember the words if they thought about them in the richer context. In our example sentences, subjects would be more likely to remember "chicken" if they thought about it in the second context than in the first.

Note that, in both of these sentences, subjects must do deep processing (thinking about the meaning of the word "chicken"), but this processing seems more elaborate, involving more connections, in the second case than in the first. Given results like these, Craik and Tulving proposed that deep processing was only one of the principles that promoted memory; another principle is **elaborate processing**. Thinking about an event's meaning (deep processing) does lead to better memory than thinking about an event's superficial appearances (shallow processing), but thinking about multiple aspects of an event's meaning (elaborate processing) helps even more. Thus, as we have already suggested, deep processing cannot be our entire story.

Most important, though, the notion of "elaborate" processing calls our attention to an important point. The Craik and Tulving experiment just described might lead you to argue this way: Maybe the "richer" sentences, the more elaborate sentences, simply involve deeper processing—more specific thinking about nuances of meaning. In that case, elaboration isn't a separate principle, it's simply more depth. Thus we could preserve our simple theory of memory, based on just a levels perspective, with no further principles needed.

HOW TO DEFINE DEPTH?

To evaluate this possibility, we need to confront a question that may already have occurred to you. What exactly *is* deep processing? Is it fair to say that both of the "chicken" sentences above involve deep processing, because they both involve the meaning of words? Or, as just suggested, are there different degrees of deep processing?

In the same vein, we can probably agree that thinking about a word's meaning is deeper than thinking about a word's typeface or size. But there are many troublesome cases. Imagine that we show subjects a series of words, and tell them we are running an experiment on aesthetics. Subjects are instructed merely to judge each word for whether it's pleasing or not (see Hyde & Jenkins, 1973). We later test subjects' memories for these words. What should we predict in this procedure? Are the subjects doing relatively shallow processing, because they are thinking about the words' appearances? Or are the subjects doing deep processing, because they are thinking about the appearances in conjunction with some principles of aesthetics? (For an interesting parallel case, see Rogers, Kuiper, & Kirker, 1977, and then Klein & Kihlstrom, 1986).

Even worse, consider some cases outside the laboratory. Did you more deeply process the news of George Bush's election, or the news of the space-shuttle disaster? We suspect the answer is open to some debate. You may well have given a lot of thought to the election, what it meant for the next four years, why Bush was popular, and so on. Yet we suspect that you remember the shuttle disaster more clearly than you remember the election. If we are to account for this contrast (or any similar case) within a levels-of-processing perspective, we would need to argue that the better-remembered event was the one more deeply (or more elaborately) processed. How could we find out if this is correct? We cannot simply say that it must be so, judging from the fact of memory, because then we have simply argued in a circle, assuming what we hoped to show.

The point of these cases should be now be clear: The usefulness of the levels-of-processing perspective (its ability to make predictions outside of the laboratory; its ability to explain new cases) seems to depend on having good definitions of deep or elaborate processing. (To see this argument spelled out in detail, see Baddeley, 1978; Nelson, 1977; Nelson, Walling, & McEvoy, 1979; Postman, Thompkins, & Gray, 1978; see also Craik & Tulving, 1975.) A number of psychologists therefore sought to develop definitions of these terms, and means of measuring how deep or elaborate the processing was. If we could measure how deeply or elaborately you thought about the space shuttle, and the election, then we could find out if memory was predictable from these considerations.

The search for definitions (or measures) of deep processing has been remarkably unsuccessful. There are several factors that turn out to be reasonable rules of thumb as the sought-after indices of processing, but it is easy to find exceptions to the rules. In many cases, for example, deep processing takes more time than shallow processing, so we can use length of time spent in processing as our index of depth. (In the experiments described earlier, judgments about uppercase and lowercase tend to be appreciably quicker than judgments about the semantic relations between words.) But it is easy to find deep tasks that are quick and shallow ones that are slow. Consider, for example, asking subjects: "Does this word have more consonants than vowels, or vice versa?" This is a shallow task, but nonetheless rather time consuming. Likewise, deep processing tends to be more difficult or more effortful than shallow processing, and so we might hope to use difficulty or effort as our measure of depth. Once again, though, it is easy to find exceptions to the rule. (The more-consonants-or-more-vowels task again serves as an example.)

Alternatively, one might argue this way: Maybe "shallow" processing refers to that which is done when a stimulus is first presented; deep processing therefore always follows shallow processing in the natural sequence of information processing. For example, when you first encounter a stimulus (let's say a word), you first judge what it looks like, in order to identify the letters; you next use the letters to figure out what word it is; you next think about the word's meaning. Note that there seems to be a fixed sequence of events here, and we might try to define depth in terms of this sequence. (We would have to take steps to identify just what this sequence is, but once that was done, we could use this sequence as a way of assessing depth.) Unfortunately, though, the claim that there is a fixed shallow-to-deep sequence of processing is itself unfounded. Much evidence indicates that the order of mental events can be rather flexible, and that many processes go on simultaneously (in "parallel" with each other), and not in sequence at all! (See, for example, Baddeley, 1978; Hinton &

Anderson, 1981; Marcel, 1983; Posner, 1978; Rumelhart & McClelland, 1986; McClelland, 1979.)

In addition, there is yet another problem that confounds the attempt to measure depth of processing. Imagine that we ask you to learn a new fact about one of your favorite topics. If you happen to be a musician, we teach you a new fact about music; if you happen to be a football fan, we teach you something new about football; and so on. Odds are that you will very quickly and easily understand this new fact, see its implications, and realize what it means. This all will be far less likely if we teach you a new fact in some relatively unfamiliar area, say, a new fact about the retinal mechanisms of color vision. Correspondingly, it will almost certainly be much easier to remember a new fact in your favorite area than a fact about color vision.

In fact, these observations provide powerful suggestions about memory functioning. This broad theme will be our primary focus in Chapter 9. For now, though, note what these observations imply about the measurement of deep or elaborate processing. How quickly or easily someone will do processing of a given type, and in what sequence they will do their processing, may depend to some extent on the individual—specifically, on the individual's prior expertise in the area of the to-be-remembered material. Individual A may glance at a page of text only briefly; individual B might pore over the same page. Perhaps individual A has failed to process the page deeply, or perhaps A has some relevant expertise and so has been very efficient at deep processing. To know which of these is correct, we would need to know what is on the page, and also what prior knowledge A and B have. This will gradually push us to a person-by-person, topic-by-topic measurement of depth, rather than a more general measure, like speed or effort of processing. This is surely more complicated than we would like our theory to be, and is certainly pushing us away from a universally valid, easily measurable definition of depth.

For all of these reasons, researchers started to turn away from the levels-of-processing perspective. Perhaps there is a consistent definition to be found for deep processing, and a way to measure depth, but such a definition and measurement process have so far eluded researchers. Where does this leave us? We would argue that there is an important and correct insight at the heart of the levels view: Finding meaningful connections between what you know and what you learn is a very important aspect of learning. Conversely, thinking about what you learn in superficial ways tends not to promote learning. As our discussion continues, these points will grow in importance, rather than fade. Likewise, finding many connections (elaborate processing) between what you know and what you learn is also immensely helpful for learning. However, this still leaves us without firm definitions of the key terms in this perspective, and, for the reasons already discussed, this lack of definitions makes it impossible to apply the levels perspective to a great many cases.

In addition, the last page or so has introduced a new point, a point of great importance. To put it simply, knowing more helps you to learn. (As they say, the rich get richer.) This point is implicit in the levels perspective. After all, deep processing means thinking about meaning, and that certainly depends on what you already know. If you didn't speak English, could you do deep processing for verbal materials presented in English? If you knew nothing about chemistry, could you do deep processing for a complex argument about chemistry? This point, however, needs to be made explicit and examined closely; it will be our primary focus in Chapter 9. As it turns out, if we are going to predict learning, or predict the accuracy and completeness of memory, we will need to consider both the circumstances of learning and the prior knowledge of the learner. That is, not only do we need to look at the various "boxes" that constitute memory, and not only do we need to look at the strategies or intentions of the learner, we also need to consider what prior knowledge the learner brings to the situation.

Once again, we are forced to a familiar theme: Our study of memory is not going to yield simple and separate principles; it is instead drawing us more and more toward considering memory as a richly interwoven system. This theme is very much echoed in the next chapter.

Summary

Across the 1960s, much memory research was framed in terms of the "modal model," a conception of memory that included sensory memories, a short-term memory, and a long-term memory. When information first reaches our eyes or ears, it takes a moment for us to interpret the input. Sensory memories make this possible by preserving a record of the raw data of sensation. These memories are very short-lived, but last long enough to allow interpretation and recognition of incoming information.

Information can be recoded from sensory memory into short-term memory. Short-term memory is small in size, containing only 7 ± 2 "chunks." However, subjects seem to have considerable flexibility in what can be included in a chunk, so that a great deal of information can be packaged into the 7 chunks of short-term memory. Information in short-term memory is readily and easily available. Hence this memory plays an important role in preserving information directly pertinent to whatever one is currently thinking about.

The modal model also includes a long-term memory. Long-term memory is vast in size, but information can be entered into long-term memory only through the expenditure of some time and effort. The distinction between short-term memory and long-term memory is easily seen in data from list-learning experiments. In these experiments, subjects tend to remember the beginning and end of the list, and to perform more poorly in remembering the list's middle. This is attributed to the fact that the list's last few words are recalled from short-term memory, while the remainder of the list is recalled from long-term memory. The first few words on the list received more time and attention than any other words, and so are most likely to have been stored in long-term memory. This interpretation is supported by several lines of evidence, indicating that factors that influence memory for the list's end (the so-called recency effect) are different from the factors that influence memory for the remainder of the list.

Further support for the short-term/long-term distinction comes from cases of amnesia. Early data indicated that amnesiacs had intact short-term memories and intact long-term memories, but seemed unable to transfer information from short-term into long-term storage. However, later data have complicated this picture somewhat.

While the modal model does seem to capture important truths about memory's structure, we need to elaborate the model in order to account for the role of subjects' strategies in memory experiments. In rehearsing the to-be-remembered materials, subjects have the option of either maintenance rehearsal or elaborative rehearsal. Maintenance rehearsal appears to maintain information in short-term memory, but not to facilitate transfer into long-term storage. Elaborative rehearsal does place material in more permanent storage. Elaborative rehearsal can be done at any of several levels, with deep processing (thinking about meaning) leading to better memory retention than shallow processing (thinking about appearances).

The levels-of-processing perspective is supported by many studies. However, the usefulness of this perspective is limited by the absence of a clear definition for "deep processing." This term has been difficult to define for several reasons, including the fact that depth of processing depends both on the subject's goals and intentions and on the expertise that the subject brings to the learning situation.

8 Interconnections between Acquisition and Retrieval

I t is clear that putting information into long-term memory helps us only if we can retrieve it later on. Otherwise, it would be like putting money into a savings account from which no withdrawals are possible, or like writing books that could never be read. And it is equally clear that there are different ways to retrieve information from memory: We can try to *recall* the information ("What was the name of your 10th-grade homeroom teacher?") or to *recognize* it ("Was the name perhaps 'Miller'?"); if we try to recall the information, a variety of cues may or may not be available (we might be told, as a hint, that the name began with an "M," or rhymed with "tiller," etc.).

In Chapter 7, we ignored these variations in retrieval. We talked as if material either was well established in memory or was not, with no regard to how the material would be retrieved from memory. We talked about deep processing, for example, as promoting a better or stronger memory, as though this were true independent of how the memory will be used, what cues or hints will be available to help you retrieve it, and so on.

Is this a sensible way to think about learning? Can we formulate a "recipe" for good memory by speaking purely in terms of *acquisition*? Or is it instead the case that learning that serves as a good preparation for one type of test may be different from the learning that prepares us for a different kind of test? In this last case, we might not be able to talk about "good" or "strong" or "effective" learning without considering what the learning is for.

Consider the following experiment, reported by Tversky in 1973. Tversky told subjects to study materials for an upcoming test. Half were told, "This is an experiment in memory for pictures [and] their names. . . . Afterward, your task will be to write down the names of as many of the objects as you can." This is a **recall** test, similar to the procedures we considered in Chapter 7. This test is analogous to an essay test, or fill-in-the-blank test. Subjects in this group were told in addition that the best way to prepare for this test was to attempt to find relations among the words presented. The other half of the subjects were given a **recognition** test. They were told that, after seeing the to-be-remembered pictures, they would be shown test pictures, some of which would be from the earlier group and some of which would be new. Their task would be to discriminate which of the test pictures they had seen before, and which they had not. This is analogous to a multiple-choice test.

When the time came for the test, half of each group got what they expected; half did not. Hence we end up with four groups: subjects who expect recall and get it; ones who expect recognition and get it; some who expect recall and get recognition; and some who expect recognition and get recall.

The results (Figure 8–1) indicated that subjects did best if they received the form of the test they had been expecting, and for which they had prepared. That is, subjects who got the recall test did better if they had prepared for a recall test (62% versus 40%); subjects who got the recognition test did better if that is what they were expecting (87% versus 67%). (Note, actually, that two separate effects are evident in Figure 8–1. In addition to the effect just described, it also turns out that recognition

| | Test Used: | |
	Recall	Recognition
Subjects Expect: Recall	62%	67%
Subjects Expect: Recognition	40%	87%

FIGURE 8–1. *Memory Performance with Two Different Types of Tests and Two Different Types of Expectations.* Half of the subjects in this study were led to expect a recall test; half expected a recognition test. Half of each group got the test they expected; half did not. In the left-hand column of data, we see that subjects did better with a recall test if this is what they expected. Likewise, in the right-hand column, subjects did better with a recognition test if this is what they had been led to expect. (After Tversky, 1973.)

testing led to better performance overall than recall testing; therefore scores in the right column tend to be better than scores in the left column. This is simply superimposed on the "it helps to get what you expect" pattern just described.)

We will not try to draw strong conclusions from this study by itself, but what seems to be going on is that what counts as "good learning" or "effective learning" depends on how memory is tested. Strategies that prepare you for one form of test turn out to be less successful if a different kind of test is given. As we will see, this is indeed the pattern of things.

Encoding Specificity

We bring a group of subjects into the laboratory and ask them to memorize a list of words. Midway down the list is the word JAM, and, by manipulating the context, we arrange things so that subjects are likely to understand the word as indicating the kind of jam one makes from strawberries or grapes. (This can be done in various ways; at the simplest, we can precede the word JAM with a word like JELLY or FRUIT. In this situation, the context "primes" subjects to understand JAM as we intend. We will discuss how this "priming" works in Chapter 11.) Some time later, we test memory by presenting various items and asking whether or not these appeared on the previous list. JAM is presented, but now we arrange context so that JAM is understood as in "traffic jam." Under these circumstances, subjects typically will say that the word was not on the previous list, even though their memory for the list seems to be quite good. That is, subjects are quite likely to remember accurately most of the other words on the list.

This kind of demonstration has been reported in numerous forms by Endel Tulving; he refers to these experiments as showing **encoding specificity** (Tulving, 1983; see also Hunt & Ellis, 1974; Light & Carter-Sobell, 1970). The notion of encoding specificity, roughly, is that one learns more than just the word; one learns the word together with its context. In this case, the context would include what one thinks and understands about the word. When subjects are later presented with the word in some other context, subjects in essence ask themselves, "Does this match anything I learned previously?" and answer *correctly*, "No." And we emphasize that their answer is indeed correct. By analogy, it is as if subjects learned the word "other" and were later asked whether they had been shown the word "the." In fact, "the" does appear as part of "other," or, more precisely, the letters t-h-e do appear within "other." But it is the "whole" that subjects learned, not the parts. Said differently, "the" might have been contained in an item on the list, just as a "4" and an "A" are contained in Figure 8–2. But the 4 and the A are not easily

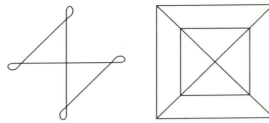

FIGURE 8–2. *Embedded Figures.* A "4" is embedded in the left-hand figure, but is usually not perceived by subjects until it is pointed out. Likewise, an "A" is embedded in the right-hand figure.

visible; geometrically they are present, but psychologically they are not. In this sense, "the" is not psychologically present in the word "other," no more than "he" and "her" are (even though these letters, too, are contained within "other"). If we showed "other," and later asked the subjects if they had seen "the" or "he" or "her," we would probably expect them to deny having seen these words, and we would probably count their denials as correct. The point Tulving is making is that a word is no more separable from its context than "he" or "her" is from "other." Subjects learn the whole, and we need to consider what the whole *is.* The letters J-A-M were contained in what subjects learned, just as t-h-e is contained in "other," but, in both cases, what was learned was the broader, integrated experience—the word as the perceiver organized it, the word as the perceiver understood it.

Although this point may seem obvious, it contains an important general lesson: At several points in our discussion, we will need to contrast the physical stimulus, the thing an experimenter puts in front of the subject's eyes or ears, and the psychological stimulus, what the subject notices, thinks about, or understands from the physical stimulus. In the "jam" case, the physical stimulus is the same in the two contexts ("strawberry" and "traffic"); the psychological stimulus is not, and it is the psychological stimulus that seems to matter for memory.

A different sort of example may help to make this clear, and will also help to show the range of contexts to which these concerns apply. We can show subjects the shape shown in Figure 8–3, and arrange things so that subjects perceive the shape as a white vase on a black background. (As before, we can use a "priming" procedure, perhaps previously showing subjects pictures of other vases, or other white figures on black backgrounds.) We take the picture away, and then, a few minutes later, show the picture again. This time, however, we prime subjects so that they will see two profiles against a white background. We now ask subjects whether they have ever seen this figure before. Subjects will typically claim that they have not seen the figure before, even though this exact same geometric configuration was before their eyes just minutes earlier (see

FIGURE 8–3.   *The Ambiguous "Vase/Profiles" Figure.* This figure can be perceived either as a white vase against a black background or as two black profiles against a white background.

Kanizsa, 1979; Rock, 1983). Apparently, as with words, it is the "stimulus-as-understood" that matters for memory, the psychologically defined stimulus, not the geometrically defined picture itself.

You might object, though, that we're playing a trick here. After all, "jam" is not an ordinary word; it happens to be a word with two distinct meanings. Perhaps encoding specificity can be demonstrated with ambiguous words (ball, tank, fly), but only with ambiguous words. Likewise, the vase/profiles figure is specifically designed to be an ambiguous stimulus; perhaps "ordinary" stimuli will not show the same pattern. As it turns out, though, these suppositions are not correct: For example, Tulving and Thomson (1973; also Watkins & Tulving, 1975; Flexser & Tulving, 1978) showed subjects a list of to-be-remembered words, with each word accompanied by a context word. For example, subjects might see "grasp–BABY," with "BABY" being the to-be-remembered item. In the next step of the procedure, subjects were shown a new list of words, and were simply asked to write down what these new words called to mind. For example, subjects were shown "infant," and, not surprisingly, many subjects wrote down "baby" in response. Finally, subjects were asked to look over their own responses and to circle any of their responses that they recognized as having occurred in the previously seen input list. In many cases, subjects did not recognize "baby" as a list word! That is, by virtue of changing the context in which this word appeared, memory seems to have been significantly disrupted: Subjects do recognize "baby" as familiar in the context of "grasp" (the word present in the study phase); they do not recognize it in a different context.

Thus we note the first regard in which there is an interaction between the process of placing information into memory and the process of bringing that information back out. How a stimulus or event is understood (how it is interpreted and thought about) seems to shape in important ways what is experienced. And what is experienced governs what is placed in memory. If the stimulus or event is later presented a second time, but is understood differently, then it is, psychologically speaking, a new stimulus and is likely not to be recognized as familiar. From the standpoint of the physical stimulus, this is anomalous; from the standpoint of the psychological stimulus, it is perfectly sensible. Therefore, if we wish to ask how likely a subject is to remember a prior event, we should not ask merely how well or how firmly the item is learned. Even if an item is "well learned," that learning may not be detected if the item is understood differently when the time for test arrives.

Retrieval Hints and Cues

In the examples we have just considered, the success or failure of memory seems to depend on how the to-be-remembered material is understood and, in particular, on the degree of match between how the material is understood at the time of learning and how it is understood at the time of test. A closely related effect can be seen if we observe the impact of various retrieval cues.

Again, we begin with a concrete example. Fisher and Craik (1977) presented their subjects with a series of word pairs. Subjects were instructed to learn the second word in each pair, and to use the first word in each pair "as an aid to remembering the target words." For half of the words presented, subjects were led to think about the words' meanings: That is, the context word was semantically associated with the target word. For example, if subjects were shown "cat," they were also shown the context word "dog." (In the language of Chapter 7, these subjects were led to do "deep" processing.) For the other word, subjects were instructed to think about the word's sound. Concretely, these words were presented together with a rhyming context word (for example, if shown "cat," they were also shown the context word "hat").

When the time came for test, the subjects were tested in either of two ways. Subjects were given either a hint concerning meaning ("Was there a word on the list associated with dog?") or a hint concerning sound ("Was there a word on the list associated with hat?"). Table 8–1 shows the results. Note, first, the column all the way to the right (averaging together trials with meaning hints and trials with sound hints). Consistent with the data in Chapter 7, thinking about meaning generally leads to better memory, in this case with an impressive 30.5 to 21.5 advantage. That is, subjects who thought about meaning at the time of learning remembered about 50% more than subjects who thought about sound. But now look at the two other columns. If subjects thought about meaning at the time of

Table 8–1.   Percentage of Words Recalled on Testing after Prior
              Association with Either Meaning or Sound

	Type of Hint		
	Meaning	Sound	Both Combined
Type of processing at time of learning			
Meaning	44%	17%	30.5%
Sound	17%	26%	21.5%

After Fisher & Craik, 1977.

learning, they do considerably better in the test *if* the cues provided by the experimenter concern meaning. Likewise for sound: If subjects thought about sound at the time of learning, then they do better with a cue concerning the word's sound. In fact, the table shows two separate influences on memory working at the same time: an advantage for thinking about meaning (overall, performance is better in the top row) and an advantage for "matched" learning and test conditions (overall, performance is best in the "main diagonal" of the table). In the top left cell of the table, these effects combine, and here performance is better than in any other condition. These effects clash in the column showing the results of the sound cue. The advantage from thinking about meaning favors the top cell in this column; the advantage from "matched" learning and test favors the bottom cell. As it turns out, the "match" effect wins over the levels-of-processing effect: That is, "deep but unmatched" (17%) is inferior to "not so deep, but matched" (26%). The advantage for "deep processing" is simply overturned in this situation.

On an everyday level, we can continue to claim that deep processing is preferable in general because, as always, deep processing produced better memory overall. This emerges in the table as the overall advantage for the top row over the bottom row. But, at the same time, it seems that other considerations can outweigh processing level. More specifically, note that the implication of this Fisher and Craik study is quite similar to that of the encoding specificity studies (see also Bransford, Franks, Morris, & Stein, 1979; Morris, Bransford, & Franks, 1977; Tulving & Osler, 1968). In encoding specificity studies, we explicitly change how an item is understood between learning and test, and memory suffers. In the present case, we are simply changing what aspect of an item (its sound or its meaning) is emphasized, and the result is the same.

STATE-DEPENDENT LEARNING

A broadly similar point can be made with a different class of studies, known collectively as **state-dependent learning** studies (Eich, 1980;

Overton, 1985). The design of these is similar to that of the Fisher and Craik experiment: There are two different learning situations, and two different tests; one of the test formats is matched to one of the learning situations, and one to the other. Hence we end up with what psychologists call a "2 × 2 design," like that used by Fisher and Craik. As one example, subjects had to learn a list of words either after smoking a cigarette containing marijuana materials or after smoking a cigarette without marijuana. Four hours later, subjects were tested under either marijuana or control conditions (Eich, Weingartner, Stillman, & Gillin, 1975). Table 8–2 shows that performance was better overall if subjects were tested while not under the influence of the drug. That is, performance is better overall in the left-hand column of the table (22.5 versus 18). Superimposed on this, however, is a state-dependency effect: Subjects did best if learning and test took place in the same state; they did worse if learning and test took place in different states. Similar data have been reported with other procedures and other species, using such drugs as alcohol, amphetamines, and caffeine (Bliss, Sledjeski, & Leiman, 1971; Overton, 1964; Sachs, Weingarten, & Klein, 1966; Weingartner, Adefris, Eich, & Murphy, 1976). In each case, there is a performance advantage if the physiological state at the time of test matches the state at the time of learning.

These results concern internal states, but comparable results can be obtained with manipulations of external states. For example, deep-sea divers' memories were tested both underwater and on land for material learned either underwater or on land (Godden & Baddeley, 1975). As with other results mentioned in this section, material is best remembered if tested under circumstances similar to those of learning (see Table 8–3). There is a report of similar data if learning and testing simply take place in different rooms (Smith, Glenberg, & Bjork, 1978).

These last few examples may remind you of a data pattern we described in Chapter 3 (pp. 115–17). We there discussed cases of Pavlovian conditioning in which the context itself served as the conditioned stimulus. That is, associations were formed between the sights, sounds, and smells

Table 8–2.   Percentage of Words Recalled in a Memory Test Designed to Show State-Dependency Effects from Marijuana

	Retrieval Condition	
Encoding Condition	Placebo	Marijuana
Placebo	25	14
Marijuana	20	22
Overall	22.5	18

After Eich, Weingartner, Stillman, & Gillin, 1975.

Table 8–3.   Percentage of Words Recalled in a
Memory Test Designed to Show State-Dependency
Effects from the Physical Setting

Encoding Condition	Retrieval Condition	
	Land	Underwater
Land	38	24
Underwater	23	32
Overall	30.5	28

After Godden & Baddeley, 1975.

of the conditioning chamber and the US. In such cases, learning will be displayed when the organism returns to the context of learning. That is, we will observe a CR when the organism is again exposed to the CS of the context itself, in accord with the principles of Pavlovian conditioning. The parallels between this and state-dependent learning should be clear.

One final example of state dependency returns us to internal states: Bower (1981) reported many studies examining state dependency of learning in which the state being manipulated is the subject's mood. There are many ways to do this, including a hypnotic procedure for placing subjects in a happy mood or a sad one, or by letting subjects read a series of statements designed to lift or to depress their spirits. The design is by now familiar, and the results yield a familiar pattern. Subjects learn material either while happy or while sad; they are later tested while either happy or sad. Memory is best if the mood state at test matches the mood state in learning. The results of one of these mood and memory studies are shown in Figure 8–4. This state-dependency effect with mood has a number of very interesting implications. Among them, this memory phenomenon may serve to keep our moods stable: When we are happy, we are better able to think of experiences and events we learned about while happy, and this helps to keep us happy. Unfortunately, the same pattern holds when we are depressed.

It is worth saying, though, that, unlike other state-dependency effects, the "mood and memory" effects have proven to be somewhat unreliable. That is, several experiments have sought to reproduce the findings just described, but with no success (Bower & Mayer, 1985; Isen, Shalker, Clark, & Karp, 1978; Wetzler, 1985). We hasten to say, however, that other studies have confirmed the pattern just described (e.g., Bower, Gilligan, & Monteiro, 1981; Gilligan & Bower, 1984; Leight & Ellis, 1981; Teasdale & Russell, 1983; Teasdale & Taylor, 1981). At least for now, it is unclear why this particular variety of state dependency sometimes does appear in the results and sometimes does not. (For a discussion of these issues, see Blaney, 1986; Eich & Metcalfe, 1989; Ellis, 1985; Hasher, Zacks, Rose, & Doren, 1985; Isen, 1985; Mayer & Bower, 1985.)

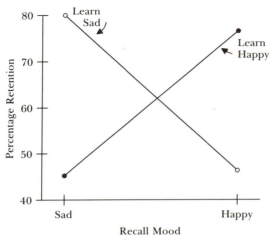

FIGURE 8–4.   *State-Dependency Effects from Mood.* Half of the subjects in this study learned a word list while in a happy mood; half learned it while sad. Half of each group was tested while in a happy mood, half while sad. Being in the same mood during the learning and during the test improved memory performance. (After Bower, 1981.)

Over and over, then, we see that we probably should not speak of something like "good" learning (or "less good" learning). What will be good learning depends on later events—good learning in preparation for testing under one set of circumstances may turn out to be less good if the testing comes in a different setting. Deep processing (as described in Chapter 7) turns out to help, *all other things being equal,* but the benefits of deep processing can sometimes be smaller than the benefits of having a matched emphasis or orientation in learning and in test.

Different Forms of Memory Testing

Our theory of memory is growing in complexity, but it is complexity demanded by the data. In order to predict when remembering will succeed, and when it will fail, we need to consider subjects' intentions and strategies (for example, their intention to do maintenance or elaborative rehearsal, or to do shallow or deep processing). We also need to consider subjects' understanding of the to-be-learned material (because of the encoding specificity data), and, moreover, we need to consider their understanding both at the time of learning and at the time of test. We also need to consider the context, both internal and external, at the time of learning and at the time of test. This list, though, still needs to be expanded by one, and this addition is, we believe, the *coup de grâce* for the claim that we can simply speak about good learning by itself, independent of considerations about how the learning will be tested.

REMEMBERING THE SOURCE VERSUS FAMILIARITY ALONE

So far, all of the cases of remembering we have discussed are of a certain sort: We have asked subjects what words they can remember from the prior presentation (a recall test), or whether a particular word was or was not presented on the earlier list (recognition), and so on. Note that not only are we asking subjects what looks or seems familiar, we are also asking subjects to identify the context in which they previously encountered the specific item. To put it differently, virtually all of the to-be-remembered materials in these studies are already quite familiar to the subjects. Usually, the to-be-remembered items are words that are common in the subjects' vocabulary, words that the subject routinely encounters in conversation or in reading. Hence the subject cannot merely say, "Yes, I know this word" or "This word is familiar to me; I have seen it before." That will be true for all of the words, both those presented on the to-be-remembered list and those presented in the test that were not on the earlier list. Therefore the subject instead has to say something much more specific—to say, in essence, "The last time I met this word was on the previous list." The subject cannot merely remember having encountered a word before (since all the words have been encountered *somewhere* before); the subject must remember the particular time and place this encounter took place, in order to tell if the word is from the previously presented list.

Once we frame things this way, one might start to think that perhaps we have underestimated what subjects actually do remember. Consider a fairly common experience: You are walking down the street, or perhaps you turn on the television, and you see a familiar face. Immediately, you know that the face is familiar, but, tantalizingly, you are unable to say just why the face is familiar. Is it the man who served you in the butcher shop? Is it someone you saw in a movie last month? Is it the driver of the bus you often take? You are at a loss to answer these questions; all you know is that the face is for some reason familiar.

Note that, in this case, you are failing to remember *if* we define memory as we do in the experiments discussed so far. It is as if you said to the experimenter, "Yes, the test word is extraordinarily familiar to me, but I haven't a clue where I last saw it, and I haven't a clue whether it was on that stupid list you showed me." If we require you to remember the connection between an item and the context of a previous encounter, then you have failed.

But this seems too harsh. Clearly you are not totally failing to remember; you do obviously remember something about the face. You know that it is familiar; you probably also know that the face is usually encountered in some context sharply different from the current one. We therefore need to say something about this intense feeling of familiarity, this confident feeling of knowing.

Remembering of this sort has been extensively investigated, with a great deal of the work done by George Mandler (1980; Graf & Mandler, 1984). Mandler's proposal, in essence, is that there are two rather separate memory processes we must consider. First, there are the processes involved in remembering the *source* of one's memory, the reasons for the familiarity. We will refer to this simply as **source memory**. Second, there is the feeling of familiarity by itself, perhaps bereft of any knowledge about where the familiarity comes from; we will refer to this simply as **familiarity**.

Mandler suggests that these two kinds of remembering, source versus familiarity, are tapped differently by the different questions we might ask of the remember. A *recall* test ("Write down as many words as you can from the prior list") requires that memory be searched with the prior context as the reference point, and so explicitly demands recovery of the connection between items and context. Therefore recall must draw on remembering of the first sort, that is, memory for source. A *recognition* test ("Which of these items were on the prior list?"), however, can actually be done in either of two ways: If one remembers the event of seeing this or that word on the prior list, then this will guide your responding in a recognition test. If, on the other hand, a word seems extremely familiar, you are quite likely to infer that you have seen it very recently, even if you cannot remember the actual encounter. In this case, guided by your inference, you will probably respond "Yes" on the recognition test. For convenience, let us call these two routes "source memory" and "familiarity plus inference about source." To rephrase Mandler's point using this language: Recall tests always demand source memory, but recognition tests can be done via source memory *or* familiarity plus inference. (Related conceptions of recognitions tests have been offered by Atkinson & Juola, 1974; Glucksberg & McCloskey, 1981; Jacoby & Brooks, 1984.)

Mandler also proposes that different kinds of learning set the basis for source memory and for familiarity. To keep things simple, we can stick with the Craik and Lockhart terminology. (Mandler's own terminology is slightly different.) Recall that Craik and Lockhart separate "elaborative rehearsal" from "maintenance rehearsal"; the former, they claim, serves to place materials into long-term memory (or, in their terminology, into "secondary" memory). Maintenance rehearsal, they suggest, merely serves to maintain material in short-term ("primary") memory, with no long-term consequences.

Mandler agrees with the first part of this conception: If you anticipate a memory test, you are likely to do elaborative rehearsal. This will create memory connections between the to-be-remembered item and other bits of knowledge already in your memory, helping to tie the to-be-remembered item to its context—to other things you were thinking about at the time, to other items on the to-be-remembered list, to various features of the physical situation you were in, and so forth. This will surely aid the remembering of the item plus its context, and so will leave you well prepared for any task that requires source memory. If, on the other hand, you anticipate no memory test, you will presumably shift to the (easier) maintenance rehearsal. No connections will be sought, nor will any be made. Hence the context (what else one was thinking about at the time, what else was present in the environment) will not be encoded (or remembered). (If these other aspects of the situation are remembered, you will not have thought about, and so will not remember, any connection between these and the to-be-remembered material.) But here Mandler parts company with Craik and Lockhart: On Mandler's view, the sheer exposure to the item does have its effect—you will be objectively more familiar with an item, and, consequently, the item will feel familiar. (We will have more to say in a little while about just what this "feeling" might mean.)

EVIDENCE FOR MANDLER'S CONCEPTION

Some of the relevant evidence will help us both to see what this claim is all about and to see why this proposal is worth taking seriously. In an experiment reported by Bartz (1976), subjects were shown a word list; half of the subjects were led to believe that they needed to memorize the words because a memory test would occur later on. Let us call these subjects, who think they must remember the words, the "remember" group. The other subjects were simply told to make a series of judgments about the words, with no expectation of later memory needs. Let us call these subjects, who think they can forget the items the moment they have completed their judgments, the "forget" group. Of course, memory was tested for both groups, in either of two ways: Half of the subjects in each group were asked to recall the items (asked to write down as many of the words as they could); half were asked to recognize the items (shown a new list, and asked which had occurred in the previous batch, which had not). Finally, as one last complication, some items on the initial list occurred only once in that list; other items on the initial list were repeated.

Consider first the subjects who had no expectation of the memory test, that is, the "forget" group (Figure 8–5). These subjects presumably had no reason to do elaborative rehearsal; their passing contact with the words would simply be the equivalent of maintenance rehearsal. With no connections established between these words and other words on the list, or between the words and other thoughts, there is little in memory to facilitate moving from "context" to the words. Hence subjects are not prepared to remember source, and *recall* performance will be quite poor.

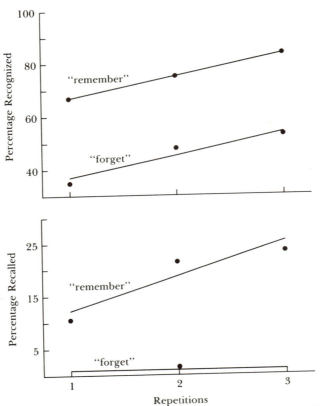

FIGURE 8–5.   *The Relationship between Strategy and Form of Testing.* Half of the subjects were told to memorize a word list; half were shown the list, but told they could forget what they had seen. Half of each group was tested with a recognition procedure (top graph), half with a recall test (bottom graph). Subjects in the "remember" group presumably did elaborative rehearsal, preparing them for either form of test; the more rehearsal they did (that is, the more repetitions), the better performance was. Subjects in the "forget" group probably did maintenance rehearsal, which did not prepare them for a recall test, even with repetitions. However, this form of rehearsal did prepare subjects for a recognition test. (After Mandler, 1981.)

This will be true even if the items were actually repeated in the initial presentation—it does not help to do nothing over and over! *Recognition performance*, in contrast, does not depend on establishing these connections between an item and its context, and so the absence of the connections is not fatal. Recognition can instead proceed purely on the basis of familiarity. Thus, even with maintenance rehearsal, the prior encounter will increase the familiarity of an item, and so prepare this group of subjects for successful performance on a recognition test. The repetitions of the item during learning will also pay off: Each encounter serves to increase familiarity a little bit more; the more familiarity, the more likely the subject is to succeed at recognition.

For subjects in the "remember" group, expecting the memory test, strategies will be quite different, and so will be our predictions. In this group, elaborative rehearsal is likely. These subjects will lay down memory connections between the item and context, will be able to remember the source, and so will be able to recall the items. The repetitions will lead to more and more connections, making recall more and more likely. This increased likelihood of source memory will also help in the recognition test, because, as we have said, recognition can be done either on the basis of familiarity or on the basis of memory for the specific prior encounter, and it is presumably the latter route which is in place here.

We now have our predictions: The "forget" group will do poorly in recall, with or without repetitions of the item; they will do all right in recognition, and here repetitions will help. The "remember" group will do fine in recall and in recognition, and repetitions will help in both cases. This pattern is exactly what the data show. (Similar data, confirming these claims, have been reported by Glenberg & Adams, 1978; Glenberg, Smith, & Green, 1977; Woodward, Bjork, & Jongeward, 1973.)

All of this also fits with the data discussed in Chapter 7. Rundus showed us that repetitions with the intent to memorize had a beneficial effect on recall; Craik and Watkins (in their "B" word experiment) showed that repetitions with no intent to memorize had no impact. The Bartz data just discussed (and several other studies in addition) indicate that this is the pattern for *recall* tests, but is not the pattern for recognition: If subjects do not need to locate the word in memory, if they instead can merely make a familiarity judgment, then repetitions help no matter what they were or were not thinking about in the process of repeating the items. (It should be mentioned that, in some procedures, maintenance does seem to improve recall as well as recognition: Dark & Loftus, 1976; Darley & Glass, 1975; Maki & Schuler, 1980; Rundus, 1980.)

By way of summing this up, look at what has happened to the question with which we began the chapter: We asked at the outset whether it made sense to speak of a good memory, or a strong memory, or a well-established memory, independent of how memory would be tested. We have now seen many indications that the answer to this question is no: We cannot speak of the quality or strength of learning without taking into account how that learning will be tested, how the memory will be used. Mandler brings us to a striking version of this: Sheer repetition leads to familiarization with materials, but not to the establishment of memory connections. Hence sheer repetition will be a fine mode of learning if a recognition test (dependent on familiarity plus inference) will be used. On the other hand, sheer repetition will create rather poor memory if we test learning via some procedure dependent on source memory—for example, by a recall measure.

Note, once again, that recognition does not need to rely on familiarity. One will also answer correctly on a recognition test if one remembers the particular episode in which an item was recently encountered. Recognition, then, seems to be a "hybrid" task—one can correctly recognize an item as being from the prior list in either of two ways, familiarity or source memory. The suggestion is that subjects sometimes use one route and sometimes the other. Or subjects may try both strategies at the same time, and decide on the basis of whichever route (memory for source or inference from sheer familiarity) yields an answer most quickly.

If a recognition procedure is a hybrid, then, this might lead us to ask if there is a "pure" familiarity task, one that can be done *only* by means of the familiarity of the items being presented. The standard recall procedure, after all, provides a pure assessment of how well one remembers source; familiarity per se will not be enough to guide responding in a recall measure. Can we find the inverse case, for familiarity? The answer to this seems to be a simple yes, and itself opens a fascinating line of exploration.

MEMORY WITHOUT AWARENESS

We begin with an illustrative experiment. Jacoby and Dallas (1981, Experiment 1) ran subjects through an incidental learning procedure. Subjects were shown a series of words. For some of the words, subjects were led to think about the meanings of these words (deep processing); for other words, subjects were led to think about the word's sound ("Does it rhyme with . . . ?"; medium processing); for the remaining words, subjects were led to think about the word's spelling pattern ("Does the word contain an 'L'?"; this is shallow processing). Two kinds of data were collected. Half of the subjects were tested with a recognition procedure; that is, they were shown a series of words and asked whether each had (or had not) appeared in the earlier session. The data (Table 8–4) showed the usual pattern, with memory performance at its best after deep processing and at its worst after shallow processing (95% correct versus 72% versus 51%).

The other half of the subjects were tested in a rather different fashion. They were seated in front of a tachistoscope—the same device we met in Sperling's sensory (iconic) memory studies—and shown a series of briefly presented words. Subjects' task was simply to say what the words were. As it turns out, some of the words they were shown were words from the list they had studied; our focus is on how identification of these words compares to that for other words not recently seen.

To explain this experiment, we need to say a few words about word identification under very brief, "tachistoscopic" exposures. First, this is a difficult task, provided that we make the exposure brief enough, and that we take some steps to interfere with the sensory memory. (This

Table 8–4.   Level of Processing Influences Recognition Memory, but Not Perceptual Recognition

Form of Memory	Question Type			New Words
	Spelling	Rhyme	Semantic	
Recognition memory				
Percentage recognized	51	72	95	—
Tachistoscopic test				
Percentage identified	78	82	80	65

After Jacoby & Dallas, 1981.

simply involves immediately following the test stimulus with some other pattern, known as a **mask**, something like "X$M%@." The mask immediately enters sensory memory, bumping out the previous stimulus.) Second, performance is improved if a word is repeated. That is, if the eighth word, say, in the sequence happens to be a word recently encountered (perhaps the same as the first word in the sequence, or maybe even a word that appeared in the experiment's instructions), subjects are much more likely to recognize the tachistoscopically presented word. This advantage is referred to as **repetition priming**.

In the Jacoby and Dallas study, subjects showed a large repetition priming effect independent of how they had processed the material on the initial encounter. In the tachistoscopic procedure, subjects were able to identify 65% of new words (words not included in the prior session). Subjects were able to identify 80% of the words for which they had previously done semantic (deep) processing. This benefit (80% versus 65%) is what one would expect from repetition priming. For words for which subjects did shallow processing in the initial encounter, 78% were identified in the tachistoscopic presentation; subjects recognized 82% of the words for which they had thought about sound. Apparently, therefore, level of processing has no impact on repetition priming (80% versus 82% versus 78%).

A further study by Jacoby and Witherspoon (1982) takes this a step further. Subjects were first shown a list of words and were then tested in two ways: with a recognition procedure, followed by a tachistoscopic task. This procedure is like that run by Jacoby and Dallas except that Jacoby and Witherspoon tested the *same* subjects in the two different ways. This allows us to compare the tachistoscopic and recognition performances. To help keep this straight, we will refer to the tachistoscopic performance as *identification,* and use *recognition* to mean subjects' answers to the question "Did you see this word in the previous list?" In these terms, we can look at tachistoscopic identification of three different categories of words:

First, there are words that were presented in the initial list and were also recognized by the subject as being from the list; second, there are words that were presented but apparently forgotten by the time of the recognition test; third, there are words that were not presented in the initial list. It is the standard recognition measure that allows us to separate the first category of words from the second, so obviously these differ with regard to memory. Yet these two categories of words behave identically in the tachistoscopic task. The results do show a clear repetition priming effect: Words presented tachistoscopically were much more likely to be recognized if these words had appeared on the prior list. (That is, subjects were much better at identifying the first two categories of words than they were in identifying the third category.) But this was true *whether or not* the subject had "forgotten" these words (as judged by the recognition performance). To put it simply, the priming effect was exactly the same for words seen before and remembered and for words seen before but forgotten.

We are therefore seeing a benefit of prior experience that seems independent of being able to recognize that prior experience. In other words, in these procedures, it would appear that subjects simultaneously do and do not remember the words from the list presented earlier. If we assess memory by performance on the recognition test, subjects seem to have forgotten many of the words. On the other hand, performance on the tachistoscopic task indicates that subjects are still being influenced by the previously seen words, even the specific words that they seem to have "forgotten." That is, if we test memory *directly*, by asking subjects what they remember, subjects (in this case) fail the test. If we test memory *indirectly*, by asking whether subjects are still influenced by the past, subjects do remember.

Results like these have led psychologists to distinguish two types of memories. **Explicit memories** are those revealed by direct memory testing, and are typically accompanied by the conviction that one is remembering a specific prior episode. **Implicit memories** are those revealed by indirect testing. In this form of testing, one's current behavior or current judgments are demonstrably influenced by some prior event, but one may be quite unaware of this. In fact, one may have forgotten that the prior event even occurred. In the Jacoby and Dallas design, the recognition test is a direct test, designed to assess explicit memory; tachistoscopic identification is an indirect test, revealing an implicit memory.

There are many questions to be asked about the relation between these two types of memory. Note that we will speak of *direct* and *indirect* when we are describing experimental procedures for testing memory, and *explicit* and *implicit* memories when we are speaking of what subjects display, that is, the memories subjects seem to have. (Our terminology here follows the lead set by Graf & Schacter, 1985, Johnson & Hasher, 1987, and Richardson-Klavehn & Bjork, 1988.) In direct tests, subjects realize that they are in fact remembering; that is, after all, what the test requires. In indirect tests, subjects are usually completely unaware that their memories are being tested.

THE BREADTH OF IMPLICIT MEMORY

How broad a phenomenon is implicit memory? Is it revealed only in tachistoscopic performance, or in other tasks as well? Our answer to this will become clear as we proceed; as we will see, implicit memory is demonstrable in a broad range of phenenomena and procedures. We also will need to ask about the mechanisms behind implicit memory. Do implicit and explicit memories tap into the different memory "records," or do they just tap into a single sort of memory, but in different ways?

This latter question—the mechanisms behind implicit memory—will be the focus of our next section. First, though, we need to say more about how implicit memory feels from the subject's point of view, and this will tie us back into our discussion of familiarity and source memory.

Let us say that we show subjects a picture and then, sometime later, show them the same picture again. Let us say further that we arrange things so that subjects have no explicit memory for the previous encounter, but they do have an implicit memory. (The Jacoby and Dallas procedure suggests one way to arrange this; other experiments in this section suggest other ways.) The evidence indicates that subjects' reactions to the picture, in that second encounter, will depend a great deal on the context. The picture is likely to feel in some ways "special." We have several expressions in English that seem to capture this specialness: We sometimes say that something "rings a bell" or that it "strikes a chord." We sometimes say that you "resonate" to an input. But exactly what this means, and exactly how this feels, seems to depend on your circumstances.

Two experiments will help to illustrate this point. One presented subjects with a list of names to read out loud. Subjects were told nothing about a memory test; they thought that the experiment was concerned with how quickly and accurately they could pronounce the names. This cover task was designed to make sure that subjects attended closely to the names. Some time later subjects were given the second step of the procedure: They were shown a new list of names, and asked to rate each person named on the list according to how famous they are. This list included some real, very famous people; some real but not-so-famous people; some made-up names which had occurred on the prior list; and some new made-up names (Jacoby, Kelley, Brown, & Jasechko, 1989).

The names we are interested in are the ones that were made up but familiar—that is, taken from the prior list. How subjects responded to these names depended very much on how much time had elapsed between presentation of the two lists. If the two were presented back-to-back, it is as if subjects said to themselves, "This name rings a bell, but that's because I just saw it on the previous list." In the terms we have been using, the subjects have the feeling of familiarity, but also remember the source. If, however, the two lists were presented 24 hours apart, things are quite different. At this delay, the implicit memory, the familiarity, still remains. (We know from tachistoscopic studies that repetition priming, a good index of implicit memory, lasts for several days—see, for example, Jacoby, 1983a.) However, memory for the source of the familiarity has now faded, so the subject is unable to attribute the familiarity. Now, it is as if the subjects were saying to themselves, "This name rings a bell, and I have no idea why. I guess this must be a famous person." We have, of course, made up these thoughts allegedly running through subjects' minds, but the data are real: After a 24-hour delay, subjects do rate the made-up names as being the names of famous people.

Why is the implicit memory misattributed to fame? Everything in the experiment serves to point the subject in this direction—the experiment is described as being about fame, and other names on the list are indeed those of famous people. It is a reasonable inference on the subjects' part, given these supporting circumstances, that any name that "rings a bell" belongs to a famous person. Therefore, if the subjects cannot remember correctly the real source of the implicit memory, these circumstances make it extremely likely what the subjects' hypothesis will be instead. Critically, though, this misattribution is possible only if we allow memory for the actual source to become less prominent; this is accomplished by the 24-hour delay. Hence Jacoby refers to this experiment playfully as his "how to become famous overnight" experiment.

A different example will strengthen this point. Robert Zajonc (1980) has done a series of experiments on the **mere-exposure effect**. There are many ways to demonstrate this effect, and here is one: Moreland and Zajonc (1977) brought subjects into the laboratory and showed them a series of Japanese ideograms (the complex characters used in Japanese writing); none of their subjects was familiar with Japanese. The subjects were shown a series of 80 figures. Actually, only 10 different figures were shown, but some figures were shown one time and others were repeated several times. The instructions to subjects told them merely to look at the figures; no other instructions were given. Half of the subjects in this procedure were then given a memory test. Subjects were shown a new series of slides and had to rate each on a 7-point scale, ranging from "I am certain this slide was in the earlier group" to "I am certain this slide was not in the earlier group." The other half of the subjects rated the test slides on how much they *liked* the figures, again on a 7-point scale (from strongly like to strongly dislike).

Many of the slides shown in the first series were not recognized as familiar, even though in some cases the slide had been presented 27 times. (These are, after all, complex, perceptually similar figures.) Of special interest is subjects' liking of just those stimuli not recognized as familiar. The results show a strong influence of exposure on liking, with figures liked more if they were seen more often. That is, exposures to a stimulus made that stimulus seem preferable, even in the absence of any explicit memory of those exposures!

In each of these experiments, subjects are clearly being influenced by the fact that they recently encountered the test stimuli. Therefore, subjects must have some memory for the earlier encounter—an *implicit* memory. Said differently, we are seeing various consequences of the fact that the test stimuli are, objectively, familiar to the subject. However, the implicit memory may not produce *subjective* familiarity; that is, it may not produce a *feeling* of familiarity. Whether or not this feeling is present seems to depend on how subjects interpret the implicit memory.

For some procedures, of course, it does not matter how subjects interpret their implicit memories. For example, in the Jacoby and Dallas procedure described earlier, we do not care whether subjects think of the previously seen words as being familiar or as being "famous," or "preferable," or whatever. Presumably, the implicit memory would facilitate tachistoscopic recognition no matter how subjects think about the stimuli. In the "famous" procedure, in contrast, everything depends on subjects' interpretation of the implicit memory. Subjects do apparently register that some of the names are somehow different, but if they attribute this feeling to the previous encounter then the effect will not work. (That is why we get the "famous" effect only if we run the procedure's two steps separated by a day.) In Zajonc's procedures, subjects again register that some of the stimuli are "special," but they experience this "specialness" as a feeling of preference, not as a feeling of familiarity!

ATTRIBUTING IMPLICIT MEMORY TO THE WRONG SOURCE

Generally, it seems that an implicit memory will produce a subjective feeling of familiarity only if one attributes the memory to a specific prior episode ("That picture strikes me as special because I saw it last Tuesday . . ."). Even in this case, however, there is still an interesting opportunity for error. Let us consider one last example. Brown, Deffenbacher, and Sturgill (1977) reported an experiment designed to examine a decision handed down by the United States Supreme Court. We will not present the Brown et al. experiment; we will instead present the Court's concern, and suffice it to say that the data show the Court's suspicion to be correct.

What the Court was concerned about was the following situation: You are witness to a crime. Some time later, thanks to various clues, the police form a suspicion about who the culprit is. The police bring you a photograph of this person and ask if this was the perpetrator of the crime, and you indicate that this photograph does indeed show the perpetrator. Your identification in this situation is not persuasive as evidence. After all, the police showed you only one photograph; perhaps you are so eager to see the perpetrator caught that you will be strongly inclined to say yes no matter who the photo shows. Perhaps the photo shows someone similar to the real culprit. If the culprit and the person in the photo were seen side-by-side, you might easily detect which is which, but, seeing this single photo in isolation, you might be confused. A fairer test would be the police lineup, in which you view several similar people and pick out the one that you believe was the perpetrator. That's exactly what happens next: Based on your positive identification of the photograph, the police arrange a lineup, and now you make what seems to be a fairer identification.

The worry about this procedure should be obvious to you, given the parallel with Jacoby's study. At the time of the lineup, we are supposing the eyewitness to be saying, "Yes, I remember seeing the fourth person from the left at the time of the crime." What the eyewitness may instead be (covertly) saying is, "The fourth person from the left looks highly familiar; I infer that this is the person from the crime." In our terms, the implicit memory is detected, that is, the person is registered as being somehow special. This feeling is then attributed to a previous encounter. This is a reasonable inference, given the circumstances. But, of course, the implicit memory may actually be coming from a different source: The person might look familiar because his was the photograph seen earlier. In this case, the eyewitness is correct about the familiarity, but is drawing the wrong inference. Given this possibility, the Supreme Court rejected identifications done in this way as being equivocal (*Simmons et al. v. United States*, 1968). And, as we indicated at the outset, the Brown et al. data indicate that this confusion about source can and does easily occur.

Apparently, implicit memory does influence a wide range of effects— from judgments about fame, to judgments about preference, to judgments about guilt. To mention another impact of implicit memory, we can test memory (indirectly) with a **lexical decision task**. In this task, subjects are shown strings of letters ("STAR," "LAMB," "HIRL"); the task is to indicate (by pressing one button or another) whether the string of letters is or is not a word in English. Lexical decisions are appreciably quicker if subjects have recently seen the test word, even if subjects have no (explicit) memory for the previous encounter (Oliphant, 1983).

Other experiments have shown that implicit memory can influence how subjects pronounce words (for example, how they pronounce "read"; see Jacoby & Witherspoon, 1982), how subjects complete word stems ("Name a word that begins "c-l-a . . ."; see Graf, Mandler & Haden, 1982), and how loud a noise seems to be (see Jacoby, Allan, Collins, & Larwill, 1988), to name just a few. (Richardson-Klavehn & Bjork, 1988, offer other tasks influenced by implicit memory. See also Brown & Murphy, 1989; Graf & Mandler, 1984; Reber & Allen, 1978; Schacter, 1987.)

Apparently, we are often influenced by specific episodes in our past, even when we are quite unaware of this influence. Or (as in the fame case, or the Supreme Court case) we are being influenced by one episode while we mistakenly believe we are being influenced by a totally different episode!

To return to our main agenda, recall that Mandler's proposal was that standard recognition tasks are in fact a "hybrid" task, with either familiarity or memory for source being sufficient to guide a response. We now have a more specific proposal about what familiarity amounts to—it comes from the feeling one gets from implicit memory. However, implicit memory by itself is not enough to produce a feeling of familiarity, and it is not enough for the judgment required in a recognition procedure. Instead, these depend both on implicit memory *and* on how subjects understand that implicit memory—specifically, whether they attribute the implicit memory to a specific prior episode. And, as we have seen, this step of attribution is far from infallible: It can fail altogether, as in the case of "I know her, but I can't figure out from where"; it can lead us to conclude mistakenly that a made-up name belongs to someone famous; or, in the case of the Supreme Court ruling, it could lead us to conclude that someone innocent is *in*famous.

WHAT IMPLICIT MEMORY IS

A very important idea has been developing over these last few pages. More and more evidence points to a distinction between two separate kinds of memory, two separate kinds of remembering. On the one hand, we can remember in the sense of consciously recollecting a prior encounter. This form of memory is not produced by exposure, but seems to depend on how we approach material at the time of learning. What we called "source memory" falls into this category; judgments of familiarity fall into this category when we make the conscious inference that the familiarity should be attributed to a specific prior encounter.

On the other hand, we can also remember in the sense of displaying some detectable influence of past experience, but with no conscious sense that we are remembering. In this type of remembering, we have no conscious recollection of the source of our knowledge. We may not even be aware that our familiarity comes from a specific prior exposure. Most extreme, we may have no suspicion that there *was* a prior exposure. Nonetheless, aware or not, our current actions and beliefs are being influenced by the prior exposure.

Implicit remembering may not seem like what we ordinarily mean by remembering. How can we speak of "remembering" when you have no idea or awareness that you are remembering, when you may even deny that you are displaying an effect of prior experience? Nonetheless, implicit memory plays an important part in our overall account of learning and memory. If we define learning by referring to the influence or the benefits of past experience, then implicit memory is clearly a case of learning. And while we have considered some cases in which implicit memory leads to memory errors (that is, cases with a misattribution of the implicit memory), it is certain that implicit memory also plays a central role in our correct use of the past. Often, the attribution is likely to be correct; in many cases (such as tachistoscopic tasks), the attribution (that is, coming up with the implicit memory's source) is simply irrelevant.

Interestingly, implicit learning may play a role in building the bridge between the human research that dominates the latter part of this book and the animal research that filled most of the earlier chapters. When we speak of animals learning or remembering the past, what we often mean is simply the animals' revealing the past's influence in their present actions. In humans, this is close to what we are now calling implicit learning. Explicit learning—being able to comment on the past's influence, describe the specific past event, and so on, being able to explain the familiarity, and being able, so to speak, to consciously relive that prior event—may conceivably be a uniquely human form of remembering, or at least a form of remembering found only in very complex organisms, perhaps apes and dolphins. Implicit learning is typically "memory without awareness" (this is the term used by Jacoby & Witherspoon, 1982); subjects in these studies usually have no idea they are displaying a strong influence of past exposures. Conversely, then, explicit learning might be defined as "memory with awareness." This tie to awareness of one's self, of the sources of one's actions and thoughts, may also be a signal that this is a very special form of learning, perhaps unique to humans. (For further discussion of these issues, see Fivush, 1988; Nelson, 1988; Oakley, 1983.)

This still leaves us to ask about the mechanisms that lie behind implicit memory, and here, in fact, there is some disagreement in the field. However, before we can turn to the theoretical claims, we need a few more facts about how implicit memory functions, and that is our next topic.

THE TIE BETWEEN IMPLICIT MEMORY
AND PERCEIVING

One striking feature of implicit memories is the degree to which these memories are tied to the *perceptual* form of the original event. Implicit memories seem to be **modality specific**. For example, implicit memory effects are much reduced if subjects *hear* the to-be-remembered material, but then *see* the test items (or vice versa). Conversely, implicit memory effects are maximized if we use the same sense modality for both the initial encounter with the stimulus and also the test items—that is, if subjects read both, or if they hear both (Jacoby & Witherspoon, 1982; Kirsner, Milech, & Standen, 1983; Roediger & Blaxton, 1987a, b). In fact, the evidence indicates that implicit memory effects are diminished if we even change the format of the materials—for example, presenting the to-be-remembered items in CAPITAL letters and the test items in small letters (Jacoby & Hayman, 1987; Jacoby & Witherspoon, 1982).

This pattern stands in contrast to most studies on explicit memory. With explicit memory, performance may be diminished somewhat if we change the form or format of the materials, but the impact of this change is small in comparison to that observed with implicit testing.

The importance of perceiving the to-be-remembered items is even clearer in another study by Jacoby (1983b). Subjects in this experiment were shown words in three different ways: In the "No Context" condition, subjects were shown a word without a context (subjects saw "XXXX, DARK" on the computer screen; subjects had to read "dark" aloud). In the "Context" condition, subjects saw the word with a context—the word was presented along with its antonym ("HOT, COLD"; subjects had to read "cold" aloud). In the "Generate" condition, subjects saw the antonym only ("LOW, ????") and had to say out loud what the target word was. Note that the Generate condition involves the most activity from the subject. The Context condition invites subjects to think about the word's meaning, and so seems to involve an intermediate level of activity. In the No Context condition, subjects have no reason or encouragement to think about the word's meaning, and are likely to read the word without thinking about it. This assessment of subjects' activity in each of the conditions is consistent with subjects' performance on a *direct* memory test (namely, a recognition test): Performance was best in this test if words had been presented in the Generate condition; performance was a little worse in the Context condition, and worst in the No Context condition (Figure 8–6).

It is possible, though, to assess these conditions in terms of what subjects see, rather than what they think about. Subjects obviously see the words in the No Context condition, and do not in the Generate condition. The Context condition again takes an intermediate position: Given the context, subjects do not need to look at the word with any great care. Having seen "hot," a quick glance will confirm what the next word ("cold") must be. That is, subjects can use their expectations (based on the antonym) to supplement what they see on the computer screen; we would say that they can use **concept-driven processing** (that is, using their knowledge and expectations) to supplement the **data-driven processing** (that is, their inspection of the input itself).

This assessment of subjects' perceptions of the words turns out to be consistent with the results of an *indirect* memory test. When subjects' memories were tested indirectly (via tachistoscopic identification), performance was best when words were viewed in the No Context condition, worse in the Context condition, and worst in the Generate condition. This is exactly the opposite of the pattern in the direct test!

The results seem to indicate that explicit memory is best created by

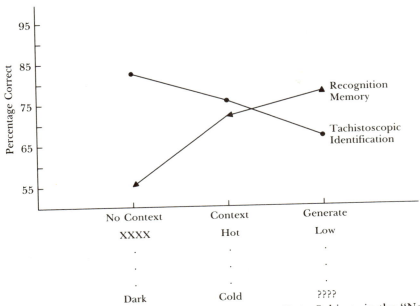

FIGURE 8–6. *Preparation for Direct and Indirect Memory Tests.* Subjects in the "No Context" condition saw words and read them aloud; subjects in the "Generate" condition had to generate the words (antonyms) on their own (and did not see them). Subjects in the "Context" condition saw the words, but had a meaningful context (antonyms) and so only had to glance at the words in order to identify them. The "Generate" condition was the best preparation for a direct test ("Are these the words you saw before?") but worst for an indirect text (tachistoscopic identification). (After Jacoby, 1983.)

concept-driven processing (that is, thinking about the words' meanings and associations, an idea that is quite consistent with Chapter 7). Implicit memory, on the other hand, seems to be created by data-driven processing, with close and careful seeing preferable to a quick glance.

WHAT TRIGGERS IMPLICIT MEMORY?

Our concern so far has been with what creates explicit and implicit memories. As it turns out, parallel claims can be made for what triggers an explicit or implicit memory. A recent experiment by Blaxton (1989; Roediger & Blaxton, 1987a, b) will bring the central points into view. The experiment is complicated, but makes several important points. The first part of Blaxton's procedure is similar to the experiment by Jacoby just described. Subjects were shown a series of words. Some words were read without context ("No Context" condition) and some were read with a context ("Context" condition). Once again, we assume that subjects must look closely at words in the first category, and will only glance at words in the second category. For still other words, subjects were shown only the context, and had to generate the word themselves ("Generate" condition). In this case, the word is not perceived, but is actively thought about.

The test phase of the experiment involved four different types of tests. Some subjects were asked simply to recall the words presented earlier (*free recall*). This is an obviously direct memory test (since it directs subjects to recall a particular prior episode), but provides no perceptual cues. Therefore, this test favors concept-driven processes. Other subjects were asked to recall the words presented earlier (again a direct test), but were given a perceptual cue (*cued recall*); this will bias things toward data-driven processes. For instance, subjects were asked whether any of the earlier words was similar in appearance to CHOPPER, with the target word being "copper." Subjects were explicitly told that the cue resembled the target word, but was distant in meaning from the target; this encouraged subjects to think only about perceptual features of the words.

The remaining two tests were indirect, but, again, one provided perceptual cues (data driven), and one did not (concept driven). The indirect tests, of course, made no mention that memory for the earlier materials was being tested. (By definition, this must be true for an indirect memory test.) Some subjects were told that they were taking a test of "general knowledge." For example, subjects were asked "What metal makes up 10% of yellow gold?" If subjects have an implicit memory for having recently read "copper," this should increase the likelihood of their responding "copper" (in this case, the correct answer). This procedure provides no perceptual cues for memory, and so is a concept-driven task. Finally, other subjects were given an indirect test but with a perceptual cue—a **word-fragment completion** test ("What's the first word that comes to mind beginning with the letters c-o-p . . . ?"). These various tests are summarized in Table 8–5.

The data, shown in Table 8–6, are straightforward. Of the three "study" conditions, the Generate condition turned out to be the best preparation for the free-recall test and for the general knowledge test. The No Context condition provided rather poor preparation for these two tests. In contrast, the No Context condition provided the best preparation for the cued-recall and word-fragment completion tests. Performance was worst in these two tests if subjects had encountered the words in the Generate condition.

As in Jacoby's (1983b) study, we are seeing a mirror-image pattern of results: Preparation that is best for some tests is worst for other tests, and vice versa. As in Jacoby's findings, a "standard" direct test (free recall) is helped most if subjects are actively engaged in thinking about the words' meanings when the words are first encountered (Generate condition). Also as in Jacoby's findings, a "standard" indirect test (word-fragment completion) is helped most if subjects just looked at the test words with some care.

Table 8–5. Tests Used in Blaxton's Procedure

Type of Test	Test Used	Example Question
Direct test, conceptual cue	Free recall	"What was on the list?"
Direct test, perceptual cue	Cued recall	"Was there a word on the list that resembles CHOPPER?"
Indirect test, conceptual cue	General knowledge	"What metal makes up 10% of yellow gold?"
Indirect test, perceptual cue	Word-fragment completion	"What's the first word that comes to mind beginning with the letters C-O-P . . . ?"

After Blaxton, 1989.

Table 8–6. Summary of Blaxton's Results: Percentage of Words Correctly Identified on Test

Type of Test	Study Condition		
	Generate	Context	No Context
Conceptually driven			
Free recall	30	16	19
General knowledge	50	38	33
Data driven			
Cued recall	34	40	45
Word-fragment completion	46	62	75

After Blaxton, 1989.

The key, though, lies in the other two conditions. If explicit memories are triggered by direct tests, then the pattern of results for cued recall should look similar to the pattern for free recall—namely, that performance will be best following the Generate condition and worst following the No Context condition. Likewise, if implicit memories are triggered by indirect tests, then the pattern for the general knowledge questions should follow the pattern for word-fragment completion: Performance should be best following the No Context condition and worst following the Generate condition.

This is not what the data show, however. The data instead suggest that there is a species of memory created by perceiving words (data-driven processing). This species of memory is well established by the No Context condition and poorly established by the Generate condition. Also, this species of memory is best revealed when we give subjects something to perceive at the time of test—either a word fragment to complete or a perceptual cue to guide their recall. Notice that one of these (word-fragment completion) is an indirect test and one (cued recall) is direct; apparently, direct versus indirect is not the critical factor here. Likewise, the data suggest that there is a separate species of memory created by thinking about words (concept-driven processing). This type of memory is well established by the Generate condition and poorly established by the No Context condition. This type of memory is best revealed when subjects are not thinking about perceptual cues at the time of test (free recall, a direct test, or the general knowledge test, an indirect test).

In the next section, we will consider how these data should be explained. Before we do that, let us reiterate the central findings:

1. Both Blaxton's and Jacoby's procedures show that implicit memories are created by carefully inspecting the to-be-remembered (TBR) material, rather than by thinking about the material. The opposite is true for explicit memories.

2. Many procedures have shown that implicit memories are tied to perception in another way: These memories are modality specific. That is, implicit memories show less of an influence on performance if the TBR material is presented visually and the test is auditory (or vice versa). In contrast, explicit memories show much smaller effects from these changes in sensory modality.

3. With regard to revealing implicit memories, the Blaxton data show that implicit memories are triggered if the test itself provides perceptual cues, rather than meaningful, conceptual cues. The opposite is true for explicit memories.

IMPLICIT MEMORY: A HYPOTHESIS

How should we think about the data just presented? We should begin by saying that this is a domain in which researchers disagree. The data themselves are clear, but there is still controversy about how these data should best be explained.

Some authors have proposed, to put it roughly, that explicit memories are memories for specific episodes, while implicit memories are memories of a more general sort. This is consistent with the claim that explicit memories are characterized by knowledge about a memory's source, while implicit memories are not. It is also consistent with the fact that explicit memories are usually revealed by direct memory tests (asking about a specific episode), while implicit memories are usually revealed by indirect tests (making no mention of an episode).

The best-known statement of this position comes from Endel Tulving, whose work we have met earlier in this chapter. (Related but different views have been offered by Squire & Cohen, 1984; Baddeley, 1982a, b.) Tulving (1972) proposed that, for many reasons, we need to distinguish between memory for specific episodes and memory for more general information (not tied to any particular episode). In the first category, which Tulving calls **episodic memory**, can be found your memory of your last birthday, or yesterday's dinner, or how you spent your last vacation. In the second category, **semantic memory**, is your memory that red is a color, that one buys food, not clothing, in restaurants, and so on. (We return to the contrast between episodic and semantic memory in Chapter 10.) On this view, explicit memories draw on episodic memory; implicit memories draw on semantic memory.

We believe, however, that this approach does not fit with the data reviewed in the previous section. Blaxton's data indicate that implicit memories can be evoked by direct tests, provided the cues are of the right sort. In addition, the tie between implicit memory and perception implies that implicit memory does preserve information about particular episodes. That is, subjects apparently do implicitly remember (for example) that the words were seen and not heard, were capitalized and not in small letters. We know that these factors have a strong influence on implicit memory performance. If subjects had no (implicit) memory for these superficial details, this influence could not be easily explained. Therefore, implicit memories do preserve details about specific episodes. For these reasons, then, we would argue that implicit memories are not any more abstract or general than explicit memories, and are not less well tied to specific episodes than explicit memories.

A different approach seems more promising. The proposal (Blaxton, 1989; Jacoby, 1988; Jacoby & Dallas, 1981; Roediger & Blaxton, 1987a, b) is this: When we encounter a stimulus or event, we usually identify it quickly and easily ("Oh, that's the word ALBATROSS"; "It's a picture of a chair"; "It's my cousin, Gladys"). This identification, even if quick, still requires some mental steps or processes. Critically, these processes are improved (or warmed up or strengthened) with practice. Therefore, having once perceived a stimulus, it will be easier to perceive that same stimulus in the future, because the relevant processes will now run more smoothly and efficiently.

An analogy to exercise may help here: Using a muscle makes that muscle stronger, and makes it easier to use that muscle in the future. Thus, the next time you need to use that muscle, you will enjoy the benefits of the earlier exercise. In addition, exercise produces specific effects: Exercising your legs makes your legs stronger, not your arms. In the same way, an opportunity to perceive a stimulus improves your ability to perceive that stimulus. To return to our earlier example, the next time you encounter a chair or the word "albatross" or a picture of your cousin Gladys, you will be able to identify them more quickly and easily, thanks to the earlier encounter. In Jacoby's terms, the experience of having identified a stimulus produces an increase in **perceptual fluency**, and this will make it easier to identify that stimulus the next time it's encountered.

The hypothesis we want to consider is this: Perhaps implicit memory may just be the name we give to this increase in perceptual fluency. That is, we should think about implicit memory as being more of a "skill" than a memory per se, a skill, as it turns out, of perceiving. How this skill will influence subjects' performance varies from task to task. For some tasks, the increase in perceptual fluency is enough to improve subjects' performance. Specifically, tasks that simply require identification will be facilitated by increased fluency. (Jacoby & Dallas, 1981, refer to these tasks as "perceptual identification" tasks, to emphasize that what is at stake in this identification is merely labeling what the thing before you is—a chair or the word "apple" or whatever.) A tachistoscopic recognition task, such as the one used by Jacoby and Dallas, would be an example of this kind of task.

For other tasks, an increase in perceptual fluency will not be enough to change performance. In addition, subjects must attribute the fluency to the correct source. This assumes subjects are sensitive to the degree of perceptual fluency—that is, realize that there is something to be attributed! When a subject detects an increase in fluency, however, she must make a decision about the source of the fluency—one knows that a stimulus "feels special," but needs to decide why this is. In a recognition test, subjects will say, "Yes, this stimulus was on the earlier list" only if they attribute the fluency to the earlier learning episode. (And, as we have seen, subjects may not attribute the fluency to that episode; they may instead attribute it to fame, or to the stimulus being particularly pretty, or whatever.)

Oddly enough, the opposite case can also occur: a decrease in perceptual fluency, rather than an increase. To arrange this, we would start with an objectively familiar stimulus and modify it slightly, to diminish the familiarity. Consider what happens when someone you know well changes his hairstyle, or gets new glasses, or shaves his beard. In such cases, one often has the uncomfortable feeling that something is new or changed, but cannot figure out what! In our terms, there is a decrease in fluency, because the stimulus has in fact changed. This lack of fluency is detected, producing a "something is new" feeling. But the attribution step fails—one cannot identify what produced this feeling. This is the mirror image of the cases we have been considering, in which something "rings a bell" but one cannot say why.

If "implicit memory" is the name we give for increased perceptual fluency, then we must ask: When will this increase be detectable? The obvious answer is: at the next encounter with the relevant stimulus. By analogy, how does one discover that practice at tennis has improved one's tennis skill? Answer: by noting that one's current tennis performance is better than (more fluent than?) previous performance. One makes this discovery the next time one is on the tennis court. By the same token, if one has become more perceptually fluent with stimuli of a certain sort, this will come into play the next time stimuli of that sort are encountered.

This claim is, of course, consistent with Blaxton's experiment, described in the last section. In that experiment, implicit memories were created when subjects looked at (rather than thought about) the to-be-learned materials, and were revealed when subjects were shown perceptual cues in the test, whether the test was direct or indirect. This clearly fits with the hypothesis we are developing.

We again emphasize, though, that this is a controversial domain. Many in the field would endorse this "perceptual fluency" view (or a variation on it). Others, however, would offer different interpretations of implicit memory (see, for example, Baddeley, 1984; Cohen & Squire, 1980; Schacter, 1987; Tulving, 1986; for a review, see Richardson-Klavehn & Bjork, 1988). This is simply a new and fast-moving research area, and no consensus explanation has yet emerged.

Nonetheless, it should by now be extremely clear how we must answer the central question of this chapter, namely, whether we can separately discuss the process of "loading" memory (encoding) and the process of "unloading" memory (retrieval). Mere exposure to a stimulus is poor preparation for explicit remembering, but it is critical for implicit remembering. Deep or elaborative processing is critical for explicit, but irrelevant for implicit. Hence we will run into serious troubles if we try to speak simply of information being firmly or strongly encoded in memory, if we try to speak about what it is that optimally places information in memory. Instead, we need to speak about what it is that prepares the rememberer for recollection *of a certain sort.* This echoes and amplifies our conclusions from earlier in the chapter, from considerations of encoding specificity or retrieval hints: Learning and remembering play their roles as part of a complicated, integrated system.

ANOTHER LOOK AT AMNESIA: WHAT KIND OF MEMORY IS DISRUPTED?

In Chapter 7, we considered some of the classical data for Korsakoff's amnesia, typically defined as an anterograde amnesia and often described as showing a separation between short-term and long-term memory. Now, with a more sophisticated eye, we can return to the amnesia data with a critical question: It is clear from casual observation of the amnesiac that remembering is disrupted. But if we separate explicit and implicit remembering, we need to ask whether both of these are disrupted in the amnesiac. If it were the case that short-term and long-term memories were somehow separated, then no new information should enter long-term storage, and so both explicit and implicit remembering should suffer. As we will see, this is not the case.

One of the central observations on this point is in fact an old observation. In 1911, Edouard Claparède (1911/1951) reported the following incident: He was introduced to a young woman suffering from Korsakoff's amnesia, and he reached out to shake the patient's hand. Claparède had secretly positioned a pin in his own hand, so that when they clasped hands the patient received a painful pinprick. (It is worth mentioning that respect for patients' rights would prevent any modern physician from doing this experiment.) The next day, Claparède returned and reached to shake hands with the patient. Not surprisingly for a Korsakoff's amnesiac, the patient initially gave no indication that she recognized Claparède or remembered anything about the prior encounter. Nevertheless, when the time came to clasp hands, the patient at the last moment abruptly withdrew her hand, and would not shake hands with Claparède. Claparède asked her why this was, and, after some confusion, the patient simply said vaguely that "sometimes pins are hidden in people's hands."

One might suggest that this patient had no explicit recollection of the prior encounter. She did not volunteer a report on this encounter in explaining her strange refusal to shake hands; when questioned closely about the prior encounter, she indicated no knowledge of it. Nonetheless, some sort of memory was retained. Mysteriously, the patient knew about the previous day's mishap, but could not report on the knowledge. In some ways, she seemed not to know that she knew; she seemed to remember but not to know that she remembered!

As mentioned, for obvious ethical reasons Claparède's demonstration is not an experiment one would repeat over and over! However, other versions of this peculiar kind of remembering can be easily demonstrated in Korsakoff's patients. For example, the following experiment has been reported (Schacter, Tulving, & Wang, 1981). Korsakoff's amnesia patients were asked a series of trivia questions. For each question, possible answers were offered, and the patient had to choose which was the right answer. If the patient did not know the answer, he was told it, and then (unbeknownst to the subject) the question was replaced in the stack. As the game continued, the patient was again asked the same question, and this time was quite likely to get it right. Did the patient "remember" the trial from, say, twenty minutes earlier? We would expect not in an amnesia patient, and, indeed, the patients were consistently unable to explain why their answers were correct. They did not say "I know because I met this item just twenty minutes ago." Instead, they were likely to say things like "I read about it somewhere" or "My sister once told me about it." Patients do seem to retain something about the prior encounter. In our new language, there seems to be an implicit memory of the prior encounter. What is missing is the attribution of this implicit memory to a specific episode. The correct item "rings a bell," as we say, but patients cannot identify the source of this feeling. Patients can pick out the correct response as being in some way special, but consistently fail to recall the prior encounter in any conscious way.

In fact, a great many results indicate that Korsakoff's amnesiacs suffer a disruption of explicit remembering, not implicit (e.g., Cohen & Squire, 1980; Graf & Schacter, 1985; Moscovitch, 1982; Kinsbourne & Wood, 1975; Schacter & Tulving, 1982a, b; Warrington & Weiskrantz, 1978). To take just one more example, in another experiment (Johnson, Kim, & Risse, 1985) Korsakoff's amnesiacs heard a series of brief melodies. Some time later, they were presented with a new series and told that some of the tunes in the second batch were repeats from the earlier presentation. The amnesiacs' assignment was to tell which were the repeats and which they were hearing for the first time. At the same time, the amnesiacs were asked to express their preferences among the tunes. As expected, the amnesiacs showed no evidence of remembering which of the tunes they had heard earlier, and their responses on this point were simply random. Remarkably, though, the amnesiacs uniformly preferred the tunes they had heard before—so they showed not an explicit memory, but an implicit memory. In this case, the implicit memory (just like in Zajonc's data, described earlier) led to the tunes having an enhanced aesthetic appeal.

It would appear that Korsakoff's amnesiacs seem to be showing a disruption of explicit memory while their implicit memory remains relatively intact. To return to our overarching message, if we ask "Have the amnesiacs lost their ability to learn?" our answer must begin, "Well, it depends on how the learning is to be tested . . ."

The last few sections have raised a host of questions: What are the limits of this unconscious knowing evident in implicit memory? How does it influence us, in addition to the ways we have seen? When we guess about things that we believe we do not know, are we drawing on implicit knowledge? Or is some guessing truly guessing? These questions have generated considerable excitement in the recent study of memory and, as we have seen, have led to some intriguing findings.

In addition, what about the main agenda of this chapter? One way to sum up where we are is to ask, given the full set of data, whether an "ideal" learning procedure can be formulated; that is, whether there is a "recipe" for good memory. In Chapter 7, we offered some steps toward such a "recipe"; for example, it helps to think about an event's meaning. We will consider some further, related principles in the next chapter. But it is easy to find exceptions to such rules. It is easy to arrange the circumstances of a memory test to change what would have been a good learning strategy into a bad one, or vice versa.

Nonetheless, the results of both this chapter and the previous one do point toward a "preferred" way to learn. The key, quite simply, lies in diversity. Different preparations are optimal for different tests. If one knows the form of the test, or if one knows what cues will be available during the test, then one can adjust one's learning strategy appropriately. However, most often one cannot predict the test in these ways. Therefore, if one doesn't know whether it will be source memory or familiarity that will help later responding, one should prepare for both (by elaborating and by repetition, respectively). If one cannot predict how one will think about the material at the time of the test (whether the cues available at the test will involve meaning or sound), then one's best bet is to study the material by thinking about it in multiple ways. Remembering turns out to be complex enough to demand various and multiple forms of learning if a good memory is to be assured.

Summary

In this chapter, we have seen a clear pattern of interdependence between memory acquisition and memory retrieval. In study after study, learning that is good preparation for one type of memory test may not be good preparation for other tests; learning that is poor preparation for one type of test may be good preparation for other tests. This is evident, for example, in the phenomenon of encoding specificity. In encoding specificity experiments, subjects are led to understand the to-be-remembered material in one way during learning, but in another way at the time of test. This change in understanding causes subjects not to recognize the items in the test, and so subjects appear not to remember what they had previously learned. As we have seen, though, one can argue that subjects do remember what they learned, but what was learned (that is, what was actually recorded in memory) was the stimulus-as-it-was-understood, and not the stimulus itself.

A similar conclusion can be drawn from studies that manipulate the hints and retrieval cues available to subjects. If the hints lead subjects to think about a word's meaning at the time of learning, then memory performance will be best if subjects think about meaning at the time of the test. Likewise, if subjects are led to think about the word's sound during the learning phase, they will perform best if they are given a cue concerning the word's sound at the time of the test.

Finally, the same pattern emerges if we look at the physical circumstances of learning—either circumstances external to the learner or circumstances internal (such as intoxication or changes in mood). Once again, memory retention seems best if learning is tested under circumstances similar to the circumstances of learning. This phenomenon has been demonstrated in many ways, and is generally known as the phenomenon of state-dependent learning.

The most powerful demonstrations of the interrelation between acquisition and retrieval arise from the different procedures we can use to test memory. It appears that some forms of learning lead to good "source memory," that is, memory for the episode of learning itself. Other forms of learning lead to "familiarity" with the stimuli encountered during learning. Source memory seems to be maximized by what we earlier called elaborative rehearsal; source memory is good preparation for either a recall test or a recognition test. Familiarity, on the other hand, seems to be maximized by sheer exposure to the to-be-remembered materials, and is good preparation for recognition testing. Thus recognition appears to be a hybrid task: Recognition judgments can be made either on the basis of source memory or on the basis of familiarity.

Source memory plays a key role in so-called explicit memory, while familiarity is implicated in so-called implicit memory. Explicit memories are those typically accompanied by the conviction that one is actually remembering a specific prior episode; implicit memories are revealed when one's current behavior is influenced by some prior event, even if one has no conscious recollection of that prior event.

Implicit memories turn out to be quite modality specific. For example, implicit memory effects are much reduced if subjects hear the to-be-remembered material but then see the test items, or vice versa. In addition, implicit memories seem to be created when subjects actually view the to-be-remembered material; these memories seem not to be influenced by how subjects think about the to-be-remembered material during learning.

According to one explanation of implicit memory phenomena, subjects' "fluency" in recognizing a stimulus—essentially their skill in perceiving—is enhanced by contact with a stimulus. It is this skill that is labeled an implicit memory. Subjects seem able to discriminate whether a stimulus was perceived easily or not, and seek to attribute this fluency to some source. It is this step of attribution that causes implicit memories to have the diverse influences they do in different task settings.

We also examined evidence concerning the nature of clinical amnesias—specifically, Korsakoff's amnesia. The evidence indicates that Korsakoff's patients do perform reasonably well, despite their amnesia, if memory is tested indirectly. We concluded that it is explicit remembering that is disrupted in these amnesiacs, not implicit remembering.

9 The Role of Prior Knowledge in Learning

In Chapter 8, we saw that it is difficult to separate claims about learning from claims about memory retrieval: Learning that is a good preparation for some forms of retrieval may not be good preparation for other forms of retrieval. In this chapter, we pursue a related issue, namely, the difficulty of separating claims about learning from claims about what we already know. The key observation here was mentioned in Chapter 7: It is easier to learn new facts and new information in a domain that we already know. Once we know some chemistry, it is far easier to learn new facts about chemistry; a musician easily learns new facts about music; and so on.

This observation will be our central focus in this chapter. Our first order of business is to ask whether the observation is *correct*. Our next steps will be to ask why it is that prior knowledge helps us to learn, and what this tells us about the learning and remembering processes.

Organizing and Memorizing

In the next several pages, we will be considering two separate claims. Simply stated, they are: (1) The better we understand something, the better we remember it; (2) what we remember is the product of our interpretation, not the "raw" data themselves. As we will see, the first of these is clearly correct; the second has been somewhat controversial. We will also see that these two assertions will lead us back to familiar ground, as both claims fit nicely into the perspective we established in Chapters 7 and 8.

Much recent theorizing about memory echoes the content of two books published over 40 years ago. The first of these was by German psychologist George Katona, and is entitled *Organizing and Memorizing*. (The second, by a British psychologist named Frederick Bartlett, we will meet in a while.) Katona's central point was that the two processes named in the book's title are inseparable: We memorize well when we discover the order within material; likewise, if we find (or impose) an organization, we will easily remember.

Katona's book reports many experiments, but the most famous is this one. We ask subjects to learn the following string of digits:

$$1 \ 4 \ 9 \ 1 \ 6 \ 2 \ 5 \ 3 \ 6 \ 4 \ 9 \ 6 \ 4 \ 8 \ 1 \ 1 \ 0 \ 0 \ 1 \ 2 \ 1$$

The data follow a familiar pattern. Subjects remember well the first two or three digits (a primacy effect) and the last few (recency), but cannot easily remember the full list. We then point out to the subjects that the list follows a simple pattern. First, we add some punctuation:

$$1, \ 4, \ 9, \ 16, \ 25, \ 36, \ \ldots$$

In this form, you probably recognize the series as being $1^2, 2^2, 3^2, 4^2, 5^2, 6^2, \ldots 11^2$. Once subjects see this, the results are rather different. Subjects can now remember the entire list perfectly and, in fact, can remember the list even if we extend it ($\ldots 1 \ 4 \ 4 \ 1 \ 6 \ 9$).

You may very well object that this is a trick, not a fair test. Subjects at first were memorizing a list of 21 items, then they were asked to memorize only one item, namely, a rule. Of course, the second is easier. And once the rule was understood, subjects were not "remembering" the digits; they were generating them from the rule. It's not fair to compare this to the case in which they *really* memorized the digits.

On Katona's view, this is not an objection, this is the point. The only bit of confusion in the preceding paragraph is the notion of what it means to memorize something "really." In general, when we understand something, we find the principle or principles that hold it together, the rules that provide the unity beneath the diversity. If no organization can be found, we invent one, imposing an order on the materials. Once this is done, it's this organized "whole" that enters memory, an organized unit, rather than diverse and separate materials.

MNEMONICS

Evidence in support of this view can be found in the various techniques people have invented as means of "improving" their memories. People have been interested in such techniques for thousands of years. The "technology" of memory was discussed as early as ancient Greece, and the Greeks invented a variety of techniques for improving memory, techniques known as **mnemonic strategies**. There are actually many different mnemonic strategies, but most of them involve a straightforward key: Organization helps.

Let us take a concrete case. You want to remember a list of largely unrelated items, perhaps the entries on your shopping list, or a list of questions you want to ask when you next see your adviser, or something like that. You might try to remember this list using one of the so-called **peg-word systems**. Peg-word systems begin with a well-organized structure, such as this one:

One is a bun.
Two is a shoe.
Three is a tree.
Four is a door.
Five is a hive.
Six are sticks.
Seven is heaven.
Eight is a gate.
Nine is a line.
Ten is a hen.

Not great poetry, but highly memorable, since you already know the numbers, and the rhyme scheme makes the sentences easy to reconstruct (Bower, 1970; Higbee, 1977; Roediger, 1980). The rhymes provide ten "peg words"—bun, shoe, tree, and so on. To memorize, say, your topics for your adviser, form an association between each topic you wish to discuss and one of the peg words. Therefore, if you want to discuss your unhappiness with your chemistry class, you might form an association between chemistry and bun—you might, for example, form a mental image of a hamburger bun floating in an Erlenmeyer flask. If you also want to discuss possible graduate school plans, form an association between some aspect of those and shoe—perhaps you might think about how you hope to avoid paying your way in graduate school by selling shoes, and so on through the list. When the time comes to meet with your adviser, all you have to do is think through that silly rhyme again. When you think of "one is a bun," it is highly likely that the image of the flask (and therefore of chemistry lab) will come to mind. When you think of "two is a shoe," you'll remember the prospect of being a shoe salesperson, and so on.

In the next chapter, we will consider why these systems work. Our point for now, though, is simply that these systems do work. The ancient Greeks primarily used one such system, called the **method of loci**, to remember speeches they were to give in the Forum. In this method, the pegs are not words, but places. One thinks of a walk one often takes, and associates the to-be-remembered items with various conspicuous locations along the walk. Not only does this help in remembering the items, it also keeps them in proper sequence. Hundreds of variations of these systems are available; some are taught in self-help courses (you've probably seen the ads—"How to Improve Your Memory!"), some are presented by corporations as part of management training, and on and on. All employ the same basic scheme. To remember a list with no apparent organization, impose an organization on it by employing a skeleton or scaffold that is itself tightly organized. If firm associations can be made between the to-be-remembered material and the scaffold, then remembering is likely to succeed. (For further details, see Bower, 1972; Bower & Reitman, 1972; Christen & Bjork, 1976; Ross & Lawrence, 1968; Yates, 1966.)

RECALL AND CLUSTERING

We have now seen that one can improve memory by imposing order. This is clear in Katona's evidence; the imposition of order is also at the heart of peg-word systems. But you might object: These are tricks and unusual strategies one might employ, perhaps if especially motivated to remember. What do these have to do with "ordinary" remembering? In addition, we began by talking about the role of understanding in remembering, but we have instead been emphasizing the role of *organizing*. In this section, we deal with the first of these concerns; we then move on to the next.

It is easy to show that subjects spontaneously use organizing schemes to help them remember, without special instruction to do so and without extraordinary motivation. A lot of the evidence comes from experiments similar to those discussed in Chapter 7. Subjects are given lists of 25 to 35 words to learn; subjects hear the words once, and repeat them back immediately. It turns out that subjects' performance is considerably better if the words are not chosen completely at random, but fall into categories. Subjects will perform quite well, for example, with this list: apple, plum, cherry, pear, apricot, shoe, pants, shirt, belt, sofa, chair, . . . In addition, we do not have to present the list category by category. If we take the same items and scramble the sequence, the availability of a categorization scheme still seems to help subjects. In fact, if the items are scrambled together in presentation, they will be "unscrambled" when the subject reports them back. That is, we can present subjects with this list: apple, shoe, sofa, plum, cherry, chair, belt, . . . Subjects are likely to report back one category of items (perhaps the furniture), then pause, then report back one of the other categories, and so on. This highly reliable pattern is referred to as **clustering** in free recall. The recall is "free" since we have allowed the subjects to report back the items in any sequence they choose. (See Bousfield, 1953; Bower, Clark, Lesgold, & Winzenz, 1969; Cofer, Bruce, & Reicher, 1966.)

You might still object that these are artificial materials, since they fall so neatly into categories. Perhaps this by itself is what triggers a clustering strategy. That objection also quickly falls, through experiments on **subjective organization**. There are actually several ways to run these experiments (cf. Buschke, 1977; Tulving, 1962); here is one. Tulving presented subjects with a list to learn, as described already. In this experiment, though, there were no obvious categories of material in the list; the list was instead randomly chosen, with no apparent structure or order. Subjects were tested on this list three times. They were asked to report back the items immediately after the presentation, as is normal in these experiments. Some time later, subjects were tested a second time and asked to report as much as they could about the earlier-presented list. Then, after another delay, subjects were tested a third time on this same list.

Tulving reasoned that subjects were probably spontaneously organizing the list of randomly chosen words. With no obvious order in the list, the organization subjects would choose would be idiosyncratic, with each subject finding his or her own pattern. We could nonetheless find out how successful subjects had been in finding an organization by comparing the results of the first and second tests. We simply look at the sequence of report, and ask what items were reported close together and what items were not. If a subject has tightly organized the list, we might expect an absolutely identical order of report in the first two tests. If the subject has found no organization, there is no reason to expect the order of report on the second testing to match that of the first.

Tulving uses a statistical assessment of match between the orderings as a measurement of the degree of "subjective organization" that has been imposed by the rememberer on the list. If organization is critical for remembering, then we make the following prediction: The more agreement between the first order of report and the second, that is, the greater the degree of inferred subjective organization, the better subjects will do on the third, and final test. In short, the earlier stability of organization should pay off in better remembering. This is exactly what the data show. With no coaching, with no special instructions, and with materials that are deliberately randomly chosen, subjects seem to rely spontaneously on an organizational strategy, and the better they can organize, the better they can remember (cf. Bower, Clark, Lesgold, & Winzenz, 1969; Buschke, 1977; Mandler & Pearlstone, 1966).

Understanding and Memorizing

Once again, it is worth surveying where we are: Organizing material helps memory. If an organizational scheme is prominent in the to-be-remembered material, subjects will employ it. If a scheme is not prominent, subjects seem to find their own scheme; the more fully they can do this, the better memory will be. Finally, at least some organizational schemes clearly draw on understanding. To recode numbers into a number rule, one needs to understand some arithmetic; to cluster things into categories, one needs to know what those categories are; and so on. Yet this still leaves us far from arguing that memorizing is intimately tied up with understanding. Organizational schemes like the peg-word systems, for example, do not require any real understanding of the material being memorized. Hence our next step will be to look directly at the importance and the influence of understanding.

THE ROLE OF KNOWLEDGE IN UNDERSTANDING

Some of our discussion in Chapter 7 implied a simple conception of how new knowledge flows into the mind: Stimuli arrive, they are channeled through this or that process, interpreted, the interpretation is channeled to the next process, and so on. All of this sounds somewhat like a one-way street—earlier processes feed later ones. In the language we introduced in Chapter 8, this overemphasizes the "data-driven" processes (or **bottom-up processes**, as they are often called). Considerable evidence, however, indicates the importance of "concept-driven" processes (or **top-down processes**). That is, the individual's assumptions about meaning, beliefs about context, and prior knowledge all play a role in governing how stimuli are responded to, even at very early levels of processing.

Some of the best examples of concept-driven processing come from our ordinary understanding of language. Consider the following two sentences:

A. John wanted to take Bill to the movies, but he didn't have enough money.
B. Sally put the vase on the table, and it broke.

In Sentence A, *who* has insufficient money? In B, *what* broke? You would probably answer "John" and "the vase," for a simple reason: You bring to these sentences a wealth of prior knowledge, including who pays for whom in our culture when you "take someone to the movies," and including which is more easily broken, a vase or a table. But there's nothing rigid about these interpretations; things will go differently if we precede Sentence A with a little bit of context:

A'. John only socializes with rich people. It makes him feel important. Yesterday, John wanted to take Bill to the movies, but he didn't have enough money.

Now, "he" is interpreted as referring to Bill, not John. Likewise, Sentence B will be interpreted differently in this case:

B'. Sally has just gone to the cellar seeking a hammer and nails; she had put the vase on the table, and it broke.

Thanks to one's knowledge in each of these cases, one draws different inferences about the pronouns. And that is the point: One's advance knowledge is clearly influencing how the sentences are understood.

This point is by no means limited to pronouns. Consider this little story (adopted from Charniak, 1972):

Betsy wanted to bring Jacob a present. She shook her piggy bank. It made no sound. She went to look for her mother.

No one has any trouble understanding this tale, but reflect for a moment on how this is possible. We understand even this simple tale by virtue of our also knowing:

1. The things one gives as presents are often things bought for the occasion, rather than things already owned. Otherwise, why did Betsy go to her piggy bank at all? (Surely you did not think she intended to give the piggy bank as the present, or its contents!)

2. Money is kept in piggy banks. This money is usually coins. One often does not keep track of how much money is in the bank, and one cannot simply look into a piggy bank to learn its contents. Without all of these facts, how could we explain why Betsy *shook* the bank?

3. Piggy banks are made out of hard material. Coins make noise when they contact hard material. Otherwise, why would it be informative that the bank made no sound?

By now the point is clear: The story is comprehensible, indeed, it is coherent, only because of the knowledge we bring to it. Without this knowledge, someone from another culture or a computer would be unable to see why the second sentence of the story is a logical sequel to the first, why the third sentence conveys information, and so on.

There is an obvious but important moral to all of this: The world as we experience it and understand it is not merely a function of the objective events in the world, of the physical stimuli that reach us. Instead, the world as we experience it represents the joint contributions of information from the world and information we supply.

HOW KNOWLEDGE RESHAPES INPUT

Not only does our knowledge supplement the input, it actually can reshape the input. This is true, for example, in our assigning meaning to ambiguous stimuli (such as the pronouns in Sentences A and B); likewise it influences how you interpret the letters in Figure 9–1. But these effects are not limited to cases of ambiguous input. Consider the familiar task of proofreading one's own writing, to correct spelling or grammatical errors. As you no doubt realize, this is not an easy thing to do—one often misses words that are clearly misspelled. Everything in the sentence "looks right," but some other reader (for example, your professor) spots the errors. Why is this? We won't pursue this issue in detail, but much evidence indicates that, in proofreading, we are simply seeing the consequence of a process that serves to make ordinary reading extremely efficient. In a nutshell, the idea is that our language is quite redundant—many of the letters of a wrd are completely predictable from contxt, and often the same is true for words within a sentnce. You can therefore gain efficiency in reading by exploiting this redundancy. There's simply no reason to take the time to look at every letter or every word. Since you can infer, for example, what must be the second letter in "letter," you can save time by only scanning the word and filling things in with an inference. The evidence indicates that this efficient strategy is exactly what a skilled reader does (Crowder, 1982).

This inference about letters in ordinary reading is so well practiced that it can easily go unnoticed. In essence, one fails to notice the difference between letters actually seen and letters only inferred. And this is the key to proofreading. The proofreader draws on the same skills that she uses in ordinary reading. This is an efficient strategy for most purposes, but it is also a bad strategy in reading for spelling errors. If one glances at only a few letters within a word, one might still be able to decide (from the context) what the word is, but one will miss a variety of spelling errors.

And this, at last, brings us back to our theme: We are active participants in the interpretation, identification, and understanding of the stimuli and events in the world. In the case of reading, a word's appearance is literally shaped by our expectations, expectations based on a combination of spelling rules, our implicit understanding of syntax, and the thread of the prose itself. Thanks to our prior knowledge, misspelled words "look right," because we are imposing our expectations on them.

All of this has clear implications for our overall study of memory. First, note what is included in the knowledge we all carry around with us: We seem to have an understanding of the rules of spelling and of syntax, and

FIGURE 9–1. *Context Influences Perception.* One is influenced by the fact that THE is a commonly observed sequence of letters; TAE is not. Likewise, CAT is often encountered; CHT is not. Given this knowledge, one is likely to read this sequence as THE CAT, reading the middle symbol as an "H" in one case and as an "A" in the other. [After Selfridge, 1955 © 1955 IRE (now, IEEE)]

knowledge about social relations (needed for understanding Sentence A, above), and about piggy banks, and so on. In each case, this is knowledge that we have at some point learned, and knowledge that must reside in memory. To say the least, our storehouse of information seems vast, and learning and memory seem correspondingly impressive.

In addition, all this information must be stored in some way that makes it easily accessible. One does not puzzle over what is kept in piggy banks; one does not pause to figure out why Betsy shook the bank. Whatever the means of locating this information in long-term memory, the process does not seem difficult. Given the scope of what is in LTM, and given how much is in this "warehouse," the efficiency of locating needed information is a remarkable achievement, and will require our attention.

It is the third point, though, that is our immediate concern. What does all this imply for the learning process? If we are active participants in understanding the stimuli and events of our world, what does this say about what we learn, and how well we learn? It is to this set of concerns that we now turn.

MEMORY AND UNDERSTANDING

We have already seen that memory is helped when we can find an organization in the to-be-remembered material or, if that is not possible, if we can create or impose an organization. It is correspondingly easy to show that memory is helped when we can understand the to-be-remembered material. Two things have already pointed us in this direction. First, we noted before that at least some ways that we might organize material require us to understand the material. Second, the benefits of understanding follow more or less directly from the levels-of-processing perspective discussed in Chapter 7. With tests of explicit memory (as discussed in Chapter 8), deep processing (thinking about meaning) helps memory, and so does elaborate processing (thinking about the material in lots of different ways). The best bet, then, would be to combine these: to think about the material's meaning, in lots of different ways. This clearly sounds like memory will be best when understanding is best.

There are many ways to show that this is true. In general, the research plan is this: One gives subjects a sentence or a paragraph to read, tests their comprehension, and then, some time later, tests their memory for the material. Comprehension can be probed by asking subjects questions about the material, or asking them to paraphrase the material, and so on. This is, of course, related to what we do in a typical levels-of-processing experiment. In those, we ask subjects to think about the material's meaning, and we essentially assume they will be able to do this. In a typical comprehension experiment, the material is difficult enough so that understanding, finding the material's meaning, is not guaranteed. This allows us to look at different degrees of success in understanding, and to ask how these influence memory.

The results are straightforward: If subjects understand a sentence or a paragraph, they will better remember it. If their paraphrase is more accurate or more complete, so will be their report from memory, whether we give the memory test 10 minutes later or 10 days later. If subjects could accurately answer questions immediately after reading the material, they will probably be able to remember the material after a delay. (For reviews of the relevant research, see Baddeley, 1976; Bransford, 1979.)

As a variation on this procedure, we can experimentally manipulate the hints or cues we give subjects about a passage, so that we can control whether understanding will or will not occur. In an often-quoted experiment by Bransford and Johnson (1972), for example, subjects read the passage shown below:

> The procedure is actually quite simple. First you arrange items into different groups. Of course one pile may be sufficient depending on how much there is to do. If you have to go somewhere else due to lack of facilities that is the next step; otherwise you are pretty well set. It is important not to overdo things. That is, it is better to do too few things at once than too many. In the short run, this may not seem important but complications can easily arise. A mistake can be expensive as well. At first, the whole procedure will seem complicated. Soon, however, it will become just another facet of life. It is difficult to foresee any end to the necessity for this task in the immediate future, but then, one never can tell. After the procedure is completed one arranges the materials into different groups again. Then they can be put into their appropriate places. Eventually they will be used once more and the whole cycle will then have to be repeated. However, that is part of life.

You are probably puzzled by this passage; so are most subjects. The story is easy to understand, though, if we give it a title: "Doing the Laundry." In the experiment, some subjects are given the title before reading the passage; others are not. The first group easily understands the passage, and is able to remember it after a delay. The second group, reading the same words, is not confronting a meaningful passage. That is, the physical stimulus is the same for the two groups, but the psychological stimulus is not. The second group fails to understand, and does poorly on the memory test.

Our examples so far have all concerned memory for verbal materials (see also Bransford & Franks, 1971; Sulin & Dooling, 1974). These effects are not limited, however, to experiments with sentences and stories. Consider, for example, the picture shown in Figure 9–2. This picture at first looks like a bunch of meaningless blotches; with some study, though, you may discover that a familiar object is depicted. Wiseman and Neisser (1974) tested subjects' memories for this picture. Consistent with what we have seen so far, subjects' memories were good if they understood the picture, and bad otherwise (see also Bower, Karlin, & Dueck, 1975; Mandler & Ritchey, 1977; Rubin & Kontis, 1983).

You may object to all these studies in the same way as you did to the

FIGURE 9–2. *Comprehension Also Aids Memory for Pictures.* Subjects who perceive this picture as a pattern of meaningless blotches are unlikely to remember the picture. Subjects who perceive the "hidden" form do remember the picture. (After Wiseman & Neisser, 1974.)

Katona number study: Subjects do not need to remember the words in the passage about laundry; in essence, they only need to remember the passage's title. Given their prior knowledge about how one washes clothes, that would almost be enough to allow them to reconstruct the passage at the time of the test. Likewise for pictorial materials: Remembering a one-word summary (for example, "dalmatian") might be enough to guide performance in the memory test. Our answer to these concerns is just as it was before: This is not an objection; this is instead a hypothesis about why understanding helps memory. But this leads us quickly to our next question: When we remember an understood passage, what is it we are remembering? Are we remembering the passage itself, or our understanding of it?

GIST, DISTORTIONS, AND SELECTIONS

Frederick Bartlett's book, *Remembering,* was published in 1932, but is in many ways still current. Bartlett gave his subjects passages to remember, and examined in detail not just how much or how well they remembered, but also what was remembered. Here is his most famous to-be-remembered passage, taken from the folklore of American Indians, and then a subject's memory for the passage after a 6-week delay.

The War of the Ghosts

One night two young men from Egulac went down to the river to hunt seals, and while they were there it became foggy and calm. Then they heard war-cries, and they thought: "Maybe this is a war-party." They escaped to the shore, and hid behind a log. Now canoes came up, and they heard the noise of paddles, and saw one canoe coming up to them. There were five men in the canoe, and they said:

"What do you think? We wish to take you along. We are going up the river to make war on the people."

One of the young men said: "I have no arrows."

"Arrows are in the canoe," they said.

"I will not go along. I might be killed. My relatives do not know where I have gone. But you," he said, turning to the other, "may go with them."

So one of the young men went, but the other returned home.

And the warriors went on up the river to a town on the other side of Kalama. The people came down to the water, and they began to fight, and many were killed. But presently the young man heard one of the warriors say: "Quick, let us go home: that Indian has been hit." Now he thought: "Oh, they are ghosts." He did not feel sick, but they said he had been shot.

So the canoes went back to Egulac, and the young man went ashore to his house, and made a fire. And he told everybody and said: "Behold I accompanied the ghosts, and we went to fight. Many of our fellows were killed, and many of those who attacked us were killed. They said I was hit, and I did not feel sick."

He told it all, and then he became quiet. When the sun rose he fell down. Something black came out of his mouth. His face became contorted. The people jumped up and cried.

He was dead.

And here is the subject's report of the passage:

The War of the Ghosts

Two youths went down to the river to fish for seals. They perceived, soon, coming down the river, a canoe with five warriors in it, and they were alarmed. But the warriors said: "We are friends. Come with us, for we are going to fight a battle."

The elder youth would not go, because he thought his relations would be anxious about him. The younger, however, went.

In the evening he returned from the battle, and he said that he had been wounded, but that he had felt no pain.

There had been a great fight and many had been slain on either side. He lit a fire and retired to rest in his hut. The next morning, when the neighbours came round to see how he was, they found him in a fever. And when he came out into the open at sunrise he fell down. The neighbours shrieked. He became livid and writhed upon the ground. Something black came out of his mouth, and he died. So the neighbours decided that he must have been to war with the ghosts.

Consider several things about this report. The subject does roughly remember the story. The memory for gist seems reasonably accurate.

Nonetheless, the details of the report depart in many regards from the original. Some amount of selection has occurred. Some of the details of the original story have simply disappeared; these tended to be details that made little sense to Bartlett's subjects. Other material is either added to the original or changed. Errors in which subjects add material to the story are called **intrusion errors**, and these, like the distortions and the omissions, are rather systematic. In the subjects' reports, aspects of the story that were unfamiliar were changed into aspects more familiar; steps of the story that seem inexplicable are supplemented to make the story seem more logical, more coherent.

All of these observations are common in Bartlett's data, as well as in many other experiments. A great deal of evidence indicates that memory for gist is excellent, and that memory for details is not. Moreover, understanding seems to guide what is remembered and what is not. Once more, some classical data come from experiments by Bransford and Johnson (1972, 1973). We ask subjects to read the passage shown below:

Watching a Peace March from the Fortieth Floor
The view was breathtaking. From the window one could see the crowd below. Everything looked extremely small from such a distance, but the colorful costumes could still be seen. Everyone seemed to be moving in one direction in an orderly fashion, and there seemed to be little children as well as adults. The landing was gentle, and luckily the atmosphere was such that no special suits had to be worn. At first there was a great deal of activity. Later, when the speeches started, the crowd quieted down. The man with the television camera took many shots of the setting and the crowd. Everyone was very friendly and seemed glad when the music started.

As you read this, one sentence ("The landing was gentle . . .") probably seemed out of place. If asked to recall this story later on, subjects are likely to do quite well, but to forget this sentence altogether. If subjects do remember this peculiar sentence, they are likely to remember it in a transformed manner: Perhaps they might remember reading "In the relaxed mood, no special clothing was required" (and omit the puzzling "landing").

Things are quite different if subjects read the same story but with a different title, namely, "Space Trip to an Inhabited Planet." In this situation, subjects will probably not be jarred by the "landing" sentence, are likely to remember it, and are *un*likely to transform it as just described.

What is going on here seems similar to what we saw in Bartlett's experiments. What fits with subjects' understanding is more likely to be remembered. What does not is likely either to be lost or to be transformed. If we can change subjects' understanding of the story, we are likely to change what they remember.

A similar point was made in an experiment by Anderson and Pichert (1978). In their study, subjects read a story about two boys playing in one of their homes. Half of the subjects were told to read the story and the description of the home pretending that they were potential homebuyers; half read the passage from the perspective of a potential burglar. The story had been constructed so that it included information particularly relevant to a burglar, and also information particularly useful for a potential buyer. When subjects' memories were tested, those reading from the "burglar" perspective recalled more of the burglar information; those reading from the "buyer" perspective recalled more of the information useful to a home buyer.

REMEMBERING THINGS THAT NEVER TOOK PLACE

Perhaps the most striking aspect of this pattern is the intrusion errors. Subjects in these memory experiments will often confidently claim to remember things that never happened, provided that the item in question fits with their understanding of the material. To take one last set of examples, consider these cases (from Johnson, Bransford, & Solomon, 1973). One group of subjects heard the following sentences:

> John was trying to fix the birdhouse. He was pounding the nail when his father came out to watch him and to help him do the work.

A second group heard these sentences:

> John was trying to fix the birdhouse. He was looking for the nail when his father came out to watch him and to help him do the work.

Some time later, subjects were asked whether this was among the sentences they heard:

> John was using the hammer to fix the birdhouse when his father came out to watch him and to help him do the work.

If the subjects were in the first group ("pounding the nail"), they were likely to say (incorrectly, but often confidently) that they had heard this sentence earlier. If the subjects were in the second group ("looking for the nail"), they were less likely to recall having heard the test sentence. In the one case, the sentence invited subjects to assume a hammer was part of the scene; after all, John had to have been using something to "pound the nail." That hammer seems to have become part of the remembered material. In the other case, the hammer was not suggested, and so does not become part of the remembered event (see also Bower, Black, & Turner, 1979).

Once again, we should emphasize that these effects are not limited to experiments with sentences or stories. In an experiment by Brewer and

Treyens (1981), subjects were asked to wait briefly in the experimenter's office, prior to the procedure's start. After 35 seconds, subjects were taken out of the room and told that there was no experimental procedure. The study instead concerned memory for the office in which they had briefly waited (Figure 9–3)! Subjects' memories were excellent for items consistent with their expectations: 29 of 30 subjects, for example, correctly remembered that the office had a chair and a desk. Subjects were less good at remembering items that were not so predictable. For example, only 8 of 30 subjects remembered the bulletin board. Subjects' performance was worst for items they expected, but did not see. Almost one-third of the subjects (9 of 30) remembered seeing books in the office, when, in fact, there was none! (Although see also Pezdek, Whetstone, Reynolds, Askari, & Dougherty, 1989.)

SCHEMA THEORY

Let us sum up where we have been so far. The process of understanding itself draws heavily on prior knowledge. This knowledge supplements and shapes what we actually hear or see or read; we seem not to realize how much we ourselves are contributing, nor do we easily detect it when our contribution actually distorts our impression of what is in front of our

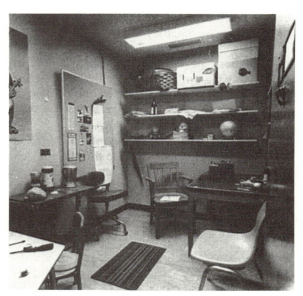

FIGURE 9–3. *The Office Used in the Brewer and Treyens Study.* No books were in view in this office, but subjects, biased by their expectations for what should be in a scholar's office, often remembered seeing books! (After Brewer & Treyens, 1981.)

eyes. In some cases, this can lead us to remember things that never happened.

The words of Bartlett (1932) serve us well here: We do not merely serve as passive recorders of the world. Instead, we are engaged in what Bartlett called "an effort after meaning." In our interactions with the world, we are constantly seeking to understand what is before us, constantly trying to make sense of what we hear and observe. It is immensely difficult, in fact, to be neutral about experience. In his book *Stranger in a Strange Land,* Robert Heinlein describes a character who is a "Fair Witness." One can ask a Fair Witness, "What color is that house over there?" and the reply will be, "The side that is facing this way appears to be white." Heinlein exploits the fact that this response seems unnatural— assuming far too little, interpreting far too little. Our point is the same: Ordinary experience incorporates a great deal of assumption and interpretation, as we make the "effort after meaning" and coherence.

In Bartlett's terms, what this effort seeks to accomplish is the fitting of the incoming material into a familiar conceptual scheme. Bartlett used the Greek word **schema** (and the plural schemata), and we will use these terms here. Schemata reflect the fact that there is a certain amount of redundancy in our experiences—virtually all kitchens have refrigerators; when one goes into a restaurant, one almost always eats something; when one pounds in a nail, one almost always uses a hammer; and so forth. A schema summarizes this redundancy, and so represents what it is that is generally true about kitchens, what it is that is generally true about eating in restaurants, and so on. Note that our schematic knowledge includes knowledge about places and things, and also about how events unfold (such as going to a restaurant). Many psychologists use the term **script** to refer to this dynamic knowledge about events, and use *schema* to refer to more static knowledge, such as that about places and things. (For further discussion of schemata and scripts, see Abelson, 1981; Friedman, 1979; Mandler, 1984; Rumelhart & Ortony, 1977; Schank, 1982; Schank & Abelson, 1977.)

Hence we might have a kitchen schema that specifies that a refrigerator is almost certain to be present, as is a stove; a coffeemaker is likely to be present; a dishwasher might be, but cannot be counted on; a sofa, on the other hand, is quite unlikely. Given all this, the next time one walks into a kitchen, one needs only to glance at the refrigerator. This is enough to tell you that you are indeed in a kitchen, and, based on this glance, you already know a great deal about the room. It is this kind of knowledge that would be helpful to you in understanding a description of a kitchen, in reading a story about a kitchen, and so on. That is, this is just the kind of knowledge that would help us in cases like the piggy-bank story discussed above, a story presumably drawing on something like a schema that captures what we know in general about children and their savings.

On this view, the world as we experience it is the "schematized" world. What it means to understand is to fit information into a schema, and, once this is done, our understanding consists of the information *and* this context. Information that does not fit in will be ignored or distorted to make it fit; information that is not present in the experience but which (according to the schema) should be present will be *assumed* as present. Even if you do not see the kitchen's refrigerator, you are likely to assume its presence (cf. Spiro, 1977; Zangwill, 1972).

Moreover, on Bartlett's view, the world as we remember it is also the "schematized" world. If some aspect of a situation is not relevant to our schema, we may not pay attention to it; as a result, this aspect of the situation will not be remembered. If certain facts do not fit with our schema, we will distort these facts to make them fit. Hence these facts will be misunderstood at the time of the experience, and will later on be misremembered. Likewise, aspects of the situation that we ourselves supplied will be remembered as present.

This last point actually fits with a theme of Chapter 8. In that chapter, we looked at many cases in which subjects experience a feeling of familiarity without being able to identify the source of the familiarity. We pointed out that we can sometimes be better at remembering that something is familiar than at remembering *why* it is familiar. This opens the door to errors about "source," and so-called **source confusion** can create the kinds of intrusion errors we have been considering. Subjects remember thinking about the hammer, for example, and mistakenly believe they thought about it because it was mentioned in the sentence. In memory, one's own contribution is inextricably interwoven with the facts actually presented by the world.

Not only do schemata play a key role in understanding and in learning, they also play a part when the time comes to remember what one has learned. In essence, one "reconstructs" according to one's schemata. One does not need to remember what was in the kitchen. One can simply remember that there was a kitchen, and then, based on schematic knowledge, one can recreate what objects or appliances were almost certainly present and which were almost certainly absent. In the same vein, one does not have to remember in detail what happened at one's last birthday party. This, too, is reconstructable from schematic knowledge, from a birthday *script.* If your birthday is of the traditional sort, you had a party with friends, cake was served, presents were brought and unwrapped, and so on. (Your birthday script may not match this traditional pattern, but, in that case, you could reconstruct according to your own script.) All this may go on quite unwittingly: One believes that one is remembering a specific episode when, in fact, one is actually reconstructing the episode by thinking about the more general case.

This clearly differs from the way that we usually conceive of memory. We tend to think of learning and remembering as being akin to storing and then retrieving books from a library. When we learn, it is as if the library acquired a new book. The book then sits on the shelf until we need it. Perhaps some erosion occurs (books fade with the passage of time, and so on). If the erosion does not occur, though, the book is still there when we need it, and so we can search for the book, with good fortune find it, and read what is written there.

The schema view is different from this conception. Rather than recording the data into memory, the claim is that we record primarily that which fits with our expectations and prior knowledge. That is, we record the *gist* of our experiences. When the time comes to remember, we do not retrieve information from the library but instead reconstruct how we believe the past to have been, fleshing out the remembered gist, guided by our present beliefs and prejudices. In short, we rewrite history to make it consistent with what we now think (see, for example, Spiro, 1977, 1980a,b).

A great deal of evidence fits within this theoretical framework. All of the evidence surveyed so far in this chapter clearly points this way; so does much of the evidence presented in Chapter 7. The evidence of Chapter 8 also blends in smoothly: We have already noted that source confusion will contribute to the likelihood of memory intrusions or, as they are sometimes called, **schematic errors**. Moreover, schema theory also provides an explanation of why memory will be best if the circumstances and understanding at time of learning match those at the time of test. If learning and recalling are both guided by schemata, then it will help if they are guided by the same schemata (although see Anderson & Pichert, 1978).

Is the Past Really "Lost"?

There is a good news and a bad news side to the view of memory we have been developing. On the good news side, a schematic organization to memory would, first of all, be very efficient. The world is a repetitive place, so there is usually no need to look at every detail, examine every aspect. We can achieve considerable savings of time and energy if we can exploit our prior experiences in the ways we have sketched. (This echoes our comments about proofreading, in which we suggested that inference from partial information is an essential aspect of smooth, fast, skilled reading.)

Second, and perhaps more important, a schematic organization to memory may be the key to solving a problem we mentioned briefly earlier on. Once we acknowledge how much information seems to be drawn on even in routine understanding, we need to consider how this information might be stored and organized to make it accessible when one needs it. We will return to this issue in Chapter 10, but for now the point simply is that a schematic organization of knowledge may help solve this problem, with new information immediately being "filed" or schematized into the existing system.

Now for the bad news. To put it badly, schemata convey a self-fulfilling quality to memory. What fits with our schemata will be noticed and remembered; what does not will be lost or distorted. We will reconstruct according to our prejudices, rather than remembering The Facts. Our memories for the objective facts of what actually occurred will be good only if our schemata happen to concur with the objective facts. And, of course, if our understanding of an event or scene is wrong or biased or incomplete, this view of memory implies that our memories will be, too.

On a schema-based view of memory, our prior knowledge both serves us and shelters us from the objective world, the world as we might describe it in the language of geometry or physics. Instead, the world we experience, the "psychologically real" world, is a world that reflects both information from the "outside" (what we earlier called data driven) and information from the "inside" (concept driven). Objective reality itself is never experienced, and never remembered. It is the "world-as-understood" that is experienced and remembered.

We have put this conception as strongly as possible, although many psychologists are adherents of even these very strong statements. As we indicated at the outset, though, we are now entering somewhat controversial ground. There is no quarrel about the data we have presented so far: It is easy to show the influence of prior knowledge and belief on what is remembered, on what is forgotten, and on what memory errors occur. The difficulty, though, comes when we try to specify exactly what lies behind these data.

In addition, one question we must answer is how to combine these findings revealing memory inaccuracy and distortion with a variety of other observations indicating the accuracy and completeness of memory. We know, just for one example, that actors learn the exact phrasing of their lines, and not just the gist of what they are to say. The actors are not, in other words, merely remembering the schematic content of their speeches; they are instead remembering the specific words in which this content is expressed. Is this just a special case, in individuals with special memory skills? Or is it the case that sometimes we do remember the objective facts, and not just our understanding of those facts? Likewise, there are many laboratory demonstrations of highly accurate memory, including memory for an event's details as well as its gist. (We turn to some of these demonstrations below.) How can we integrate these findings with the various schema findings already presented?

As it turns out, it is not difficult to see how observations like these can be integrated with the schema view. One might claim, as we just did, that much of what goes into memory is the world-as-understood, and that what happens in remembering is often a process of reconstruction. However, claiming that this is *often* true is obviously not the same as claiming that this is always true. Perhaps one does truly remember some aspects of the past. In fact, this seems necessary if we want to argue that reconstructions of the past are not pure fantasy or fiction. The truly remembered aspects of the past can provide the "seeds" around which one reconstructs, so that, even if reconstruction is central to the remembering process, the reconstruction is constrained by some historically correct aspects of the original event. In short, we do objectively remember some things, even if much of our remembering is reconstruction.

Alternatively, one might claim that memory is for the most part accurate and faithful to the objective facts, all contrary to Bartlett's suggestions. How, therefore, could we explain the schema effects we have just reviewed? All we need to argue is that memory is not systematically biased or schematic, but is, instead, simply less than perfect. That is, what we notice is less than 100% of what lies in front of our eyes; what we remember is less than 100% of what we once knew. This creates a gap-filled record, and the rememberer may well be aware of these gaps ("I remember that he was in a rush, but I don't remember why," "I remember that they did something before going to school, but I don't remember what," and so on). Now we just need one more step: Subjects do their best to fill in these gaps, in order to be able to give a full and coherent report of their earlier experience. Thus, on this view, reconstruction effects do occur in memory, and these may well be based on one's general knowledge of the world (in our examples, why people sometimes feel rushed, or what one does before school). Using this perspective, schema-based reconstruction is not the heart of remembering; it is instead the backup system, used only when the normally accurate, normally complete memory does not work.

These alternative conceptions differ in their emphases, but clearly have much in common. On both views, there is some genuine remembering; on both views, part of our knowledge of the past is based on after-the-fact reconstruction. Framed in this way, we probably do not want to ask "Is the schema view correct?" Instead, we want to ask how much we remember, and how much we reconstruct. What circumstances favor remembering, and what circumstances favor reconstruction? And last, but perhaps most important, how accurate is our remembering? The schema view leaves considerable room for memory inaccuracy, particularly with regard to the details of how an event unfolded, and we need to ask whether such inaccuracies really are observed.

REMEMBERING ACTUAL PHRASING VERSUS REMEMBERING "GIST"

On the schema view, what is placed in memory is subjects' schematized understanding of the world. For example, if subjects hear a sentence about John "pounding a nail," then it is their understanding of this sentence that is remembered. If subjects are later tested with paraphrases of this sentence ("was hammering the nail," "was hitting the nail with a hammer"), these will mesh with what is in memory just as well as the original sentence does.

As an alternative view, we might argue that what is placed in memory is indeed the actual words heard, the actual scenes witnessed. These may even still be in memory, perhaps in eroded form. Hence we might expect certain privileges to be associated with the actual words heard, in comparison to some inference from those words. If subjects really heard that John was "pounding the nail," then these exact words should be just a bit more familiar than the paraphrases of this sentence. The paraphrases fit with the gist of the sentence, but the original sentence has the additional advantage of having been experienced, of having been once placed in memory.

How would this memory for the original words manifest itself? Perhaps subjects might say "Yes, these were the words I heard" to all three versions of the phrase, but might respond a tiny bit *faster* for the original words. Or perhaps subjects might be a tiny bit more *confident* in their recognition of the original words; they might reveal this if we ask them directly, or they might reveal it if we urged them to say "Yes, this is familiar" *only if* they are quite certain about their judgment.

Experiments based on this kind of logic have been done with a variety of materials—sentences, like the one we have been using as our example, as well as paragraphs like the ones we considered earlier. For example, Potts (1972, 1974) had subjects memorize sentences like "The lion is to the left of the bear," "The lion is to the left of the giraffe," "The bear is to the left of the moose," and so on. In constructing these sentences, Potts began with a single left-to-right ordering—for example, an order of "lion, bear, giraffe, moose. . . ." All of the sentences presented to subjects fit with this ordering. No sentence conveys the entire ordering, since each sentence only mentions two of the animals in the series. However, the sentences were chosen so that the ordering could be reconstructed by integrating information from the full set of sentences. Subjects were then tested for their understanding of this left-to-right ordering, via a true–false test. For example, subjects might be presented with "The lion is to the left of the moose" and would have to answer "True" as quickly as possible.

We can compare the speed and accuracy of subjects' responses for two types of test sentences—ones that were actual duplicates of sentences presented in training, and ones that were compatible with the training but were being presented for the first time. That is, sentences in this latter category are consistent with the left-to-right ordering that lies behind the sentences; it just happens that sentences in this latter category were not among the sentences actually used in conveying this ordering. Potts found no advantage (in speed or accuracy) for the objectively familiar sentences. That is, in terms of subjects' memory, there is no difference between actually heard sentences and legitimate inferences from these sentences. This is consistent with the claim that what subjects remembered was an integrated understanding of the sentences, and not the sentences themselves.

In general, results indicate that, if tested soon after the to-be-remembered materials are presented, subjects do show a memory advantage for the exact stimulus, in comparison to paraphrases of the stimulus or to legitimate inferences from the stimulus information. After a small amount of time has elapsed, though, this advantage disappears. What subjects then seem to remember is their understanding of the stimulus materials. Sentences actually heard are compatible with this understanding, but so are paraphrases or inferences from these sentences. As a consequence, many studies have found no difference in memory performance between actually heard sentences and legitimate inferences from these sentences. Consistent with the schema view, it appears that the true, objective past is not what is remembered. What seems to be preserved is instead the past-as-understood, with no advantage for the exact event as it actually unfolded (Begg & Wickelgren, 1974; Bransford, Barclay, & Franks, 1972; Bransford & Franks, 1971; Brewer, 1977; Fischoff, 1977; Paris & Lindauer, 1976; Potts, 1973, 1976, 1977; Sachs, 1967; Sulin & Dooling, 1974; Thorndyke, 1976; but see also Alba & Hasher, 1983, for a critical review).

WHEN REMEMBERING IS ACCURATE

We have reviewed a number of cases in which memory is accurate with regard to the *gist* of an episode, but not with regard to the details of how the episode unfolded. Subjects seem to remember the meaning of the stories and sentences presented to them, but not the exact wording or format of these stimuli. In addition, we have considered several studies in which subjects' memories are poor when they cannot place the incoming material in a schematic frame (for example, Bartlett's ghost story, or the laundry story). Last but surely not least, we have seen evidence for "intrusion errors," when subjects "remember" things that were likely to have occurred, but which, in fact, did not occur. All of this is consistent with the idea that subjects assimilate episodes and stimuli into a schema or script, and then later on reconstruct the original materials based on this schematic knowledge.

However, it is not difficult to find experiments that yield a different pattern of results. For example, consider the studies showing subjects' poor recall for stories they did not understand—that is, stories for which no schema was available. We saw this in Bartlett's original data (with stories from another culture), as well as in the experiments by Bransford and Johnson (1972), and in a very early experiment by Dooling and Lachman (1971). However, Alba, Alexander, Hasher, and Caniglia (1981) have shown that subjects do seem to remember these very same materials if memory is tested via a recognition procedure, instead of recall. In their procedure, apparently, the original materials were preserved in memory, as reflected by recognition performance. Alba and

Hasher (1983) review a broad range of other, related cases, in which various changes in testing procedure can turn around the schema data.

Even with recall measures, at least some of the effects of schematic knowledge depend on subjects' strategies and understanding of their task. For example, Hasher and Griffin (1978) presented subjects with a story about a man walking through the woods. Subjects read the story together with an appropriate title (for example, "Going Hunting"). Some of the subjects were given this same title at the time of the recall test. Hasher and Griffin expected that this would encourage subjects to rely on the title itself in reconstructing the story. This, they predicted, would lead to many schematic errors. Their data confirm this prediction. Thus, when subjects have reason to believe their understanding of the story's gist is correct, they rely on this gist, and use it to reconstruct the story.

The main interest, however, lies in the experiment's other subjects. At the time of the recall test, these subjects were told that an error had occurred, and that they had been inadvertently given the wrong title for the story. They were given a new title ("An Escaped Convict") that was, in fact, consistent with the story's contents. Hasher and Griffin reasoned that these subjects, now convinced that their prior understanding of the story was incorrect, would try to set aside this understanding and to recall the exact story as it actually was presented. On this basis, Hasher and Griffin predicted that subjects in this group would recall the story accurately, and that is what the results show. Note that this implies, first, that subjects remember both the gist of the story and the actual sentences that made up the story. Second, these data also indicate that subjects have some degree of control over whether they will reconstruct a story or try to reproduce it faithfully.

Finally, other results speak directly to the overall accuracy of memory. Since schematic knowledge is general knowledge (about kitchens in general, about birthday parties in general), one should, on a schema-based view, be relatively poor in remembering the details of a specific kitchen one has entered, or a specific birthday party one has attended. We have seen several studies that confirm this prediction, but the overall pattern of evidence is mixed. For example, Bates, Masling, and Kintsch (1978) tested recognition memory for sentences that subjects had heard as part of a television soap opera. Subjects were presented with original sentences and also close paraphrases of the originals and were asked which of these they had actually heard. Subjects' performance in this test was surprisingly good: Subjects apparently remembered the exact wording of these sentences, and not just their gist.

Likewise, subjects also seem relatively good at remembering the locations of objects they have seen. As one interesting example, one sometimes has the feeling, after reading a book or an article, that one remembers seeing a certain sentence on the lower half of the right-hand page, or in the middle of the left-hand page, and so on. Several studies have shown that this feeling is often correct: If we check the accuracy of this memory, subjects' memories are often correct (Zechmeister & McKillip, 1972; Rothkopf, 1971).

What should we make of all this? We seem to be seeing a contradictory pattern. On the one hand, the influences of schematic knowledge are easy to document, as we saw in the prior sections. On the other hand, subjects also seem to remember more than we would expect on schematic grounds. They remember specific information about individual episodes; they remember even information that did not fit into a schema at the time of learning. As we indicated early on, it looks like both reconstruction and bona-fide remembering do take place.

WHEN DO WE REMEMBER, WHEN DO WE RECONSTRUCT?

All of this leads us to ask when schema effects occur, or, more realistically, what factors increase their likelihood and what factors instead favor genuine remembering. The available data indicate a simple pattern: Reconstruction is most likely to occur when there are gaps in the memory record. As it turns out, though, several different factors need to be considered in understanding when these gaps will occur. For example, one important factor depends on subjects' attention. Consider an experiment by Keenan, MacWhinney, and Mayhew (1977). They began their study by tape-recording a luncheon discussion by a group of psychology researchers. (The participants in the discussion knew they were being tape-recorded, but were not aware of the purpose.) One day later, subjects were given a recognition test for sentences uttered during this discussion; subjects had to choose between sentences actually spoken and close paraphrases of these sentences.

Critically, the sentences from the conversation had been categorized in terms of their "interactional content," that is, whether the sentence had been phrased in a way that was itself important for the conversation. A sentence with "high interactional content" is one in which the exact phrasing of the sentence conveys important information about the speaker's intentions or her relations to the listener. Such a sentence might be particularly rude, for example, or witty, or elegant.

Subjects were asked to classify the test sentences as either "old" (presented previously) or "new" (not presented previously). With the low-interactional sentences, subjects had considerable difficulty distinguishing actually spoken sentences from paraphrases or new-content sentences—that is, we get results consistent with the schema view (Table

9–1). With the high-interactional-content sentences, however, subjects were rather accurate in remembering exactly the phrasing of the earlier sentences.

In this study, it seems that subjects remembered exact phrasing of a sentence (contrary to the schema claims) when the phrasing caught their attention—that is, when the sentence was said in a particularly noteworthy way. Conversely, this implies that schema effects are most likely when we try to remember events or stimuli that we did not attend to closely at the time of learning. This is perhaps not surprising: Things that we notice are remembered; things that we do not notice are not remembered, leaving a gap in the memory record and inviting reconstruction (see also Bartlett, Till, & Levy, 1980; Loftus & Kallman, 1979; Nakamura, Graesser, Zimmerman, & Riha, 1985).

Another factor that invites reconstruction seems to be interference. That is, schema effects seem most easily demonstrated when subjects have a large quantity of similar materials to remember (e.g., Brewer, 1988). Under these circumstances, the to-be-remembered materials seem to "blur" together, making accurate memory less likely and reconstruction more likely. We will have more to say about interference effects in Chapter 13, when we discuss forgetting, as well as in the next section.

Yet another factor is the passage of time itself: Inferential errors like the ones we have described are most likely when much time passes between the original learning and the test (e.g., Anderson & Pichert, 1978; Dooling & Christiaansen, 1977; Spiro, 1977). The obvious interpretation of this is that, with the passage of time, less and less is remembered. Subjects then use a reconstruction process to "fill in" the gaps in their memories; with more time, there are more gaps, and so more reconstruction.

Thus schema effects seem to some extent predictable, although we must consider factors at the time of learning and also factors subsequent to the to-be-remembered event. We turn next to one last factor, which also depends on what happens subsequent to the to-be-remembered event. As it turns out, the data here are quite striking, but rather controversial.

Table 9–1. Percentage of "Old" Responses Given by Subjects (an "Old" Response Meaning the Sentence Had Been Heard Before)

	Target	Paraphrase of Target	New Content
High interactional content	56	18	2
Low interactional content	19	18	8

After Keenan, MacWhinney, & Mayhew, 1977.

ACCOMMODATIVE DISTORTION—DO WE REWRITE HISTORY?

Imagine that you experience an event and place in memory your understanding of what you have experienced, as schema theory claims. Imagine further that your understanding of the event subsequently changes—if, perhaps, you acquire further information. Now the time comes to remember. According to schema theory, you will reconstruct according to the information you currently have. You will therefore report the past according to your present view, and thus rewrite history (Bruner, 1986; Fischoff, 1977; Loftus, 1979; Neisser, 1982; Spiro, 1977, 1980a,b; Wood, 1978).

A number of results indicate that just this effect does occur. We have already seen one example related to this, when we talked about the Supreme Court ruling in Chapter 8 (Brown, Deffenbacher, & Sturgill, 1977; *Simmons et al. v. United States,* 1968). In that example, the event of seeing a photograph after a crime had occurred changed the eyewitness's recollection of who was present at the crime. In that case, what changed was not what subjects believed or understood about the prior event; what changed instead was what seemed familiar, and that in turn changed how the past was reconstructed.

Many of the examples relevant to this issue concern what happens when people are eyewitnesses to crime. The most famous research in this area has been done by Elizabeth Loftus and her colleagues (Loftus, 1975, 1979; Loftus, Miller, & Burns, 1978) and focuses in particular on the effects of "misleading" questions. Here is one of Loftus's experiments, by now something of a classic (Loftus & Palmer, 1974): Subjects watch a series of projected slides depicting an automobile collision. Some time later, subjects' memories are probed. Some of the subjects are asked "How fast were the cars going when they hit each other?" Other subjects are asked "How fast were the cars going when they smashed into each other?" The difference between these (hit versus smashed) is enough to bias subjects' estimates of speed—subjects in the first group estimate the speed to have been 34.0 mph; subjects in the second group estimate 40.8 mph. But what is critical comes next: One week later, subjects are asked whether or not they saw any broken glass in the slides they saw. In truth, none was visible. Subjects who were asked the "hit" question are less likely to remember any glass (14% say there was glass present) than subjects asked the "smashed" question (32%). Not only did the question directly bias their answer about speed, it also seems to have adjusted their memory, bringing it in line with this response.

Loftus has reported a number of variations on this basic experiment, offering many refinements and extensions to the basic findings. For example, in one remarkable experiment, Loftus showed subjects a video sequence in which a car ran past a stop sign, and then subsequently misled them by asking them about the car's speed when it passed a *yield* sign. When later asked about the scene, subjects remembered quite clearly having seen the (fictitious) yield sign, choosing it when given a choice between (a) stop, (b) yield, and (c) one-way. Loftus then told subjects directly that their response was incorrect, and asked them to choose their answer from the remaining two. Now subjects were equally likely to choose the (correct) stop sign and the (out-of-nowhere) one-way sign. Even given this "second-guess" option, subjects showed no signs of remembering the original event as it actually occurred!

One additional example indicates the breadth of these effects. Spiro (1977) presented subjects with descriptions like this one: "Bob and Margie are engaged to be married. Bob strongly desires not to have children." Half of the subjects were told that Margie shares this desire; the other subjects were told that Margie very much wants to have children. Near the end of the experiment, subjects were given further information. Half of each group were told that, in actuality, Margie and Bob did get married and are still happily together. Half of each group were told that Bob and Margie subsequently broke off their engagement. Thus we have some subjects for whom the initial account fits with the later information: Neither partner wants children and they stay together, or there is a conflict over children and they break up. For other subjects, the initial account does not fit so well with the later information (conflicting desires but stay together anyway; consonant desires but break up).

Spiro's subjects were later asked to recall the description of Bob and Margie, as accurately as they could. The data show that subjects' memories for the original materials were influenced by knowing Bob and Margie's current status. For those subjects believing that Bob and Margie stayed together, the conflict over children was remembered as being relatively minor. For those subjects believing that Bob and Margie eventually broke up, the conflict was remembered as being serious. In short, later information seemed to alter memory for earlier information. Knowing the story's end, subjects seem to misremember the story's beginning, to bring it better into line with the story's end!

In all these experiments, recollection of the past seems to be influenced by events that occur after the remembered event. The memory seems to be "updated," as we rewrite history to accommodate new information. That is why these errors are often referred to under the banner of **accommodative distortion**.

THE CONTROVERSY OVER "UPDATING"

The experiments described in the last section have grown increasingly controversial in the last few years. The central concerns were expressed by McCloskey and Zaragoza in 1985. The McCloskey and Zaragoza argument is essentially in two parts. First, they argued that the data of the previous section are actually ambiguous: There are several ways to explain the data, some of which do not involve memory updating. Therefore, we simply cannot draw conclusions from these data, since we do not know what lies behind them. Perhaps the data reveal updating or accommodative distortion, and perhaps they do not.

To see how this argument unfolds, let us consider a concrete case. An eyewitness to a theft observes a workman steal a calculator, pick up his hammer, and then leave the room. Later, the witness reads a printed account of the crime, but this account mentions that the worker picked up a *wrench* before leaving. Finally, the witness is asked, "In the original event, did you see the worker pick up a hammer or a wrench?" As we have seen, the witness is likely to report (incorrectly) seeing a wrench, that is, will report the misleading information, not the original.

This **misinformation effect** is not controversial; it has been reproduced in many laboratories, with many variations on the basic procedure. Loftus's original proposal was that the results reflect the fact that the original memory (for the hammer) has been replaced or "overwritten" by the subsequent misleading information (the wrench). This is the idea of memory updating.

McCloskey and Zaragoza, however, note that other explanations for misinformation effects are possible. For example, perhaps subjects never noticed the hammer in the first place, or perhaps they did notice it but forgot about it for reasons quite separate from the misleading information. Either of these will leave a gap in the memory record. When the misleading information arrives, there is nothing in memory to contradict it, and so the misleading information is accepted as true. On this view of things, no memory updating has taken place, since there was no memory for the hammer to be updated!

As a different account, perhaps subjects remember both the hammer and the wrench. When the test arrives, they reason this way: "I remember seeing a hammer, but I know I just read about a wrench. I guess my memory must therefore be wrong!"

There has come to be wide agreement that these various possibilities are compatible with the original misinformation results. (For still other possible explanations of these results, see Lindsay & Johnson, 1987.) The question we then need to ask is which of these possible mechanisms is the actual source of the data. We mentioned that the McCloskey and Zaragoza argument was in two parts; the second part involves their own experiments, attacking just this question. In particular, they seek to show that the accounts just described, and not memory updating, lie behind the misinformation effect.

In designing their own experiments, McCloskey and Zaragoza begin by noting that we get little information by asking subjects questions like "Did the worker pick up a hammer or a wrench?"—that is, a choice between the *original* information and the *misinformation.* As we have seen, there are several reasons why subjects might choose the misinformation alternative (the wrench in this case). As a consequence, if subjects do make this choice, we can conclude nothing about memory updating. McCloskey and Zaragoza therefore employ a different testing procedure: Subjects initially see (let us say) the workman pick up a hammer; they are later given misinformation that the workman picked up a wrench; then, in the test, the subjects are asked: "Did you see the worker pick up a hammer or a screwdriver?" That is, subjects are given a choice between the original information and a completely novel item.

If the misinformation actually erodes memory for the original materials, then misled subjects have had their memory of the hammer eroded, and should be less likely to choose "hammer" relative to control subjects who were not misled. However, this procedure should not be influenced by the other effects that misinformation might have. For example, consider a subject who remembers both seeing the hammer and also reading about the wrench. As we have already seen, this subject is likely to be confused by the "standard" test procedure ("was it a hammer or a wrench?") and, as a result, may perform poorly in this test. This same subject will not be confused by the McCloskey and Zaragoza modified test ("hammer or screwdriver?") and should choose correctly.

Therefore, if misinformation genuinely causes memory updating, then we should detect a misinformation effect in the McCloskey and Zaragoza procedure. If misinformation influences subjects in some other fashion, then we should not observe a misinformation effect in this procedure. As it turns out, McCloskey and Zaragoza do not find a misinformation effect in their modified test, arguing against the claim of memory updating.

While the McCloskey and Zaragoza data seem to indicate that memory updating does not occur, their data and those of subsequent studies remain the subject of debate. Although it is too soon to know how this debate will end, the current evidence indicates an intriguing conclusion: There is at least some support for each of the possible mechanisms described above. In some procedures, genuine memory updating does seem to occur. In other procedures, misinformation seems to have its effects when subjects remember both the original information and the misinformation, and become confused about which was which. Thus all of these mechanisms may potentially be operating simultaneously! (For more detailed discussion, see Belli, 1989; Loftus & Hoffman, 1989; McCloskey & Zaragoza, 1985; Tversky & Tuchin, 1989; Zaragoza & Koshmider, 1989; Zaragoza & McCloskey, 1989).

There are two morals to draw from this. First, on any of these accounts, subjects' remembering is not merely a matter of placing something in memory and then, later on, "opening" the relevant "file" and reading out its contents. In all the various hypotheses offered for the misinformation effect, subjects are integrating information, using new information to fill "gaps" in their recollection, making decisions about the sources of their information ("Did I see this or read it?"), and so on. These various accounts clearly share an emphasis on the active nature of remembering and on the complex interactions between memories for a specific episode and memories for other things that one knows!

Second, and most striking, subjects in these experiments seem to believe that they are reporting a faithful rendition of the originally experienced event. For example, subjects' confidence in their incorrect responses, responses influenced by the misleading information, can be quite high in these procedures. Thus, at the theoretical level, we may be uncertain about whether the misleading information "erases" or "replaces" earlier information, for reasons just explained. At the pragmatic level, though, what subjects report about an event is clearly influenced by the misleading information, with subjects seeming to be oblivious to the dynamic we have described. We can debate the mechanisms through which misinformation has its effect, but there is no doubt that misinformation does have a strong impact on how the past is described and, it seems, on how the past is remembered.

EVIDENCE THAT "IT'S ALL IN THERE SOMEWHERE"

Before we leave this section, we need to consider several other pieces of evidence that seem relevant to the questions under scrutiny. As it turns out, though, we will see that there is less to this evidence than meets the eye. We need to consider, first, reports of people who are hypnotized to remember "everything" about an event, including aspects of the event they did not even notice (much less think about and interpret) at the time. This hypnotized remembering seems to indicate that memory is actually full and detailed and complete, and these results seem incompatible with the claims we have made about reconstruction.

Many laboratory studies have questioned what hypnosis does to remembering, and the evidence is quite consistent: Hypnotized subjects who are instructed to remember do their very best to comply, and this means that they will give a full and detailed reporting of the target event. However, it is not the case that subjects remember more. Instead, they simply *say* more, in order to be cooperative. By saying more things, subjects will (perhaps just by chance) say some things that happen to be true. But most of the memory report by hypnotized subjects turns out not to be true, and, worse, the hypnotized subjects cannot tell you which of the reported details are correct and which are made up or are guesses. In other words, hypnosis does not improve memory; it just changes the willingness to talk (Dywan & Bowers, 1983; Hilgard, 1968; Smith, 1982). The often-made claim that hypnosis can reveal a rich, detailed, complete recollection of prior events is therefore simply false. These days, few courtrooms allow evidence based on hypnotically induced recollections.

What about cases of people receiving stimulation directly to the brain who often suddenly remember a scene out of childhood in clear and remarkable detail? These cases also seem to imply a remarkably complete and long-lasting memory and again seem incompatible with schema claims. As it turns out, though, the "brain-stimulation" work falls roughly the same way as the hypnosis data. The relevant data come from several neurosurgeons, but primarily from Wilder Penfield, who has done brain surgery on a large number of patients (Penfield & Roberts, 1959). This surgery is done under local anesthesia, so that the reports and judgments of the awake patient can be used to map the brain. (As different parts of the brain are mechanically pressed or are weakly stimulated, subjects will see light flashes or show bits of movement and so on. This functional mapping is then used as a means of guiding the necessary surgery. It is also important to mention that the brain itself does not have any sensitivity to these touches and pressures, so the patient feels no discomfort from this mechanical prodding.)

Some number of Penfield's patients do report vivid recollections in response to brain stimulation, although this number is quite small. These patients report immensely vivid reliving of prior experiences, often experiences from early on in life, and usually experiences that have not been remembered for many, many years. The trick, though, is that we have no way of knowing whether these are *memories.* These experiences might, for example, be hallucinations of some sort. Or, in fact, these experiences might be very vivid reconstructions. Because this evidence comes from an extreme circumstance, it has been immensely difficult to track down the historical facts to confirm (or disconfirm) these patients' recollections. Until this is done, we have no evidence that they are even remembering, much less remembering accurately, and so no view of memory can count on these observations as support. (See also Sacks, 1987, for similar cases, also without documentation about whether the remembering is bona fide.)

Thus neither the hypnosis data nor the brain stimulus work will serve as a rebuttal to the schema claims. Both of these sources of evidence seem, at first inspection, to imply strong claims about memory, something like "It's all in there somewhere, if only you knew where or how to look!" However, neither of these arguments turns out to be very persuasive when closely examined.

Putting the Pieces Together

In this chapter, we have seen two ways that learning and remembering are influenced by prior knowledge. On the one hand, memory is improved when we can understand incoming material, when we can see how the material meshes with things we already know. If we cannot find meaning or order in the input, we can often impose an order that we have created, and this too improves memory.

On the other hand, there is a sense in which prior knowledge also works against memory: We remember poorly that which we cannot understand. In some circumstances, we seem to distort things in memory, to bring them into line with our understanding. In other circumstances, we "remember" things that did not occur, if our understanding expects them to have occurred.

A study by Owens, Bower, and Black (1979) puts these points nicely in view. Half of the subjects in their experiment read the following passage:

Nancy arrived at the cocktail party. She looked round the room to see who was there. She went to talk with her professor. She felt she had to talk to him but was a little nervous about just what to say. A group of people started to play charades. Nancy went over and had some refreshments. The hors d'oeuvres were good but she wasn't interested in talking to the rest of the people at the party. After a while she decided she'd had enough and left the party.

The other half of the subjects read the same passage, but with a prologue that set the stage:

Nancy woke up feeling sick again and she wondered if she really were pregnant. How would she tell the professor she had been seeing? And the money was another problem.

All subjects were then given a recall test, in which they were asked to remember the sentences as exactly as they could. As can be seen in Table 9–2, subjects recalled more when they had a meaningful context for the story. At the same time, subjects also made five times as many intrusion errors in this condition, importing elements into the story that had never been mentioned.

This pattern is what we would expect on a schema view. The presence of a schema improves memory for materials that fit the schema, and works against memory for materials that do not fit. This means we will be less likely to remember elements that were present but incongruent with the schema, and more likely to add elements that were absent but congruent with the schema.

Table 9–2.   Number of Propositions Remembered by Subjects

	Theme Condition	Neutral Condition
Studied propositions (those in story)	29.2	20.2
Inferred propositions (those not in story)	15.2	3.7

After Owens, Bower, & Black, 1979.

However, as we have seen, other facts do not fit so well with the schema view. We sometimes remember the exact form and format of our experiences, and not just their schematic content. Schema-based memory errors appear in many experiments, but not all. These errors seem less likely with recognition procedures than with recall and less likely when there is a short delay between learning and test rather than a longer interval. Schema errors are also less likely when subjects specifically notice the inputs' format or phrasing, or when the to-be-learned materials are easily distinguishable from each other, minimizing interference.

All of this makes it clear that schemata and scripts do play a central role in remembering, but are not the whole story. To see how these pieces get put together, we must return to issues addressed very early in this chapter. When we read, or when we look at a picture or survey a scene, we do not scrutinize every detail. Research on subjects' eye movements shows that they look selectively, and fill in the rest with inference and supposition, presumably guided by schematic knowledge. This increases the likelihood of error (if the inferences are wrong), but gains two things: efficiency, and access to a wealth of knowledge with which to supplement the incoming information.

In these and many other cases, what we see and hear are supplemented by our interpretation and by what we expect, and what we expect is guided by our prior knowledge. The knowledge supplied by the observer is as much a part of the event as the sensory stimulation itself. It is the combination of the two that is experienced, and it is the experience that is recorded into memory. Thus we place in memory neither the "objective event" nor a "schematic event"; we remember something that seamlessly combines both of these.

The same words can be said about getting information *out* of memory. The data provided by memory itself are often selective, and we can fill in the gaps with plausible inference. Even when one's memory is relatively complete, it may be quicker, or less effortful, to make a plausible inference about the past, rather than seeking out the relevant memory (cf. Reder, 1982; Reder & Ross, 1983). For these reasons, retrieval from memory, just like the learning process itself, will be heavily supplemented by inference based on general knowledge.

Thus, at every step of the way, we "go beyond the information given" (a phrase coined by Jerome Bruner, 1957, 1973). This was the point of Figure 9–1; it was the point of our proofreading discussion; it is a prominent theme in memory as well. We remember well when we can make "connections" between incoming material and what we already know, but this often makes it difficult to keep separate what was the new information in the episode and what was supplied by us. As a result, memory will often be true to the facts, but memory errors will predictably occur.

WHY SHOULD MEMORY BE THIS WAY?

Why should we rely on a strategy that reliably leads to errors? The answer to this is in two parts: The gains from this strategy are considerable, and the costs are low. We have already mentioned some of the gains: If we assume that inferences can be made quickly and with low effort, we gain efficiency when we use inference in place of data gathering.

Why does efficiency matter? The world potentially provides us with an overabundance of information. There are an incredibly vast number of things in our environment that we could notice, and there are a vast number of things we could think about in response to the incoming information. Figure 9–4 is silly, but makes a profound point: We need

FIGURE 9–4. *The Importance of Schemata in Guiding Our Attention.* Our world is rich with information, far more information than we could use. Worse, much of this information is not useful for many of our purposes. We therefore need some means of making intelligent selections from the overall information available to us. Guidance of this sort seems to be exactly what this corporate spy is missing.

some guide or strategy that will protect us from this potential overload by helping us to focus on useful information, not irrelevances.

We have discussed how schemata supplement the input. Schemata also provide guides in selecting input. Our background knowledge for a situation seems literally to guide our eye movements when we examine a picture (e.g., Friedman, 1979) and in general to guide our attention. The Anderson and Pichert "home buyer versus burglar" experiment (p. 337) makes the same point. Schematic information keeps us informed about what is important in a situation and what is not, allowing us to focus on the useful information.

In all of these ways, we are helped by schemata in our intellectual commerce with the world. What about the errors and mistakes produced by schemata? One could argue, first, that these will be the exception, not the rule. After all, schemata capture what is regular and redundant about the world, that is, what is true more often than not. In addition, one might argue that schematic errors are rather unimportant errors; that is, in some ways, remembering particular events may be something of a luxury. If you are a wildebeest trying to remember where the nearest waterhole is, does it matter if you recall the particular occasion on which you visited the waterhole? Or does it instead matter just that you remember the location of the waterhole, how to get there, and so on? If you are a chimpanzee trying to remember which members of your troop are aggressive toward you, does it matter how you came to this belief? Or does it just matter that you get the facts right, no matter how you learned them? We would think that what matters for survival in these and other cases is generic knowledge, derived from the prior experiences but quite separate from the details of how the experiences actually unfolded.

If one takes this perspective, then the memory errors we have seen are not particularly consequential. We need to remember the meaning of our experiences; we need, in other words, to learn what lessons there are to be learned, but it may not matter for many purposes how those lessons were packaged. Indeed, in Chapter 13, when we discuss forgetting, we will argue that there are serious advantages to forgetting, and our logic will build on considerations like those just offered.

A similar argument can be made for the effects we labeled "accommodative distortion." Why should we want to remember what we once believed? Consider the fact that we tend not to save our rough drafts of papers. For example, the rough drafts of the chapter you are now reading are long gone. And there was no reason to keep them—the newer version is in many ways better, and neither you nor the authors need to recall what a less-good job we had once done. This "updating" of the records, keeping only the most current, most complete, best version, is a sensible thing in the case of rough drafts, and memory might well be the same. Note that this notion of updating puts these effects in a much more positive light, in contrast to speaking about "accommodative distortion."

Having made this argument, however, we immediately note that there are exceptions to it. An eyewitness in a courtroom, we would hope, is remembering the actual event, not the interpreted event. A nuclear engineer, we would hope, is remembering the exact instructions on how to run the reactor, not some distorted version of them. The patient answering the doctor's questions about symptoms ("Has the pain increased or decreased in the last week?") is also, we hope, remembering the actual events, and not reconstructing.

WHAT IS AN ACCURATE MEMORY?

Notice that there is ambiguity here about what we should mean by an "accurate" memory. For many purposes, accurate memory for the gist of an event is just what we want, even if this gist incorporates our interpretation of the event. For other purposes, an accurate memory is one that records the exact event, as it happened, with a minimum of our own interpretation.

This invites a list of questions. What determines which aspects of a scene we notice and remember and which aspects are "filled in" by plausible inference? We have mentioned some factors that tip the scales toward or away from schema influence; what other factors are there? Are there certain learning circumstances that favor a more "objective" memory record? Certain kinds of testing? How do people differ from one another with regard to remembering detail versus remembering gist?

These questions are obviously of importance to police investigators, and physicians, and college professors, all of whom have reason to care about eyewitnesses', patients', and students' memories. We have partial answers to these questions, as we have seen. But a full account simply awaits further data.

Let us close by circling back to the questions that opened this chapter. It is now clear that we cannot separate discussion of the learning process from a discussion of the learner. When one learns, one brings a wealth of information to bear on this process, supplementing, shaping, and selecting the input. The learner's prior knowledge is critical in determining whether materials will be remembered or not and in determining what will be included or excluded from the record.

Summary

Much of this chapter's discussion has focused on two claims: that the better we understand something, the better we remember it, and that what we remember is the product of our interpretation, not the raw data themselves. The experimental data indicate that the first of these claims is clearly correct; the second appears to capture some important truths, but at the same time to overstate the facts.

Evidence for the role of understanding in memorizing comes from many sources. Subjects can understand number series or word lists better when they can discover a pattern in the series or in the list. When there is no pattern, memory is improved by imposing an organizational scheme on the to-be-remembered materials; this is the heart of many "mnemonic" strategies, including the method of loci and various peg-word systems. The impact of these various strategies is visible in various ways: Subjects remember more of the material when they have discovered or imposed an organizational scheme; they also remember the material in a sequence governed by the organizational scheme.

Perhaps most important, subjects' memory accuracy for stories can be predicted on the basis of how fully and accurately subjects understood the stories when they first heard them. Stories that are better understood will be better remembered. Parts of the story that did not fit with the subjects' understanding will be omitted from memory or distorted to make them fit. "Intrusion errors" will occur as subjects add elements to the remembered story in order to make it a more coherent, more comprehensible account.

These data are often understood as reflecting the operation of memory "schemata." Subjects learn by assimilating new material into general patterns of knowledge or schemata. When trying to remember, subjects reconstruct what the past must have been by drawing on schematic knowledge. On this view, what is placed in memory is not the event as it occurred, but the event as it was understood, complete with whatever distortions and selections accompanied that understanding.

A variety of findings fit with this claim, including the fact that subjects are often unable to discriminate sentences they have actually heard before from sentences that are new but compatible in meaning with sentences they have heard before. However, while these results have been obtained in many studies, other procedures yield evidence of more accurate, more objective remembering.

Overall, the evidence indicates that some remembering is truly remembering of the past as it actually occurred. Other (seeming) remembering is reconstruction of what the past must have been, based on subjects' current knowledge and beliefs. Reconstruction effects seem most likely when there are gaps in the memory record, with these gaps created by factors such as (a) inattention to detail as the event was unfolding, (b) memory interference, if the subject is trying to remember just one of a series of similar events, and (c) the passage of time in between the to-be-remembered event and the effort at remembering. Reconstruction also seems evident if subjects learn new information about an event after the event has already occurred. Results in this latter category are reliable and robust, but there has been considerable controversy over how these results should be understood. In particular, it was initially argued that new information caused the erasure or destructive updating of prior memories; however, other mechanisms have been proposed that seem to account for the available data. At present, the status of destructive updating is unclear.

As we have seen, this general pattern of data reflects broad features of cognition. In many aspects of our commerce with the world, what we see and hear are supplemented by our interpretations and expectations. The fact that we "go beyond the information given" indicates that cognitive processes sacrifice some accuracy or objectivity, in order to gain efficiency. This efficiency, in turn, seems demanded by the overabundance of information available to us, both in the world and in our memories. Hence our strategy of supplementing memory with schematic knowledge may be an inevitable and broadly applicable feature of cognition.

PART 4

DESCRIBING

KNOWLEDGE

10 Concepts and Generic Knowledge

When we speak about memory, we usually mean memory for specific events in the past. We speak of remembering a birthday, or remembering a particular conversation, or remembering what we did on vacation, and so on. In these cases, one is remembering a particular episode, tied to a particular time and place, an event that is part of our personal history.

Much of our discussion so far has focused on this sort of memory. In many of the experiments we have reviewed, subjects have been asked directly about materials learned on this or that occasion; in Chapter 8, we called these tests of source memory. The "source" is obviously the occasion on which the information was acquired, so that these tasks clearly require memory for a specific occasion, a specific event.

In Chapter 9, we began to move away from these **episodic memories** (to use Tulving's term). We were led to the important contribution of a different sort of memory: In discussing how we understand simple sentences, it became clear that we supply important bits of knowledge that are not tied to any particular episode—we contribute knowledge about what various words mean, or about what things break more or less easily, or about what is kept in piggy banks, and so on. This information must be stored in the mind somehow, and therefore is memory of a sort, yet it is not in any obvious way memory for an episode or an occasion. Tulving (1983) has called such memories **semantic memories**, but we will use the more general term, **context-free** or **generic memories**, to emphasize that these memories are not tied to any particular event, to any particular time or place. They are memories for facts rather than memories for occasions; they are, so to speak, memories of timeless truths.

One way of phrasing the view of the schema theory, described in Chapter 9, is that much of our episodic memory may turn out to be only *apparently* episodic; it may instead be a construction based on a variety of context-free knowledge—knowledge about what kitchens do or do not contain, knowledge about how one builds a birdhouse, knowledge about how events unfold when one visits a restaurant, and so on. In a sense, the key idea of schema theory is that memories for the particular, when closely examined, often turn out to be memories for the generic.

Our primary agenda for this chapter is to consider what form this generic knowledge takes. What is generic information? What information and what facts are stored in the mind? Our initial focus will be on knowledge that we might call "conceptual" knowledge—the knowledge each of us has about the concepts we use all the time, concepts like "dog," and "chair," and "tree." These do not seem very glamorous or complicated, but, as we will see, describing these concepts turns out to be more difficult than one might initially guess.

Two points are worth making before we begin. First, one might reasonably ask whether one's understanding of the concept "dog" is a legitimate topic for a text on learning and memory. Surely this is not the sort of remembering one has in mind when one wishes for a better memory, nor is this the kind of thing we usually mean when we speak of our "storehouse" of memories. But, as we mentioned a moment ago, this kind of knowledge is clearly stored in the mind, and therefore is by definition a memory of a sort. In addition, our discussions of the last chapter should have made clear just how closely tied this kind of knowledge is to more episodic memories. For these reasons, this kind of conceptual knowledge plays a central part in our overall account and explanation of memory, and more than merits our attention in this chapter.

Second, it is clear that each of us understands and knows about a great diversity of concepts—concepts of things ("cat," "movie star," "sitting Supreme Court Justice"), about actions ("walking," "wanting," "waltzing"), about events ("birthday party," "trip to the zoo," "taking an examination"). It is not obvious at the outset that one theory, or one form of representation, will serve for this broad range of concepts. Nonetheless, we will proceed on the assumption that one theory will do the job; we will see how far we can get with this assumption.

Definitions: What Do We Know When We Know What a Dog Is?

We all obviously know what a dog is. If someone sends us to the pet shop to buy a dog, we are sure to succeed. If someone tells us that a particular disease is common among dogs, we know that our pet terrier is at risk, and so are the foxes in the zoo. We can answer questions about dogs, and on and on. Clearly, our store of remembered information contains knowledge that supports these not-very-exciting achievements. What is that knowledge?

The obvious answer to this is that we know something akin to a dictionary definition. That is, what we know is of the form: "A dog is the creature that is (a) mammalian, (b) has four legs, (c) barks, (d) wags its tail, (e) . . ." This definition (however it gets filled out) would presumably serve us well. When asked whether a candidate creature is a dog, we could use our definition as a checklist, scrutinizing the candidate for the various defining features. When told that "A dog is an animal," we would know that we had not learned anything new, since this is, as they say, true by definition. If we were asked what dogs, cats, and horses have in common, we could scan our definition of each looking for common elements, and so on.

All of this seems uncontroversial, and could presumably be broadened to account for more complicated knowledge, such as what a kitchen is, or what a schizophrenic is, or what an injustice is. The difficulty, however, comes when we try to spell out just how these terms are defined. The relevant argument here comes not from a psychologist, but from an important twentieth-century philosopher, Ludwig Wittgenstein. Wittgenstein (1953) noted that philosophers had been trying for thousands of years to define terms like "virtue" and "knowledge." There had been some success, inasmuch as various features had been identified as important aspects of these. However, even after thousands of years of careful thought, these terms were still without accepted, full definitions.

One might think that this is unsurprising, since after all these are subtle, philosophically rich terms, embedded in a complex web of human activities, and so naturally resistant to definition. However, Wittgenstein wondered if this really was the problem. He wondered in fact whether we could find definitions even for simple, ordinary terms, for example, the word "game."

What is a game? Consider, for example, the game of hide-and-seek. What makes hide-and-seek a game? Hide-and-seek (a) is an activity most often found in children, (b) is engaged in for fun, (c) has certain rules, (d) involves multiple people, (e) is in some ways competitive (that is, there are winners and losers), (f) is played during periods of leisure, separate from the routines of one's life. All these seem like plausible attributes of games, and so we seem well on our way to defining "game." But are these attributes really part of the definition of "game"? Consider (a) and (b): What about the Olympic games? The competitors in these games are not children, and runners in marathon races do not look like they're having a great deal of fun. Yet nonetheless we call the Olympics "games." Consider (d) and (e): What about card games played by one person? These are played alone, without competition, yet, again, we call these "games." Consider (f): What about professional golfers?

For virtually any characteristic of games, one can find an exception to the rule: an activity that we call a game that does not have that characteristic. And the same is true for most any concept: We might define "dog" in a way that includes four-leggedness, but what about a dog who has lost a limb in some accident? We might specify "communicates by barking" as part of the definition, but what about the African basenji, which has no bark? Quite consistently, our most common terms, terms denoting concepts that we use easily and often, resist being defined. When we do come up with a definition, it is all too easy to find exceptions to it.

To put this more precisely, what it means to "know a term" or "know a concept" is apparently not to "know a definition." Definitions can be found for some of our terms, but this is a separate matter from whether or not we, the "concept-holders," know and use these definitions. That is, there may be a definition for "dog," perhaps in terms of a particular genetic pattern. Nonetheless, this definition is unknown to most of the people who know the concept of dog, and who use the term "dog" correctly. If asked to define "dog," these concept-holders are unlikely to spell out the correct genetic pattern. Instead, they will list plausible dog features, but, once again, we can easily find exceptions to their proposed definitions.

FAMILY RESEMBLANCES

There is an obvious conclusion one might draw from these points. Perhaps what concept-holders have is not a firm, "works-every-time" definition, but instead something less rigid: Since exceptions to definitions seem so common, perhaps we need to devise definitions in a way that will allow us to handle the exceptions. Wittgenstein's proposal is roughly along these lines. His notion was that members of a category (all of the dogs, or all of the games) have a **family resemblance** to each other. Consider the ways that members of a family resemble each other: Some features are common in the family (a particular hair color, a particular shape of nose), but this does not mean that everyone in the family has these features. You might resemble your mother because you both have the same body type; you might resemble your sister because you both have the same eye shape (which your mother does not share); you might resemble your brother because of yet some other features. There may be no feature that we can point to as being definitive of a family's appearance. Nevertheless, members of the family do resemble each other, and we can identify family members when we meet them for the first time.

Likewise there may be no definition of categories like dog, because there may be no attributes that are shared by all dogs (so-called **necessary conditions**) and there may be no attributes that are unique to dogs (so-called **sufficient conditions**). This does not mean, however, that the category of "all dogs" is a random assembly. Instead, any two or three dogs we might consider are likely to have a great deal in common, just as you and your brother have a great deal in common, or your brother and your father. The specific communality may be a shifting one (just as the features you and your brother share may be different from the features shared by your brother and your father). Hence there will be resemblance among the members of the category; the only problem comes when we try to specify what it is that all members of the category (all family members) have in common. Possibly, there is nothing that all members of the set share, but the point of family resemblance is that there might still be common threads inside of the set—a thread that unites members A, B, and C of the family, a different thread that unites B, C, and D, a thread that unites C, D, and A, and so on (Figure 10–1).

There are a number of ways we might translate this notion into a psychological theory. One immensely influential translation was proposed by Eleanor Rosch, in the mid-1970s (Rosch, 1973, 1978; Rosch & Mervis, 1975; Rosch, Mervis, Gray, Johnson, & Boyes-Braem, 1976), and it is to her perspective that we now turn.

Prototypes: An Alternative to Definitions

One way to think about definitions is that they set the "boundaries" for a category: If a test case has such-and-such attributes, then it is "inside"

"Attention, everyone! I'd like to introduce the newest member of our family."

Drawing by Kaufman © 1977 The New Yorker Magazine, Inc.

FIGURE 10–1. *What Attributes Define a Chair?* Some chairs have four legs, some three, some none. Most chairs can be sat upon, but some are too small for sitting. It seems that chairs instead have a "family resemblance," and not a definition.

the category (*is* a dog, or *is* a game, and so on). If the test case fails this "test," that is, does not have the defining attributes, then it is outside the category, *not* a member of the set. (For a review of this "classical" view, see Smith, 1988; Smith & Medin, 1981.)

Prototype theory begins with a different tactic: Perhaps the best way to identify a category, to characterize a concept, is to specify the *center* of the category. Perhaps the concept of "dog" is not represented in the mind by a definition of a dog (the boundaries) but by some representation of the "ideal" dog, the **prototype** dog. In this view, judgments about dogs are made with reference to this ideal. Categorization, for example, involves a comparison between a test case (the furry creature currently before your eyes) and this ideal. If there is minimal similarity between these, then it is a good bet that the creature before you is not a dog; if there is considerable similarity, then you draw the opposite conclusion.

What is a prototype? For present purposes, we can think of a prototype as an "average" of the various category members one has encountered. Thus the prototype will be of average color, age, size, and so forth. When averaging is not appropriate, the prototype's attributes will match the most frequent attributes in the category. Thus the prototype for "family" will be of average age and average education level and average income, but will have 1 child, not (the average of) 1.19! (For some of the complexities in defining prototypes, see Armstrong, Gleitman, & Gleitman, 1983; Barsalou, 1987; Neuman, 1977.)

The suggestion, in essence, is that categories are represented in the mind by means of an example. We hasten to add, though, that the example is of a special sort, namely, one abstracted from the pattern of our experience. Notice, therefore, that different individuals will have different prototypes: For an American, for example, the prototypical "house" has one form; for someone from another continent, the prototype might be rather different.

On the prototype view, we were simply asking definitions to do the wrong job. Defining the set of all dogs (locating the boundaries) may be impossible except by appeal to some experts; defining the prototype dog, though, is entirely possible. The attributes or features mentioned in a definition were certainly not irrelevant; they are exactly the attributes that matter for deciding about "doghood." The problem, though, is that these attributes are just not shared by all dogs. Dogs that have many of these attributes will be quickly and easily recognized as being dogs; dogs that have fewer of these will probably cause us uncertainty about their identity.

FUZZY BOUNDARIES AND GRADED MEMBERSHIP

The hypothesis before us is this: What it means to "know" a concept, to represent a concept in the mind, is to represent a prototype for that concept; all judgments about the concept, all reasoning about the concept, are done with reference to this prototype. Consider therefore the simple task of categorization: As we sketched before, one might categorize objects by comparing them to prototypes stored in memory. Thus, in deciding that a particular ceramic vessel is a cup and not a bowl, you might compare the vessel to your cup prototype and to your bowl prototype. By discovering that the vessel is more similar to one than to the other, a decision is reached.

This sounds plausible enough, but has an odd implication. Imagine a range of vessels, each one further and further removed from the cup prototype. The first might, for example, be the shape and size of a teacup, and white in color. The second might be the same shape and size, but shocking pink in color. The third might be shocking pink, and twice the size of a normal teacup; the next might be all these things, and also made of lead, and so on. According to a definition view (the "classical" view), our cup definition (if we could find one) would tell us that some of these cases do count as cups, and others do not. That is all. The category of cups has a boundary somewhere, and each test case is either on one side of the boundary or the other. All of the cups, inside the boundary, are "equal citizens," each one fully and legitimately entitled to be called a cup. All of the non-cups are also "equal citizens," each one fully and equivalently not a cup. You are a cup, or you're not a cup. End of story.

The prototype view would allow us to say none of this. We could certainly say that some of the vessels under consideration are closer to the prototype than others, and that the ones closer to the prototype are more likely to be cups while the ones further from it are less likely. But at no point is there a boundary between "inside" the category and "outside." Instead, the category of cup has a **fuzzy boundary**, with no clear specification of membership and nonmembership. Congruent with this, not all cups are equal; instead, some are "cup-ier" than others, namely, the ones nearer the prototype.

To put this more generally, prototype-based categories will have both fuzzy boundaries and **graded membership**, with some dogs being "better" dogs than others, some plants being "better" plants than others, and on through the other categories in your repertoire. The graded-membership notion, therefore, is a striking and important implication of the prototype view.

TESTING THE PROTOTYPE NOTION

Consider the following task (after Smith, Rips, & Shoben, 1974): Subjects sit at a computer screen and are presented with a succession of sentences; the task is to indicate (by pressing the appropriate button) whether the sentences are true or false. The sentences are simple in form: "A sparrow is a bird." "A chair is furniture." "A collie is a cat." For these, of course, the subject would respond *true*, *true*, and *false*.

Subjects' speed in this **sentence-verification task** depends on several factors. Subjects are faster for true sentences than for false, faster for familiar categories, but, most important for our purposes, the speed of response varies from item to item within a category. For example, response times are longer for sentences like "A penguin is a bird" than for "A robin is a bird," longer for "An Afghan hound is a dog" than for "A German shepherd is a dog."

Why should this be? According to a prototype perspective, subjects make these judgments by comparing the thing mentioned (penguin, for example) to their prototype for that category (in this case, their bird prototype). When there is much similarity between the test case and the prototype, subjects can make their decisions more quickly; judgments about items more distant from the prototype take more time. Given the results, it seems that penguins and Afghans are more distant from their respective prototypes than are robins and German shepherds.

But this is a circular argument. We are concluding that penguins are more distant from the prototype because the sentence about penguins is verified more slowly. We are then turning around and arguing just the reverse: The sentence is verified more slowly because subjects perform this task by consulting their prototypes, and penguins are further from that prototype, slowing down the decision.

This draws us to an important point in the logic of testing the prototype view. This view makes many predictions for how efficiently or easily subjects will reason about cases close to their prototypes, and for how efficiently or easily subjects will reason about cases distant from the prototype. The problem, however, is that we do not know at the outset which cases are close to, and which distant from, the prototype. If we use the data to decide this, we cannot use the same data to support our perspective.

The escape from this circle is easy to find. We can use experiments like the sentence-verification task to identify which category members seem (on this basis) to be close to the prototype. We can then use this information to predict the results of other studies. For example, we can simply ask subjects to name as many birds as they can, or as many dogs (cf. Mervis, Catlin, & Rosch, 1976). On a prototype view, these mental categories are represented via a prototype. Therefore, in this task, subjects should begin their memory search for birds or dogs by locating the prototype, and then asking themselves (implicitly) what resembles this prototype; as a result, they will in essence start with the center of the category, and work their way outward from there. (We will have more to say about this sort of memory search in the next chapter.) Thus, birds close to the prototype should be mentioned first, birds further from the prototype later on. More concretely, the first birds to be mentioned in this **production task** should be the birds that yielded fast response times in the verification task; the birds mentioned later in production should have yielded slower response times in verification, and so on. And this is exactly what happens.

This sets the pattern of evidence for prototype theory: Over and over, in category after category, members of a category that are "privileged" on one task (for example, yield the fastest response times) turn out also to be privileged on other tasks (for example, are most likely to be mentioned). That is, various tasks **converge** in the sense that each task yields the same answer, each task picks out the same category members as special. (See Table 10–1 for an example with "fruit" and "bird" as categories, with subjects rating each item presented for how "typical" it was for that category.)

This notion of **converging evidence** provides two important benefits for us. First, as we indicated, it escapes the circle we mentioned just before. Second, and perhaps most important, consider what it *means* to study concepts: Concepts presumably constitute the knowledge we draw on for a variety of purposes—we use our "fish" concept to identify fish, to talk about fish, to draw inferences about fish, etc. In other words, a variety of tasks are presumably based on the same underlying conceptual knowledge. Therefore, if we are trying to study the concept of "fish" (or any other concept), we are less interested in how subjects do this or that particular task, and more interested in what these various tasks have in common; we are less interested in the processes or strategies involved in the task, and more interested in the knowledge that supports the task.

Table 10–1.   Subjects' Typicality Ratings for the Category "Fruit" and the Category "Bird"

Fruit	Rating	Bird	Rating
Apple	6.25	Robin	6.89
Peach	5.81	Bluebird	6.42
Pear	5.25	Seagull	6.26
Grape	5.13	Swallow	6.16
Strawberry	5.00	Falcon	5.74
Lemon	4.86	Mockingbird	5.47
Blueberry	4.56	Starling	5.16
Watermelon	4.06	Owl	5.00
Raisin	3.75	Vulture	4.84
Fig	3.38	Sandpiper	4.47
Coconut	3.06	Chicken	3.95
Pomegranate	2.50	Flamingo	3.37
Avocado	2.38	Albatross	3.32
Pumpkin	2.31	Penguin	2.63
Olive	2.25	Bat	1.53

Note: Ratings were made on a 7-point scale, 7 corresponding to the highest typicality.
After Malt & Smith, 1984.

Given this, the idea that we are getting data from a spectrum of tasks, and that these data are converging on the same answer, gives us reason to believe that we are not "merely" studying how subjects do a particular task. Instead, this idea gives us reason to believe that we are studying knowledge of a broadly useful, fundamental sort, exactly the kind of knowledge that we would expect concepts to provide.

THE CONVERGING EVIDENCE FOR PROTOTYPES

We have mentioned two lines of experiments with converging data patterns, but there are many more. We list six of these here, to give you a sense of the evidence:

1. *Sentence verification:* As indicated, items close to the prototype are more quickly identified as category members. This presumably reflects the fact that category membership is determined by assessing the similarity to the prototype (Rosch, Simpson, & Miller, 1976; although see Smith, 1978, Glass, Holyoak, & Kiger, 1979, McCloskey & Glucksberg, 1979, and Smith, Rips, & Shoblen, 1974, for some complications in the sentence-verification procedure).

2. *Production:* As indicated, items close to the prototype are the earliest and the most likely to be mentioned in a production task. This presumably reflects the fact that the memory search supporting this task begins with the prototype and "works outward" (Barsalou, 1983, 1985; Barsalou & Sewell, 1985; Mervis, Catlin, & Rosch, 1976).

3. *Picture identification:* This task is similar to the sentence-verification task. Subjects are told that they are about to see a picture that may or may not be a dog (for example); they are asked to hit a "yes" or "no" button as quickly as they can. Pictures of dogs similar to the prototype (for example, German shepherd or collie) are more quickly identified, while pictures of dogs less similar to the prototype (for example, Chihuahua or dachshund) are more slowly identified (Figure 10–2). The same result can be obtained with pictures of birds, or of furniture, and so forth (Rosch, Mervis, Gray, Johnson, & Boyes-Braem, 1976; Smith, Balzano, & Walker, 1978).

4. *Explicit judgments of category membership:* Rosch (1975; also Malt & Smith, 1984) explicitly asked subjects to judge how typical various category members were for the category. In these **typicality** studies, subjects are given instructions like

FIGURE 10–2. *Typicality Also Influences the Identification of Pictures.* American subjects are quicker in identifying pictures of German shepherds or collies as dogs than they are in identifying pictures of Chihuahuas or dachshunds. This is what one would expect if subjects make these identifications by comparing each picture to their mental prototype for the category "dog."

these: "We all know that some birds are birdier than others, some dogs are doggier than others, and so on. I'm going to present you with a list of birds or of dogs, and I want you to rate each one on the basis of how birdy or doggy it is." Subjects initially express some surprise and amusement at this task, but then are easily able to render judgments. Quite consistently, subjects rate instances as being very "birdy" or "doggy" when these instances are close to the prototype (as determined in the other tasks). Subjects rate instances as being less "birdy" or "doggy" when these are further from the prototype. This suggests that subjects perform this task by comparing the test item to the prototype.

5. *Induction:* An interesting result involves subjects' willingness to extrapolate from current information. In one study, subjects were told a new fact about robins and were willing to infer that the new fact would also be true for

ducks; if subjects were told a new fact about ducks, they would not extrapolate to robins (Rips, 1975). Apparently, subjects will make inferences from the typical to the whole category, but will not make inferences from the atypical to the category.

6.   *Tasks asking subjects to "think about" categories:* The procedure here has three steps in it (after Rosch, 1977). First, we simply ask subjects to make up sentences about a category. Thus, if the category were "birds," subjects might make up such profoundly interesting sentences as "I saw two birds in a tree" or "I like to feed birds in the park." Next, the experimenters rewrite these sentences, substituting for the category name the name of either a prototypical member of the category (for example, robin) or a not-so-prototypical member (for example, penguin). Thus, in our example, we would get "I like to feed robins in the park" and "I like to feed penguins in the park." Finally, we take these new, edited sentences to a different group of subjects, and ask this group to rate how silly or anomalous the sentences seem.

The hypothesis is that, when we ask subjects to think about a category, they are in fact thinking about the prototype for that category. Therefore, in making up the sentences, subjects will come up with statements appropriate for the prototype. The sentence's sensibility will thus be pretty much unchanged if we substitute a prototypical member for the category name, since that will be close to what the subject had in mind in the first place. Substituting a nonprototypical member, on the other hand, may yield an anomalous proposition. This is essentially what the data show. When the new group of subjects rates these sentences, they rate as being quite ordinary the sentences into which we have placed a prototypical case (for example, "I saw two robins in a tree") and reject as silly the sentences into which we have placed a nonprototypical case ("I saw two penguins in a tree").

Are Our Concepts Really Prototypes?

The evidence just considered shows that a spectrum of tasks reflects the "graded membership" of mental categories. Some members of the categories are "better" than others; the better members are recognized more readily, mentioned more often, judged more typical, and so on. This pattern is what we would expect if mental categories are represented via prototypes, and if these tasks are performed with this prototype as a reference point.

All this seems to indicate that prototypes, or something like them, play an important role in the mental representation of concepts. One might still ask, however, whether this is all there is. After all, it might be the case *both* that we use prototypes in many tasks and that there is more to conceptual knowledge than prototypes. That is, we might know about the "center" of the category, and also the category's boundaries. It's true, for example, that robins might strike us as being closer to the typical bird than penguins do, consistent with a prototype perspective. But we still believe with certainty that both robins and penguins are birds, as though the category of birds does have a clear boundary. On the prototype view, judgments about category membership depend on judgments about typicality, and so these two kinds of judgments (about typicality and boundaries) should be closely linked. Yet, with robins and penguins, we seem able to make independent assessments of category membership and typicality. And there is nothing special here about robins and penguins. Moby Dick was definitely not a typical whale, but he certainly was a whale; George Washington was not a typical American, but he was an American, and so on.

ODD NUMBER, EVEN NUMBER

Several lines of evidence tell us that typicality is not the same thing as category membership. For example, subjects judge whales to be more typical of the concept "fish" than sea lampreys are, even though they know that sea lampreys are fish and whales are not (McCloskey & Glucksberg, 1978)!

In a study by Armstrong, Gleitman, and Gleitman (1983), subjects were asked to do several of the concept tasks we have been discussing. For example, subjects were asked to offer explicit judgments about whether individuals were typical or not for their category (like judging how "doggy" a Chihuahua is). The twist, though, is that Armstrong et al. used categories for which there clearly is a definition—for example, the category "odd number." As a subject, therefore, you might be asked, "We all know that some numbers are odder than others. What I want you to do is to rate each of the numbers on this list for how good an example it is for the category 'odd.'" As you might imagine, subjects felt that this was a rather silly task. Nevertheless, subjects were able to render these judgments and, interestingly, were just as consistent with one another using these stimuli as they were with categories like "dog" and "bird" and "fruit" (Table 10-2).

The obvious response to this experiment is that subjects knew the

Table 10–2. Subjects' Typicality Ratings for
Well-Defined Categories

Even Number		Odd Number	
Stimulus	Typicality Rating	Stimulus	Typicality Rating
4	5.9	3	5.4
8	5.5	7	5.1
10	5.3	23	4.6
18	4.4	57	4.4
34	3.6	501	3.5
106	3.1	447	3.3

Note: Subjects rated each item for how "good an example" it was for its category. Ratings were on a 0 to 7 scale, with 7 meaning the item is a "very good example." Subjects rated some even numbers as being "better examples" of even numbers than others, although, mathematically, this is absurd: Either a number is even (divisible by 2 without a remainder) or it is not.
After Armstrong, Gleitman, & Gleitman, 1983.

definition of "odd number," but were somehow "playing along" in response to the experimenters' request. In fact, it is not difficult to figure out what subjects did to play along. Numbers like 7777 are "very odd," while numbers like 2467 are "less odd." It looks like subjects are basing these judgments on superficial grounds, even though they know that only the right-most digit is pertinent.

The results here carry several morals. First, the *presence* of "graded-membership" results cannot imply the *absence* of a firm definition for the category. In cases like "odd number," we have both: There is a definition, and yet the data clearly show graded membership. It is possible, therefore, that prototypes are an important part of conceptual knowledge but, perhaps, only part.

Second, the data carry the suggestion that prototypes may be getting at superficial characteristics of a category. It is perceptual characteristics, how the number looks, that seem to influence typicality judgments, and not the "deeper" characteristics that "really" matter for determining category membership.

Third, while the Armstrong et al. data might be read as undermining the prototype view, these data also convey the opposite message: Apparently, our ability to think in terms of typicality is so powerful that we can think in these terms even when this is not customary, not practiced, and not even legitimate. The ease and the consistency with which subjects judged the typicality of odd numbers, "overruling" what they really knew about "oddness," are themselves important. Concretely, one might interpret these facts as indicating that typicality may be a fundamental feature of the strategies we use in our intellectual commerce with the world. We will return to this point when we bring all these data together later in this chapter.

LEMONS AND COUNTERFEITS

Perhaps we should not generalize from the case of odd numbers. After all, mathematical or other technical terms might be special cases since definitions are available for these, while this is not an option for many other concepts. However, it is easy to show that the issue is a broad one, and that exemplariness or typicality is not the same as category membership. We will first make this point informally, by means of two examples, but we will see more evidence for this point as we proceed.

Consider a lemon. Paint the lemon with red and white stripes. Is it still a lemon? Most people believe that it is. Now inject the lemon with sugar water, so that it has a sweet taste. Then run over the lemon with a truck, so that it is flat like a pancake. What have we got at this point? Do we have a striped, artificially sweet, flattened lemon? Or do we have a non-lemon? Once again, most people still accept this poor, abused fruit as a lemon, but consider what this entails: We have taken several steps to make this object more and more distant from the prototype, but this seems not to shake our faith that the object remains nonetheless what it was—a lemon. To be sure, we have a not easily recognized lemon, an exceptional lemon, but still a lemon. If you think about what it is that qualifies this object for "lemonhood," you are likely to say something about the object's history, the fact that it grew on a lemon tree, is genetically a lemon, and so on. This is, we believe, an important observation, but we hold it to the side for a moment while we consider a different case.

With the lemon, category identity was preserved despite considerable distance from the prototype. Here is the opposite case. Consider a really perfect counterfeit $10 bill. This bill will be enormously similar to the prototype for a real $10 bill, yet we still count it as counterfeit, not real. Apparently, then, similarity to the prototype is not enough to qualify this bill for membership in the category of real money!

In fact, think about the category "perfect counterfeit." One can certainly imagine the prototype for this category, but, of course, the prototype would have to be very similar to the prototype for the category "real money." The obvious suggestion, therefore, is that there must be more to these categories than just the prototypes. If there weren't more, then we would often be confused in our thinking about real versus counterfeit bills, since the prototypes for these two (and therefore, on this view, the two concepts) would be so hard to distinguish. And yet, while we might be perceptually confused about this distinction, we certainly have no trouble remembering what is true of one of these categories and what is true of the other.

The critical difference between the real $10 bill and the counterfeit one is, of course, the history of each. After all, one of these was printed by the government in very special circumstances, and one was printed in a crook's basement. In addition, the counterfeit bill was probably printed with nefarious intentions (that is, was intended for use in the marketplace, not for playing Monopoly). We also know that one of these may have been given to us by a dishonest person (or someone who got the bill from a dishonest person); we make no such presumption for the other.

In both the lemon case and the counterfeit case, we see the separation of typicality (that is, closeness to the prototype) and category membership. The abused lemon is very different from a typical lemon, but is still a lemon. The counterfeit bill is very similar to a typical authentic bill, but is nonetheless not authentic. Thus one can have category membership without typicality, and typicality without category membership. Therefore, category membership must be based on something beyond typicality.

Of course, one could argue that the abused lemon does resemble the lemon prototype in one important regard: history. The abused lemon grew on a lemon tree, and so did the prototype lemon. But this will not help us here: Apparently, the abused lemon does have one point of resemblance to the prototype (history), but it has many points of difference (color, taste, shape). Thus the abused lemon is still rather far from being typical. And so typicality is not the same as category membership.

LESS SOPHISTICATED CONCEPT-USERS?

One might still worry about whether these are special cases. After all, we are all sophisticated concept-users. Maybe our examples, and maybe the Armstrong et al. procedure, all lead us to play with concepts in an unnatural way. It seems worth asking whether we can draw comparable claims by examining "ordinary" concepts and "ordinary" concept-holders.

Relevant evidence for this point comes from work by Keil (1986). Keil was particularly interested in how children come to have concepts, and what children's concepts do or do not include. For our purposes, this is ideal, since it will allow us to ask about concept-holders who are not "contaminated" by education in technical or specialized ways.

In one of Keil's studies, preschool children are asked what it is that makes something a "coffeepot" or a "raccoon" and so on. In one aspect of the procedure, the children are asked whether it would be possible to turn a toaster into a coffeepot. Children will often acknowledge that this may be possible. One would have to widen the holes in the top of the toaster, and fix things so that the water would not leak out of the bottom, and put in a place for the coffee grounds, etc. But it could be done. On the other hand, children will steadfastly deny that the same is true for a skunk and a raccoon. That is, if we dye the skunk's fur, teach it to climb trees, and the like, the children insist that it would still be a skunk, just a peculiar one.

This looks similar to the cases of the lemon and the counterfeit bill. Being a skunk, on the child's view, is not merely a function of having skunk features; there is something deeper than that. This something, in the eyes of the child, is likely to be expressed in terms of having a skunk mommy and a skunk daddy and so on. That is, a skunk (just like lemons and counterfeit money) is defined in part by virtue of its history; this history is relevant by virtue of a web of other beliefs about how biological creatures (as opposed to coffeepots or toasters) are created, the role of inheritance in biological creatures (as opposed to artifacts), and so on.

CONTEXT DEPENDENCY

If prototypes are representations of our concepts, then one would expect stability in prototypes. That is, the concept of "giraffe" that I have today is presumably the same as the concept I had yesterday (assuming that I haven't learned any new facts about giraffes). Likewise, the concept of "giraffe" that I use when speaking to a 6-year-old is presumably the same concept I have in mind when speaking to a peer (although I'll choose different things to talk about, and use different language). This echoes our earlier point about converging evidence: Concepts supposedly provide the core information drawn on by a range of tasks in a range of circumstances; the knowledge being used is supposedly the common element to various concept tasks, and this is why we expected the data from various concept tasks to converge.

There are strong indications, though, that prototypes are not stable in these ways, and that the content of a prototype changes drastically and appropriately from one context to another. In an early study, Labov (1973) showed that context has a strong influence on categorization: What subjects call a "cup" rather than a "bowl" or a "vase" depends very much on the circumstances in which the object is encountered. For example, the wider objects in Figure 10–3 were categorized by subjects as cups if they appeared in someone's hands; they were categorized as bowls if they were filled with mashed potatoes. Likewise for the other shapes shown in the figure; which of these were identified as "cups" depended heavily on the context.

Recent work by Barsalou speaks more directly to prototype issues. Barsalou (1988) notes that the prototypical animal from the point of view of a pet-store owner might well be different from the prototypical animal from the point of view of a zookeeper; the prototypical gift might be different from the vantage point of a college student than it would be for a college professor; and so on. This follows from the fact that prototypes

FIGURE 10–3. *Stimuli that May Be Either Cups or Bowls.* Subjects' identification of these figures as "cups," "bowls," or "vases" was influenced by context. Object 1 was likely to be called a cup no matter what its context. Object 4 was more likely to be called a cup if subjects imagined the object in someone's hands. However, Object 4 was likely to be called a bowl if subjects thought about it as sitting on a table, filled with mashed potatoes. (After Labov, 1973.)

are hypothesized to reflect the experience of each individual. What Barsalou has shown, however, is that we can adopt one another's perspective, and change our prototypes accordingly.

These shifts in perspective are easily demonstrated: All we need do is repeat the original set of prototype demonstrations (for example, the sentence-verification tasks, or the explicit judgments of typicality) and instruct subjects to take this or that point of view. When this is done, subjects easily shift perspective, and give rather different answers as their vantage point changes. For instance, subjects instructed to take an American point of view rate "robin" and "eagle" as being highly typical birds; the same subjects taking a Chinese point of view rate "robin" and "eagle" much lower, and now rate "swan" and "peacock" as being more typical (Barsalou & Sewell, 1984). Likewise, students rating the prototypical faculty gift do a reasonable job of reflecting what the faculty themselves judge to be a typical gift, and vice versa.

Again, this research indicates that our concepts include more than a prototype, since apparently we also have some knowledge that allows us to adjust our prototype to fit the new perspective. One could, however, try to read these data in a different way. We have been claiming that subjects adjust, or perhaps even invent, their prototypes as needed in these procedures. But one could argue that subjects just have a great many prototypes, and draw on each as appropriate. That is, subjects might arrive in the laboratory with a Chinese-bird prototype, and a separate American-bird prototype, and a student-gift prototype, and a faculty-gift prototype, and so on. Barsalou's procedures are simply urging subjects to move from one concept to another as they do the various tasks.

This line of argument has several problems attached to it. Just how many prototypes do we have? One for each potential context? This could be an enormous number. And if our Chinese-bird prototype and our American-bird prototype represent different concepts, how is it that we see the close relation between them? Beyond these questions, though, Barsalou (1988) also offers another line of data that speaks against this view of things. Almost all of the conceptual categories we have been considering involve the meanings of single words (for example, "bird" or "gift"). But Barsalou notes that there are also (in his terms) *goal-derived categories* and completely *ad hoc categories*. In the first of these, we might include *things to eat on a diet, things to carry out of your house in case of a fire;* in the latter group we might include *things that could fall on your head,* and so on. Interestingly, these categories also turn out to have a graded membership: Subjects easily identify some category members as being more typical than others, more quickly recognize the typical ones, and so forth. The implication is that these categories also have prototypes, and these prototypes are surely made up on the spot. This last claim derives from the fact that one can proliferate categories like these endlessly. (There is, for example, the category of *gifts to give one's former high school friend who has just had her second baby.* And then there is the category of . . .) Unless one wishes to argue that subjects arrive in the laboratory with an infinite stockpile of prototypes, one is forced to conclude, as we have been suggesting, that these prototypes are just constructed as needed.

It seems that we need to supplement prototypes with other kinds of knowledge, telling us how to construct or adjust our prototypes. What is this other knowledge? We will return to this problem later in the chapter. For now, though, we underline a key point, a point we have already met: It is striking that even Barsalou's made-up categories have graded membership, implying that these categories also have prototypes. Thus we are simultaneously getting two messages about prototypes. On the one hand, the use of prototypes seems to be a fundamental and pervasive characteristic of how we deal with categories. On the other hand, prototypes cannot be "The" representations in the mind of conceptual knowledge. Before we are through, we will need to figure out how these two messages get put together.

ANALOGIES FROM EXEMPLARS

Let us summarize where we are so far. People generally cannot define many of their concepts; when definitions are offered, it is easy to find exceptions to them. Apparently, therefore, one can "know a concept" without knowing a definition for that concept. This implies that concepts are not represented in the mind via definitions. As an alternative, perhaps concepts are represented in the mind via prototypes; judgments about the category can then be made with reference to this prototype. As we have seen, a considerable quantity of laboratory evidence favors this view.

At the same time, however, other evidence indicates that the prototype view, by itself, is incomplete, and that our knowledge about concepts goes beyond that contained in a prototype. A number of different arguments lead to this claim. For one, subjects are able to make judgments about category membership quite separately from judgments about resemblance to a prototype. This would not be possible if prototypes were all we had to go on in judging category membership. Second, subjects seem able to adjust and create prototypes as the task demands. This seems to require some additional knowledge beyond the prototype itself, with this knowledge providing the basis for the adjustment and creation of prototypes. We will have much more to say about this other knowledge before we are done. In the meantime, though, we must address a different concern: We have been looking at evidence that we must supplement prototypes with some knowledge that is more abstract than the prototype, knowledge that goes beyond the easily recognized, perceptual features that seem to constitute the prototype. Oddly enough, we may also need to supplement prototypes with something less abstract, something more concrete.

Imagine that we place a wooden object in front of you and ask, "Is this a chair?" You might (on the classical, definition view) decide by consulting your chair definition, and asking if the candidate object has the appropriate features or aspects. On a prototype account, you might call up your chair prototype from memory, and compare the candidate to it. If the resemblance is great, you announce, "Yes, this is a chair." If not, you announce, "No."

But there is one more way you might make this decision: You might notice that this strange object is very similar to a strange object that sits in your Uncle Jack's living room, and you know that the object in Uncle Jack's living room is indeed a chair. After all, you've seen Uncle Jack sitting in the thing, reading his newspaper, over and over. If Jack's possession is a chair, and if the new object resembles Jack's, then it is a safe bet that the new object is a chair, too.

The proposal here is that, in some cases, categorization draws on knowledge about specific category members, rather than on more general information about the overall category. In our example, the categorization is supported by memories of a specific chair, namely, Uncle Jack's chair, rather than remembered knowledge about chairs in general. This is referred to as an *exemplar-based approach,* with an **exemplar** defined as a specific remembered instance—in essence, an example. Notice that this approach overlaps with the prototype view in one key regard. According to both of these views, we categorize by making comparisons to a mentally represented example of the category. On the prototype view, this example will be a special example, one abstracted from the various instances of the category that we have encountered. On an exemplar view, the example we use is one drawn from our memories of specific category members. One of these category members will be remembered, and this will serve as basis for categorization.

It should be clear, though, that these two views diverge on some key points. For one, the prototype conception implies that reasoning about concepts will always draw on the same "example" of the concept, namely, the prototype itself. According to the exemplar view, however, this need not be true—it is quite possible that different examples will come to mind on different occasions, and this will influence our performance.

An illustration will help show how this matters, and will also show us how far an exemplar approach might be extended. A young child, learning to read, encounters a new word, and struggles to figure out the word's pronunciation. Or, for that matter, you are reading along, and encounter the novel word TAVE. How to pronounce this letter string? You might call to mind the rules of English spelling, which tell you, in this case, that the pattern of consonant, vowel, consonant, "e" demands a long vowel. Therefore, the word is pronounced as though it rhymes with "save" or "cave."

Alternatively, you might look at the word TAVE and be reminded not of a rule, but of other words, such as "save" or "cave." By analogy with these, you would pronounce TAVE with a long vowel. In this way, you would arrive at the same decision as via the rule. But this process of find-an-instance-and-draw-an-analogy leaves open another possibility: TAVE might also remind you of "have," and, in this case, the analogy would lead you to a short-vowel pronunciation. And, interestingly enough, college students, asked to pronounce this letter string, do on occasion come up with the short-vowel pronunciation, a peculiar finding if they are using the rule, but easily explained if they are using instances + analogies (Baron, 1977).

Our confidence that this is what's going on is increased by the fact that we can prime subjects in a simple way: Subjects read down a list of words, some of which are real words and some of which are made up. Word No. 23 on this list might be "have." Word No. 26 is the test word "tave." It turns out that this recent "activation" of "have" makes the short-vowel pronunciation much more likely. We will have more to say about such priming effects in the next chapter, but for now note that this is just what we would expect on an instance + analogy account: If the instance "have" is made more likely to come to mind, it is more likely that it (and not "save" or "cave" or "rave") will be the basis for the analogy, and so, by manipulating memory availability of "have," we influence how the analogy will turn out.

EXPLAINING TYPICALITY DATA WITH AN EXEMPLAR MODEL

The proposal, then, is that many judgments about concepts are made via analogies based on specifically remembered instances (Brooks, 1978, 1987; Estes, 1972, 1973, 1976; Hintzman, 1986; Medin, 1975, 1976; Reed, 1972). We note an ironic point here: When we considered memory for episodes in Chapter 9, a central theme was that memory for specific events is heavily influenced by generic knowledge. In short, the particular was assimilated into the generic; that was what led to the inquiry that fills this chapter. The notion of exemplar-based categorization indicates that the reverse can also be true: Tasks that, on the surface of things, depend on generic information might be influenced by memory of a much more specific sort.

Several lines of evidence and argument support the exemplar proposal, including the fact that exemplar-based approaches can explain much of the evidence we have reviewed in this chapter. For example, consider a task in which we show subjects a series of pictures and ask the subjects to decide whether each picture shows a fruit or not. We already know that subjects will respond more quickly for typical fruits (orange, apple) than for less typical fruits (honeydew, date).

We have seen how this "typicality" result is handled by a prototype account. How could an exemplar model explain this finding? Subjects will make their judgments by comparing the pictures to mentally represented examples. The set of examples in memory, however, is a biased set— there are likely to be more memories of oranges and apples and fewer of other fruits, simply because oranges and apples are frequently encountered in our culture.

Given this assumption about what is in memory, the typicality result is easily explained. There are more memories of apples and oranges than memories of dates. Therefore, if one reaches into memory for a fruit exemplar, one is more likely to find a memory of "apple" or "orange" than a memory for "date." That is, the exemplars that come to mind are likely to be exemplars of typical fruits. For a subject making judgments about pictures, "apple" and "orange" will be categorized quickly, because the exemplars coming to mind will often be memories of other apples and oranges. Dates and honeydews will be judged more slowly, because the exemplars coming to mind are likely not to be dates and honeydews.

Several variations on this account are possible (cf. Hintzman, 1986; Smith & Medin, 1981; Reed, 1972). With accounts like this one, most of the prototype data turn out to be compatible with an exemplar account.

DIRECT SUPPORT FOR THE EXEMPLAR VIEW

Several results point directly to the role of exemplars in concept tasks. For example, subjects in one study were taught about a fictitious disease, "burlosis"; subjects learned about this disease by examining a series of hypothetical case studies of burlosis patients (Medin, Altom, Edelson, & Freko, 1982). After the subjects had examined these case studies, they were presented with pairs of descriptions of other patients and asked which patient within each test pair was more likely to be the one with burlosis.

How might subjects make this diagnosis? On a prototype account, subjects learning about burlosis will represent the category via a prototype abstracted from the case studies used in training. The prototype will reflect the average or most frequent symptoms in the case studies. If Symptoms A, B, C, and D were commonly associated with burlosis in the case studies, then the prototype for burlosis would display all of these symptoms. On this view, subjects would compare the test cases to this prototype. Within each pair of test cases, whichever case more closely resembled the prototype would be the case more likely to have burlosis.

According to an exemplar approach, subjects diagnose test cases by comparing these to known exemplars of burlosis patients, that is, to their memories of the case studies presented in training. The cases presented in training tended to have Symptoms A, B, C, and D. These are the cases placed in memory. The exemplars used in diagnosis are drawn from these memories, and so it follows that the exemplars used in diagnosis are likely to have these symptoms. Thus a test case with many of these symptoms is likely to resemble an exemplar drawn from memory, and a test case with few of the symptoms will not resemble the exemplar.

We now have two hypotheses available to us. Both hypotheses predict, for example, that a patient with Symptoms A, B, C, and D is more likely to be diagnosed as having burlosis than a patient with only Symptom A. On the prototype view, the former patient has more in common with the prototype. On the exemplar view, the former patient has more in common with many of the remembered exemplars. How, therefore, can we tell which hypothesis is correct?

This experiment contained an additional layer of complexity that allows us to distinguish between the prototype and exemplar predictions. In the case studies presented to subjects, Symptoms A, B, C, and D were all commonly associated with burlosis. In addition, Symptoms C and D were correlated with each other. That is, if a patient had either of these, the patient was certain to have the other. On the other hand, Symptoms

C and A were uncorrelated: A patient with burlosis might have both of these symptoms, or one without the other, or neither.

When subjects were given test cases, some of these had symptoms in line with this correlated pattern, and others did not. For example, we might present subjects with two patients, Jack, who has Symptoms A, C, and D but not Symptom B, and Jill, who has Symptoms A, B, and D but not Symptom C. Which of these is more likely to have burlosis? Jack's symptoms are consistent with the correlation in the training cases—he has both Symptom C and Symptom D. Jill's symptoms are not consistent with the training cases—she has D but not C. Therefore, even though both of these patients have three of the four burlosis symptoms, Jack is more likely to have the disease.

If subjects are basing their diagnosis on a burlosis prototype, then we would not expect this correlation to influence subjects' judgments. If the prototype merely represents the average of the various case studies, then it will not preserve information about which symptoms were correlated with which others. If, on the other hand, subjects are basing their diagnosis on exemplars, then they should be influenced by the correlation. Both Jack and Jill resemble the average of the test cases, namely, the prototype, since they each have three of burlosis's four symptoms. Jack, on the other hand, resembles many individuals known to have burlosis, since his symptoms are in the same configuration as theirs. This is not true for Jill. Jack therefore resembles the exemplars more than Jill does (Table 10–3).

The data show that subjects are influenced by the correlation information. That is, subjects tended to choose the case that preserved the correlation among symptoms over the case that broke the correlation. This remains true even if the case that breaks the correlation has more of the disease symptoms. (That is, we can give subjects a choice, say, between David, who has three burlosis symptoms in the correlated pattern, and Doris, who has four symptoms but not in the correlated pattern. Doris, with more of the symptoms, is more "typical" of the average of burlosis sufferers, but David is more similar to specific individuals with burlosis. Given this choice, subjects reliably choose David as the one more likely to have burlosis.)

Thus it appears that subjects learning this new category do so by placing exemplars in memory, and then using these for later categorizations. Apparently, therefore, at least some categorization tasks are guided by exemplars, rather than by a prototype abstracted from the training cases.

EXEMPLAR VIEW—AN OVERVIEW

Given the evidence of the previous section, should we abandon the prototype account in favor of exemplars? This issue has been debated in the literature, and disagreements remain. At the moment, it appears that

Table 10–3. Training and Test Cases for Diagnosis of "Burlosis"

	Symptoms			
	Swollen Eyelids (A)	Splotches on Ears (B)	Discolored Gums (C)	Nosebleed (D)
Training Cases: All of these cases have burlosis.				
R.C.	Yes	Yes	Yes	Yes
R.M.	Yes	Yes	Yes	Yes
J.J.		Yes		
L.F.	Yes	Yes	Yes	Yes
A.M.	Yes		Yes	Yes
J.S.	Yes	Yes		
S.T.		Yes	Yes	Yes
S.E.	Yes			
E.M.			Yes	Yes
Test Cases: Within each pair, which case is *more* likely to have burlosis?				
Pair 1: A (Jack)	Yes		Yes	Yes
B (Jill)	Yes	Yes		Yes
Pair 2: X				Yes
Y		Yes		

Note: Subjects learned about the disease "burlosis" by examining the nine case studies. Each of the symptoms occurs in 6 of 9 training cases; therefore, these symptoms are all indications of burlosis. The prototypical burlosis sufferer, therefore, would probably have all of these symptoms. In addition, discolored gums and nosebleeds are correlated symptoms: If a patient has one of these symptoms, he or she has both. In the test cases, which patient in each of the pairs is more likely to have burlosis? The number of symptoms is the same for both members of each pair; however, one patient in each pair has the symptoms in the correlated pattern and the other does not. Subjects typically choose the patients with correlated symptoms, evidence of an exemplar approach.
After Medin, Altom, Edelson, & Freko, 1982.

both prototypes and exemplars are used in various category tasks. Both of these, it seems, are part of our overall conceptual knowledge. (Brooks, 1987, and Hintzman, 1986, provide recent discussions.)

We should stress, though, that there are limits on the exemplar claims, just as we have already discussed limits on the prototype claims. Most centrally, it is highly unlikely that concepts could be represented in the mind by nothing more than specific memories. Why not? The relevant arguments here are not new, but were discussed in detail in the eighteenth century by philosophers such as David Hume and Bishop George Berkeley. The first concern is lodged in the fact that one can think about a category, and also think about specific members of the category, and these are clearly different thoughts. One can think about a particular fish, or all the fish one has ever encountered, or one can think about fish in general. These three cases would clearly involve different thoughts, yet, if the concept "fish" is represented in the mind by memories of various specific cases, how do we avoid becoming confused about which we are considering at any point?

The second relevant concern lies in the processes through which one uses exemplar information. Remember, the proposal is that a case before one's eyes *reminds* one of a case in memory, and then one *draws an analogy* based on this remembered case. But consider for a moment how this reminding or this "analogizing" proceeds. Imagine, for the sake of argument, that a furry creature now stands before me and I reason, "This creature reminds me of the thing I saw in the zoo yesterday; the sign indicated that the thing in the zoo was a gnu, so this is one, too." Of course the creature before my eyes is not a "perfect match" for the gnu in the zoo. I might say to myself, "The gnu in the zoo was a different color, but I bet that does not matter. Despite the new hue, this is a gnu, too."

But how did I know that it was legitimate to ignore hue? Consider a different case: "This stone in my hand reminds me of the ruby I saw yesterday; therefore, I bet this is a ruby, too. Of course, the ruby I saw yesterday was red, and this stone is green, but . . ." Of course, one would not draw this analogy, because, in this case, we know that it is wrong to ignore hue. Thus, we have knowledge about which features to pay attention to and which we can safely ignore, and that knowledge depends on what category we are considering.

In other words, in order to use the exemplars in these two cases, one first has to have some understanding of the relevant concepts—that for rubies color is a critical aspect, and that for gnus it is not. More generally, it will always be true that a test case before one's eyes does not exactly match stored exemplars. In deciding whether the match is "good enough," one needs to know something about the concept in question. A match for a ruby is not good enough if the case before one's eyes is the wrong color; for other categories, color matters far less. For some categories, size is essential; for others, it is not; and so on. (For evidence that we do have knowledge about variation within categories, see Fried & Holyoak, 1984; Nisbett, Krantz, Jepson, & Kunda, 1983.)

In the same spirit, once we have come up with an exemplar from memory, how do we know which analogies to draw from this memory and which analogies not to draw? Here is an analogy we might draw: "This creature reminds me of the gnu in the zoo; the gnu in the zoo likes to eat oats; therefore I suspect this creature likes to eat oats." Here is an analogy we would not draw: "This creature reminds me of the gnu in the zoo; the gnu in the zoo expects to get its oats daily at 3 P.M. from a red-haired zookeeper; therefore I suspect this creature now before me expects to get oats at 3 P.M. from . . ."

Put more generally, when an exemplar comes to mind, one will remember both "generalizable" facts, like eating oats, and "not-generalizable" facts, like having a red-haired zookeeper. In order to make sensible use of the exemplar information, one must somehow know which facts are the generalizable ones and draw analogies only from these. And, once again, this seems to require some understanding of the concepts in question, in order to use the exemplar information.

These examples show us that, while exemplars are of great usefulness in guiding categorization, or in guiding inferences, they cannot do this job on their own, so to speak. In deciding that a test case "matches" a stored exemplar, we need to use knowledge about the relevant category. In drawing analogies from exemplars, we need to use knowledge as a guide to which analogies are legitimate and which are not. To make exemplars do their job, we need further knowledge that is not contained in the exemplars themselves. And thus we conclude that exemplars do not contain all of the knowledge that we have about a given category.

One more point before we get back onto our main path: The observations just offered apply with equal force to prototypes. When one compares a stimulus to a prototype, there will once again rarely be a perfect match. So, once again, we need some means of deciding when the match is good enough. Why is it that a wrong-colored gnu seems similar to the gnu prototype, while a wrong-colored ruby seems distant from its prototype? The concern here is identical to the concern with exemplars. This leads us to a familiar message: Prototypes (like exemplars) have great usefulness, but there is more and more reason to ask what other knowledge must be added so that we may use prototypes (and exemplars) in concept tasks.

WE KNOW MORE THAN PROTOTYPES

Again, let us summarize where we are. The knowledge we draw on in categorization, or in reasoning about concepts, or in talking about concepts, seems to involve multiple components. Some of our performance in concept tasks indicates that we are using something like a prototype. Other arguments strongly suggest that our knowledge is not limited to prototypes. This led us to a theory in which concepts are mentally represented by a prototype plus some other information. However, we have now seen that this two-part theory might not be enough. The role of exemplars (that is, specifically remembered instances or occasions) suggests that we may need a three-part theory of concepts, with concepts being represented in the mind by a prototype + some set of specifically remembered cases + some further abstract information. And, finally, we also need these parts to interact in order to explain similarity judgments and drawing of analogies. What you know about the concept seems to help govern what properties will be emphasized and what properties ignored in judging similarity to a prototype or in calling up exemplars from memory, and so forth.

All this tells us something very important: Our hopes for an elegant, slim theory of concepts and categorization are likely to be vain hopes. This by itself is an interesting conclusion, but it leaves many questions unanswered. High on the list, what is this "further abstract information" we have repeatedly mentioned? How do these various components of conceptual knowledge fit together? Which component is used for what? It is to these issues that we now turn.

Assembling the Elements of Conceptual Knowledge

The claims reviewed in the previous sections are well established and widely accepted among psychologists. There is still room for disagreement, however, about how all these pieces fit together. To put it differently, we know a great deal about the "ingredients" that make up human conceptual knowledge, but the role played by each ingredient and how the ingredients are related to each other remain subjects of debate. The following sections, therefore, should be read as being more tentative than the claims made earlier in this chapter.

PROTOTYPES AS HEURISTICS

While concepts cannot be fully represented by prototypes, prototypes do have an important function. Several theorists have suggested that prototypes serve as very efficient identification procedures. The idea, roughly, comes in two steps. First, the information that the world presents to us and the information that we bring to a situation (thanks to our terrific memories) are both vast. In contrast, we do not have vast amounts of time, or attention, or working memory to devote to each and every decision we make or each and every idea that crosses our mind. For these reasons, there is a strong pressure for **cognitive economy**, that is, to preserve the precious resources of time, attention, and working memory by using strategies or shortcuts that are as efficient as possible.

The notion of cognitive economy played a key role in the arguments in Chapter 9; there we argued that the pressures of cognitive economy lead to memory strategies that sacrifice some accuracy in order to gain efficiency. The idea of cognitive economy is equally important here. It will be useful to borrow some vocabulary from the field of computer science: Often a problem can be solved or a decision reached by a laborious, step-by-step procedure that is guaranteed, eventually, to yield the correct answer. Such a procedure is called an **algorithm**; an example would be trying to choose the best next move in a game of chess by considering each and every one of the options, then to think through what your opponent might do in response to each of these, then to think through what you would do next, etc. Needless to say, this would quickly mount up to an enormous number of possibilities, and would be as exhausting as it is exhaustive. As a far more efficient alternative, you might seek a strategy that allows you to decide quickly which are the five or six most likely moves, so that you only need to consider these. You might, for example, only consider moves that involve major pieces or that involve the center of the board. Such a strategy would buy efficiency, but at a cost: It might be that the best move involves a pawn moving at the edge of the board. Your strategy, while efficient, would not lead you to see this option. This would be intolerable if this option were often desirable, but, more often than not, the best chess moves do involve the major pieces and the middle of the board. Hence the risk of missing a brilliant move is low, and the efficiency might be worth taking this risk. This kind of strategy is called a **heuristic**. Heuristics are not guaranteed to be perfect; they may miss some options, but they are efficient and, if well chosen, are right more often than not.

With this as context, the proposal should be obvious: Prototypes serve an important heuristic function. Specifically, not all tasks drawing on, say, our knowledge about gorillas require the same information. On some occasions, your reasoning about gorillas might have to be done quickly. You are visiting the zoo with your kid sister. You turn away for only a moment, and she wanders off. Suddenly, you realize that she has entered one of the cages, and you need to decide fast which cage she's in . . . In cases like this a rough-and-ready, let-me-check-quickly strategy will suffice. There is no reason in this case to drag out all of your gorilla knowledge, and, in fact, doing so would probably take more time or effort than you want to spend. In this case, a categorization heuristic is just what you want.

Prototypes are well suited to this heuristic function. First, insofar as prototypes represent the average or the most common features of a category, they will be representative of the category's members more often than not. Second, as we mentioned, prototypes seem to involve perceptual features rather than more abstract knowledge about a category, and this probably means that comparisons to a prototype can be made quickly and efficiently, as a heuristic demands. Third, if prototypes can be fine-tuned to the context, as Barsalou's evidence indicates, this would further serve to make the prototype a situationally appropriate, efficient categorization device.

As an example, think about what you would do if I gave you a message to deliver to Robin's grandmother. (The example is borrowed from Landau, 1982.) If I told you that the grandmother works at the day-care center down the block, you might go to the day-care center and glance about quickly, looking for a gray-haired, smiling woman with twinkly eyes, preferably sitting in a rocking chair, dispensing brownies (or cookies or knishes or whatever). Any individual in the room who resembles this prototype would be speedily identified and, so, with no effort, you have located the grandmother. Alternatively, if I told you the grandmother spends her days at the senior-citizens' center, then the heuristic strategy just described will not work. Instead, you might need to make inquiries about who is the female parent of a parent, a strategy that is clearly more time consuming, but both less prone to error than the former strategy and appropriate to this situation.

A different way to put all of this involves some terminology we introduced earlier. Much of our discussion has indicated that we can not equate "goodness of example" with "membership in a category." We saw this in the fact that an individual (for example, the abused lemon) can be a member of a category even if it is a poor example of the category; likewise, an individual can closely resemble a category's ideal, but not be in the category (for example, a perfect counterfeit). At the same time, though, we should preserve a central insight of the prototype approach: "Membership" and "exemplariness" are different from each other, as we have seen, but they are still related, and this is critical for the heuristic idea. Prototypes can serve as heuristics thanks to the fact that good examples of a category are likely to be in the category; extremely bad examples are likely not to be in the category. Thus one can use exemplariness as a fast and efficient basis for judging membership. (See also the discussion in Chapter 6, page 236, for why natural concepts seem more readily learned than artificial, sharply defined concepts.)

Reasoning via exemplars may serve the same heuristic function. The idea here is that, for many tasks, we are "mental opportunists," using whatever information comes to mind in order to make judgments, or to reach decisions, as quickly and as efficiently as possible. As Brooks (1987) has discussed, a case before our eyes—a picture to be classified, a word to be pronounced—may call a prototype to mind, or it may call some specific prior instance to mind. Either of these will support a categorization judgment, and so one should be prepared to use whichever is available. This flexibility will maximize efficiency, and so maximize cognitive economy.

Indeed, as we suggested before, the process will be roughly the same in these two cases: An object or scene before one's eyes calls to mind a representation of prior experience, and one compares the current input to this representation. If there is a good "match," one concludes that things true of the representation are probably true of the new case. When the representation called up from memory happens to be a memory for some specific instance, we call this *reasoning via exemplars*. If the representation called up from memory happens to be a prototype, we call this *classifying via prototypes*. Given this clear parallel in process, it should be no surprise if both of these mental representations could serve the same heuristic function.

PROTOTYPES + WHAT ELSE?

The previous section gives a picture of what role prototypes and exemplars serve, and therefore why these are so important. We will classify via these heuristics (1) when speed is needed in performing concept-based tasks, (2) when the decision is not an important one and so great effort is not warranted, or (3) when a decision is already mostly made, so that further examination of the issue is only playing a confirmatory role.

Thus, prototypes are part of the "identification procedure" associated with a concept and not part of the "core" of the concept itself (cf. Armstrong, Gleitman, & Gleitman, 1983; Osherson & Smith, 1981). But this still leaves us to ask: If neither prototypes nor exemplars are the core of concepts, what is? What is it that, for example, allows us to adjust a prototype, to make the prototype appropriate to the context? How do we create prototypes, as in Barsalou's "ad hoc" categories? How do we make decisions when the conditions just listed, favoring the use of the heuristic, do not apply, and thus when we are not relying on prototypes? What knowledge were Keil's subjects using when they made decisions (for example) about whether a skunk could be turned into a raccoon?

We have already seen a broad set of hints about how these questions must be answered: One concern about prototypes (and, for that matter, an aspect of definitions as well) is that they try to characterize a concept more or less in isolation; they do not carry information about how a concept is related to other concepts. Yet, in our discussion of the concept of counterfeit bill, and in Keil's studies, it was clear that subjects' reasoning about concepts drew heavily on the subjects' knowledge about how various concepts are interrelated. To understand what a "counterfeit bill" is, one needs to know what "real money" is, what "crime" is, how money is printed, and so on.

Perhaps our understanding of concepts demands a more holistic analysis than what we have been trying so far. Our various concepts and terms may take their meaning by virtue of how they are interconnected with other concepts and terms. That is, it may not be possible to characterize concepts one by one; we may need to characterize each by characterizing the network in which it is embedded. The question then becomes how to flesh out this vague proposal. We will return to this issue in a moment; first, though, we need to lay some groundwork.

What Happens with the Harder Cases?

It is ironic that our discussion has grown so complicated, since after all we have been looking at the supposedly easy cases—simple, everyday concepts for the most part, concepts like "dog" and "fish" and "table" and "chair." These are the concepts for which definitions seemed unavailable and for which a prototype seemed important but not fully adequate. And these are the concepts for which a full characterization may require a broad theory about how our ideas are related to each other, rather than a theory of individual concepts.

MENTAL MODELS

If these are the conclusions we meet in considering simple concepts, what happens with more complex concepts? In at least some cases, the kind of network notion we have just hinted at seems inevitable. Consider the concept "blood pressure." It would be surprising if this concept could be characterized in isolation from a set of other terms, terms such as "circulation," "heart," and "arteries." To understand blood pressure, one must understand these other terms, and one seems to need a web of beliefs about how these various terms are interrelated (cf. Banks, Thompson, Henry, & Weissmann, 1986; Carey, 1985).

There have been several proposals for how this web of beliefs should be characterized. Neisser (1987) has proposed that these beliefs can be thought of as an implicit "theory" about the relevant subject matter—a theory that the individual holds (perhaps without being able to articulate it) about how the various terms are interconnected. Lakoff (1987) has offered a related notion defined as an "idealized cognitive model." Several psychologists have explored the idea of a "mental model" (e.g., Gentner & Stevens, 1983). The idea throughout, to stay with the example of blood pressure, is that we all have a set of beliefs about how blood pressure is defined, what causes blood pressure to be higher or lower, and so forth. Although far less sophisticated (and probably far less accurate) than a medically correct, scientific model, our mental model seeks to perform the same function as the scientific one: It embodies a set of beliefs that, overall, provide a cause-and-effect account that corresponds to our understanding of the process, and all of the terms participating in this model (including blood pressure) are defined by virtue of how they fit into this cause-and-effect account.

Mental models seem essential for describing complex concepts such as "blood pressure." It may turn out that we also need mental models to describe seemingly simpler concepts. Consider, for example, the term "bachelor." This noun seems easily defined: A bachelor is an unmarried adult male. Even this noun, however, can be understood only in the context of certain expectations about marriage and marriageable age, as the examples shown below (taken from Fillmore, 1982) help make clear. As you read these examples, think about what guides your judgments.

Various potential bachelors:
Alfred is an unmarried adult male, but he has been living with his girlfriend

for the last 23 years. Their relationship is happy and stable. Is Alfred a bachelor?

Bernard is an unmarried adult male, and does not have a partner. But Bernard is a monk, living in a monastery. Is Bernard a bachelor?

Charles is a *married* adult male, but has not seen his wife for many years; Charles is earnestly dating, hoping to find a new partner. Is Charles a bachelor?

Donald is a married adult male, but lives in a culture that encourages males to take two wives. Donald is earnestly dating, hoping to find a new partner. Is Donald a bachelor?

(and so forth!)

The suggestion is that your judgments depend on a rich understanding of who is eligible to marry, and who is likely to marry. Thus, understanding even a term like "bachelor" may depend on a mental model, in this case a model that encompasses your understanding of matrimonial customs within our culture. (Further examples are provided by Fillmore, 1982; Lakoff, 1987; Neisser, 1987.)

SCHEMA THEORY REVISITED

We began this chapter by noting that episodic memories were heavily influenced by generic information, specifically in the form of schemata or scripts. Yet our discussion of generic knowledge has said little about schemata. As it turns out, though, it is a small step from where we are to schema theory.

It will take us a bit of discussion to explain the proposal, but, in a nutshell, the suggestion is this: As we saw in Chapter 9, schemata provide a means of representing general knowledge; this knowledge is used both in learning new materials and in reconstructing what one has previously learned. The knowledge represented by schemata includes knowledge about objects and about situations, and often involves the interrelations among diverse concepts. Framed in these terms, we see that the contents of a schema are not very different from the contents of what we have called, in this chapter, a mental model. In fact, what we are suggesting is that schemata and mental models are roughly the same thing. More precisely, schemata provide the means through which these models are represented in the mind.

While a schema contains general information, it also provides a base from which to create more specific knowledge. This was critical when we discussed how schemata can guide the recollection of specific prior episodes. For example, one uses generic knowledge about birthday parties to help in remembering a specific party; one uses generic knowledge about offices to help in remembering a particular office; and so on. In these examples, one uses a schema to reconstruct a specific, previously encountered case. As we will see, one can also use the schema to generate an "idealized" case, representing the "average" of previously encountered cases. In short, one can use a schema to create a prototype.

The proposal, then, is that schemata capture the general knowledge we have been discussing under the banner of mental models. Schemata also provide a base from which to generate prototypes. How does all this work? Within the schema view, what it means to understand new information is to fit that information into a schematic frame. This implies that the schema has slots or openings, into which the new information can be placed. This is usually viewed as possible by virtue of the fact that the schema contains *variables*, not fixed information (see Rumelhart & Ortony, 1977). In the case of the kitchen schema, for example, there is no representation of a specific stove, but a marker standing for some to-be-specified stove; likewise a marker standing for some to-be-specified counter-top appliance, a marker standing for some to-be-specified kitchen table, and so on. When we are thinking about, or looking at, a specific kitchen, these variables are filled in to reflect the particular kitchen under scrutiny. When we are thinking about kitchens in general, these variables will be left open.

The variables within a schema do not have equal status. Some (for example, the stove) are "obligatory"—they are more or less necessary; they must be filled in when we are thinking about a particular kitchen, or recognizing a room as a kitchen. Presumably, this is an important part of how we recognize the room as a kitchen. The obligatory features are presumably also the features that give the schema its identity. This is why we would say that kitchen-without-a-toaster is still a kitchen; it is, so to speak, only a minor variation on "kitchenhood" because "toaster" is assumed not to be obligatory. Kitchen-without-a-place-to-prepare-food, however, is a contradiction in terms. Note, however, that we cannot be rigid when we speak of these variables as "obligatory." Just as definitions are hard to find, because one can routinely find exceptions, so also are "obligatory" features hard to name. Hence "obligatory" here needs to be toned down to "extremely likely."

Other variables, such as the counter-top appliance, are "optional"—they may or may not be filled in when we are thinking about a specific kitchen, or exploring a new kitchen. Finally, other variables have **default** values—values we automatically fill in unless we have some reason to the contrary. For example, it is a good bet that a kitchen table is present, although not all kitchens have tables. Hence this is a variable with a default value—assume a kitchen table of standard size, unless otherwise informed.

REPRESENTATION OF SCHEMATIC KNOWLEDGE

Schemata contain variables rather than specific information; this allows schemata to represent the general case rather than a specific instance. How this information is actually represented in the mind is complex enough to demand a chapter of its own; this will be the topic of Chapter 11. For now, though, a few points about knowledge representation are relevant to our discussion.

Most current proposals describe the representation of knowledge as involving a **network of associations** (Anderson, 1976, 1980; Collins & Loftus, 1975; Rumelhart & McClelland, 1986). The idea of a network serves us well in the present context—it allows us to interconnect the various aspects of the kitchen schema with other bits of knowledge and in this way build our way toward a fabric of connections that could constitute a mental model.

In addition, a prominent idea about long-term memory is that knowledge is stored in the form of **propositions**, with a proposition defined as the smallest unit of knowledge that can possess a truth value—that is, be true or false (Anderson, 1976, 1980; Anderson & Bower, 1973; Kintsch, 1974; Reder & Anderson, 1980). Thus, for example, "Kitchens have stoves" and "People eat food" are simple propositions, while "a blue kitchen" is not a proposition, since what would it mean for this phrase to be true or false? In Anderson's (1976) model, propositions are represented in terms of associations among ideas, shown graphically in Figure 10–4; the proposition depicted is "Dogs chase cats." Notice that the associations are **labeled** in this case, allowing us to distinguish the agent and object of a relationship. In this way, we can make sure to represent "Dogs chase cats," rather than "Cats chase dogs."

These associations make it possible to represent a variety of relationships; this looks like just what we need to represent the web of cause-and-effect connections within a mental model. Figure 10–5 shows a hypothesized portion of a network representation of "dog" (after Anderson, 1980). It is easy to see how this network could be extended and elaborated upon to fill in the other knowledge we have about dogs (although see Smith, Adams, & Schorr, 1978; Wexler, 1978; Rumelhart & McClelland, 1986).

There is disagreement in the field over the status of propositional theories—for example, what form these should take or whether an entirely different approach is preferable (see Chapter 11). For our present purposes, propositional theories illustrate one way we might flesh out conceptual knowledge. Whether other approaches are more promising remains to be seen.

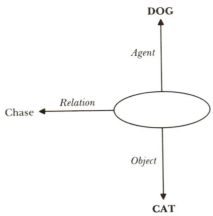

FIGURE 10–4. *Network Representation of the Proposition "Dogs Chase Cats."* The ellipse denotes a proposition; the ellipse is, in essence, the "meeting point" for the elements of the proposition. Three nodes are involved in this proposition—"dog," "cat," and the action, "chase." The arrows indicate associations among the nodes; labels on the arrows specify the nature of the association. (After Anderson, 1980.)

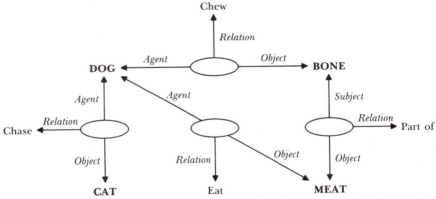

FIGURE 10–5. *Network Representation of Some of the Concepts Associated with "Dog."* One's understanding of dogs—what dogs are, what they are likely to do—is represented by an interconnected network of propositions, with each proposition indicated by an ellipse. Thus one's understanding involves the propositions "Dogs chase cats," "Dogs eat meat," and "Dogs chew bones," and so on. A complete representation of knowledge about dogs would of course include a far greater number of propositions. (After Anderson, 1980.)

HOW TO TIE PROTOTYPES TO THIS LARGER FRAME?

As we have seen in previous sections, conceptual knowledge seems to include a web of cause-and-effect knowledge—knowledge about an object's history and knowledge about how the object is related to a variety of other concepts. The claim is that a network of labeled associations is a plausible way to represent this knowledge. The various beliefs that constitute a mental model can be described in terms of propositions, and these propositions can be represented via labeled associations. By using variables within this network, we can allow the associations to represent generic knowledge, rather than specific cases. When we encounter a specific case, or when we wish to think about a specific case, we can replace the variables with particular values (a particular stove, a particular sink) and in this fashion link our general knowledge to a specific instance.

How can we tie this proposal back to prototypes? Remember that variables within a schematic frame have a "default" value, a value taken if no other information is available. Default values presumably represent the typical, or the most often expected, way a variable is filled in. By filling in variables with these default values, we are describing the typical form for the schema or script, and this will represent the prototype.

This approach easily allows us to explain how subjects can adjust their prototypes to fit one situation or another or to change perspective. If prototypes are generated by replacing the variables with specific values, then adjustments are possible by simply choosing different values, rather than the default values. Thus the flexibility of prototypes derives from the fact that concept knowledge is framed in terms of variables, and so the prototype can be shifted into other forms simply by choosing to set the variables to one value or another.

We therefore end with a somewhat tidy account, although, to be sure, an account that is considerably less specific than we would like. This approach seems to do justice to the fact that concepts involve interwoven beliefs; it also provides a basis for the pliability that we know exists in concepts, particularly with regard to generating new prototypes. These, once generated in a form appropriate to the situation, provide heuristic measures through which we can use our conceptual knowledge as efficiently as possible.

The Source of Generic Knowledge

We have covered much ground in this chapter, but there is one last point we should touch on before leaving the topic of generic knowledge. Interestingly enough, this will bring us back to where we began, namely, the connection between episodic and generic memories.

The question before us, simply, is where generic knowledge comes from. In the case of episodic knowledge, this was not a problem, since episodic knowledge, by definition, is knowledge of a particular episode, and therefore the source of that knowledge is clear. But where does "context-free" generic knowledge come from?

Our discussion has not addressed this topic directly, but we have surveyed lots of information pertinent to this issue. First, as we have seen, at least some categorization (and at least some thinking about categories) is done with reference to specific cases encountered earlier. This guarantees that these cases will be thought about in conjunction with new cases pertaining to that category, serving to unite these cases in memory. Second, we have seen that source confusion is fairly common in episodic memory, as shown in many of the studies in Chapters 8 and 9. Without memory for specific sources, there is nothing to prevent information from different cases from blurring together.

There is in fact independent evidence that this blurring occurs. Neisser (1981) has examined in detail a specific case of remembering—an instance in which an important public event occurred and then subsequently one of the participants in the event tried to report the details of the event, with close questioning by a panel of investigators. Finally, it came to light that the whole affair had been tape-recorded, so the witness's testimony could be assessed for accuracy. The public event in question was the Watergate scandal that ended the Nixon presidency. As the scandal unfolded, it became clear that Nixon's advisers had committed a series of illegal acts. There was uncertainty, however, about Nixon's own role in the planning or the cover-up of these crimes. In investigating Nixon's role, the Watergate Committee of the United States Senate carefully interrogated John Dean, former counsel to Nixon, about conversations that had taken place in the Oval Office. In his testimony, Dean did not realize that his reports would later be checked against the tapes Nixon made of all Oval Office conversations.

Neisser reports that Dean's testimony is quite accurate in its gist (consistent with the evidence in Chapter 9), but it is often off on the details. The errors, however, were not random. Instead, Dean often reported snippets of conversation as having taken place in one context when, in fact, they took place in a slightly different context. In other words, the individual episodes were, indeed, being blurred together. Neisser argues that this is extremely likely for repeated and related episodes, and proposes the name **repisodes** for our memories of these Repeated EPISODES. Other evidence (for example, several of the studies considered in Chapter 9) fits with this pattern: Memory for detail is likely to suffer when episodes are similar, as details get exchanged from one episode to another.

This repisodic blurring guarantees that information from different cases will be combined into some sort of summary case. In addition, we have reason to believe that one's own thoughts and reflections will be combined into this summary as well. This is indicated by the evidence on accommodative distortion and updating, reviewed in Chapter 9.

Thus we see one more important tie between episodic and generic memory. The normal working of episodic memory draws on the resource of generic memory; that is what schema effects are all about. Tasks that seem to draw on generic memory are often influenced by specific memories; this is the heart of the exemplar claim. It now turns out that the normal workings of episodic memory make it likely that individual episodes, individual encounters, will be summarized and blurred together. It seems a reasonable claim that it is from this blurring that a great deal of our generic knowledge is created.

We do not wish to imply, however, that this creation is a simple process. Imagine, for example, taking every circle you have ever seen and combining them by piling each on the others—each a slightly different size, each a slightly different line thickness, each with its center in a slightly different place. What would the compilation look like? It would obviously be just a hodge-podge (Figure 10–6). To combine the circles, one needs to know that size is not really relevant to "circlehood," nor is line thickness and so on. Hence the essential properties can be abstracted away from these attributes, and must be in order to allow the compilation. (This obviously echoes our points about the drawing of analogies from exemplars, in which one also had to separate somehow the essential information from the rest.) However, this puts us in a bind: In order to combine the circles, we need to know something about what is essential and what is not. Therefore, we cannot find out what a circle essentially is by merely combining all the circles we have seen—we must combine them in the right way, and we must ignore certain irrelevant features.

A full account, then, of how this conceptual development takes place would require a book unto itself. (You might look at, for example, Carey, 1985, or Keil, 1979.) Tackling this problem would clearly take us far afield from our central agenda. Our point, therefore, is a modest one:

FIGURE 10–6.   *How Are Concepts Created?* One cannot learn what a circle is merely by combining together all of the circles one has ever seen. If one did, something like this would result—a hodge-podge, not a concept of a circle. Instead, one has to combine the individual cases in the right way—lining up the centers, ignoring size and attending only to shape, and so on.

Much of the evidence of episodic memory says that combination of episodes is a key to the origin of generic knowledge. However, this combination is not a simple process of addition or accumulation; it is instead interestingly selective.

In this chapter, we have encountered both many mysteries and firm answers. The details of what a mental model is, or what a mental model includes, remain to be filled out. The process through which a mental model allows you to generate a prototype, or to adjust a prototype for a new context, remains unspecified. The process by which mental models are derived from experience also has been put to the side.

Against this background, though, we should not lose sight of the important and firm conclusions the evidence will allow. If we had to select a single one of these as most important, it is this: Even for the simplest cases, the simplest examples, human generic knowledge is impressively complex. To put it bluntly, none of the questions we might ask about generic knowledge receives a simple, one-part answer. Considering that our use of this knowledge seems effortless and ubiquitous, this gives us an indication both of the complexity of cognitive processes in general and of the remarkable complexity of the human species.

Summary

The previous chapter made it clear that both our learning and our remembering are guided by general knowledge, knowledge about the objects and events in our world. What is the nature of this "generic" knowledge? What exactly do we know about the various concepts and categories that we know and use?

One obvious possibility is that our knowledge about concepts amounts to a series of definitions, one for each of the concepts in our repertoire. However, even everyday, commonsense notions, notions like "dog" and "game," turn out to be difficult to define. It is easy to come up with plausible definitions, but it is equally easy to come up with exceptions to these proposed rules—for example, dogs that do not fit the definition but are still dogs.

An alternative approach seeks to define the "ideal" or prototype for each concept, and to use this prototype as a basis for reasoning about that concept. The prototype approach implies that categories will have "fuzzy boundaries" and "graded membership," and a great deal of research is consistent with these two claims. That is, in task after task, certain members of a category seem to be better members of that category; these members are presumably those that closely resemble the category's prototype.

However, other evidence indicates that our knowledge about concepts extends beyond the information contained in a prototype. At least some tasks, apparently drawing on conceptual knowledge, are influenced by specific memories of particular category members. Hence our prototype knowledge is apparently accompanied by memories for specific "exemplars" of the category.

In addition, a number of lines of evidence indicate that, in some cases, subjects can make independent judgments about whether an instance is a member of a category, and whether the instance is typical for that category. In some cases (for example, counterfeit bills), an object can be typical for a category, but not in the category; in other cases (for example, abused lemons), the reverse is true. All of this contradicts the claim that judgments about category membership are based on an assessment of typicality. Once again, therefore, it seems that our conceptual knowledge must include information other than information about prototypes and typicality.

Finally, other evidence indicates that our prototypes change from one context to another, and that new prototypes can be easily created if one's task demands this. All of this suggests that we have some other, perhaps more abstract, knowledge about concepts and categories. This other knowledge can then be used as a basis for adjusting or creating prototypes as needed.

We proposed that prototypes serve an important role as identification heuristics. That is, prototypes allow us to make fast and efficient categorization judgments. As with all heuristics, this efficiency is purchased at the price of possible inaccuracy. As we have discussed, however, there are circumstances in which this trade of efficiency for accuracy is appropriate.

How is our more abstract knowledge about concepts represented in the mind? We explored the possibility that this knowledge is best thought of as a network of associations that defines a concept, in essence, by specifying how that concept is related to a variety of other concepts. This notion is sometimes referred to as a mental model, explaining a set of conceptual terms. One way to represent mental models is by means of a schema. Schemata contain variables, and this allows them to represent the general case—that is, generic knowledge. These variables can also be filled in with specific values; if we use the most typical (or default) variables, this will specify the most typical form for that schema, that is, the prototype.

Finally, where does generic knowledge come from? We have suggested that generic knowledge is created by the blurring together of knowledge about many specific individuals. A variety of evidence indicates that this blurring does occur, especially when one is exposed to a series of similar objects or events. This blurring together cannot be, however, a simple process of adding or superimposing each case on the others; instead, this blurring seems to be guided by some understanding of the concepts in question.

11 The Network Approach to Memory

We have already commented on the vastness of memory's contents. We have made references to memories for episodes and memories for mundane facts, memories for verbal passages as well as for pictures, memories for meaningful materials and memories for superficial appearances. Our memories contain schemata, and scripts, and an immense quantity of commonsense information about a diversity of objects, actions, and events. The scope of memory seems even greater when we include the unconscious, "implicit" memories, described in Chapter 8.

If memory contains so much, how do we ever find anything in this vast warehouse? In fact, we emphasized in Chapter 9 how "seamlessly" we combine remembered information with current environmental input. We are often not even aware that we have supplemented the actual input with information from memory. All this indicates that not only do we manage to locate the sought-after information in memory, we do so with relative speed and ease. How does this happen?

In the same vein, what kind of filing system, or organizational scheme, do we use for assembling this information? We have seen a number of hints for how the information is assembled, but these need to be fleshed out. For example, in the earlier chapters of this book, we spoke repeatedly of "forming associations" between stimuli, or between stimuli and responses. In Chapters 8 and 9, we mentioned that memory is improved when one makes "connections" between to-be-learned materials and things one already knows or between to-be-learned materials and aspects of the learning context. In Chapter 10, we explicitly discussed how schemata, scripts, or mental models might be represented as a "network of associations" among ideas.

In this chapter, we examine the network notion directly. We will ask how the network functions when we learn, and how we use the network to locate information in memory. There have been several proposals about how the network represents knowledge, and we will examine these. Finally, we will consider some of the objections and concerns that have been expressed about the network approach.

The Network Notion

The idea that memory can be represented by some sort of network of associations is hardly new. The idea has been discussed, both in philosophy and in psychology, for several centuries (see Chapter 1). Our initial focus in this chapter will be on the versions of the 1970s and early 1980s, although we will say a few words about how these versions differed from their predecessors. We will then turn to the most recent version of associative theorizing, a particularly sophisticated treatment known as "connectionism."

As we proceed, you should bear in mind that there is disagreement about many of the details of network models. Our presentation of network ideas is heavily influenced by the theorizing of Collins and Loftus (1975) and Anderson (1976, 1980; Anderson & Bower, 1973). However, other versions of the network are possible, and so our presentation should be understood as describing how the network *might* be fleshed out, rather than as a rigid proposal.

HOW MIGHT THE NETWORK WORK?

The essence of an associative network is straightforward. The claim is that we can explain a great range of data if we think about memory as being a vast web of ideas (remembered episodes, remembered facts, remembered sights and smells, etc.) connected to one another in an orderly fashion. We will speak of the ideas as being **nodes** within the network, and then the connections from one node to the next as being **associations** or **associative links**.

To put this in metaphorical terms, think of the nodes as being akin to cities on a map, and associations as being the highways that link the cities. Learning, within this metaphor, would be akin to finding or creating a connection—building a highway between two cities, or perhaps improving an existing highway, so that it is more easily and quickly traveled. Alternatively, you can think of the nodes as being small electronic devices, each storing an idea or a memory, and the associations as being the cables among these devices.

On this view, what it means to "search" through memory is to begin at one node (one "city") and to travel via the connections until the target information is reached. Critically, not all associations are of equal strength. Some of the "cities" are linked by superhighways, others only by country roads. Other "cities" are not linked to each other at all, but you can get from one to the next by traveling via some intermediate cities. This will immediately provide part of our account for why some memories are easily called up while others are not: If you are asked, for example, your birthday, you quickly and easily answer. This would be captured, presumably, by the fact that there is a strong connection between the BIRTHDAY node and the node representing a specific birthdate. This connection has presumably been established by the fact that this date and the idea of birthdays have frequently been thought about in conjunction with each other, creating an easily traveled path from one to the other. (Throughout this chapter, we will use small capital letters when we are referring to a NODE in memory; we will use normal type when referring to the word or stimulus represented by that NODE.)

Even at this early stage of presentation, we reach a point in which modern versions of associative nets differ from older versions. According to philosophers like John Locke and George Berkeley, ideas in one's mind are linked by associations, but these associations are "stamped in" by the environment. If you have often experienced a date and the word "birthday" in close contiguity, this will cause these to be firmly associated. This is, as we have seen, in conflict with the data: In Chapter 3, we saw that Pavlovian associations are created when there is *contingency* between stimuli, and not just *contiguity*. Likewise, in Chapter 7, we saw that merely thinking about something over and over in a mechanical fashion *(maintenance rehearsal)* seems not to lay down associations in memory; associations are instead created by the more active process of *elaborative rehearsal.*

Modern network views incorporate the evidence just mentioned by requiring a more active role for the learner. Associations are not passively stamped in; they are instead established by the learner's thinking about the items together. For example, consider the levels-of-processing view, introduced in Chapter 7. On that view, good retention results from "deep" and "elaborate" processing. In terms of the network, these forms of processing aid memory by laying down **retrieval paths** from the context to the to-be-remembered (or TBR) items themselves. That is, the retrieval paths will run from a node in memory representing THAT LIST FROM BEFORE, or THE OCCASION IN WHICH THE EXPERIMENTER HAD ME MEMORIZE ITEMS, to the nodes representing the TBR material. In essence, one is building new highways, or perhaps improving paths that already exist. When later asked "What words were on the list I read you before?" subjects begin their memory search with the **context node**, representing the event itself (that is, learning the list). If the connections are in place, subjects can move easily from this node to nodes representing more specific memories about the list's contents.

On this view, elaborative processing—thinking about many connections—helps because it creates many retrieval paths, maximizing the chances of reaching the nodes representing the TBR material. Why is deep processing preferable to more superficial processing? One possibility is that deep processing leads to more *distinctive* coding. If one studies a word list by looking, say, at whether the items are in CAPITALS or not (a clear case of shallow coding), then the words will not be thought of in distinctive ways. All the capitalized words will be lumped together, and so will all the noncapitalized words. If one instead thinks about the words' meanings (deep processing), more attention will be paid to how the words differ from each other. Think about the associative connections each of these will create: Having an association between THE LIST I STUDIED EARLIER and SOME CAPITALIZED WORDS will not lead you to a response. Having an association between THE LIST I STUDIED EARLIER and A WORD MEANING ABLE TO WRITE EQUALLY WELL WITH LEFT OR RIGHT HAND would.

SPREADING ACTIVATION

Most theorists speak of a node becoming **activated** when it has received a strong enough input signal. This implies that what travels through the associative links is something like energy or activation. When one node is "activated," energy will spread out via the associations radiating from this node, and this energy will in turn activate the nodes at the ends of these connections.

This idea of **spreading activation** allows us to deal with a key issue. How does one choose within the network which paths or which associations to follow? If one starts a search at one node, how does one decide where to go from there, especially if we assume that most nodes have many associative links radiating out from them? The answer to this turns out to be that we do not "choose" or "decide." Instead, we essentially take all roads at once, by letting activation spread out in all directions simultaneously.

This is not to say that all pathways will be equally effective in carrying the activation. Recall that some associative links, thanks to recent or frequent use, are particularly effective, while others are less so. Perhaps other associations are "built in," that is, are innately strong. In any of these cases, effective links will more efficiently carry activation, and so will be more successful at activating subsequent nodes. Hence the spread of activation may start out uniform, but will be selectively carried, traveling furthest and most strongly on already well-traveled routes.

The activation of nodes is assumed to be a **graded effect**. That is, activation is a "more or less" affair, rather than "all or none." What *is* all or nothing is this: Once the activation level of a node is high enough, this triggers some other mechanism that summons attention, or perhaps transfers the node's contents to short-term memory. Informally, activation above this threshold level causes us to be *aware* of the activated node. This is what it means to "find" a node.

Activation levels below the response threshold, so-called **subthreshold activation**, have an important role to play: Activation is assumed to accumulate, so that if a node has been partially activated recently and now receives new input, the node is already "warmed up," and so even a weak input may be sufficient to bring the node to the threshold needed to summon attention.

Evidence Favoring the Network Approach

We now have a preliminary description of the network: *Spreading activation* causes different *activation levels* of the network's *nodes*. The activation may not reach *threshold* immediately, but *subthreshold activation* can accumulate. When a node's activation does reach threshold levels, this summons attention. In addition, once a node is activated to threshold levels, it will serve as a source for further spreading activation, exciting still other nodes.

This still leaves much unspecified, but is sufficient for us to begin considering the relevant data. We begin by discussing some of the results that we have already seen, showing how these are encompassed by the network. This approach will allow us to illustrate how the network functions and to document the power of this mode of thinking.

HINTS

Why do hints help us to remember? Why is a free-recall procedure ("What was on the list?") more difficult than cued recall ("Was there a word on the list that rhymed with 'glove'?")?

In a recall test, one's entry point for memory search is the node representing memory of the context of learning. One presumably remembers general facts about the learning episode—that there was a list, that the list took place in a certain time and place—and the nodes representing these facts provide the starting point for search through the network. Once these context nodes are activated, the activation spreads via associative links to the nodes representing the TBR (once again, "to-be-remembered") material.

However, the associations between these "context markers" and the TBR material may not be strong, in which case insufficient activation will reach the target nodes from this source. That is, the target nodes will receive only subthreshold activation, and so will not be "found." However, with hints or cues, we can feed the target nodes activation from two different sources. If subjects hear a hint like "the word sounds like 'glove'," this will cause activation of the GLOVE node, and so activation will spread out from this source. If the word "shove" was on the list, its node can now receive activation both from the context markers and from the rhyme cue. The combined activation received from these two sources will be more likely to raise the target node to threshold levels (Figure 11–1).

MNEMONICS

In Chapter 9, we saw that mnemonic devices (such as the "method of loci") clearly improve memory. In a mnemonic, one takes advantage of an already existing strong set of associations. Rather than creating new associations to bind words together, one uses a skeleton already in place. In the method of loci, one exploits associations among familiar places; in the rhyming mnemonic we presented in Chapter 9, one takes advantage of the associations already existing among the numbers. Those strong

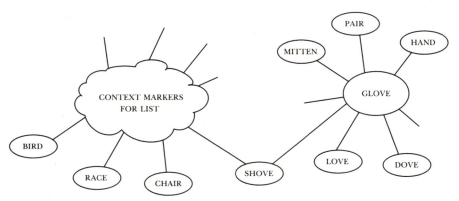

FIGURE 11–1. *Activation of a Node from Two Sources.* A subject is asked, "Was there a word on the list that rhymed with 'glove'?" This activates nodes representing context markers for the list, and also the GLOVE node. The context markers are linked with various nodes, including nodes representing the words on the list. The GLOVE node is linked to various nodes, including words with similar sounds. If activation spreads from both GLOVE and the context markers, then the sought-after word ("shove") will receive activation from both sources, so this node is likely to be activated. In this sketch, words within ellipses represent individual nodes; no attempt has been made here to depict the propositions represented in the network.

associations then provide the glue that holds the list together. To use our metaphor from before, rather than building new highways among the TBR items, one can simply tie the items to cities (nodes) that are themselves already well connected to each other.

The underlying assumption here is that activation may spread more efficiently through very well established, *indirect* connections than it will via direct, but less well established connections. Thus it is in the memorizer's interest to let new connections be "parasitic" on old ones, linking words (or whatever) together by hanging them onto an already well connected frame. Moreover, if one activates any part of the mnemonic's frame, then all of the other parts will be activated as well, thanks to the strong connections among the mnemonic's parts. Therefore, in hunting through memory, all one has to do is find any piece of the mnemonic. Once the first piece is found, the connections will virtually guarantee that the rest of the mnemonic (and the material it is carrying) will be found as well (Figure 11–2).

STATE DEPENDENCY

As we saw in Chapter 8, if one learns materials while sad, or while intoxicated, or while underwater, there will be an advantage to retention

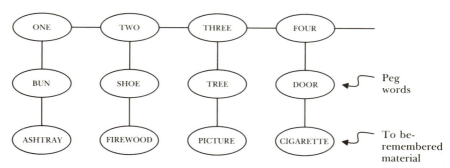

FIGURE 11–2. *Connections among Nodes in a Mnemonic Strategy.* A subject memorizes a series of words ("ashtray," "firewood," "picture". . .) using a mnemonic strategy. The mnemonic is based on the rhyme "one is a bun, two is a shoe, three is a tree. . . ." The rhyme is easily learned, given the links already in place between ONE and TWO, TWO and THREE, and so on, and also the strong connections between the rhymes ("one" and "bun," "two" and "shoe," etc). In learning the word list, subjects make connections between each word and its *peg*—for example, between "bun" (the peg) and "ashtray." (The subject might think of a hamburger bun filled with ashes and cigarette butts.) With these connections, subjects easily remember which word was in each place on the list, or which was associated with "tree" and so on. Subjects will perform less well if asked what word followed "picture" on the list, since there is no connection between picture and its successor (cigarette).

while sad, or while intoxicated, or while underwater. Why is this? The hypothesis is that these states have a particular set of nodes connected to them. Perhaps there is literally a SAD node that is activated when one is sad; perhaps there is a set of thoughts that often occur when one is sad, and so the nodes representing these thoughts will be activated once one is in a sad state. If these nodes were active during learning, associations may have been formed between them and the nodes for the TBR material (cf. Gilligan & Bower, 1984; Bower, 1981).

At the time of test, the nodes for the state would work the same way that hints do: Imagine that the nodes for the TBR material are receiving subthreshold activation from context markers. In addition, the nodes affiliated with sadness (or intoxication or being underwater) are activated. If these nodes were activated during the learning episode, there is likely to be an associative link between these nodes and those for the TBR material. Thus the nodes for the TBR material will also receive activation from these "state" nodes. This state activation will combine with the activation arriving from the nodes representing the context, and so will fully activate the sought-after nodes (Figure 11–3).

More Direct Tests of the Network Claims

The network seems to provide a natural way to bring together the evidence presented in the last several chapters. This by itself suggests that the network notion is a coherent and useful way to think about

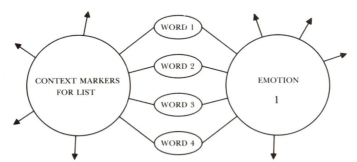

FIGURE 11–3. *A Network Representation of State-Dependent Retrieval.* A subject learns a word list while in a specific context (a particular room, a particular time of day) and also while in a specific mood. Associations are therefore strengthened between the nodes representing the words and the nodes representing the context, *and also* between nodes representing the words and nodes representing the emotion. If the subject is in the same mood during the memory test, then the word nodes will be receiving activation from this mood source as well, making it more likely that the sought-after nodes will be activated. (Adapted from Bower, 1981.)

memory—a single framework into which we can bring many different claims and findings. But, in addition, the network approach leads directly to several specific predictions about memory. In this section, we look at evidence designed to assess some of these predictions, and therefore the assumptions and claims built into the network idea.

SPREAD OF ACTIVATION AND PRIMING

A key idea of an associative net is that activation spreads through links to activate nodes, and that activation can "accumulate" if, for example, activation reaches a node from more than one source. Evidence that directly supports this claim comes from several paradigms, one of which is the **lexical-decision task**.

In a lexical-decision experiment, subjects are shown a series of letter sequences on a computer screen. Some of the sequences spell words; others *look like* words, but are in fact made up (for example, "blar" or "plome" or "tuke"). Subjects' task is to hit a "yes" button if the sequence spells a word, and a "no" button otherwise.

The idea behind this procedure is that subjects perform this task by "looking up" these words in their "mental dictionary." If subjects recognize a word as one they know—that is, if they find it in the dictionary— then they will respond "yes." We can therefore use subjects' speed of response in this task as an index of how quickly subjects can locate the word in their memories.

Meyer and Schvaneveldt (1971; Meyer, Schvaneveldt, & Ruddy, 1972, 1974) presented subjects with pairs of letter strings like those shown in Table 11–1; subjects had to decide whether each letter string was a word or not. Notice that the procedure contains several different kinds of pairs—sometimes both are words, sometimes both are not. Sometimes it

Table 11–1. Stimuli and Results from a Priming Experiment

Positive Pairs		Negative Pairs		
Unrelated	Related	Nonword First	Nonword Second	Both Nonwords
Nurse	Bread	Plame	Wine	Plame
Butter	Butter	Wine	Plame	Reab
940 msec	855 msec	904 msec	1087 msec	884 msec

Note: Subjects must respond "yes" if both stimuli in the pair are words ("positive" pairs); subjects respond "no" if either stimulus in the pair is not a word ("negative" pairs). Within the positive pairs, some pairs are semantically related ("bread," "butter"), while others are not ("nurse," "butter"). Thanks to the spread of activation, responses are quickest for the related pairs.

After Meyer & Schvaneveldt, 1971.

is the first string that is a word, but not the second; sometimes the reverse is true. Our main interest, though, is with the first two types of pairs: For these, both strings are words, but for some the words are semantically related, while for others they are not.

Consider what will happen if we give subjects a "related" pair, for example, "bread, butter." Subjects first respond "yes" to "bread," presumably having located the BREAD node in memory. That is, the BREAD node has been activated to threshold level, leading to the subject's response. But if that node has been activated, then a spread of activation should have begun, and so other nodes linked to the BREAD node should receive some of this activation. It seems likely that the association from "bread" to "butter" is a strong one, and therefore the BUTTER node has received some of this activation.

Having made a decision about "bread," the subject now turns her attention to the second word in the pair, namely, "butter." To reach a response, the subject must activate the BUTTER node to threshold levels. But in this case, the process is already begun, since the node has just received some activation from the previous decision. Therefore, it will require less *additional* activation to bring the BUTTER node to threshold, and it seems a fair bet that it will therefore require less *time* for the BUTTER node to reach threshold. Hence we expect quicker responses to "butter" in this context, compared to a context in which "butter" is preceded by some unrelated word, or by a nonword.

As Table 11–1 shows, this **priming** result is in fact what occurs. Subjects' lexical-decision responses were faster if the present stimulus word was preceded by a semantically related word, as we would expect based on spreading activation and accumulating activation levels. Priming effects are easy to demonstrate and, in fact, can be used as a way to try and "map" the network. That is, we can discover how closely associated two nodes are by assessing the degree to which activation of one primes the other. By repeating this for many pairs of nodes, we can begin to outline the patterns and organizations of memory. (For related results, see Fischler, 1977a, b; Neely, 1977; Quillian, 1969; Ratcliff & McKoon, 1981.)

SENTENCE VERIFICATION

When one searches through the network, activation spreads from node to node to node. Search through the network, therefore, is like travel, and the farther the distance one must travel, the longer it will take to reach one's destination. In a classic experiment, Collins and Quillian (1969) tested this claim, using the sentence-verification task introduced in Chapter 10. Subjects were shown sentences on a computer screen such as "A robin is a bird," "A robin is an animal," "Cats have claws," or "Cats have hearts." Mixed together with these obviously true sentences were a variety of false sentences ("A cat is a bird") and subjects simply had to hit a "true" or "false" button as quickly as they could.

Collins and Quillian reasoned as follows: Subjects perform this task by searching through memory for an associative bridge from, say, "robin" to "bird." If the two nodes are directly linked by an association, as robin and bird probably are, it will require little time to traverse the distance between them, and subjects will quickly answer "true." If the two nodes are connected only indirectly (like "robin" and "animal"), it will take more time to establish that there is a link between them, and so responding will be slower. Therefore, we would expect slower responses to sentences that require a "two-step" connection than to sentences that exploit a single connection. "A robin is a bird" is a case of the latter sort; "A robin is an animal" is a case of the two-step sort.

In addition, Collins and Quillian supposed that, in the interests of economy, memory does not store redundant material. That is, there is no point storing "Cats have hearts" *and* "Dogs have hearts" *and* "Squirrels have hearts" and so on; likewise for "Squirrels eat food" and "Cats eat food" and so on. Instead, Collins and Quillian supposed, memory might contain associations from DOG or CAT or SQUIRREL to the node for "animal" and then associations from ANIMAL to the nodes for HEART and EATS FOOD and the like. That way, the heart information would be entered into the network just one time, rather than over and over. On this logic, we would expect relatively slow responses to "Cats have hearts" (since, to choose a response, a subject must locate the linkages from CAT to ANIMAL to HEART) and relatively quick responses to "Cats have claws." Here there would be a direct connection, since not all animals have claws, so this information could not be entered at the higher level (Figure 11–4).

These predictions were all borne out in the Collins and Quillian data, as can be seen in Figure 11–5. Responses to sentences like "A canary is a canary" take approximately 1000 msec (1 second). This is presumably the time it takes just to read the sentence, to move one's finger on the response button, and so on. Sentences like "A canary can sing" are hypothesized to require an additional step of traversing one link in memory, and in fact yield slightly slower responses. Sentences like "A canary can fly" are hypothesized to require traversing two links, from CANARY to BIRD and then from BIRD to CAN FLY, and in fact are correspondingly slower.

The picture presented in the Collins and Quillian data is remarkably clear cut: All we need, to predict response times, is to count the number of associative steps that must be traversed to support a response. In addition, the evidence fits with the claim that material is not stored redundantly. That is, information seems to be stored as high as possible in the hierarchy.

However, some research challenges both of these claims (e.g., Conrad, 1972; McCloskey & Glucksberg, 1978; Smith, Rips, & Shoben, 1974; Rips, Shoben, & Smith, 1973). Collins and Quillian are correct that re-

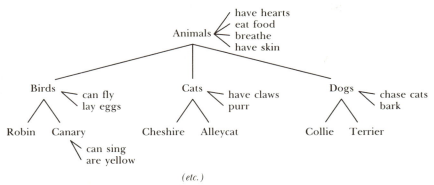

FIGURE 11–4. *Hypothetical Memory Structure for Knowledge about Animals.* Collins and Quillian proposed that memory has a hierarchical structure. This system avoids redundant storage of connections between CATS and HAVE HEARTS, and between DOGS and HAVE HEARTS, and so on for all the other animals. Instead, HAVE HEARTS is stored as a property of all animals. To confirm that cats have hearts, one must therefore traverse two links: from CAT to ANIMAL, and from ANIMAL to HAVE HEARTS. This should take more time than it would to confirm, say, that cats have claws and that cats purr, which require traversing only one link. (After Collins & Quillian, 1969.)

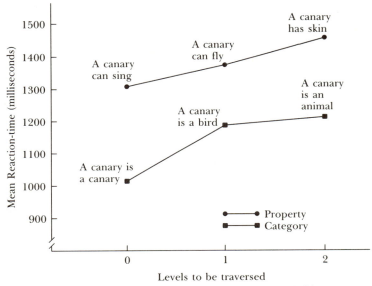

FIGURE 11–5. *Time Needed to Confirm Various Semantic Facts.* Subjects must answer "true" or "false" to sentences, such as "A canary is a bird." The graph shows the relation between the type of sentence and how long it took subjects to respond to each sentence (response time, or RT). Subjects were fastest when no links in the network had to be traversed, slower when the necessary ideas were separated by one link, and slower still if the ideas were separated by two links. (After Collins & Quillian, 1969.)

sponse times are influenced by the number of associative steps traversed, but this is not the whole story. We have already seen that other factors enter into the speed of travel within the network, including, of course, recency and frequency of use of a specific pathway (Conrad, 1972; Glass, Holyoak, & O'Dell, 1974).

For example, we saw in Chapter 10 that subjects are quicker to assent to "Robin is a bird" than to "Penguin is a bird" (Rosch, 1973, 1975; Smith, Rips, & Shoben, 1974). If we simply count nodes, these are both one-step connections, yet one is much quicker than the other. This is not difficult to explain: These typicality effects, within the network conception, might be due to frequency of association (higher for "robin" and "bird" than for "penguin" and "bird"). But this does make clear that things are somewhat more complicated than Figure 11–4 might imply.

Finally, evidence suggests that the principle of economy envisioned by Collins and Quillian does not always hold. For example, from the standpoint of economy, the property of "having feathers" should be associated with the BIRD node rather than (redundantly) with the ROBIN node and the EAGLE node and so forth. Therefore there should be a two-step connection from any particular bird to FEATHERS, producing (relatively) slow responses. However, subjects are likely to respond very quickly to a sentence like "Peacocks have feathers." This is because, in observing peacocks or speaking of peacocks, one often thinks about or refers to their prominent tail feathers (cf. Conrad, 1972). Thus, even though it is informationally redundant, a strong association between PEACOCK and FEATHERS is likely to be established.

For these and other reasons, psychologists have moved away from the specific model proposed by Collins and Quillian (1969) in which the network of associations has a hierarchical form, as shown in Figure 11–4. The Collins and Quillian data do tell us that we can predict memory access by counting the number of nodes subjects must traverse in answering a question *all other things being equal.* But we cannot neglect the "all other things" phrase. Speed of memory access depends on a number of factors—the efficiency of specific associations, the existence of special connections, and something referred to as the "degree of fan."

"DEGREE OF FAN"

Imagine a sentence-verification task in which a subject confronts (on separate trials) the following two sentences: "A robin has wings" and "An aardvark has legs." The associations between ROBIN and its properties are likely to be stronger than those between AARDVARK and its properties, simply because subjects in these experiments have encountered more robins than aardvarks. In addition, though, there are probably a great many more associations radiating out from ROBIN than there are from AARDVARK. For example, we can think of only a few aardvark properties, but can think of many things true of robins. As illustrated in Figure 11–6,

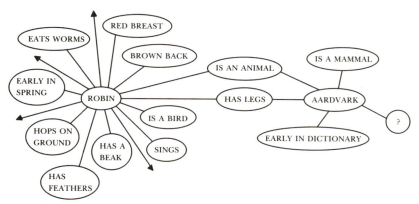

FIGURE 11–6. *Degree of Fan for Two Nodes.* One knows many facts about robins, and so there are many linkages radiating out from the ROBIN node—a high degree of fan. In contrast, one knows relatively few facts about aardvarks, and so few linkages radiate out from the AARDVARK node—a low degree of fan.

this implies that the ROBIN node will look like the hub of a many-spoked wheel, and the AARDVARK node will not. In the standard terminology for this, ROBIN has a "high degree of fan" (many things fanning out from it), while AARDVARK has a "low degree."

The notion of "fan" has been extensively explored by Anderson and his associates (Anderson, 1974, 1976; Lewis & Anderson, 1976; also Peterson & Potts, 1982; Thorndyke & Bower, 1974). Why should degree of fan matter? The answer to this depends on how one conceives of spreading activation. We have already assumed that the spread of activation goes in all directions at once. That is, once a node is activated, the links radiating out from this node will all receive activation energy simultaneously—the links will be activated in **parallel** with each other, rather than in some **serial** order. In addition, it seems sensible to assume that the quantity of activation is limited—there is just so much to go around, and the more ways it is divided, the less will go to each recipient. Thus a certain amount of activation going into the AARDVARK node will be divided (say) only five ways, while the activation going into ROBIN will be much more thinly divided.

Does degree of fan matter for memory retrieval? This question is difficult to ask with "robin" and "aardvark," precisely because there is a difference between both degree of fan and strength of association. Imagine that we ask subjects to verify two sentences: "Aardvarks have legs" and "Robins have wings." The prediction is that the ROBIN node has a greater degree of fan, and this will slow down verification of its sentence. At the same time, the links radiating out from ROBIN are likely to be more efficient, thanks to frequency of use, and this will speed up verification of its sentence. Hence we have two effects on the scene, working in opposite directions, and potentially canceling each other out.

To ask whether degree of fan matters, we need to find a case in which two nodes differ *only* in degree of fan. One way to do this is to start, so to speak, from scratch. For example, Anderson (1974) taught subjects a set of sentences about people in locations: "The doctor is in the bank"; "The fireman is in the park"; "The lawyer is in the church"; "The lawyer is in the park"; and so on. In the full set of sentences, some subjects (for example, the doctor) appeared in only one location (the bank); other subjects (the lawyer) appeared in two locations. Likewise, some locations (the church) contained only one person; other locations (the park) contained two. In this way, Anderson controlled the degree of fan from the nodes representing each of these terms—there was greater fan for PARK than for CHURCH, greater fan for LAWYER than for DOCTOR, and so on.

At the same time, all of these were new facts for the subjects, since Anderson had just made them up. Therefore, the strength of the association for these sentences started out at zero. By controlling the learning process, he controlled the growth of association strength and, in particular, made certain that association strength was the same for all of the sentences. In this way, Anderson ended up with a set of nodes that differed in degree of fan, but not in the strength of their connections to other nodes.

Once subjects had memorized these sentences, they were given a recognition test in which a series of test sentences was presented. Subjects had to decide as quickly as possible whether each of these test sentences had been presented as part of the learning set. As Table 11–2 shows, subjects' speed of response was influenced by degree of fan: Response times were fastest when only one sentence from the learning set had mentioned a specific person or a specific place; response times were slowest when two sentences named a specific person or place. This is

Table 11–2.   Influence of Degree of Fan on Decision Time

Number of Sentences Using a Specific Location	Number of Sentences about a Specific Person	
	1 Sentence	2 Sentences
1 Sentence	1.11 sec	1.17 sec
2 Sentences	1.17 sec	1.22 sec

Note: Subjects were slower in recognizing sentences that involved nodes with a higher degree of fan and faster with sentences that involved a lower degree of fan. The sentences were of the form "The lawyer is in the park." Fan was manipulated by varying how many facts the subjects knew about the lawyer (that is, whether the lawyer appeared in only one of the sentences that had been learned or in two), and also how many facts the subjects knew about the park (that is, whether the park had been mentioned in one of the sentences or in two). The effect observed in this experiment is not large (for example, a 0.06-second difference in the left-hand column), but this is probably because we are considering only small differences in degree of fan (1 versus 2).
After Anderson, 1974.

exactly what we would expect if activation were a fixed quantity, and so, the more ways divided, the less to each recipient. The less to each recipient, the longer it takes for the target node to be fully activated and so, finally, the longer for the response to be chosen.

IS THERE A COST TO KNOWING "TOO MUCH"?

Note an odd consequence of this experiment, and of the notion of fan. In a sense, there is a cost attached to knowing "too much." If one knows only one fact about aardvarks, for example, then this fact will be easily remembered whenever one thinks about aardvarks. That is because, with such a low degree of fan, all the activation from the AARDVARK node will spread down this single association. However, as one learns more and more about aardvarks, the degree of fan increases and so less and less activation will spread down any particular association.

This observation is in line with some of the phenomena we discussed in earlier chapters, but seems to conflict with other phenomena we have encountered. We saw in Chapter 3 that Pavlovian conditioning proceeds most quickly in the early trials, and more slowly in later trials. That is, the learning of simple associations seems to proceed most quickly when the learning has just begun; as the organism learns more and more, the pace of learning becomes slower and slower. This seems consistent with the idea that knowledge somehow *impedes* learning, just as in the fan effect.

On the other hand, much of Chapter 9 argued that learning is facilitated when we understand the to-be-remembered material—that is, when we can fit the TBR material into things we already know. This indicates that knowledge helps learning, contrary to the observations just described.

How do we resolve this seeming paradox? One possible solution is this: Consider the simple bit of network shown in Figure 11–7. At an early stage of learning, there is one association radiating out from Node A; therefore all of A's activation will be channeled to Node B. This is Situation 1 in the figure. At a later stage of learning (Situation 2), the degree of fan from Node A has increased; now Node B receives only one-tenth of A's activation. If we are studying the learning of some isolated fact (such as an association between CS and US) then this is all that is going on.

But what if the learning concerns a more complex domain, such as the learning that you are doing right now, as you read this chapter? In this case, one is not just learning a bunch of facts about a single node (not just adding new associations to Node A, for example); instead, the learning is leading to a whole network of new connections. New connections might be made between Node C and Node B, and between Node D and Node B, and so forth. This is Situation 3 in the figure. In this case, thanks to the effects of fan, B receives less input from A than it did at the outset.

Situation 1

Situation 2

Situation 3

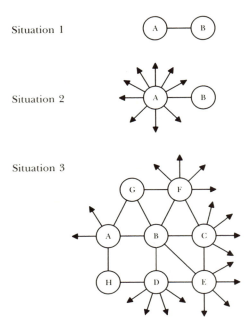

FIGURE 11–7. *Degree of Fan versus the Number of Retrieval Paths.* Early in learning (Situation 1), a subject may know only a single fact about A, namely, that it is associated with B. Later in learning (Situation 2), the subject may have learned more about A. Thanks to the increased fan, less of A's activation spreads to B. This makes it more difficult to activate Node B in Situation 2 than in Situation 1. As an alternative, the subject may learn a rich network of interconnected facts (Situation 3). In this case, A's degree of fan is increasing, so that less of A's activation spreads to B. At the same time, B is receiving activation from many new sources. As a result, B will be *easier* to activate in this case than in Situation 1.

At the same time, B is also receiving input from many other sources. This increase in the number of sources is likely to compensate for the decrease in activation arriving from any individual source. As a result, Node B will be easier to activate; that is, it will be easier to locate in Situation 3 (within the network) than it was in Situation 1. Thanks to fan, B receives more activation from A in Situation 1 than it does in Situation 2 or 3. But Situation 3 has an even greater advantage: the advantage created by the existence of multiple retrieval paths.

Retrieving Information from a Network

So far, things look good for the network model. We have easily encompassed a large set of prior findings; the data also look positive for the claims about spreading activation and fan. In addition, the network idea holds the promise of explaining how we search through memory so quickly and easily.

SEARCHING THROUGH THE NETWORK VIA ASSOCIATIVE LINKS

To see the advantages of the associative net in memory search, let's begin with a familiar case. Imagine that you are searching through a book, but do not know quite how the sought-after material was indexed. For example, perhaps you are trying to locate the passage in this book that defined "episodic" and "semantic" (or "context-free") memory. Unfortunately, you do not remember quite what the terms were, and so you might initially look in the index under "source memory." Close, but not quite. This term is in our index, and will guide you to material related to what you seek, but will not guide you to what you seek. Now what? With most indexing systems, it is no help that you have gotten halfway to your goal—that is, located related material. You would have no option but to go back to the index and try again. And if you still do not remember the term "episodic memory," you will not be able to use the index very successfully.

The problem, roughly, is that an index is an all-or-none affair. If the index leads you to your goal (the sought-for information), you are done. If the index brings you only part way to your goal (that is, to a related topic), the index provides no way to take advantage of this; you must start again with a new lead from the index.

Of course, in reality, there is something you can do instead of returning to the index: If you find a topic related to what you seek, you might look one page earlier, and one page later, taking advantage of the fact that most writers put related material together. Once you are in the vicinity, it pays to search the neighborhood.

This helps, but is a limited strategy. It is just not possible to put all related material together. A given topic might be related to a large number of other topics and themes and, with limitations of space, not all of these can be put into the same physical vicinity. But this is easily solved: What we could do is put notes in the book's margins, along the lines of "For related information, see page X and page Y." In this case, we could link together related topics both by physical proximity and by these pointers; this will allow a much richer set of interconnections.

With these pointers in place, the index only needs to lead you approximately to the right location. Once there, you are presented with a set of pointers, all relevant to the topic at hand. Obviously, this will narrow things down appreciably. These pointers might lead to the target information; if not, they would lead to other, related topics that may in turn lead to your goal.

All depends on having the right pointers. It is also advantageous to have neither too few pointers nor too many. If too few pointers, one will not take full advantage of the system—bridges may be omitted between related topics. If too many pointers, though, some of the advantages of this system may be lost. Imagine that the index sends you to page 191 of this book, and on that page you find some useful materials and also the message "For related information, see all of the rest of this book." In our earlier terms, this would be an infinitely high degree of fan, and, as Harry Nillson (1985) remarked, "A point in every direction is the same as no point at all!"

All of this is easily translated into network terms. Associative links guide search through memory just as the "See also" pointers can guide search through a textbook. In both cases, this greatly facilitates the search. As long as the search begins in roughly the right neighborhood, the network of associations will gradually lead to the sought-after information.

Our earlier discussion of hints and state dependency indicates a further aspect of the network that will help the search along. Consider what happens if one tries to remember "a word from the previous list" that is also "the name of a fruit." To continue our metaphor, this is like searching memory with more than one "index" listing. This will, in essence, provide two separate "See also" lists, one starting from the context markers and one from FRUIT. Then all one has to do is to find what item or items are mentioned on both lists. Spreading activation will accomplish this by spreading out from both of these entry points and "converging" on the sought-after node.

FINDING ENTRY NODES

The preceding section concerned how associative links guide a search from an "entry point" in the network to the sought-after information. But what starts this process? How does one get to the entry point in the first place? We mentioned an "index," but how serious a suggestion could this be?

On reflection, an "index" system for memory seems enormously unlikely. If each node were somehow named in the index, then there would be as many index entries as there are nodes. In that case, all we have done is substitute one problem for another—instead of searching through the nodes, we now must search through the index.

How, then, do we enter the associative net, if not through an index? This turns out not to be a difficult problem to solve. Why not link the network directly to the mechanisms of perception? Thus some nodes within the net are "input nodes." In terms of overall functioning, these nodes will be like any others. That is, these nodes will have a varying activation level, and they will be connected to other nodes via associative connections. Once activated, these nodes will send activation energy to the associated nodes. What is special about these input nodes is that they receive most of their input activation from appropriate **detectors**, with these in turn connected to the eyes, ears, and so on.

Consider, for example, the portion of a network shown in Figure 11–8. We will discuss the details of figures like this one in a moment. For now, though, notice that this portion of the network includes ties between APPLE and certain perceptual inputs, in this case, perceptual inputs of various colors. These would be tied in the appropriate way to the visual system, so that the presence of the specified colors would lead to the activation of these input nodes, which in turn would lead to the activation of the APPLE node. Needless to say, this example leaves out a great deal, since apples are not merely a certain color, they are also a certain shape and size and so on. However, these other attributes could be similarly tied, on the one side, to the APPLE node and, on the other side, to the mechanisms in vision.

In a slightly more complicated case, imagine a subject in a lexical-decision experiment. The word "leash," let us say, appears as one of the test items, and since this is obviously a word of English, the subject

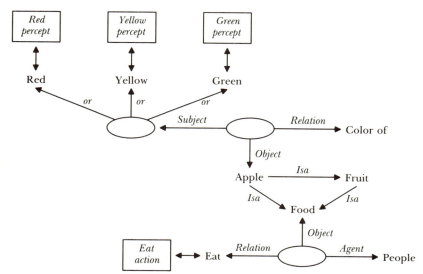

FIGURE 11–8. *A Propositional Network Capturing Some of One's Knowledge about "Apple."* Some of the nodes in this bit of network are tied directly to the mechanisms of perception, so that the presence of a red stimulus, or a yellow one, or a green one will contribute activation to nodes within the network. In this way, perceptual processes can directly activate nodes. The actual network would be much more complicated than this, since apples are not merely a certain color, they are also a certain size, shape, and so on. Details of this network will be discussed in the next two sections of this chapter. (After Anderson, 1980.)

should press the "yes" button. How does the subject locate the node for "leash" in memory? As a partial hypothesis, we might suppose that the subject has an "L" detector, an "E" detector, and so on, all part of the mechanisms of perception. When these are simultaneously activated, this activates the LEASH node. This would, in turn, activate nodes representing the sound of the word, some semantic representation, and so on (Figure 11–9; for a much more complete view of how this might work, see McClelland & Rumelhart, 1981).

What triggers the various letter detectors? An obvious suggestion is that the "L" detector, for example, is triggered by two lower-level detectors, one triggered by the presence of a horizontal line and one by the presence of a vertical line. In this way, simple visual features are detected by the visual system, and these trigger higher-level nodes such as letter nodes, and then these trigger still higher-level nodes. Thus we have a hierarchical system, tied at one end to the visual input and at the other end to the full associative network.

Entry into the system for other purposes or for other tasks would be described in the same terms. If the experimenter asks whether there was a name of a fruit on an earlier-presented list or a word that rhymed with "horse," then "fruit" or "horse" would be recognized via a process similar to the one just described. In these cases, we would have "auditory

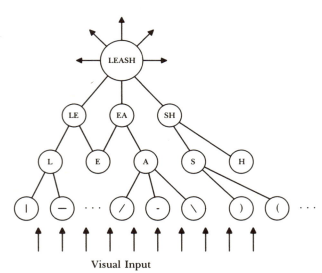

Visual Input

FIGURE 11–9. *A Network of Nodes and Detectors to Recognize the Printed Word "Leash."* The visual input triggers nodes specialized to detect horizontal lines, verticals, and curves of certain shapes. These nodes, once activated, send activation to a different group of nodes, each representing a letter. These nodes would serve as "letter detectors," and would be triggered whenever the appropriate letter is present. These nodes would then activate other nodes and so on, until finally the node for LEASH is activated.

feature detectors," rather than detectors for (say) horizontal and vertical lines. The auditory detectors might respond to features such as certain vowel sounds, or abrupt loudness changes, and so on. In all other ways, the auditory inputs would work much as visual inputs do. Activation would spread from the nodes associated with these detectors, initiating the search. If the experimenter merely says "Recall the list from before," then this would be the initial cue. The word "list" would be recognized through the input process; this would in turn lead to the activation of various context markers associated with the recently studied list. And this, in turn, would lead to the items on the list.

We should note, however, some apparent limitations to this approach: Memory hints and requests for information are likely to be delivered in the form of declarative sentences and questions, and we have said nothing about how the syntax of these might be handled. And the syntax is clearly important. We would want to respond differently to these two memory questions: "Tell me what the mouse ate for dinner yesterday" and "Tell me what ate the mouse for dinner yesterday." These two questions use the same words, and so differ only in syntax. If we are going to retrieve the appropriate information from memory, we must have a means of discriminating between these two requests! The process we have so far sketched, unfortunately, does not provide a ready means of making this discrimination.

Our point for the moment, then, is a modest one. How do we enter the memory network? How do we begin a search through memory? For at least some stimuli, a relatively mechanical process of entry does seen possible. For more complex stimuli, we will need a more elaborate process. Nonetheless, the central point remains: We can seek to hook up the network directly to the mechanisms of perception. In this way, the task of identifying an input is the same as the task of identifying that input's node in the network.

Unpacking the Nodes

We have so far spoken of nodes as representing "ideas" or "memories." But what does this mean? Could a node contain, for example, "my full memory of last summer's vacation"? A node such as this would create two problems for us. First, this node would itself contain a great deal of information. We would then need to figure out how one searches through the information *inside* of a node, in addition to the problem of how one finds nodes in the first place. Second, if we build information into a node, we invite a worry about how one "interprets" or "reads" the information in a node. If each node contained a book-length description of an event or episode, we would need to incorporate into our theorizing some device capable of reading and interpreting this corpus of material. The simpler we keep the node's informational content, the more readily we can define an interpretive device.

Within the associative network, nodes are assumed to represent single, simple concepts, consistent with the examples we have used. In these examples, nodes have stood for simple concepts such as "birthday," or "chair," or "doctor." But how, then, do we represent within the network slightly more complex ideas, such as "George Washington was the first president" or "My favorite movie is *Casablanca*"? How do we represent very complex ideas, such as "Last summer, I went hiking in the mountains and we camped out, and the weather was great, and we went swimming in the lake, and . . ."?

More complex ideas are represented, on the network view, with more network. As a first approximation, an associative link may exist between "George Washington" and "first president," and a set of links may tie together "movie" and "favorite" and "*Casablanca*," and so on. But this is too simple. How, for example, would one represent the contrast between "Sam has a dog" and "Sam is a dog"? Early theorizing sought to distinguish these by introducing different *types* of associative links, with some links representing equivalence or partial-equivalence relations, and other links representing possessive relations. These links were termed **isa** links, as in "Sam isa dog," and **hasa** links, as in "A bird hasa head" or "Sam hasa dog" (Norman, Rumelhart, & Group, 1975).

There are clear limits, however, on what we can encompass with these labeled associations. We would like to get by with a relatively small number of types of links. Otherwise, we would need, once again, to add an "interpreter" or "reader" to understand the links themselves. At the same time, if our set of possible types of links is too small, we will not be able to represent the full range of relationships. For example, it seems certain that we cannot represent relations like "is diametrically opposed to" and "is an appropriate metaphor for" in terms of *isa* and *hasa* connections.

PROPOSITIONAL NETWORKS AND ACT

Researchers have proposed a number of ways that network models might represent complex ideas. These proposals share certain assumptions, but differ in many details. One of these is a model developed by Anderson (Anderson, 1976, 1980; Anderson & Bower, 1973; Reder & Anderson, 1980). We encountered this model briefly at the end of Chapter 10; the background provided in the present chapter will allow us to take a closer look at this important proposal.

Central to Anderson's conception is the idea that human knowledge is represented in the mind in the form of **propositions**. It is propositions that are encoded in the network, and they provide the means through which the network can represent complex ideas and relationships.

Propositions are defined as the smallest unit of knowledge that can be either true or false. For example, "Children love candy" is a proposition, but "children" is not. Propositions are easily represented as sentences, but this is merely a convenience. In fact, the same proposition can be represented in a variety of different sentences: "Children love candy," "Candy is loved by children," and "Kinder lieben Bonbons" all express the same proposition. For that matter, this same proposition can also be represented in various nonlinguistic forms, including a structure of nodes and linkages, and that is exactly what Anderson's model does.

Anderson's theory is embodied in a computer program known as ACT (and, in later versions, as ACT*—see Anderson, 1983). Within ACT, complex ideas are built up out of simpler propositions, and these propositions are represented in terms of associations among nodes. For example, Figure 11–10, which we first met in Chapter 10, shows the simple proposition "Dogs chase cats." The ellipse identifies the proposition itself; the associations radiating out from the ellipse connect to the ideas that are the proposition's constituents. The associations are labeled, but only in general terms. That is, the associations are identified in terms of their syntactic role within the proposition.

This simple network can be expanded to represent more complex bits of knowledge. Figure 10–5 in Chapter 10 (p. 400) shows the proposition "Dogs chew bones" in the context of other propositions about dogs, with the overall structure then serving as part of our knowledge about what a dog is and how it behaves. Figure 11–8, earlier in this chapter (p. 425), shows a portion of the network representing our knowledge about apples. In Chapter 10, we suggested that networks like these could plausibly

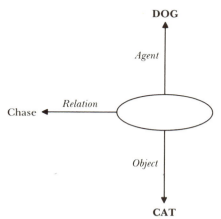

FIGURE 11–10. *Network Representation of the Proposition "Dogs Chase Cats."* The ellipse denotes a proposition; the ellipse is, in essence, the "meeting point" for the various elements of the proposition. Three nodes are involved in this proposition: "dog," "cat," and the action, "chase." Arrows indicate associations among the nodes; labels on the arrows specify the nature of the association. (After Anderson, 1980.)

serve as the mental representation for our schematic knowledge; in these examples, for our dog schema and our apple schema.

As a different example, Figure 11–11 shows how propositions can be interconnected to represent other relationships. This figure depicts the propositional representation of the sentence "Children who are slow eat bread that is cold." Sentences like these have been used to test one aspect of the propositional network. Weisberg (1969) had subjects memorize sentences like this one. Later, subjects were given a single word from the sentence and asked to respond with the first word from the sentence that came to mind. Subjects' responses were in line with the propositional structure of the sentence (as shown in Figure 11–11). That is, if cued with the word "slow," subjects were more likely to respond with words close to "slow" in the propositional representation, rather than with words close to "slow" in the original sentence ("eat," "bread"). These data indicate that subjects' memory representations for this sentence do correspond to the propositional representation.

We have mentioned how ACT represents general knowledge, but how does it represent more specific memories? In the terminology of Chapter 10, our examples so far have centered on *semantic* or *generic* knowledge, rather than on *episodic* knowledge—that is, knowledge about what terms mean and what dogs eat, rather than knowledge about specific events and occasions in our lives. Likewise, we have provided no means for ACT to distinguish between knowledge about, say, dogs in general (as in Figure 11–10) and knowledge about a specific dog, say, Beth's dog, Cerberus.

This problem is easily solved. First, ACT shares with many network models a distinction between **type nodes** and **token nodes**. "Type" refers to a general category, and type nodes are embedded in propositions true for the entire category. A "token" is a specific instance of a category, and token nodes are therefore found in propositions concerning specific events and individuals. Note that type and token nodes are typically connected to each other, as shown in Figure 11–12.

In addition, the ACT model needs to incorporate a means of marking which propositions represent claims about continuing activities, such as

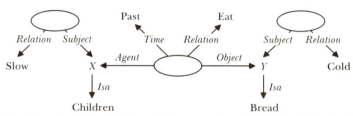

FIGURE 11–11. *Propositional Network Representation of "Children Who Are Slow Eat Bread that Is Cold."* Ideas that are closely linked in this representation turn out to be closely linked in subjects' memories, even if these ideas were not positioned closely together in the original sentence. (After Anderson, 1985.)

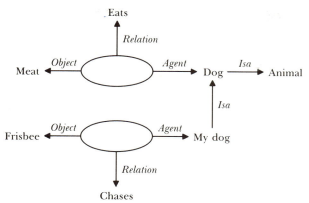

FIGURE 11–12. *Networks Contain Information about Categories and about Individuals.* This fragment of a network contains a "type node," representing dogs in general, and a "token node," representing a specific dog ("my dog"). The type node is linked to propositions true for all dogs; the token node is linked to propositions true only for "my dog." That is, all dogs eat meat. Not all dogs chase Frisbees, although "my dog" does. The type node and token node are linked to each other, indicating that "my dog" is a member of the category "dogs."

"Jacob feeds the ducks," and which propositions represent specific statements, such as "Yesterday, Jacob fed the ducks in the park." ACT addresses this by incorporating time and location nodes as part of propositions. That is, in addition to marking the subject and object of a proposition, ACT marks when and where the proposition was true, and in this fashion can represent facts about specific episodes (Figure 11–13).

In summary, the ACT model shares many claims with other network models: Nodes are connected by associative links. Some of these links are

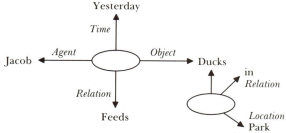

FIGURE 11–13. *Representing Episodes within a Propositional Network.* In order to represent episodes, the propositional network includes time and location nodes. This fragment of a network represents two propositions—the proposition that Jacob yesterday fed ducks, and the proposition that the ducks are in the park. Note that no time node is associated with the proposition about the ducks being in the park. Therefore, what is represented is that the feeding of the ducks was yesterday, but the ducks are generally in the park.

stronger than others, with the strength of the link depending on how frequently and recently the link has been used. Once a node is activated, the process of spreading activation causes the nearby nodes to become activated as well. ACT is distinctive, however, in its attempt to represent knowledge in terms of propositions, and the promise of this approach has attracted the support of many researchers in this area.

Evaluating Network Models

Network models have generated much excitement and much research in the field, and strike many as our best hypothesis about how knowledge is represented in the mind. These models have attempted to characterize both our semantic or generic knowledge and our knowledge about specific episodes.

At the same time, however, these models have been controversial. In this section, we will review some of the concerns that have arisen about network models, in an attempt to ask whether these models do represent a productive way to theorize about memory.

HOW TO TEST NETWORK MODELS?

Before we consider possible concerns about network models, we should address a preliminary question: How should we go about testing these models? Network models are large and complicated since, after all, they are designed to encompass an enormous amount of knowledge. Our experiments can examine this or that portion of the network, and, to be sure, these experiments yield evidence that something like an associative network plays a role in memory.

But these experiments cannot tell us how the entire network will function, or whether the network will be able to deliver what is promised. For example, we have offered an account of how search through the network proceeds. Key parts of this account are supported by evidence—for example, evidence for the influence of fan and evidence for spreading activation. What this evidence shows, though, is that these mechanisms are involved in memory search. The evidence does not show whether these mechanisms are, by themselves, enough "to get the job done." Bear in mind just how vast our memories seem to be. This leads one to ask: Will spreading activation by itself support a search through a huge number of nodes, with a very high degree of fan? Or will we need to add other mechanisms to support and perhaps guide the search?

Perhaps the best way to tackle these questions might be simply to give it a serious try. If one has a theory of memory and memory organization, a powerful test of the theory would be to build a "working model," based on the theoretical claims, and to examine how well the model performed as an information storage and retrieval device. This is, in fact, one of the main ways that psychologists have attempted to assess the potential of the associative network.

How should this "working model" be created? One way is to design a computer system that functions according to the rules and procedures specified in our theory, and, as we mentioned earlier, theories such as ACT have been embodied in computer programs. This allows us to see how well the computer does in "learning," in storing new information, in retrieving facts based on some cue or hint, and so forth. If the computer fails in these tasks, or does less well than humans do, we know that something is missing (or wrong) in the theory. What if the computer succeeds? This would indicate that the processes and strategies programmed into the computer are sufficient to accomplish the tasks of learning and remembering. This computer success would not by itself show that humans use the same processes and strategies. It would, however, be a strong argument that the theory must be taken seriously as a potential account of human performance.

It would take us rather far afield to evaluate these modeling efforts in any detail. To make a long story short, though, it is not currently possible to point to a full working model of an associative network and say, "See? Here is a successful simulation of human memory prowess." That is to say, all of this is "work in progress." The available models work reasonably well, but have various blemishes, and typically work only on a scale far more modest than "all of knowledge." At this stage, it is not yet possible to interpret the status of network models. One could argue that the limitations of current models reflect deep inadequacies in the network approach. But one could also argue that the limitations merely reflect the early state of the models' evolution. With further work and refinements, perhaps these weaknesses will be overcome.

For present purposes, then, the moral is a simple one: Computer implementation of psychological models provides a potentially powerful tool for testing the models. The evidence so far indicates limits on what these models can accomplish, but there is room for disagreement about what these limits are telling us (see Charniak & McDermott, 1985; Johnson-Laird, Herrmann, & Chaffin, 1984; Smith, Adams, & Schorr, 1978; Wexler, 1978; Winston, 1984).

In considering why this might be so, our plan is not to look at the models themselves. Instead, we will look at some of the potential "trouble spots" for this modeling effort. We will first present the concerns, and then circle back to ask how we might address these concerns.

RETRIEVAL BLOCKS AND PARTIAL RETRIEVALS

One attractive feature of the associative net is that activation spreads more or less in all directions, more or less automatically. If this were not the case, we would need to add to our theorizing some means of "directing" the activation, or supervising the search. As we mentioned before, spreading activation removes this problem altogether. One does not *choose* which of the many associations to travel, in moving out from one's starting point in the network; one just lets the activation travel wherever the connections lead.

But do things always work in a fashion consistent with this "automatic" view? Try to think of the word that means a type of carving done on whale bone, often depicting whaling ships or pictures of whales. Try to think of the name of the navigational device used by sailors to determine the positions of stars. Try to think of the name of the ancient Greek orator who taught himself to speak clearly by practicing his speeches with pebbles in his mouth. Chances are that, in at least one of these cases, you found yourself in a frustrating state—certain you knew the word, but unable to come up with it. The word was, as they say, right on the "tip of your tongue," and, following this lead, psychologists refer to this as the **T.O.T.** phenomenon. Subjects in the T.O.T. state often know correctly that the word is somewhere in their vocabulary; they often correctly remember what letter the word begins with, how many syllables it has, and approximately what it sounds like. Thus a subject might remember "It's something like Sanskrit" in trying to remember "scrimshaw," or "something like secant" in trying to remember "sextant" (Brown & McNeill, 1966; James, 1890/1950; Read & Bruce, 1982; Reason & Lucas, 1984; by the way, the Greek orator who practiced with pebbles in his mouth was Demosthenes).

In addition, many people report that, when in the T.O.T. state, the best thing to do is not to try and remember the word. Instead, one should simply try to think about something else for a while, and, in a few minutes, the word will "come to you." In the available research, this seems to be true, but not all the time. If one is in the T.O.T. state and keeps coming up with the wrong word (for example, Sanskrit), then one is best served by giving up for a while and trying again later. If one is in the T.O.T. state (that is, knows that the word is in one's vocabulary, but can't think of it) and nothing is coming to mind (no "false leads"), then one seems better served by continuing to search memory for the word (Reason & Lucas, 1984).

A related finding was reported by Hart (1965, 1967). Hart used a three-step procedure in his study. First, in a recall test, subjects were asked a variety of questions, such as "What is the name of the largest planet in our solar system?" Second, if subjects could not recall the answer, they were asked if they thought they would recognize the correct answer if it were shown to them. Third, subjects were given a recognition test on the same information—for example, "Is the largest planet Pluto, Venus, Earth, or Jupiter?" Hart's data show that subjects were able to predict their own recognition performance with some accuracy. That is, subjects were more likely to choose the correct answer for questions for which they had indicated that they knew the unrecalled item, compared to questions for which they claimed they did not know the answer. In Hart's terms, when subjects had a **feeling of knowing** the answer, they typically did know it.

These results do not easily fit with the network view. Clearly, a subject in the T.O.T. state has reached the vicinity of the sought-after word, as is true for a subject with a "feeling of knowing." Otherwise, in the T.O.T. case, we have no explanation of how the subject comes up with the starting letter and number of syllables. And, presumably, there is much activation in this vicinity—especially given the time and effort and concentration one spends in trying to find the word. But the activation seems not to spread to the word node itself, or, if it does, the activation of this word node is not being recognized or acknowledged. We will need to complicate our story somewhat to explain this sort of "near-miss retrieval failure." At the least, it looks like we cannot conceive of spreading activation as a purely mechanical process whose success is guaranteed once one is in the correct memory vicinity. It would seem instead that some other sort of control structure, in this case *undermining* memory search, is on the scene. (For a fuller discussion of these "retrieval blocks," and how they might be accommodated within a network view, see Roediger & Neely, 1982.)

FINDING MORE DISTANT CONNECTIONS

Our second concern is, in a sense, the mirror image of the points just raised. The problem of T.O.T. phenomena suggests that we sometimes fail to locate memories despite close connections and plenty of activation. We can equally well worry about *success* in locating memories when there do not seem to be close connections, or when the connections are indirect.

The crux of the issue here is part psychology, part arithmetic. Consider first the range of jobs we want associative links to do for us—they tie together episodic memories, they tie together generic memories, they tie together aspects of our concepts (for example, the "possession of feathers" is presumably part of, or closely tied to, our concept of "bird," and the linkage between these is, once again, an association). Given all this, it becomes clear that the number of associative linkages radiating out from any individual concept—that is, the realistic degree of fan—will be very high indeed.

We have already said that only some of the links radiating out from a node will be efficient—namely, those used frequently or recently. But, realistically, what is the number of these likely to be? How many strong associations does one have, say, to "water"? Is, say, 100 a halfway plausible number? We suspect that this is a gross underestimate, but it will serve for the moment. Using this estimate, think about what happens when activation spreads outward from the WATER node. One hundred other nodes each receive some activation (Figure 11–14). If the sought-for information is directly associated with the WATER node, things will now go well: One only has to choose which among these 100 is the node one seeks. (We stand silent on how exactly this choice occurs; perhaps one simply reacts to whichever node is most highly activated.)

What if the sought-for node is *not* directly tied to WATER? What if it is tied by means of one intermediate step? In this case, 100 nodes receive activation directly from WATER, and then activation spreads out from these. If each of these is connected to 100 more nodes, we end up with activation reaching $100 \times 100 = 10,000$ nodes. How among these do we find the sought-for information? We cannot search through them one by one, but then how? And, of course, if the sought-for node is still one more step removed, we need to let activation spread once again, so that now activation reaches $100 \times 100 \times 100$ nodes, an even million. We earlier spoke of the associative pointers leading us to the right vicinity, but now, when we think about it, the vicinity may be very large indeed, *still leaving us* with a search problem!

Clearly, we must steer a path between two dangers. One danger is that the spreading activation will spread too far. In this case, too many nodes will be activated, and we will lose the selective guidance we hoped for in

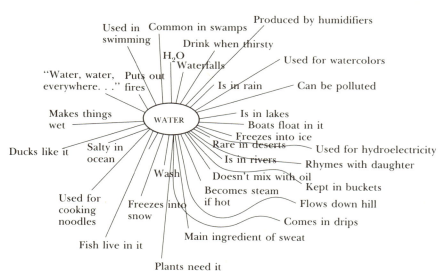

FIGURE 11–14. *How Many Associations Are There to "Water"?* There are probably a huge number of linkages radiating out from each node; we have shown here only some of the ideas associated with the node for WATER. Each of these associations leads to some other node, and there are many linkages radiating out from those other nodes. If activation spreads out just one step, a large number of nodes will be activated. If activation spreads out two steps, how many nodes receive activation?

the first place. The opposite danger is that we could let the spreading activation get weaker and weaker as it moves outward from its source. If this **dampening** happens quickly enough, we will avoid the risk of activating too many nodes, but we risk not finding the node we seek.

The same tension can be framed differently, in terms of degree of fan: If each node is connected to every other node—that is, a very high degree of fan—we lose the selective guidance that linkages were supposed to provide. As we remarked earlier, a point in every direction is the same as no point at all. If, on the other hand, we decrease the fan at each node, then it becomes likely that our entry and target nodes will be connected only indirectly. In this case, we are forced to rely on more steps from entry to target so that each time we let the activation go another step, we multiply again the number of nodes reached. Too high a degree of fan is problematic, and so is too low a degree of fan. Whether there is a middle value that escapes this worry simply remains to be seen.

THE HOMUNCULUS

One of the great advantages of the associative net is that it involves no complex, ill-understood, mysterious processes. Differential activation levels and spreading activation are simple, more or less mechanical processes, easily translated into precise models. The advantage of this is plain—it gives us a model which can (we would think) be firmly and fully spelled out and tested. But the disadvantage of the associative net is also now in view. It is this same mechanical, automatic spread of activation that gives rise to the worries of the previous section: It was the apparent *failure* of the automatic spread of activation that gave rise to the puzzlement over the T.O.T. effect.

Why not let things be a little less mechanical? Imagine, for the sake of argument, that some process "supervised" the spread of activation. If one is trying to remember the chemical formula for water, it will do no good to think of *all* the memory associations for water. One would not want to be reminded, for example, of the poet Coleridge's lines "Water, water, everywhere, / Nor any drop to drink," or of the fact that, when traveling in certain countries, one is warned about drinking the water; nor would one want to be reminded of all the words that rhyme with "water," or of one's last vacation on the lake, or. . . . It would be handy if one could somehow "shut down" these various associations, and let activation spread only in the productive directions, or at least only in those directions with some likelihood of being productive. In this way, one would activate nodes much more selectively, much more *intelligently,* and so not risk activating a vast number of nodes.

Indeed, something like this seems to be going on in the T.O.T. evidence. In the T.O.T. state, it is as if you were systematically guiding activation in the direction expected to be productive, but the expectation, as it turns out, is incorrect. Given this, you keep coming up, over and over, with the wrong word (although a sound-alike word). Once in this state, your best bet is to give up, and to let the word eventually "come to you." Informally, we might say, you need to be more "passive" in the memory search, consistent with the idea that you were blocking retrieval in the first place by virtue of some activity of (mis)directing the search.

It is not hard to see the difficulty in arguments like this. If someone or something "chooses" which nodes to pursue, if someone "directs" the search, then who is it? How does this choice, or this direction, occur? What processes underlie it? How are these processes to be described, and claims about them to be tested?

The worry here is one with a long history. In explaining the overall efficiency of memory search, it is tempting to say that some efficient process or mechanism must guide this search. More broadly, in explaining the intelligence of behavior, it is tempting to say that there must be some processes in the mind that are themselves intelligent, strategic, and foresightful. But this simply postpones an explanation. It is like saying that we act intelligently because we are guided by an intelligent little "person in the head." This explains nothing, because the little person or **homunculus** (as this person is classically called) would itself need to be explained.

We first met this problem in Chapter 1, and again in Chapter 4. There we noted that human behavior (and, in fact, the behavior of many species) seems generally intelligent, reasonable, and governed by strategies and judgment. If we explain this by reference to processes that are intelligent and reasonable, we have simply created a new problem for ourselves, namely, explaining these processes. This has led many scholars to argue that *un*intelligent processes must lie behind the intelligent behaviors we observe. That is, scholars have looked for relatively mechanical processes which, if appropriately set up, might lead to intelligent outcomes. Darwin's theory of natural selection is a proposal in this direction, as is the law of effect (for further discussion, see Chapter 1).

It seems important to appreciate this argument but also not to get carried away with it. The problem with "homunculus" explanations, in essence, is that they are not really explanations. Instead, they are I.O.U.s, a promise of an explanation to come. But this is not a disaster if one is prepared to "pay up" on the I.O.U.; that is, if one can provide an explanation of how the homunculus functions (cf. Rozin, 1976).

To see how this works, let us return to the problem of memory retrieval. It seems desirable that we try to explain as much as we can with relatively passive processes, such as the spread of activation we have been considering throughout this chapter. These processes can be explicitly described; they require no appeal to mysterious Directors or unexplained Guides; they involve no I.O.U.s. But what if we cannot handle all the data in these terms? As we have seen, the T.O.T. effect and the ability to find information despite distant connections suggest that something does guide the memory search. If this evidence is taken at face value, it seems that the spread of activation is not as mechanical or as automatic as our discussion has implied. In short, it looks like we may need a homunculus.

The trick, though, is not to rest content with this as our final account. If there is a Director or Guide, we need to explain how this Director works. We will have more to say about this before we are through, but first we need to consider one last important topic. Before we get to that topic, however, let us review where we are so far. We have seen a quantity of evidence that associations and spreading activation play a role in memory; we have seen a plausible proposal that knowledge can be represented in terms of propositions, and that propositions can then be represented in terms of a network. This invites us to ask if these terms might be all we need to account for the full range of memory successes and memory failures. In that context, we sketched how the network notion explains search and also entry to the network. This sketch, however, could not by itself tell us whether the network is enough "to get the job done." We briefly noted that one attempt to tackle this issue, by generating computer models to implement network claims, has met with mixed success. We then looked at several concerns that might give us some indications about possible trouble spots. Those led us, finally, to the temptation of adding another constituent to our theorizing—namely, some more active agency to guide the memory search. The temptations of this direction are clear. The principal danger of this move is that we simply do not have a good and full theory of how this agency might function.

The Newest Chapter: Connectionism

In the last dozen years or so, an important descendant of the associative network idea has appeared on the intellectual scene, and has generated enormous excitement in psychology as well as in computer science and philosophy. This development seeks to address (among other things) exactly the worries we have just been considering. Rather than addressing these issues by adding a more intelligent component, this new approach goes in the opposite direction, and tries to show just how much we can accomplish with network and more network.

DISTRIBUTED PROCESSING, DISTRIBUTED REPRESENTATIONS

A small number of important innovations have spurred this new wave of associative theorizing, a wave referred to as **connectionism**, or **PDP**. The PDP initials stand for **parallel distributed processing**, and by spelling out what these terms mean we can put the theoretical proposal in view. (For detailed descriptions of PDP proposals, see Ackley, Hinton, & Sejnowski, 1985; Hinton & Anderson, 1981; McClelland & Rumelhart, 1986; Rumelhart & McClelland, 1986.)

One difficulty in the "standard" associative net lies in finding *the* node which carries a particular content. If there is only one target, the target may be difficult to locate. If there were many copies of the target—one here, one there, another there—it would be much easier to come across any one of them. If you photocopy a dozen copies of your shopping list and scatter these around your house, you'll have far less trouble locating the shopping list when you need it.

The PDP approach takes this idea and goes considerably farther with it. In the standard network approach, what it means to "think about" or "remember" a particular idea is to activate the node for that idea. This view of "one idea per node," or "one content per location," is referred to as the idea of **local representation**. Within a PDP network, there are no local representations. There are no nodes that can be spoken of as representing a particular content—no BIRTHDAY node, no GRANDMOTHER node, no node at all to which we can attach a single label.

In a PDP system, contents are represented by widespread patterns of activation. The suggestion, roughly, is that entertaining thoughts about, say, birthdays would correspond to the simultaneous activation of Node 1432 and Node 27,456 and Node 24,478 and a thousand others that we would have to specify. This combination would uniquely correspond to (and thus represent) ideas about birthdays. These same nodes, in different combinations, will also be part of the patterns representing other contents. In other words, the activation of Node 1432 has no intrinsic meaning by itself; we can learn what is being represented only by looking at many other nodes simultaneously, to find out what *pattern* of activation currently exists.

This mode of representation is referred to as **distributed representation**, rather than local representation, and we now have the "DP" in PDP: The PDP networks employ Distributed Processing to represent, and thus to act on, mental contents. This is in some ways a radical idea, and so it is worth spending a moment to make it clear. A metaphor will help. Think about a complicated spy novel. The Master Spy has a plan that involves many operatives. The Master Spy gives Operative X her instructions, thus putting a small piece of the plan into motion. Ditto for Operative Y, and Z, and on through the group. No one of the operatives knows about or can even figure out the entire plan, since she only knows about her small part of the operation. (This is, of course, desirable from the perspective of the Master Spy, since it makes detection of the plan difficult!) The plan is only known to the Master Spy, who oversaw the implementation of the plan's many parts.

Now imagine, as a plot twist, that the Master Spy is killed in a chance accident, immediately after giving the last operative his instructions. Has the plan ceased to exist? There is no longer a "local representation" of it—no one place where the plan exists and is represented in a unitary form. Nonetheless, the plan does continue to exist in a larger sense—in the collective actions of the full set of operatives. The plan is there to be perceived if only we could get a broad enough view—if only we could somehow take a large step back and "view the whole," seeing the actions of these various individuals and seeing the consequences of and the relations among their individual actions. The plan still exists in a "distributed" mode, and would only be detected if we view the action at the aggregate level, not at the level of the parts.

In implementing the Master Spy's plan, there may be various decisions to be made: How the overall plan unfolds will depend on new information coming in; later stages of the plan may depend on how earlier stages went, and so on. This decision-making is not done, however, by a centralized authority. Instead, all decision-making is done at the local level. Each operative makes decisions and takes actions, but, as we have said, each has no idea about how these actions fit into the plan, and therefore there is no way for decisions to be based on considerations of the full pattern. Each operative is able to make only small-scale decisions, about her part in the operation, based on her information.

Thus, not only is the plan itself distributed across the set of operatives, so is the processing: With each operative making only specific, small-scale decisions, the large-scale, "visible" decisions—how the plan responds to contingencies, how the plan reacts to new information—are contained only in the aggregate actions of all the operatives, and so are distributed across the set.

It is critical that all of the operatives go about following their instructions simultaneously, since it is in their collective actions that the plan takes form. Each cannot wait for the others; each cannot depend on the others. In fact, each does not even know the others exist. All of the operatives are working in parallel, and we now meet the final third of the PDP label. What is critical for PDP theorizing is *parallel* distributed processing.

Connectionism may be the ultimate "grass-roots" enterprise. Representations are distributed—the job of representing this or that content is accomplished by the aggregate activities of many units. Processes are also distributed—the job of making decisions, choosing actions, or getting any particular task done is, once again, accomplished by the aggregation of processes operating on a small level, each working only with information that is locally available.

We should make clear, however, the limitations of the metaphor we have been using. The problem, simply, is that the spy network is not distributed enough! The operatives are themselves individuals with knowledge and intelligence. Even if each is ignorant about the overall plan, each is able to contemplate ideas and meanings in his actions and his decision-making. Compared to the nodes within a PDP network, this is far too much processing going on in a single place—that is, too much local processing.

It would be more accurate, although less kind, to describe a PDP network as a vast army of idiots, not spies. This would require that the tasks assigned to each operative be extremely simple, so that the tasks would be within the idiots' very limited competence. This is, however, precisely the proposal of PDP. With enough idiots connected together in the right ways, and with each idiot doing the appropriate, very simple tasks, the aggregate activity of the network will reproduce the full intelligence of which the mind is capable.

Is this absurd? Think about the brain. Individual neurons are structurally and biochemically complicated, but their function is not: Inputs reach the neuron; activation accumulates; when the activation gets to a high enough level, the neuron fires. A simple plan, idiotically simple one might say, yet many millions of these idiots, when connected together in the right ways, do produce the full intelligence of which the mind is capable. Advocates of the PDP approach have in fact argued that PDP networks work in a fashion closely akin to the brain's functioning, and this is viewed as an interesting point in favor of our taking this approach seriously (see many of the contributions to McClelland & Rumelhart, 1986; but also see Crick, 1989).

WHO RUNS THE SHOW?

Who is it that takes the large-scale view of the network's activity, in order to perceive the aggregate pattern and so take action on it? And who takes the role of Master Spy, in order to set up the pattern? Bearing in mind our earlier concerns about avoiding a "homunculus," the answer, not surprisingly, is that no one plays either of these roles. Let us first consider how the pattern gets read and translated into action.

The problem of "reading" the network seems formidable. After all, a lot of the network may be contributing to each (distributed) representation, and so one must survey the entire network's activities to discover what is being represented at any point in time. The suggestion, though, is that this frames the situation in the wrong way. The idea of reading the network implies that the distributed representation will be examined by some centralized authority, and the pattern will then be summarized in some way. That is, a local representation will be generated as the product of reading the broad distributed pattern. But this raises a question: What do we gain by this translation from a distributed representation into a local one?

Think back to our discussion of how one enters a network. The idea was that some nodes are connected directly to perceptual inputs, and so activation of the nodes by the inputs was tantamount to perceptual identification. Thus there was no question of first understanding the stimulus, and then looking it up in the system. That is, we do not use the process depicted in the top of Figure 11–15. Instead, the processes of understanding and look-up are one and the same: The process of understanding the word *is* the process of looking it up, as shown in the bottom of the figure.

The answer to reading a PDP network is analogous. The idea we are rejecting is shown in the top of Figure 11–16; here the net is read, and then this is used as the basis for action. In place of this, why not connect the network directly to "output" nodes, just as we connected it, at the

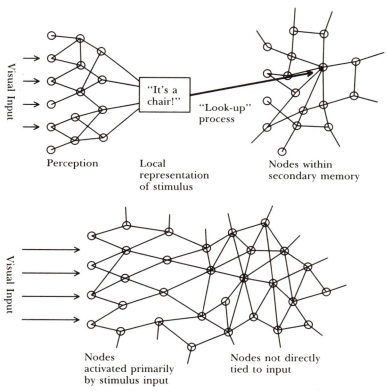

FIGURE 11–15. *Two Views of Entry into the Memory Network.* In the top panel, the processes involved in perception lead to a local representation of the stimulus. That representation identifies what the stimulus is, specifies its size, shape, and so on. A further process would be needed to find the memory representation corresponding to this stimulus. Many network theorists, however, would reject this conception in favor of that shown in the bottom panel. On this view, the memory network is directly connected to the processes of perception (as indicated in Figures 11–8 and 11–9). There is no local representation of the input, and no separate process of "look-up." Instead, stimulus identification and "network look-up" are simply different names for the same process.

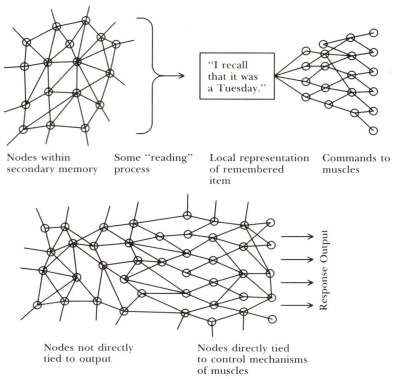

Nodes within   Some "reading"   Local representation   Commands to
secondary memory   process   of remembered   muscles
                                          item

Nodes not directly   Nodes directly tied
tied to output   to control mechanisms
                                  of muscles

FIGURE 11–16. *Two Views of How Network Activation Is Translated into Behavior.* In the top panel, the broad pattern of activation within the network is "read," leading to a summary of the network's status (that is, a local representation). This is then translated into commands to the muscles, causing the actual response. Most network theorists, however, prefer the conception in the bottom panel. No summary of the network is "read" from the pattern of activations. Instead, the nodes within the network are directly tied to control mechanisms for the muscles. When sufficient activation accumulates in the appropriate pattern, a response is produced.

other end, to "input" nodes? Output nodes receive input from the network via the same spreading activation as any other nodes. When the right configuration of activations is on the scene, this will bring the output nodes to some threshold level of activation, and this will in turn trigger a response.

As an example, we might ask subjects, "What does one call the offspring of a dog?" As described above, this input leads to the activation of the many nodes that comprise the distributed representation of "dog," and those that comprise the distributed representation of "offspring." Activation will spread from these to many other nodes—namely, those that represent the various ideas and concepts associated with "dog" and "offspring." One set of nodes, though, will receive activation from both of these sources: The nodes that comprise the distributed representation of "puppy" will receive activation both from the "dog" nodes and from the "offspring" nodes. As a result, the many nodes representing "puppy" will themselves become strongly activated. Each of these nodes will in turn send activation to output nodes, but each, by itself, sends only a weak signal. When all the nodes involved in representing "puppy" send their signals at the same time, then the output nodes do receive a sufficient input, and so do become activated. And, finally, the output nodes send activation to the control system for the muscles, causing the subject to utter a response.

In sum, this is a "grass-roots" recognition of the input leading to a "grass-roots" selection of an answer leading to a "grass-roots" production of the actual response. Nowhere in this process does a light bulb come on indicating "puppy." Nowhere is there a local summary of the input, used as the basis for "looking" here or there in the system. And at no point is there a local summary of the network's activity, to be used as the basis for the next action. The distributed pattern is never summarized in some central place, and so no Master Spy is needed either in setting up or in reading the network pattern. The system is, start to finish, concerned with distributed representations; there is no "executive," no "supervisor."

LEARNING AS THE SETTING OF "CONNECTION WEIGHTS"

On a connectionist account, how does learning take place? What sets up the pattern of the network in the first place? First, we need to be clear about what it means, within this framework, to "know something." When one knows a fact or a rule, or remembers an event, how is this represented? In the connectionist scheme, knowledge is literally contained within the connections themselves. We already saw a step in this direction when we discussed the "unpacking" of the nodes—that what it means to know "George Washington was a president" is to have a connection between a node for GEORGE WASHINGTON and a node for PRESIDENT.

This is, of course, phrased in terms of *local* representations, but the same idea is echoed in PDP approaches. What it means to know this fact about Washington is to have a pattern of connections between the many nodes that together represent "Washington" and the many nodes that together represent "president." Once these connections are in place, activation of either of these distributed representations will lead to the activation of the other. Notice that knowledge, therefore, is not contained in the activation patterns themselves. One might know that Washington was a president but have neither of these representations active at the moment. Knowledge, instead, amounts to being in a particular state of readiness: If the "Washington" pattern of activations happens to occur, the connections are in place to lead to the "president" pattern of activations, and vice versa.

Bear in mind that connections within the network can be strong or weak; PDP shares this idea with other versions of network theorizing. What it means to learn, therefore, is to adjust the various connection strengths so that activation will "flow" in the right way, so that activating the "Washington" pattern will lead to the "president" pattern and not the "queen of England" pattern. Likewise, we need to adjust the connection strengths so that a specific input pattern will, via the flow of activation, eventually lead to the appropriate output pattern. The process of learning is therefore a process of adjusting the strengths of connections, or, in the connectionists' jargon, of adjusting the **connection weights**. What it means to know something (a proposition, for example) is, in these terms, to have the appropriate connection weights.

Consistent with other aspects of PDP theorizing, the adjustment of connection weights is not done via some executive's intervention, nor is it done by some powerful computational technique that might require an executive or supervisor. Instead, connection weights are adjusted by means of computational techniques that are all on a small scale, all on the local level, so that learning, like other events in this scheme, is a distributed process.

At the level of individual nodes, locally available information, in the form of other nodes' activation levels, will cause local changes in this or that connection weight. This will, in turn, influence how strongly a node is activated by various inputs to that node, and it will influence how strongly that node activates various other nodes. From outside of the network, we observe the overall process of improvement, the overall process of learning. If we take a closer look, though, what we observe is merely the sum of lots of little changes in individual nodes, with each of the changes governed entirely by what is happening in the immediate vicinity of that node.

This is, in some ways, an amazing proposal. Hundreds of thousands of microscopic changes take place in the network, each quite independent of the others. Nonetheless, these changes, when taken as a group, add up to all of the intelligent learning of which organisms are capable, ranging from the processes of Pavlovian conditioning through the learning of a new language. Needless to say, though, the trick is to say exactly how this happens, and here, finally, is the last in the series of intellectual innovations that is driving connectionism forward. Connectionists have offered a number of powerful computing schemes, called "learning algorithms," that seek to accomplish learning within the PDP setup. The learning typically requires a large number of learning trials, and some sort of feedback about the correctness or appropriateness of the response. But given this, connectionists have offered schemes with names like the "delta rule" and "back propagation" that accomplish learning on the local level, without an executive, and that seem to make the entire system grow gradually and impressively smarter.

In simple terms, these algorithms cause connection weights to increase or decrease whenever specific, locally described configurations are present. As a simple example, we might set things up so that the connection weight between two nodes will increase whenever the two nodes are both activated, or both not activated; the connection weight will decrease when either is activated but the other is not. With this rule in place, the connection weight will be determined by the correlation between the activation levels of the two nodes. If the correlation is strong, that is, if Node A tends to be activated whenever Node B is activated, the connection weight will often be incremented, and will end up fairly strong. If the correlation is weak, that is, if A is often activated without B, or B without A, the connection weight will often be decremented, and will end up weak.

As a different example, consider the Rescorla–Wagner theory, which we discussed in Chapter 3. This theory summarizes the process of classical conditioning through a mathematical formula. The formula describes changes in simple associations between stimuli, but manages to explain a variety of complex phenomena, including how animals assess the informativeness or predictiveness of potential CSs (see pp. 101–12).

It is not difficult to set up a connectionist model implementing the Rescorla–Wagner logic (cf. Gluck & Bower, 1988; Sutton & Barto, 1981). For our purposes, notice that the Rescorla–Wagner theory has many of the properties we want in a connectionism learning algorithm. First, look at what the Rescorla–Wagner formulation involves: Strength of association between CS and US is adjusted on the basis of local considerations, namely, what has happened on the most recent trial. In addition, learning is governed by a simple comparison between the current strength of association and the strength of association that the US will support. This comparison is formalized within the model by subtracting one of these from the other (see Chapter 3). This comparison might be implemented within the network using a setup related to the "correlation detector" described above.

At the same time, look at what the Rescorla–Wagner mechanism accomplishes: Although influenced only by local, trial-by-trial considerations, the mechanism manages to reflect patterns of contingency and predictiveness across many trials. Although driven by a simple comparison between two terms, this mechanism generates "expectations," and learns only when stimuli are "informative" or "surprising." In network terms, this mechanism is extremely simple if we examine what the nodes are doing, and can be mechanically implemented with no problem. If we instead look at what an organism "equipped" with this mechanism would accomplish, we see what looks like sophisticated and intelligent learning. Clearly, a great deal here depends on one's point of view—whether one looks at the mechanism, which is relatively simple, or at what the mechanism accomplishes, which is relatively complex. And indeed this is a consistent message of connectionism: Behaviors that look complicated from the outside can be produced by the combined actions of vastly many very simple mechanisms.

We leave the details of connectionism's learning algorithms aside, both because they are mathematically complex and because, when we talk about the state of the art, anything we say will be quickly out of date. The questions, though, are what these uncomplicated learning mechanisms can accomplish, and what limits there may be to what can be accomplished in this way.

POSSIBLE LIMITS ON PDP NETWORKS

We mentioned earlier in this chapter that psychologists are divided in their assessments of network models—some view networks as an important step forward; others argue that network models are inadequate as accounts of memory and that we should be pursuing other approaches. The field is no less divided about PDP models. While there are articulate advocates for this approach, there are also severe critics. (For advocates of the PDP approach, see many of the contributions to Rumelhart & McClelland, 1986; for more critical views, see Fodor & Pylyshyn, 1988; Holyoak, 1987; Lachter & Bever, 1988; Pinker & Prince, 1988.)

What arguments might incline us for or against the PDP approach? To some extent, this approach must be evaluated in terms of what PDP networks can and cannot accomplish. That is, the test here is just like the one we described for network modeling in general: If one has a correct theory of how learning happens, or of how knowledge is represented and used, then one should be able to use the theory to create a working model for these accomplishments. This is exactly what the connectionists have been seeking to do.

Much connectionist research has focused on the learning process, and connectionist models have been built for aspects of language learning, for parts of learning to read, and for learning to play strategic games such as backgammon. (Many of these accomplishments are summarized in papers in Rumelhart & McClelland, 1986.) While there have been conspicuous successes in these projects, there has also been controversy over what limits there may be to this learning, and whether this learning matches the learning that humans do (see, for example, Pinker & Prince, 1988; McCloskey & Cohen, 1989).

The state of the art, therefore, resembles that which we saw with networks in general: Some mental processes have been successfully modeled, but the number of successful models is still quite small. And questions have been raised about the nature of these models, so controversy remains. In short, we get no strong answers on this front, which has lead many in the field to adopt a wait-and-see attitude about what PDP modeling will eventually accomplish.

Even at this early stage, some problems are already in view, and it is too soon to tell how, or whether, these can be resolved. For example, the existing PDP models have dealt with only small pieces of cognition; that is, they have modeled one or another specialized task. Most connectionists realize that these small pieces of the network cannot simply be glued together, to form one huge, amorphous network. Some overall structure or plan seems needed to assemble these smaller pieces, but this raises many questions: How will these pieces of the network communicate with each other? How will various inputs get routed to the right piece of the network so that sentences are dealt with by the language net and not the arithmetic net? And so on.

Note that we are flirting here with a familiar problem: In discussing the conventional nets, we asked whether a supervisor might be needed to run the net, realizing that the function of this supervisor would need spelling out. In some ways, we may be forced to the same concern in confronting the issues just raised. It is simply too soon, however, to say how these questions will be answered. We are now literally in a domain in which this month's challenges are next month's accomplishments, and only time will tell us what connectionist theorizing can and cannot accomplish.

For what it is worth, it is our own expectation that the success of the PDP approach will be uneven. A number of psychological problems may well be explained via connectionist theorizing, including the central problem of this chapter, namely, the organization of secondary memory. But this is not to say that the entire PDP proposal is correct. The proposal offered by connectionists is that the entire mind can be modeled in PDP terms, from "input nodes" to "output nodes," with only distributed processes in between these and, in particular, with no local representations. At the moment, we see no strong argument in favor of this very ambitious proposal, and several persuasive philosophical arguments have been raised on the opposite side (e.g., see Fodor & Pylyshyn, 1988). This in no way makes the PDP program of research less interesting; it simply says that PDP is not going to be the answer to all of psychology's mysteries.

Our discussion in this chapter has been proceeding on two levels. On one level, we have seen that network theorizing (either in a traditional version or in PDP) gives us a broad and powerful way to describe memory functioning. In addition, such key notions as spreading activation and fan are well supported in the data. Our success at this level, and the power of this framework in organizing the evidence, invites the second level of discussion. At this more ambitious level, the question becomes whether network theorizing may not be part of the story, but instead the entire story.

For now, this more ambitious argument seems best viewed as "too soon to tell." This cautious message has come up several times in this chapter and in many other chapters. We cannot yet say whether the network will be able to account for the speed and ease with which we search through the vast warehouse of our knowledge. We mentioned some potential trouble spots for a network account of memory search, and we do not know yet how readily these can be addressed. It also remains to be seen what the limits might be on distributed processing, and when (if ever) some local process might be demanded.

It is the same issue coming up in each of these cases. In discussing search, we specifically considered whether a supervisor might be needed, to guide the spread of activation. Likewise, what is striking (and controversial) about the PDP proposal is its claim that we can explain all in terms of distributed processing and representations; that is, that we need no centralized director.

The key issue seems to be: Can we get by without a homunculus? If so, how? If not, then how is the functioning of the homunculus to be explained? These are thorny issues, and of central importance within both psychology and computer science. To tackle these issues directly would require a book by itself. What we have done, therefore, is to try and sketch one avenue into the debate—how one might try to get by without a central processor (or with limited demand for one), what the advantages are of such an approach, and what the possible problems are.

If you have uncertainties about this argument, you are in good company—so do many in the field. There is widespread agreement that memory does draw on associative processes and spreading activation, but there is far more uncertainty about whether these by themselves can explain all of mental functioning. This whole area is still "work in progress" on an immensely complex and subtle topic—merely the task of describing All of Knowledge. Moreover, we can take considerable comfort from the fact that, unsolved mysteries or no, we seem to have at least a part of the puzzle under control. Our theorizing is allowing us to handle a lot of data, and leading us to new discoveries. This is, on anybody's account, a positive and promising sign.

Summary

Considering how much is in memory, how do we ever find information in this vast warehouse? What organizational scheme is used for filing information within memory? In this chapter, we have explored the hypothesis that memory is arranged as a vast network, with individual ideas being the "nodes" within the net and with these nodes connected to each other via "associative links." When a node is activated, this activation energy spreads out to neighboring nodes, causing them to become activated. If neighboring nodes become activated to "threshold" levels, this will initiate a response and cause activation to spread out from this new source. At the same time, "subthreshold activation" also plays a role, since subthreshold activation can accumulate. In addition, some of the associations in the network are strong and others weak (consistent with our discussion in Chapters 2 and 3); this is presumably caused by several factors, including the recency and frequency with which a particular connection has been activated. As a result, activation energy will spread more efficiently and more quickly through strong associations than through weak ones.

This account provides an easy explanation for a variety of memory phenomena, including hints, the power of mnemonic strategies, and state-dependency effects. In addition, several lines of evidence speak directly in favor of claims made within the network approach. For example, once a node has been activated, this does cause partial activation of nearby nodes (the priming effect).

Likewise, the network view claims that search within the network is like travel, and the farther one must travel, the longer it will take. This prediction has been confirmed by sentence-verification experiments.

The network view also predicts that search through memory will be slower if activation energy spreads in many directions. In this case, the activation energy will be finely divided, with not very much going in any single direction. This prediction has been confirmed in experiments manipulating the "degree of fan" from target nodes. Consistent with predictions, memory searches are slower if based on nodes with a higher degree of fan.

Given the network's ability to handle this range of data, we were motivated to ask just how much we can accomplish in network terms. In this vein, we examined how memory search might be initiated in the network conception, and then how this search would proceed through the network.

How is complex knowledge represented within the network? We discussed one possible answer to this question—namely, the claim that complex knowledge can be analyzed into a series of propositions, and that propositions can, in turn, be represented as associations among nodes.

Finally, we turned to several results that seemed not to fit so well with the network conceptions, including cases in which memory retrieval fails despite the fact that one has reached the correct memory vicinity, and cases in which memory retrieval succeeds even though one begins the search at some distance from the target node. We noted that such cases seem to imply that search through the network is guided by some active director, rather than spreading passively as the notion of spreading activation implies. Problems with this "homunculus" proposal were discussed.

We turned next to the newest version of network theorizing, a proposal known as connectionism, or parallel distributed processing (PDP).

Within the PDP view, ideas and memory contents are represented not by a single node, but by a pattern of activation across a wide number of nodes. Likewise, processing is also distributed, with a large number of very simple operations being summed together to create the observed inferences, associations, and decisions. Learning, on this view, is also a distributed process, with a large number of adjustments to "connection weights" being the process underlying the learning we observe.

12 The Varieties of Memories

We began Chapter 11 by commenting on how much is in secondary memory. It is no less remarkable what a diversity of memories fills this storehouse. There are memories for verbal passages as well as for pictures, memories for meaningful materials and memories for superficial appearances, memories for particular episodes and memories for facts.

Is all this information lodged in one vast warehouse? Or might it be that we have one warehouse containing episodic information and another containing more general ("generic") information? Perhaps we have one warehouse for verbal and meaningful materials and another for pictorial and appearance information. Or, to make sure that we consider all possibilities, maybe our memories are organized into a great many individualized compartments. Perhaps we have a joke memory separate from our face memory separate from our psychology facts memory. On this view, the great warehouse of our knowledge is divided into a large number of rooms, each containing the knowledge pertinent to a particular topic or situation.

These questions will be our concern in this chapter. How many memories are there? We first met this question in Chapter 7, when we considered the evidence that led psychologists to distinguish "sensory memories" from "working memory," and "working memory" from "secondary memory." The question now before us is whether we need still further distinctions. In the first part of the chapter, we will look at the question of whether we need to consider multiple working memories. We will then turn to the same question with regard to secondary memory.

How Many Working Memories?

The early theorizing about working memory came from William James, at the end of the nineteenth century. James's (1890/1950) term for this memory was **primary memory**, and he argued that primary memory was inseparable from the current stream of thought. To put it loosely, whatever you are thinking about right now and whatever you are attending to are by definition represented in primary memory.

One can obviously think about, or attend to, a vast variety of events or stimuli or ideas. If we take the proposal in the previous paragraph at face value, then working memory must be capable of holding this diversity of contents. Indeed, there has to be somewhere that all these contents can be brought together "under one roof"; how else could we think about *combinations* of pictures and words, of abstract ideas and concrete ones, and about all of the other combinations we can entertain?

This looks like an argument that there must be a single working memory, capable of holding a rich diversity of contents. Before we accept this, though, it seems wise to examine this diversity more closely. We will therefore look first at evidence indicating that working memory relies heavily on a speech-like mode of representation. Next, we will turn to research on mental images. Images seem to be a special form our thoughts can take and therefore a different sort of content that can be held in working memory. We will then return to our main question: Given this survey of the contents held in working memory, do we need to theorize that there are multiple working memories, or, in keeping with James's view, just one?

WORKING MEMORY AS A SPEECH-BASED STORE

Many results indicate that working memory relies heavily on a speech-like mode of representation. First, what happens if subjects are presented with, say, a series of letters and asked immediately to echo this series? In the terminology of Chapter 7, this **digit-span task** simply requires subjects to place the letters briefly in working memory and then to read out this memory's contents a moment later.

In this task, subjects often report that it helps them to repeat the letters to themselves as the letters are presented; if the test is delayed, subjects report that it helps to continue repeating the letters over and over until the test arrives. This is, of course, the rehearsal process described in Chapter 7 (cf. Rundus, 1980), and implies an important role for speech in this working-memory task. More precisely, subjects are not speaking out loud, so the speech is covert, or, in the proper terminology, subjects are **subvocalizing**.

In addition, when subjects make mistakes on working-memory tasks, they often make "sound-alike" errors and not "look-alike" errors. For example, subjects are likely to remember "D" instead of "B," "F" instead of "S," but not "F" in place of "E," or "Q" in place of "O" (cf. Baddeley, 1966a; Conrad, 1964; Conrad & Hull, 1964; Sperling, 1960; Sperling & Speelman, 1970). This is true even if the list was initially shown to the subjects so that they saw it rather than heard it. This implies that the memory for this list is drawing on processes akin to hearing, and is vulnerable to the same confusions as hearing.

A related observation concerns the so-called **word-length effect**. Consider a memory-span task in which subjects are given lists of, say, 7 words to remember for just a short period. The subject might hear, "Light, button, hair, egg, apple, camp, car." The subject hears the list once, perhaps read at the rate of one word per second, and then, after a short delay, the subject reports these back. This task is easy with lists of about 7 words, but errors start creeping in if the list is made longer than this.

Exactly how many words can be remembered in this fashion (whether 6 or 7 or 8) depends on several factors, including how quickly the words can be pronounced. It is not the length of the word in number of letters or number of syllables that matters; it is literally the pronunciation time. For example, subjects can remember slightly more words with lists like "tip, pack, cat . . ."; these happen to be words that can be pronounced very quickly, in comparison to lists like "fine, wish, lob . . .," all of which take slightly longer to say. This is true even if the words are *seen* initially. This seems to imply that *saying the words* has a key role in working memory, again implying a speech-like mode of representation (Baddeley, Thomson, & Buchanan, 1975; Ellis & Henneley, 1980).

As a final bit of evidence, Baddeley (1966b; Baddeley & Dale, 1966; Dale & Baddeley, 1969) had subjects memorize either lists of similar-sound materials (tube, tub, tab, top) or lists of similar-meaning materials (bush, shrub, tree, plant). Hand in hand with the above results, subjects did more poorly with the similar-sound list in short-term testing. In long-term testing, the pattern reversed, so that subjects did more poorly with the similar-meaning materials.

In sum, speech seems implicated in many working-memory tasks. Some psychologists read these findings as indicating that working memory is, at its essence, a "phonological" storage system. Yet this seems to conflict with the function of working memory envisioned by James and others, a function that requires a great diversity of contents in working memory. We will sort this out in a little while, but first we need to look at a different form that the contents of working memory can take.

MENTAL IMAGES

The study of mental imagery is one of the great success stories of modern cognitive psychology. We know a great deal about mental images, although most of what we know concerns visual images, rather than images in other sensory modalities (see, e.g., Kosslyn, 1980, 1983; Shepard & Cooper, 1982; although see also Reisberg, 1990). Images are often constructed by drawing on knowledge in secondary memory, but the image itself is an active representation, held in working memory. Therefore an understanding of imagery seems crucial for our understanding of working memory's contents.

Many results show striking parallels between visual images and actual, out-in-the-world pictures. As an entry to this evidence, think about how pictures themselves are different from, say, verbal descriptions. Consider what would happen if you were asked to write a paragraph describing a cat. It seems likely that you would mention the various distinctive features of cats—their claws, their whiskers, and so on. It probably would not occur to you to mention that cats have heads, since this is so obvious that it seems not worth mentioning. Now consider, in contrast, what would happen if we asked you to draw a sketch of a cat. In this format, the cat's head would be prominent, for the simple reason that the head is relatively large and up front. The claws and whiskers might be less salient, because these features are small, and so would not take up much space in the drawing. Apparently, then, what information is included and what information is prominent are to some extent dependent on the mode of presentation, putting us in the position to ask what information is available in a visual image. Is it the pictorially prominent features, or the verbally prominent ones?

In an experiment by Kosslyn (1976), subjects were asked to form a mental picture of a cat and were then asked a series of yes/no questions about their picture: "Does the cat have a head?" "Does the cat have claws?" Subjects responded to these questions quickly, but, strikingly, responses to the "head" question were quicker than those to the "claws" question. This suggests that information quickly available in the image follows the rules for pictures, not paragraphs. For contrast's sake, a different group of subjects was asked merely to think about cats (with no mention of imagery). These subjects, asked the same questions, gave quicker responses to the "claws" question than to the "head" question, the reverse pattern of before. Apparently, the initial pattern is specific to inspection of an image, just as we would expect.

Here is a different experiment, making a related point (Kosslyn, Ball, & Reiser, 1978). Subjects were asked to memorize the fictional map shown in Figure 12–1 and, in particular, to memorize the locations of the various landmarks—the well, the straw hut, and so on. The experimenters made sure subjects had the map memorized by asking them to draw

FIGURE 12–1. *Map of a Fictional Island Used in Image-Scanning Experiments.* Subjects in the study first memorized this map, including the various landmarks (the hut, the well, the patch of grass, and so on). Subjects then formed a mental image of this map for the scanning procedure. (After Kosslyn, 1983.)

a replica of the map from memory; once they could do this, the main experiment began. Subjects were asked to form an image of the island and to point their "mind's eye" at a specific landmark; let us say the well. Another landmark was then mentioned, perhaps the straw hut. Subjects were instructed to imagine a black speck moving in a straight line from the first landmark to the second. When the speck "reached" the target, subjects pressed a button, stopping a clock. This provides a measure of how long it takes to **scan** from the well to the hut. The same was done for the well and the palm tree, the hut and the rock, and so forth, for all of the various pairs of landmarks. Our question, then, is how these scanning times compare to the scanning distances.

Figure 12–2 shows the remarkably clear results. What seems to be going on is that subjects scan across their image at a constant rate, and, critically, it seems that the image really does preserve the various distance relationships, and therefore the layout, of the original map. In essence, we get a pattern of results identical to what we would expect if subjects were scanning across an actual picture with some sort of pointer. This data pattern, once again, only occurs if we encourage subjects to do this task via imagery: Kosslyn et al. had a different group memorize the map, and answer these same questions, but with no mention that they should employ an image in determining their responses. Data from these subjects show no relation between response time and distance on the original map.

One last result will drive the point home. Consider the display shown in Figure 12–3A. In a series of experiments by Shepard, Cooper, and Metzler, subjects were asked to decide whether displays like this one showed two different shapes, or just one shape, viewed from two different perspectives. That is, is it possible to "rotate" the form shown on the left

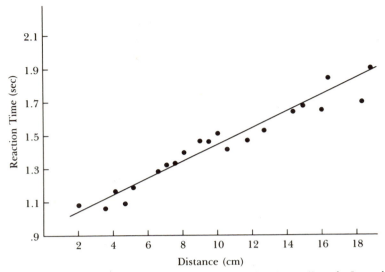

FIGURE 12–2. *Relationship between Reaction Time and "Distance" on the Imaged Map.* Subjects had to "scan" from one point on their mental image to another point; they pressed a button to indicate when their "mind's eye" had arrived at its destination. Response times in this task were closely related to the "distance" subjects had to scan across on the image, implying that mental images are similar to actual pictures in how they represent positions and distance. (After Kosslyn, 1983.)

in 12–3A, so that it will end up looking just like the form on the right? Likewise for the two shapes shown in 12–3B, and the two in 12–3C, and so on.

How might subjects do this task? One option is that subjects literally imagine one of the shapes rotating so that it is oriented in the same way as the other shape, and only then respond. This step of imagining will presumably take some time. Specifically, we might suppose that the farther subjects must imagine the shape rotating, in order to "line up" the forms, the longer this will take (Cooper & Shepard, 1973; Shepard & Metzler, 1971).

Figure 12–3 also shows the results. Subjects' response times are directly proportional to how far the forms had to be rotated to bring them

FIGURE 12–3. *Stimuli and Data from a Mental Rotation Experiment.* Subjects had to judge whether the two stimuli shown in Panel A are the same as each other, but viewed from different perspectives, or actually different forms; likewise for the pairs shown in B and C. Subjects seem to make these judgments by imagining one of the forms rotating until its position matches that of the other form. If they must imagine only a small rotation, response times are fast; as the angle of rotation increases, so does response time. (After Shepard & Metzler, 1971.)

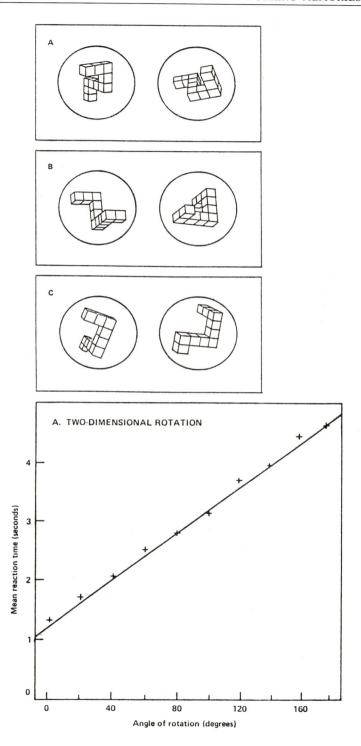

A. TWO-DIMENSIONAL ROTATION

Mean reaction time (seconds)

Angle of rotation (degrees)

into "alignment." This is what we would expect if subjects imagine rotations at a constant velocity (just as they seemed to scan their images at a constant velocity) and if the spatial properties of imagery fully mimic the spatial properties of the external world. Thus, in the external world, 15° is half of 30° is half of 60°, and images respect these relations. Thus imaging a rotation through 15° seems to take half as much time as imaging a rotation through 30°, etc. (The total time for responding, though, is much longer than this, thanks to the fact that the task involves several steps beyond the rotation itself—for example, reaching a decision once the rotation is completed, actually making the response, and so on.)

SELECTIVE INTERFERENCE WITH IMAGERY

The results just cited indicate that visual images and actual pictures are closely related—information availability, linear distance relationships, and angular distance relationships all seem to work in images just as they do in pictures. Given these results, one might expect some overlap between the processes of imagery and those of perception. Segal and Fusella (1970, 1971) asked their subjects to detect either very dim visual stimuli or very soft tones. The subjects' task was merely to indicate, on each trial, whether the faint signal had or had not been presented. Subjects did this in either of two conditions: while forming a visual image before their "mind's eye," or while forming an auditory image before their "mind's ear." Thus we once again have a 2 × 2 design—two types of signals to be detected, and two (potentially) interfering activities.

The results given in Figure 12–4 show that forming a visual image did interfere with seeing. That is, subjects were less successful in detecting

	Percentage Detections			Percentage False Alarms	
	Visual signal	Auditory signal		Visual signal	Auditory signal
While visualizing	61%	67%	While visualizing	7.8%	3.7%
While maintaining an auditory image	63%	61%	While maintaining an auditory image	3.6%	6.7%

FIGURE 12–4. *Can One Visualize and See at the Same Time?* Subjects were less successful in detecting a weak visual signal if they were simultaneously maintaining a visual image than if they were maintaining an auditory image. (The effect is small, but highly reliable.) The reverse is true with weak auditory signals: Subjects were less successful in this detection if maintaining an auditory image than if visualizing. In addition, visual images often led to "false alarms" for subjects trying to detect visual signals; auditory images led to false alarms for auditory signals. (After Segal & Fusella, 1970.)

the light while visually imagining (although the difference is not great); likewise, forming an auditory image interfered with hearing. This fits with the claim that imaging and perceiving draw on overlapping processes or structures, and so there is competition if the subject tries to do both at once (see also Farah & Smith, 1983).

DIFFERENCES BETWEEN IMAGES AND PICTURES

As we have just seen, subjects reasoning with mental images show a distinctive data pattern, a pattern different from what we observe when imagery is not on the scene. In addition, it seems that the processes through which we manipulate, create, and maintain images overlap with the processes used in perceiving (see also Finke, 1980; Farah, 1985).

Some in the field read these data as reflecting the fact that mental images are a distinct form of mental representation and, as such, must be displayed or manifested in the mind in a special way. Thus Kosslyn argues that imagery is represented in a special **image medium**, a medium different, for example, from that in which propositional information is represented (Kosslyn, 1981; Kosslyn, Pinker, Smith, & Schwartz, 1979; see Chapter 11 for discussion of mental propositions). However, others dispute these claims (e.g., Pylyshyn, 1981, 1984), and many in the field regard the issue as still unsettled.

In addition, a further note of caution is needed in understanding the imagery data: Quite plainly, to show that images share *some* properties with pictures still leaves us to ask if there are other properties *not* shared by images and pictures. Here is one important way in which images and pictures seem to differ: A picture exists in the physical world, while an image exists only in the mental world. How might this matter? If we encounter a picture, we must interpret it. The picture provides the "raw material," and we reach the best understanding of this raw material we can. Sometimes, though, we misinterpret the picture, and that is what geometric illusions are all about. And it is also possible that more than one interpretation might be compatible with the information in a picture, so that a picture can be ambiguous. For example, the cube at the left of Figure 12–5, the so-called Necker Cube, is ambiguous—it can be perceived as a version of either Cube A or Cube B. This is possible because the raw material of the picture itself is separable from what interpretation we place on this raw material, and so we can set our initial interpretation aside and reinterpret the picture. The same is true for the so-called duck/rabbit figure, shown on the right. Subjects initially perceive this form as either a duck or a rabbit, but are able to set aside this interpretation and discover the other interpretation of the shape.

Is the same true for images? Is there some raw material, akin to the picture, or akin to the optical input to the eye, onto which we place an interpretation, just as in perception? Some psychologists have endorsed this position (e.g., Finke, 1980; Kosslyn, 1983), but there is reason to

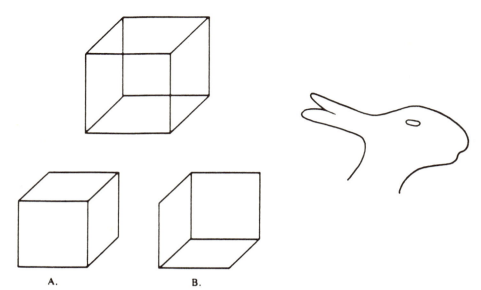

A.   B.

FIGURE 12-5.   *The Necker Cube, and the Duck/Rabbit.* This cube can be perceived either as if viewed from above or as if viewed from below. The right-hand picture can be seen either as a duck or as a rabbit. Subjects readily find both interpretations of these figures. However, if subjects imagine one of these figures, they have great difficulty finding a different interpretation of their image. For example, if subjects imagine the figure on the right and think of it as a duck, they have great difficulty discovering the rabbit.

believe this is not the case at all. Unlike a picture, which exists independently of what we happen to believe about it, a mental image seems to exist only via our understanding of it, and is consequently inseparable from that understanding. That is, there is no raw material to which an interpretation is added; there is instead a unity of geometric or pictorial layout plus the interpretation from the very start.

Seeing how this plays out for a specific case may help to understand the proposal, and also to see how this matters. We know that pictures are reinterpretable; that was the point of our comments about the Necker cube and the duck/rabbit. One can separate the raw material (the picture itself) from the interpretation initially put on it, and find a new interpretation—for example, discovering that both Cube A and Cube B are possible interpretations of the cube drawing. Is the same true for images? Given the claims in the previous paragraph, it should not be true. There is no way to set aside one's understanding in order to reinterpret the raw material of an image, because there is no image separate from the understanding—no neutral stimulus event, existing independent of the imager's intentions.

Consider the following studies by Chambers and Reisberg (1985). Subjects in these studies were briefly shown a drawing of an ambiguous figure (such as the Necker cube or the duck/rabbit). These subjects were then asked to form a mental image based on that drawing. All of the subjects had previously been trained so that they understood what was meant by an ambiguous figure, and had successfully reinterpreted a series of practice figures. Subjects were then asked if they could reinterpret their image, just as they had reinterpreted the practice figures. For example, if subjects had initially perceived the duck/rabbit figure as a duck, they were asked to form a mental image of the duck and then asked if they could reinterpret that image.

The results are easily summarized: Across several experiments, no subjects succeeded in reinterpreting their images. Perhaps subjects did not understand the task, or did not remember the figure. To rule this out, immediately after their failure at reinterpreting their images, subjects were given a blank piece of paper and asked to draw the figure, based on their image. Now, looking at their own drawings, all of the subjects were able to reinterpret the configuration in the appropriate way. Thus we have 100% failure with images and 100% success, a moment later, with the drawings. (See also Reisberg & Chambers, 1989, but also Finke, Pinker, & Farah, 1989. For related data with auditory images, see Reisberg, Smith, Baxter, & Sonenshine, 1989.)

These data suggest that images are saturated with meaning, carrying the imager's intentions, and are not at all neutral (and open to reinterpretation) the way a picture is (cf. Casey, 1976; Fodor, 1975; Kolers & Smythe, 1979, 1984). With a picture of the cube, for example, we can separate the geometry itself from the way the geometry is understood; that is what we do when we reinterpret an ambiguous drawing. In imagery, the geometry and our understanding of it seem inseparable. Oddly enough, this suggests that we may be able to learn things from a picture that we cannot learn from the corresponding image, just as subjects in the experiments described above succeeded in the one case and failed in the other (Reisberg, 1987).

Other evidence also indicates that visual imagery is not as intimately tied to vision as some have suggested. For example, we have described how imagery experiments (such as the rotation of images or scanning across images) turn out if we use sighted subjects. It is interesting to note that these experiments yield a similar data pattern if done with subjects who have been blind since birth (Carpenter & Eisenberg, 1978; Jonides, Kahn, & Rozin, 1975; Kerr, 1983; Marmor & Zaback, 1976; Paivio & Okovita, 1971; Zimler & Keenan, 1983). It seems safe to assume that the blind subjects are not using a visual mode of representation in performing imagery tasks, and therefore a visual representation seems unnecessary for these tasks. Several other pieces of evidence point in the same direction (e.g., Baddeley & Lieberman, 1980; Kerr & Neisser, 1983; Neisser & Kerr, 1973; although see also Keenan & Moore, 1979; Keenan, 1983). This has led many psychologists to argue that we should be speaking of **spatial imagery**—that is, imagery for spatial relations and spatial layout—rather than *visual imagery* (Reisberg, Culver, Heuer, & Fischman, 1986; Reisberg & Heuer, 1990).

None of this takes any force away from the results showing substantial parallels between images and pictures. Images do have many properties in common with pictures, and, just as important, images have properties that seem not to be shared by other forms of representation. We should be cautious, though, in what we conclude from these data, given the complications discussed above. (See also Pylyshyn, 1981, and Kosslyn, 1981, for further discussion of whether the imagery data require the existence of a separate medium of representation.)

A WORKING MEMORY *SYSTEM*

Let us take stock of what we have so far. Our initial question was whether we needed to hypothesize more than one working memory. We have seen three considerations that speak to this point. First, there is a functional argument that working memory must hold many different contents, all "under one roof," in order to allow us to bring these contents together into varying combinations. Second, in seeming contrast to this, we have seen evidence that working memory has a very strong inclination toward a specific kind of content, one drawing on a speech-like code. Third, we have also seen evidence that images in working memory seem genuinely different from other forms of representation. For example, in the "cat's whiskers/head" study, we get one data pattern when subjects use imagery, and a different pattern when they just think about cats. Likewise, the processes that operate on images in working memory also seem special to images.

How can we put these various pieces together? One possibility comes from a hypothesis offered by Baddeley and his colleagues (Baddeley, 1986; Baddeley & Hitch, 1974; Salame & Baddeley, 1982)—namely, that we must speak of a **working-memory** *system*, containing several components. One component is the **central executive**, a multipurpose processor capable of running many different operations on many different types of materials. In addition, there are a small number of specialized **slave systems**.

Baddeley's initial proposal involved two slave systems: a **rehearsal loop** and a **visuospatial scratchpad**. Baddeley later refined this proposal, arguing that the rehearsal loop actually involves two separate components working together. Here is the overall proposal: When one operates on or works with one's ideas the central executive of working memory is needed for the many active aspects of processing. The executive is not needed, however, for mere storage. As an example, we might ask subjects to do a bit of mental multiplication, say, 23 times 18. One first multiplies 3 times 18, getting 54; this partial product must then be remembered temporarily while one multiples 20 times 18, and then the product of this

(360) is added to the (stored) 54. The operation of multiplying itself requires the executive, but the storage of the interim result (that is, 54) can be turned over to a less sophisticated subordinate, serving the function of an internal "scratchpad."

To make this concrete, try reading the next few sentences while "holding on to" this list of numbers: 1, 4, 6, 4, 9. Got them? Now read on. You are probably repeating the numbers over and over to yourself, cycling them, so to speak, through your inner voice. But this turns out to require very little effort, so that you can easily continue to read while recycling the numbers in this fashion. And, of course, the moment you need to recall the numbers (what were they?), they are immediately available to you.

In Baddeley's view, one performs tasks like this by maintaining the numbers in the articulatory rehearsal loop. This leaves the central executive free to continue reading. The rehearsal loop is composed of two parts, which are informally referred to as the **inner ear** and the **inner voice**. To remember the list of numbers, or an interim result, the executive uses the "inner voice" to pronounce the words. The activity of speaking is of course immensely well practiced, and so the inner voice is highly skilled. As a result, the central executive can initiate this inner speech relatively quickly and easily.

The inner voice pronounces the materials; that is, the materials are subvocalized, with no sound actually produced. The subvocalization causes a record of these pronunciations to be loaded into the inner ear; that is, an auditory image is created. This image will gradually fade away, and, when it does, the cycle must be restarted: The executive is again briefly needed to initiate action in the inner voice, but then the inner voice and inner ear carry out their functions without further supervision. Thus, the executive is needed periodically, but while the inner voice is pronouncing the materials, and then before the image has faded from the inner ear, the executive is free to work on other matters, at least until the cycle must be restarted (Figure 12–6).

This account immediately explains why speech-like effects are often observed in working memory. The executive often relies on the inner voice and the inner ear. Errors reflecting acoustic confusions are made, Baddeley proposes, as a consequence of using the inner ear. In addition, the use of the inner voice is what produces the word-length effect—that is, the observation that one can remember more words if one can say them more quickly.

On this proposal, one should be able to manipulate the presence of the word-length effect, by manipulating the availability of the inner voice. To deny subjects use of the inner voice, experimenters ask subjects to remember word lists while simultaneously saying "Ta, ta, ta, ta . . ." out loud. By tying up the speech apparatus, subjects are unable to speak to themselves. When this is done, the word-length effect does not appear in the data, as predicted (Vallar & Baddeley, 1982).

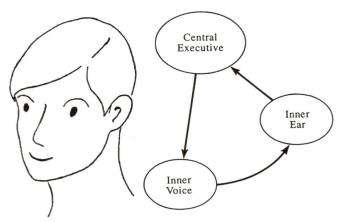

FIGURE 12–6. *The Working-Memory System.* The central executive of working memory can deal with only a small amount of information at a time. However, the executive can initiate a rehearsal process, by instructing the "inner voice" to pronounce the to-be-remembered (TBR) materials. These instructions are quickly given, and so, while the inner voice is carrying out this task, the executive is free to work on other tasks. This covert (subvocal) pronunciation creates an auditory mental image, "heard" by the "inner ear." The image gradually fades, but the executive can take note of the image and restart the cycle.

Whether this manipulation also removes phonological confusions depends on how the to-be-remembered material is presented. The key here is that there are two ways to enter the inner ear. If one actually *hears* the to-be-remembered material, this provides direct access to the inner ear. On the other hand, if one initially *sees* the to-be-remembered material, the material must enter the inner ear via a different route: With visual presentations, subjects' usual strategy would be to use the rehearsal loop. That is, they would pronounce the items to themselves, using the inner voice; this would provide the input for the inner ear. Once in the inner ear, phonological confusions could arise.

Note, then, that the inner voice is needed to load the inner ear with visual presentations. Therefore, if we use visual presentations *and* block the use of the inner voice, then the to-be-remembered material should never reach the inner ear, and so no phonological confusions should be detected in the data. However, the inner voice is not needed to load the inner ear with auditory presentations. Therefore, phonological confusions should occur with these presentations, even if subjects are blocked from using the inner voice (Figure 12–7). This pattern is exactly what the data show.

By similar logic, we should be able to prevent phonological confusions if we prevent subjects from using the inner ear. We can do this by having subjects do our memory tests while hearing, via headphones, some other

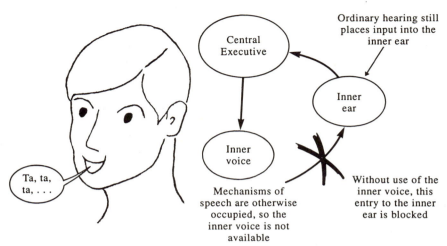

FIGURE 12–7. *Manipulations of the Rehearsal Loop.* Because the inner voice is related to actual speaking, pronunciation speed influences its function. This creates the "word-length effect." Use of the inner voice can be blocked, however, if subjects are required to make simultaneous use of their actual ("outer") voice. This eliminates the word-length effect. If the to-be-remembered (TBR) materials are presented visually, phonological confusions are also eliminated, since there is now no way for the TBR materials to reach the inner ear. However, phonological confusions still occur if subjects actually hear the TBR materials.

voices. Even though subjects are not attending to these other voices, if the outer ears (that is, the real ears!) draw on the same processes as the inner ear, this will diminish the use of the inner ear. (The logic of this parallels that of the Segal and Fusella studies mentioned above.) When we do this, phonological confusions vanish from the data, whether presentation of the to-be-remembered materials is visual or auditory.

This is a somewhat complex pattern of results, but the evidence clearly favors Baddeley's view. Other evidence also favors the existence of another slave system, the visuospatial scratchpad. The visuospatial scratchpad seems certain to play a critical role in supporting the various visual imagery processes we have described; it is presumably the medium in which imagery happens. As with the inner ear and the inner voice, the visuospatial scratchpad is limited in its function—it merely serves as the store, or the medium, holding on to information used by the central executive. Hence the metaphor of a "scratchpad" seems quite apt—a scratchpad does not do any work for you; it merely holds on to the information until the executive (you in this case) is ready for it.

In working memory, then, the question of this chapter gets both a "yes, separate memories" and a "no, one memory" answer. There does seem to be one system of memories, sharing certain characteristics, since all depend on a single central executive. But, within this system, there are isolatable subcomponents. These are specialized, but merely slave systems, and so limited in the ways we have described.

Is There More than One Long-Term Memory?

What about secondary memory? Do we have just one secondary memory, or do we have separate, specialized memories, with each corresponding to one of the types of things we remember—perhaps a language memory and a picture memory and an autobiographical memory, and so on?

It is clear that we do remember a broad diversity of materials—memories for general facts and also specific episodes, memories for verbal materials and also sights and smells and tastes. But this diversity by itself cannot convince us to divide up secondary memory. After all, it is possible that secondary memory is one large storehouse that simply holds different types of contents. By analogy, libraries contain books on many topics and in many languages, and often contain tape and video recordings and works of visual art. Nonetheless, all of these are in the same cataloging system, all are physically accessed in the same fashion, and so on.

If different contents do not argue for multiple memories, then what would? Our best way to confront this question is by considering concrete proposals about how secondary memory might be divided. Then we will be in a position to gather specific evidence and arguments with which to assess the proposal. Several such proposals have in fact been offered, but one in particular has received considerable attention, and is tied in with the topics we have been considering: Do we have one secondary memory for verbal materials and a different one for images and nonverbal materials?

How could we place both images and verbal materials in a single memory network? As we saw in Chapter 11, verbal materials lend themselves to analysis into propositions, and the propositions can then be represented as connections among network nodes. Can we provide a similar analysis for memories of sights and smells and sounds? If so, this would help in building an argument for a unified secondary memory, holding both verbal and nonverbal materials.

As it turns out, nonverbal memories are easily represented in network terms. For one, recall that the network contains nodes that are directly connected to the perceptual apparatus. These nodes played an important role in our account of how memory search begins, of how one "enters" the network (see Chapter 11, pp. 424–27). In perceiving, these nodes receive their activation from the mechanisms of vision or hearing and so on; we can speak of this as *data-driven* (or "bottom-up") activation. In remembering appearances, or in forming an image, these nodes can receive their activation from other nodes within the network; this would be *concept-driven* (or "top-down") activation. In this way, there is no difficulty including nodes in the network for particular colors, or musical timbres, or smells.

One might extend this proposal to include intact visual images. In essence, one might have nodes containing entire pictures, or **templates**, and these nodes could be triggered by either data-driven or concept-driven processes. However, evidence indicates that this is unnecessary. Kosslyn and his associates have done research on how subjects go about generating images in working memory (much of this research is reviewed in Kosslyn, 1980, 1983). Their results indicate that images are not created by activating intact templates. Instead, images are generated piece by piece in a systematic fashion. Kosslyn has proposed that what is stored in secondary memory is an **image file**, containing information, first, about the image's **frame** (that is, the image's overall outline and structure) and, second, about various details that can be placed on this frame to create a full and elaborate image.

Kosslyn has proposed that the contents of an image file can be thought of, in essence, as a set of instructions, or a "recipe," for creating an image. These instructions are not in any way pictorial, although they do lead to the creation of something picture-like. The instructions are very much like propositions, and can easily be analyzed in network terms. On this view, images do have special status once activated; that is, once an image is created in working memory. After the image is constructed, it contains certain information, is operated on with certain processes, and may even demand a separate representational medium, all differing from the status of other forms of thought. However, in secondary memory, images do not have special status. Image files can be stored in exactly the same fashion as other materials (for example, as propositions) and so place no new demands on secondary memory.

DO WE REMEMBER, OR TRANSLATE, NONVERBAL MATERIALS?

The previous section suggests an interesting possibility. The suggestion was that secondary memory may not contain images, but may instead contain instructions for creating images, or, equivalently, descriptions of images. Could this, in general, be the way we remember sights and sounds and smells and so on? To see the issue, consider this observation: We show subjects a picture, or perhaps just a color, or perhaps a smell. Some time later, we present subjects with several pictures (or colors or smells) and ask which of these was the one shown earlier. The subjects respond with high confidence, and in fact choose correctly. Does this demonstrate the existence of nonverbal memories?

One way to do the task just described does not require nonverbal memory. One might, when presented with a picture, describe it to oneself. ("Oh, this is a picture of a cow standing in front of a barn, with the farmer visible in the background.") This description could be placed in memory and then later retrieved and used to guide responding in a subsequent memory test. Several pieces of evidence indicate that something like this is what subjects do a lot of the time. One persuasive finding is a half-century old: Carmichael, Hogan, and Walter, in 1932, showed their subjects drawings like the ones in Figure 12–8. For the top drawing, for example, half of the subjects were told, "This is a picture of eyeglasses." Half were told, "This is a picture of barbells." Subjects were later required to reproduce, as carefully as they could, the picture they had seen earlier. Subjects who had understood the picture as spectacles produced distorted drawings resembling spectacles; subjects who had understood the picture as weights distorted their drawings appropriately. This is what one would expect if subjects had memorized the description, rather than the picture itself, and were recreating the picture based on this description.

This result is actually very similar to many of the findings described in Chapter 9. Subjects appear to be assimilating the pictorial information into a schema, and then remembering the schematic content of the picture, in essence the picture's gist, rather than remembering the picture itself (see also Bartlett, 1932).

A different set of results makes roughly the same point. For some years, psychologists were intensely interested in a hypothesis put forward by the anthropologist Benjamin Whorf that our thinking is shaped by the language we speak. Many experiments were done to investigate Whorf's (1956) claim, mostly focusing on the perception of color. Some languages have many words for describing and categorizing colors; others have only a few words. Does this influence how speakers of a language perceive color? To make a long story short, the results indicate that one's language does influence the experimental outcome, but that this is not a perceptual effect. It seems that all humans (except those who are color-blind) perceive color in essentially the same way. However, it is easier to remember a color if one has a label for it, so that individuals with large "color vocabularies" have better color memories (Brown & Lenneberg, 1954; Rosch, 1977). Again, this is what one would expect if it were not the color itself that was memorized, but instead the description.

These data show that *sometimes,* when we ask subjects to remember pictures or colors or appearances, the subjects place some sort of description in memory, rather than a "copy" of the to-be-remembered materials. This is in many ways consistent with the findings in Chapter 9, which showed that what we remember is often our understanding of stimulus events, and not the events themselves. To the extent that this happens, we are led to a familiar conclusion: Remembering nonverbal information places no special demands on the contents or organization of secondary

Subjects'   Labels   Original   Labels   Subjects'
Drawings   Supplied   Figure   Supplied   Drawings

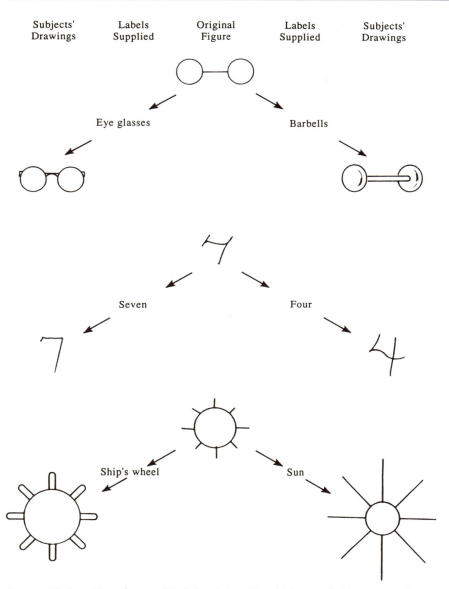

FIGURE 12–8. *The Influence of Verbal Labels on Visual Memory.* Subjects were shown the figures in the middle column. If the top figure was presented with the label "eyeglasses," subjects were likely later on to reproduce the figure as shown on the left. If the figure was presented with the label "barbells," subjects were likely to reproduce it as shown on the right. (And so on for the other figures.) One interpretation of these data is that subjects were remembering the verbal label and not the drawing itself, and then, at time of test, reconstructed what the drawing must have been based on the remembered label.

memory, and we have no reason to subdivide secondary memory to accommodate this information.

ONE SECONDARY MEMORY WITH DIVERSE CONTENTS?

Much of the preceding discussion is based on a premise that should be made explicit: We wish to keep our theorizing about memory as simple as possible, and a theory with multiple, specialized secondary memories is more complicated than a theory with only one secondary memory. That is, we should stick to the "one warehouse, many contents" argument unless the evidence forces us away from this view.

This "one warehouse" view has fared well so far. We know that people can remember diverse contents (colors as well as sounds, smells as well as feelings). However, it seems that at least some nonverbal materials are remembered via translation into a descriptive format. If this turns out to be a broad pattern, then there may be a diversity in *what* is remembered, but not in *how* it is remembered. That is, perhaps one descriptive mode of representation will suffice for all.

There are other ways, however, that we might seek to argue for multiple secondary memories. In Chapter 7, what convinced us that working memory differed from secondary memory was a pattern of functional differences—working memory worked in one way, secondary memory in another; working memory was influenced by one set of variables, secondary memory by another set; and so on. Can we find comparable differences among types of secondary memories?

IMAGERY MNEMONICS

Much evidence indicates that imagery plays an important role in long-term remembering. Popular books on memorizing often urge the use of image mnemonics as a powerful tool in aiding memory, and evidence indicates that this advice is well founded. For example, experimenters asked subjects to learn pairs of words. Some subjects were instructed to study the pairs by rehearsing each pair silently. Other subjects were instructed to make up a sentence for each pair of words, linking the words in some sensible way. Finally, other subjects were told to form a mental image for each pair of words, with the image combining the words in some interaction. The results showed that the imagery group performed considerably better on a recall test. The group that generated the sentences recalled more words than the rehearsal group, but fewer than the imagery group (Bower & Winzenz, 1970).

In the Bower and Winzenz study, subjects were encouraged to make their images as elaborate or as bizarre as they liked. Several authors have argued that, in fact, bizarre images are better remembered than more mundane images. For example, in another study, subjects learned word pairs such as PIANO, CIGAR, with each pair illustrated by a line drawing. Four kinds of drawings were used, as shown in Figure 12–9. The drawings depicted the objects either interacting in some way or separate, and either in a bizarre fashion or in a nonbizarre fashion. The results, though, show no memory impact of bizarreness. Memory was considerably improved, however, when the objects were shown in some interaction, rather than when the objects were shown separately (Wollen, Weber, & Lowry, 1972; see also Einstein, McDaniel, & Lackey, 1989; Kroll, Schepeler, & Angin, 1986).

We should also briefly mention that imagery instructions have comparable effects with subjects who have been blind since birth. These subjects benefit from instructions to remember words by forming images, just as sighted subjects do (Jonides, Kahn, & Rozin, 1975). This echoes a point we made earlier: So-called visual images may not be visual in any direct way.

Noninteracting, nonbizarre

Noninteracting, bizarre

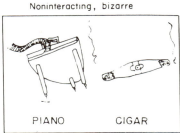

Interacting, nonbizarre

Interacting, bizarre

FIGURE 12–9. *The Effects of Bizarreness on Memory.* Subjects were required to memorize word pairs (for example, the pair PIANO, CIGAR). The pairs were accompanied by drawings that were either nonbizarre (left column) or bizarre (right column), and that involved the two items either not interacting in any way or interacting. Memory was improved if the two items were shown as interacting; bizarreness had no effect. (After Wollen, Weber, & Lowry, 1972.)

DUAL-CODING THEORY

The impact of imagery on long-term remembering can also be shown by manipulating the to-be-remembered materials, rather than the instructions to subjects. Paivio and his associates presented college students with a list of nouns and asked students to rank the nouns on a 1 to 7 scale for how readily the noun evoked an image, that is, "a mental picture, or sound, or other sensory picture" (Paivio, 1969; Paivio, Yuille, & Madigan, 1968). Examples of words receiving high ratings are "church," with an average rating of 6.63, and "elephant," rated at 6.83. Words receiving much lower ratings included "context" (2.13) and "virtue" (3.33).

We can now ask whether these imagery ratings generated by one group of subjects can be used to predict memory performance with a new group of subjects. Thus, new subjects are brought into the laboratory and asked to memorize lists of words, using the words for which we have imagery ratings. Subjects more readily learn high-imagery words than low-imagery words (Paivio, 1969). If asked to learn word pairs, subjects perform best if both words in the pair are high-imagery words, perform worst if both are low-imagery words, and perform at intermediate levels if one word in the pair is a high-imagery word and the other is not (Paivio, Smythe, & Yuille, 1968; but also see Marschark & Hunt, 1989).

These and related results led Paivio (1971; see also Paivio & Csapo, 1969; Yuille, 1983) to propose a view called **dual-coding theory**, and this brings us back to the main questions of this chapter. Paivio's claim is that two different components comprise secondary memory: One, a verbal system, stores memories via units called **logogens**, after the Greek term for "word," *logos*, and this is the primary memory repository for verbal materials. In addition, a separate imagery system stores memories via units called **imagens**; it is here that nonverbal materials are stored. On this view, instructions to subjects to form images lead to two records of the to-be-remembered material, one in each memory system. If we assume that one's chances of finding two memory records are better than one's chances of finding one record, we can explain why this double storage yields better memory performance. Likewise, imageable sentences will be doubly coded, and so also will be better remembered (Figure 12–10).

Paivio goes on to argue that these two memory systems differ in their functioning, and that is critical both for his theory and for our present agenda. Remember that it is not enough to show that there are different species of memory *contents;* that by itself would allow us to argue for a single secondary memory holding different kinds of information. In order to claim we have more than one secondary memory, we need in addition to show that these contents follow different rules.

Paivio argues that we can find these functional contrasts for the imagen

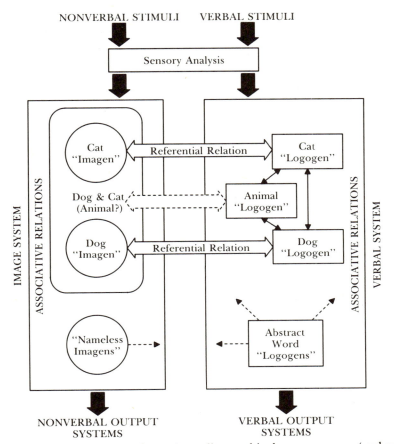

FIGURE 12–10. *Dual-Coding Theory.* According to this theory, memory (and cognition in general) is divided into a verbal system, containing representations called "logogens," and a nonverbal system, containing "imagens." These systems are separate, but there are connections between them, allowing us to place names on pictures and pictures on names. (After Paivio & Begg, 1981.)

and logogen systems. Access to the logogen system, he claims, is easiest if one starts with a word, as in: "Do you know the word 'squirrel'?" Access to the imagen system, in contrast, will be easiest if one begins with a picture: "Do you recognize this pictured creature?" Moreover, some types of information (for example, semantic associations) are stored in the logogen system, while other types of information (for example, size and shape) are more readily accessed from the imagen system.

Putting these suggestions together, we are led to a prediction (te Linde, 1983). Subjects were shown pairs of items to be judged; some of the pairs were words (for example, "duck-car"), other pairs were pictures (for example, picture of a duck, picture of a car). For half of the procedure, the subjects' task was to indicate whether there was a close association between the items in the pair. For example, shown the word pair "mouse–cheese," subjects should press the "yes" button; shown the pair "car–tomato," subjects should press the "no" button. This abstract, semantic information is hypothesized to be one of the kinds of information stored in the verbal system.

The other judgments in this study, in contrast, drew on the nonverbal, imagen system: In the other half of the procedure, subjects had to indicate whether the two items in the pair were of similar size in real life. For example, subjects would respond "yes" to "thimble–acorn," and "no" to "key–dress." Of course, when these items were presented as pictures, the pictures themselves were the same size. This way, the subject could not respond on the basis of which *picture* was bigger; instead, the subject had to respond on the basis of remembered information (Figure 12–11).

We therefore have another 2 × 2 design—two types of stimulus information, and two types of questions. (The design actually contained other conditions as well, but these are not critical for our purposes.) Before we turn to the data, though, we need to add a complication. There is reason to believe that, overall, simple pictures are recognized more quickly than words, perhaps because pictures are more distinctive from each other than words are (Friedman & Bourne, 1976). This effect will therefore be

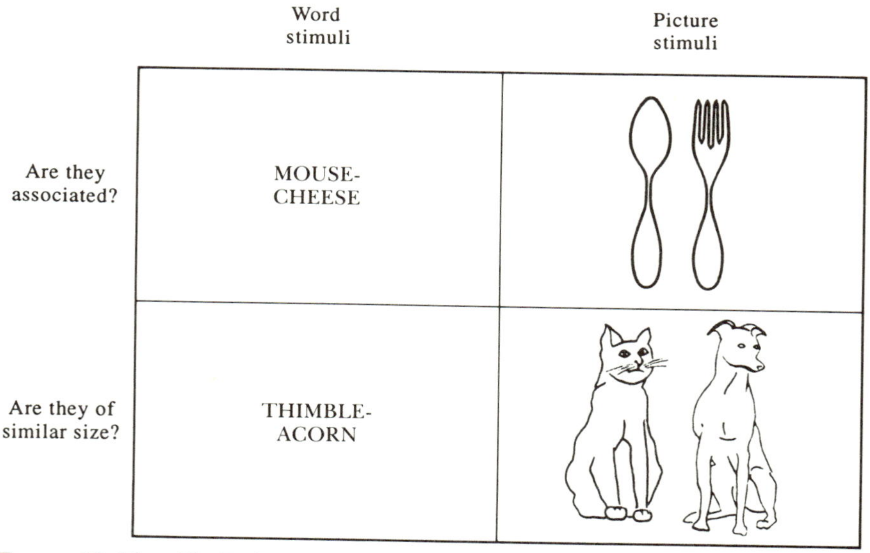

	Word stimuli	Picture stimuli
Are they associated?	MOUSE-CHEESE	
Are they of similar size?	THIMBLE-ACORN	

FIGURE 12–11.   *The Tasks and Stimuli for te Linde's Dual-Coding Experiment.* Subjects were asked either a question about association (presumably requiring information from the verbal system) or a question about size (presumably tapping the nonverbal system). Half of the questions were presented in word form (providing easier access to the verbal system) and half in pictorial form (easier access to the nonverbal system).

superimposed on the effect we are after—namely, the advantage of pictures as cues in accessing imagens, and the advantage of words as cues in accessing logogens. Think about what this means for te Linde's results. With questions about size, subjects should be quicker with pictures for two reasons: Pictures are quicker overall, and pictures are also just the right input with which to access size information. In answering questions about semantic associations, pictures have the advantage of being quickly recognized in general, but they also have the disadvantage of being an inappropriate input for accessing the desired information. These two effects should cancel each other, yielding no difference between pictures and words with the semantic association questions.

As you can see in Figure 12–12, the results are as predicted. The size questions were answered most quickly when test items were presented as pictures. Responses times were much slower if test items were presented as words. This fits with the claim that these questions are best answered with information from the imagen system, and that the imagen system is best accessed via pictures, rather than words.

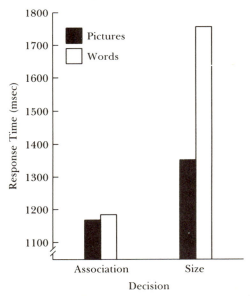

FIGURE 12–12. *Results from a Dual-Coding Experiment.* Size questions are answered by drawing on the nonverbal system; therefore responses should be faster with picture stimuli (that is, short response times with picture stimuli, long response times with word stimuli). This prediction is confirmed. With questions about association, the information is coming from the verbal system, and so we expect faster responses with word stimuli. However, this effect is offset by the general advantage of picture stimuli over word stimuli. These two effects "cancel" each other, leaving us with no difference between picture and word stimuli for the association decision. (After te Linde, 1983.)

The association questions, on the other hand, yield a very different pattern. These questions should be answered with information from the logogen system, and this system is best accessed with words. As predicted, however, this effect is masked by the overall quickness of pictures. With this task, we therefore observe no difference between picture and word stimuli.

THE SYMBOLIC-DISTANCE EFFECT

As further evidence for the dual-coding view, consider the following. We begin with some perception data: Subjects are shown drawings of various objects, and asked which of the depicted objects is larger. This time, though, the drawings are each to the same scale—both 1/100th of their actual size, or both 1/200th. This means that the ratio between the sizes of the pictures will be the same as the ratio of the sizes of the actual objects. It turns out that these judgments are, not surprisingly, easy to make, but yield a consistent pattern. If the sizes are similar (for example, a drawing of a rhinoceros and a drawing of a refrigerator, both drawn to the same scale), responses are relatively slow. If the sizes are rather different (for example, mouse versus flea), responses are very fast.

An analogous procedure can be run as a memory experiment (Moyer, 1973; Moyer & Bayer, 1976; Paivio, 1980). Rather than showing subjects pictures of the test items, subjects were shown words naming the test items. Subjects must now respond on the basis of the remembered size. Subjects in this task yield the same pattern of results as in the perceptual case—the smaller the difference in sizes, the slower the response. More specifically, the data in this memory task parallel quite closely the data with perceived objects—in both cases, the relationship between response times and sizes is an inverse logarithmic function (Figure 12–13). This so-called **symbolic-distance effect** is just what we would expect if the process of drawing on the imagen system were closely akin to the process of perceiving, and if the process of inspecting mental images were like the process of inspecting visual stimuli.

MULTIPLE SECONDARY MEMORIES

Are we finally seeing evidence of two different types of secondary memory? We believe we are not. The efficacy of imagery mnemonics, or the memory advantage for imageable materials, can be explained without recourse to a two-memory system. Even with a single secondary memory, we would still expect that double encoding is better than single encoding, and, indeed, it would be no surprise if diverse encoding were better than homogeneous encoding. That would tie the to-be-remembered material

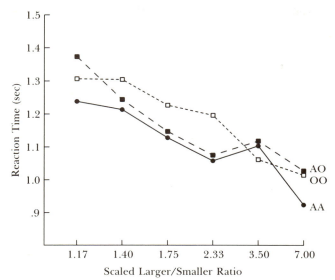

FIGURE 12–13. *The Symbolic-Distance Effect.* Subjects were shown pairs of words and had to indicate which of the named objects was bigger. Subjects' response times were related to the actual difference between the objects' sizes. If the ratio between the sizes was large ("moose/flea"), responses were fast. If the ratio was small ("rhinoceros/refrigerator"), responses were slower. The test pairs included pairs of animals (AA), pairs of objects (OO), and pairs made up of one animal and one object (AO). The results were roughly the same for all three types of pairs. (After Paivio, 1975.)

to a greater variety of nodes, providing more retrieval paths or more entry points from which the material could be found, all consistent with our discussion in Chapter 11.

Moreover, the greater accessibility of some material via pictures, and the greater accessibility of other material via words, is also no problem for a single network. Remember that we proposed that some nodes within the network were directly tied to perceptual systems, so that activation from the environment, so to speak, would more or less directly activate the target nodes. This said, it is clear that different nodes will need different connections to the environment. After all, we want the TIGER node to be activated when a pattern of inputs appropriate for a tiger is on the scene, and we want the FLY BALL node to be activated when its inputs are around, and so on. Therefore we already need to individualize the input connections to each node, and so it poses no additional problems if we individualize the connections so that some nodes are more readily activated by a configuration of inputs corresponding to a pictorial stimulus, and some by a configuration corresponding to a verbal stimulus.

Finally, what about the symbolic-distance effect? This refers, once again, to the finding that when subjects make comparisons (for example, size comparisons) based on remembered information, we find that the less similar the items being compared (that is, the more distance between them), the faster the response. Thus subjects more quickly verify "house is bigger than mouse" than they do "cat is bigger than bat"; this result matches what we get with actual perceptual comparisons.

There are two things to say about this result. First, notice that this task seems to require that the memories of, say, cats and bats first be activated, then images formed, and then these images compared. In this case, we are looking at a working-memory effect, since that, after all, is where this comparison must be taking place. Thus, while this finding might tell us about working memory's function, it cannot be an argument for separate secondary memories.

In addition, recent data call into question whether imagery is in fact the source of the observed data pattern in the symbolic-distance effect. Consider the following experiment (Paivio, 1978): Subjects are shown pairs of names of objects, like HOUSE, CHAIR. Subjects are instructed to press the left button if the object named on the left is worth more money, and the right button if the object named on the right is worth more. This procedure, oddly enough, yields a symbolic-distance effect: the more dissimilar the actual monetary values, the quicker the response. Thus subjects respond quickly to pairs like HOUSE, CHAIR, and more slowly to pairs like HOUSE, SHIP. In another study, subjects were shown pairs of animal names and had to decide which animal in each pair was "more intelligent." Once again, a symbolic-distance effect was obtained, with faster response times to pairs that differed sharply in "intelligence" (WORM, CHIMPANZEE), and slower response times to pairs that were similar in "intelligence" (SQUIRREL, MOUSE) (Banks & Flora, 1977).

We could try to read this result as showing that monetary worth, or intelligence, is judged by a comparison between images; that would bring this result into line with the other symbolic-distance findings (cf. Paivio, 1980; also Banks, 1977; Banks & Flora, 1977; Kerst & Howard, 1977). However, it is rather difficult to see how or why this could be. Properties such as monetary worth and intelligence are not properties one can perceive directly; it therefore seems odd to argue that these properties are judged by inspecting images. Alternatively, one might conclude that the symbolic-distance effect is not necessarily an imagery effect, in which case we should draw no conclusions about imagery from symbolic-distance data.

How to sum all this up? The data make it clear that there are different types of memory content; that is, we remember different kinds of materials, in apparently different formats. It also seems clear, at least in working memory, that imagery employs different operations and processes than other representations do. However, the data do not demand separate secondary memories. It seems that we can continue treating secondary memory as one big warehouse.

HOW WE REMEMBER PICTURES

We are claiming, therefore, that the memory in which we store verbal materials is the same as the one in which we store images. This implies that the principles we uncovered in previous chapters should be general principles, so that memories for things like pictures, or facial appearances, will follow the same general rules we have laid out in previous chapters. To find out if this is true, we will take a brief look at what is known about picture memory in this section, and then face memory in the next section.

How well do we remember pictures? One might think we would not remember them well, given our arguments so far. In Chapter 7, for example, we suggested that attention just to appearances leads to poor retention. One might think that looking at pictures is a case in which attending to appearances is exactly what one does. Therefore, picture memory should be poor. However, the response to this is easy to find: Just as we can attend to the details of how a word is printed (*shallow processing*) or to the meaning of what is represented by the printed word (*deep processing*), we can also do either with pictures: We can attend to the shape of specific contours, whether the lines are thick or thin and so forth, *or* we can think about the meaning of what is depicted by the picture. For that matter, we could even do deep processing about the contours or lines themselves; for example, we could think about why the artist chose to use thick lines rather than thin. This draws our attention once more to the difficulty of defining deep and shallow processing, a point we discussed in Chapter 7 (pp. 282–86). That to the side, though, it should be clear that there is no essential connection between shallow processing and the perception of pictures.

When we think about the meaning of a picture, what does this involve? One possibility is that we seek to assimilate the pictorial information into a schematic frame, as described in Chapters 9 and 10. And, in fact, it is easy to demonstrate schema effects, related to those reviewed in Chapter 9, with pictures. For example, Friedman (1979) showed subjects pictures of scenes, such as a typical kitchen or a typical barnyard. In addition, the pictures also contained objects that did not fit particularly well with the scene. For example, the kitchen picture included such obvious things as a stove and a toaster, but also included items less often found in a kitchen, such as a fireplace. Subjects were later given a recognition test in which they had to discriminate between the pictures previously seen and versions of these pictures in which something had been changed. For example, subjects might be shown a test picture in which a different kind of stove appeared in place of the original stove, or one in which the toaster on the counter had been replaced by a radio. In either of these cases, subjects were to respond that the picture was new, that is, not the same as the one shown in training.

Friedman's data show that subjects rarely noticed changes to the familiar objects in the pictures. In the examples just given, subjects tended (incorrectly) to respond "old" even when the stove was replaced by a different stove, or the toaster by the radio. This is sensible on schema grounds: Both the original and altered pictures were fully consistent with the kitchen schema, and so both would be compatible with a schema-based memory.

On the other hand, subjects almost always noticed changes to the unexpected objects in the scene. For example, if the originally viewed kitchen had a fireplace, and the test picture did not, subjects consistently detected this alteration. Again, this is predictable on schema grounds: The fireplace did not fit with the kitchen schema, and therefore drew special notice and was likely to be specifically noted in memory. In fact, Friedman recorded subjects' eye movements during the original presentations of the pictures. Her data showed that subjects tended to look twice as long at the unexpected objects as the expected ones—clearly these objects did catch subjects' attention!

In essence, what Friedman's subjects seemed to remember was that they had seen something we might label "kitchen + a fireplace," a description that both identifies the relevant schema and notes what was special about this particular instance of the schema. If recognition memory is tested with a kitchen without a fireplace, subjects spot this discrepancy easily, since this picture does not fit with the remembered description. If tested with a kitchen plus or minus a radio, this still fits with the "kitchen + a fireplace" description, and so the alteration is likely not to be noticed. (See also Pezdek, Whetsone, Reynolds, Askari, & Dougherty, 1989.)

This finding echoes a result mentioned earlier in this chapter; namely, that memory for appearances seems often to draw on a remembered description of the previously viewed scene. The cases we considered earlier involved single-word labels for simple objects. Friedman's evidence shows that we get parallel effects with memory for complex scenes; the only difference is that subjects are influenced in this case by schematic knowledge, rather than by single words.

Is this all there is to picture memory? Do we remember pictures by remembering descriptions, and nothing more? Further evidence indicates that there is more to picture memory than this. In an early study by Shepard (1967), subjects viewed a series of 612 pictures. Subjects were then given a recognition test, in which they were shown pairs of pictures, one of which was from the previous set and one of which was completely new. Subjects' task was to decide which picture in each pair had been previously presented. When this testing was immediate, subjects were 98% accurate; with a week's delay, accuracy dropped to 90%. Other experiments have reported comparable results when there were literally several thousands of pictures in the initial series (e.g., Nickerson, 1968;

Standing, Conezio, & Haber, 1970; Standing, 1973). Given Friedman's results, we know that these subjects are not remembering every detail of the pictures they have seen. However, subjects are remembering enough to distinguish the previously seen pictures from novel ones, even with enormous numbers of pictures in the to-be-learned set.

What is going on here? On the one side, we are seeing schema effects, as though subjects encoded a picture's meaning or gist. On the other side, it seems difficult to believe that a schematic representation would support the high levels of performance just mentioned. It is not surprising, therefore, that several theorists have proposed two-part theories of picture memory. For example, one hypothesis is that we separately remember *general visual information* and then *specific detail* (Loftus & Bell, 1975). Another proposal speaks of memory for a picture's schema and memory for other information specifying what visual form the schema took (Mandler & Ritchey, 1977).

Several pieces of evidence support these proposed distinctions. Loftus and Bell (1975) found that memory for pictorial details is predictable from subjects' eye movements when they first inspect the picture. This should not be surprising: If subjects look directly (say) at the fire hydrant, then they are likely to remember the detail that there was a fire hydrant. Subjects' memories for "general visual information," on the other hand, are not directly predictable from eye movements. Mandler and Ritchey (1977) report that these types of information also differ in longevity: Subjects seem to remember schematic information about a picture long after they have forgotten specific information about the picture's appearance.

Finally, in one of the earlier experiments in this area, Bahrick and Boucher (1968) showed subjects pictures of common objects, then tested for both recall of the objects' names and recognition. Bahrick and Boucher hypothesized that memory for schematic or descriptive information would be enough to support performance in the recall test. In the recognition test, however, subjects had to pick out the previously viewed picture from among choices all in the same category. For example, subjects had to choose which of several pictured coffee cups was the one they had previously been shown. For this test, memory for schematic information will not be enough, since all of the test items fit within the same schema. Instead, the recognition choice could only be made on the basis of memory for specific visual details.

The expectation, therefore, is that these two tests require different kinds of memory from the subject—schematic memory on the one hand, and detail memory on the other. Consistent with this, Bahrick and Boucher found that recognition performance and recall performance were independent of each other—one could not predict a subject's recall score by knowing her recognition performance, and vice versa (see also Nickerson & Adams, 1979).

MEMORY FOR FACES

For many years psychologists believed that our abilities to perceive and recognize faces drew on highly specialized skills, involving specific brain structures whose sole function was to support recognition of faces. However, more recent evidence has challenged this "faces are special" view. In this section, we look briefly at the evidence on both sides.

In some ways it would not be surprising if face recognition was served by a separate, biologically specialized mechanism. It is easy to imagine evolutionary reasons why humans and other social species need to recognize their friends and family, and to distinguish these from foes. Evolution might therefore have favored the development of great skill in this discrimination, and this in turn might have demanded the development of specialized "neural machinery," functioning in its own particular way, in order to get this job done as well as possible.

Note the parallel between this suggestion and our discussion of biologically specialized learning in Chapters 1 and 2. In those early chapters, we considered the possibility that, while some principles of learning are truly general, there may also be cases of specialized learning, learning that is specific to a certain species or a certain situation. The best-known case of this is taste aversion learning, described in Chapter 2 (Garcia & Koelling, 1966; Revusky & Garcia, 1970; Rozin & Kalat, 1971). The question to be asked is whether face memory also falls into this category of specialized learning.

Several pieces of evidence support the claim that face memory is served by specialized structures and mechanisms. One indication comes from individuals who have suffered brain strokes. Depending on where exactly in the brain these strokes occur, patients can develop a striking variety of very specific symptoms. In particular, patients who suffer damage to the occipital cortex sometimes develop a syndrome called **prosopagnosia**: They lose their ability to recognize faces, even though their other visual abilities seem to be relatively intact. This implies the existence of a special neural structure involved almost exclusively in the recognition and discrimination of faces (Alexander & Albert, 1983; Damasio, Damasio, & Van Hoesen, 1982; Hecaen, 1981).

Second, recognition of faces seems highly dependent on orientation. It is generally difficult to recognize things if they are presented at a novel orientation (for example, upside down), but this effect is particularly pronounced with faces. We can make this point in either of two ways. Experimentally, Figure 12–14 shows the results of an experiment by Yin (1969). Four categories of stimuli were considered: right-side-up faces, upside-down faces, right-side-up pictures of common objects other than faces (such as houses), and upside-down pictures of common objects. As can be seen, performance suffered for all of the upside-down stimuli. However, this effect is much larger for faces than it is for other kinds of stimuli.

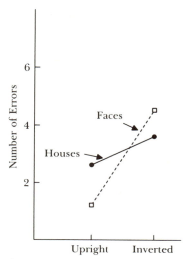

FIGURE 12–14. *Memory for Faces Presented Upright or Upside Down.* Subjects' memory for faces is quite good, compared with memory for other pictures (in this case, pictures of houses). However, subjects' performance is very much disrupted when the pictures of faces are inverted. Performance with houses is also worse with inverted pictures, but the effect of inversion is far smaller. (After Yin, 1969.)

The same point can also be made informally. Figure 12–15 shows two upside-down photographs of British prime minister Margaret Thatcher (from Thompson, 1980). You can probably detect that something is odd about these, but now try turning the book upside down, so that the faces are right side up. As you can see, the difference between these faces is immense, and yet this large and rather fiendish contrast is mostly lost when the faces are upside down. This fits with Yin's finding that our perception of faces is strikingly different when we view the faces upside down.

The degree to which face recognition suffers with disoriented stimuli implies that face recognition draws on processes somehow different from those involved with other stimuli. Likewise, the existence of prosopagnosia seems to imply that a portion of the brain is specialized for face recognition. However, we need to complicate this picture in at least two ways.

First, our understanding of prosopagnosia has grown more complex as a greater number of cases have been examined. There is a well-documented report of a prosopagnosic farmer who not only lost the ability to recognize faces, he also lost the ability to discriminate among his *cows.* Likewise, there is a case of a prosopagnosic bird-watcher who has, it seems, lost both the ability to discriminate faces and the ability to discriminate *warblers* (Bornstein, 1963; Bornstein, Sroka, & Munitz, 1969). Damasio et al. (1982) describe a patient who lost the ability to tell cars apart, and was able to locate her car in a parking lot only by reading all

FIGURE 12–15. *Perception of Upside-Down Faces.* The left-hand picture looks some-what odd, but the two pictures still look relatively similar to each other. Now try turning the book upside down (so that the faces are upright). In this position, the left-hand face (now on the right) looks ghoulish, and the two pictures look very different from each other. Perception of upside-down faces is quite different from our perception of upright faces. (From Thompson, 1980.)

the license plates until she found her own! Thus, prosopagnosia seems to involve a disorder in the ability to make fine discriminations, or to discriminate individuals within a category. Prosopagnosia does not seem to be strictly a disorder of face recognition.

The evidence about the "upside-down effect" goes the same way. It is not only face recognition that is severely disrupted by disorientation; it is also the fine discrimination of individuals within a category. The evidence for this point comes from an experiment by Diamond and Carey (1986). In their experiment, the subjects were either ordinary college students or highly experienced judges from dog shows; that is, people who know a particular breed extremely well. These judges are able to make fine discriminations among the individuals in that breed, based on tiny details of body shape, leg form, tail hairiness, and so forth.

Diamond and Carey compared how well these subjects recognized right-side-up and upside-down stimuli in each of two categories: faces and dogs in the familiar breed. Not surprisingly, performance was much worse with upside-down faces than with right-side-up faces, replicating Yin's findings. The critical result, though, is that for the expert judges performance also suffered just as much with upside-down pictures of dogs (Figure 12–16). The college students were very much disrupted by the inversion of the faces, but were not disrupted by the inversion of the pictures of the dogs.

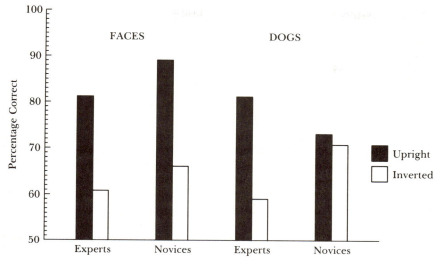

FIGURE 12–16.   *Recognition of Upright and Inverted Pictures.* All subjects were much worse at recognizing inverted (upside-down) faces, in comparison to upright faces. Expert dog judges showed the same effect in recognizing pictures of dogs. The "novice" subjects (college students), less familiar with dogs, were affected far less by inversion of the dog stimuli. (After Diamond & Carey, 1986.)

Apparently, then, the "upside-down effect" is not limited to faces. Instead, the effect appears when subjects are making fine discriminations among individuals within a highly familiar set. It is the same fine discriminations that are at risk in prosopagnosia. Thus we seem to be seeing evidence of a specialized skill, although it seems to be more a skill of perceiving and discriminating among individuals, rather than a specialization of learning or remembering. Moreover, this specialized skill is not a skill for recognition of faces alone; we have seen that other stimuli can also engage this highly refined ability. (For further research on memory for faces, see Baddeley, 1982a,b; Bower & Karlin, 1974; Davis, Ellis, & Shepard, 1978; Patterson & Baddeley, 1975; Woodhead, Baddeley, & Simmonds, 1979.)

SUMMARY OF MEMORY FOR VISUAL MATERIALS

One question at stake throughout this chapter has been, in essence, whether we can generalize the results presented in previous chapters—whether the patterns that have emerged for certain types of stimuli, certain types of to-be-remembered materials, hold up when we examine a broader range of materials. Specifically, do the memory principles we have uncovered apply to memory for nonverbal materials and, in particular, to memory for visual appearances?

In some regards, visual memories are special: There are claims we can make about visual memories that we cannot make about other memories, and vice versa. This is most clearly evident in working memory, in which the properties of visual images seem different from those of other forms of representation. In addition, visual memories themselves turn out to be a diverse set, so we need to make further, finer subdivisions. That was part of the point in our discussion of face memory. Face memory seems to have special characteristics, not shared by all visual memories—that is, face recognition is supported by a specific part of the brain, and face recognition is particularly disrupted if the stimuli are disoriented. However, these characteristics are not unique to face memory; they are shared by other memories in a category we might label as "visual memories for discriminating individual members of a highly familiar set."

All of this leaves us with a three-part conclusion. First, the evidence is consistent with the argument that we have only one secondary memory, holding diverse materials, and only one working memory, although it is a working memory with multiple, specialized components. Second, while there is but a single secondary memory, its contents do not constitute a homogeneous domain: Claims that are true for some sorts of memory may not be true for other sorts of memory. This seem clearest in the case of face memory, but may turn out to be true for other species of memory as well. Thus, even if all memories were stored in a single storage system, different types of memories may have different properties.

Third, and perhaps most important, our review of visual memories has also pointed toward many communalities between visual memories and memories in general. Schema effects were as easily detected here as in the memories we have of stories and events. Visual memories seem improved by "deeper" processing (e.g., Bower & Karlin, 1974) just as verbal memories are (see Chapter 7). Subjects show "primacy" and "recency" effects when they learn a series of pictures (Tabachnick & Brotsky, 1976), just as they do when they learn a list of words (Chapter 7). There is also reason to believe that network theorizing applies to picture memory just as it applies to verbal memory, and that phenomena such as spread of activation and priming can be demonstrated with nonverbal materials (e.g., Kroll & Potter, 1984) just as they can be demonstrated with verbal materials. In short, the communalities between visual memories and other memories seem just as important as the contrasts.

Other Categories of Memories

Our question at the outset of this chapter was whether memory needed to be subdivided, with different types of materials held in different memory stores. But we have closely examined only one way we might seek to subdivide memory, namely, a division between verbal and nonverbal memories. For that matter, we have focused primarily on a single type of nonverbal memory, namely, visual memory.

Might we have reached different conclusions if we had considered other memory divisions? One might ask, for example, whether memories for smells are somehow in a separate store, or memories for tastes, or sounds. Alternatively, one might ask whether memories for generic information are stored separately from memories for specific episodes and events. (For discussion, see McKoon, Ratcliff, & Dell, 1986; Tulving, 1983, 1989.)

Other types of memories are also worth considering, and certainly seem rather different from the memories we have discussed in this book. What about memories for skills? This would include both muscular skills, like knowing how to ski, and intellectual skills, like knowing how to solve crossword puzzles. This kind of knowledge is sometimes referred to as **procedural** knowledge, knowledge of how to do various activities, as opposed to **declarative** knowledge, knowledge that certain facts are true. Is procedural knowledge stored in memory in a fashion similar to declarative knowledge? Procedural knowledge is clearly different in its content from declarative knowledge, but we believe it is too soon to draw conclusions about whether this difference in content places special demands on the organization or functioning of memory (see Baddeley, 1982a,b; Cohen, 1984; Squire & Cohen, 1984).

For another possibility, much research indicates that the two halves of the brain—more technically, the two cerebral hemispheres—differ with respect to many aspects of cognition. Is there a "right-hemisphere memory" separate from the "left-hemisphere memory"? So far, little evidence speaks for or against this intriguing suggestion.

To mention one last and very different possibility, Zajonc (1980) caused some controversy when he proposed that emotions and emotionality operate in a mental system separate from so-called cold cognitions (that is, dispassionate and calm memories or thoughts) and that emotions follow separate principles. This proposal has evoked interesting discussion (Lazarus, 1982, 1984; Zajonc, 1984), but, once again, we believe it is too soon to tell what implications this has for claims about memory.

One could plausibly argue that each of these distinctions may demand further subdivisions of memory, perhaps further branches within the working-memory system, or even a separate and distinct secondary memory. But so far the available data will not yet support firm answers on either side of these questions. Nonetheless, we hope it is clear that the logic and methods we have pursued in this chapter could easily be applied to any of these proposed distinctions. In fact, the agenda for this chapter has been as much methodological as it has been substantive. We have tried to show by example both what it would mean to propose a separate memory system and how one might go about investigating that proposal.

The number of subdivisions one might still propose remains large, and we look forward to seeing the evidence as it accumulates.

Summary

We clearly remember a great diversity of materials—verbal passages and pictures and complex episodes, memories for specific occasions and memories for general information. Is all this information stored in one large memory? Or do we have separate memories, each specialized for a certain type of content?

For primary memory, considerations of function lead us to argue that a single primary memory must be used to store diverse contents. At the same time, a variety of evidence indicates that primary memory often relies on a speech-like mode of representing information, as if subjects, trying to remember materials for a short term, literally speak to themselves. This is evident in the errors subjects make in short-term memory tasks, often errors in which "sound-alike" items ("bell" and "ball," "tap" and "tack") are substituted for each other.

A separate line of evidence indicates that primary memory can also hold mental images. These images, at least in the case of visual imagery, seem to have many properties in common with actual pictures. Information that is prominent in a picture (as opposed to a verbal description) turns out to be prominent in a mental image as well. Mental images also seem to preserve distance relationships and spatial arrangements. It also appears that the psychological processes used for evaluating images overlap to some extent with the processes of perception. This is demonstrated in the fact that subjects have difficulty in perceiving if they are simultaneously forming a mental image, with the implication that both of these tasks draw on (and therefore compete for) the same mental resources.

At the same time, a number of considerations also point to contrasts between visual images and pictures, in addition to the many similarities between them. For example, subjects can easily reinterpret a picture of an "ambiguous figure," setting aside one interpretation of the figure and finding a new one. Subjects seem not able to do this with visual images of the same figure. This is interpreted as indicating that visual images are inherently meaningful, and not separable from how the person holding the image understands that image.

Given all of this evidence, we explored the claim that working memory actually consists of a system of interconnected components. At the center of this system is a "central executive," able to combine together information of different forms and different formats. This executive can draw on a number of "slave systems," which serve to hold on to information for a brief moment while the executive works on other matters. One slave system, employed for imagery, is the visuospatial scratchpad. Another slave system is the articulatory rehearsal loop, which can be divided into an "inner voice" and an "inner ear." In using this loop, one pronounces the to-be-remembered items to oneself. Once initiated, this pronunciation is automatic enough so that it requires minimal attention, freeing the executive for other functions. This pronunciation creates an auditory image, which then gradually fades. Once this happens, the executive is again needed to reinitiate the cycle.

What about secondary memory? Are there separate secondary memories, each specialized for containing a particular species of information? We examined whether our memory for verbal materials is separate from our memory for nonverbal materials. Some nonverbal materials appear to be remembered via a description into a verbal or propositional format; this sort of remembering clearly places no special demands on memory. Likewise, the advantages of imagery mnemonics, and the ease with which we remember concrete terms (which are easily imaged), are also compatible with the claim that there is only one secondary memory, holding diverse types of material.

One line of theorizing, however, has challenged the claim that verbal and nonverbal materials are stored in a single memory system. According to dual-coding theory, verbal materials are stored in one system and are represented by "logogens"; nonverbal materials are stored in another system and are represented by "imagens." Within this view, these systems can be distinguished in several ways. The verbal system is most easily accessed with words as memory cues; the nonverbal system with pictures. The verbal system holds semantic information, while the nonverbal system holds information about appearances.

Several lines of evidence were presented in favor of this view, including the fact that subjects can make semantic judgments more quickly if the questions are posed verbally rather than in picture form; this is not the case when subjects are asked to make judgments about sizes or shapes. However, this finding turns out to be compatible with the claim that there is only one secondary memory, able to hold many kinds of contents. Some of these contents are more easily accessed with one sort of cue while other contents are more easily retrieved with different cues, but this by itself does not argue for separating secondary memory into smaller, more specialized storehouses.

If a single secondary memory holds information about both verbal and nonverbal materials, then we would expect similarities between how we remember these different kinds of materials. This implies that the principles described in previous chapters, principles derived largely from research with verbal materials, should also apply to memory for other sorts of information. Consistent with this, schema effects are easily demonstrated in picture memory, just as they were with memory for paragraphs and stories. At the same time, evidence indicates that picture memory is composed of two elements, one being the schematic content or gist of a picture and the other being memory for the specific details and layout of the picture.

We also considered indications that memory for faces was highly specialized, and functioned differently from memories for other sorts of material. One line of evidence for this claim is the severe disruption in memory performance when faces are viewed upside down, which is far greater than the disruption observed when other visual stimuli are viewed upside down. In addition, a certain form of brain damage appears to disrupt face memory and only face memory, implying that face memory is served by a specific and specialized portion of the brain.

However, recent findings have disputed both of these claims. Face memory is disrupted if stimuli are viewed upside down, but so is memory for other highly familiar stimuli, particularly stimuli for which one is making fine-grained discriminations among individuals. Likewise, brain damage that disrupts face memory also disrupts the ability to make discriminations among other cases—for example, the damage also disrupts the ability to tell species of birds apart, or to tell different cars apart. Apparently a portion of the brain is specialized for these tasks, but the specialization seems to be a skill for making fine discriminations among individuals, and not a specialization for face memory.

In sum, the main question of this chapter gets a mixed answer. In primary memory, there is one single memory, but it has diverse constituents, with some of these (the slave systems) specialized for holding certain kinds of information. For secondary memory, the evidence is consistent with arguing for a single, vast memory that happens to hold diverse contents. Certain principles seem to apply to all of these contents—the role of deep processing, the role of schemata, and so on. Other principles seem to apply only to certain memory types—for example, memories used for making fine discriminations. This is, once again, consistent with there being but a single secondary memory (hence the common principles), but holding a truly heterogeneous set of contents (hence the more specialized principles).

PART 5

LOSING

INFORMATION,

USING

INFORMATION

13 Forgetting

O ne topic has been largely absent from our discussion so far, namely forgetting. Why do we forget? What sorts of things do we forget? Can one arrange things so that one forgets less? For that matter, would it be desirable to forget less? In this chapter, we will consider these questions, examining various theories of forgetting and how these are related to the memory principles developed in the previous chapters.

Before we examine theories of forgetting, though, there is a question that must be asked, one that provides a central theme in this chapter. The question is this: Does forgetting exist?

Does Forgetting Exist?

In some ways, it seems obvious that forgetting exists. One forgets two of the items on one's shopping list. One forgets appointments. One forgets facts one has learned (and usually discovers this loss in the middle of taking an exam). Clearly, therefore, our question is not whether the *phenomenon* of forgetting exists. Unmistakably it does.

Our question is subtler: Does a *process* of forgetting exist? What is usually meant by forgetting is that material was once available in memory, but is no longer available. The question is why this should be. As one possibility, the information might not come to mind because it has vanished from memory. Perhaps the sought-after information has faded because of the passage of time, or perhaps it has been displaced by newer information. In these cases, forgetting would involve a genuine loss of information from memory; our theories would need to include mechanisms to account for this loss.

Alternatively, perhaps there is no actual loss. Perhaps there is no "exit" from memory; material, once in, stays in. On this view, when we seem to forget, we simply are failing to locate the sought-after information within the vast storehouse of memory. The information is still in storage; we are just suffering a **retrieval failure**, an inability to find the sought-after material.

We have ample reason to believe that retrieval failure accounts for some forgetting; the question here is whether retrieval failure might account for all forgetting. If this were the case, then we would need to postulate no process of forgetting. The normal processes of memory can succeed, in which case we remember, or the normal processes of memory can fail, in which case we seem to have forgotten. And there are a large number of reasons why the processes of memory, and retrieval in particular, can fail. We may have been given an inadequate retrieval cue, or no retrieval cue. The degree of fan from the retrieval cue may be very large, so that insufficient activation travels from the cue's node to the target node (see Chapter 11). We may have changed our understanding of the to-be-remembered material, and so we may have activated an inappropriate schema. And so on.

In each of these cases, we explain retrieval failure by means of mechanisms introduced in earlier chapters. Thus no new theorizing is needed to account for retrieval failures, and no new theorizing is needed, on this view, to explain forgetting. Forgetting is just the absence of successful remembering; forgetting involves no processes or mechanisms of its own.

We confronted an issue just like this, earlier in the text. Think about our discussion of inhibition and inhibitory learning, in Chapter 2. In that context, we considered what evidence would speak in favor of a single force, present or absent, underlying learning, and what would speak in favor of two separate forces, one promoting a response and one working against a response, each with its own rules and with its own existence. As it turns out, we found reasons to believe that inhibition was a separate process from excitation; both can be on the scene at the same time in something like a tug-of-war. Is the same true for remembering and forgetting?

The Advantages of Forgetting

Before we examine the evidence about forgetting, a preliminary point should be made. Many people regard forgetting as something undesirable, and express a wish for a "better" memory. In some ways, it is clear what motivates this: It is frustrating to be taking an examination and realize that one cannot recall material studied the night before. It is likewise annoying to forget the birthdays of loved ones, or the names of people one has met, or any of the thousands of things that we routinely fail to remember.

At the same time, however, there are also considerable advantages to forgetting. One might suppose that these concern the forgetting of unpleasant facts and events, as a means of protecting ourselves from unhappy or painful memories. These are not, however, what we mean. As we will see later in the chapter, it is far from clear whether forgetting serves this kind of self-protective function. Instead, the advantages to forgetting are of a subtler sort.

In an extraordinary short story entitled "Funes the Memorious," Jorge Luis Borges (1964) describes a character named Funes, who has a perfect memory. Funes never forgets anything, but, rather than being pleased or proud of this capacity, is immensely distressed by his memory prowess. "My memory, sir, is like a garbage heap," he complains. Funes's problem, though, was that "he was . . . almost incapable of ideas of a general, Platonic sort. Not only was it difficult for him to comprehend that the generic symbol *dog* embraces so many unlike individuals of diverse size and form; it bothered him that the dog at 3:14 (seen from the side) should have the same name as the dog at 3:15 (seen from the front)."

This story is, of course, a work of fiction, but Funes is remarkably similar to an actual person. Luria (1968) describes a case of a man, identified only as "S," who, like Funes, never forgets anything. Luria's observations of S closely parallel Borges's description of Funes. S, just like Funes, is not served well by his extraordinary memory. In tests of intelligence, S does not do well; he is often distracted, it would seem, by the rich detail of his own recollections.

Why should this be? In Chapter 9, we discussed the role of generic knowledge in guiding our intellectual commerce with the world; we proposed that this knowledge is created by blurring together various episodes and particulars we have encountered. Likewise, in Chapter 10, we noted that comparisons between present circumstances and remembered exemplars will never yield a "perfect match." To draw on remembered exemplars, one must overlook these points of contrast, and this will be more difficult if one remembers every distinctive aspect of the object or event.

In short, the suggestion is that the absence of forgetting would be an impediment to generalization, and to abstract thinking. To think abstractly, one must overlook many concrete details; forgetting seems to help make this possible. In order to generalize, one must ignore the points of difference between various episodes; again, forgetting facilitates this. S, the real character, complains about his "perfect" memory, just as Funes did. Apparently, whether or not one might wish for a better memory, a perfect memory, with no forgetting, is far from desirable.

We should be careful about what is being suggested here. There are intellectual advantages attached to not having a perfect memory. But this does not commit us to claiming that a bona-fide forgetting process exists. In order to obtain the advantages just described, all we need is some sort of flaw in the processes of learning and memory, to make these processes less than perfect. For example, a flaw in memory retrieval could serve this function. We are therefore still left to ask: Does forgetting exist as a process? Are memories ever lost from secondary storage? Or is it the case that once information enters memory it is permanently in place, although potentially not located because of inadequacies in the remembering process?

The Decay Theory

The **decay theory** of forgetting states simply that, with the passage of time, memories fade or erode. Why might this be? For one possibility, the relevant brain cells might gradually die off. For another, network connections might require a steady stream of new inputs in order to maintain their strength. If no new input comes in, the connection weight will gradually drop.

DECAY OF ACTIVATION WITHIN THE NETWORK VIEW

We have already appealed to something like decay theory, when we suggested that network connections benefit from both frequency and recency of activation. The idea was that an associative link that has been recently used would still be warmed up, and so activation would more rapidly and efficiently flow through this connection. With the passage of time, this activation would no longer be recent and so would no longer provide a memory advantage.

This decay is necessary, if priming is to do its job. The purpose of priming, presumably, is to prepare us for likely events. Given the redundancy of the world, many inputs or stimuli are repetitive, and so recently experienced inputs are likely to be experienced again. Thus priming via recency prepares us for these frequently encountered inputs. It is critical, though, that this preparation dissipate after a while. Imagine what would happen if the priming lasted merely one day. By the end of 24 hours, all of the nodes activated during that day would still be primed, and this is a large number indeed. In this case, one would lose the selective advantage supposedly inherent in priming. Being ready for everything may be better than its opposite (whatever that is), but it is less effective than anticipating a particular event or input.

Does this settle the issue about forgetting? Is a decay theory of forgetting therefore correct? We have reason to believe that decay does exist in the form of dissipation of priming. But, unfortunately, this comes nowhere close to supporting a decay theory of forgetting, and it is not hard to see why. Figure 13–1 illustrates this species of decay. When a node is activated, or when an associative link is traversed, some residual activation is left behind; this is what makes recency priming possible. Then this activation decays. But decays to what? At the end of the decay, there is still a residual benefit. This must be the case, since we know that there is an effect of both recency *and* frequency. That is, each individual activation must leave something behind, so that these can accumulate to create the frequency advantage. Thus the decay cannot be back to zero, because otherwise we would get no accumulation. This does not seem at all like the mechanism needed to account for a loss of memory. The decay does erode a short-term privilege, but actually leaves the activation levels higher than they were at the very beginning.

Moreover, the time course of priming's decay seems wrong if we are to use decay as an explanation of forgetting. One would want an explanation of forgetting to account for memory losses over months and years; yet the dissipation of priming or fluency happens far more quickly than that. Once again, these mechanisms, while describable in decay terms, do not fit the bill for a theory of forgetting.

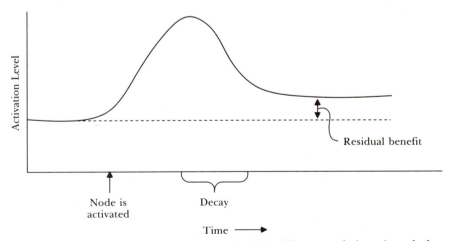

FIGURE 13–1. *Decay of Activation for a Single Node.* When a node is activated, the activation level of that node increases. However, this is temporary; the activation then decays. But the decay brings the activation down to a level somewhat higher than it was at the outset. This allows accumulation with other activations later on, eventually leading to a "frequency" effect.

TESTING THE DECAY NOTION

If considerations of priming and its dissipation do not support the decay notion, perhaps other evidence will. What kind of evidence do we need? We might seek evidence that memories from long ago are less clear, or less accurate, than memories of more recent events. This would be consistent with decay claims, but, by itself, will not be enough. To see why, consider a different hypothesis, the hypothesis of forgetting from **interference**. According to this view, forgetting occurs because new learning works against, or interferes with, older learning. We will examine this hypothesis in more detail in the next section, but for now notice that this view also predicts that less will be remembered about older events than about recent events. On an interference account, this is not because of the corrosive effects of time, but because more learning has come between older events and the present time than between newer events and the present. Hence, both interference and decay predict this disadvantage of older materials, and so, if we find such a result, it will be consistent with either hypothesis, and "proof" of neither.

A stronger test of decay theory is easy to design, but rather difficult to carry out. All we need to do is teach subjects something, then have them spend time neither learning new material nor thinking about anything nor attending to anything. Then, after a time spent in this fashion, we test subjects' memories. If interference arises from events subsequent to learning, then this design allows no opportunity for interference. If interference arises both from events prior to the learning and from events after the learning, then at least this design eliminates one source of interference (that is, interference from events after learning). In any case, these manipulations should not matter for the time-dependent mechanisms of decay. On an interference view, therefore, a period of inactivity subsequent to learning should diminish forgetting. On a decay view, a period of inactivity should not diminish forgetting: Time is still passing, and, according to the decay claim, it is the passage of time, not interference, that leads to forgetting.

Needless to say, this experiment is difficult to implement, if not impossible. How could we get subjects to do nothing, think about nothing, attend to nothing? The experiments that come closest to this logic have been done with animals, not humans. These procedures take advantage of the fact that many animals do spend long periods of time seemingly doing nothing, or close to it. Therefore, it seems a reasonable suggestion that these animals will suffer little interference from new learning, allowing us to test the decay claim.

For example, many experiments have been done with cockroaches, exploiting the fact that roaches, once they enter a warm, dark, dry place, will lie still for many minutes (e.g., Minami & Dallenbach, 1946). We can therefore teach the cockroach a simple response, using the avoidance paradigm described in Chapter 4. We then provide a warm, dark, dry place, and wait. If we wait a short time, then, on the decay hypothesis, little forgetting will have taken place. If we wait a longer interval, forgetting should be correspondingly greater.

In studies like these, the passage of time turns out to be a poor predictor of forgetting. Forgetting does occur, however, if we allow the cockroaches to crawl about in the interval between learning and test. In other words, the data favor the interference hypothesis, not decay. In some ways, these results were inevitable, given our earlier comments about what does and does not produce *extinction* in Pavlovian or operant conditioning (Chapter 2, pp. 45–46, and Chapter 4, pp. 122–23). It is not the passage of time that leads to extinction. Instead, extinction occurs when the animal experiences CSs without USs, or when the animal makes responses without reinforcement. Once again, this speaks against a decay theory of forgetting.

We do not have exactly comparable data from humans, but we do have an approximation: Many studies have looked at learning just before sleep in comparison with learning just before a day's activities. There is unquestionably some mental activity during sleep, but there is surely less during sleep than during the day. Therefore in this study we are comparing "less interference" with "more," rather than "no interference" with "interference."

In a classic study by Jenkins and Dallenbach (1924), two subjects learned lists of nonsense syllables, like BIV or ZAR. The subjects were then tested after **retention intervals** of 1, 2, 4, or 8 hours. Critically, subjects sometimes slept during the retention interval, and sometimes were awake. Figure 13–2 shows the data. In both conditions, performance dropped as the interval between learning and test increased. However, this drop was much more pronounced if subjects were awake during the retention interval. That is, 1 hour with much interference produced more forgetting than 1 hour with minimal interference; likewise for 2 hours or 4 or 8. (See also Ekstrand, 1967, 1972; Hockey, Davies, & Gray, 1972.) Thus time seems not to be the crucial factor; instead it seems to be mental activity that leads to forgetting.

Baddeley and Hitch (1977) offer yet another way of getting at this question. They asked rugby players to recall the names of the teams they had played against over the course of a rugby season. Not all players made it to all games, because of illness or injuries or schedule conflicts. This allows us to compare, let us say, players for whom "two games back" means 2 weeks ago with players for whom "two games back" means 4 weeks ago. Thus we can look at the effects of retention interval (2 weeks versus 4 weeks) with the number of intervening events held constant. Likewise, we can compare players for whom the game a month ago was "three games back" with players for whom a month means "one game back." Now we have the retention interval held constant, and we can look at the effects of intervening events. In this setting, Baddeley and Hitch

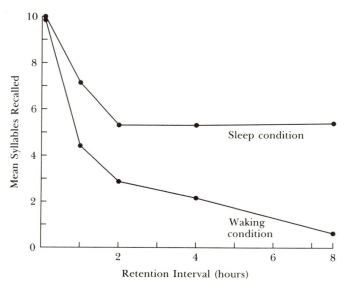

FIGURE 13–2. *Forgetting after Time Spent Awake or Asleep.* Subjects learned a series of nonsense syllables and were tested either after a period of time spent asleep or after a period of time spent awake. Forgetting was greater after time awake, presumably because during that time subjects were thinking about and learning new things, leading to memory interference. (After Jenkins & Dallenbach, 1924.)

report that the mere passage of time accounts for very little; what really matters is the number of intervening events (Figure 13–3).

None of these tests is perfect. One might worry about extrapolating from cockroach memory to that of other species; one might worry about what other things were going on in the lives of Baddeley and Hitch's rugby players. For example, a player for whom the previous game was long ago is obviously a player who missed many games. Why is this? Frequent illness? A schedule filled with other things? Could these influence the pattern of data? With these questions unanswered, we must be cautious in interpreting the Baddeley and Hitch data.

Nevertheless, a consistent message is emerging from these studies: There is a strong relationship between forgetting and the arrival of new information and new events; hence it appears that we do need an interference mechanism as part of our account of forgetting. But does this speak against the decay claim? Here a neutral answer seems appropriate. On the negative side, we have no firm evidence in favor of the decay claim. Moreover, as we will see later in this chapter, there are at least some cases of excellent memory even at very long delays; this is contrary to decay claims. On the positive side, the decay view is correct in its prediction that, overall, remembering tends to be worse after long intervals than after short intervals. Unfortunately, this observation is ambiguous. It could be due to decay, or to interference, or to a combination of these.

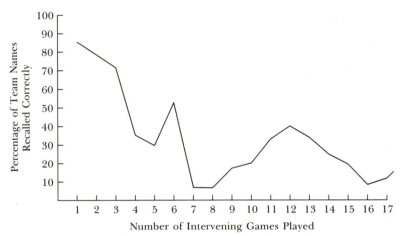

FIGURE 13–3. *Forgetting from Interfering Events.* Members of a rugby team were asked to recall the names of teams they had played against. Subjects' performance was influenced by the number of games that had intervened between the to-be-recalled game and the attempt to remember. This fits with an interference view of forgetting. (After Baddeley & Hitch, 1977.)

As we have discussed, a completely unambiguous test of decay does not exist. We have no reason to argue that the mere passage of time produces forgetting, but we cannot say firmly that the decay claim is wrong.

The Interference Theory of Forgetting

Our examination of decay theory quickly led to the notion of interference as the cause of forgetting. The idea of memory interference actually has a long history. Most of the data derive from two tasks: **serial learning** and **paired-associate learning**. In serial learning, subjects are given lists of words or nonsense syllables to memorize; we first met this task in Chapter 7, in our discussion of the modal model. In paired-associate learning, the experimenter says or shows one word, and the subject has to learn the response word. Then the experimenter says or shows another word, and the subject has to learn the response for it, and so on. Thus the experimenter might say "hair," and the subject must say "light." The experimenter says "rock," and the subject must say "card," etc. The first couple of times through the list, the experimenter provides the responses for the subject, but soon the subject is able to anticipate the response before the experimenter says it.

To demonstrate interference, once this paired-associate learning has occurred, the subject begins learning a new list. For half the subjects, we reuse the same cue words. Now when the experimenter says "hair," the subject must say "apple." When the experimenter says "rock," the subject must say "power," etc. For the other half of the subjects, we use new cue words (and new responses) on the second list.

The results reliably show that subjects have a harder time on this task if the cue words are kept the same for both lists than if the cue words are changed. In the terms shown in Table 13–1, performance is worse in the so-called A–B, A–D design than in the A–B, C–D design, where A and C refer to the cue words and B and D to the responses. Thus prior learning seems to retard new learning. This impact of old-on-new is labeled **proactive interference**, or **PI**. In addition, we can circle back and retest the subject on the first list, with no additional opportunity for learning. In the A–B, A–C design, we find relatively poor retention of the original list.

Table 13–1.   The Paired-Associate Paradigm

A–B, A–D Design			
Subjects first learn:	*List A words*		*List B words*
Each time you hear:	hair	Respond with:	light
Each time you hear:	rock	Respond with:	card
etc.			
Subjects then learn:	*List A words*		*List D words*
Each time you hear:	hair	Respond with:	apple
Each time you hear:	rock	Respond with:	power
etc.			
A–B, C–D Design			
Subjects first learn:	*List A words*		*List B words*
Each time you hear:	hair	Respond with:	light
Each time you hear:	rock	Respond with:	card
etc.			
Subjects then learn:	*List C words*		*List D words*
Each time you hear:	tree	Respond with:	apple
Each time you hear:	lamp	Respond with:	power
etc.			

Note: In the "A–B, A–D" design, subjects first learn to associate a word from List B with each word from List A. Next, they learn a new list of words (from List D), with each of these also associated with one of the List A stimuli. In the "A–B, C–D" design, subjects also first learn to associate words from List B with words from List A. But then, in the procedure's second step, subjects learn to associate words from List D with words from List C. Interference is much greater in the A–B, C–D design. In both designs, learning the first series of pairs interferes with learning the second series of pairs; this is proactive interference. Likewise, because of retroactive interference, learning the second series of pairs makes it harder to remember the first series of pairs.

That is, there is also an impact of new-on-old, labeled **retroactive interference**, or **RI**. The interference we considered in examining the decay notion was RI, since the interference was produced by experiences after the initial learning, that is, during the retention interval.

There is much research on the characteristics of PI and RI. PI seems weakest, for example, if testing occurs soon after the learning; this interference grows worse with the passage of time. RI, on the other hand, is maximal right after learning the second list (that is, the list that produces the interference); RI seems to diminish with time. Both forms of interference are maximized when the stimulus (cue) words on the two lists are very similar. The A–B, A–C design, with identical cue words on the two lists, is simply the extreme case of this. In addition, both forms of interference are increased if the quantity of interfering material is increased. That is, RI is greatest when there is a great deal of material interpolated between learning and test (e.g., Melton & Irwin, 1940); PI is greatest when a great deal of material has preceded learning (e.g., Underwood, 1957).

For our purposes, though, we now have two strands of evidence. First, in our studies of decay, it looked like it was ongoing activity that led to forgetting, and not the mere passage of time. Now, we have further evidence that interference can be demonstrated in the laboratory, and seems to be at its strongest when one is trying to make different associations to the same root idea. Do we now have indications of a bona-fide mechanism of forgetting? Not quite. We still need to ask why interference occurs. After all, it's not obvious that interference has to occur. Why don't the old learning and new learning peacefully coexist? We therefore turn to theories of interference.

RESPONSE COMPETITION AND UNLEARNING

Two mechanisms were proposed early on to explain the interference in paired-associate learning. The first of these, **response competition**, is, in a sense, not a theory of forgetting. The idea of response competition is that subjects retained both the original association and the newly formed one. When the experimenter called for a response, both associations were on the scene, but only one response was allowed. Therefore, subjects were, so to speak, pulled in two directions at once and, often enough, were pulled away from the correct answer (McGeoch, 1942).

There are several ways to test this claim. Most centrally, this idea leads to a prediction about errors. If subjects give a wrong response, they do so because they are pulled off by the previously correct response. Therefore, their incorrect answer should be that response. This prediction was tested in a classic study by Melton and Irwin (1940). Melton and Irwin had their subjects learn a list of nonsense syllables; the same subjects then studied a different list and were retested on the original list. Control subjects learned a list, then simply rested in the interval between learning and retest. The contrast between the two groups, therefore, provides a measure of RI.

As Figure 13–4 shows, RI was greater when the interpolated list was repeatedly presented. What is critical is that Melton and Irwin also looked at subjects' errors, asking how many of the errors were intrusions from the previous list. As the figure shows, this number is much too small to be the source of RI. That is, while some errors were intrusions, many were not. In addition, the curve showing intrusions is of a different form than the curve showing RI; this also argues that intrusions cannot be the sole source of RI. Melton and Irwin argued from this that some other factor, which they dubbed "Factor X," must also be on the scene. Factor X's contribution is determined by subtracting the number of intrusions from the measure of RI, showing us, in essence, how much RI is unexplained by the intrusions.

What is Factor X? This brings us to the second conception of interference. Think back for a moment to the idea of extinction of a learned response (Chapter 2). What produces extinction? Unreinforced trials. If the conditioned stimulus occurs but no unconditioned stimulus follows,

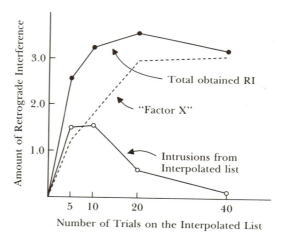

FIGURE 13–4. *Evidence for "Factor X."* Subjects learned a list of nonsense words (List 1), then learned a new list (List 2), and then were retested on List 1. Control subjects learned List 1, rested, and then were retested. By comparing the groups, we assess the amount of retroactive interference (RI). The black dots in the figure show that, with more training on List 2, there is a greater amount of interference with List 1. The white dots in the figure show the number of intrusion errors— responses from List 2 that were offered by subjects trying to remember List 1. The amount of overall interference is far greater than the number of intrusions. This implies that another factor, Factor X, must also be on the scene. Factor X's contribution is estimated by subtracting the intrusion errors from the total interference. (After Melton & Irwin, 1940.)

or if the subject emits the operant but no reinforcement happens, this gradually undoes the learning. Now think about the paired-associate paradigm. If the subject has previously learned the pair "hair–light," and now "hair" is cued with no opportunity during the learning phase for "light," this is akin to an unreinforced trial. By this logic, these reinforced trials should produce gradual extinction, or **unlearning**.

Thus Melton and Irwin argued for a "two-factor" theory of interference, with both response competition (since we did find some evidence for it) and unlearning (since response competition is apparently not all). But Melton and Irwin's work was some time ago; what has happened since?

EVIDENCE AGAINST INTERFERENCE CLAIMS

For many years, the interference theory dominated discussions of forgetting; in fact, it dominated all discussions of memory. The hope was that notions like unlearning and response competition would account for all of the facts of what we remember, what we forget, when memory mistakes happen, and what these mistakes will be. Moreover, the notions of unlearning and response competition are easily translated into the paradigms of animal learning, such as those reviewed earlier in this book. Therefore, the conception promised to unify a great deal of evidence.

However, a number of findings emerged that did not fit neatly into this package. For example, most early studies of interference had employed one of two methods—learning of lists or paired-associate learning. Both of these methods involve a test of subjects' recall of earlier items. In one method, this recall is cued only by the list itself ("What was on the list I showed you earlier?"); in the other, recall is cued by the single item paired with the test word ("What word went with the syllable DROX?").

While these methods reliably yield evidence of interference, other methods do not. Interference is much reduced, or not observed at all, with various recognition tests. In a **matching procedure**, for example, subjects are given a list of cue words, a list of response words, and asked which went with which. In a **forced-choice procedure**, subjects are given a cue word, and then two or three response words, and must choose which of these was paired with the cue during training. Many studies have compared these methods to the more standard recall tests and have consistently found little RI with these recognition procedures (McGovern, 1964; Postman & Stark, 1969).

Note, first of all, that this implies that interference is largely irrelevant to recognition testing. Thus we will need some other mechanism to account for forgetting in recognition paradigms. In addition, this evidence can be read as indicating that interference does not actually cause forgetting. In the terms we have been using, the suggestion seems to be that interference renders the prior learning less accessible, less easily located in memory. With a sufficiently strong cue, as in a recognition test, the memory can be retrieved.

A powerful demonstration along these lines was provided by Tulving and Psotka (1971). Tulving and Psotka had their subjects memorize lists of 24 words each. Each list consisted of six categories of words, with four words per category. For example, one list was "hut, cottage, tent, hotel, cliff, river, hill, volcano, captain, corporal, sergeant, colonel, ant, wasp, beetle. . . ." Some subjects learned only one of these lists; others learned two, three, four, five, or six lists. Finally, subjects were tested several times.

To measure the original learning, subjects were tested just after learning each list. As can be seen in Figure 13–5, performance is quite good in this condition. Subjects were also given a recall test at the end of all the lists. In other words, the procedure is: Learn List 1, test on List 1; learn List 2, test on List 2; and so on, and then, at the end, a final recall test on all the lists. As the figure shows, the final recall test yields clear evidence of RI—performance very much depends on the number of lists interpolated between learning and this test; with more interpolated lists, performance is worse. Finally, subjects were given one last test, but were this time provided with cue words, namely the categories into which the studied words had fallen. For example, for the above list, subjects might be given the cue "rank" or "insect." Figure 13–5 also shows the results for this group: Performance was excellent, and shows little indication of retroactive interference.

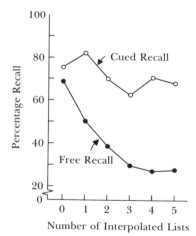

FIGURE 13–5. *Memory Cueing Effectively Eliminates RI.* In a free-recall test, subjects' ability to remember the test words strongly depended on the amount of interfering material. If no list was interpolated between the original learning and the test, subjects remembered almost 70% of the words. With 3 or 4 lists interpolated between the learning and the test, recall dropped to less then 30%. However, if subjects were given memory cues, performance did not depend on the number of interpolated lists. (After Tulving & Psotka, 1971.)

This result implies once again that interference is largely inapplicable to some procedures. Thus we need some other mechanism to account for forgetting in these procedures. In addition, the Tulving and Psotka findings show that interference plays little role if subjects have a good cue with which to search memory. The clear implication is that interference ordinarily works by rendering prior materials difficult to locate in memory.

One last study will drive this point home. Many studies have shown that an item is more difficult to remember if the item appeared on a long list rather than on a short list (Deese, 1960; Murdock, 1962). In interference terms, this is because a long list surrounds a test item with many other items, maximizing interference. But there is another way to think about this finding: On a long list, one must search through a great deal to find the sought-after item, and there may be difficulties in this search process that undermine memory performance.

Shiffrin (1970) designed a clever way to ask which explanation is correct—the one in terms of search or the one in terms of interference. Subjects learned a series of lists of words; some lists were long, and some were short. Subjects were asked to recall the list *preceding* the list just presented. What should we expect if, for example, subjects heard a short list (say, 5 words) followed by a long list (20 words)? On the search hypothesis, subjects' task requires them to search through a short list, and so performance should be quite good. According to the interference hypothesis, however, the short list was followed by many words, namely, the 20-word list, and so we should expect much RI and, consequently, poor performance.

Shiffrin's data unambiguously support the search hypothesis, and not the interference hypothesis. Subjects' recall performance was clearly influenced by the length of the list being recalled. However, and contrary to interference predictions, there was no effect of the length of the list following the list that was recalled. Once again, the data seem best understood in terms of memory search and memory access, rather than in terms of the mechanisms proposed by interference theory.

MODERN ALTERNATIVES TO INTERFERENCE THEORY

Despite psychology's great hopes for interference theory, the theory has largely been abandoned by the field. What caused the decline of this seemingly powerful theory? A major concern was in the data themselves. As research progressed within the interference framework, findings emerged that challenged interference theory's claims. To accommodate these findings, the once-simple theory became increasingly complex and, correspondingly, less and less attractive. (For reviews of these developments, see Crowder, 1976, 1982; Hulse, Egeth, & Deese, 1980; Postman & Underwood, 1973.)

The previous section described some of the troublesome evidence. As it turns out, other lines of evidence point in the same direction—for example, studies of interference from sources *outside* of the laboratory (Postman, 1969; Mandler, 1962; Underwood & Ekstrand, 1966; Underwood & Postman, 1960) and also fine-grained analyses of interference (DaPolito, 1966; Greeno, James, & DaPolito, 1971; Martin, 1971).

In addition to these concerns, interference theory also suffered from one more problem: Competitor theories started to appear, and these did a better job of explaining the evidence than interference theory did. Many of these competitors draw on the network theorizing introduced in Chapter 11. In a way, these theories incorporate many of interference theory's ideas but translate them into more modern terms. Once this translation is done, we see that there is nothing distinctive about the interference phenomena: They are simply a consequence of the normal processes of memory functioning.

For example, consider the ideas of spreading activation and degree of fan, introduced in Chapter 11 (cf. Anderson & Bower, 1974; Anderson, 1976). If the degree of fan from a node is high, activation will spread out from this node in many directions. As a result, less activation will go in each direction. To put it differently, each time a new associative link is added, the degree of fan increases, causing old links to get a smaller fraction of the total. In a sense, therefore, old and new learning "compete" with each other, as new learning "takes away" activation from old learning. Hence the network approach contains a notion quite similar to response competition.

In addition, frequent or recent use will firmly establish an associative link, allowing activation to travel swiftly down this link. This makes it more likely that this link will be the one to trigger a response, and so makes it correspondingly less likely that old linkages will govern responding. Thus, relatively speaking, there will be a decline in the influence of old associations as new associations arrive on the scene. This loss of relative position by the old linkages provides an analog of unlearning.

One could say that this merely translates interference claims from one vocabulary into another, out of the terminology of response competition and unlearning and into network terminology. What do we gain by this translation? We gain the power and breadth of network theorizing. Network ideas allow us to explain the interference data, since the network incorporates mechanisms analogous to response competition and unlearning. At the same time, the network also allows us to explain a wide range of further phenomena, as discussed in Chapter 11.

In particular, we noted in Chapter 11 that network ideas let us tackle the problem of how search through secondary memory proceeds. This is essential if we are to understand the interference phenomena, because, as we have now seen, the data indicate that interference results from problems in memory search; interference is minimized when search is facilitated. Thus, in order to understand interference, we need to understand search. An understanding of search in turn depends on an understanding of how secondary memory is organized. Proposals about response competition and unlearning, by themselves, provide little help with these questions. However, by translating interference ideas into network terms, we can go to work on this problem.

Where does all this leave us with regard to the main themes of this chapter? We began the chapter by asking whether we needed a process of forgetting, separate from the possibility of "malfunction" in the ordinary processes of remembering. We considered decay as one such process, but the evidence suggested that interference, not decay, led to memory loss. We have now seen that the facts of interference can be assimilated into the broad framework of earlier chapters, and in particular into network terms. This still leaves us with a "non-theory" of forgetting: Interference seems to result from retrieval failure, rather than from a bona-fide loss of information from storage. It still seems that we can understand forgetting in terms of the same mechanisms as remembering; we need no additional theory.

Repression

We are still left asking, might there be some other mechanism through which we forget? If the evidence for decay is thin, and if interference can be explained without reference to a separate process, might there be other means through which memory is "undone"? This brings us at last to what may be the most famous theory of forgetting, the theory of repression proposed by Sigmund Freud.

FREUD'S HYPOTHESIS

Freud claimed that many aspects of our mental lives—certain memories, certain wishes—provoke considerable anxiety and fear, and that a mechanism was needed to shield the conscious mind from this emotional pain. The primary mechanism for this is **repression.** When memories and wishes are repressed, Freud claimed, they are denied access to the conscious mind, but, critically, they are not erased. The repressed material remains on the scene, and, by virtue of the emotion attached to this material, the repressed thoughts and wishes keep trying to rise to the surface. Sometimes they make it to the surface in disguised form, as when we try to say one thing but "slip" and end up saying what we really mean—that is, express the repressed memory or repressed wish. The repressed material can also make it to the surface when our guard is down, such as when we are tired, or ill, or dreaming. One way or another, the repressed material pushes its way into our thoughts and actions. (For an excellent review of Freud's repression theory, and the pertinent evidence, see Erdelyi, 1985; Erdelyi & Goldberg, 1979.)

At the heart of this proposal are two separate claims. First, Freud claimed that much of forgetting is brought about by motivation and, more specifically, by self-protection. Thus forgetting is particularly likely for emotional materials, but most of all for emotionally unpleasant materials. Second, this motivated forgetting is hypothesized to take a particular form—not erasure, but a covering over. And, at that, not a fully successful covering over, but one that allows the possibility that repressed material will return, usually in disguised form.

THE "RETURN OF THE REPRESSED"

As just described, Freud's repression claims can be thought of in two parts: as a claim about what will be forgotten, and as a claim about the form of forgetting. Although Freud clearly viewed these claims as interrelated, we will consider them separately, examining the evidence for each. We focus first on Freud's claims about the form that forgetting takes.

On Freud's account, repressed memories are not erased; they are instead "hidden," and reemerge in a variety of forms. This reemergence is referred to as the **return of the repressed** and three lines of evidence are relevant to this "return." Two of these come from clinical data, and one from the laboratory.

If repressed material returns in disguised form, then we can discover this material if we somehow penetrate the disguise. This is typically done by close consideration of a case study, often a study of a patient undergoing therapy. A slip of the tongue, or a momentary lapse of conversation, or a dream, is interpreted as revealing the repressed wish or memory. The material extracted below (from Erdelyi's 1985 summary of a case reported by Freud in 1901 in *The Psychopathology of Everyday Life*) presents one such case, much of it taken from Freud's own writings (note that internal references have been deleted). This is a casual report by Freud, rather than one of his clinical studies, but it does give a clear sense of how the evidence goes, and how repressed contents can be uncovered:

> Freud was taking a vacation when he fell into a conversation with a young academician who was familiar with some of his theories. The young man was exceedingly dispirited about the state of the world in general and was embittered in particular about his own bleak prospects in academe. Not only were there few opportunities, but his Jewish background virtually guaranteed professional failure in those times. He sought to punctuate his outrage at the injustice by quoting a line from Virgil's *Aeneid*, in which the wronged Dido prays for revenge:

Exoriar aliquis nostris ex ossibus ultor.
(Let someone arise from my bones as an avenger.)

However, the young man had made a mistake; he had omitted the word *aliquis* (someone), saying: *"Exoriar . . . ex nostris ossibus ultor."* Immediately aware of the error, he tried to correct it, but he just could not remember the fugitive word, and finally had to ask Freud to supply it. Rather put out by his failure, the young man tried to turn the table on Freud. He reminded Freud of his . . . theory that such senseless miscues had meaning—"that one never forgets a thing without some reason"—and now challenged Freud to prove his theory.

Freud promptly took up the challenge, but on the condition that the young man follow the basic rule of psychoanalysis, "to tell me, *candidly* and *uncritically,* whatever comes into your mind if you direct your attention to the forgotten word without any definite aim". . . . The young man accepted and began his free associations:

"There springs to mind the ridiculous notion of dividing the word *aliquis* like this: *a* and *liquis.*" The next word to come to mind was *"reliquiem"* (relic); then: "liquefying," "fluidity," "fluid". . . . Then a somewhat strange association arose:

"I am now thinking of *Simon of Trent,* whose relics I saw two years ago in a church at Trent. I am thinking of the accusation of ritual blood-sacrifice which is being brought against the Jews again just now. . . ." (The original event took place in the fifteenth century. Simon had been a two-and-a-half-year-old child whom the Jews had been accused of killing for the purpose of blood ritual. As a result, Simon was declared a martyr and a saint. Only centuries later did the Catholic Church exonerate the Jews, since confessions of the crime had been extracted under torture.)

The young man's next association was that he had recently read an article in an Italian newspaper entitled "What St. Augustine Thinks of Women." Then: "I am thinking of a fine old gentleman I met on my travels last week. He was a real *original,* with all the appearance of a huge bird of prey. His name was Benedict. . . ."

At this point Freud broke into the subject's free associations: "Here are a row of saints and Fathers of the Church: St. *Simon,* St. *Augustine,* St. *Benedict,* [and] the Church Father . . . *Origen*". . . .

The next free association was, "St. *Januarius* and the miracle of his blood". . . .

Freud again interposed a comment: "Just a moment: St. *Januarius* and St. *Augustine* both have to do with the calendar. But won't you remind me about the miracle of his blood?"

The young man then explained:

"They keep the blood of St. Januarius in a phial inside the Church of Naples, and on a particular holiday it miraculously *liquefies.* The people attach great importance to this miracle and get very excited if it is delayed as happened once at a time when the French were occupying the town. So the general in command—or have I got it wrong? Was it Garibaldi?—took the reverend

gentleman aside [the priest in charge of the church] and gave him to understand with an unmistakable gesture towards the soldiers posted outside that
he *hoped* that the miracle would take place very soon. And in fact it did take
place. . . ."

And then something interesting happened. The free associations stopped
and a look of consternation came over the face of the young academician. "Why
do you pause?" asked Freud. The young man replied: "Well, something has
come into my mind . . . but it's too intimate to pass on. . . . Besides, I don't
see any connection, or any necessity for saying it". . . .

Now Freud knew that he had him: "You can leave the connections to me. Of
course I can't force you to talk about something that you find distasteful; but
then you mustn't insist on learning from me how you came to forget your
aliquis". . . .

Finally, the young man reluctantly continued: "I have suddenly thought of
a lady from whom I might easily hear a piece of news that would be very
awkward for both of us". . . .

At this point Freud delivered his interpretation, in the form of a question:
"That her periods have stopped?" The young man was startled. "How could
you guess that?" . . .

Freud replied:

"That's not difficult any longer; you've prepared the way sufficiently. Think
of *the calendar saints*; *the blood that starts to flow on a particular day*; *the disturbance
when the event fails to take place*; the open threats that the *miracle must be
vouchsafed or else*. . . . In fact you have made use of the miracle of St. Januarius
to manufacture a brilliant allusion to women's periods." . . .

The young man's muted reaction was, "I certainly was not aware of it."

Freud then elaborated on his interpretation: The prefix *a* often means no;
liquis means liquid. The young man was trying to reject from consciousness the
frightening idea *"a-liquis,"* no-liquid, that is, no menstruation—she's pregnant!
Also the young man might already have begun to feel guilty over a possible
solution to the problem other than marriage, namely abortion, alluded to by
St. *Simon*, who had been *sacrificed as a child*, and so on.

The young man asked Freud to stop: "I hope you don't take these thoughts
of mine too seriously, if indeed I really had them. In return I will confess to
you that the lady is Italian and that I went to Naples with her. But mayn't all
this just be a matter of chance?"

Some people react to such evidence with skepticism: The interpretation is contrived, they say, capitalizing on coincidences. Indeed, they say,
one could probably weave a tale around any set of observations, maybe
even several different tales. Freud's response to this would be, simply,
"Show me." Freud would agree that an individual observation, a single
slip of the tongue or lapse or dream, is open to many interpretations.
(Ironically, Freud would therefore disapprove of the game we play of
trying to interpret so-called Freudian slips.) It is a *pattern* of evidence,

Freud would argue, that we must consider. An incorrect interpretation might fit with this or that observation, but not with the full fabric of data, and so it is only by considering the fabric that we can find the true interpretation.

With this method, one can find many observations consistent with the Freudian account. Freud's writings present many case studies, most of them more elaborate than the informal one we have presented. In addition, Freud's followers have presented case after case in which one seems able to make sense of a patient's personality, and slips, and symptoms, and dreams, by appeal to the processes of repression and repressed material.

What should we make of this? Many psychologists argue that the Freudian theory fits with the data because the theory would fit with *any* data. That is, the theory is so flexible that it cannot be put to a serious test. To see why this is, consider the forms that repressed material can take. If, for example, one is repressing a wish to murder one's father, this wish is likely to surface only in disguised form. The "disguise" may be a wish to kill someone else, or a claim of really loving one's father, or in the form of being convinced that someone else wishes to kill one's father. In Freudian terms, these would be referred to as defenses via **displacement, sublimation,** and **projection,** respectively. But with this range of options, almost anything can be interpreted as revealing this repressed wish, and so almost any data pattern could be explained in these terms!

Concerns like these make many researchers skeptical about this line of evidence. The attempt to penetrate repression's "disguises" requires an interpretation process, and it is often difficult to know if we have discovered the "right" interpretation. This leads us to ask whether some more objective demonstration can be found to show that repressed materials are hidden, rather than truly lost.

"HYPERMNESIA"

Repression does not erase memories; it hides them. This opens the possibility that people may be able to recover these memories, if only the repression could be "lifted." Consistent with this suggestion, patients often remember little about their childhoods, or about the start of their current troubles, at the beginning of therapy. As the therapy progresses, patients remember more, just as we would expect if the therapy were lifting the repression. This is a process we might call *un*forgetting, as previously forgotten materials now become available. The technical term for this process is **hypermnesia,** the opposite of amnesia.

Clinical hypermnesia is difficult to interpret, for two reasons. First, we often do not know whether a patient's reports about the past are true. Before we claim that a memory was repressed and then later recovered, we need to know what the historical facts are; otherwise we have no idea what there is to be remembered! Second, if a patient remembers little at the start of therapy and remembers more later on, can we conclude that repression was initially on the scene and is now lifted? As a different possibility, perhaps the patient has always remembered his past, but was initially unwilling to discuss painful aspects of the past with the therapist. As therapy continues, the patient might feel more and more comfortable with the therapist, and therefore more willing to discuss memories. In this case, we could explain the hypermnesia with no mention of repression.

These concerns have been addressed in various laboratory versions of hypermnesia. For example, subjects can be shown complex pictures, then asked to recall the pictures' contents. In a standard memory procedure, subjects are tested only once. In hypermnesia procedures, subjects are asked to continue trying to remember, sometimes for a period of many minutes, sometimes for several days. Remarkably, as subjects continue their efforts at remembering, they are able to recover more and more of the initial materials. The results from one such study are shown in Figure 13–6 (Erdelyi & Kleinbard, 1978). If we judge by subjects' early recall efforts, they had forgotten a great deal; if we examine subjects' continuing efforts, this forgetting steadily dissipates (see also Erdelyi & Becker, 1974; Erdelyi, Buschke, & Finkelstein, 1977; Erdelyi, Finkelstein, Herrell, Miller, & Thomas, 1976; Roediger & Payne, 1982, 1985; Roediger & Thorpe, 1978). There is some controversy over the details of hypermnesia—for example, whether hypermnesia is less likely for verbal materials than for pictures. However, there is no doubt that hypermnesia can be demonstrated.

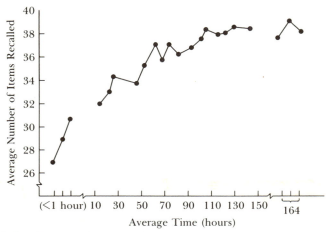

FIGURE 13–6. *Hypermnesia or "Unforgetting."* Subjects in this experiment continued, over the period of one week, to try remembering materials they had learned. As the figure shows, subjects' efforts were rewarded: With more time and effort spent on trying to remember, subjects actually remembered more and more. (After Erdelyi & Kleinbard, 1978.)

The hypermnesia data do support part of the Freudian account: that we can have memories we do not know about, that we can consciously think we have forgotten when in fact we have not. Also consistent with the Freudian account, it often takes some work to bring these memories back to the surface. Note, though, that these data fall short of establishing the full Freudian claim. The claim is not merely that memories can be "consciously forgotten but still remembered." The claim instead is that repressed ideas try to assert themselves in various disguised ways. This stronger claim, critical for Freud's theorizing, has not been demonstrated in any laboratory studies.

Emotion and Remembering

We have so far focused on Freud's claims about the nature of forgetting. As we have seen, Freud seems correct that "forgotten" material is often "hidden" and not truly lost; this is most evident in the hypermnesia data. What about the other side of Freud's claim, that repression is a motivated act, designed to shield us from unpleasant memories and thoughts? Is it the case that we remember unpleasant things less well? A number of studies have asked this question, and the evidence runs counter to Freud's claims. As we will see, however, the relationship between memory and emotion is somewhat complex.

VIVID MEMORIES FOR EMOTIONAL EVENTS

On Freud's view, we should remember unpleasant events less well than we remember pleasant or emotionally neutral ones. Much evidence indicates that this is not the case. Inside the laboratory, several studies have sought to make subjects feel anxious or guilty about a particular experience, and then have assessed memory for this experience (Eriksen & Pierce, 1968; Holmes, 1974; MacKinnon & Dukes, 1964). Such experiences do seem to be remembered less well, but it is unclear whether this represents a genuine memory loss or merely an unwillingness by the subject to talk about this unpleasant event! We mentioned this problem as a concern about the clinical evidence for repression; it is no less of a problem for some laboratory studies.

Other research has examined memory for events outside of the laboratory, that is, the events of our day-to-day lives. These studies indicate that pleasant and unpleasant events are remembered equally, and, in fact, both are better remembered than emotionally neutral events. For example, in one study, subjects were asked how clearly they remembered certain episodes in their lives—"death of a favorite pet," "getting one's driver's license," and so on. Subjects were also asked how emotional these events had been. The data clearly show that the most vividly remembered events were also the most emotional events. And it did not seem to matter what the emotion was. Unemotional events were by and large not remembered, but events that made subjects sad were remembered as well as events that made them afraid or angry or happy (Reisberg, Heuer, McLean, & O'Shaughnessy, 1988; also Rapaport, 1942; for a different view, see Matlin & Stang, 1978). There does not seem to be what Hollingworth (1910) called an "oblivescence of the disagreeable."

The extreme of this pattern comes from a class of memories that Brown and Kulik (1977) dubbed "flashbulb memories." To understand the label, think about what it is like to sit in a darkened room and have a picture taken by flashbulb. The scenes just prior to and just after the flash are difficult to make out. The moment of the flash, however, stands out in stark clarity. You often feel, minutes after the flash, like you can still "see the scene in your mind's eye" in full detail.

Flashbulb memories are rather like that. When Brown and Kulik introduced the notion of flashbulbs (in 1977) they pointed, as a paradigm case, to the memories people have of first hearing the news of John F. Kennedy's assassination in November 1963. This example is somewhat dated for many readers, but memories of comparable clarity have been reported for other events, such as the January 1986 space-shuttle disaster, the 1985 assassination attempt on Ronald Reagan, and John Lennon's assassination in December 1980 (Pillemer, 1984; Rubin & Kozin, 1984).

In flashbulb memories, subjects remember a great deal about the event. Interestingly, they often remember little of the "plot" itself; for example, the kinds of details that would be recorded in history books or that were reported on the news. Instead, they remember personal circumstances—where they were, what they were doing, and who they were with at the time of the event. Many people describing flashbulb memories include such details as the clothing worn by the people around them, people's positions within the room, the exact words uttered, and so on.

We should be cautious, however, in what we conclude about these memories. It is possible, for example, that these memories are not completely accurate. Instead, subjects may be offering plausible and vivid reconstructions of these past events. Some recent data on this point were collected by McCloskey, Wible, and Cohen (1988). Subjects filled out a questionnaire three days after the space-shuttle disaster, describing where they were and what they were doing when news of the disaster arrived. The same subjects answered similar questions nine months later. McCloskey et al. found that many of their subjects report the stark vividness associated with flashbulb memories. Nonetheless, the nine-month reports were often at odds with the reports given immediately after the event, indicating that these memories are far from flawless. (For further discussion of this study, see Schmidt & Bohannon, 1988; Cohen, McCloskey, & Wible, 1988. For related data, see Christianson, 1989; Neisser, 1982, 1986; Thompson & Cowan, 1986.)

Apparently, flashbulb memories can contain inaccuracies. And the data indicate that flashbulbs do not constitute a special "class" of memory, contrary to Brown and Kulik's initial suggestion. Instead, flashbulb memories seem to represent only the extreme of the range of memory vividness and memory clarity. Despite all this, flashbulb memories still stand as evidence that we often do remember a great deal about unpleasant events we have experienced. More strongly, flashbulb memories fit into a pattern of evidence that memory is enhanced by emotion at the time of an event, so that emotional events will be better remembered than neutral events. As we will see, however, some further data indicate that emotion's contribution to memory is more complex than that.

THE EASTERBROOK HYPOTHESIS AND "WEAPON FOCUS"

Studying emotion's contribution to memory turns out to be somewhat tricky. One could study emotion as it naturally occurs in people's lives, but, in this case, how will we evaluate the completeness and accuracy of memory? With no objective record of the event itself, we have nothing against which to compare subjects' reports of the event. Alternatively, we can try to induce emotion in a laboratory setting. Now we can easily assess the memory, because the to-be-remembered materials or events are under experimental control. However, we now have a different worry—is the emotion we have induced comparable to emotions in daily life?

Investigators seek to deal with these concerns by the use of converging lines of evidence. Each line of evidence might be somehow flawed, but it would be a striking coincidence if all the flaws turned out to have the same impact on the results. Therefore, if various studies, drawing on various paradigms, all give us the same answer, it seems likely that we are seeing bona-fide effects and not the accidental by-products of flawed research. With that said, we turn to the data.

One place in which emotion's role has been examined is the domain of eyewitness testimony. It goes without saying that eyewitnesses to crimes are often emotionally aroused, usually afraid, or excited, or angry. Much depends on the eyewitness's ability to remember accurately how events unfolded, what the perpetrators looked like, and so on.

One common observation about eyewitnesses, particularly eyewitnesses to violent crimes, concerns the phenomenon of **weapon focus.** The idea, roughly, is that the witness seems to "zoom in" on some critical detail, to the exclusion of much else. The paradigm case is one in which a witness remembers the perpetrator's gun, and remembers it with great clarity, but remembers little else about the crime.

Attorneys and police officers widely agree about the reality of the weapon focus, but should we be convinced by this? We have no "historical record" of the actual event, of the crime itself, and so we have no way to assess the eyewitness's memory. We do, however, have a different line of evidence that seems to converge on the weapon-focus idea. Across the 1950s, several researchers examined the effects of arousal on learning. The details of these studies need not concern us here. The evidence, though, is summarized in a claim known as the **Easterbrook hypothesis** (after Easterbrook, 1959). The hypothesis is that arousal causes a narrowing of the "range of attention." At low arousal, a great breadth of information is taken in, including information relevant to the task at hand, as well as distractors. With more arousal, less information is taken in, and this actually improves performance, since it leads to the exclusion of distraction. With even more arousal, however, performance starts to erode, since now some of the needed information is excluded as well (Bahrick, Fitts, & Rankin, 1952; Bruner, Matter, & Papanek, 1955; Bursill, 1958; Calloway & Stone, 1960; Cornsweet, 1969; Eysenck, 1982; Mandler, 1975; Loftus, 1982; Mendelsohn & Griswold, 1967; Walley & Weiden, 1973, 1974).

The Easterbrook hypothesis is well supported by animal learning data, and points to an obvious prediction about memory. If arousal leads to a narrow focus of attention, then all of one's attention will be focused on just a few aspects of an emotional event. These few attended-to aspects will therefore be firmly placed into memory, but little else about the event will be. As a result, subsequent memories will be impoverished—good memory, perhaps, for an event's "center," but poor memory for anything else about the event. This fits with the weapon-focus claim, in which the emotional arousal associated with the crime has narrowed attention considerably—little is noticed but the weapon, and little is remembered but the weapon.

THE MULTIPLE EFFECTS OF EMOTION ON MEMORY

How shall we fit together the data of the two previous sections? The Easterbrook claim suggests that emotional arousal works against memory. More precisely, emotional arousal might serve to promote memory for a few aspects of an event or scene, but at the cost of little memory for much else in the event. In a sense, this fits with one part of the Freudian claim, since emotion is hypothesized in both frameworks to work against memory. On the other hand, flashbulb memories, and vivid memories in general, seem most likely for emotional events. What makes these memories vivid is the inclusion of a great many peripheral details, just the kinds of details that should be excluded if the weapon-focus effect is operating.

There are several ways to resolve this seeming dilemma. We could seek to undermine the Easterbrook claim, although we would then need some account of the data that support this claim. Alternatively, we might worry about the correctness of vivid memories. Perhaps the Easterbrook claim is right, so that relatively little is taken in during the emotional events. In this case, what is "remembered" is a vivid reconstruction, with no guarantee that the reconstruction is correct.

There is, however, another possibility. Perhaps the Easterbrook claim is true under some circumstances, and the opposite (a beneficial effect of emotion) is true under other circumstances. Specifically, in the Easterbrook cases, or the weapon-focus cases, not only are subjects emotional while the learning takes place, they are still emotional at the time they are remembering. In the flashbulb case, in contrast, the event itself was emotional, but one seems to be fully calm at the time of remembering. Could this matter?

A number of studies indicate that this contrast is important. For example, in one study, subjects had to learn to associate words and numbers, using a paired-associate procedure. Some of the words were relatively neutral ones; others had strong emotional impact (for example, "rape," "vomit"). Thus emotionality was manipulated here by the words themselves. Subjects' memory for these words was tested after various intervals. As shown in Figure 13–7, at short intervals memory was poorer for the emotional words, consistent with the Easterbrook claim that arousal undermines memory. At longer intervals (for example, a week), retention was better for the emotional materials, consistent with the claim that

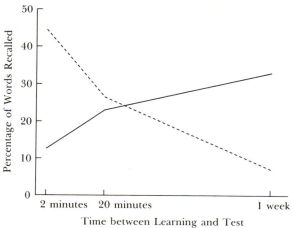

FIGURE 13–7. *Emotion Hurts Memory in the Short Run, but Helps in the Long Run.* Subjects learned to associate words with numbers; some of the words were emotional words ("rape," "vomit"). When memory was tested 2 minutes after the learning, subjects performed less well with the emotional words than with the neutral words. When memory was tested a week after the learning, the pattern reverses: Subjects were more likely to remember the emotional words. (After Kleinsmith & Kaplan, 1963.)

arousal somehow benefits memory (Kleinsmith & Kaplan, 1963, 1964; also Clark, Milberg, & Ross, 1983).

Similar results were reported by Baddeley (1982a). Subjects were shown words and were asked to say what other words these prompts called to mind. Some of the prompts were neutral in content ("tree," "cow"), and others were emotional ("quarrel," "angry"). After this was done, subjects were then given the same set of prompts and asked to reproduce their original responses. Half of the subjects were tested immediately; these subjects did more poorly in remembering their responses to the emotional words than they did in remembering their responses to the neutral words. Half of the subjects were tested 4 weeks later; these subjects did better in remembering their responses to the emotional words.

Why should emotion have opposite effects on short-term and long-term remembering? Several hypotheses are possible, and no data, at present, distinguish among these hypotheses. As one option, emotion may promote learning but disrupt retrieval. With short-term testing, the emotionality of the event is still present during the memory test. Therefore, emotionality will undermine the memory retrieval, making it difficult to determine what was learned and, in particular, potentially hiding from view emotion's facilitation of learning. With long-term testing, subjects are calm at the time of retrieval, and so emotion's disruption of retrieval is irrelevant to this case. Thus the beneficial effects of emotion on the learning itself become visible. As a different option, emotion may have disruptive effects initially, but also lead to hypermnesia, the "unforgetting" discussed earlier. Perhaps one initially remembers only that an episode was emotional; this may be enough to spur greater efforts at remembering, and therefore hypermnesia.

Whatever the mechanism behind this effect, we need one more step to fill out the picture. As we noted earlier, the Easterbrook claim is not just that emotion disrupts memory; instead, the claim is concerned with emotion's impact on the *breadth* of attention, and thus the breadth of memory. Likewise, what is striking about flashbulb memories is the quantity of seemingly peripheral detail that is apparently retained. The data just cited, concerned with memory for word lists and the like, do not really speak to this issue of memory breadth.

Several studies, however, do fill this gap (e.g., Christianson, 1984; Christianson & Loftus, 1987; Christianson, Loftus, & Nilsson, 1987). For example, in a study by Heuer and Reisberg (1990), subjects were shown a filmed episode. For some subjects, the story was emotionally neutral; other subjects, though, saw a story similar in structure and complexity, but designed to be emotionally arousing. Two weeks later, subjects in both groups were given an unexpected memory test, examining memory both for the story's plot and for tiny details about the story and the pictures. For example, subjects were asked whether the figures in the story were standing in front of a green door or a blue door; whether the pictures showed the figures from the knees up or from the waist up; and so on.

After the 2-week delay, subjects who saw the emotional story did better in both memory for plot and memory for detail compared to the group that watched the neutral story. The "arousal" group also outperformed a different group that watched the neutral story but with explicit instructions to memorize as much as they could. This latter group did well in remembering plot, but not the details.

In summary, emotion seems to have multiple effects on memory. In the short term, emotion seems disruptive of remembering and, according to various data, particularly undermines memory for inessential details, details at the edge of an episode. In the longer term, emotion seems to aid memory, both for the gist of what happened and for inessential details. This is not to say that emotion creates flawless remembering; as we have seen, even very vivid flashbulb memories can contain errors. In addition, we noted in Chapter 8 that emotion produces a state-dependency effect: Happy subjects seem better able to remember happy past events; sad subjects seem better able to remember sad past events (e.g., Blaney, 1986; Eich & Metcalfe, 1989; Gilligan & Bower, 1984). Thus any understanding of emotionality and memory must take all of these diverse effects into account.

Where does all this leave us with regard to Freud's claims about forgetting? Freud seems correct that some "forgetting" is not true information loss; instead, "forgotten" material is simply unavailable to the conscious mind. This is consistent with our overall suggestion that much forgetting is largely a question of retrieval failure. Freud's claims about "return of the repressed" are supported by clinical evidence, but the status of this evidence is far from clear. No laboratory evidence speaks in favor of the "return" notion. Finally, the evidence makes it difficult to argue that forgetting serves a self-protective function. Subjects seem well able to remember emotionally painful events; in fact, they seem to remember these better than they remember emotionally neutral events. (For a Freudian view of this evidence, see Erdelyi, 1985.) In sum, several elements of Freud's view are well supported by evidence, but key elements of the view are not; as a result, most contemporary psychologists do not regard repression as a promising theory of why and what we forget.

Remembering in the Very Long Term

When we study forgetting in the laboratory, our procedures usually involve relatively short time spans: The interval between learning and test, that is, the **retention interval,** is typically measured in minutes or, at most, days. Yet this seems not to correspond to the remembering that we do, and the forgetting that we do, in our daily lives. Outside of the laboratory, we might try to remember events from last month, from last year, or even from years ago.

This leads to an obvious question: How accurate or complete is memory over these longer time spans? We have mentioned some studies that bear on this issue, but the question of very-long-term remembering seems to merit closer attention. In this section, therefore, we will describe two lines of investigation pertinent to this topic.

CHILDHOOD AMNESIA

Many researchers have noted how difficult it is to remember events that took place before one's third or fourth birthday (Dudycha & Dudycha, 1941; Meudell, 1983; Nelson, 1988; Rubin, Wetzler, & Nebes, 1986; Wetzler & Sweeney, 1986; White & Pillemer, 1979; Winograd & Killinger, 1983). Individuals can sometimes remember an event or two from this period in their lives, but, by and large, memory is poor for the initial few years of life. This is known as **childhood amnesia.** For example, when college students are asked to describe their earliest remembered experience, the average age of these experiences is about 3.5 years (Dudycha & Dudycha, 1941). Likewise, Waldfogel (1948) asked college students to write down a list of all their memories dating from before their 8th birthday. The resulting data are shown in Figure 13–8; as you can see, subjects remember little from before their 4th birthday.

Why should this be? One obvious factor is that infancy was a long time ago. If it turns out that memories do decay with the passage of time, there has been much opportunity for this to happen. There has also been much opportunity for interference from new learning. However, neither of these accounts fits with the available data. We can compare, for example, an 18-year-old remembering her childhood with a 34-year-old remembering his college days. Both of these individuals would be remembering events from about 16 years back. If the passage of time erodes memories, through decay or interference, neither individual should remember very much. Likewise, we can compare an 18-year-old remembering her childhood and a 34-year-old remembering his childhood. If the passage of time is what erodes memories, the 34-year-old should remember far less. None of these predictions is supported by evidence.

For these reasons, neither a decay nor an interference hypothesis seems applicable to childhood amnesia. A different hypothesis comes from Freud. Freud argued that childhood is filled with many painful events, and, as a result, most memories from this period of life are repressed. There is little firm evidence with which to evaluate this claim, although several considerations speak against Freud's account. For one, childhood amnesia has also been demonstrated in rats (Spear, 1979)! It seems unlikely that rats have an emotional makeup similar to humans,

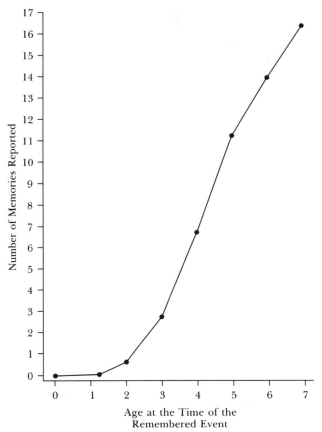

FIGURE 13–8. *Evidence for Childhood Amnesia.* College-age students were asked to list as many events as they could from before their 8th birthday. Subjects reported few memories from the first 3 years of life. (After Waldfogel, 1948.)

making it difficult to apply the Freudian account to them. Second, and far more important, researchers have proposed other explanations of child-hood amnesia, rather different from Freud's. These other explanations are directly supported by data, making them preferable to Freud's ac-count.

The first few years of life are obviously years of enormous intellectual growth and development. The child is learning new facts about the world, and new ways to conceptualize and organize these facts. These uncon-troversial observations provide the core of several proposals about child-hood amnesia (Neisser, 1976; Nelson, 1988; Schachtel, 1947; White & Pillemer, 1979). On these views, the child lacks the schematic framework that guides and structures adult memory (see Chapter 9). In this case, we would expect the child to store poorly organized or poorly integrated memories. Alternatively, the child may employ a schematic framework rather different from the adult's. Therefore, the child will simply store memories in a rather different fashion than adults do. It is no surprise, therefore, if the adult has little access to these early memories. On this view, childhood amnesia derives from mechanisms similar to those involved in encoding specificity or state dependency (both described in Chapter 8).

Framed in these terms, it is clear that several lines of evidence support the claim that childhood amnesia results in large measure from this intellectual development. First, the phenomena of encoding specificity and state-dependent learning are well established, as described in Chapter 8. Second, we have also reviewed the evidence showing that one's current knowledge influences how one learns and how one remembers (Chapter 9). Thus the elements of our account of childhood amnesia are already in place. In addition, several studies have looked directly at how young children organize and remember the events of their daily lives (e.g., Nelson, 1988). Not surprisingly, these studies document that children's understanding of life events is often rather different from that of adults, as we would expect on this account of childhood amnesia.

In sum, two points should be made about childhood amnesia. First, our best current account of this amnesia lies in the conceptual change that takes place from infancy to adulthood (although see also Jacobs & Nadel, 1985; Nadel & Zola-Morgan, 1984). Second, this account borrows heavily from concepts presented in earlier chapters. This interrelationship clearly strengthens our belief that these concepts are useful ones in understanding "real-world" remembering.

TESTING MEMORY AFTER LONG INTERVALS

A number of recent studies have examined how well subjects remember events from very long ago. Before looking at the data, we once again need to flag some methodological issues. For one, if an episode is remembered from very long ago, we need to ensure that the episode has not been reencountered in the meantime. If, for example, you remember your second birthday, this might be because you have heard the event discussed in the family, seen the photos in the album, and so on. In this case, we would not know if you truly remember the event from long ago. And, once again, we also need some way to verify the memory. The issue of verification is not trivial, inasmuch as most of us are not followed around by film crews or biographers, making it difficult to know what the historical truth really is.

There are ways around these problems, although these often involve circumstances that are special in one way or another. Bahrick and his colleagues have looked at several such cases. In one study, Bahrick, Bahrick, and Wittlinger (1975) tracked down the graduates of a particular high school—people who were graduated last year, and the year before, and the year before that, and, ultimately, people who were graduated 50 years before. All of these graduates were shown photographs from their own high school yearbook. For each photo, they were given a group of names and had to choose the name of the person shown in the picture. The data show remarkably little forgetting—performance was approximately 90% correct if tested 3.3 months after graduation, the same after 1 year, the same after 7 years, and the same after 14 years! Performance was still excellent in some versions of the test after 34 years (Figure 13–9).

Other subjects were also shown the pictures and asked to come up with the names on their own; this recall performance was worse, but still rather impressive: Subjects were able to name 70% of the faces when tested 3.3 months after graduation, and 60% after 9.3 months. Remarkably, subjects were still able to name 60% after 7 years. (It is not clear what causes the dip in the curve at 1 year, 11 months; this seems likely to be just a statistical fluke.)

This may be a special case, inasmuch as the names and faces of one's high school classmates are things one knows well. Will less well-learned facts show the same pattern? Bahrick (1984) has also looked at how well college teachers remember the names and faces of students who had taken one of their courses. (Students who took subsequent courses from the same instructor were not included in the study.) Recognition was still high if tested after 1 year: Instructors could choose the correct name for 60% of the students. Performance dropped to approximately 40% within 4 years.

Similar results come from an extraordinary study by Linton. Linton (1975, 1978, 1982, 1986; also Wagenaar, 1986) has been keeping careful notes for many years on the events that fill each of her days, sort of like keeping a detailed diary. After certain intervals, she selects events from the diary and tests her own memory for what transpired; this memory can then be checked against the written record. Linton reports reasonably impressive memory for such mundane events—over 65% remembered after 3 years, and roughly the same after 4 years. In addition, Linton often retests her memory for a given event. This way, we can ask about the effects of rehearsing these memories, since, after all, the experience of testing memory constitutes a reencounter with the original episode. Rehearsal turns out to have enormous impact. For those events tested (rehearsed) only once before, forgetting after 3 years was cut in half, from 32% forgotten with no rehearsals to 16% with one rehearsal (Figure 13–10).

These data confirm some not so surprising facts. Loss of memories

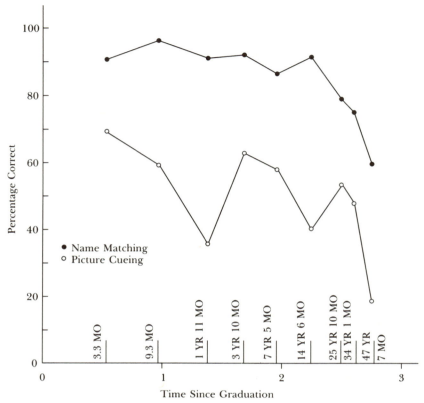

FIGURE 13–9. *Memory over the Very Long Term.* Subjects were tested for how well they remembered names and faces of their high school classmates. In one version, subjects were given a group of names and had to select which name belonged to the face shown. In this task ("name matching"), subjects were 90% correct even 14 years after graduation. In a different version, subjects were shown the pictures and had to come up with the names on their own ("picture cuing"). In this test, subjects were still 60% accurate after 7 years. (After Bahrick, Bahrick, & Wittlinger, 1975.)

does occur, and gets progressively worse with the passage of time. In addition, well-learned facts are lost less rapidly than less well-learned materials. Recognition memory seems to outlast recall, and this may account for why Linton's performance is below that of Bahrick's subjects.

However, what is most notable about these data is how little is forgotten, and these studies should make us cautious about speaking about the ravages of time on memory. Linton is remembering a considerable amount, even with no rehearsals, and a single rehearsal has a large impact on her retention. Thus forgetting might seem to be a less dramatic force than one might initially have guessed. In addition, these studies by them-

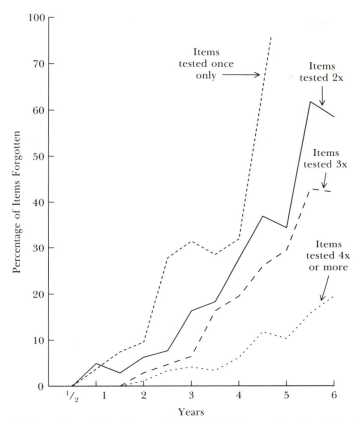

FIGURE 13–10. *Remembering Events in One's Life.* The subject in this study recorded, each day, what had happened during that day. At various later times she tested her memory for different events. Some events were tested only once; two-thirds of these were still remembered after 3 or 4 years. Other items were tested multiple times; each test served to remind the subject of the event, and so "refreshed" the memory. Even a single "refresher" can markedly decrease forgetting. (After Linton, 1978.)

selves do not speak to *why* forgetting might be happening—decay, or interference, or some other force.

How Shall We Think about Forgetting?

Let us sum up. We do forget. Sometimes, our forgetting is just a momentary lapse—this is most visible in the T.O.T. effect (Chapter 11), or when we are unable to remember something until a hint comes along and then we remember easily. In other cases, our forgetting seems to be a lapse of a more interesting sort. This is the case of hypermnesia: We fail to remember despite hints and effort, but, with the passage of time and the expenditure of effort, we can recover the "forgotten" material.

These cases are what we might call "temporary forgetting." If we look at "forgetting proper," it is striking how little we forget. Bahrick's subjects, and Linton in her own studies, remember a great deal despite the passing years. What forgetting there is seems easy to avoid—even a single rehearsal is enough to slow the forgetting appreciably. And, when there has been much rehearsal, remarkably little forgetting occurs.

How should we conceive of forgetting in these various cases? We maintain that none of the evidence reviewed so far demands additional mechanisms or processes beyond the memory processes reviewed in previous chapters. Concretely, three effects, all of which appeared in earlier chapters, seem enough to handle the available data.

RETRIEVAL FAILURE

First, there is the notion we have been considering all along, namely retrieval failure. The suggestion here is that memory lapses may be more typical of forgetting than one might think. Information does not disappear from memory; it simply becomes more and more difficult to locate. This can be so for several reasons, all fully compatible with the network theorizing offered in Chapter 11.

This hypothesis fits with the fact that relatively little forgetting is evident in the data if we test memory via recognition. This was clear, for example, in the Bahrick data; we encountered the same observation in studies of interference. If "forgotten" material is in memory, but merely not found, then we should be able to lift the forgetting with a suitable hint, and the best hint for finding a memory of something is the thing itself. Of course, even a recognition test will eventually show some forgetting. This is because recognition, with suitable delays, depends on memory search, just as recall does (see Chapter 8). Even with a terrific cue to guide this search, success in locating the sought-for material is not guaranteed. Thus even recognition eventually shows forgetting.

The retrieval-failure hypothesis is also consistent with Linton's finding of the degree to which a few rehearsals can preserve a memory. If memories were decaying because of the passage of time, or dissolving through interference, then it would be remarkable if a few "refreshers" could bring the memory back to near full strength. If, on the other hand, memories were simply becoming harder and harder to find (thanks to the accumulation of new memories and new associations), then it is not so strange that rehearsals help. Each new rehearsal will create new linkages between the memory and the present context, and will also strengthen prior associations. With old retrieval paths renewed, and with new retrieval paths created, each new rehearsal can appreciably ease the process of locating a memory in the network.

SCHEMA THEORY AND MEMORY FAILURE

Beyond retrieval failure, a second explanation for forgetting derives from the schema theorizing introduced in Chapter 9. Recall that much of the experimental evidence for the schema view came from memory failures and omissions predictable on schematic grounds. That is, one is likely to omit from memory the aspects of a scene or event that did not fit with the frame. One is likely to "import" into one's memory aspects that were absent, but that were highly probable according to the schema. Finally, if one's schemata change, so does the "past." We considered evidence for these claims in Chapter 9, although we did not refer to these results as "forgetting" then. However, the net impact of such mechanisms will be indistinguishable from what we ordinarily do call "forgetting."

REPISODIC BLURRING

A third source of "forgetting" also came up in Chapter 9. The phenomenon of "repisodic blurring" refers to the fact that memories for Repeated EPISODES seem to blur together into one; elements are correctly recalled, but are mixed together in ways departing from the historical sequence. This suggests that, even if memories are permanent, there is nothing to hold them together as units, nothing to keep them from fragmenting.

Why should this be? With repeated, similar episodes, there are likely to be strong associations between elements in one episode and elements in another; these associations between episodes may even be stronger than associations within an episode. Thinking of an element in Episode 1, therefore, will weakly activate other elements in that episode, but strongly activate elements in other episodes, and so bring the "wrong" elements to mind. (They will be "wrong" only if one is seeking to remember a single episode.) Thus, without any forgetting, episodes will dissolve into each other. In the extreme, remembering elements of episodes may remain easy, but remembering intact episodes may be very difficult.

Which of these—retrieval failure, schematic forgetting, and repisodic blurring—is most important in "ordinary forgetting"? We believe that each has a role to play, with the centrality of that role shifting from case to case. The main point, though, remains the same: Our theory of remembering does not contain a specific forgetting mechanism, but forgetting is virtually guaranteed by the theory. While we have concentrated in this chapter on retrieval failure as the chief factor in forgetting, other factors enter as well.

Is the Past Lost?

Toward the end of Chapter 9, we considered a hypothesis that we might refer to as the claim of "It's all in there somewhere." This is the claim that everything you have ever seen, heard, or felt, and so on is still somewhere in your memory, even if it would take extraordinary measures to bring the relevant recollection to light. There is a strong version of this claim that is almost certainly false: You are extremely unlikely to retain memories of things that were in front of your eyes but which received no attention, or sentences that you heard but which you totally failed to comprehend. That is, you are extremely unlikely to retain memories of something that never really entered your experience.

The more interesting case, though, is the case of something you once knew—once were aware of, once thought about, once remembered. Are all of memories of this sort "in there somewhere"? Are all these memories "permanent"—once in, never out? As we have seen, the available evidence can be explained without recourse to processes like decay or unlearning. Therefore, to keep our theorizing as simple as possible, we should not include these options in our accounts. In other words, the evidence is fully compatible with the "it's all in there" suggestion. Memories are never lost and gone forever; they are merely not found. Old memories do not die; they merely become immensely difficult to locate.

Many people find this implausible. After all, think about Jacob, who drives to work each day, and who drives to the store, and to many other places. Each time Jacob parks his car, he must remember where he has parked, sometimes only for 10 or 15 minutes, if he is making a brief stop, but often for longer periods. Thus we know that the car's location was in memory once. Does this mean the location is recorded forever? Is this true for each and every parking location Jacob has used in his lifetime? Is it true for all the shopping lists Jacob remembered long enough to get to the store? Likewise, every joke Jacob once knew? This is what one is committed to if there is no process of forgetting. Many events in our lives go by without our giving them much thought; these presumably do not make it into memory at all. But vastly many events are remembered, at least for a short time. If there is no decay, and no unlearning, then these memories will stay with us (albeit not be findable) for life.

If you worry about the plausibility of this, so do we. In fact, we are willing to believe that some future data may force us to include something like decay in our theorizing. For now, though, it seems appropriate to close with two observations that may make the "it's all in there somewhere" claim more palatable. First, note that this claim seems most implausible for the large numbers of repetitive, ordinary events in our lives, such as driving to work or the store. Yet these are the events for which repisodic blurring seems most likely, guaranteeing, if not true memory "loss," then at least a form of forgetting, as described in the previous section.

Second, we close with one last set of observations. These are not data from the laboratory, but from various observations of "real-world" remembering. As Neisser (1986) has argued, memory performance in non-laboratory settings is often remarkable, for both the completeness and the longevity of the memory record. For example, there are performers in Yugoslavia who recite long poems from memory. Some of these poems literally take all night to recite, and an individual performer might know as many as 30 of these poems (Lord, 1960). In the same vein, the anthropologist Gregory Bateson (1958) has described masters of totemic knowledge in New Guinea who are able to recall the names of thousands of significant totems. Closer to home, the conductor Toscanini apparently had memorized the complete scores of a huge number of works of music, and could remember details of each score with ease (Marek, 1975).

One could argue that each of these is a special case in one way or another, and that we must not try to generalize from these remarkable feats of memory. Perhaps these are special people, each with a particularly good memory, or perhaps we are seeing what extraordinary amounts of practice or rehearsal can do for memory. But one can also read these cases as indicating just how much human memory can encompass, both in terms of quantity of material and in terms of the number of years over which a memory can endure. These cases, together with the laboratory data we have presented, lend some plausibility to the suggestion that maybe our memories are permanent, after all. Maybe, once we set aside retrieval failures, and schematic mistakes, and repisodic blurring, it *is* "all in there somewhere."

Summary

It is obvious that we forget many things—shopping lists, materials we have studied for an examination, names of people we have met. What causes this forgetting? A principal theme of this chapter has been the possibility that these cases of forgetting can best be explained as malfunctions of the normal processes of remembering. On this view, forgetting is not a process with properties of its own; forgetting is merely the absence of successful remembering.

In this chapter, we have looked at three views of forgetting, each arguing that forgetting is not merely the absence of remembering. One such view is the decay theory, which states that memories decay with the passage of time. Decay theory is consistent with the fact that recent events are better remembered than more distant events. However, this fact by itself does not show the decay theory to be correct. As an alternative, perhaps older memories are more difficult to remember because of memory "interference."

This notion is at the center of a second theory of forgetting, the interference theory. On an interference account, forgetting occurs because new learning interferes with older learning (and vice versa). If distant events are remembered poorly, on this view, this is because more learning has come between older events and the present time than between newer events and the present.

A number of studies have tried to separate the influences of time and interference, and these studies consistently indicate that it is interfering information, and not the passage of time, that leads to forgetting. For example, forgetting is greater after a period of time spent awake than after a period of time spent asleep; forgetting is much reduced if, with various organisms, we arrange a period of nearly complete inactivity; and so on.

If it is interference rather than decay that causes forgetting, what causes interference? Why is memory (seemingly) unable to store both old and new information together? In laboratory studies of interference, two species of interference are distinguished: retroactive interference (RI), in which subsequent learning interferes with previously learned materials, and proactive interference (PI), in which earlier learning interferes with subsequently learned materials.

Two mechanisms have been proposed to account for RI and PI. According to the "response-competition" view, subjects do remember both old and new materials, but must choose between these in responding to a memory question. Because of this competition between (potential) responses, subjects will appear to have forgotten.

Available evidence indicates that response competition does contribute to interference, but is not a complete account. Instead, a separate mechanism, called "unlearning," has been proposed. Unlearning is closer to what we generally call forgetting; on an unlearning claim, new learning actually causes old material to be "unlearned." The specific mechanisms through which this is alleged to occur resemble mechanisms of extinction, as described in operant and Pavlovian conditioning.

Interference theory was for many years the dominant theory of forgetting, but has largely been set aside by memory researchers. One reason for this is the accumulating evidence that simply does not fit with interference claims. For example, while interference is readily demonstrated in a recall paradigm, interference is usually not detected with recognition testing. This implies that interference may work merely by rendering prior materials difficult to locate in memory. In short, interference leads to retrieval failures, not to forgetting.

A third view of forgetting was proposed by Sigmund Freud. Freud argued that much of forgetting served a self-protective function, in which we "repress" memories of emotionally painful episodes in our past. Repression is hypothesized to take a specific form—not erasing memories, but pushing them out of conscious awareness. These repressed memories attempt to reenter consciousness, but, according to Freud, this reentry is often possible only when our guard is down, or when the memories take on a disguised form that is more acceptable to the conscious mind.

Much research has sought to evaluate Freud's proposal. Some of this research has taken the form of clinical studies, in which a patient's dreams, slips of the tongue, and symptoms are all interpreted as revealing repressed wishes or memories. However, this research is regarded by many as unpersuasive, as more than one interpretation of a patient's behavior is often possible.

A different line of evidence for the Freudian view is so-called hypermnesia, or a process of "unforgetting", as (allegedly) repression is lifted. This hypermnesia is often observed during psychotherapy: The patient is able to remember more later in the therapy than at the outset. However, this observation is ambiguous. It is unclear, for one, whether the patient is truly remembering (that is, whether the reported episodes match the actual history). In addition, it is possible that patients are simply willing to report more later in therapy than at its beginning.

These problems have been addressed by various laboratory studies of hypermnesia, and in the laboratory hypermnesia can be readily demonstrated. Thus this aspect of Freud's theory is well grounded in evidence. However, this establishes only that memories can be "lost" and then "found again." The evidence falls short of establishing either that it is emotionally painful material that is repressed or that repressed materials seek to reemerge in consciousness. These latter claims, however, are central for Freud's view.

Is it the case that we fail to remember emotionally painful materials? A number of studies have examined this issue, and they indicate that emotional material is, in general, well remembered, whether the emotion attached to the material is positive (happiness, pride, relief) or negative (sadness, fear, anger). This is particularly clear in so-called flashbulb memories, memories that are singularly vivid and detailed and which are also often memories for emotionally painful events.

Emotion's contribution to memory turns out, however, to be a complex one. According to the Easterbrook hypothesis, emotion leads to a narrowing of attention, and therefore to impoverished memories. A number of studies have confirmed this claim. However, this seems to be the case only if memory is tested soon after the emotional event. With longer testing delays, emotion seems to lead to rather complete memories, memories that include a large number of details seemingly peripheral to the remembered event.

Finally, we turned to studies of memory at very long intervals, memories for events that happened many years ago. Much of this research concerns "childhood amnesia," the apparent inability to remember events that took place before one's third or fourth birthday. This form of amnesia is well documented, and appears to be the result of the vast intellectual changes that take place between childhood and adulthood. The child lacks the schematic framework that guides and structures adult memory, leading the child to store poorly organized or poorly integrated memories. In addition, the child's understanding of the world is often very different from that of the adult. Therefore the child stores memories in a fashion different from an adult, making many of these memories inaccessible when the child becomes an adult.

Other recent research has examined memory for specific target events many years in the past. For example, some studies have examined subjects' ability to remember the names of their high school classmates, years after graduation. Other studies have involved careful record keeping of the events in the subject's life, and then subsequent testing of the subject, based on those records. These studies are most remarkable for how little forgetting they show. Performance is often excellent even after years have passed between the remembered episode and the memory test.

We argued in conclusion that there is no persuasive evidence for a process of forgetting. Instead, the forgetting that we observed is likely to come from three sources: failure to locate information in memory, memory errors produced by the influence of knowledge schemata (as described in Chapter 9), and the blurring together of similar episodes (also described in Chapter 9). Thus forgetting seems best explained in terms of the mechanisms of normal remembering; no further theory of forgetting seems required.

14 Memory and the Decision-making of Everyday Life

We each make decisions and draw conclusions all the time. We decide which of two restaurants will serve us a better meal; we decide what courses to register for, or what to major in. We draw conclusions about our friends: "Does she really like me?" "Why was Fred in such a bad mood yesterday?" And then we take action based on these conclusions.

Notice that these decisions and conclusions rest to a large extent on memory: Our restaurant choice will be influenced by what we recall about past meals at various restaurants, and also by our recollections of friends' comments about these restaurants. Our conclusions about Fred will depend on what we know about Fred's likes and dislikes, about his temperament, and so on, all information supplied to us by memory.

Much of the remembering we all do is in the service of endeavors like these. When we try to make a decision, or draw a conclusion, we do our best to remember the relevant evidence. To the extent that our memories are complete and accurate, this will support our deciding, concluding, and judging. To the extent that our memories are biased, or contain gaps, this may seriously compromise our reasoning performance. It follows that the ordinary functioning of memory can play a decisive role in shaping our everyday commerce with the world.

In this chapter, we seek to show that both the successes and failures of practical reasoning can often be explained by means of the memory principles introduced in previous chapters. In addition, this final chapter also seeks to bridge a gap between the animal evidence surveyed earlier in this book and the human evidence in the last few chapters. Consider the tasks we set for human and animal subjects: Humans in a memory experiment are not asked to discover anything new, or to draw any conclusions. They are given certain materials and are expected to commit these to memory. In contrast, in an operant or Pavlovian procedure, animals are not given something to "memorize." Instead, the animals are given a problem to solve, a question to answer. They are put into a novel situation, and must learn how to behave in that situation. In a sense, the animals' task is like that of a researcher: The animal is able to do "experiments" and make "observations." What happens when the lever is pressed? What occurs after the buzzer? Learning depends on the animals' discerning the pattern behind these experiments and these observations.

In this chapter, we examine how humans perform in this other, more "research-like" sort of learning. We ask how well humans learn from evidence, how well we interpret the evidence, and how well we draw conclusions.

The Availability Heuristic

When we make decisions or draw conclusions, what evidence do we use? The answer should be obvious: We use the information and evidence available to us. How could it be otherwise? Let us look at an example. It is not a deeply interesting case, but will make our point. (This example, like many others in this chapter, is drawn from the research of Daniel Kahneman and Amos Tversky.)

Are there more words in the dictionary beginning with the letter "r" or more words with an "r" in the third position? Most people, after thinking about this for a moment, suspect that there are more words beginning with "r," although the reverse is true, and strongly so. In a computer count for this chapter, words with "r" in the third position were twice as frequent as words beginning with "r"; other samples of written materials yield comparable data (Tversky & Kahneman, 1973, 1974). Why do people get this wrong, and by so much?

In answering this question, subjects have at least two strategies open to them. One strategy would be to invest the effort in searching through a dictionary, or through some randomly selected book page. If subjects used this latter strategy, they would come up with the correct answer. A different strategy would be to scan through memory quickly and to see how many words one can come up with in the two categories (red, rose, rabbit, race versus careful, for, strategy, error). As it turns out, a first-letter cue seems to allow a more effective memory search than a third-letter cue. This presumably is telling us something about memory's organization, but, for present purposes, it means that it will be easier to come up with words in the first group than in the second. That is, words in the first group are more **available**, producing a bias in what is retrieved from memory. If one uses this strategy, therefore, and relies on the sample that comes easily to mind, this will lead to error. Since we know that subjects in fact answer incorrectly, it seems clear that they are using something like the second, misleading, strategy and not the first, accurate, strategy.

A different experiment conveys the same point: Tversky and Kahneman (1973) presented subjects with a list of names of known personalities; subjects were later asked to judge whether the list contained more names of men or more names of women. As it turns out, some of the names on the list were very famous (for example, Richard Nixon, Elizabeth Taylor) and others were less famous (for example, William Fulbright, Lana Turner). Tversky and Kahneman reasoned that famous names would be easier to recall later on, and this would bias subjects' assessments of the list's membership. If the list contained names of famous women but not-so-famous men, then the women's names would be better remembered, and this would bias subjects toward believing that the list contained more women's names than men's. Likewise, if the list contained names of famous men but not-so-famous women, this would, by the same logic, bias subjects toward believing that the list contained more men's names than women's. The data confirm these predictions.

Note that there is a trade-off here: In the "r" case, going out to collect full information will avoid error, but is more cumbersome than merely using the easily available information. Likewise in the case just cited: A more careful memory search might avoid the "fame" bias, but would certainly be more effortful than a casual scan through memory. These trade-offs should sound familiar: We are again seeing the contrast between a heuristic and an algorithm, first introduced in Chapter 10. Tversky and Kahneman (1973, 1974) in fact speak of the **availability heuristic**, a strategy of using information that is readily at hand. The idea is that using this strategy is easy and efficient, and likely to succeed more often than not. The gain in efficiency from such a strategy is presumably large; this justifies tolerating the occasional errors produced by this strategy.

AVAILABILITY IN MEMORY

Is it true that this strategy works more often than not, as a heuristic requires? To put it differently, does "availability in memory" correspond to "frequency in the world"? The answer to this is yes in many cases: We know that frequency of encounter leads to stronger memories, and therefore to greater availability. This point first came up in Chapter 7, when we noted that frequency of rehearsal was a good predictor of recall. The point came up again in consideration of the network model, in which activation was (in part) dependent on frequency of prior use.

What went wrong in the "r" case? Frequency of encounter does lead to good retention, but retention is not all one needs. Having information in memory is not the same as having that information active and influencing you. In the "r" case, we know the relevant words—that is, the words are in our vocabularies. What is critical, though, is whether we can think of these words when we need them.

There is an obvious but enormously consequential point to these data: It is not what you know that counts; it is what you can think of when you need it. At some level, this cannot be news, since we all have had more or less the following experience: You study really well for an examination. You take the exam, and do a reasonable job on the essay questions. You leave the room, and then, in a flash of insight, you realize that three other examples should have been introduced to support the claims just made. You obviously knew the materials, since you were able to come up with them *after* the fact. The extra examples were, apparently, in your memory. But you simply did not "make the connection," as they say, at the time of the exam. Having the examples in memory is not enough to get them into the exam answer; you also have to realize that the examples are applicable.

Observations such as this one are almost inevitable, thanks to a single, important fact: The retrieval of information from memory is not a trivial process, and is by no means guaranteed to succeed. This was critical in our discussion of forgetting (Chapter 13); it was embedded in our discussion of hints, and the contrast between cued recall and recall (Chapter 11); it was also implicit in our discussion of state-dependent learning and encoding specificity (Chapter 8). In each of these cases, we saw that one can know something but not be able to remember it. That is, having the information stored in memory is not enough; one also must be able to retrieve that information.

This point may be theoretically obvious, especially since failures in memory retrieval can happen for many different reasons. Nonetheless, the consequences of this are easy to overlook. We therefore shift to a brief detour on these points, and then return to our main agenda.

ENLIGHTENMENT EFFECTS

We have often emphasized in this book the ease and efficiency with which memory works, so it may be important to balance the perspective. Not everything you know is instantly available to you, influencing your decisions, informing your actions, all the time. Knowledge has to be activated, has to be brought into play. Knowledge that lies dormant has no direct effects.

Here is one example of how important this is. There is a finding in social psychology known as "bystander apathy." This is not the place to survey all the data on this theme, but the essence is this: If you witness a crime, or see someone who appears to need help, will you assist? Or will you be apathetic—stand idly by and do nothing? The answer, strikingly, is that a great deal depends simply on how many people are around. If you are the lone witness, you are far more likely to respond. If you are one of many witnesses to the event, chances are good that you will reason something like this: "Someone else will act, so I don't have to get involved." In a group there is a **diffusion of responsibility**, so no one person feels responsible, and no one acts (Bickman, 1972, 1975; Darley & Latane, 1968; Darley & Batson, 1973).

All this is merely the setting for the issue we are after. Our question is this: Now that you know about diffusion of responsibility, will it influence you? The next time you are part of a crowd and witness a crime, will you be dissuaded from action by the mere fact of being in a crowd? Or will your newly acquired knowledge render you immune to the diffusion of responsibility? Is the "group-size effect" smaller among people who know about the group-size effect?

Several studies have looked for these so-called **enlightenment effects** (Beaman, Barnes, Klentz & McQuirk, 1978; Klentz & Beaman, 1981; Rayko, 1977). The procedure is in two steps. First, we "enlighten" subjects by telling them about research on bystander apathy, including the effects of group size on bystander intervention. The experiment is then ostensibly over, and the subjects leave the room. Out in the corridor, however, we have arranged for a miniature crisis—perhaps someone drops her books, or perhaps there is the sound from behind a closed door of someone falling. The question is: How will the subjects react? And, of course, we arrange things so that sometimes a subject is alone when the "crisis" happens, and sometimes the subject is part of a crowd, so that we can look for the usual result that larger crowds somehow inhibit action.

The results of these studies are mixed, but in many cases enlightenment effects are not observed (e.g., Bermant & Starr, 1972; Katzev & Averill, 1984). That is, subjects who have just learned about the effects of crowd size still show the usual effects of crowd size. This is so despite the fact that the subjects often express surprise and distress when they learn about these effects, and may even have expressed the fervent wish that they would never act in such an "irresponsible" manner. On the surface of things, then, it looks like "enlightenment" often does not change behavior, and, alas, we may have discovered the limits of what education can accomplish.

But is this conclusion correct? We suggest that the problem here is one of availability. Merely knowing about diffusion of responsibility does not prevent the diffusion. What we need to do is get the subject to see the connection between what they have just learned and the situation they are now in. There are many ways to do this. At the simplest, we might say to the subject: "Aren't you now acting the same way most people do?" or even "Doesn't this situation remind you of something you recently learned about?" With these triggers to activate the newly acquired knowledge, subjects will show the influence of enlightenment. It is not that we fail to act in accord with our beliefs; it is instead that we sometimes fail to realize which beliefs apply to which situation.

A different way to put this reflects some of the themes of Chapter 8: Memory works best if subjects understand the test situation the same way they understood the learning situation. To stick with our bystander example, subjects have learned something about how to act in a certain set of situations, namely, situations in which one is a bystander to a crisis. In schema terms, this learning has been assimilated into the "bystander to crisis" schema. If subjects are subsequently in a situation they perceive to be a crisis, this same schema will be activated, and so the new knowledge will be brought to bear. If subjects are subsequently in a situation they perceive as a non-crisis, then a different schema will be employed. Since there may be no connections between this schema and the newly acquired knowledge about crises, we will see no impact of this new knowledge. In short, it is available knowledge that matters, and availability hinges both on what one has learned and on what one activates.

STATE DEPENDENCY AND AVAILABILITY

Let us review. We began with a perfectly innocuous claim: The information we use in reasoning is the information that is available to us. We have seen that the information currently available to us is only a subset of what might be available to us, thanks to the fact that we might not activate relevant knowledge when we need it. In this way, the success of *reasoning* does indeed depend on the functioning of *memory*.

In the enlightenment case, a failure to activate a memory simply means that useful information is omitted, and is not brought to bear on the current situation. We can also find cases in which a great deal is remembered, but the memories are *selective*. One class of demonstrations derives from the phenomenon of state dependency, introduced in Chapter 8. Consider the following instance. Let us say, for the sake of argument, that you are getting a stomach flu and, as a result, you wake up one morning feeling rather crummy. You might lie in bed asking yourself, "Why do I feel so bad? Do I have reason? What's going on?" You sift through the evidence, realize that things have not been going well for you lately, and decide, incorrectly, that your mood is caused by recent emotional events. You conclude that you feel crummy because you are depressed, and that your depression has full cause.

This is potentially an instance very much prone to availability bias. The phenomenon of state dependency tells us that it is easier to remember happy events when happy and easier to remember sad events when sad. Therefore, if you wake up feeling bad, and try to remember what has filled your last few days, there will be a bias toward remembering not-very-happy events. From this biased data set, you might be reasonable in drawing the conclusion that the world has recently turned against you. The conclusion itself is warranted from the memory evidence, but we might worry about the quality of the evidence.

A similar, well-documented case is provided by Lewinsohn and Rosenbaum (1987). They studied a group of 2000 people over a period of 3 years, seeking to ask several questions about the nature of depression. Among their other results, they found that currently depressed people tended to recall their parents as being rejecting and unloving. Is this a correct recollection? If so, it would imply that depression may be caused, in part, by past relations with one's parents.

However, some further data suggest a different interpretation: Lewinsohn and Rosenbaum also studied the recall of parental behavior by **remitted** depressives, that is, people who had been depressed but were no longer depressed at the time of the recall. They also examined the recall of **predepressives**, that is, people who were not depressed at the time of recall but who became depressed later on during the study. The results show that these groups did not differ from control subjects in how they recalled their parents' attitudes or behavior.

In other words, just before subjects become depressed, they remember their parents as being normal and loving. While subjects are depressed, they remember their parents as being unloving. Just after depression, subjects again remember their parents as being normal and loving. These data imply that there is not a strong linkage between parental behavior and being prone to depression. Instead, there is a link between how parental behavior is remembered, on the one hand, and being currently depressed, on the other. In short, these results fit with a state-dependency interpretation: If one feels unhappy, one is better able to remember unhappy things, leading to a biased recollection of past events.

The point, once again, is that evidence from memory is vulnerable to any inaccuracies or biases that may influence memory. If one tries to reason or draw conclusions based on this evidence, one's conclusions may be compromised by memory's inaccuracies. This is not to say that reasoning or memory will always be faulty. On the contrary, we believe that remembering is likely to be accurate more often than not. But it does imply that what appears to be valid reasoning may sometimes be valid reasoning from *false premises*. We have tried in this section and the previous one to give some illustrations of just how important this is.

CAN WE AVOID AVAILABILITY ERRORS?

What if one wished to avoid the various errors described above? As we see it, there are several options. One could, for example, decide not to rely on available evidence, but to dig deeper. If investigating how many words there are with a particular spelling pattern, one could choose to sit down with the dictionary and count. Of course, this method has a cost attached to it, in time and in effort, which is what made the *heuristic* desirable in the first place. Sometimes, though, this effort will be worth the trouble, particularly if one is alert to the likelihood of availability errors.

Alternatively, one could do something much more general. Once one acknowledges the possibility of availability bias in judgments, one could try to compensate for that bias. One could, for example, add a note of caution to one's conclusions, or one could add a "margin for error." However, a separate tendency, known as **anchoring**, turns out to work against this strategy. Once an answer to a question is on the scene, subjects seem very much influenced by it. Rather than setting the initial answer to the side, in order to come up with a new estimate, subjects seem to hold on to the first answer, to use it as an "anchor" and to make some adjustment to this anchor. And subjects do this even when the initial answer is clearly not worth trusting.

In a demonstration of anchoring, Tversky and Kahneman (1974) asked subjects to estimate what proportion of nations in the United Nations are African nations. (The correct answer is 35%.) Subjects first watch while the experimenter spins a wheel marked with numbers from 1 to 100. The wheel is rigged, so that for half of the subjects it stops at "10" and for half it stops at "65." Subjects are asked whether the actual percentage is above or below this first "estimate," and then give their own estimate. The results show that subjects who saw the wheel stop at 10 offer, on average, an estimate of 25%. Subjects who saw the wheel stop at 65 offer, on average, an estimate of 45%. Even in this case, subjects are apparently taking the wheel's seemingly random "selection" as a reference point when making their own best estimate.

The anchoring effect is important for several reasons, but, for our purposes, it indicates that once an error is made, from availability or from any other source, it may be difficult for subjects to set the error to the side and start again.

AVAILABILITY BIASES FROM OTHER SOURCES

Our discussion so far has focused on availability created by memory factors. Availability biases can also arise from other sources. Imagine, for example, that you are advising the government on research designed to save lives. You want to spend your efforts on the more frequent causes of death, rather than investigating rare problems. Now the question: Should we spend more on preventing death from motor vehicle accidents, or death from stomach cancer? Which is more common? Should we spend more on preventing homicides, or diabetes? Again, which is more common? People reliably assert that motor vehicle accidents and homicide are the more frequent in each pair, although the opposite is true both times (Combs & Slovic, 1979; Slovic, Fischhoff, & Lichtenstein, 1982); see Table 14-1. Why is this?

Table 14–1.   Availability Bias in Estimates of Frequency
of Death from Various Causes

Most Overestimated	Most Underestimated
All accidents	Smallpox vaccination
Motor vehicle accidents	Diabetes
Pregnancy, childbirth, and	Stomach cancer
abortion	Lightning
Tornadoes	Stroke
Flood	Tuberculosis
Botulism	Asthma
All cancer	Emphysema
Fire and flames	
Venomous bite or sting	
Homicide	

Note: Subjects estimated how many deaths are caused by each of these factors. Subjects were clearly influenced by how often each factor is reported in the media: Stomach cancer is usually not reported; homicide and death from fires are often reported.
   From Slovic, Fischhoff, & Lichtenstein, 1982.

It turns out that people's estimate of the likelihood of events is closely tied to the frequency with which such events are reported in the news. Homicide makes the front page; diabetes usually does not. Once again, this is an availability issue: Just as some information is less available to us via the selectivity of memory, some information is less available via the selectivity of the media. If it is available data that people use, this bias is as important as the memory bias.

A related case comes from social perception. We all tend to notice people who stand out from a group, people who are different from those who surround them. It seems reasonable to think that this will make us more likely to remember distinctive characters. This will in turn increase the availability of memories about distinctive people, and so influence our social judgment. To see how this works, consider research by Taylor and her colleagues (Taylor, 1982; Taylor, Fiske, Etcoff, & Ruderman, 1978). In these studies, subjects observed a videotape showing an informal discussion among a group of six persons. Some subjects saw a group that included one male and five females; other subjects saw a group that included one female and five males. Subjects were then asked to report their impressions of the individuals in the group.

The results indicate that subjects' attention was caught by the "socially isolated" figure, the lone male or the lone female. More was recalled of this "solo" figure's behavior than was recalled about the other participants in the group; the solo was also judged to have talked more and to have influenced the discussion more than others in the group. Last but not least, the solo person's behavior was evaluated more extremely. As Taylor (1982, p. 194) puts it, "an obnoxious person was perceived as even more so when a solo; a nice person was perceived as even nicer when a solo."

Thus availability can also be biased by our attention: Because we are more likely to notice and think about salient members of a group, we create a bias in how the group is remembered and how the group is evaluated. More information is available about the solo group member, with a clear impact on social perception and social judgment. (For other availability effects in social judgments, see Ross & Sicoly, 1979.)

A different availability bias is subtler. Again, an example from Tversky and Kahneman's (1973) work will make the point. Subjects are asked the following question: We have 10 people on a committee. We need to select 2 of these to form a subcommittee. How many possible subcommittees are there? If we call the committee members A, B, C, and so on, then the possible subcommittees are A + B, A + C, A + D, . . . , B + C. . . . How many possibilities? What if we need to form a larger subcommittee of, say, 8? How many of these subcommittees are there? Subjects tend to estimate the first number as higher than the second, although the answer in both cases is the same (45). In fact, the answer must be the same: When we form a subcommittee of A + B, we have, in essence, simultaneously formed a subcommittee of the remaining (all but A + B) 8. Whenever we pick out a subcommittee of 2, we have also formed a subcommittee of the residual 8.

Why do subjects believe there are more potential pairs than octets? Apparently, subjects can easily think of many pairs, just as we began to; subjects less easily think of octets. Pairs come easily to mind; octets do not. Thus, we have another case of availability, this time availability to the imagination rather than availability to memory.

This committee example may not seem very important, but other evidence points toward a similar availability-to-the-imagination effect in various judgments. For example, Kahneman and Tversky (1982) argue that we are often influenced by this sort of availability when we try to reason about future events. For example, if civil war breaks out in Saudi Arabia, what are the likely consequences? If marijuana is legalized, will this increase or decrease use of this drug? Or, for a more mundane example, if we invite Herbert and Harry to dinner on the same evening, will they get along?

Kahneman and Tversky claim that, in reasoning through questions like these, we tend to construct scenarios about how the hypothesized events will unfold. Scenarios that come easily to mind tend to be judged as more plausible; scenarios that must be contrived are judged to be less plausible, and therefore less probable.

It seems likely that this strategy will often be successful. One possible reason is this: Scenarios that come easily to mind are likely to be those that resemble events frequently encountered in the past. Events frequently encountered in the past, in turn, are likely to be reasonable predictors of future events. In this case, this reasoning strategy should lead to a sensible judgment. Whether or not this strategy will often work, however, it is apparently often used, and its use provides yet another way in which availability, in this case availability to the imagination, can influence a broad range of judgments about upcoming events.

Representativeness

Our main focus in this chapter is on how, and how well, we learn from evidence. Our first concern was with the evidence itself—what evidence do we use? We turn now to the next step: In evaluating evidence, how do we reason back and forth between the particulars contained in our experience, or contained in our memory, and the universals of the world at large? When, and on what basis, do we draw conclusions about "all" from our experience with "some"? How fully do we expect the properties of "all" to be reflected in our experience with "some"?

Note that these issues are fundamental to our understanding of the learning process itself. Think about what is happening when one learns, for example, that Susan is a reliable person, or that Joe's Cafe serves a good dinner, or, for that matter, that a CS is reliably followed by a US. In each case, one is drawing a conclusion from evidence; one is basing a broad claim on a limited sample of observations. Do we tend to be reasonable in drawing these conclusions, or do we jump to premature conclusions? How sensibly do we generalize from the evidence we have gathered?

These questions lead us to another heuristic strategy that seems to characterize much of people's reasoning. We first met this heuristic in Chapter 10, when we proposed that subjects often categorize by use of prototypes. This strategy exploits the fact that while "typicality" is different from "membership in a category," these qualities do overlap: Something that resembles a "typical bird" is likely to be a bird when closely inspected. And this allows us all to use typicality as an efficient, usually successful categorization strategy.

In Chapter 10, we argued that categorization by typicality is a powerful, efficient, and broadly used strategy. It turns out, though, that this strategy is merely a special case of an even broader heuristic, namely, the **representativeness heuristic**. This heuristic can be summarized in this way: In general, assume that instances of a category tend to resemble the ideal or prototype, and that the prototype likewise resembles each instance. Said differently, this is an assumption of homogeneity of categories. If one makes this assumption of homogeneity, a number of consequences follow—strategies one can use, inferences one can make. The categorization strategy is one of these consequences, but we will look at some others as well. As we will see, this assumption helps us more often than not, but can lead to error. We begin with the errors, and then circle back to the help.

REASONING FROM THE POPULATION TO AN INSTANCE

If we operate on the assumption that each instance resembles the prototype, then we should expect each instance to show the properties that we expect in the category overall. This expectation is clearly visible in something called the "gambler's fallacy." Most people (and many gamblers) believe that, after a coin has come up heads five or six times in a row, it is more likely to come up tails on the next toss. Likewise, if a pair of dice has not come up with a 12 for many rolls (let us say no 12 in the last 50 rolls), then 12 is judged to be more likely on upcoming rolls. The "logic" in these cases seems to be that, if the coin is fair, then we expect a set of tosses to contain equal numbers of heads and tails. If no tails have appeared for a while, then some are "overdue" to bring about this balance. (And likewise for the dice.)

But how could this be? The coin has no "memory," so it has no way of knowing how long it has been since the last "tails." More generally, there simply is no mechanism through which the history of the previous tosses could influence the current one. Therefore, the likelihood of a tail on Toss No. 7 is 50–50 (that is, 0.50), just as it was on the first toss, and as it is on every toss. Where, then, does our belief come from, and where does it go wrong? The answer lies in our assumption that instances resemble prototypes, and vice versa. We know that, over the long haul, a fair coin will produce equal numbers of heads and tails. And if we toss the coin many, many times, we will approach that ideal. But, if we toss the coin only a few times, we may stray rather far from a 50–50 split. Nonetheless, subjects seem to expect the 50–50 division (a property of the whole set, or of the ideal) even in a short run of tosses (the instance of the category).

A different way to say this appeals to standard notions of sampling and statistics. If we examine a large number of cases (that is, if we look at a big sample of data), we will find patterns close to those in the population at large. This is what statisticians refer to as the "law of large numbers." There is, however, no "law of small numbers"; that is, there is no tendency for small samples to approximate the pattern of the population. But people seem not to appreciate this. Here is an example to make the point, from another study by Tversky and Kahneman (1974).

Subjects are given the following problem:

In a small town nearby, there are two hospitals. Hospital A has an average of 45 births per day; Hospital B is smaller, and has an average of 15 births per day. As we all know, overall the number of males born is 50%. Each hospital recorded the number of days in which, on that day, at least 60% of the babies born were male. Which hospital recorded more such days: (a) Hospital A, (b) Hospital B, (c) both equal?

The majority of the subjects chose (c), both equal, but this answer is statistically unwarranted. All of the births in the country add up to a 50–50 split between male and female babies. The larger the sample one examines, the more likely one is to approximate this ideal. Conversely, the smaller the sample one examines, the more likely one is to stray from this ideal. Days with 60% male births, straying from the ideal, are therefore more likely in the smaller hospital, Hospital B. If you don't see this, compare Hospitals C and D. Hospital C has 1000 births per day; D has exactly 1 birth per day. How often does Hospital D have "at least 60% male births"? Approximately every other day, when, in fact, it has 100% male births—1 out of 1. In contrast, 100% male births at Hospital C, all 1000, would be a remarkable event indeed.

In the hospital problem, just like in the gambler's fallacy, subjects seem not to take sample size into account. This is what one would expect if subjects make the blanket assumption that each instance of a category, or, in this case, each subset of a larger set, should show the properties associated with the entire set.

REASONING FROM AN INSTANCE TO THE POPULATION

In the cases just described, subjects expect each individual in a category to have the properties of the category overall. The reverse error can be demonstrated: If subjects believe that category prototypes resemble instances, then they should be willing to extrapolate from instances to the entire category. The evidence indicates that subjects do this, even when they are explicitly given information that the instance is not representative of the larger group! For example, Hamill, Wilson, and Nisbett (1979) showed subjects a videotaped interview in which a person identified as a guard at a state prison discussed his job. In one condition, the guard was compassionate and kind, and expressed great concern for rehabilitation. In the other condition, the guard was just the opposite—he expressed contempt for the prison inmates, referring to them as "animals," and he scoffed at the idea of rehabilitation. Before seeing either of these videotapes, some subjects were told that this guard was quite typical of those at the prison; other subjects were told that he was quite atypical, chosen for the interview precisely because of his extreme views. Still other subjects were given no information about whether the interviewed guard was typical or not.

Subjects were later questioned about their views of the criminal justice system. The data indicate that subjects were clearly influenced by the interview they had seen: Subjects who saw the humane guard indicated that they believed prison guards to be decent people in general; subjects who saw the inhumane guard reported much more negative views of prison guards in general. What is remarkable, though, is that subjects seemed largely to ignore the information about whether the interviewed guard was typical or not. Subjects who were explicitly told the guard was atypical were influenced by the interview just as much, and in the same way, as subjects who were told the opposite—that the guard was typical.

These data and other laboratory findings (e.g., Hamill, Wilson, & Nisbett, 1979, 1980) make it clear that subjects are quite willing to draw conclusions from a single case, even when they have been explicitly warned that the single case is not representative. This is exactly what we would expect if subjects are using the representativeness heuristic. If one makes a blanket assumption that categories are homogeneous, then it is reasonable to extrapolate from one observation to the entire category, and that seems sadly close to what subjects are doing.

Similar data are easily observed outside of the laboratory. Consider what Nisbett and Ross (1980) have referred to as "man who" arguments. You are shopping for a new car. You have read various consumer magazines and decided, based on their reports of test data and repair records, that you will buy a Smacko brand car. You report this to your father, who is aghast. "Smacko?!? You must be crazy. Why, I know a man who bought a Smacko, and the transmission fell out two weeks after he got it. Then the alternator went. Then the brakes. . . . How could you possibly buy a Smacko?"

What should you make of this argument? The consumer magazines tested many cars and reported (let us say) that 5% of all Smackos break down. In your father's "data," 100% of the Smackos (1 out of 1) break down. Should this "sample of one" outweigh the much larger sample tested by the magazine? Your father presumably believes he is offering a persuasive argument, but what is the possible basis for this? The only basis we can see is the presumption that the category will resemble the instance; only if that were true would reasoning from the instance be appropriate.

Our world (and, for that matter, the news) is filled with "person who" stories. Just for one more example, in 1981, the U.S. Congress was examining whether the drug laetrile should be marketed as a cancer cure. Many people in the country were convinced that laetrile, an apricot-pit derivative, was effective, but the scientific evidence said otherwise. In June 1981, *Science* magazine reported a conversation between Congresswoman Paula Hawkins (R–Fla.), a member of the investigative subcommittee, and a researcher testifying before the subcommittee. Hawkins noted, "I know of a person who had skin cancer, who was diagnosed as a terminal case. The person took laetrile and she's alive 2 years later." (*Science* reports that the researcher replied, quietly but firmly, "Individual cases don't make a generality.")

In part, these "person who" cases reflect further evidence for an availability bias. These concrete cases, often presented in vivid terms, will be likely to capture one's attention, and will likely be remembered. Thus an availability advantage is one reason why "person who" arguments are often successful. However, availability cannot be the entire story here. In many "person who" cases, the statistical information and the single, vivid instance are both readily available—discussed in the same conversation, considered in the same context. In these cases, availability is not an issue, but the single, vivid instance is still given far more weight than it deserves.

Detecting Covariation

Once one has collected a set of facts, a list of data, what next? A great many questions we might ask of these data turn out to be questions about what **covaries** with what. "Covaries" has a technical meaning, but, for our purposes, we can unpack it as follows: X and Y "covary" if X tends to be on the scene whenever Y is, and if X tends to be absent whenever Y is absent. X might also covary with the *absence* of Y—X is likely to be present when Y is absent, and vice versa. Finally, if X and Y are more or less quantities, rather than all or none, covariation means there will tend to be a lot of X around when there is a lot of Y, and so on.

For example, height and weight covary—people that have a "lot" of one (that is, people who are tall) tend to have a lot of the other (are heavy). Owning phonograph records and going to concerts also covary, although less strongly than height and weight. (Some people own many records but rarely go to concerts.) Note, then, that covariation is a matter of degree. Having a disease symptom and having the disease covary, not surprisingly, since one is an index of the other's presence. And, finally, high temperatures and increased thirst covary, also not surprisingly, since one is the cause of the other.

These examples should start to give you an idea of why we care about covariation. Covariation is what we look at in assessing the quality of a diagnostic technique. Can we learn something about you by examining your descriptions of ink blots? If so, aspects of your descriptions should covary with some aspects of your personality. Covariation is also what we look at to test a hypothesis about cause and effect. Does education lead to a higher-paying job? If so, then degree of education and salary should covary. And, finally, covariation is what we might look at to determine if a particular therapy works, a different sort of cause and effect. Does taking aspirin prevent heart attacks? If so, then aspirin use and heart attacks should covary negatively, with the presence of one being associated with the absence of the other.

Assessing covariation is therefore a fundamental skill, drawn on by many different sorts of data analyses. In fact, once again, skill in detecting covariation turns out to be critical for learning. In Pavlovian conditioning, for example, the organism is learning about a covariation between CSs and USs, namely, that when the first occurs, the second is likely to follow. The same can be said for operant conditioning, although here the covariation is between the response and reinforcement (Chapter 4, pp. 132–38). In addition, many cases of more complex learning can also be described in these terms. When we learn that Chez Jose serves a good dinner, we are learning about the covariation between going to Chez Jose and having a satisfying meal. When we learn that Fred gives good advice about movies, we are learning about covariation between Fred's judgment and our own. Thus, if we hope to understand learning, it seems that we must first understand how we do in assessing covariation.

We know that humans can assess covariation when they have access to the appropriate computational tools—that's no trick. But how well do people do in assessing covariation in more day-to-day issues? Does my colleague at work act in a friendlier fashion when I'm formal or when I'm casual? Does "playing hard to get" work? Can one study better if one has a period of physical exercise during the day? These are all questions of a sort that we frequently ask, and these questions are addressed through an examination of covariation. So how well do we do?

"ILLUSIONS" OF COVARIATION

Psychologists interested in personality have developed a wide set of "assessment instruments," tests designed to measure personality characteristics or behavioral inclinations. One well-known assessment tool is the **Rorschach test**. In this test, the subject (or patient) is shown inkblots, is asked to describe them, and then these descriptions are examined, looking for certain patterns. For example, responses that mention humans in motion are said to indicate imagination and a rich inner life; responses that describe the white spaces around the inkblot are taken as an indication of rebelliousness.

Is this valid? That is, do specific responses, or **signs**, as they are called, really covary with certain traits or symptoms? And how astutely do clinicians (or anyone else) detect this covariation? This question was examined by Chapman and Chapman (1971). Their study begins in the library, not in the laboratory: The Chapmans reviewed previous research to ask which signs and traits really do covary and which do not. Specifically, they asked which Rorschach responses were valid indicators of homosexuality. It is important to mention that the Chapmans' research was done two decades ago, at a time when many psychologists viewed homosexuality as a "problem" to be diagnosed. Psychologists have long since abandoned this view. We discuss the Chapmans' research because it is a classic study of covariation; we emphasize that this research tells us nothing about homosexuality.

As it turns out, at least 20 different Rorschach signs had been hypothesized as indicators of homosexuality, but only 2 of these signs were supported by the data. For example, various authors had claimed that homosexuals were more likely to perceive buttocks in the inkblots. To test this, researchers had examined the Rorschach responses from homosexuals and heterosexuals, and had statistically asked whether "buttocks" responses were more likely from one group rather than the other. In actuality, the two groups do not differ in the likelihood of this response; that is, there is no covariation between sexual orientation and use of this response. Therefore this is not a valid indicator of homosexuality. Similar research examined the other proposed signs. Overall, the data indicated that 18 of the hypothesized responses were (contrary to prediction) equally likely in both groups; only 2 of the signs turned out to be valid.

Nonetheless, the Chapmans found that many clinicians continued to use all of these signs in reaching their "diagnoses" of homosexuality. In fact, the clinicians were quite convinced, based on their extensive experience with patients, that these signs were valid indicators of homosexuality. According to the clinicians, there *was* covariation between these signs and homosexuality, despite the research data to the contrary.

Who should we believe? Are the clinicians right, and the research muddled? The Chapmans found evidence to indicate that this was not the case. The Chapmans created a number of Rorschach **protocols**, that is, written transcripts of a subject's responses to the patterns. The protocols were actually fictional, made up for this study, but were designed to resemble real subjects' responses. The Chapmans also made up a number of descriptions of the people who had supposedly offered these responses: One description, for example, was of someone who "has sexual feelings toward other men"; another description was of someone who "believes other people are plotting against him"; and so on. These protocols and descriptions were randomly paired with each other: one protocol and one description, the next protocol and a different description, and so on. Thanks to the random pairing, we know that, in this set of data, there was no covariation between protocols and descriptions, between signs and traits.

The Chapmans took these randomly assembled protocol–profile pairs and showed them to a group of undergraduates, students who had no prior history with the Rorschach test and who did not know the theory behind the test. These students were asked to inspect the protocol–profile pairs and then to determine what signs covaried with homosexuality in these data. We know that there is no objective covariation in these data, thanks to the random pairing. Nonetheless, the students reported seeing a pattern of covariation. Certain signs, they reported, seemed consistently good indicators that the respondent was a homosexual. And the signs they mentioned were the same ones the clinicians reported using. For example, the subjects erroneously mentioned that buttocks responses were more common among homosexuals, in line with the clinicians' claims. Apparently, this pattern of covariations is "observed" whether it is present in the data or not.

Finally, the Chapmans went to a new group of students and simply asked how strongly the word "homosexuality" tended to call various ideas to mind. There was no mention, for this group, of the Rorschach data. Subjects' responses were merely based on their own intuitions and expectations. These subjects tended to agree with one another about what ideas had a strong verbal association with homosexuality. And, oddly enough, these verbal associations corresponded to the Rorschach signs that had been "observed" to covary with homosexuality. For example, subjects in this study rated as strong the association between "homosexuality" and "buttocks." Apparently, there is a strong, intuitive connection between these ideas, quite independent of any Rorschach data, random or otherwise.

How shall we read these findings? The obvious conclusion is that subjects expect certain patterns and certain thoughts to be associated with homosexuality. These expectations can be observed in the "verbal association" responses, responses not guided by any Rorschach data. Lo and behold, other subjects "observe" this association (in the form of covariation) in the Rorschach data, even when, objectively, there is no covariation. It would appear that the subjects are simply projecting their own biases into the data.

Laboratory subjects "observe" covariation in the Rorschach responses when we know the data are random. Trained clinicians observe the same covariation in their own studies, even though the research says that these observations, like the laboratory data, contain no covariation. It would seem that highly trained, highly experienced professionals are as vulnerable to these illusory covariations as undergraduates are.

THEORY-DRIVEN AND DATA-DRIVEN DETECTION OF COVARIATION

The clear message of the Chapmans' data is that covariation detection is influenced by prior expectations. The suggestion, essentially, is that the clinicians saw what they expected to see, and what they expected to see was what seemed sensible to them from the very beginning.

We are not surprised if such errors happen to someone very dogmatic—for example, to the sexist who believes all women are intellectually incompetent (that is, expects to see, and "sees," covariation between gender and competence) or to the racist who believes all blacks are lazy (again, a covariation claim). We expect that these ugly beliefs might be supported only by evidence of the flimsiest sort, by arguments that will not stand up to scrutiny. But we are a bit more surprised, and unhappy, to discover the same patterns of prejudice in ourselves.

A key study here was done by Jennings, Amabile, and Ross (1982). Their study employed a group of college students, and examined their performance in two types of situations: situations in which the students had no prior expectations or biases, and situations in which students did have prior beliefs. In the "prior-belief" (or "theory-based") case, subjects were asked to estimate the covariation between pairs of traits. The experimenters chose traits for which it seemed likely that subjects would have some expectations or beliefs about the covariation. For example, subjects were asked to estimate how strong the covariation is between (a) children's dishonesty as measured by false report of athletic performance and (b) children's dishonesty as measured by amount of cheating in solving a puzzle. If a child is dishonest according to one of these indices, is she also dishonest according to the other? Or, as a different example, subjects estimated the covariation between (a) how highly a student rated U.S. presidents' performances in the last decade and (b) how highly the student rated business leaders' performances in the last decade. If you think highly of our presidents, do you also think highly of the business community?

Subjects presumably made these judgments by reflecting on their prior experience and their intuitions; no new data were presented in the experimental procedure. Subjects expressed these judgments by selecting a number between 0 and 100, where 0 indicated that the two traits were unrelated, did not covary, and 100 indicated that the traits covaried perfectly. Subjects could also use negative values (to −100) to indicate the belief that the two traits covary, but with the presence of one guaranteeing the absence of the other.

The subjects were also asked to make a comparable judgment in a "no-prior-belief" (or "data-based") case, that is, with variables they had never met or considered before. For example, subjects were shown 10 pictures, each showing a man holding a walking stick. The heights of the men varied in the pictures, as did the length of the walking stick, and subjects had to judge whether these two variables covaried, again choosing some value between −100 and +100.

The data are easy to describe. As Figure 14–1 shows, subjects' estimates were reasonably regular in the data-based cases: the stronger the covariation, the stronger the estimate. Subjects also tended to be rather conservative; their estimates exceeded +30 (on the 0–100 scale) only when the objective correlation was very strong. Figure 14–2 shows a very different picture for the theory-based cases. Subjects tended to be far more extravagant in these estimates, with estimates of +50 and +60 and +80. Subjects were also far less regular in the theory-based cases, with only a weak relation between the magnitude of the estimated covariation and the magnitude of the actual covariation. For example, the "children's dishonesty" pair, mentioned earlier, is shown as the black square in Figure 14–2. In this case, the objective correlation, statistically measured, is fairly small. That is, children who are dishonest in one context are often

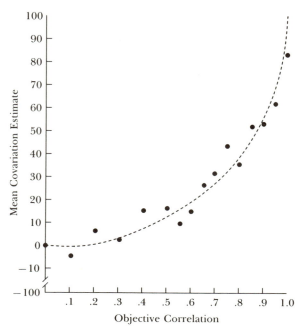

FIGURE 14-1. *Assessments of Covariation in the Absence of Expectations.* When subjects enter a situation with no expectations about the data, their estimates of covariation are quite orderly: The estimates grow stronger and stronger as the actual (objective) correlation grows stronger and stronger. In addition, subjects give low estimates unless the actual correlation is very strong. (After Jennings, Amabile, & Ross, 1982.)

honest in other contexts! Subjects estimated this covariation to be quite large, though, with an average estimate of +60. For the "presidents and business leaders" case (the black star in the figure), the objective correlation is much stronger than the "children's dishonesty" pair, but subjects estimated it to be much weaker.

At the very least, subjects are performing differently in the theory-based and data-based judgments. More strongly, the theory-based judgments tend to be extravagant; the data-based judgments tend to be conservative. The data-based judgments track the objective facts fairly well; the theory-based judgments do not. It is difficult to avoid the conclusion that theory biased what subjects "saw" in the data, and led them to see much stronger (or weaker) covariation than was there.

WHY ANIMALS ARE MORE ACCURATE THAN PEOPLE

You may have noticed a peculiar contrast: In the previous sections, we described how easily humans go astray in assessing covariation. In Chap-

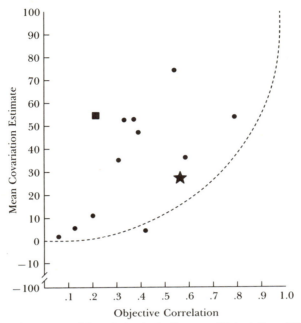

FIGURE 14–2. *Assessments of Covariation in the Presence of Expectations.* When subjects enter a situation with expectations about the data, their estimates of covariation are often inaccurate. In this instance, subjects were asked to assess the covariation in 16 cases. The square and the star indicate the two cases discussed in the text. Subjects often estimated the covariation as strong even when it was quite weak, or as being weak even when it was strong. The systematic pattern observed in Figure 14–1 is clearly absent here. (For purposes of comparison, this figure includes the curve describing the data from Figure 14–1.) (After Jennings, Amabile, & Ross, 1982.)

ters 3 and 4, however, we indicated that laboratory animals, rats or pigeons, for example, are quite adept in assessing covariation! Recall a few facts about Pavlovian conditioning: It is not the *contiguity* of a conditioned stimulus and unconditioned stimulus that leads to conditioning. Instead, animals seem sensitive to *contingency*. Conditioning occurs when the conditioned stimulus is informative, or, more precisely, when the probability of the US, given that the CS has occurred, is different from the probability of the US in the absence of the CS. When this is true, then it pays to notice the CS, because it gives information about things to come.

Much evidence, reviewed in earlier chapters, indicates that contingency is what drives conditioning, that learning occurs when the CS is informative. But this is a straightforward claim about covariation: If the CS is informative, this is because the CS and US covary—the presence of one tells you something about the likelihood of the other, and the absence of one tells you something as well. Therefore, if laboratory animals are sensitive to what we earlier called *contingency,* then they are demonstrating sensitivity to *covariation.*

Should we conclude that animals are more sensitive to covariation than humans are? The Jennings et al. data, described in the previous section, point toward a different view, a view developed in some detail by Alloy and Tabachnik (1984). As we saw in the Jennings et al. study, human sensitivity to covariation depends very much on whether one enters the situation with prior expectations (with a theory). When subjects assess covariation in a "theory-based" case, covariation is often misjudged. In the extreme, subjects confidently detect covariation when there is absolutely none. This seemed to be the case in the Chapman and Chapman study of Rorschach protocols. In sharp contrast, when human subjects assess covariation in a "data-driven" case, one in which they have no prior expectations, subjects' estimates do track the data reasonably well. Which of these should we compare to animal performance? Presumably, a laboratory animal has no expectations prior to an experimental procedure about the connection between bell and food, or lever press and water. Therefore, this seems likely to be a "data-driven" case, and in data-driven cases animals and humans both detect covariation with reasonable accuracy.

Humans are led astray when they have prior expectations about covariation; is the same true for laboratory animals? Alloy and Tabachnik suggest that one such case is provided by the phenomenon of "learned helplessness" (introduced in Chapter 4). In the learned helplessness paradigm, the animal first experiences a setting in which events and outcomes are independent of the animal's actions. Evidence indicates that the animal seems to learn that there is no contingency in this situation, and the animal therefore ceases to act—it instead sits passively and does nothing. Note that the animal has correctly detected the null covariation; that is how the learning takes place.

Our concern, though, is with the next step: We now change the situation, so that the animal's actions do have consequences—do produce a reward, for example. In this case, the animal shows a learning deficit—the prior history with null covariation seems to make it much harder for the animal to learn a case of covariation. There are several ways to think about this result, but Alloy and Tabachnik point to the obvious parallel between this finding and human theory-based learning: The learned helplessness procedure leads the animal to the "expectation" (or "theory") that its actions have no consequences; this expectation biases what the animal learns from later data. Thus, on this view of things, it appears that the pattern of covariation detection by animals is the same as that by humans: reasonably accurate detection when not misled by prior expectations, but relatively poor sensitivity to covariation when prior expectations are on the scene.

A similar point can be made about *taste aversion learning,* described in

Chapter 2. In this phenomenon, rats (for example) behave as if they have the "theory" that stomach illness is usually caused by eating novel foods, and not by familiar foods or other environmental events. Thanks to this "theory," rats are better able to learn associations between novel tastes and illness, and are less sensitive to associations between other stimuli and illness. In either case, rats are selective in what they will learn; they are, so to speak, less objective about the facts. While this lack of objectivity, in this case, will usually lead rats to the correct "conclusion," this does not undermine the general point that in the presence of a "theory" organisms are less accurate in judging covariation between events.

ILLUSORY COVARIATION: ANOTHER AVAILABILITY EFFECT?

There is some disagreement about what causes subjects to see covariation that is not there. We know that subjects are less accurate when they have a prior theory, but why is this? How does having a theory cause subjects to misjudge covariation? One possibility is that subjects are simply dogmatic: It's the situation of "I've already made up my mind; don't distract me with the facts." This strikes us as likely to be true on some occasions, but unpromising as a general explanation: In the experiments we have considered (and many others just like them), subjects certainly seem to be taking their task seriously—carefully examining the Rorschach responses, for example, and giving every indication that they are weighing the evidence as well as they can. Hence we do not believe subjects simply ignore the facts in these experiments. Why, then, do subjects still go astray?

We propose that at least part of the explanation should be cast in familiar terms—namely, availability. (Our proposal follows that offered by Jennings, Amabile, & Ross in accounting for their own data.) How does one assess covariation the proper way? One takes pairs of observations—be they height and walking-stick length, or Rorschach responses and personality traits—and feeds these into a calculator or computer; the calculator cranks through the relevant formulas and gives the answer. One might think that *we* do nothing like this in making our informal estimates; after all, most of us do not even know the appropriate formulas. Perhaps, then, errors in estimating covariation come from use of the "wrong formulas," or, more realistically, some estimation strategy that bears little resemblance to the correct formulas.

This cannot be the problem. If it were, then subjects' performance in judging covariation should be uniformly poor. That is not the case: Subjects do reasonably well in judging covariation in data-driven cases, when they don't have a prior theory. Apparently, subjects' estimation strategy is close enough to the correct formula to provide the right answer some of the time.

There is, however, one crucial difference between a calculator or computer assessing covariation and human subjects trying to do the same: A calculator or computer takes all the data as its input, whether 4 or 8 or 100 observations. Do we do the same? Could we do the same? The answer to this hinges on a point raised earlier in this chapter. In assessing how many words have an "r" in the third position ("part," "merry," "throat," etc.), we *could* do a time-consuming, relatively complete search of our vocabularies, and in this way find the right answer. Or we could just use the words that come quickly to mind, and so reach an answer much more quickly. As we have seen, evidence indicates that subjects use the latter approach; that is, they rely on information that is readily available. By the same token, in judging covariation, we could spend the time and effort to think about all of the relevant cases that we can. Or we could rely on the cases that come easily to mind. Given what we know about the "r" case, it seems a safe assumption that subjects will use the more efficient route, and consider only the available data.

This still leaves us to ask, though, which observations subjects are likely to consider; that is, which observations are available. Will it be a random set? A representative sample? Or perhaps a biased sample? To answer this, we need some further theory telling us what factors cause an observation to catch one's attention and what factors cause an observation to be overlooked. In fact, the relevant theory is not hard to find: Much evidence indicates that one's attention is likely to be caught by "confirming" instances, instances that fit with one's beliefs. This tendency has been dubbed a **confirmation bias,** and can be demonstrated in various ways (see Nisbett & Ross, 1980; Tweney, Doherty, & Mynatt, 1981).

We presented some of the evidence relevant to confirmation bias in Chapter 9, in our discussion of schema theory: The evidence indicates that inputs consistent with subjects' schemata will be easily remembered. Inputs that are inconsistent may be overlooked or forgotten. Worse still, information that does not fit with one's schema can be distorted in memory, to bring it into line with the schema! Overall, this will help to preserve in memory information that confirms one's prior beliefs and will help to undermine information that challenges one's beliefs.

The notion of confirmation bias provides our account for why theory-based estimates of covariation are often inaccurate, and very often are too high. Let us say, for example, that you have the belief that big dogs tend to be vicious. When thinking about dogs, or looking at dogs, the confirmation bias will lead you to notice big dogs that are, in fact, vicious, and little dogs that are friendly. Your memory schemata will also help you to remember episodes that fit with this belief, and these schemata will work against remembering counterexamples to the belief. Thus a biased sample of dogs will be available to you. If you are then asked to estimate covariation between dog size and temperament, you will overestimate the covariation, thanks to this biased sample. Imagine, though, that you have no prior beliefs about dog size and viciousness. Then, your attention and memory will not be biased in this regard, giving you a less biased sample to think about and allowing a more accurate covariation estimate.

The pattern of this argument should by now be familiar: Reasoning and judgment can be quite accurate in many cases, and so the ability to reason and judge well is apparently within our capacity. However, reasoning and judgment are often based on what we notice and what we remember, and these are vulnerable to a number of biases. Hence, in some substantial number of cases, our reasoning may be accurate, but based on faulty or incomplete data.

How often does this kind of error happen? We do not know, but it seems worth some concern. We have mentioned sexist hypotheses that depend on "observed covariation" for their support, and racist hypotheses in the same boat. There is also the hypothesis that smoking marijuana leads to the use of hard drugs, another covariation claim. And there are many medical hypotheses that hinge on covariation—we have already considered a case involving psychological testing, and we will turn shortly to a case involving diagnosis of cancer. In short, the stakes are often very high in judgments involving covariation. If misjudging covariation merely meant missing out on a great meal at Chez Jose, then we might not worry very much when such errors occur. But, alas, the cost of these errors is potentially far higher than this.

"CODABILITY" OF THE DATA

Confirmation bias is one factor that can cloud our judgments of covariation, but, we should emphasize, there are other relevant factors as well. An additional factor concerns the clarity of the data themselves. Holland, Holyoak, Nisbett, and Thagard (1987) discuss this in terms of the **codability** of the data—that is, how readily one can categorize, or quantify, the evidence being considered.

For example, consider a study by Kunda and Nisbett (1986). Subjects were asked to judge covariation with two different types of cases: Some of the judgments were made about easily codable events—things like athletic performance or academic achievement. These are easily quantified in terms of points per game or test scores and so on. Other judgments were made about less easily coded events. For example, subjects made judgments about things like friendliness and honesty. As Holland et al. put it (p. 212), "Such events are manifestly difficult to code reliably. . . . Even the . . . appropriate unit to code is problematic. Should friendliness be measured in smiles per minute, 'good vibrations' per encounter, or what?" In addition, there remains a problem in evaluating individual cases: "Was John being friendly to you just now, or was he being ingratiating, or was he simply responding in kind to your pleasant overtures?"

Kunda and Nisbett predicted that subjects would be reasonably accurate in their assessments of covariation involving codable data, like athletic performance, and far less accurate in their assessments with cases that are difficult to code, like social behaviors. The data clearly support this prediction. Once again, we are led to a familiar conclusion: Reasoning processes work well, if these processes are given accurate, unbiased input. The quality of the input, it now seems, depends on multiple factors: memory availability, the presence or absence of a confirmation bias, and, it turns out, subjects' ability to code the data in a clear and informative fashion.

Base Rates

Consider the following problem (after Kahneman & Tversky, 1973; Nisbett & Ross, 1980):

> The present authors have a friend who is a professor. He likes to write poetry, is rather shy, and is small in stature. Which of the following is his field: (a) Chinese studies or (b) psychology?

Most subjects suspect that this friend is in Chinese studies. In a sense, this fits the idea of a representativeness heuristic: In this example, we have described someone close to many people's stereotype of a Chinese scholar, and so subjects draw the appropriate conclusion. Once again, subjects seem to categorize by making comparisons to a prototypical case, embodying the stereotype for the category.

What this does not take into account, however, is this: As you can probably guess, the number of psychologists in this country vastly outnumbers the number of scholars in Chinese studies. To see how this matters, let us assume, just for the sake of argument, that virtually all Chinese scholars fit the stereotype—let us say 90%. Let us assume further that only 5% of the psychologists fit the stereotype. In this case, "fitting the stereotype" would be what is called high-quality **diagnostic information**.

But now we need to factor in how many psychologists there are, and how many Chinese scholars. If there are relatively few Chinese scholars, then even if 90% of these fit the description this is still 90% of a small number. If merely 5% of the psychologists fit the description, this will be 5% of a much larger number. Just for example, let us say there are 10,000 Chinese scholars in this country, but 200,000 psychologists. In this case, 9000 Chinese scholars fit the description (90% of 10,000). But 10,000 psychologists fit the description, too (5% of 200,000). In this way, the total *number* of psychologists who fit the description may be greater than the total number of Chinese scholars fitting the description. This is per-

fectly consistent with the observation that the *proportion* of Chinese scholars fitting the description is much larger than the proportion of psychologists (90% versus 5%).

To put this more generally, in order to make judgments like this, one
needs two types of information: the diagnostic information and the **base
rates**, or, as they are sometimes called, the **prior probabilities**. Prior to
any other information, prior to hearing the sketch of our friend, you knew
something about the relative numbers of scholars in psychology and in
Chinese studies. This base-rate information can offset the diagnostic
information: In our example, a "small percentage of a big number"
turned out to be larger than a "large percentage of a small number."
Thus, the diagnostic information by itself appeared to favor the conclusion of "Chinese studies." However, the diagnostic information *in conjunction with* base rates can point toward a different conclusion.

BASE RATES AND DIAGNOSTIC INFORMATION

Here is a different base-rate problem, also drawn from the research of
Kahneman and Tversky. Subjects are given the following instructions:

> A panel of psychologists has interviewed and administered personality tests to
> 30 engineers and 70 lawyers, all successful in their respective fields. On the
> basis of this information, thumbnail descriptions of the 30 engineers and 70
> lawyers have been written. You will find on your forms five descriptions, chosen
> at random from the 100 available descriptions. For each description, please
> indicate your probability that the person described is an engineer, on a scale
> from 0 to 100 [Kahneman & Tversky, 1973, p. 241].

The "thumbnail descriptions" provided were actually carefully designed so that some were compatible with subjects' "engineer" stereotype but not with their "lawyer" stereotype; other descriptions were
compatible with a lawyer stereotype but not an engineer. For example,
a description favoring the engineer stereotype described a man whose
hobbies include home carpentry, sailing, and mathematical puzzles, and
who has no interest in political or social issues.

How should subjects respond in this task? Subjects who read about
someone resembling the lawyer stereotype should combine this information with the fact that 70% of the people in the group were lawyers. The
base-rate information should in this case strengthen the estimate that the
person described is a lawyer. In contrast, subjects who read about someone resembling the engineer stereotype should temper their estimate,
given the fact that less than one-third of the people in the group were
engineers. In short, subjects should combine the diagnostic information,
contained in the description, with the base-rate information.

The results indicate that subjects base their responses entirely on the degree of resemblance between the individual described and the stereo-type of a lawyer or an engineer. That is, subjects paid careful attention to the diagnostic information and ignored the base-rate information. In fact, for half of the subjects, the base-rate information was reversed in the experiment: For these subjects, the original group was described as con-taining 70% engineers, rather than 70% lawyers. This made no differ-ence at all in subjects' judgments, confirming that subjects were by and large ignoring the base rates.

Do subjects believe that the base-rate information is irrelevant to their task? Subjects in a different condition of the study were asked to perform the same task (with 70% lawyers, 30% engineers) but were given no personality information. They were merely asked to estimate the proba-bility that "an individual chosen at random from the sample" was an engineer. In this case, subjects had no diagnostic information; hence the only information to guide responding was the base rates. Under these circumstances, subjects did pay attention to the base rates, and, in fact, gave an estimate of 30%. This is, of course, the correct answer.

Apparently, subjects do pay attention to base rates in the absence of diagnostic information; subjects therefore do know that base rates are relevant to their task. However, the moment diagnostic information is available, subjects ignore base rates, rather than combining these two relevant sources of information.

"DILUTION EFFECTS"

A further line of research helps to clarify how subjects approach this task. We have already seen that if subjects' only information is the base rates, they use base rates. If subjects are also given diagnostic informa-tion, subjects choose to ignore base rates. What happens if we go a step further, and give subjects even more information? In a study by Nisbett, Zukier, and Lemley (1981), subjects were asked to make predictions about their fellow students, including predictions about movie attend-ance. Some subjects were given diagnostic information, such as whether the target student was majoring in the sciences or the humanities. (Sci-ence majors were predicted to go to about half as many movies as humanities majors!) Other subjects were given this diagnostic informa-tion plus some irrelevant information—for example, the target individ-ual's hometown. This irrelevant information clearly influenced subjects: It caused them to pay less attention to the diagnostic information! In Nisbett et al.'s terms, the irrelevant information *dilutes* the diagnostic information, diminishing its impact. Thus, just as diagnostic information causes subjects to set aside base rates, the irrelevant information causes subjects to discount diagnostic information (see also Zukier, 1982).

As we have just seen, irrelevant information dilutes diagnostic informa-tion. It turns out that irrelevant information also can dilute base-rate information. In the lawyers/engineers study, subjects use base-rate information if this is all the information they have. For example, if subjects are told only that an individual was drawn from a group of 30 engineers and 70 lawyers, subjects (correctly) believe that there is a 30% chance that the individual chosen will be an engineer. In contrast, we have already mentioned the finding that if subjects have base-rate information *and* diagnostic information, they ignore base rates and use only the diagnostic information. What happens if subjects have base-rate information and also some uninformative information?

In one study, subjects were told that a particular group contained 30 engineers and 70 lawyers; they were told in addition that the individual chosen from this group "is a 30-year-old man . . . married with no children . . . well liked by his colleagues." This obviously tells nothing about whether the person being described is a lawyer or an engineer. If one only had this information and no more (no base-rate information), and if one had to decide if this person is a lawyer or an engineer, then one would estimate that there is a 50–50 chance of this person being an engineer. But in this procedure one also has the base-rate information. In fact, given that the description of this individual is entirely uninformative, the base rate is the only information here that is in any way useful. Thus one's prediction should, in this case, be based solely on the base rates.

In this procedure, one should predict that there is a 30% chance that the person described is an engineer. Instead, given the worthless information, subjects seem to pay attention only to the worthless information and to ignore the base rates. As a result, subjects estimate that there is a 50–50 chance of this individual being an engineer (Kahneman & Tversky, 1973; but see also Ginosar & Trope, 1980; Manis, Dovalina, Avis, & Cardoze, 1980; Wells & Harvey, 1977).

Holland, Holyoak, Nisbett, and Thagard (1987) have proposed a way to think about this broad pattern of data. On their view, subjects have a preference for "specific-level evidence." Given this preference, subjects seek to think about people and situations in the most specific way they can. If subjects are merely told an individual was "chosen at random" from a group, they have minimal information, and so they can only think about this individual as being a faceless, anonymous figure. The only thing the subjects know for certain is that the individual is from the group, and so information about the group is applied. That is, subjects consider base rates.

If, however, subjects are given more information about this individual, they can begin to think about him as an actual person. The diagnostic information is in fact designed to suggest that the individual is a member of a particular category—lawyer or engineer, humanities major or science major. This leads subjects to think of this individual in terms of that category. As we have already seen, subjects thinking about categories are likely to use the representativeness heuristic, and so, as a result, subjects are likely to understand this individual in comparison to their prototype for the category. The individual is categorized according to her resemblance to the prototype; likewise, the individual is assumed to have the properties associated with the prototype.

What is striking, though, is that thinking about the individual in this fashion seems to interfere with thinking about the individual in other ways. Specifically, thinking about the individual with reference to the prototype seems to exclude thinking about the individual with reference to the more "abstract" group information. As a consequence, once subjects are thinking in terms of the category, they use the diagnostic information to assess similarity to the prototype, but they effectively ignore the base rates.

Finally, if subjects are given still more information about the individual, they start to think about him as a specific character, with specific traits, and not merely as an exemplar of a larger category. In this case, neither the category information (the prototype) nor the group information (the base rates) is applied. Instead, the individual is thought of as just that: an individual. This individual is still a member of a group, but this is no longer considered. This individual is still a member of certain categories, but this also is ignored. These other considerations about this person are disregarded or, in the terms we have been using, diluted.

The Holland et al. proposal clearly fits with claims we have offered in previous chapters. We argued in Chapter 9 that the demands of cognitive economy encourage us to think about events and stimuli in schematic terms, in terms of a specific framework. This guides our attention, guides our memory, and in general eases our intellectual commerce with the world. The Holland et al. proposal carries this claim two steps further: First, we have a preference for using the most specific schema that we can, and, second, thinking about a situation within one schematic frame leads us to ignore or exclude information in other schematic frames.

It remains to be seen whether the Holland et al. proposal is the best way to think about these data. One way or the other, though, one point should be clear. It is easy to demonstrate in laboratory studies that subjects underutilize base-rate information. When more specific information becomes available, subjects do not combine this with base-rate information; they simply jettison the base rates and attend only to the specific information. In the laboratory, this can easily lead to judgments or conclusions not warranted by statistics or logic. Unfortunately, as we will see, the same can be demonstrated outside of the laboratory.

BASE RATES IN THE REAL WORLD

There has been much discussion over the last decade about the importance of early detection of cancer. Cancer, detected early, can often be treated more easily, more fully, and with greater chance of long-term survival than if detected only later on. Happily, we have reasonably accurate diagnostic procedures. For breast cancer, for example, a mammogram is 79% accurate. This is the likelihood of a positive test if cancer is on the scene. If there is no cancer, there is a 90% chance the test will correctly come back negative; that is, the possibility of a **false positive** is just 10%. These estimates and this example come from Eddy's (1982) unsettling essay, "Probabilistic Reasoning in Clinical Medicine."

What, therefore, should one conclude if a mammogram comes back indicating that cancer is present? One might well schedule surgery as quickly as possible, given the apparent reliability of the test and the great value of taking action early. However, once again, there is a question of base rates. Let us assume that, for a particular patient group (a certain age, a certain family history, a certain diet, and so forth), the statistics show overall a 1% likelihood of cancer. This is the base rate, the probability we estimate prior to any diagnostic testing. We now receive a mammogram indicating cancer, and we know the mammogram to be quite accurate, detecting 79% of the cancers, with only a 10% likelihood of false positive.

How should all this information be combined? The mammogram is known to be quite reliable, and so the mammogram being mistaken is, *proportionally,* an unlikely outcome. Thanks to the base rates, though, there are a great many opportunities for this unlikely event to occur. That is, the test will falsely show positive in just 10% of the non-cancer cases. But there are many non-cancer cases—99% of the population, according to the base rates. Hence the proportion of false positives will be low (10%), but the *number* of false positives will be high, since this is 10% of a large number.

Let us make this concrete. The top part of Table 14–2 shows the accuracy of the mammogram in proportional terms. Of all the cancer cases, 79% will be correctly diagnosed; 21% will be misdiagnosed. Of all the non-cancer cases, 90% will be correctly diagnosed; 10% will be misdiagnosed.

But now let us place *number* of occurrences in the table, rather than

Table 14–2.   Mammogram Reliability Figures (Top) and
Mammogram Response Frequencies (Bottom)

	Mammogram Indicates		
	Cancer	No Cancer	Total
Cancer present	79%	21%	100%
Cancer absent	10%	90%	100%
Cancer present	790	210	1000
Cancer absent	9900	89,100	99,000

Note: See text for discussion.
After Eddy, 1982.

percentages. The base rates, we have said, show a 1% likelihood of cancer for the patient group we are considering. This means there are 99 patients in the bottom row (cancer absent) for every 1 in the top row (cancer present). To make our arithmetic more straightforward, let us imagine that there are 99,000 patients not having cancer and 1000 having cancer. Of these 1000 patients, we know that 79% will be correctly diagnosed by the mammogram, so that the mammogram will indicate cancer in 790 cases, and no cancer in 210 cases. Of the 99,000 patients not having cancer, the mammogram will be correct for 90% of them, or a total of 89,100 patients. The mammogram will be incorrect, though, for 10%, a total of 9900 patients.

We are now in a position to ask what it means if a mammogram indicates cancer. In the bottom part of Table 14–2, a positive mammogram result places us in the left-hand column. But note that, within this column, the "cancer absent" cases far outnumber the "cancer present" cases, by a margin of 9900 to 790, or more than 10 to 1. In short, a mammogram indicating cancer is *wrong* more than 10 times as often as it is right. This is not because the mammogram is a poor test. Just the opposite: We have already commented that mammograms are, overall, very accurate as diagnostic tools. A mammogram's being correct is, proportionally, much more likely than a mammogram's being incorrect. But, given these base rates, there are many more opportunities for the less likely event to occur, with the result evident in the table.

All we have done so far is to show how important it is, in understanding this diagnostic information, to take base rates into account. If one looks only at the mammogram's reliability as a test, one might conclude that a positive test on a mammogram is a sure sign of cancer. If one looks at both the mammogram and the base rates, one might draw a rather different conclusion. What we need to ask now, though, is whether medical professionals are sensitive to these issues. We have already seen that laboratory subjects do poorly on base-rate problems, but one might hope that doctors, trained in the subtle points of using diagnostic information, might do better. In fact, this is not the case. Evidence suggests that doctors, just like the rest of us, do not take base-rate information into account when evaluating evidence (Eddy, 1982; Dawes, 1988). Doctors (and other medical professionals) show the same patterns and errors of reasoning that we have already observed in laboratory subjects—errors, in this case, that can lead to serious misassessments of a patient's status.

Schema-based Reasoning

Let us sum up where we are. We entered this chapter by asking whether the ordinary functioning of memory had an influence on reasoning. Said differently, in the previous chapters, we had examined remembering more or less in isolation—we had asked laboratory subjects to remember certain materials, as though this were an end in itself. In this chapter, we are asking whether remembering follows the same rules, functions the same way, when it is embedded in the context of other mental tasks.

The answers to these questions should by now be clear. Our principles of memory do have a direct bearing on the likelihood of success in reasoning, whether we are considering everyday practical reasoning, or reasoning in the social domain, or reasoning among medical practitioners. This is most obvious in the phenomenon of availability, but we have seen other cases as well. For example, the notion of schemata came up repeatedly in our discussions of memory (for example, Chapters 9, 10, and 11); it has been no less central here. Schemata played a part in our account of covariation detection; they also play a key role in Holland et al.'s proposal about why subjects fail to use base rates, thanks to subjects' strong preference for "specific-level evidence."

The Four-Card Problem

This section explores another example of schema-based reasoning, this time an inquiry into subjects' performance in deductive reasoning. Much of this research has employed a single paradigm, so we begin with it (Wason, 1966).

Subjects are shown four cards, as in Figure 14–3. Subjects are told that each card has a number on one side, and a letter on the other. Their task is to evaluate this rule: *If a card has a vowel on one side, it must have an even number on the other side.* Which cards must be turned over to put this rule to the test?

You might think about this for a moment before reading further. Many subjects assert that the "A" card must be turned over, checking for an even number. Other subjects assert that the "6" card must be turned

FIGURE 14–3. *The "Four-Card Problem."* Each card has a letter on one side, and a number on the other side. Which cards must be turned over to check this rule: *If a card has a vowel on one side, it must have an even number on the other side.*

over, checking for a vowel. Other subjects assert that both of these must be turned over. In Wason's early research, here is how the data turned out: 46% of the subjects turned over the "A" and the "6"; 33% turned over just the "A." The remaining subjects gave various other answers, with only 4% of the subjects giving the correct answer—turning over the "A" and the "7."

Why is this the right answer? If we turn over the "A" card and find an even number, this would fit with the rule. If we find an odd number on the reverse, this would contradict the rule. Hence there is information to be gained by turning over this card. The rule makes no claims about what is on the flip side of a consonant card, so we gain nothing by turning over the "J." How about the "6"? If we find a vowel on the reverse side of this card, this would fit with the rule. If we find a consonant on the reverse, this also fits, since the rule makes no claims about what is on the reverse of a consonant card. Thus there is nothing to be learned by turning over this card. Finally, if we turn over the "7" and a vowel is on the other side of this card, this would disprove the rule. If we turn over the "7" and find a consonant, this would be compatible with the rule. Therefore we do want to turn over this card.

In brief, performance is atrocious in the four-card problem, with the vast majority of subjects giving wrong answers. This basic finding has been replicated by a number of researchers. However, some studies, using variations on this problem, have found better performance. For example, Johnson-Laird, Legrenzi, and Legrenzi (1972) showed Italian subjects a drawing like the one in Figure 14–4 and asked them to test this rule: "If a letter is sealed, then it has a 50-lire stamp on it." In this version of the task, the correct response would be to turn over the sealed envelope (if it does not have a 50-lire stamp, then the rule is violated) and the envelope with the 40-lire stamp (if it is sealed, then the rule is violated). As it turns out, subjects did rather well in this version of the test (88% correct, versus 8% correct in a control condition similar to the original problem, with letters and numbers). This is an impressive difference, especially when we consider that, in its form, the "envelope" version of the test is identical to the original four-card problem.

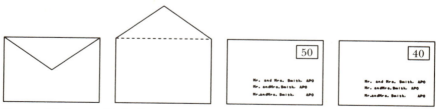

FIGURE 14–4. *An Easier Version of the Four-Card Problem.* Which envelopes would you need to turn over to find out if this rule is true: *If a letter is sealed, then it has a 50-cent stamp on it.* Subjects have an easier time with this problem than with the standard four-card problem (see Figure 14–3), even though the two problems are identical in form. (After Wason & Johnson-Laird, 1972.)

Several theories have been proposed to explain performance both on the envelope problem and on the original vowel/even-number problem. One very influential account centers on the role of schemata, and how they guide reasoning (Cheng & Holyoak, 1985; also Cheng, Holyoak, Nisbett, & Oliver, 1986; Holland, Holyoak, Nisbett, & Thagard, 1987). We begin with some background.

ABSTRACT REASONING, CONCRETE REASONING, AND SCHEMATIC REASONING

There has been much argument over the last century about how "abstract" the rules of thought are. Consider an example: I tell you, "If you love me, you'll stop being so mean." According to some views, we reason about such cases by using rules similar to the abstract rules proposed by logicians (e.g., Braine, 1978; Braine, Reiser, & Rumain, 1984; Rips, 1983). These rules make no mention of content or specifics; instead, they consider only the "form" or "syntax" of the assertions being considered. For example, the rule of **modus ponens** states that, given the assertions "If P then Q" and also "P," it is valid to conclude "Q." The rule applies to any assertion of the form "If P then Q," no matter what P is, and no matter what Q is. Since the "if you love me" example is of this form, modus ponens could potentially be used here.

Other psychologists, however, have taken a rather different view (e.g., D'Andrade, 1982; Griggs & Cox, 1982; Manktelow & Evans, 1979; Reich & Ruth, 1982). They claim that we do not have abstract reasoning rules; instead, we have knowledge of a much more concrete sort. One knows a lot, for example, about love and lovers, and about being mean or not being mean, and this very concrete knowledge will guide reasoning about the "if–then" statement in the previous paragraph. Notice that this specific knowledge will help with this particular "if–then," but not with some other. Unlike modus ponens, which applies to any if–then statement, this use of content-specific knowledge will be sharply limited in its application. (For further discussion of these two views of reasoning, see Henle, 1962; Holland, Holyoak, Nisbett, & Thagard, 1987; Lehman, Lempert, & Nisbett, 1988.)

However, a third view is also possible, effectively splitting the difference between the two perspectives just sketched (Cheng & Holyoak, 1985). On this view, much deductive reasoning is done via **pragmatic-reasoning schemata**. These schemata are derived from experience, just like schemata in general, and so summarize that which is redundant and repetitive in our world. Pragmatic-reasoning schemata are defined in terms of goals, or event relationships. Hence we have a "cause-and-effect" schema that summarizes our experiences with cause-and-effect relations, and which we use in reasoning about causal relations. We also have an "obligation" schema, which we use in reasoning about social relations of the appropriate sort; we also have a "permission" schema; and so on.

These schemata embody rules that are quite similar to the rules of logic, and so these schemata can be used in a fashion similar to logical reasoning. For example, the *permission schema* includes rules like "If one wishes to take a certain action, then one must have permission" and "If one has permission to take a certain action, then one may take the action." These rules will support various inferences, and so resemble the rules of logic. Unlike formal logic, though, these schemata are influenced by content and meaning, and not solely by logical form. Thus reasoning schemata are far more concrete than logical rules. At the same time, pragmatic-reasoning schemata apply to broad classes of situations—for example, any situation involving permission. Thus the schemata are more widely usable than memories of specific experiences would be.

REASONING SCHEMATA AND THE FOUR-CARD PROBLEM

How does all of this help in understanding the four-card problem? Note that the standard version of this problem contains no practical or meaningful relations: The rule of "if a vowel, then an even number" is an arbitrary rule. The problem is therefore unlikely to invoke a pragmatic-reasoning schema. This leaves subjects at a loss, since these schemata usually play a pivotal role in their deductive thinking. That is, for most subjects, the rules of formal logic are simply not available. Thus, with their primary reasoning strategy not in play, no wonder subjects do poorly on this task.

On this view, we should be able to improve performance on the four-card task simply by altering the problem so that it will trigger a pragmatic-reasoning schema. Then subjects will be able to employ their usual means of reasoning, and so should perform quite well. To test this prediction, Cheng and Holyoak (1985) gave subjects several versions of the basic four-card problem. For example, subjects were given the version of the problem illustrated in Figure 14–5; subjects' task was to decide which cards to turn over to test the rule "If the form says ENTERING on one side, then the other side includes cholera among the list of diseases." So far, this resembles the standard four-card problem, with a seemingly arbitrary rule.

For half of the subjects, the cholera problem was given with no further rationale. The prediction here is that no schema is likely to be invoked by this problem, and so performance should be quite poor. The other half of the subjects, however, were given a rationale for this problem designed to trigger the permission schema. These subjects were told that the cards listed diseases against which airline passengers had been inoculated. In

| ENTERING | TRANSIT | CHOLERA | OTHER |

FIGURE 14–5.   *The Role of a "Rationale" in the Four-Card Problem.* Subjects were asked which cards they would need to turn over to find out if this rule is true: *If the form says ENTERING on one side, then the other side includes cholera among the list of diseases.* Subjects perform well on this problem if they are provided with a rationale; otherwise they perform poorly.

addition, they were told that cholera inoculation was required of all passengers seeking to enter the country. These subjects were given the same rule as stated above, but now the rule can be understood in permission terms, something like "If a passenger wishes to enter the country, he or she must first receive a cholera inoculation." With this rationale in view, the problem should trigger a schema, and so subjects should perform quite well.

Subjects were also given the envelope version of the problem, with the rule: "If an envelope is sealed, then it must have the higher-value stamp." Half of the subjects were given no rationale; half were told that first-class mail was always sealed, and that the post office charged a higher rate for first-class mail. Finally, as it turns out, half of the subjects in this study were students living in Michigan; half were students living in Hong Kong. (We will see the relevance of this in a moment.)

As can be seen in Figure 14–6, subjects did rather well with the rationale versions of these problems, averaging about 85–90% correct. Without rationale, subjects did quite poorly (about 60%). The figure shows one exception to this pattern: Subjects run in Hong Kong did quite well with the envelope problem, even when no rationale was provided by the experimenters. This result is not difficult to understand: Residents of Hong Kong were familiar with an actual postal rule similar to the one described within the experiment. Thus these subjects had no trouble coming up with the rationale on their own—the problem involved a familiar case. In essence, these subjects were in the rationale group, although the rationale was supplied by the subjects themselves, not the experimenters.

If subjects were reasoning about these problems by use of logical rules, then we should have observed equivalent performance in all conditions. In terms of their form, all versions of the problem are identical, involving inferences about an "if–then" rule. This clearly is not the pattern we observe in Figure 14–6.

If subjects were reasoning about these problems by reflecting on their own concrete experiences, then we should have observed low levels of

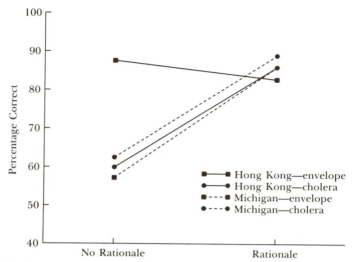

FIGURE 14–6. *Logical Reasoning When a Rationale Is Provided.* Subjects were tested with the "envelope" problem (Figure 14–4) and the "cholera" problem (Figure 14–5). When a rationale was provided, subjects performed well with both problems. When no rationale was provided, only the Hong Kong subjects working on the envelope problem did well. These subjects, familiar with the envelope rule, could provide a rationale for themselves. (After Cheng & Holyoak, 1985.)

performance with all versions of the problem except the Hong Kong–envelope condition. This condition presented a familiar problem to subjects; all other conditions presented totally unfamiliar problems. Again, this is not the pattern we observe. Performance is good in the Hong Kong envelope condition, but it is equally good in several other conditions.

If, finally, subjects were reasoning by using pragmatic schemata, then we should expect good performance when the schemata are called into play and poor performance without the schemata. In this case, we predict high performance either with a concretely familiar case or with a case accompanied by a rationale triggering a specific schema. This is, of course, exactly what the data show.

Memory and Decision-making: Conclusions

In most laboratory studies of memory, we divorce memory from the context of other mental events. We ask subjects to remember purely for the sake of reporting the remembered information; we typically do not ask them to do anything with the remembered information beyond taking some sort of memory test. In contrast, remembering in our day-to-day lives is often embedded in a rich web of other activities. When we reach a conclusion, or make a decision, we may not even notice that we are drawing on remembered information. The retrieval of information is done tacitly; the remembered information is immediately put to use in evaluating alternatives, assessing hypotheses, and so on.

If our theories of memory are good and useful theories, then they should tell us something about remembering in this richer context— remembering in the context of using the remembered information, not just reporting it. As we have seen in this chapter, our theories of memory meet this challenge rather well. We have seen that reasoning employs an availability heuristic; in examining this availability, we immediately meet standard phenomena of remembering. In this way, how we remember seems to shape how we reason. Likewise, many judgments seem influenced by a representativeness strategy, in which we assume resemblance between properties of a category and properties of an instance. This also meshes with our earlier discussion, insofar as a version of this heuristic played a key role in our description of concepts and generic knowledge. Covariation detection likewise seems to hinge on availability—in particular, on availability as determined by consistency between the data being considered and one's schemata. The importance of schemata also came up in our understanding of when subjects do and do not pay attention to base-rate information, and in our understanding of how subjects approach problems involving deduction.

At the same time, our survey in this chapter has also pointed toward a rather unsettling conclusion. We have seen many places in which our strategies of reasoning may, in fact, lead us astray, both in making day-to-day decisions about restaurant choices or about how to interpret a friend's actions and also in much more serious domains, such as cancer diagnosis. The problem is not that we use poor reasoning or employ unwise strategies. As we have seen, the choice of strategies is often dictated by demands of cognitive economy; reasoning is often done well, but is unwittingly based on incomplete or biased information.

For the moment, it is not clear what defense to offer against these potential reasoning errors. Several psychologists are exploring educational programs that might improve reasoning (e.g., Baron, 1988; Baron & Sternberg, 1987); it remains to be seen how broadly effective these will be. At the present time, our best hope may lie in publicizing the potential problems in reasoning, with chapters like this one. (See also volumes by Nisbett & Ross, 1980, and by Dawes, 1988, which are considerably more elaborate than the present chapter.) Clearly there is a hope here that forewarned is forearmed!

Summary

Much of the remembering we do is in the service of other intellectual tasks, like making decisions and reaching conclusions. How are these processes influenced by the functioning of memory? Much evidence indicates that human reasoning relies on a number of "heuristic" strategies. One such strategy is the availability heuristic: We rely on the information that comes quickly and easily to mind, rather than doing time-consuming and effortful searches of memory. For example, in judging how common or typical an event is, we do a quick search of memory; if examples of the event come quickly to mind, we conclude that the event is one that is frequently encountered.

As we have seen, this strategy can lead us astray because availability in memory does not always accurately reflect frequency of occurrence in our world. We discussed several factors that bias availability, all of them rooted in the memory theory of previous chapters. For example, state-dependency effects can influence memory availability, potentially creating a bias in the information available for making decisions and drawing conclusions.

Cases in which knowledge seems not to influence behavior can also be understood in these terms. The relevant knowledge is in memory, but is it not retrieved in response to the situation one is in. Thus the relevant knowledge, not readily available, does not influence one's understanding of the situation.

Another commonly used reasoning strategy is the representativeness heuristic. This heuristic centers on an assumption commonly made by subjects that categories are relatively homogeneous. This leads subjects to draw conclusions about the entire category based on only a few data points; it also makes subjects expect properties associated with the category to appear in all individuals in that category. This strategy is a more general version of a strategy we met in Chapter 10, in our discussion of concepts. That is, when subjects categorize according to prototypes, they are using a specific version of the representativeness strategy.

The representativeness heuristic can be demonstrated in many ways. One is the "gambler's fallacy," in which people expect properties of an entire population to emerge even if we look at only a small number of individuals from that population. Another is subjects' willingness to draw conclusions about a category based on a small sample of evidence.

A different skill of reasoning is the ability to assess covariation among the events and stimuli we encounter. Subjects are vulnerable to "illusions" of covariation, seeing covariation when there is none. These illusions seem to occur when subjects have prior expectations about the data before evaluating the data. If subjects have no expectations about the data, detection of covariation seems quite accurate. As we have seen, this contrast between "data-based" and "theory-based" evaluations of covariation is detectable both in humans and in animals: In both cases, "data-based" evaluations of covariation seem accurate, but "theory-based" evaluations are often incorrect.

We explored the possibility that illusions about covariation reflect, in part, another availability effect. Subjects have a "confirmation bias," that is, a tendency to attend to and to remember evidence that confirms their views, rather than evidence that challenges their views. This bias is to some extent inevitable, given the role of schemata in remembering. Given the confirmation bias, information that is available to someone judging covariation is likely to be biased if the person has prior expectations about the covariation. In this case, the person may draw a reasonable conclusion about covariation from a lopsided sample of evidence drawn from memory.

In evaluating evidence, one needs to consider both diagnostic information and base rates. Evidence indicates that subjects do take base rates into account if no other information is available. Once other information is provided, subjects largely ignore the base rates. If subjects are given diagnostic information, this information is used. However, if subjects are given both diagnostic and irrelevant information, the irrelevant information is not ignored; it instead dilutes the diagnostic information.

Finally, we examined how well subjects perform in tasks designed to draw on deductive reasoning. In one such task, the four-card problem, subjects perform at extremely low levels. With minor variations on this task, however, subjects' performance is much better. We examined one hypothesis concerning this pattern of results, namely, the hypothesis that subjects solve these problems with "pragmatic-reasoning schemata." These schemata reflect subjects' knowledge about classes of familiar events, defined in terms of a goal. Reasoning schemata include, for example, a schema about cause-and-effect relations, another about actions requiring permission, and another about obligations.

Pragmatic-reasoning schemata include rules that will allow certain inferences, and in this way these schemata resemble a system of logic. At the same time, pragmatic-reasoning schemata are specifically defined around certain pragmatic situations, and so are much more concrete than the laws of logic. Evidence indicates that subjects will perform well on reasoning problems only if the problems elicit a pragmatic-reasoning schema.

References

Abelson, R. P. (1981). Psychological status of the script concept. *American Psychologist, 36,* 715–729.

Abramson, L. Y., Seligman, M. E. P., & Teasdale, J. (1978). Learned helplessness in humans: Critique and reformulation. *Journal of Abnormal Psychology, 87,* 49–74.

Ackley, D. H., Hinton, G. E., & Sejnowski, T. J. (1985). A learning algorithm for Boltzmann machines. *Cognitive Science, 9,* 147–169.

Ainslie, G. (1975). Specious reward: A behavioral theory of impulsiveness and impulse control. *Psychological Bulletin, 82,* 485–489.

Ainslie, G., & Herrnstein, R. J. (1981). Preference reversal and delayed reinforcement. *Animal Learning and Behavior, 9,* 476–482.

Alba, J. W., Alexander, S. G., Hasher, L., & Caniglia, K. (1981). The role of context in the encoding of information. *Journal of Experimental Psychology: Human Learning and Memory, 7,* 283–292.

Alba, J. W., & Hasher, L. (1983). Is memory schematic? *Psychological Bulletin, 93,* 203–231.

Alexander, M. P., & Albert, M. L. (1983). The anatomical basis of visual agnosia. In A. Kertesz (Ed.), *Localization in neuropsychology.* New York: Academic Press.

Allan, L. G., & Jenkins, H. M. (1980). The judgment of contingency and the nature of the response alternatives. *Canadian Journal of Psychology, 34,* 1–11.

Allison, J. (1983). *Behavioral economics.* New York: Praeger.

Alloy, L. B., & Abramson, L. Y. (1979). Judgment of contingency in depressed and non-depressed students: Sadder but wiser? *Journal of Experimental Psychology: General, 108,* 441–485.

Alloy, L. B., & Seligman, M. E. P. (1979). On the cognitive components of learned helplessness and depression. In G. H. Bower (Ed.), *Psychology of learning and motivation* (Vol. 13). New York: Academic Press.

Alloy, L. B., & Tabachnik, N. (1984). Assessment of covariation by humans and animals: The joint influence of prior expectations and current situational information. *Psychological Review, 91,* 112–149.

Amsel, A. (1962). Frustrative non-reward in partial reinforcement and discrimination learning. *Psychological Review, 69,* 306–328.

Amsel, A. (1967). Partial reinforcement effects on vigor and persistence. In K. W. Spence & J. T. Spence (Eds.), *The psychology of learning and motivation* (Vol. 1). New York: Academic Press.

Anderson, D. C., O'Farrell, T., Formica, R., & Caponegri, V. (1969). Preconditioning CS exposure: Variation in the place of conditioning and presentation. *Psychonomic Science, 15,* 54–55.

Anderson, J. R. (1974). Verbatim and propositional representation of sentences in immediate and long-term memory. *Journal of Verbal Learning and Verbal Behavior, 13,* 149–162.

Anderson, J. R. (1976). *Language, memory, and thought.* Hillsdale, N.J.: Lawrence Erlbaum Associates.

Anderson, J. R. (1980). *Cognitive psychology and its implications.* San Francisco: W. H. Freeman.

Anderson, J. R. (1983). *The architecture of cognition.* Cambridge, Mass.: Harvard University Press.

Anderson, J. R. (1985). *Cognitive psychology and its implications,* 2nd ed. New York: W. H. Freeman.

Anderson, J. R., & Bower, G. H. (1972). Recognition and retrieval processes in free recall. *Psychological Review, 79,* 97–123.

Anderson, J. R., & Bower, G. H. (1973). *Human associative memory.* Washington, D.C.: Winston & Sons.

Anderson, J. R., & Bower, G. H. (1974). *Human associative memory.* New York: Hemisphere Publishing.

Anderson, R. C., & Pichert, J. (1978). Recall of previously unrecallable information following a shift in perspective. *Journal of Verbal Learning and Verbal Behavior, 17,* 1–12.

Anger, D. (1963). The role of temporal discrimination in the reinforcement of Sidman avoidance behavior. *Journal of the Experimental Analysis of Behavior, 6,* 477–506.

Annau, Z., & Kamin, L. J. (1961). The conditioned emotional response as a function of the intensity of the US. *Journal of Comparative and Physiological Psychology, 54,* 428–432.

Arkes, H. R., & Harkness, A. R. (1985). Estimates of contingency between two dichotomous variables. *Journal of Experimental Psychology: General, 112,* 117–135.

Armstrong, S. L., Gleitman, L. R., & Gleitman, H. (1983). What some concepts might not be. *Cognition, 13,* 263–308.

Atkinson, R. C., & Juola, J. F. (1974). Search and decision processes in recognition memory. In D. H. Krantz, R. C. Atkinson, & P. Suppes (Eds.), *Contemporary developments in mathematical psychology.* San Francisco: W. H. Freeman.

Atkinson, R. C., & Shiffrin, R. M. (1968). Human memory: A proposed system and its control processes. In K. W. Spence & J. T. Spence (Eds.), *The psychology of learning and motivation* (Vol. 2), pp. 89–105. New York: Academic Press.

Atthowe, J. M., & Krasner, L. (1968). A preliminary report on the application of contingent reinforcement procedures (token economy) in a "chronic" psychiatric ward. *Journal of Abnormal Psychology, 73,* 37–43.

Auge, R. J. (1974). Context, observing behavior, and conditioned reinforcement. *Journal of the Experimental Analysis of Behavior, 22,* 525–533.

Averbach, E., & Coriell, A. S. (1961). Short-term memory in vision. *Bell System Technical Journal, 40,* 309–328.

Ayllon, T., & Azrin, N. H. (1968). *The token economy: A motivational system for therapy and rehabilitation.* New York: Appleton-Century-Crofts.

Baddeley, A. D. (1963). A Zeigarnik-like effect in the recall of anagram solutions. *Quarterly Journal of Experimental Psychology, 15,* 63–64.

Baddeley, A. D. (1966a). The influence of acoustic and semantic similarity on long-term memory for word sequences. *Quarterly Journal of Experimental Psychology, 18,* 302–309.

Baddeley, A. D. (1966b). Short-term memory for word sequences as a function of acoustic, semantic and formal similarity. *Quarterly Journal of Experimental Psychology, 18,* 362–365.

Baddeley, A. D. (1976). *The psychology of memory.* New York: Basic Books.

Baddeley, A. D. (1978). The trouble with "levels": A reexamination of Craik and Lockhart's framework for memory research. *Psychological Review, 85,* 139–152.

Baddeley, A. D. (1982a). *Your memory: A user's guide.* New York: MacMillan.

Baddeley, A. D. (1982b). Domains of recollection. *Psychological Review, 89,* 708–729.

Baddeley, A. D. (1984). The fractionation of human memory. *Psychological Medicine, 14,* 259–264.

Baddeley, A. D. (1986). *Working memory.* Oxford: Clarendon Press.

Baddeley, A. D., & Dale, H. C. A. (1966). The effect of semantic similarity on retroactive interference in long- and short-term memory. *Journal of Verbal Learning and Verbal Behavior, 5,* 417–420.

Baddeley, A. D., & Hitch, G. J. (1974). Working memory. In G. Bower (Ed.), *Recent advances in learning and motivation* (Vol. 8). New York: Academic Press.

Baddeley, A. D., & Hitch, G. J. (1977). Recency re-examined. In S. Dornic (Ed.), *Attention and performance* (Vol. 6), pp. 646–667. Hillsdale, N.J.: Erlbaum.

Baddeley, A. D., & Lieberman, K. (1980). Spatial working memory. In R. Nickerson (Ed.), *Attention and performance* (Vol. 8), pp. 521–539. Hillsdale, N.J.: Erlbaum.

Baddeley, A. D., Thomson, N., & Buchanan, M. (1975). Word length and the structure of short-term memory. *Journal of Verbal Learning and Verbal Behavior, 14,* 575–589.

Bahrick, H. P. (1984). Semantic memory content in permastore: 50 years of memory for Spanish learned in school. *Journal of Experimental Psychology: General, 113,* 1–29.

Bahrick, H. P., Bahrick, P. O., & Wittlinger, R. P. (1975). Fifty years of memory for names and faces: A cross-sectional approach. *Journal of Experimental Psychology: General, 104,* 54–75.

Bahrick, H. P., & Boucher, B. (1968). Retention of visual and verbal codes of the same stimuli. *Journal of Experimental Psychology, 78,* 417–422.

Bahrick, H. P., Fitts, P. M., & Rankin, R. E. (1952). Effect of incentives upon reactions to peripheral stimuli. *Journal of Experimental Psychology, 44,* 400–406.

Baker, A. G. (1976). Learned irrelevance and learned helplessness: Rats learn that stimuli, reinforcers and responses are uncorrelated. *Journal of Experimental Psychology: Animal Behavior Processes, 2,* 130–141.

Baker, A. G., & Mackintosh, N. J. (1977). Excitatory and inhibitory conditioning following uncorrelated presentations of CS and US. *Animal Learning and Behavior, 5,* 315–319.

Baker, A. G., & Mackintosh, N. J. (1979). Pre-exposure to the CS alone, US alone or CS and US uncorrelated: Latent inhibition, blocking by context, or learned irrelevance? *Learning and Motivation, 10,* 278–294.

Baker, L. M., Best, M. R., & Domjan, M. (Eds.) (1977). *Learning mechanisms in food selection.* Waco, Texas: Baylor University Press.

Baker, T. B., & Tiffany, S. T. (1985). Morphine tolerance as habituation. *Psychological Review, 92,* 78–108.

Balsam, P. D., & Tomie, A. (Eds.) (1985). *Context and learning.* Hillsdale, N.J.: Erlbaum.

Banks, W. P. (1977). Encoding and processing of symbolic information in comparative judgements. In G. H. Bower (Ed.), *The psychology of learning and motivation.* New York: Academic Press.

Banks, W. P., & Flora, J. (1977). Semantic and perceptual processes in symbolic comparisons. *Journal of Experimental Psychology: Human Perception and Performance, 3,* 278–290.

Banks, W. P., Thompson, S., Henry, G., & Weissmann, T. (1986). Mental models of physiological function in health and illness. Presentation at the 27th annual meeting of the Psychonomic Society, New Orleans.

Baron, J. (1977). Mechanisms for pronouncing printed words: Use and acquisition. In S. J. Samuels (Ed.), *Basic processes in reading: Perception and comprehension.* Hillsdale, N.J.: Erlbaum.

Baron, J. (1988). *Thinking and reasoning.* Cambridge: Cambridge University Press.

Baron, J. B., & Sternberg, R. J. (1987). *Teaching thinking skills: Theory and practice.* New York: W. H. Freeman.

Barsalou, L. W. (1983). Ad hoc categories. *Memory and Cognition, 11,* 211–227.

Barsalou, L. W. (1985). Ideals, central tendency, and frequency of instantiation. *Journal of Experimental Psychology: Learning, Memory, and Cognition, 11,* 629–654.

Barsalou, L. W. (1987). The instability of graded structure: Implications for the nature of concepts. In U. Neisser (Ed.), *Concepts and conceptual development.* Cambridge: Cambridge University Press.

Barsalou, L. W. (1988). The content and organization of autobiographical memories. In U. Neisser & E. Winograd (Eds.), *Remembering reconsidered.* Cambridge: Cambridge University Press.

Barsalou, L. W., & Sewell, D. R. (1984) *Constructing representations of categories from different points of view.* Emory Cognition Project Report #2, Emory University, Atlanta.

Barsalou, L. W., & Sewell, D. R. (1985). Contrasting the representation of scripts and categories. *Journal of Memory and Language, 24,* 646–665.

Bartlett, F. C. (1932). *Remembering: A study in experimental and social psychology.* Cambridge: Cambridge University Press.

Bartlett, J. C., Till, R. E., & Levy, J. C. (1980). Retrieval characteristics of complex pictures: Effects of verbal encoding. *Journal of Verbal Learning and Verbal Behavior, 19,* 430–449.

Bartz, W. H. (1976). Rehearsal and retrieval processes in recall and recognition. *Bulletin of the Psychonomic Society, 8,* 258.

Bates, E., Masling, M., & Kintsch, W. (1978). Recognition memory for aspects of dialogue. *Journal of Experimental Psychology: Human Learning and Memory, 4,* 187–197.

Bateson, G. (1958). *Naven.* Stanford: Stanford University Press.

Batson, J. D., & Best, M. R. (1981). Single element assessment of conditioned inhibition. *Bulletin of the Psychonomic Society, 18,* 328–330.

Baum, M. (1969). Extinction of avoidance response following response prevention: Some parametric investigations. *Canadian Journal of Psychology, 23,* 1–10.

Baum, M. (1970). Extinction of avoidance responses through response prevention (flooding). *Psychological Bulletin, 74,* 276–284.

Baum, W. M. (1975). Time allocation in human vigilance. *Journal of the Experimental Analysis of Behavior, 23,* 43–53.

Baum, W. M. (1981). Optimization and the matching law as accounts of instrumental behavior. *Journal of the Experimental Analysis of Behavior, 36,* 387–403.

Beaman, A., Barnes, J., Klentz, B., & McQuirk, B. (1978). Increasing helping rates through information dissemination: Teaching pays. *Personality and Social Psychology Bulletin, 4,* 406–411.

Beatty, W. W., & Shavalia, D. A. (1980). Rat spatial memory: Resistance to retroactive interference at long retention intervals. *Animal Learning and Behavior, 8,* 550–552.

Bedford, J., & Anger, D. (1968). Flight as an avoidance response in pigeons. Paper presented to the Psychonomic Society, St. Louis.

Begg, I., & Wickelgren, W. A. (1974). Retention functions for syntactic and lexical vs. semantic information in sentence recognition memory. *Memory and Cognition, 2,* 353–359.

Belli, R. F. (1989). Influences of misleading postevent information: Misinformation interference and acceptance. *Journal of Experimental Psychology: General, 118,* 72–85.

Benedict, J. O., & Ayres, J. J. B. (1972). Factors affecting conditioning in the truly random control procedure. *Journal of Comparative and Physiological Psychology, 78,* 323–330.

Bermant, G., & Starr, M. (1972). Telling people what they are likely to do: Three experiments. In *Proceedings of the 80th annual convention of the American Psychological Association,* pp. 171–172. Washington, D.C.: American Psychological Association.

Bernstein, I. L. (1978). Learned taste aversions in children receiving chemotherapy. *Science, 200,* 1302–1303.

Bernstein, I. L., & Webster, M. M. (1980). Learned taste aversions in humans. *Physiology and Behavior, 25,* 363–366.

Best, M. R. (1975). Conditioned and latent inhibition in taste-aversion learning: Clarifying the role of learned safety. *Journal of Experimental Psychology: Animal Behavior Processes, 1,* 97–113.

Best, P. J., Best, M. R., & Henggeler, S. (1977). The contribution of environmental non-ingestive cues in conditioning with aversive internal consequences. In L. M. Baker, M. R. Best, & M. Domjan (Eds.), *Learning mechanisms in food selection.* Waco, Texas: Baylor University Press.

Bickman, L. (1972). Social influence and diffusion in responsibility in an emergency. *Journal of Experimental and Social Psychology, 8,* 438–445.

Bickman, L. (1975). Bystander intervention in a crime: The effect of a mass-media campaign. *Journal of Applied Social Psychology, 5,* 296–302.

Bjork, R. A., & Whitten, W. B. (1974). Recency-sensitive retrieval processes. *Cognitive Psychology, 6,* 173–189.

Blaney, P. H. (1986). Affect and memory: A review. *Psychological Bulletin, 99,* 229–246.

Blaxton, T. A. (1989). Investigating dissociations among memory measures: Support for a transfer-appropriate processing framework. *Journal of Experimental Psychology: Learning, Memory, and Cognition, 15,* 657–688.

Bliss, D. K., Sledjeski, M., & Leiman, A. (1971). State dependent choice behavior in the rhesus monkey. *Neuropsychologia, 9,* 51–59.

Bobrow, S., & Bower, G. H. (1969). Comprehension and recall of sentences. *Journal of Experimental Psychology, 80,* 455–461.

Bolles, R. C. (1970). Species-specific defense reactions and avoidance learning. *Psychological Review, 77,* 32–48.

Bolles, R. C. (1985). A cognitive, nonassociative view of inhibition. In R. R. Miller & N. E. Spear (Eds.), *Information processing in animals: Conditioned inhibition.* Hillsdale, N.J.: Erlbaum.

Bolles, R. C., Moot, S. A., & Nelson, K. (1976). Note on the invariance of response latency in shuttlebox avoidance learning. *Learning and Motivation, 7,* 108–116.

Borges, J. L. (1964). *Labyrinths.* New York: New Directions.

Bornstein, B. (1963). Prosopagnosia. In L. Halpern (Ed.), *Problems of dynamic neurology.* Jerusalem: Hadassah Medical Organization.

Bornstein, B., Sroka, H., & Munitz, H. (1969). Prosopagnosia with animal face agnosia. *Cortex, 5,* 164–169.

Bottjer, S. W. (1982). Conditioned approach and withdrawal behavior in pigeons: Effects of a novel extraneous stimulus during acquisition and extinction. *Learning and Motivation, 13,* 44–67.

Bousfield, W. A. (1953). The occurrence of clustering in the recall of randomly arranged associates. *Journal of General Psychology, 49,* 229–240.

Bouton, M. E. (1984). Differential effect of context in the inflation and reinstatement paradigms. *Journal of Experimental Psychology: Animal Behavior Processes, 10,* 56–74.

Bower, G. H. (1970). Analysis of a mnemonic device. *American Scientist, 58,* 496–510.

Bower, G. H. (1972). Mental imagery and associative learning. In L. W. Gregg (Ed.), *Cognition in learning and memory.* New York: Wiley.

Bower, G. H. (1981). Mood and memory. *American Psychologist, 36,* 129–148.

Bower, G. H., Black, J. B., & Turner, T. J. (1979). Scripts in memory for text. *Cognitive Psychology, 11,* 177–220.

Bower, G. H., Clark, M. C., Lesgold, A. M., & Winzenz, D. (1969). Hierarchical retrieval schemes in recall of categorized word lists. *Journal of Verbal Learning and Verbal Behavior, 8,* 323–343.

Bower, G. H., Gilligan, S. G., & Monteiro, K. P. (1981). Selectivity of learning caused by affective states. *Journal of Experimental Psychology: General, 83,* 421–430.

Bower, G. H., & Karlin, M. B. (1974). Depth of processing pictures of faces and recognition memory. *Journal of Experimental Psychology, 103,* 751–757.

Bower, G. H., Karlin, M. B., & Dueck, A. (1975). Comprehension and memory for pictures. *Memory and Cognition, 3,* 216–220.

Bower, G., & Mayer, J. (1985). Failure to replicate mood-dependent retrieval. *Bulletin of the Psychonomic Society, 23,* 39–42.

Bower, G. H., McLean, J., & Meachem, J. (1966). Value of knowing when reinforcement is due. *Journal of Comparative and Physiological Psychology, 62,* 184–192.

Bower, G. H., & Reitman, J. S. (1972). Mnemonic elaboration in multilist learning. *Journal of Verbal Learning and Verbal Behavior, 11,* 478–485.

Bower, G. H., & Winzenz, D. (1970). Comparison of associative learning strategies. *Psychonomic Science, 20,* 119–120.

Braine, M. D. S. (1978). On the relation between the natural logic of reasoning and standard logic. *Psychological Review, 85,* 1–21.

Braine, M. D. S., Reiser, B. J., & Rumain, B. (1984). Some empirical justification for a theory of natural propositional logic. In G. H. Bower (Ed.), *The psychology of learning and motivation.* New York: Academic Press.

Bransford, J. D. (1979). *Human cognition: Learning, understanding and remembering.* Belmont, Calif.: Wadsworth Publishing Co.

Bransford, J. D., Barclay, J. R., & Franks, J. J. (1972). Sentence memory: A constructive versus interpretive approach. *Cognitive Psychology, 3,* 193–209.

Bransford, J. D., & Franks, J. J. (1971). The abstraction of linguistic ideas. *Cognitive Psychology, 2,* 331–350.

Bransford, J. D., Franks, J. J., Morris, C. D., & Stein, B. S. (1979). Some general constraints on learning and memory research. In L. S. Cermak & F. I. M. Craik (Eds.), *Levels of processing in human memory.* Hillsdale, N.J.: Erlbaum.

Bransford, J. D., & Johnson, M. K. (1972). Contextual prerequisites for understanding: Some investigations of comprehension and recall. *Journal of Verbal Learning and Verbal Behavior, 11,* 717–726.

Bransford, J. D., & Johnson, M. K. (1973). Considerations of some problems of comprehension. In W. G. Chase (Ed.), *Visual information processing.* New York: Academic Press.

Brewer, W. F. (1977). Memory for the pragmatic implications of sentences. *Memory and Cognition, 5,* 673–678.

Brewer, W. F. (1988). Memory for randomly sampled autobiographical events. In U. Neisser & E. W. Winograd (Eds.), *Remembering reconsidered.* Cambridge: Cambridge University Press.

Brewer, W. F., & Treyens, J. C. (1981). Role of schemata in memory for places. *Cognitive Psychology, 13,* 207–230.

Brimer, C. J. (1970). Inhibition and disinhibition of an operant response as a function of the amount and type of prior training. *Psychonomic Science, 21,* 191–192.

Broadbent, D. E. (1958). *Perception and communication.* London: Pergamon Press.

Brogden, W. J. (1939). Sensory pre-conditioning. *Journal of Experimental Psychology, 25,* 323–332.

Brooks, L. R. (1978). Non-analytic concept formation and memory for instances. In E. Rosch & B. Lloyd (Eds.), *Cognition and categorization.* Hillsdale, N.J.: Erlbaum.

Brooks, L. R. (1987). Decentralized control of categorization: The role of prior processing episodes. In U. Neisser (Ed.), *Concepts and conceptual development.* Cambridge: Cambridge University Press.

Brown, A. L. (1979). Theories of memory and the problems of development: Activity, growth, and knowledge. In L. S. Cermak & F. I. M. Craik (Eds.), *Levels of processing in human memory.* Hillsdale, N.J.: Erlbaum.

Brown, A. S., & Murphy, D. R. (1989). Cryptomnesia: Delineating inadvertent plagiarism. *Journal of Experimental Psychology: Learning, Memory and Cognition, 15,* 432–441.

Brown, E., Deffenbacher, K., & Sturgill, W. (1977). Memory for faces and the circumstances of encounter. *Journal of Applied Psychology, 62,* 311–318.

Brown, J. (1958). Some tests of the decay theory of immediate memory. *Quarterly Journal of Experimental Psychology, 10,* 12–21.

Brown, J. S., & Jacobs, A. (1949). The role of fear in the motivation and acquisition of responses. *Journal of Experimental Psychology, 39,* 747–759.

Brown, P., & Jenkins, H. M. (1968). Autoshaping of the pigeon's keypeck. *Journal of the Experimental Analysis of Behavior, 11,* 1–8.

Brown, R., & Kulik, J. (1977). Flashbulb memories. *Cognition, 5,* 73–99.

Brown, R., & Lenneberg, E. H. (1954). A study in language and cognition. *Journal of Abnormal and Social Psychology, 49,* 454–462.

Brown, R., & McNeill, D. (1966). The "tip of the tongue" phenomenon. *Journal of Verbal Learning and Verbal Behavior, 5,* 325–337.

Bruner, J. S. (1957). *Contemporary approaches to cognition.* Cambridge, Mass.: Harvard University Press.

Bruner, J. S. (1973). *Beyond the information given.* New York: W. W. Norton.

Bruner, J. S. (1986). *Actual minds, possible worlds.* Cambridge, Mass.: Harvard University Press.

Bruner, J. S., Goodnow, J., & Austin, G. (1956). *A study of thinking.* New York: Wiley.

Bruner, J. S., Matter, J., & Papanek, M. L. (1955). Breadth of learning as a function of drive level and mechanization. *Psychological Review, 42,* 1–10.

Bugelski, B. R. (1938). Extinction with and without sub-goal reinforcement. *Journal of Comparative Psychology, 26,* 121–134.

Burkhardt, P. E., & Ayres, J. J. B. (1978). CS and US duration effects in one-trial simultaneous fear conditioning as assessed by conditioned suppression of licking in rats. *Animal Learning and Behavior, 6,* 225–230.

Bursill, A. E. (1958). The restriction of peripheral vision during exposure to hot and humid conditions. *Quarterly Journal of Experimental Psychology, 10,* 123–129.

Buschke, H. (1977). Two-dimensional recall: Immediate identification of clusters in episodic and semantic memory. *Journal of Verbal Learning and Verbal Behavior, 16,* 201–215.

Calloway, E., & Stone, G. (1960). Re-evaluating the focus of attention. In L. Uhr & J. G. Miller (Eds.), *Drugs and behavior.* New York: Wiley.

Cannon, D. S., Best, M. R., Batson, J. D., & Feldman, M. (1983). Taste familiarity and apomorphine-induced taste aversions in humans. *Behaviour Research and Therapy, 21,* 669–673.

Carey, S. (1985). *Conceptual change in childhood.* Cambridge, Mass.: Bradford/MIT Press.

Carmichael, L. C., Hogan, H. P., & Walters, A. A. (1932). An experimental study of the effect of language on the reproduction of visually perceived form. *Journal of Experimental Psychology, 15,* 73–86.

Carpenter, P. A., & Eisenberg, P. (1978). Mental rotation and the frame of reference in blind and sighted individuals. *Perception and Psychophysics, 23,* 117–124.

Carter, D. E., & Werner, T. J. (1978). Complex learning and information processing by pigeons: A critical analysis. *Journal of the Experimental Analysis of Behavior, 29,* 565–601.

Casey, E. (1976). *Imagining: A phenomenological study.* Bloomington, Ind.: Indiana University Press.

Catania, A. C. (1963). Concurrent performances: A baseline for the study of reinforcement magnitude. *Journal of the Experimental Analysis of Behavior, 6,* 299–301.

Catania, A. C., & Reynolds, G. S. (1968). A quantitative analysis of the responding maintained by interval schedules of reinforcement. *Journal of the Experimental Analysis of Behavior, 11,* 327–383.

Chambers, D., & Reisberg, D. (1985). Can mental images be ambiguous? *Journal of Experimental Psychology: Human Perception and Performance, 11,* 317–328.

Chapman, L. J., & Chapman, J. (1971). Test results are what you think they are. *Psychology Today,* November, 18–22, 106–110.

Charniak, E. (1972). Toward a model of children's story comprehension. Unpublished doctoral dissertation, M. I. T.

Charniak, E., & McDermott, D. (1985). *Introduction to artificial intelligence.* Reading, Mass.: Addison-Wesley.

Charnov, E. L. (1976). Optimal foraging, the marginal value theorem. *Theoretical Population Biology, 9,* 129–136.

Chase, W. G., & Ericsson, K. A. (1978). Acquisition of a mnemonic system for digit span. Paper presented at the meeting of the Psychonomic Society, San Antonio, Texas.

Chase, W. G., & Ericsson, K. A. (1979). A mnemonic system for digit span: One year later. Paper presented at the meeting of the Psychonomic Society, Phoenix.

Chase, W. G., & Ericsson, K. A. (1982). Skill and working memory. In G. H. Bower (Ed.), *The psychology of learning and motivation.* New York: Academic Press.

Cheng, P. W., & Holyoak, K. J. (1985). Pragmatic reasoning schemas. *Cognitive Psychology, 17,* 391–416.

Cheng, P. W., Holyoak, K. J., Nisbett, R. E., & Oliver, L. M. (1986). Pragmatic versus syntatic approaches to training deductive reasoning. *Cognitive Psychology, 18,* 293–328.

Chi, M. T. H. (1976). Short-term memory limitations in children: Capacity or processing deficits? *Memory and Cognition, 4,* 559–572.

Christen, F., & Bjork, R. A. (1976). On updating the loci in the method of loci. Paper presented at the meeting of the Psychonomic Society, St. Louis.

Christianson, S.-A. (1984). The relationship between induced emotional arousal and amnesia. *Scandinavian Journal of Psychology, 25,* 147–160.

Christianson, S.-A. (1989). Flashbulb memories: Special, but not so special. *Memory and Cognition, 17,* 435–443.

Christianson, S.-A., & Loftus, E. (1987). Memory for traumatic events. *Applied Cognitive Psychology, 1,* 225–239.

Christianson, S.-A., Loftus, E., & Nilsson, L. (1987). Memory for emotional events. Paper presented at the annual meeting of the Psychonomic Society, Seattle.

Chung, S. H., & Herrnstein, R. J. (1967). Choice and delay of reinforcement. *Journal of the Experimental Analysis of Behavior, 10,* 67–74.

Churchland, P. M. (1984). *Matter and consciousness.* Cambridge, Mass.: M.I.T. Press.

Claparède, E. (1951). Reconnaissance et moiité. In D. Rapaport (Ed.), *Organization and pathology of thought.* New York: Columbia University Press.

Clark, M. S., Milberg, S., & Ross, J. (1983). Arousal cues arousal-related material in memory: Implications for understanding effects of mood on memory. *Journal of Verbal Learning and Verbal Behavior, 11,* 671–684.

Cofer, C. N., Bruce, D. R., & Reicher, G. M. (1966). Clustering in free recall as a function of certain methodological variations. *Journal of Experimental Psychology, 71,* 858–866.

Cohen, N. J. (1984). Preserved learning capacity in amnesia: Evidence for multiple memory systems. In L. R. Squire & N. Butters (Eds.), *Neuropsychology of memory.* New York: Guilford Press.

Cohen, N. J., McCloskey, M., & Wible, C. G. (1988). There is still no case for a flashbulb-memory mechanism: Reply to Schmidt and Bohannon. *Journal of Experimental Psychology: General, 117,* 336–338.

Cohen, N. J., & Squire, L. R. (1980). Preserved learning and retention of pattern analyzing skill in amnesics: Dissociation of knowing how and knowing that. *Science, 210,* 207–210.

Cohen, S. L., Calisto, G., & Lentz, B. E. (1979). Separating the reinforcing and discriminative properties of brief-stimulus presentations in second-order schedules. *Journal of the Experimental Analysis of Behavior, 32,* 149–156.

Collier, G. H. (1983). Life in a closed economy: The ecology of learning and motivation. In M. D. Zeiler & P. Harzem (Eds.), *Advances in the analysis of behavior.* Vol. 3: *Biological factors in learning.* Chichester, England: Wiley.

Collier, G. H., Hirsch, E., & Hamlin, P. H. (1972). The ecological determinants of reinforcement in the rat. *Physiology and Behavior, 9,* 705–716.

Collier, G. H., Johnson, D. F., Hill, W. L., & Kaufman, L. W. (1986). The economics of the law of effect. *Journal of the Experimental Analysis of Behavior, 46,* 113–136.

Collins, A. M., & Loftus, E. F. (1975). A spreading activation theory of semantic processing. *Psychological Review, 82,* 407–428.

Collins, A. M., & Quillian, M. R. (1969). Retrieval time from semantic memory. *Journal of Verbal Learning and Verbal Behavior, 8,* 240–247.

Colwill, R. M., & Rescorla, R. A. (1985a). Postconditioning devaluation of a reinforcer affects instrumental responding. *Journal of Experimental Psychology: Animal Behavior Processes, 11,* 120–132.

Colwill, R. M., & Rescorla, R. A. (1985b). Instrumental responding remains sensitive to reinforcer devaluation after extensive training. *Journal of Experimental Psychology: Animal Behavior Processes, 11,* 520–536.

Colwill, R. M., & Rescorla, R. A. (1986). Associative structures in instrumental learning. In G. H. Bower (Ed.), *The psychology of learning and motivation* (Vol. 20). New York: Academic Press.

Combs, B., & Slovic, P. (1979). Causes of death: Biased newspaper coverage and biased judgments. *Journalism Quarterly, 56,* 837–843, 849.

Conrad, C. (1972). Cognitive economy in semantic memory. *Journal of Experimental Psychology, 92,* 149–154.

Conrad, R. (1964). Acoustic confusion in immediate memory. *British Journal of Psychology, 55,* 75–84.

Conrad, R., & Hull, A. J. (1964). Information, acoustic confusion and memory span. *British Journal of Psychology, 55,* 429–432.

Cooper, L. A. & Shepard, R. N. (1973). Chronometric studies of the rotation of mental images. In W. G. Chase (Ed.), *Visual information processing.* New York: Academic Press.

Cornsweet, D. J. (1969). Use of cues in the visual periphery under conditions of arousal. *Journal of Experimental Psychology, 80,* 14–18.

Cowles, J. T. (1937). Food-tokens as incentive for learning by chimpanzees. *Comparative Psychology Monographs, 14,* No. 5.

Craik, F. I. M. (1977). Age differences in human memory. In J. E. Birren & K. W. Schaie (Eds.), *Handbook of the psychology of aging.* New York: Van Nostrand.

Craik, F. I. M., & Lockhart, R. S. (1972). Levels of processing: A framework for memory research. *Journal of Verbal Learning and Verbal Behavior, 11,* 671–684.

Craik, F. I. M., & Tulving, E. (1975). Depth of processing and the retention of words in episodic memory. *Journal of Experimental Psychology: General, 104,* 268–294.

Craik, F. I. M., & Watkins, M. J. (1973). The role of rehearsal in short-term memory. *Journal of Verbal Learning and Verbal Behavior, 12,* 599–607.

Crick, F. (1989). The recent excitement about neutral networks. *Nature, 337,* 129–132.

Crocker, J. (1981). Judgment of covariation of social perceivers. *Psychological Bulletin, 90,* 272–292.

Crowder, R. G. (1976). *Principles of learning and memory.* Hillsdale, N.J.: Erlbaum.

Crowder, R. G. (1982). *The psychology of reading.* New York: Oxford University Press.

Dale, H. C. A., & Baddeley, A. D. (1969). Acoustic similarity in long-term paired-associate learning. *Psychonomic Science, 16,* 209–211.

Damasio, A. R., Damasio, H., & Van Hoesen, G. W. (1982). Prosopagnosia: Anatomic basis and behavioral mechanisms. *Neurology, 32,* 331–341.

D'Amato, M. R. (1973). Delayed matching and short-term memory in monkeys. In G. H. Bower (Ed.), *The psychology of learning and motivation* (Vol. 7). New York: Academic Press.

D'Amato, M. R., & Salmon, D. P. (1982). Tune discrimination in monkeys *(Debus apella)* and in rats. *Animal Learning and Behavior, 10,* 126–134.

D'Andrade, R. (1982). Reason versus logic. Paper presented at the symposium on the Ecology of Cognition: Biological, Cultural, and Historical Perspectives, Greensboro, N.C.

DaPolito, F. J. (1966). Proactive effects with independent retrieval of competing responses. Unpublished doctoral dissertation, Indiana University, Bloomington.

Dark, V. J., & Loftus, G. R. (1976). The role of rehearsal in long-term memory performance. *Journal of Verbal Learning and Verbal Behavior, 15,* 479–490.

Darley, C. F., & Glass, A. L. (1975). Effects of rehearsal and serial list position on recall. *Journal of Experimental Psychology: Human Learning and Memory, 104,* 453–458.

Darley, J., & Batson, D. (1973). "From Jerusalem to Jericho": A study of situational and dispositional variables in helping behavior. *Journal of Personality and Social Psychology, 27,* 100–108.

Darley, J., & Latane, B. (1968). Bystander intervention in emergencies: Diffusion of responsibility. *Journal of Personality and Social Psychology, 10,* 202–214.

Darwin, C. (1859). *The origin of species.* P. Appleman (Ed.). New York: W. W. Norton, 1975.

Darwin, C. J., Turvey, M. T., & Crowder, R. G. (1972). An auditory analogue of the sperling partial report procedure: Evidence for brief auditory storage. *Cognitive Psychology, 3,* 255–267.

Davenport, D. G., & Olson, R. D. (1968). A reinterpretation of extinction in discriminated avoidance. *Psychonomic Science, 13,* 5–6.

Davis, G., Ellis, H., & Shepard, J. (1978). Face recognition accuracy as a function of mode of representation. *Journal of Applied Psychology, 63,* 180–187.

Dawes, R. M. (1988). *Rational choice in an uncertain world.* San Diego: Harcourt Brace Jovanovich.

de Villiers, P. A. (1974). The law of effect and avoidance: A quantitative relation between response rate and shock frequency reduction. *Journal of the Experimental Analysis of Behavior, 21,* 223–235.

de Villiers, P. A. (1977). Choice in concurrent schedules and a quantitative formulation of the law of effect. In W. K. Honig & J. E. R. Staddon (Eds.), *Handbook of operant behavior.* Englewood Cliffs, N.J.: Prentice-Hall.

Deese, J. (1960). Frequency of usage and number of words in free recall: The role of association. *Psychological Reports, 7,* 337–394.

Deese, J., & Kaufman, R. A. (1957). Serial effects in recall of unorganized and sequentially organized verbal material. *Journal of Experimental Psychology, 54,* 180–187.

Dempster, F. N. (1981). Memory span: Sources of individual and developmental differences. *Psychological Bulletin, 89,* 63–100.

Denny, M. R. (1971). Relaxation theory and experiments. In F. R. Brush (Ed.), *Aversive conditioning and learning.* New York: Academic Press.

Deutsch, R. (1974). Conditioned hypoglycemia: A mechanism for saccharin-induced sensitivity to insulin in the rat. *Journal of Comparative and Physiological Psychology, 86,* 350–358.

Diamond, R., & Carey, S. (1986). Why faces are and are not special: An effect of expertise. *Journal of Experimental Psychology: General, 115,* 107–117.

Dinsmoor, J. A. (1977). Escape, avoidance and punishment. Where do we stand? *Journal of the Experimental Analysis of Behavior, 28,* 83–95.

Dinsmoor, J. A. (1983). Observing and conditioned reinforcement. *Behavioral and Brain Sciences, 6,* 693–728.

Dinsmoor, J. A., Browne, M. P., & Lawrence, C. R. (1972). A test of the negative discriminative stimulus as a reinforcer of observing. *Journal of the Experimental Analysis of Behavior, 18,* 79–85.

Dinsmoor, J. A., Flint, G. A., Smith, R. F., & Viemeister, N. F. (1969). Differential reinforcing effects of stimuli associated with the presence or absence of a schedule of punishment. In D. P. Hendry (Ed.), *Conditioned reinforcement.* Homewood, Ill.: Dorsey Press.

Domjan, M. (1981). Ingestional aversion learning: Unique and general processes. In J. S. Rosenblatt, R. A. Hinde, C. Beer, & M. Busnel (Eds.), *Advances in the study of behavior* (Vol. 11). New York: Academic Press.

Domjan, M. (1983). Biological constraints on instrumental and classical conditioning: Implications for general process theory. In G. H. Bower (Ed.), *The Psychology of learning and motivation* (Vol. 17). New York: Academic Press.

Domjan, M., & Wilson, N. E. (1972). Specificity of cue to consequence in aversion learning in the rat. *Psychonomic Science, 26,* 143–145.

Dooling, D. J., & Christiaansen, R. E. (1977). Episodic and semantic aspects of memory for prose. *Journal of Experimental Psychology: Human Learning and Memory, 3,* 428–436.

Dooling, D. J., & Lachman, R. (1971). Effects of comprehension on retention of prose. *Journal of Experimental Psychology, 88,* 216–222.

Dreyfus, H. L. (1979). *What computers can't do,* rev. ed. New York: Harper Colophon Books.

Dudycha, G. J., & Dudycha, M. M. (1941). Childhood memories: A review of the literature. *Psychological Bulletin, 38,* 668–682.

Dywan, J., & Bowers K. (1983). The use of hypnosis to enhance recall. *Science, 222,* 184–185.

Easterbrook, J. A. (1959). The effect of emotion on cue utilization and the organization of behavior. *Psychological Review, 66,* 183–201.

Eddy, D. M. (1982). Probabilistic reasoning in clinical medicine: Problems and opportunities. In D. Kahneman, P. Slovic, & A. Tversky (Eds.), *Judgment under uncertainty: Heuristics and biases.* Cambridge: Cambridge University Press.

Egger, M. D., & Miller, N. E. (1962). Secondary reinforcement in rats as a function of information value and reliability of the stimulus. *Journal of Experimental Psychology, 64,* 97–104.

Egger, M. D., & Miller, N. E. (1963). When is a reward reinforcing? An experimental study of the information hypothesis. *Journal of Comparative and Physiological Psychology, 56,* 132–137.

Eich, E., & Metcalfe, J. (1989). Mood dependent memory for internal versus external events. *Journal of Experimental Psychology: Learning, Memory, and Cognition, 15,* 443–455.

Eich, J. E. (1980). The cue-dependent nature of state dependent retrieval. *Memory and Cognition, 8,* 157–173.

Eich, J. E., Weingartner, H., Stillman, R. C., & Gillin, J. C. (1975). State-dependent accessibility of retrieval cues in the retention of a categorized list. *Journal of Verbal Learning and Verbal Behavior, 14,* 408–417.

Eikelboom, R., & Stewart, J. (1982). Conditioning of drug-induced physiological responses. *Psychological Review, 89,* 507–528.

Einhorn, H. J., & Hogarth, R. M. (1978). Confidence in judgment: Persistence of the illusion of validity. *Psychological Review, 85,* 395–416.

Einstein, G. O., McDaniel, M. A., & Lackey, S. (1989). Bizarre imagery, interference, and distinctiveness. *Journal of Experimental Psychology: Learning, Memory, and Cognition, 15,* 137–146.

Ekstrand, B. R. (1967). Effect of sleep on memory. *Journal of Experimental Psychology, 75,* 64–72.

Ekstrand, B. R. (1972). To sleep, perchance to dream (about why we forget). In C. P. Duncan, L. Sechrest, & A. W. Melton (Eds.), *Human memory: Festschrift for Benton J. Underwood*, pp. 59–82. New York: Appleton-Century-Crofts.

Elias, C. S., & Perfetti, C. A. (1973). Encoding task and recognition memory: The importance of semantic encoding. *Journal of Experimental Psychology, 99*, 151–156.

Ellis, H. C. (1985). On the importance of mood intensity and encoding demands in memory: Commentary on Hasher, Rose, Zacks, Sanft and Doren. *Journal of Experimental Psychology: General, 114*, 392–395.

Ellis, N. C., & Henneley, R. A. (1980). A bilingual word-length effect: Implications for intelligence testing and the relative ease of mental calculation in Welsh and English. *British Journal of Psychology, 71*, 43–52.

Erdelyi, M. H. (1985). *Psychoanalysis*. New York: W. H. Freeman.

Erdelyi, M. H., & Becker, J. (1974). Hypermnesia for pictures: Incremental memory for pictures but not words in multiple recall trials. *Cognitive Psychology, 6*, 159–171.

Erdelyi, M. H., Buschke, H., & Finkelstein, S. (1977). Hypermnesia for Socratic stimuli: The growth of recall for an internally generated memory list abstracted from a series of riddles. *Memory and Cognition, 5*, 283–286.

Erdelyi, M. H., Finkelstein, S., Herrell, N., Miller, B., & Thomas, J. (1976). Coding modality vs. input modality in hypermnesia: Is a rose a rose a rose? *Cognition, 4*, 311–319.

Erdelyi, M. H., & Goldberg, B. (1979). Let's not sweep repression under the rug: Toward a cognitive psychology of repression. In J. F. Kihlstrom & F. J. Evans (Eds.), *Functional disorders of memory*. Hillsdale, N.J.: Erlbaum.

Erdelyi, M. H., & Kleinbard, J. (1978). Has Ebbinghaus decayed with time?: The growth of recall (hypermnesia) over days. *Journal of Experimental Psychology: Human Learning and Memory, 4*, 275–289.

Ericsson, K. A., Chase, W. G., & Faloon, S. (1980). Acquisition of a memory skill. *Science, 208*, 1181–1182.

Eriksen, C. W., & Pierce, J. (1968). Defense mechanisms. In E. Borgatta & W. Lambert (Eds.), *Handbook of personality theory and research*. Chicago: Rand McNally.

Estes, W. K. (1972). An associative basis for coding and organization in memory. In A. W. Melton & E. Martin (Eds.), *Coding processes in human memory*. Washington, D.C.: Winston.

Estes, W. K. (1973). Memory and conditioning. In F. J. McGuigan & D. B. Lumsden (Eds.), *Contemporary approaches to conditioning and learning*. Washington, D.C.: Winston.

Estes, W. K. (1976). Structural aspects of associative models for memory. In C. N. Cofer (Ed.), *The structure of human memory*. San Francisco: W. H. Freeman.

Estes, W. K., & Skinner, B. F. (1941). Some quantitative properties of anxiety. *Journal of Experimental Psychology, 29*, 390–400.

Eysenck, M. W. (1974). Age differences in incidental learning. *Developmental Psychology, 10*, 936–941.

Eysenck, M. W. (1982). *Attention and arousal: Cognition and performance*. New York: Springer-Verlag.

Fanselow, M. S., & Baackes, M. P. (1982). Conditioned fear-induced opiate analgesia on the formalin test: Evidence for two aversive motivational systems. *Learning and Motivation, 13*, 200–221.

Fantino, E. (1977). Conditioned reinforcement: Choice and information. In W. K. Honig & J. E. R. Staddon (Eds.), *Handbook of operant behavior*. Englewood Cliffs, N.J.: Prentice-Hall.

Fantino, E., & Abarca, N. (1985). Choice, optimal foraging, and the delay-reduction hypothesis. *Behavioral and Brain Sciences, 8,* 315–362.

Fantino, E., & Case, D.A. (1983). Human observing: Maintained by stimuli correlated with reinforcement but not extinction. *Journal of the Experimental Analysis of Behavior, 40,* 193–210.

Fantino, E., & Moore, J. (1980). Uncertainty reduction, conditioned reinforcement, and observing. *Journal of the Experimental Analysis of Behavior, 33,* 3–13.

Farah, M. (1985). Psychophysical evidence for a shared representational medium for mental images and percepts. *Journal of Experimental Psychology: General, 114,* 91–103.

Farah, M., & Smith, A. (1983). Perceptual interference and facilitation with auditory imagery. *Perception and Psychophysics, 33,* 475–478.

Felton, M., & Lyon, D. O. (1966). The post-reinforcement pause. *Journal of the Experimental Analysis of Behavior, 9,* 131–134.

Ferster, C. B., & Skinner, B. F. (1957). *Schedules of reinforcement.* New York: Appleton-Century-Crofts.

Fillmore, C. (1982). Towards a descriptive framework for spatial deixis. In R. J. Jarvella & W. Klein (Eds.), *Speech, place and action: Studies in deixis and related topics.* Chichester, England: Wiley.

Finke, R. A. (1980). Levels of equivalence in imagery and perception. *Psychological Review, 87,* 113–132.

Finke, R., Pinker, S., & Farah, M. (1989). Reinterpreting visual patterns in mental imagery. *Cognitive Science, 13,* 51–78.

Fischler, I. (1977a). Associative facilitation without expectancy in a lexical decision task. *Journal of Experimental Psychology: Human Perception and Performance, 3,* 18–26.

Fischler, I. (1977b). Semantic facilitation without association in a lexical decision task. *Memory and Cognition, 5,* 335–339.

Fischoff, B. (1977). Perceived informativeness of facts. *Journal of Experimental Psychology: Human Performance and Perception, 3,* 349–358.

Fisher, R. P., & Craik, F. I. M. (1977). The interaction between encoding and retrieval operations in cued recall. *Journal of Experimental Psychology: Human Learning and Memory, 3,* 701–711.

Fivush, R. (1988). The functions of event memory: Some comments on Nelson and Barsalou. In U. Neisser & E. Winograd (Eds.), *Remembering reconsidered.* Cambridge: Cambridge University Press.

Flanagan, O. J. (1984). *The science of the mind.* Cambridge, Mass.: M.I.T. Press.

Flexser, A. J., & Tulving, E. (1978). Retrieval independence in recognition and recall. *Psychological Review, 85,* 153–172.

Fodor, J. A. (1975). *The language of thought.* New York: Thomas Y. Crowell.

Fodor, J. A., & Pylyshyn, Z. W. (1988). Connectionism and cognitive architecture: A critical analysis. *Cognition, 28,* 3–71.

Foree, D., & LoLordo, V. M. (1975). Stimulus–reinforcer interactions in the pigeon: The role of electric shock and the avoidance contingency. *Journal of Experimental Psychology: Animal Behavior Processes, 104,* 39–46.

Fowler, H., Kleiman, M. C., & Lysle, D. T. (1985). Factors affecting the acquisition and extinction of conditioned inhibition suggest a "slave" process. In R.

R. Miller & N. E. Spear (Eds.), *Information processing in animals: Conditioned inhibition.* Hillsdale, N.J.: Erlbaum.

Fried, L. S., & Holyoak, K. J. (1984). Induction of category distributions: A framework for classification learning. *Journal of Experimental Psychology: Learning, Memory, and Cognition, 10,* 234–257.

Friedman, A. (1979). Framing pictures: The role of knowledge in automatized encoding and memory for gist. *Journal of Experimental Psychology: General, 108,* 316–355.

Friedman, A., & Bourne, L. E., Jr. (1976). Encoding the levels of information in pictures and words. *Journal of Experimental Psychology: General, 105,* 169–190.

Garb, J., & Stunkard, A. J. (1974). Taste aversions in man. *American Journal of Psychiatry, 131,* 1204–1207.

Garcia, J., & Koelling, R. A. (1966). The relation of cue to consequence in avoidance learning. *Psychonomic Science, 4,* 123–124.

Gemberling, G. A., & Domjan, M. (1982). Selective associations in one-day-old rats: Taste-toxicosis and texture–shock aversion learning. *Journal of Comparative and Physiological Psychology, 96,* 105–113.

Gentner, D., & Stevens, A. L. (1983). *Mental models.* Hillsdale, N.J.: Erlbaum.

Gibbon, J. (1977). Scalar expectancy theory and Weber's law in animal timing. *Psychological Review, 84,* 279–325.

Gibbon, J. (1981). The contingency problem in autoshaping. In C. M. Locurto, H. S. Terrace, & J. Gibbon (Eds.), *Autoshaping and conditioning theory.* New York: Academic Press.

Gibbon, J., Baldock, M. D., Locurto, C. M., Gold, L., & Terrace, H. S. (1977). Trial and intertrial durations in autoshaping. *Journal of Experimental Psychology: Animal Behavior Processes, 3,* 264–284.

Gibbon, J., & Balsam, P. (1981). Spreading association in time. In C. M. Locurto, H. S. Terrace, & J. Gibbon (Eds.), *Autoshaping and conditioning theory.* New York: Academic Press.

Gibbon, J. Locurto, C. M., & Terrace, H. S. (1975). Signal–food contingency and signal frequency in a continuous trials auto-shaping paradigm. *Animal Learning and Behavior, 3,* 317–324.

Gilligan, S. G., & Bower, G. H. (1984). Cognitive consequences of emotional arousal. In C. E. Izard, J. Kagan, & R. B. Zajonc (Eds.), *Emotions, cognitions, and behavior.* Cambridge: Cambridge University Press.

Ginosar, Z., & Trope, Y. (1980). The effects of base rates and individuating information on judgments about another person. *Journal of Experimental Social Psychology, 16,* 228–242.

Glanzer, M., & Cunitz, A. R. (1966). Two storage mechanisms in free recall. *Journal of Verbal Learning and Verbal Behavior, 5,* 351–360.

Glass, A. L., Holyoak, K. J., & Kiger, J. I. (1979). Role of antonymy relations in semantic judgments. *Journal of Experimental Psychology: Human Learning and Memory, 5,* 598–606.

Glass, A. L., Holyoak, K. J., & O'Dell, C. (1974). Production frequency and the verification of quantified statements. *Journal of Verbal Learning and Verbal Behavior, 13,* 237–254.

Glenberg, A., & Adams, F. (1978). Type I rehearsal and recognition. *Journal of Verbal Learning and Verbal Behavior, 17,* 455–463.

Glenberg, A., Smith, S. M., & Green, C. (1977). Type I rehearsal: Maintenance and more. *Journal of Verbal Learning and Verbal Behavior, 16,* 339–352.

Gluck, M. A., & Bower, G. H. (1988). From conditioning to category learning: An adaptive network model. *Journal of Experimental Psychology: General, 117,* 227–247.

Glucksberg, S., & McCloskey, M. (1981). Decisions about ignorance: Knowing that you don't know. *Journal of Experimental Psychology: Learning, Memory, and Cognition, 7,* 311–325.

Godden, D. R., & Baddeley, A. D. (1975). Context-dependent memory in two natural environments: On land and underwater. *British Journal of Psychology, 66,* 325–332.

Gonzalez, R. C., Gentry, G. V., & Bitterman, M. E. (1954). Relational discrimination of intermediate size in the chimpanzee. *Journal of Comparative and Physiological Psychology, 47,* 385–388.

Graf, P., & Mandler, G. (1984). Activation makes words more accessible, but not necessarily more retrievable. *Journal of Verbal Learning and Verbal Behavior, 23,* 553–568.

Graf, P., Mandler, G., & Haden, P. E. (1982). Simulating amnesic symptoms in normals. *Science, 218,* 1243–1244.

Graf, P., & Schacter, D. L. (1985). Implicit and explicit memory for new associations in normal and amnesic subjects. *Journal of Experimental Psychology: Learning, Memory, and Cognition, 11,* 501–518.

Grant, D. S. (1975). Proactive interference in pigeon short-term memory. *Journal of Experimental Psychology: Animal Behavior Processes, 1,* 207–220.

Grant, D. S. (1976). Effect of sample presentation time on long delay matching in the pigeon. *Learning and Motivation, 7,* 580–590.

Grant, D. S. (1981a). Short-term memory in the pigeon. In N. E. Spear & R. R. Miller (Eds.), *Information processing in animals: Memory mechanisms,* pp. 227–256. Hillsdale, N.J.: Erlbaum.

Grant, D. S. (1981b). Stimulus control of information processing in pigeon short-term memory. *Learning and Motivation, 12,* 19–39.

Grant, D. S. (1984). Directed forgetting and intratrial interference in pigeon delayed matching. *Canadian Journal of Psychology, 38,* 166–177.

Grant, D. S. (1986). Establishing a forget cue in pigeons using the intratrial interference procedure. *Animal Learning and Behavior, 14,* 267–274.

Grant, D. S., & Roberts, W. A. (1973). Trace interaction in pigeon short-term memory. *Journal of Experimental Psychology, 101,* 21–29.

Grant, D. S., & Roberts, W. A. (1976). Sources of retroactive inhibition in pigeon short-term memory. *Journal of Experimental Psychology: Animal Behavior Processes, 2,* 1–16.

Green, L., & Kagel, J. H. (Eds.) (1987). *Advances in behavioral economics* (Vol. 1). Norwood, N.J.: Ablex.

Green, L., Kagel, J. H., & Battalio, R. C. (1987). Consumption–leisure trade-offs in pigeons: Effects of changing marginal wage rates by varying amount of reinforcement. *Journal of the Experimental Analysis of Behavior, 47,* 17–28.

Green, L., & Rachlin, H. (1977). Pigeon's preferences for stimulus information: Effects of amount of information. *Journal of the Experimental Analysis of Behavior, 27,* 255–263.

Greeno, J. G., James, C. T., & DaPolito, F. J. (1971). A cognitive interpretation of negative transfer and forgetting of paired associates. *Journal of Verbal Learning and Verbal Behavior, 10,* 331–345.

Griggs, R. A., & Cox, J. R. (1982). The elusive thematic-materials effect in Wason's selection task. *British Journal of Psychology, 73,* 407–420.

Grosch, J., & Neuringer, A. (1981). Self-control in pigeons under the Mischel paradigm. *Journal of the Experimental Analysis of Behavior, 35,* 3–22.

Grossen, N. E., & Kelley, M. J. (1972). Species-specific behavior and acquisition of avoidance behavior in rats. *Journal of Comparative and Physiological Psychology, 81,* 307–310.

Groves, P. M., & Thompson, R. F. (1970). Habituation: A dual process theory. *Psychological Review, 77,* 419–450.

Hall, G., & Pearce, J. M. (1979). Latent inhibition of a CS during CS–US pairings. *Journal of Experimental Psychology: Animal Behavior Processes, 5,* 31–42.

Hamill, R., Wilson, T. D., & Nisbett, R. E. (1979). *Ignoring sample bias: Inferences about collectivities from atypical cases.* Unpublished manuscript, University of Michigan, Ann Arbor.

Hamill, R., Wilson, T. D., & Nisbett, R. E. (1980). Insensitivity to sample bias: Generalizing from atypical cases. *Journal of Personality and Social Psychology, 39,* 578–589.

Hamm, S. L., & Shettleworth, S. J. (1987). Risk aversion in pigeons. *Journal of Experimental Psychology: Animal Behavior Processes, 13,* 376–383.

Hammond, L. J. (1980). The effect of contingency upon the appetitive conditioning of free operant behavior. *Journal of the Experimental Analysis of Behavior, 34,* 297–304.

Hanson, H. M. (1959). Effects of discrimination training on stimulus generalization. *Journal of Experimental Psychology, 58,* 321–334.

Hanson, H. M. (1961). Stimulus generalization following three-stimulus discrimination training. *Journal of Comparative and Physiological Psychology, 54,* 181–185.

Hart, J. T. (1965). Memory and the feelings of knowing experience. *Journal of Educational Psychology, 56,* 208–216.

Hart, J. T. (1967). Memory and the memory-monitoring process. *Journal of Verbal Learning and Verbal Behavior, 6,* 685–691.

Hasher, L., & Griffin, M. (1978). Reconstructive and reproductive processes in memory. *Journal of Experimental Psychology: Human Learning and Memory, 4,* 318–330.

Hasher, L., Zacks, R., Rose, K., & Doren, B. (1985). On mood variation and memory: Reply to Isen (1985), Ellis (1985), and Mayer and Bower (1985). *Journal of Experimental Psychology: General, 114,* 404–410.

Haugeland, J. (Ed.) (1981). *Mind design.* Cambridge, Mass.: M.I.T. Press.

Haugeland, J. (1986). *Artificial intelligence: The very idea.* Cambridge, Mass.: M.I.T. Press.

Healy, A. F. (1981). The effects of visual similarity on proofreading for misspellings. *Memory and Cognition, 9,* 453–460.

Hearst, E. (1968). Discrimination learning as the summation of excitation and inhibition. *Science, 162,* 1303–1306.

Hearst, E., & Franklin, S. R. (1977). Positive and negative relations between a signal and food: Approach–withdrawal behavior to the signal. *Journal of Experimental Psychology: Animal Behavior Processes, 3,* 37–52.

Hearst, E., & Jenkins, H. M. (1974). *Sign-tracking: The stimulus–reinforcer relation and directed action.* Austin, Texas: Psychonomic Society.

Hecaen, H. (1981). The neuropsychology of face recognition. In G. Davies, H. Ellis & J. Shepard (Eds.), *Perceiving and remembering faces.* New York: Academic Press.

Hendry, D. P. (1969a). Reinforcing value of information: Fixed-ratio schedules. In D. P. Hendry (Ed.), *Conditioned reinforcement.* Homewood, Ill.: Dorsey Press.

Hendry, D. P. (Ed.) (1969b). *Conditioned reinforcement.* Homewood, Ill.: Dorsey Press.

Henle, M. (1962). On the relation between logic and thinking. *Psychological Review, 69,* 366–378.

Herrick, R. M. (1964). The successive differentiation of a lever displacement response. *Journal of the Experimental Analysis of Behavior, 7,* 311–315.

Herrnstein, R. J. (1969). Method and theory in the study of avoidance. *Psychological Review, 76,* 49–69.

Herrnstein, R. J. (1970). On the law of effect. *Journal of the Experimental Analysis of Behavior, 13,* 243–266.

Herrnstein, R. J. (1979). Acquisition, generalization and discrimination reversal of a natural concept. *Journal of Experimental Psychology: Animal Behavior Processes, 5,* 116–129.

Herrnstein, R. J. & de Villiers, P. A. (1980). Fish as a natural category for people and pigeons. In G. H. Bower (Ed.), *Psychology of learning and motivation* (Vol. 14). New York: Academic Press.

Herrnstein, R. J., & Heyman, G. M. (1979). Is matching compatible with reinforcement maximization on concurrent variable-interval, variable ratio? *Journal of the Experimental Analysis of Behavior, 31,* 209–223.

Herrnstein, R. J., & Hineline, P. N. (1966). Negative reinforcement as shock frequency reduction. *Journal of the Experimental Analysis of Behavior, 9,* 421–430.

Herrnstein, R. J., & Loveland, D. H. (1964). Complex visual concepts in the pigeon. *Science, 146,* 549–551.

Herrnstein, R. J., Loveland, D. H., & Cable, C. (1976). Natural concepts in pigeons. *Journal of Experimental Psychology: Animal Behavior Processes, 2,* 285–302.

Herrnstein, R. J., & Vaughn, W. (1980). Melioration and behavioral allocation. In J. E. R. Staddon (Ed.), *Limits to action.* New York: Academic Press.

Heuer, F., & Reisberg, D. (1990). Vivid memories of emotional events: The accuracy of remembered minutiae. *Memory and Cognition, 18,* 496–506.

Higbee, K. L. (1977). *Your memory: How it works and how to improve it.* Englewood Cliffs, N.J.: Prentice-Hall.

Hilgard, E. R. (1968). *The experience of hypnosis.* New York: Harcourt Brace Jovanovich.

Hilgard, E. R., & Marquis, D. G. (1940). *Conditioning and learning.* New York: Appleton-Century-Crofts.

Hineline, P. N. (1977). Negative reinforcement and avoidance. In W. K. Honig & J. E. R. Staddon (Eds.), *Handbook of operant behavior.* Englewood Cliffs, N.J.: Prentice-Hall.

Hineline, P. N., & Rachlin, H. (1969). Escape and avoidance of shock by pigeons pecking a key. *Journal of the Experimental Analysis of Behavior, 12,* 533–538.

Hinson, R. E. (1982). Effects of UCS preexposure on excitatory and inhibitory rabbit eyelid conditioning: An associative effect of contextual stimuli. *Journal of Experimental Psychology: Animal Behavior Processes, 8,* 49–61.

Hinton, G. E., & Anderson, J. A. (1981). *Parallel models of associative memory.* Hillsdale, N.J.: Erlbaum.

Hintzman, D. L. (1986). "Schema abstraction" in a multiple-trace memory model. *Psychological Review, 93,* 411–428.

Hockey, G. R., Davies, S., & Gray, M. M. (1972). Forgetting as a function of sleep at different times of day. *Quarterly Journal of Experimental Psychology, 24,* 386–393.

Holland, J. H., Holyoak, K. F., Nisbett, R. E., & Thagard, P. R. (1987). *Induction.* Cambridge, Mass.: M.I.T. Press.

Holland, P. C. (1977). Conditioned stimulus as a determinant of the form for the Pavlovian conditioned response. *Journal of Experimental Psychology: Animal Behavior Processes, 3,* 77–104.

Holland, P. C. (1980). Influence of visual conditioned stimulus characteristics on the form of Pavlovian appetitive conditioned responding in rats. *Journal of Experimental Psychology: Animal Behavior Processes, 6,* 81–97.

Holland, P. C. (1985). The nature of conditioned inhibition in serial and simultaneous feature negative discriminations. In R. R. Miller & N. E. Spear (Eds.), *Information processing in animals: Conditioned inhibition.* Hillsdale, N.J.: Erlbaum.

Holland, P. C. (1986). Temporal determinants of occasion setting in feature positive discriminations. *Animal Learning and Behavior, 14,* 111–120.

Holland, P. C., & Rescorla, R. A. (1975). The effects of two ways of devaluing the unconditioned stimulus after first- and second-order appetitive conditioning. *Journal of Experimental Psychology: Animal Behavior Processes, 1,* 355–363.

Holland, P. C., & Straub, J. J. (1979). Differential effect of two ways of devaluing the unconditioned stimulus after Pavlovian appetitive conditioning. *Journal of Experimental Psychology: Animal Behavior Processes, 5,* 65–78.

Hollingworth, H. (1910). The obliviscence of the disagreeable. *Journal of Philosophical and Psychological Sciences Methods, 7,* 709–714.

Hollis, K. (1982). Pavlovian conditioning of signal-centered action patterns and autonomic behavior: A biological analysis of function. In J. S. Rosenblatt, R. A. Hinde, C. Beer, & M. Busnel (Eds.), *Advances in the study of behavior* (Vol. 12). New York: Academic Press.

Hollis, K. L. (1984). The biological function of Pavlovian conditioning: The best defense is a good offense. *Journal of Experimental Psychology: Animal Behavior Processes, 10,* 413–425.

Holmes, D.S. (1974). Investigations of repression: Differential recall of material experimentally or naturally associated with ego threat. *Psychological Bulletin, 81,* 632–653.

Holyoak, K. (1987). Review of parallel distributed processing. *Science, 236,* 992.

Honig, W. K. (1965). Discrimination, generalization and transfer on the basis of stimulus differences. In D. J. Mostofsky (Ed.), *Stimulus generalization.* Stanford: Stanford University Press.

Honig, W. K. (1978). Studies of working memory in the pigeon. In S. H. Hulse, H. Fowler, & W. K. Honig (Eds.), *Cognitive processes in animal behavior.* Hillsdale, N.J.: Erlbaum.

Honig, W. K., & Urcuioli, P. J. (1981). The legacy of Guttman and Kalish (1956): Twenty-five years of research on stimulus generalization. *Journal of the Experimental Analysis of Behavior, 36,* 405–445.

Hull, C. L. (1920). Quantitative aspects of the evolution of concepts. *Psychological Monographs* (Whole No. 123).

Hull, C. L. (1943). *Principles of behavior.* New York: Appleton-Century-Crofts.

Hull, C. L. (1952). *A behavior system.* New Haven: Yale University Press.

Hulse, S. H., Egeth, H., & Deese, J. (1980). *The psychology of learning.* New York: McGraw-Hill.

Hume, D. A. (1739/1888). *Treatise of human nature.* L. A. Selby-Bigge, Ed. London: Oxford University Press.

Hunt, R. R., & Ellis, H. D. (1974). Recognition memory and degree of semantic contextual change. *Journal of Experimental Psychology, 103,* 1153–1159.

Hursh, S. R. (1978). The economics of daily consumption controlling food- and water-reinforced responding. *Journal of the Experimental Analysis of Behavior, 29,* 475–491.

Hursh, S. R. (1980). Economic concepts for the analysis of behavior. *Journal of the Experimental Analysis of Behavior, 34,* 219–238.

Hursh, S. R. (1984). Behavioral economics. *Journal of the Experimental Analysis of Behavior, 42,* 435–452.

Hursh, S. R., & Bauman, R. A. (1987). The behavioral analysis of demand. In L. Green & J. H. Kagel (Eds.), *Advances in behavioral economics* (Vol. 1). Norwood, N.J.: Ablex.

Hursh, S. R., & Natelson, B. J. (1981). Electrical brain stimulation and food reinforcement dissociated by demand elasticity. *Physiology and Behavior, 18,* 141–150.

Huttenlocher, J., & Burke, D. (1976). Why does memory span increase with age? *Cognitive Psychology, 8,* 1–31.

Hyde, T. S., & Jenkins, J. J. (1969). Differential effects of incidental tasks on the organization of recall of a list of highly associated words. *Journal of Experimental Psychology, 82,* 472–481.

Hyde, T. S., & Jenkins, J. J. (1973). Recall for words as a function of semantic, graphic, and syntactic orienting tasks. *Journal of Verbal Learning and Verbal Behavior, 12,* 471–480.

Isen, A. M. (1985). Asymmetry of happiness and sadness in effects on memory in normal college students: Comment on Hasher, Rose, Zacks, Sanft and Doren. *Journal of Experimental Psychology: General, 114,* 388–391.

Isen, A. M., Shalker, T. E., Clark, M., & Karp, L. (1978). Affect, accessibility of material in memory, and behavior: A cognitive loop? *Journal of Personality and Social Psychology, 36,* 1–12.

Jackson, R. L., Alexander, J. H., & Maier, S. F. (1980). Learned helplessness, inactivity, and associative deficits: Effects of inescapable shock on response choice escape learning. *Journal of Experimental Psychology: Animal Behavior Processes, 6,* 1–20.

Jacobs, W. J., & LoLordo, V. M. (1980). Constraints on Pavlovian aversive conditioning: Implications for avoidance learning in the rat. *Learning and Motivation, 11,* 427–455.

Jacobs, W. J., & Nadel, L. (1985). Stress-induced recovery of fears and phobias. *Psychological Review, 92,* 512–531.

Jacoby, L. L. (1978). On interpreting the effects of repetition: Solving a problem versus remembering a solution. *Journal of Verbal Learning and Verbal Behavior, 17,* 649–667.

Jacoby, L. L. (1983a). Perceptual enhancement: Persistent effects of an experience. *Journal of Experimental Psychology: Learning, Memory, and Cognition, 9,* 21–38.

Jacoby, L. L. (1983b). Remembering the data: Analyzing interactive processes in reading. *Journal of Verbal Learning and Verbal Behavior, 22,* 485–508.

Jacoby, L. L. (1988). Memory observed and memory unobserved. In U. Neisser

& E. Winograd (Eds.), *Remembering reconsidered.* Cambridge: Cambridge University Press.

Jacoby, L. L., Allan, L. G., Collins, J. C., & Larwill, L. K. (1988). Memory influences subjective experience: Noise judgments. *Journal of Experimental Psychology: Learning, Memory, and Cognition, 14,* 240–247.

Jacoby, L. L., & Brooks, L. R. (1984). Nonanalytic cognition: Memory, perception and concept learning. In G. H. Bower (Ed.), *The psychology of learning and motivation: Advances in research and theory.* New York: Academic Press.

Jacoby, L. L., & Craik, F. I. M. (1979). Effects of elaboration of processing at encoding and retrieval: Trace distinctiveness and recovery of initial context. In L. S. Cermak & F. I. M. Craik (Eds.), *Levels of processing in human memory.* Hillsdale, N.J.: Erlbaum.

Jacoby, L. L., & Dallas, M. (1981). On the relationship between autobiographical memory and perceptual learning. *Journal of Experimental Psychology: General, 3,* 306–340.

Jacoby, L. L., & Hayman, C. A. G. (1987). Specific visual transfer in word identification. *Journal of Experimental Psychology: Learning, Memory, and Cognition, 13,* 456–463.

Jacoby, L. L., Kelley, C. M., Brown, J., & Jasechko, J. (1989). Becoming famous overnight: Limits on the ability to avoid unconscious influences of the past. *Journal of Personality and Social Psychology, 56,* 326–338.

Jacoby, L. L., & Witherspoon, D. (1982). Remembering without awareness. *Canadian Journal of Psychology, 36,* 300–324.

Jacoby, L. L., Woloshyn, V., & Kelley, C. (1989). Becoming famous without being recognized: Unconscious influences of memory produced by dividing attention. *Journal of Experimental Psychology: General, 118,* 115–125.

James, W. (1890). *The principles of psychology.* New York: Dover, 1950.

Jarvik, M. E., Goldfarb, R., & Corley, J. L. (1969). Influence of interference on delayed matching in monkeys. *Journal of Experimental Psychology, 81,* 1–6.

Jenkins, H. M. (1985). Conditioned inhibition of key pecking in the pigeon. In R. R. Miller & N. E. Spear (Eds.), *Information processing in animals: Conditioned inhibition.* Hillsdale, N.J.: Erlbaum.

Jenkins, H. M., & Harrison, R. H. (1960). Effects of discrimination training on auditory generalization. *Journal of Experimental Psychology, 59,* 246–253.

Jenkins, H. M., & Harrison, R. H. (1962). Generalization gradients of inhibition following auditory discrimination learning. *Journal of the Experimental Analysis of Behavior, 5,* 435–441.

Jenkins, H. M., & Ward, W. C. (1965). Judgment of contingency between responses and outcomes. *Psychological Monographs, 79* (Whole No. 594).

Jenkins, J. G., & Dallenbach, K. M. (1924). Oblivescence during sleep and waking. *American Journal of Psychology, 35,* 605–612.

Jennings, D. L., Amabile, T. M., & Ross, L. (1982). Informal covariation assessment: Data-based versus theory-based judgments. In D. Kahneman, P. Slovic, & A. Tversky (Eds.), *Judgments under uncertainty: Heuristics and biases.* Cambridge: Cambridge University Press.

Johnson, M. K., Bransford, J. D., & Solomon, S. (1973). Memory for tacit implication of sentences. *Journal of Experimental Psychology, 98,* 203–205.

Johnson, M. K., & Hasher, L. (1987). Human learning and memory. *Annual Review of Psychology, 38,* 631–668.

Johnson, M. K., Kim, J. K., & Risse, G. (1985). Do alcoholic Korsakoff's syndrome patients acquire affective reactions? *Journal of Experimental Psychology: Learning, Memory, and Cognition, 11,* 27–36.

Johnson-Laird, P. N., Herrmann, D. J., & Chaffin, R. (1984). Only connections: A critique of semantic networks. *Psychological Bulletin, 96,* 292–315.

Johnson-Laird, P. N., Legrenzi, P., & Legrenzi, M. S. (1972). Reasoning and a sense of reality. *British Journal of Psychology, 63,* 395–400.

Jonides, J., Kahn, R., & Rozin, P. (1975). Imagery instructions improve memory in blind subjects. *Bulletin of the Psychonomic Society, 5,* 424–426.

Kahneman, D., & Tversky, A. (1973). On the psychology of prediction. *Psychological Review, 80,* 237–251.

Kahneman, D., & Tversky, A. (1982). Subjective probability: A judgment of representatives. In D. Kahneman, P. Slovic, & A. Tversky (Eds.), *Judgment under uncertainty: Heuristics and biases.* Cambridge: Cambridge University Press.

Kamil, A. C., & Roitblat, H. L. (1985). The ecology of foraging behavior: Implications for animal learning and memory. *Annual Review of Psychology, 36,* 141–169.

Kamin, L. J. (1956). Effects of termination of the CS and avoidance of the US on avoidance learning. *Journal of Comparative and Physiological Psychology, 49,* 420–424.

Kamin, L. J. (1969). Predictability, surprise, attention, and conditioning. In B. A. Campbell & R. M. Church (Eds.), *Punishment and aversive behavior.* New York: Appleton-Century-Crofts.

Kamin, L. J., Brimer, C. J., & Black, A. H. (1963). Conditioned suppression as a monitor of fear of the CS in the course of avoidance training. *Journal of Comparative and Physiological Psychology, 56,* 497–501.

Kandel, E. R. (1976). *Cellular basis of behavior.* San Francisco: W. H. Freeman.

Kandel, E. R. (1979). Small systems of neurons. *Scientific American, 241,* 66–76.

Kanizsa, G. (1979). *Organization in vision.* New York: Praeger.

Katona, G. (1940). *Organizing and memorizing.* New York: Columbia University Press.

Katzev, R., & Averill, A. (1984). Knowledge of the bystander problem and its impact on subsequent helping behavior. *Journal of Social Psychology, 123,* 223–230.

Keenan, J. M. (1983). Qualifications and clarifications of images of concealed objects: A reply to Kerr and Neisser. *Journal of Experimental Psychology: Learning, Memory, and Cognition, 9,* 222–230.

Keenan, J. M., MacWhinney, B., & Mayhew, D. (1977). Pragmatics in memory: A study of natural conversation. *Journal of Verbal Learning and Verbal Behavior, 16,* 549–560.

Keenan, J. M., & Moore, R. E. (1979). Memory for images of concealed objects: A reexamination of Neisser and Kerr. *Journal of Experimental Psychology: Human Learning and Memory, 5,* 374–385.

Keil, F. C. (1979). *Semantic and conceptual development.* Cambridge, Mass.: Harvard University Press.

Keil, F. C. (1986). The acquisition of natural-kind and artifact terms. In W. Demopoulos & A. Marras (Eds.), *Language, learning, and concept acquisition.* Norwood, N.J.: Ablex.

Keil, F. C. (1987). Conceptual development and category structure. In U. Neisser (Ed.), *Concepts and conceptual development: Ecological and intellectual factors in categorization.* Cambridge: Cambridge University Press.

Kelleher, R. T. (1958). Fixed-ratio schedules of conditioned reinforcement with chimpanzees. *Journal of the Experimental Analysis of Behavior, 1,* 281–289.

Kemler, D. G., & Shepp, B. E. (1971). Learning and transfer of dimensional relevance and irrelevance in children. *Journal of Experimental Psychology, 90,* 120–127.

Kendler, H. H., & D'Amato, M. F. (1955). A comparison of reversal shifts and nonreversal shifts in human concept formation. *Journal of Experimental Psychology, 49,* 165–174.

Kendler, H. H., & Kendler, T. S. (1962). Vertical and horizontal processes in problem solving. *Psychological Review, 69,* 1–16.

Kendrick, D. F., Rilling, M., & Stonebraker, T. B. (1981). Stimulus control of delayed matching in pigeons: Directed forgetting. *Journal of the Experimental Analysis of Behavior, 36,* 241–251.

Kerr, N. H. (1983). The role of vision in "visual imagery" experiments: Evidence from the congenitally blind. *Journal of Experimental Psychology: General, 112,* 265–277.

Kerr, N. H., & Neisser, U. (1983). Mental images of concealed objects: New evidence. *Journal of Experimental Psychology: Learning, Memory, and Cognition, 9,* 212–221.

Kerst, S. M., & Howard, J. H. J. (1977). Mental comparisons for ordered information on abstract and concrete dimensions. *Memory and Cognition, 5,* 227–234.

Killeen, P. (1978). Superstition: A matter of bias, not detectability. *Science, 199,* 88–90.

Kinsbourne, M., & Wood, F. (1975). Short-term memory processes and the amnesic syndrome. In D. Deutsch & A. J. Deutsch (Eds.), *Short-term memory.* New York: Academic Press.

Kintsch, W. (1974). *The representation of meaning in memory.* Hillsdale, N.J.: Erlbaum.

Kirsner, K., Milech, D., & Standen, P. (1983). Common and modality-specific processes in the mental lexicon. *Memory and Cognition, 11,* 621–630.

Klein, S. B., & Kihlstrom, J. F. (1986). Elaboration, organization, and the self-reference effect in memory. *Journal of Experimental Psychology: General, 115,* 26–38.

Kleinsmith, L. J., & Kaplan, S. (1963). Paired associate learning as a function of arousal and interpolated interval. *Journal of Experimental Psychology, 65,* 190–193.

Kleinsmith, L. J., & Kaplan, S. (1964). The interaction of arousal and recall interval in nonsense syllable paired-associate learning. *Journal of Experimental Psychology, 67,* 124–126.

Klentz, B., & Beaman, A. (1981). The effects of type of information and method of dissemination on the reporting of a shoplifter. *Journal of Applied Social Psychology, 11,* 64–82.

Köhler, W. (1939). Simple structural functions in the chimpanzee and the chicken. In W. D. Ellis (Ed.), *A source book of Gestalt psychology.* New York: Harcourt Brace.

Kolers, P. A., & Smythe, W. E. (1979). Images, symbols, and skills. *Canadian Journal of Psychology, 33,* 158–184.

Kolers, P., & Smythe, W. (1984). Symbol manipulation: Alternatives to the computational view of mind. *Journal of Verbal Learning and Verbal Behavior, 23,* 289–314.

Konorski, J. (1948). *Conditioned reflexes and neuron organization.* Cambridge: Cambridge University Press.

Konorski, J. (1967). *Integrative activity of the brain.* Chicago: University of Chicago Press.

Kosslyn, S. M. (1976). Can imagery be distinguished from other forms of internal representation? Evidence from studies of information retrieval times. *Memory and Cognition, 4,* 291–297.

Kosslyn, S. M. (1980). *Image and mind.* Cambridge, Mass.: Harvard University Press.

Kosslyn, S. M. (1981). The medium and the message in mental imagery: A theory. *Psychological Review, 88,* 46–66.

Kosslyn, S. M. (1983). *Ghosts in the mind's machine.* New York: W. W. Norton.

Kosslyn, S. M., Ball, T. M., & Reiser, B. J. (1978). Visual images preserve metric spatial information: Evidence from studies of image scanning. *Journal of Experimental Psychology: Human Perception and Performance, 4,* 1–20.

Kosslyn, S. M., Pinker, S., Smith, G. E., & Shwartz, S. P. (1979). On the demystification of mental imagery. *Behavioral and Brain Sciences, 2,* 535–581.

Krane, R. V., & Wagner, A. R. (1975). Taste aversion learning with a delayed shock US: Implications for the "generality of the laws of learning." *Journal of Comparative and Physiological Psychology, 88,* 882–889.

Krebs, J. R. (1978). Optimal foraging: Decision rules for predators. In J. R. Krebs & N. B. Davies (Eds.), *Behavioral ecology.* Sunderland, Mass.: Sinauer Associates.

Krebs, J. R., & Davies, N. B. (Eds.) (1978). *Behavioral ecology.* Sunderland, Mass.: Sinauer Associates.

Krebs, J. R., & McCleery, R. H. (1984). Optimization in behavioral ecology. In J. R. Krebs & N. B. Davies (Eds.), *Behavioral ecology* (2nd ed.). Sunderland, Mass.: Sinauer Associates.

Kremer, E. F. (1978). The Rescorla–Wagner model: Losses in associative strength in compound conditioned stimuli. *Journal of Experimental Psychology: Animal Behavior Processes, 4,* 22–36.

Kremer, E. F., & Kamin, L. J. (1971). The truly random control procedure: Associative or non-associative effects in rats. *Journal of Comparative and Physiological Psychology, 74,* 203–210.

Kroll, J. F., & Potter, M. C. (1984). Recognizing words, pictures, and concepts: A comparison of lexical, object, and reality decisions. *Journal of Verbal Learning and Verbal Behavior, 23,* 39–66.

Kroll, N. E., Schepeler, E. M., & Angin, K. T. (1986). Bizarre imagery: The misremembered mnemonic. *Journal of Experimental Psychology: Learning, Memory, and Cognition, 12,* 42–54.

Kunda, Z., & Nisbett, R. E. (1986). The psychometrics of everyday life. *Cognitive Psychology, 18,* 195–224.

Labov, W. (1973). The boundaries of words and their meanings. In C.-J. N. Bailey & R. W. Shuy (Eds.), *New ways of analyzing variations in English.* Washington, D.C.: Georgetown University Press.

Lachter, J., & Bever, T. G. (1988). The relation between linguistic structure and associative theories of language learning—a critique of some connectionist learning models. *Cognition, 28,* 195–247.

Lakoff, G. (1987). Cognitive models and prototype theory. In U. Neisser (Ed.),

Concepts and conceptual development. Cambridge: Cambridge University Press.

Lamon, S., Wilson, G. T., & Leaf, R. C. (1977). Human classical aversion conditioning: Nausea versus electric shock in the reduction of target beverage consumption. *Behavior Research and Therapy, 15,* 313–320.

Landau, B. (1982). Will the real grandmother please stand up? The psychological reality of dual meaning representations. *Journal of Psycholinguistic Research, 11,* 47–62.

Laudenslager, M. L., Ryan, S. M., Drugan, R. C., Hyson, R. L., & Maier, S. F. (1983). Coping and immunosuppression: Inescapable but not escapable shock suppresses lymphocyte proliferation. *Science, 221,* 568–570.

Lawrence, D. H. (1950). Acquired distinctiveness of cues. II. Selective association in a constant stimulus situation. *Journal of Experimental Psychology, 40,* 185–188.

Lawrence, D. H., & DeRivera, J. (1954). Evidence for relational transposition. *Journal of Comparative and Physiological Psychology, 47,* 465–471.

Lazarus, R. S. (1982). Thoughts on the relations between emotion and cognition. *American Psychologist, 37,* 1019–1024.

Lazarus, R. S. (1984). On the primacy of cognition. *American Psychologist, 39,* 124–129.

Lea, S. E. G. (1978). The psychology and economics of demand. *Psychological Bulletin, 85,* 441–446.

Lea, S. E. G. (1979). Foraging and reinforcement schedules in the pigeon: Optimal and non-optimal aspects of choice. *Animal Behaviour, 27,* 875–886.

Lea, S. E. G. (1984). In what sense do pigeons learn concepts? In H. L. Roitblat, T. G. Bever, & H. S. Terrace (Eds.), *Animal cognition.* Hillsdale, N.J.: Erlbaum.

Lea, S. E. G., & Ryan, C. M. E. (1983). Feature analysis of pigeons' acquisition of concept discrimination. In R. J. Herrnstein & A. R. Wagner (Eds.), *Quantitative analysis of behavior.* Vol. 4: *Discrimination processes.* Cambridge, Mass.: Ballinger.

Lehman, D. R., Lempert, R. O., & Nisbett, R. E. (1988). The effects of graduate training on reasoning: Formal discipline and thinking about everyday-life events. *American Psychologist, 43,* 431–442.

Leight, K. A., & Ellis, H. C. (1981). Emotional mood states, strategies, and state-dependency in memory. *Journal of Verbal Learning and Verbal Behavior, 20,* 251–275.

Lewinsohn, P. M., & Rosenbaum, M. (1987). Recall of parental behavior by acute depressives, remitted depressives, and nondepressives. *Journal of Personality and Social Psychology, 52,* 611–619.

Lewis, C. H., & Anderson, J. R. (1976). Interference with real world knowledge. *Cognitive Psychology, 7,* 311–335.

Light, L. L., & Carter-Sobell, L. (1970). Effects of changed semantic context on recognition memory. *Journal of Verbal Learning and Verbal Behavior, 9,* 1–11.

Lindsay, D. S., & Johnson, M. K. (1987). Reality monitoring and suggestibility: Children's ability to discriminate among memories from different sources. In S. J. Ceci, M. P. Toglia, & D. F. Ross (Eds.), *Children's eyewitness memory.* New York: Springer-Verlag.

Linton, M. (1975). Memory for real-world events. In D. A. Norman & D. E. Rumelhart (Eds.), *Explorations in cognition.* San Francisco: W. H. Freeman.

Linton, M. (1978). Real world memory after six years: An in vivo study of very long term memory. In M. M. Gruneberg, P. E. Morris, & R. N. Sykes (Eds.), *Practical aspects of memory.* London: Academic Press.

Linton, M. (1982). Transformations of memory in everyday life. In U. Neisser (Ed.), *Memory observed: Remembering in natural contexts.* San Francisco: W. H. Freeman.

Linton, M. (1986). Ways of searching and the contents of memory. In D. C. Rubin (Ed.), *Autobiographical memory.* Cambridge: Cambridge University Press.

Lockhart, R. S., Craik, F. I. M., & Jacoby, L. (1976). Depth of processing, recall, and recognition. In J. Brown (Ed.), *Recall and recognition.* New York: Wiley.

Locurto, C. M., Terrace, H. S., & Gibbon, J. (Eds.) (1981). *Autoshaping and conditioning theory.* New York: Academic Press.

Loftus, E. F. (1975). Leading questions and the eyewitness report. *Cognitive Psychology, 7,* 560–572.

Loftus, E. F. (1979). *Eyewitness testimony.* Cambridge, Mass.: Harvard University Press.

Loftus, E. F. (1982). Remembering recent experiences. In L. S. Cermak (Ed.), *Human memory and amnesia.* Hillsdale, N.J.: Erlbaum.

Loftus, E. F., & Hoffman, H. G. (1989). Misinformation and memory: The creation of new memories. *Journal of Experimental Psychology: General, 118,* 100–104.

Loftus, E. F., Miller, D. G., & Burns, H. J. (1978). Semantic integration of verbal information into a visual memory. *Journal of Experimental Psychology: Human Learning and Memory, 4,* 19–31.

Loftus, E. F., & Palmer, J. C. (1974). Reconstruction of automobile destruction: An example of the interaction between language and memory. *Journal of Verbal Learning and Verbal Behavior, 13,* 585–589.

Loftus, G. R., & Bell, S. M. (1975). Two types of information in picture memory. *Journal of Experimental Psychology: Human Learning and Perception, 104,* 103–113.

Loftus, G., & Kallman, H. (1979). Encoding and use of detail information in picture recognition. *Journal of Experimental Psychology: Human Learning and Memory, 5,* 197–211.

Logue, A. W. (1979). Taste aversion and the generality of the laws of learning. *Psychological Bulletin, 86,* 276–296.

Logue, A. W. (1985). Conditioned food aversion learning in humans. *Annals of the New York Academy of Sciences, 104,* 331–340.

Logue, A. W., Ophir, I., & Strauss, K. E. (1981). The acquisition of taste aversions in humans. *Behaviour Research and Therapy, 19,* 319–333.

LoLordo, V. M. (1979). Selective associations. In A. Dickenson & R. A. Boakes (Eds.), *Mechanisms of learning and motivation.* Hillsdale, N.J.: Erlbaum.

LoLordo, V. M., & Fairless, J. L. (1985). Pavlovian conditioned inhibition: The literature since 1969. In R. R. Miller & N. E. Spear (Eds.), *Information processing in animals: Conditioned inhibition.* Hillsdale, N.J.: Erlbaum.

LoLordo, V. M., & Rescorla, R. A. (1966). Protection of the fear-eliciting capacity of a stimulus from extinction. *Acta Biologicae Experimentalis, 26,* 251–258.

Lord, A. B. (1960). *The singer of tales.* Cambridge, Mass.: Harvard University Press.

Lubow, R. E. (1974). High-order concept formation in the pigeon. *Journal of the Experimental Analysis of Behavior, 21,* 475–483.

Luria, A. R. (1968). *The mind of a mnemonist.* Chicago: Henry Regnery.

MacKinnon, D., & Dukes, W. (1964). Repression. In L. Postman (Ed.), *Psychology in the making.* New York: Knopf.

Mackintosh, N. J. (1973). Stimulus selection: Learning to ignore stimuli that predict no change in reinforcement. In R. A. Hinde & J. S. Hinde (Eds.), *Constraints on learning.* London: Academic Press.

Mackintosh, N. J. (1974). *The psychology of animal learning.* New York: Academic Press.

Mackintosh, N. J. (1975). A theory of attention. *Psychological Review, 82,* 276–298.

Mackintosh, N. J. (1977). Stimulus control: Attentional factors. In W. K. Honig & J. E. R. Staddon (Eds.), *Handbook of operant behavior.* Englewood Cliffs, N.J.: Prentice-Hall.

Mackintosh, N. J., Bygrave, D. J., & Picton, D. M. B. (1977). Locus of the effect of a surprising reinforcer in the attenuation of blocking. *Quarterly Journal of Experimental Psychology, 29,* 327–336.

Mackintosh, N. J., & Cotton, M. M. (1985). Conditioned inhibition from reinforcement reduction. In R. R. Miller & N. E. Spear (Eds.), *Information processing in animals: Conditioned inhibition.* Hillsdale, N.J.: Erlbaum.

Mackintosh, N. J., & Little, L. (1969). Intradimensional and extradimensional shift learning by pigeons. *Psychonomic Science, 14,* 5–6.

MacLennan, A. J., Jackson, R. L., & Maier, S. F. (1980). Conditioned analgesia in the rat. *Bulletin of the Psychonomic Society, 15,* 387–390.

Maier, S. F. (1970). Failure to escape traumatic shock: Incompatible skeletal motor responses or learned helplessness? *Learning and Motivation, 1,* 157–170.

Maier, S. F., & Seligman, M. E. P. (1976). Learned helplessness: Theory and evidence. *Journal of Experimental Psychology: General, 105,* 3–46.

Maki, R. H., & Schuler, J. (1980). Effects of rehearsal duration and level of processing on memory for words. *Journal of Verbal Learning and Verbal Behavior, 19,* 36–45.

Maki, W. S., Gillund, G., Hauge, G., & Siders, W. A. (1977). Matching to sample after extinction of observing responses. *Journal of Experimental Psychology: Animal Behavior Processes, 3,* 285–296.

Maki, W. S., & Hegvik, D. K. (1980). Directed forgetting in pigeons. *Animal Learning and Behavior, 8,* 567–574.

Malott, R. W., & Malott, M. K. (1970). Perception and stimulus generalization. In W. C. Stebbins (Ed.), *Animal psychophysics.* New York: Appleton-Century-Crofts.

Malt, B. C., & Smith, E. E. (1984). Correlated properties in natural categories. *Journal of Verbal Learning and Verbal Behavior, 23,* 250–269.

Mandler, G. (1962). From association to structure. *Psychological Review, 69,* 415–427.

Mandler, G. (1975). *Mind and emotion.* New York: Wiley.

Mandler, G. (1980). Recognizing: The judgment of previous occurrence. *Psychological Review, 87,* 252–271.

Mandler, G., & Pearlstone, Z. (1966). Free and constrained concept learning and subsequent recall. *Journal of Verbal Learning and Verbal Behavior, 5,* 126–131.

Mandler, J. M. (1984). *Stories, scripts, and scenes: Aspects of schema theory.* Hillsdale, N.J.: Erlbaum.

Mandler, J. M., & Ritchey, G. H. (1977). Long-term memory for pictures. *Journal of Experimental Psychology: Human Learning and Memory, 3,* 386–396.

Manis, M., Dovalina, I., Avis, N. E., & Cardoze, S. (1980). Base rates can affect individual predictions. *Journal of Personality and Social Psychology, 38,* 231–248.

Manktelow, K. I., & Evans, J. S. B. T. (1979). Facilitation of reasoning by realism: Effect or non-effect. *British Journal of Psychology, 70,* 477–488.

Marcel, A. J. (1983). Conscious and unconscious perception: Experiments on visual masking and word recognition. *Cognitive Psychology, 15,* 197–237.

Marek, G. R. (1975). *Toscanini.* London: Vision Press.

Marmor, G. S., & Zaback, L. A. (1976). Mental rotation by the blind: Does mental rotation depend on visual imagery? *Journal of Experimental Psychology: Human Perception and Performance, 2,* 515–521.

Marschark, M., & Hunt, R. R. (1989). A reexamination of the role of imagery in learning and memory. *Journal of Experimental Psychology: Learning, Memory, and Cognition, 15,* 710–720.

Marslen-Wilson, W. D., & Teuber, H. L. (1975). Memory for remote events in anterograde amnesia: Recognition of public figures from news photographs. *Neuropsychologia, 13,* 353–364.

Martin, E. (1971). Verbal learning theory and independent retrieval phenomena. *Psychological Review, 78,* 314–332.

Martin, L., & Levey, A. B. (1978). Evaluative conditioning. *Advances in Behaviour Research and Therapy, 1,* 57–102.

Masterson, F. A., & Crawford, M. (1982). The defense motivation system: A theory of avoidance behavior. *Behavioral and Brain Sciences, 5,* 661–696.

Matlin, M. W., & Stang, D. J. (1978). *The Pollyana principle: Selectivity in language, memory, and thought.* Cambridge, Mass.: Schenkman.

Mayer, J. D., & Bower, G. H. (1985). Naturally occurring mood and learning: Comment on Hasher, Rose, Zacks, Sanft and Doren. *Journal of Experimental Psychology: General, 114,* 396–403.

Mazur, J. E. (1981). Optimization theory fails to predict performance of pigeons in a two-response situation. *Science, 214,* 823–825.

McAllister, W. R., & McAllister, D. E. (1962). Post conditioning delay and intensity of shock as factors in the measurement of acquired fear. *Journal of Experimental Psychology, 64,* 110–116.

McAllister, W. R., & McAllister, D. E. (1971). Behavioral measurement of conditioned fear. In F. R. Brush (Ed.), *Aversive conditioning and learning.* New York: Academic Press.

McClelland, J. L. (1979). On the time relations of mental processes: An examination of systems of processes in cascade. *Psychological Review, 86,* 287–330.

McClelland, J. L., & Rumelhart, D. E. (1981). An interactive model of context effects in letter perception. Part 1: An account of basic findings. *Psychological Review, 88,* 375–407.

McClelland, J. L., & Rumelhart, D. E. (1986). *Parallel distributed processing* (Vol. 2). Cambridge, Mass.: M.I.T. Press.

McCloskey, M., & Cohen, N. J. (1989). Catastrophic interference in connectionist networks: The sequential learning problem. In G. H. Bower (Ed.), *The psychology of learning and motivation* (Vol. 23). New York: Academic Press.

McCloskey, M., & Glucksberg, S. (1978). Natural categories. Well-defined or fuzzy sets? *Memory and Cognition, 6,* 462–472.

McCloskey, M., & Glucksberg, S. (1979). Decision processes in verifying category membership statements: Implications for models of semantic memory. *Cognitive Psychology, 11,* 1–37.

McCloskey, M., Wible, C. G., & Cohen, N. J. (1988). Is there a special flashbulb-memory mechanism? *Journal of Experimental Psychology: General, 117,* 171–181.

McCloskey, M., & Zaragoza, Z. (1985). Misleading postevent information and memory for events: Arguments and evidence against memory impairment hypotheses. *Journal of Experimental Psychology: General, 114,* 3–18.

McGeoch, J. A. (1942). *The psychology of human learning.* New York: Longman, Green.

McGovern, J. B. (1964). Extinction of associations in four transfer paradigms. *Psychological Monographs, 78* (Whole No. 593).

McKoon, G., Ratcliff, R., & Dell, G. (1986). A critical evaluation of the semantic/episodic distinction. *Journal of Experimental Psychology: Learning, Memory, and Cognition, 12,* 295–306.

Medin, D. L. (1975). A theory of context in discrimination learning. In G. H. Bower (Ed.), *The psychology of learning and motivation* (Vol. 9). New York: Academic Press.

Medin, D. L. (1976). Theories of discrimination learning and learning set. In W. K. Estes (Ed.), *Handbook of learning and cognitive processes.* Hillsdale, N.J.: Erlbaum.

Medin, D. L., Altom, M. W., Edelson, S. M., & Freko, D. (1982). Correlated symptoms and simulated medical classification. *Journal of Experimental Psychology: Learning, Memory, and Cognition, 8,* 37–50.

Mellgren, R. (1982). Foraging in a simulated natural environment: There's a rat loose in the lab. *Journal of the Experimental Analysis of Behavior, 38,* 93–100.

Melton, A. W., & Irwin, J. M. (1940). The influence of degree of interpolated learning on retroactive inhibition and the overt transfer of specific responses. *American Journal of Psychology, 53,* 173–203.

Mendelsohn, G. A., & Griswold, B. B. (1967). Anxiety and repression as predictors of the use of incidental cues in problem solving. *Journal of Personality and Social Psychology, 6,* 353–359.

Menzel, E. W. (1978). Cognitive mapping in chimpanzees. In S. H. Hulse, H. F. Fowler, & W. K. Honig (Eds.), *Cognitive processes in animal behavior.* Hillsdale, N.J.: Erlbaum.

Mervis, C. B., Catlin, J., & Rosch, E. (1976). Relationships among goodness-of-example, category norms and word frequency. *Bulletin of the Psychonomic Society, 7,* 268–284.

Meudell, P. (1983). The development and dissolution of memory. In A. R. Mayes (Ed.), *Memory in humans and animals,* pp. 83–133. Wokingham, U.K.: Van Nostrand Reinhold.

Meyer, D. E., & Schvaneveldt, R. W. (1971). Facilitation in recognizing pairs of words: Evidence of a dependence between retrieval operations. *Journal of Experimental Psychology, 90,* 227–234.

Meyer, D. E., Schvaneveldt, R. W., & Ruddy, M. G. (1972). Activation of lexical memory. Paper presented at the meeting of the Psychonomic Society, St. Louis.

Meyer, D. E., Schvaneveldt, R. W., & Ruddy, M. G. (1974). Functions of graphemic and phonemic codes in visual word recognition. *Memory and Cognition, 2,* 309–321.

Millar, A., & Navarick, D. J. (1984). Self-control and choice in humans: Effects of video game playing as a positive reinforcer. *Learning and Motivation, 15,* 203–218.

Miller, G. A. (1956). The magical number seven plus or minus two: Some limits on our capacity for processing information. *Psychological Review, 63,* 81–97.

Miller, G. A., Galanter, E., & Pribram, K. H. (1960). *Plans and the structure of behavior.* New York: Holt, Rinehart and Winston.

Miller, N. E. (1948). Studies of fear as an acquirable drive. *Journal of Experimental Psychology, 38,* 89–101.

Miller, R. R., & Spear, N. E. (Eds.) (1985). *Information processing in animals: Conditioned inhibition.* Hillsdale, N.J.: Erlbaum.

Milner, B. (1966). Amnesia following operation on the temporal lobes. In C. W. M. Whitty & O. L. Zangwill (Eds.), *Amnesia.* London: Butterworths.

Milner, B. (1970). Memory and the medial temporal regions of the brain. In K. H. Pribram & D. E. Broadbent (Eds.), *Biology of memory.* New York: Academic Press.

Minami, H., & Dallenbach, K. M. (1946). The effect of activity upon learning and retention in the cockroach. *American Journal of Psychology, 59,* 1–58.

Mineka, S. (1979). The role of fear in theories of avoidance learning, flooding, and extinction. *Psychological Bulletin, 86,* 985–1010.

Mineka, S. (1985). The frightful complexity of the origins of fears. In F. R. Brush & J. B. Overmeir (Eds.), *Affect, conditioning, and cognition.* Hillsdale, N.J.: Erlbaum.

Mineka, S., & Gino, A. (1979). Dissociative effects of different types and amounts of non-reinforced CS exposure on avoidance extinction and the CER. *Learning and Motivation, 10,* 141–160.

Mineka, S., & Gino, A. (1980). Dissociation between conditioned emotional response and extended avoidance performance. *Learning and Motivation, 11,* 476–502.

Minor, T. R., Jackson, R. L., & Maier, S. F. (1984). Effects of task irrelevant cues and reinforcement delay on choice escape learning following inescapable shock: Evidence for a deficit in selective attention. *Journal of Experimental Psychology: Animal Behavior Processes, 10,* 543–566.

Mischel, W. (1966). Theory and research on the antecedents of self-imposed delay of reward. *Progress in Experimental Personality Research, 3,* 85–132.

Mischel, W. (1974). Processes in delay of gratification. In L. Berkowitz (Ed.), *Advances in experimental social psychology* (Vol. 7). New York: Academic Press.

Moore, J. W. (1972). Stimulus control: Studies of auditory generalization in rabbits. In A. H. Black & W. F. Prokasy (Eds.), *Classical conditioning II.* New York: Appleton-Century-Crofts.

Moray, N., Bates, A., & Barnett, T. (1965). Experiments on the four-eared man. *Journal of the Acoustical Society of America, 38,* 196–201.

Moreland, R. L., & Zajonc, R. B. (1977). Is stimulus recognition a necessary condition for the occurrence of exposure effects? *Journal of Personality and Social Psychology, 35,* 191–199.

Moreland, R. L., & Zajonc, R. B. (1979). Exposure effects may not depend on stimulus recognition. *Journal of Personality and Social Psychology, 37,* 1085–1089.

Morris, C. D., Bransford, J. D., & Franks, J. J. (1977). Levels of processing versus transfer appropriate processing. *Journal of Verbal Learning and Verbal Behavior, 16,* 519–533.

Moscovitch, M. (1982). Multiple dissociations of function in amnesia. In L. S. Cermak (Ed.), *Human memory and amnesia.* Hillsdale, N.J.: Erlbaum.

Mowrer, O. H. (1947). On the dual nature of learning: A reinterpretation of "conditioning" and "problem solving." *Harvard Educational Review, 17,* 102–148.

Moyer, R. S. (1973). Comparing objects in memory: Evidence suggesting an internal psychophysics. *Perception and Psychophysics, 13,* 180–184.

Moyer, R. S., & Bayer, R. H. (1976). Mental comparisons and the symbolic distance effect. *Cognitive Psychology, 8,* 228–246.

Murdock, B. B., Jr. (1962). The serial position effect of free recall. *Journal of Experimental Psychology, 64,* 482–488.

Nadel, L., & Zola-Morgan, S. (1984). Infantile amnesia: A neurobiological perspective. In M. Moscovitch (Ed.), *Infant memory.* New York: Plenum.

Nakamura, G. V., Graesser, A. C., Zimmerman, J. A., & Riha, J. (1985). Script processing in a natural situation. *Memory and Cognition, 13,* 140–144.

Neely, J. H. (1977). Semantic priming and retrieval from lexical memory: Role of inhibitionless spreading activation and limited capacity attention. *Journal of Experimental Psychology: General, 106,* 226–254.

Neisser, U. (1976). *Cognition and reality.* New York: W. H. Freeman.

Neisser, U. (1981). John Dean's memory: A case study. *Cognition, 9,* 1–22.

Neisser, U. (1982). *Memory observed.* San Francisco: W. H. Freeman.

Neisser, U. (1986). Remembering Pearl Harbor: Reply to Thompson and Cowan. *Cognition, 23,* 285–286.

Neisser, U. (1987). From direct perception to conceptual structure. In U. Neisser (Ed.), *Concepts and conceptual development.* Cambridge: Cambridge University Press.

Neisser, U., & Kerr, N. H. (1973). Spatial and mnemonic properties of visual images. *Cognitive Psychology, 5,* 138–150.

Nelson, K. (1988). The ontogeny of memory for real events. In U. Neisser & E. Winograd (Eds.), *Remembering reconsidered: Ecological and traditional approaches to the study of memory.* Cambridge: Cambridge University Press.

Nelson, K. R., & Wasserman, E. A. (1978). Temporal factors influencing the pigeon's successive matching-to-sample performance: Sample duration, intertrial interval, and retention interval. *Journal of the Experimental Analysis of Behavior, 30,* 153–162.

Nelson, R. L., Walling, J. R., & McEvoy, C. L. (1979). Doubts about depth. *Journal of Experimental Psychology: Human Learning and Memory, 5,* 24–44.

Nelson, T. O. (1976). Reinforcement and human memory. In W. K. Estes (Ed.), *Handbook of learning and cognitive processes* (Vol. 3). Hillsdale, N.J.: Erlbaum.

Nelson, T. O. (1977). Repetition and depth of processing. *Journal of Verbal Learning and Verbal Behavior, 16,* 151–171.

Neuman, P. G. (1977). Visual prototype information with discontinuous representation of dimensions of variability. *Memory and Cognition, 5,* 187–197.

Newman, F. L., & Baron, M. R. (1965). Stimulus generalization along the dimension of angularity. *Journal of Comparative and Physiological Psychology, 60,* 59–63.

Newman, P. (1965). *The theory of exchange.* Englewood Cliffs, N.J.: Prentice-Hall.

Nickerson, R. S. (1968). A note on long-term recognition memory for picture material. *Psychonomic Science, 11,* 58.

Nickerson, R. S., & Adams, M. J. (1979). Long-term memory for a common object. *Cognitive Psychology, 11,* 287–307.

Nisbett, R. E., Krantz, D. H., Jepson, C., & Kunda, Z. (1983). The use of statistical heuristics in everyday inductive reasoning. *Psychological Review, 90,* 339–363.

Nisbett, R. E., & Ross, L. (1980). *Human inference: Strategies and shortcomings of social judgment.* Englewood Cliffs, N.J.: Prentice-Hall.

Nisbett, R.E., & Wilson, T. D. (1977). Telling more than we can know: Verbal reports on mental processes. *Psychological Review, 84,* 231–259.

Nisbett, R. E., Zukier, H., & Lemley, R. E. (1981). The dilution effect: Nondiagnostic information weakens the implications of diagnostic information. *Cognitive Psychology, 13,* 248–277.

Norman, D. A., Rumelhart, D. E., & Group, T. L. R. (1975). *Explorations in cognition.* San Francisco: W. H. Freeman.

Notterman, J. M., & Mintz, D. E. (1965). *Dynamics of response.* New York: Wiley.

Oakley, D. A. (1983). The varieties of memory: A phylogenetic approach. In A. R. Mayes (Ed.), *Memory in humans and animals.* Wokingham, U.K.: Van Nostrand Reinhold.

Obrist, P. A., Sutterer, J. R., & Howard, J. L. (1972). Preparatory cardiac changes: A psychobiological approach. In A. H. Black & W. F. Prokasy (Eds.), *Classical conditioning II.* New York: Appleton-Century-Crofts.

O'Leary, K. D. (1978). The operant and social psychology of token systems. In A. C. Catania & T. A. Brigham (Eds.), *Handbook of applied behavior analysis.* New York: Irvington.

O'Leary, K. D., & Drabman, R. (1971). Token reinforcement programs in the classroom: A review. *Psychological Bulletin, 75,* 379–398.

Oliphant, G. W. (1983). Repetition and recency effects in word recognition. *Australian Journal of Psychology, 35,* 393–403.

Olson, D. J., & Maki, W. S. (1983). Characteristics of spatial memory in pigeons. *Journal of Experimental Psychology: Animal Behavior Processes, 9,* 266–280.

Olton, D. S. (1978). Characteristics of spatial memory. In S. H. Hulse, H. F. Fowler, & W. K. Honig (Eds.), *Cognitive processes in animal behavior,* pp. 341–373. Hillsdale, N.J.: Erlbaum.

Olton, D. S. (1979). Mazes, maps and memory. *American Psychologist, 34,* 583–596.

Olton, D. S., Collision, C., & Werz, M. A. (1977). Spatial memory and radial arm maze performance of rats. *Learning and Motivation, 8,* 289–314.

Olton, D. S., & Samuelson, R. J. (1976). Remembrances of places passed: Spatial memory in rats. *Journal of Experimental Psychology: Animal Behavior Processes, 2,* 96–116.

Osherson, D. N., & Smith, E. E. (1981). On the adequacy of prototype theory as a theory of concepts. *Cognition, 9,* 35–58.

Overton, D. A. (1964). State-dependent or "dissociated" learning produced with pentobarbital. *Journal of Comparative and Physiological Psychology, 57,* 3–12.

Overton, D. A. (1985). Contextual stimulus effects of drugs and internal states. In P. D. Balsam & A. Tomie (Eds.), *Context and Learning.* Hillsdale, N.J.: Erlbaum.

Owens, J., Bower, G. H., & Black, J. B. (1979). The "soap opera" effect in story recall. *Memory and Cognition, 7,* 185–191.

Paivio, A., (1969). Mental imagery in associative learning and memory. *Psychological Review, 76,* 241–263.

Paivio, A. (1971). *Imagery and verbal processes.* New York: Holt, Rinehart & Winston.

Paivio, A. (1978). Dual coding: Theoretical issues and empirical evidence. In J. M. Scandura & C. J. Brainerd (Eds.), *Structural/process models of complex human behavior.* Leiden: Nordhoff.

Paivio, A. (1980). On weighing things in your mind. In P. W. Jusezyk & R. W. Klein (Eds.), *The nature of thought.* Hillsdale, N.J.: Erlbaum.

Paivio, A., & Csapo, K. (1969). Concrete image and verbal memory codes. *Journal of Experimental Psychology, 80,* 279–285.

Paivio, A., & Okovita, H. W. (1971). Word imagery modalities and associative learning in blind and sighted subjects. *Journal of Verbal Learning and Verbal Behavior, 10,* 506–510.

Paivio, A., Smythe, P. C., & Yuille, J. C. (1968). Imagery versus meaningfulness of nouns in paired-associate learning. *Canadian Journal of Psychology, 22,* 427–441.

Paivio, A., Yuille, J. C., & Madigan, S. (1968). Concreteness, imagery, and meaningfulness values for 925 nouns. *Journal of Experimental Psychology Monographs, 78* (1, Pt. 2).

Paris, S. C., & Lindauer, B. K. (1976). The role of inference in children's comprehension and memory for sentences. *Cognitive Psychology, 8,* 217–227.

Parkin, A. J. (1984). Levels of processing, context, and facilitation of pronunciation. *Acta Psychologia, 55,* 19–29.

Patterson, K. E., & Baddeley, A. D. (1975). When face recognition fails. *Journal of Experimental Psychology: Human Learning and Memory, 3,* 406–417.

Pavlov, I. (1927). *Conditioned reflexes.* Oxford: Oxford University Press.

Pearce, J. M., & Hall, G. (1980). A model for Pavlovian learning. *Psychological Review, 87,* 532–552.

Peeke, H. V. S., & Petrinovich, L. (Eds.) (1984). *Habituation, sensitization, and behavior.* New York: Academic Press.

Peeke, H. V. S., & Vino, G. (1973). Stimulus specificity of habituated aggression in three-spined sticklebacks *(Gasterosteus aculeatus). Behavioral Biology, 8,* 427–432.

Pelchat, M. L., & Rozin, P. (1982). The special role of nausea in the acquisition of food dislikes by humans. *Appetite, 3,* 215–223.

Penfield, W., & Roberts, L. (1959). *Speech and brain mechanisms.* Princeton: Princeton University Press.

Perone, M., & Baron, A. (1980). Reinforcement of human observing behavior by a stimulus correlated with extinction or increased effort. *Journal of the Experimental Analysis of Behavior, 34,* 239–261.

Peterson, C., & Seligman, M. E. P. (1984). Causal explanations as a risk factor for depression: Theory and evidence. *Psychological Review, 91,* 347–374.

Peterson, L. R., & Peterson, M. J. (1959). Short-term retention of individual verbal items. *Journal of Experimental Psychology, 58,* 193–198.

Peterson, L. R., & Potts, G. R. (1982). Global and specific components of information integration. *Journal of Verbal Learning and Verbal Behavior, 21,* 403–420.

Pezdek, K., Whetstone, T., Reynolds, K., Askari, N., & Doughterty, T. (1989). Memory for real-world scenes: The role of consistency with schema expectation. *Journal of Experimental Psychology: Learning, Memory, and Cognition, 15,* 587–595.

Pillemer, D. B. (1984). Flashbulb memories of the assassination attempt on President Reagan. *Cognition, 16,* 63–80.

Pinker, S., & Prince, A. (1988). On language and connectionism: Analysis of a parallel distributed processing model of language acquisition. *Cognition, 28,* 73–193.

Porter, D., & Neuringer, A. (1984). Music discrimination by pigeons. *Journal of Experimental Psychology: Animal Behavior Processes, 10,* 138–148.

Posner, M. I. (1978). *Chronometric explorations of mind.* Hillsdale, N.J.: Erlbaum.

Postman, L. (1964). Short-term memory and incidental learning. In A. W. Melton (Ed.), *Categories of human learning.* New York: Academic Press.

Postman, L. (1969). Mechanisms of interference in forgetting. In G. A. Talland & N. C. Waugh (Eds.), *The pathology of memory,* pp. 195–210. New York: Academic Press.

Postman, L. (1975). Verbal learning and memory. *Annual Review of Psychology, 26,* 291–335.

Postman, L., & Phillips, L. W. (1965). Short-term temporal changes in free recall. *Quarterly Journal of Experimental Psychology, 17,* 132–138.

Postman, L., & Stark, K. (1969). Role of reponse availability in transfer and interference. *Journal of Experimental Psychology, 79,* 168–177.

Postman, L., Thompkins, B. A., & Gray, W. D. (1978). The interpretation of encoding effects in retention. *Journal of Verbal Learning and Verbal Behavior, 17,* 681–705.

Postman, L., & Underwood, B. J. (1973). Critical issues in interference theory. *Memory and Cognition, 1,* 19–40.

Potts, G. R. (1972). Information-processing strategies used in the encoding of linear orderings. *Journal of Verbal Learning and Verbal Behavior, 11,* 727–740.

Potts, G. R. (1973). Memory for redundant information. *Memory and Cognition, 1,* 467–470.

Potts, G. R. (1974). Storing and retrieving information about ordered relationships. *Journal of Experimental Psychology, 103,* 431–439.

Potts, G. R. (1976). Artificial logical relations and their relevance to semantic memory. *Journal of Experimental Psychology: Human Learning and Memory, 2,* 746–758.

Potts, G. R. (1977). Integrating new and old information. *Journal of Verbal Learning and Verbal Behavior, 16,* 305–320.

Poulos, C. X., Hinson, R. E., & Siegel, S. (1981). The role of Pavlovian processes in drug tolerance and dependence: Implications for treatment. *Addictive Behaviors, 6,* 205–211.

Prelec, D. (1982). Matching, maximizing, and the hyperbolic reinforcement feedback function. *Psychological Review, 89,* 189–230.

Premack, D. (1976). *Intelligence in ape and man.* Hillsdale, N.J.: Erlbaum.

Premack, D. (1978). On the abstractness of human concepts: Why it would be difficult to talk to a pigeon. In S. H. Hulse, H. Fowler, & W. K. Honig (Eds.), *Cognitive processes in animal behavior.* Hillsdale, N.J.: Erlbaum.

Prewitt, E. P. (1967). Number of preconditioning trials in sensory preconditioning using CER training. *Journal of Comparative and Physiological Psychology, 64,* 360–362.

Pyke, G. H., Pulliam, H. R., & Charnov, E. L. (1977). Optimal foraging: A selective review of theory and tests. *Quarterly Review of Biology, 52,* 137–154.

Pylyshyn, Z. (1981). The imagery debate: Analogue media versus tacit knowledge. *Psychological Review, 88,* 16–45.

Pylyshyn, Z. (1984). *Computation and cognition.* Cambridge, Mass.: M.I.T. Press.

Quillian, M. R. (1969). The teachable language comprehender. *Communications of the Association for Computing Machinery, 12,* 459–476.

Quinsey, V. L. (1971). Conditioned suppression with no CS–US contingency in the rat. *Canadian Journal of Psychology, 25,* 69–82.

Rachlin, H. (1974). Self-control. *Behaviorism, 2,* 94–107.

Rachlin, H. (1980). Economics and behavioral psychology. In J. E. R. Staddon (Ed.), *Limits to action.* New York: Academic Press.

Rachlin, H., Battalio, R. C., Kagel, J. H., & Green, L. (1981). Maximization theory in behavioral psychology. *Behavioral and Brain Sciences, 4,* 371–388.

Rachlin, H., & Green, L. (1972). Commitment, choice and self-control. *Journal of the Experimental Analysis of Behavior, 17,* 15–22.

Rachlin, H., Green, L., Kagel, J. H., & Battalio, R. C. (1976). Economic demand theory and psychological studies of choice. In G. H. Bower (Ed.), *The psychology of learning and motivation* (Vol. 10). New York: Academic Press.

Randich, A. (1981). The US preexposure phenomenon in the conditioned suppression paradigm: A role for conditioned situational stimuli. *Learning and Motivation, 12,* 321–341.

Randich, A., & LoLordo, V. M. (1979). Associative and non-associative theories of the UCS preexposure phenomenon: Implications for Pavlovian conditioning. *Psychological Bulletin, 86,* 523–548.

Rao, G. A., Larkin, E. C., & Derr, R. F. (1986). Biologic effects of chronic ethanol consumption related to a deficient intake of carbohydrates. *Alcohol and Alcoholism, 21,* 369–373.

Rapaport, D. (1942). *Emotions and memory.* New York: International Universities Press.

Ratcliff, R., & McKoon, G. (1981). Automatic and strategic priming in recognition. *Journal of Verbal Learning and Verbal Behavior, 20,* 204–215.

Rayko, D. (1977). Does knowledge matter? Psychological information and bystander helping. *Canadian Journal of Behavioral Sciences, 9,* 295–304.

Read, J. D., & Bruce, D. (1982). Longitudinal tracking of difficult memory retrievals. *Cognitive Psychology, 14,* 280–300.

Reason, J. T., & Lucas, D. (1984). Using cognitive diaries to investigate naturally occurring memory blocks. In J. E. Harris & P. E. Morris (Eds.), *Everyday memory actions and absent-mindedness.* London: Academic Press.

Reber, A. S., & Allen, R. (1978). Analogy and abstraction strategies in synthetic grammar learning: A functional interpretation. *Cognition, 6,* 189–221.

Reder, L. M. (1982). Plausibility judgment versus fact retrieval: Alternative strategies for sentence verification. *Psychological Review, 89,* 250–280.

Reder, L. M., & Anderson, J. R. (1980). A comparison of texts and their summaries: Memorial consequences. *Journal of Verbal Learning and Verbal Behavior, 19,* 12–34.

Reder, L. M., & Ross, B. H. (1983). Integrated knowledge in different tasks: Positive and negative fan effects. *Journal of Experimental Psychology: Human Learning and Memory, 8,* 55–72.

Reed, S. K. (1972). Pattern recognition and categorization. *Cognitive Psychology, 3,* 383–407.

Reich, S. S., & Ruth, P. (1982). Wason's selection task: Verification, falsification and matching. *British Journal of Psychology, 73,* 395–405.

Reisberg, D. (1987). External representations and the advantages of externalizing one's thought. In E. Hunt (Ed.), *The ninth annual conference of the Cognitive Science Society.* Hillsdale, N.J.: Erlbaum.

Reisberg, D. (1990). *Auditory imagery.* Hillsdale, N.J.: Erlbaum.

Reisberg, D., & Chambers, D. (1990). Neither pictures nor propositions: What can we learn from a mental image? *Canadian Journal of Psychology,* in press.

Reisberg, D., Culver, C., Heuer, F., & Fischman, D. (1986). Why does vivid imagery hurt colour memory? *Canadian Journal of Psychology, 40,* 161–175.

Reisberg, D., & Heuer, F. (1990). Remembering emotional events. In E. Winograd & U. Neisser (Eds.), *Affect and flashbulb memories.* New York: Cambridge University Press.

Reisberg, D., Heuer, F., McLean, J., & O'Shaughnessy, M. (1988). The quantity, not the quality, of affect predicts memory vividness. *Bulletin of the Psychonomic Society, 26,* 100–103.

Reisberg, D., Smith, J. D., Baxter, D. A., & Sonenshine, M. (1989). "Enacted" auditory images are ambiguous; "pure" auditory images are not. *Quarterly Journal of Experimental Psychology, 41A,* 619–641.

Reiss, S., & Wagner, A. R. (1972). CS habituation produces a "latent inhibition" effect but no active conditioned inhibition. *Learning and Motivation, 3,* 237–245.

Rescorla, R. A. (1967a). Pavlovian conditioning and its proper control procedures. *Psychological Review, 74,* 71–80.

Rescorla, R. A. (1967b). Inhibition of delay in Pavlovian fear conditioning. *Journal of Comparative and Physiological Psychology, 64,* 114–120.

Rescorla, R. A. (1968). Pavlovian conditioned fear in Sidman avoidance learning. *Journal of Comparative and Physiological Psychology, 65,* 55–60.

Rescorla, R. A. (1969). Pavlovian conditioned inhibition. *Psychological Bulletin, 72,* 77–94.

Rescorla, R. A. (1973). Effects of US habituation following conditioning. *Journal of Comparative and Physiological Psychology, 82,* 137–143.

Rescorla, R. A. (1974). Effect of inflation on the unconditioned stimulus value following conditioning. *Journal of Comparative and Physiological Psychology, 86,* 101–106.

Rescorla, R. A. (1979a). Aspects of the reinforcer learned in second-order Pavlovian conditioning. *Journal of Experimental Psychology: Animal Behavior Processes, 5,* 79–95.

Rescorla, R. A. (1979b). Conditioned inhibition and extinction. In A. Dickenson & R. A. Boakes (Eds.), *Mechanisms of learning and motivation.* Hillsdale, N.J.: Erlbaum.

Rescorla, R. A. (1980a). *Pavlovian second-order conditioning.* Hillsdale, N.J.: Erlbaum.

Rescorla, R. A. (1980b). Simultaneous and successive association in sensory preconditioning. *Journal of Experimental Psychology: Animal Behavior Processes, 6,* 207–216.

Rescorla, R. A. (1982). Simultaneous second order conditioning produces S–S learning in conditioned suppression. *Journal of Experimental Psychology: Animal Behavior Processes, 8,* 23–32.

Rescorla, R. A. (1985). Conditioned inhibition and facilitation. In R. R. Miller & N. E. Spear (Eds.), *Information processing in animals: Conditioned inhibition.* Hillsdale, N.J.: Erlbaum.

Rescorla, R. A. (1987). A Pavlovian analysis of goal-directed behavior. *American Psychologist, 42,* 119–129.

Rescorla, R. A., & Furrow, D. R. (1977). Stimulus similarity as a determinant of Pavlovian conditioning. *Journal of Experimental Psychology: Animal Behavior Processes, 3,* 203–215.

Rescorla, R. A., & Gillian, D. J. (1980). An analysis of the facilitative effect of similarity on second-order conditioning. *Journal of Experimental Psychology: Animal Behavior Processes, 6,* 339–352.

Rescorla, R. A., & Holland, P. C. (1977). Associations in Pavlovian conditioned inhibition. *Learning and Motivation, 8,* 429–447.

Rescorla, R. A., & LoLordo, V. M. (1965). Inhibition of avoidance behavior. *Journal of Comparative and Physiological Psychology, 59,* 406–412.

Rescorla, R. A., & Solomon, R. L. (1967). Two-process learning theory: Relations between Pavlovian conditioning and instrumental learning. *Psychological Review, 74,* 151–182.

Rescorla, R. A., & Wagner, A. R. (1972). A theory of Pavlovian conditioning: Variations in the effectiveness of reinforcement and non-reinforcement. In A. H. Black & W. F. Prokasy (Eds.), *Classical conditioning II.* New York: Appleton-Century-Crofts.

Revusky, S. H., & Garcia, J. (1970). Learned associations over long delays. In G. H. Bower & J. T. Spence (Eds.), *The psychology of learning and motivation* (Vol. 4). New York: Academic Press.

Reynolds, G. S. (1961). Behavioral contrast. *Journal of the Experimental Analysis of Behavior, 4,* 57–71.

Richardson-Klavehn, A., & Bjork, R. A. (1988). Measures of memory. *Annual Review of Psychology, 39,* 475–543.

Richie, B. F. (1951). Can reinforcement theory account for avoidance? *Psychological Review, 58,* 382–386.

Riley, D. A. (1968). *Discrimination learning.* Boston: Allyn and Bacon.

Rilling, M. (1977). Stimulus control and inhibitory processes. In W. K. Honig & J. E. R. Staddon (Eds.), *Handbook of operant behavior.* Englewood Cliffs, N.J.: Prentice-Hall.

Rilling, M., Kendrick, D. F., & Stonebraker, T. B. (1984). Directed forgetting in context. In G. H. Bower (Ed.), *The psychology of learning and motivation* (Vol. 18). New York: Academic Press.

Rips, L. J. (1975). Inductive judgments about natural categories. *Journal of Verbal Learning and Verbal Behavior, 14,* 665–681.

Rips, L. J. (1983). Cognitive processes in propositional reasoning. *Psychological Review, 90,* 38–71.

Rips, L. J., Shoben, E. J., & Smith, E. E. (1973). Semantic distance and the verification of semantic relations. *Journal of Verbal Learning and Verbal Behavior, 12,* 1–20.

Ritchie, J. M. (1985). The aliphatic alcohols. In A. G. Gilman, L. S. Goodman, T. W. Rall, & F. Murad (Eds.), *The pharmacological basis of therapeutics,* pp. 372–386. New York: Macmillan.

Rizley, R. C., & Rescorla, R. A. (1972). Associations in higher order conditioning and sensory preconditioning. *Journal of Comparative and Physiological Psychology, 81,* 1–11.

Roberts, W. A. (1981). Retroactive inhibition in rat spatial memory. *Animal Learning and Behavior, 9,* 566–574.

Roberts, W. A., & Grant, D. S. (1976). Studies of short-term memory in the pigeon using the delayed matching to sample procedure. In D. L. Medin, W. A. Roberts, & R. T. Davis (Eds.), *Processes of animal memory.* Hillsdale, N.J.: Erlbaum.

Roberts, W. A., & Grant, D. S. (1978). An analysis of light-induced retroactive inhibition in pigeon short-term memory. *Journal of Experimental Psychology: Animal Behavior Processes, 4,* 219–236.

Rock, I. (1983). *The logic of perception.* Cambridge, Mass.: M.I.T. Press.

Roediger, H. L. (1980). The effectiveness of four mnemonics in ordering recall. *Journal of Experimental Psychology: Human Learning and Memory, 6,* 558–567.

Roediger, H. L., & Blaxton, T. A. (1987a). Effects of varying modality, surface features, and retention interval on word fragment completion. *Memory and Cognition, 15,* 379–388.

Roediger, H. L., & Blaxton, T. A. (1987b). Retrieval modes produce dissociations in memory for surface information. In D. S. Gorfein (Ed.), *Memory and cognitive processes: The Ebbinghaus Centennial Conference,* pp. 349–379. Hillsdale, N.J.: Erlbaum.

Roediger, H. L., & Crowder, R. G. (1976). The serial position effect in recall of U. S. presidents. Unpublished manuscript.

Roediger, H. L., & Neely, J. H. (1982). Retrieval blocks in episodic and semantic memory. *Canadian Journal of Psychology, 36,* 213–242.

Roediger, H. L., & Payne, D. G. (1982). Hypermnesia: The role of repeated testing. *Journal of Experimental Psychology: Learning, Memory, and Cognition, 8,* 66–72.

Roediger, H. L., & Payne, D. G. (1985). Recall criterion does not affect recall level or hypermnesia: A puzzle for generate/recognize theories. *Memory and Cognition, 13,* 1–7.

Roediger, H. L., & Thorpe, L. A. (1978). The role of recall time in producing hypermnesia. *Memory and Cognition, 6,* 296–305.

Rogers, T. B., Kuiper, N. A., & Kirker, W. A. (1977). Self-reference and the encoding of personal information. *Journal of Personality and Social Psychology, 35,* 677–688.

Roitblat, H. L. (1980). Codes and coding process in pigeon short-term memory. *Animal Learning and Behavior, 8,* 341–351.

Roitblat, H. L. (1982). The meaning of representation in animal memory. *Behavioral and Brain Sciences, 5,* 353–372.

Roitblat, H. L., Bever, T. G., & Terrace, H. S. (Eds.) (1984). *Animal Cognition.* Hillsdale, N.J.: Erlbaum.

Rosch, E. H. (1973). On the internal structure of perceptual and semantic categories. In T. E. Moore (Ed.), *Cognitive development and the acquisition of language.* New York: Academic Press.

Rosch, E. H. (1975). Cognitive representations of semantic categories. *Journal of Experimental Psychology: General, 104,* 192–233.

Rosch, E. H. (1977). Human categorization. In N. Warren (Ed.), *Advances in cross-cultural psychology.* London: Academic Press.

Rosch, E. H. (1978). Principles of categorization. In E. Rosch & B. Lloyd (Eds.), *Cognition and categorization,* pp. 27–48. Hillsdale, N.J.: Erlbaum.

Rosch, E., & Lloyd, B. (Eds.) (1978). *Cognition and categorization.* Hillsdale, N.J.: Erlbaum.

Rosch, E. H., & Mervis, C. B. (1975). Family resemblances: Studies in the internal structure of categories. *Cognitive Psychology, 7,* 573–605.

Rosch, E. H., Mervis, C. B., Gray, W., Johnson, D., & Boyes-Braem, P. (1976). Basic objects in natural categories. *Cognitive Psychology, 3,* 382–439.

Rosch, E., Simpson, C., & Miller, R. S. (1976). Structural bases of typicality effects. *Journal of Experimental Psychology: Human Perception and Performance, 2,* 491–502.

Ross, J., & Lawrence, K. A. (1968). Some observations on memory artifice. *Psychonomic Science, 13,* 107–108.

Ross, M., & Sicoly, F. (1979). Egocentric biases in availability and attribution. *Journal of Personality and Social Psychology, 37,* 322–336.

Ross, R. T., & Holland, P. C. (1981). Conditioning of simultaneous and serial feature positive discriminations. *Animal Learning and Behavior, 9,* 293–303.

Ross, R. T., & Holland, P. C. (1982). Serial positive patterning: Implications for "occasion setting." *Bulletin of the Psychonomic Society, 19,* 159–162.

Ross, R. T., & LoLordo, V. M. (1986). Blocking during serial feature positive discriminations: Associative versus occasion-setting functions. *Journal of Experimental Psychology: Animal Behavior Processes, 12,* 315–324.

Ross, R. T., & LoLordo, V. M. (1987). Evaluation of the relation between Pavlovian occasion-setting and instrumental discriminative stimuli: A blocking analysis. *Journal of Experimental Psychology: Animal Behavior Processes, 13,* 3–16.

Rosselini, R. A., DeCola, J. P., & Shapiro, N. K. (1982). Cross-motivational effects of inescapable shock are associative in nature. *Journal of Experimental Psychology: Animal Behavior Processes, 8,* 376–388.

Rothkopf, E. Z. (1971). Incidental memory for location of information in text. *Journal of Verbal Learning and Verbal Behavior, 10,* 608–613.

Rozin, P. (1976). The evolution of intelligence and access to the cognitive unconscious. In E. Stellar & J. M. Sprague (Eds.), *Progress in psychobiology and physiological psychology* (Vol. 6). New York: Academic Press.

Rozin, P., & Kalat, J. W. (1971). Specific hungers and poison avoidance as adaptive specializations of learning. *Psychological Review, 78,* 459–486.

Rubin, D. C., & Kontis, T. S. (1983). A schema for common cents. *Memory and Cognition, 11,* 335–341.

Rubin, D. C., & Kozin, M. (1984). Vivid memories. *Cognition, 16,* 81–95.

Rubin, D. C., Wetzler, S.E., & Nebes, R.D. (1986). Autobiographical memory across the lifespan. In D. Rubin (Ed.), *Autobiographical memory.* New York: Cambridge University Press.

Rudolph, R. L., & Van Houten, R. (1977). Auditory stimulus control in pigeons: Jenkins and Harrison (1960) revisited. *Journal of the Experimental Analysis of Behavior, 27,* 327–330.

Rumelhart, D. E., & McClelland, J. L. (1986). *Parallel distributed processing* (Vol. 1). Cambridge, Mass.: M.I.T. Press.

Rumelhart, D. E., & Norman, D. A. (1975). The active structural network. In D. A. Norman & D. E. Rumelhart (Eds.), *Explorations in cognition.* San Francisco: W. H. Freeman.

Rumelhart, D. E., & Ortony, A. (1977). The representation of knowledge in memory. In R. C. Anderson, R. J. Spiro, & W. E. Montague (Eds.), *Schooling and the acquisition of knowledge.* Hillsdale, N.J.: Erlbaum.

Rundus, D. (1971). Analysis of rehearsal processes in free recall. *Journal of Experimental Psychology, 89,* 63–77.

Rundus, D. (1980). Maintenance rehearsal and long-term recency. *Memory and Cognition, 8,* 226–230.

Sachs, J. D. S. (1967). Recognition memory for syntactic and semantic aspects of connected discourse. *Perception and Psychophysics, 2,* 437–442.

Sachs, E., Weingarten, M., & Klein, N.W., Jr. (1966). Effects of chlordiazepoxide on the acquisition of avoidance learning and its transfer to the normal state and other drug conditions. *Psychopharmacologia, 9,* 17–30.

Sacks, O. (1987). *The man who mistook his wife for a hat, and other clinical tales.* New York: Harper & Row.

Salame, P., & Baddeley, A. D. (1982). Disruption of short-term memory by unattended speech: Implications for the structure of working memory. *Journal of Verbal Learning and Verbal Behavior, 21,* 150–164.

Schachtel, E. G. (1947). On memory and childhood amnesia. *Psychiatry, 10,* 1–26.

Schacter, D. L. (1987). Implicit memory: History and current status. *Journal of Experimental Psychology: Learning, Memory, and Cognition, 13,* 501–518.

Schacter, D. L., & Tulving, E. (1982a). Amnesia and memory research. In L. S. Cermak (Ed.), *Human memory and amnesia.* Hillsdale, N.J.: Erlbaum.

Schacter, D. L., & Tulving, E. (1982b). Memory, amnesia, and the episodic/semantic distinction. In R. L. Isaacson & N. E. Spear (Eds.), *The expression of knowledge.* New York: Plenum.

Schacter, D. L., Tulving, E., & Wang, P. (1981). Source amnesia: New methods and illustrative data. Paper presented at the meeting of the International Neuropsychological Society, Atlanta.

Schank, R. C. (1982). *Dynamic memory: A theory of reminding and learning in computers and people.* New York: Cambridge University Press.

Schank, R. C., & Abelson, R. (1977). *Scripts, plans, goals, and understanding.* Hillsdale, N.J.: Erlbaum.

Schiff, R., Smith, N., & Prochaska, J. (1972). Extinction of avoidance in rats as a function of duration and number of blocked trials. *Journal of Comparative and Physiological Psychology, 81,* 356–359.

Schmidt, S. R., & Bohannon, J. N., III. (1988). In defense of the flashbulb-memory hypothesis: A comment on McCloskey, Wible, and Cohen (1988). *Journal of Experimental Psychology: General, 117,* 332–335.

Schneiderman, N. (1973). *Classical (Pavlovian) Conditioning.* Morristown, N.J.: General Learning Press.

Schneiderman, N., Fuentes, I., & Gormezano, I. (1962). Acquisition and extinction of the classically conditioned eyelid response in the albino rabbit. *Science, 136,* 650–652.

Schull, J. (1979). A conditioned opponent theory of Pavlovian conditioning and habituation. In G. H. Bower (Ed.), *The psychology of learning and motivation* (Vol. 13). New York: Academic Press.

Schwartz, B. (1973). Maintenance of keypecking in pigeons by a food avoidance but not a shock avoidance contingency. *Animal Learning and Behavior, 1,* 164–166.

Schwartz, B. (1974). On going back to nature: A review of Seligman and Hager's *Biological boundaries of learning. Journal of the Experimental Analysis of Behavior, 21,* 183–198.

Schwartz, B. (1980). Development of complex, stereotyped behavior in pigeons. *Journal of the Experimental Analysis of Behavior, 33,* 153–166.

Schwartz, B. (1981). Reinforcement creates behavioral units. *Behaviour Analysis Letters, 1,* 33–41.

Schwartz, B. (1982). Failure to produce response variability with reinforcement. *Journal of the Experimental Analysis of Behavior, 37,* 171–181.

Schwartz, B., & Gamzu, E. (1977). Pavlovian control of operant behavior. In W. K. Honig & J. E. R. Staddon (Eds.), *Handbook of operant behavior.* Englewood Cliffs, N.J.: Prentice-Hall.

Schwartz, B., & Lacey, H. (1988). What applied studies of human operant conditioning tell us about humans and about conditioning. In G. Davie (Ed.), *Conditioning in humans.* New York: Wiley.

Seawright, J. E., Kaiser, P. E., Dame, D. A., & Lofgren, C. S. (1978). Learned taste aversions in children receiving chemotherapy. *Science, 200,* 1302–1304.

Segal, S. J., & Fusella, V. (1970). Influence of imaged pictures and sounds in detection of visual and auditory signals. *Journal of Experimental Psychology, 83,* 458–474.

Segal, S., & Fusella, V. (1971). Effect of images in six sense modalities on detection of visual signal from noise. *Psychonomic Science, 24,* 55–56.

Seligman, M. E. P. (1966). CS redundancy and secondary punishment. *Journal of Experimental Psychology, 72,* 546–550.

Seligman, M. E. P. (1968). Chronic fear produced by unpredictable shock. *Journal of Comparative and Physiological Psychology, 66,* 402–411.

Seligman, M. E. P. (1969). Control group and conditioning: A comment on operationism. *Psychological Review, 76,* 481–491.

Seligman, M. E. P. (1970). On the generality of laws of learning. *Psychological Review, 77,* 406–418.

Seligman, M. E. P. (1975). *Helplessness.* San Francisco: W. H. Freeman.

Seligman, M. E. P., & Binik, Y. M. (1977). The safety signal hypothesis. In H. Davis & H. M. B. Hurwitz (Eds.), *Operant–Pavlovian interactions.* Hillsdale, N.J.: Erlbaum.

Seligman, M. E. P., & Hager, J. L. (Eds.) (1972). *Biological boundaries of learning.* New York: Appleton-Century-Crofts.

Seligman, M. E. P., & Johnston, J. C. (1973). A cognitive theory of avoidance learning. In F. J. McGuigan & D. B. Lumsden (Eds.), *Contemporary approaches to conditioning and learning.* Washington, D.C.: Winston–Wiley.

Seligman, M. E. P., Maier, S., & Geer, J. (1968). The alleviation of learned helplessness in the dog. *Journal of Abnormal and Social Psychology, 73,* 256–262.

Seltzer, B., & Benson, D. F. (1974). The temporal pattern of retrograde amnesia in Korsakoff's disease. *Neurology, 24,* 527–530.

Shapiro, K. L., Jacobs, W. J., & LoLordo, V. M. (1980). Stimulus–reinforcer interactions in Pavlovian conditioning of pigeons: Implications for selective associations. *Animal Learning and Behavior, 8,* 586–594.

Shapiro, K. L., & LoLordo, V. M. (1982). Constraints on Pavlovian conditioning of the pigeon: Relative conditioned reinforcing effects of red-light and tone CSs paired with food. *Learning and Motivation, 13,* 68–80.

Sheffield, F. D. (1965). Relation between classical conditioning and instrumental learning. In W. F. Prokasy (Ed.), *Classical Conditioning.* New York: Appleton-Century-Crofts.

Shepard, R. N. (1967). Recognition memory for words, sentences, and pictures. *Journal of Verbal Learning and Verbal Behavior, 6,* 156–163.

Shepard, R. N., & Cooper, L. A. (1982). *Mental images and their transformations.* Cambridge, Mass.: M.I.T. Press.

Shepard, R. N., & Metzler, J. (1971). Mental rotation of three-dimensional objects. *Science, 171,* 701–703.

Shepp, B. E., & Eimas, P. D. (1964). Intradimensional and extradimensional shifts in the rat. *Journal of Comparative and Physiological Psychology, 57,* 357–361.

Shepp, B. E., & Schrier, A. M. (1969). Consecutive intradimensional and extradimensional shifts in monkeys. *Journal of Comparative and Physiological Psychology, 67,* 199–203.

Shettleworth, S. (1972a). Constraints on learning. In D. S. Lehrman, R. A. Hinde,

& E. Shaw (Eds.), *Advances in the study of behavior* (Vol. 4). New York: Academic Press.

Shettleworth, S. (1972b). Stimulus relevance in the control of drinking and conditioned fear responses in domestic chicks *(Gallus gallus)*. *Journal of Comparative and Physiological Psychology, 80,* 175–198.

Shettleworth, S. J. (1983). Memory in food-hoarding birds. *Scientific American, 248,* 102–110.

Shettleworth, S. J. (1985). Handling time and choice in pigeons. *Journal of the Experimental Analysis of Behavior, 44,* 139–155.

Shettleworth, S. J., & Krebs, J. R. (1982). How marsh tits find their hoards: The roles of site preference and spatial memory. *Journal of Experimental Psychology: Animal Behavior Processes, 8,* 354–375.

Shiffrin, R. M. (1970). Memory search. In D. A. Norman (Ed.), *Models of human memory,* pp. 375–447. New York: Academic Press.

Shimp, C. P. (1966). Probabilistically reinforced choice behavior in pigeons. *Journal of the Experimental Analysis of Behavior, 9,* 443–455.

Shimp, C. P. (1969). Optimal behavior in free-operant experiments. *Psychological Review, 76,* 97–112.

Shurtleff, D., & Ayres, J. J. B. (1981). One-trial backward excitatory fear conditioning in rats: Acquisition, retention, extinction and spontaneous recovery. *Animal Learning and Behavior, 9,* 65–74.

Sidman, M. (1953). Two temporal parameters of the maintenance of avoidance behavior in the white rat. *Journal of Comparative and Physiological Psychology, 46,* 253–261.

Sidman, M. (1966). Avoidance behavior. In W. K. Honig (Ed.), *Operant behavior: Areas of research and application.* New York: Appleton-Century-Crofts.

Siegel, S. (1975). Evidence from rats that morphine tolerance is a learned response. *Journal of Comparative and Physiological Psychology, 89,* 498–506.

Siegel, S. (1977). Morphine tolerance acquisition as an associative process. *Journal of Experimental Psychology: Animal Behavior Processes, 3,* 1–13.

Siegel, S. (1978). Tolerance to the hypothermic effect of morphine in the rat is a learned response. *Journal of Comparative and Physiological Psychology, 92,* 1137–1149.

Siegel, S. (1979). The role of conditioning in drug tolerance and addiction. In J. D. Keehn (Ed.), *Psychopathology in animals: Research and clinical implications.* New York: Academic Press.

Siegel, S. (1983). Classical conditioning, drug tolerance, and drug dependence. In Y. Israel, F. B. Glaser, H. Kalant, R. E. Popham, W. Schmidt, & R. G. Smart (Eds.), *Research advances in alcohol and drug problems* (Vol. 7). New York: Plenum.

Siegel, S., Hinson, R. E., & Krank, M. D. (1978). The role of predrug signals in morphine analgesic tolerance: Support for a Pavlovian conditioning model of tolerance. *Journal of Experimental Psychology: Animal Behavior Processes, 4,* 188–196.

Siegel, S., Hinson, R. E., Krank, M. D., & McCully, J. (1982). Heroin "overdose" death: Contribution of drug-associated environmental cues. *Science, 216,* 436–437.

Silberberg, A., Hamilton, B., Ziriax, J. M., & Casey, J. (1978). The structure of choice. *Journal of Experimental Psychology: Animal Behavior Processes, 4,* 368–398.

Simmons et al. v. United States, 390 U. S. 377 (1968).

Simon, H. A. (1974). How big is a chunk? *Science, 183,* 482–488.

Skinner, B. F. (1938). *Behavior of organisms.* New York: Appleton-Century-Crofts.

Skinner, E. A. (1985). Action, control judgments, and the structure of control experience. *Psychological Review, 92,* 39–58.

Slamecka, N. J., & Graf, P. (1978). The generation effect: Delineation of a phenomenon. *Journal of Experimental Psychology: Human Learning and Memory, 4,* 592–604.

Slovic, P., Fischhoff, B., & Lichtenstein, S. (1982). Facts versus fears: Understanding perceived risk. In D. Kahneman, P. Slovic, & A. Tversky (Eds.), *Judgment under uncertainty: Heuristics and biases.* Cambridge: Cambridge University Press.

Smith, E. E. (1978). Theories of semantic memory. In W. K. Estes (Ed.), *Handbook of learning and cognitive processes.* Hillsdale, N.J.: Erlbaum.

Smith, E. E. (1988). Concepts and thought. In R. J. Sternberg & E. E. Smith (Eds.), *The psychology of human thought.* Cambridge: Cambridge University Press.

Smith, E. E., Adams, N., & Schorr, D. (1978). Fact retrieval and the paradox of interference. *Cognitive Psychology, 10,* 438–464.

Smith, E. E., Balzano, G. J., & Walker, J. H. (1978). Nominal, perceptual, and semantic codes in picture categorization. In J. W. Cotton & R. L. Klatzky (Eds.), *Semantic factors in cognition.* Hillsdale, N.J.: Erlbaum.

Smith, E. E., & Medin, D. L. (1981). *Categories and concepts.* Cambridge, Mass.: Harvard University Press.

Smith, E. E., Rips, L. J., & Shoben, E. J. (1974). Structure and process in semantic memory: A featural model for semantic decisions. *Psychological Review, 81,* 214–241.

Smith, M. (1982). Hypnotic memory enhancement of witness: Does it work? Paper presented at the meeting of the Psychonomic Society, Minneapolis.

Smith, S. M., Glenberg, A., & Bjork, R. A. (1978). Environmental context and human memory. *Memory and Cognition, 6,* 342–353.

Solomon, R. L. (1980). The opponent process theory of acquired motivation. *American Psychologist, 35,* 691–712.

Solomon, R. L., & Corbit, J. D. (1974). An opponent process theory of motivation. I: The temporal dynamics of affect. *Psychological Review, 81,* 119–145.

Solomon, R. L., Kamin, L. J., & Wynne, L. C. (1953). Traumatic avoidance learning: The outcomes of several extinction procedures with dogs. *Journal of Abnormal and Social Psychology, 48,* 291–302.

Solomon, R. L., & Wynne, L. C. (1953). Traumatic avoidance learning: Acquisition in normal dogs. *Psychological Monographs, 67* (Whole No. 354).

Solomon, R. L., & Wynne, L. C. (1954). Traumatic avoidance learning: The principles of anxiety conservation and partial irreversibility. *Psychological Review, 61,* 353–385.

Spear, N. E. (1979). Experimental analysis of infantile amnesia. In J. F. Kihlstrom & F. S. Evans (Eds.), *Functional disorders of memory,* pp. 75–102. Hillsdale, N.J.: Erlbaum.

Spear, N. E., & Miller, R. R. (Eds.) (1981). *Information processing in animals: Memory mechanisms.* Hillsdale, N.J.: Erlbaum.

Spence, K. W. (1936). The nature of discrimination learning in animals. *Psychological Review, 43,* 427–449.

Spence, K. W. (1937). The differential response in animals to stimuli varying within a single dimension. *Psychological Review, 44*, 430–444.

Spence, K. W. (1956). *Behavior theory and conditioning.* New Haven: Yale University Press.

Spencer, H. (1880). *Principles of psychology.* New York: Appleton-Century-Crofts.

Sperling, G. (1960). The information available in brief visual presentations. *Psychological Monographs, 74* (Whole No. 11).

Sperling, G. (1963). A model for visual memory tasks. *Human Factors, 5,* 19–31.

Sperling, G., & Speelman, R. G. (1970). Acoustic similarity and auditory short-term memory: Experiments and a model. In D. A. Norman (Ed.), *Models of human memory,* pp. 152–202. New York: Academic Press.

Spiro, R. J. (1977). Remembering information from text: The "state of schema" approach. In R. C. Anderson, R. J. Spiro, & W. E. Montague (Eds.), *Schooling and the acquisition of knowledge.* Hillsdale, N.J.: Erlbaum.

Spiro, R. J. (1980a). Accommodative reconstruction in prose recall. *Journal of Verbal Learning and Verbal Behavior, 19,* 84–95.

Spiro, R. J. (1980b). Prior knowledge and story processing: Integration, selection, and variation. *Poetics, 9,* 313–327.

Squire, L. R., & Cohen, N. J. (1984). Human memory and amnesia. In J. McGaugh, G. Lynch, & N. Weinberger (Eds.), *Proceedings of the conference on the neurobiology of learning and memory,* pp. 3–64. New York: Guilford Press.

Staddon, J. E. R. (1980a). Optimality analyses of operant behavior and their relation to optimal foraging. In J. E. R. Staddon (Ed.), *Limits to action.* New York: Academic Press.

Staddon, J. E. R. (Ed.) (1980b). *Limits to action.* New York: Academic Press.

Staddon, J. E. R. (1983). *Adaptive behavior and learning.* Cambridge: Cambridge University Press.

Staddon, J. E. R., Hinson, J. M., & Kram, R. (1981). Optimal choice. *Journal of the Experimental Analysis of Behavior, 35,* 397–412.

Staddon, J. E. R., & Motheral, S. (1978). On matching and maximizing in operant choice experiments. *Psychological Review, 85,* 436–444.

Standing, L. (1973). Learning 10,000 pictures. *Quarterly Journal of Experimental Psychology, 25,* 207–222.

Standing, L., Conezio, J., & Haber, R. (1970). Perception and memory for pictures: Single-trial learning of 2500 visual stimuli. *Psychonomic Science, 19,* 73–74.

Starr, M. D., & Mineka, S. (1977). Determinants of fear over the course of avoidance learning. *Learning and Motivation, 8,* 332–350.

Stephens, D. W., & Krebs, J. R. (1986). *Foraging theory.* Princeton: Princeton University Press.

Sulin, R. A., & Dooling, D. J. (1974). Intrusion of a thematic idea in retention of prose. *Journal of Experimental Psychology, 103,* 255–262.

Sumby, W. H. (1963). Word frequency and serial position effects. *Journal of Verbal Learning and Verbal Behavior, 1,* 443–450.

Sutherland, N. S., & Mackintosh, N. J. (1971). *Mechanisms of animal discrimination learning.* New York: Academic Press.

Sutton, R. S., & Barto, A. G. (1981). Toward a modern theory of adaptive networks: Expectation and prediction. *Psychological Review, 88,* 135–171.

Switalski, R. W., Lyons, J., & Thomas, D. R. (1966). Effects of interdimensional training on stimulus generalization. *Journal of Experimental Psychology, 72,* 661–666.

Tabachnick, B., & Brotsky, S. (1976). Free recall and complexity of pictorial stimuli. *Memory and Cognition, 4,* 466–470.

Taylor, S. E. (1982). The availability bias in social perception and interaction. In D. Kahneman, P. Slovic, & A. Tversky (Eds.), *Judgments under uncertainty: Heuristics and biases.* Cambridge: Cambridge University Press.

Taylor, S. E., Fiske, S. T., Etcoff, N., & Ruderman, A. (1978). The categorical and contextual bases of person memory and stereotyping. *Journal of Personality and Social Psychology, 36,* 778–793.

Teasdale, J. D., & Russell, M. L. (1983). Differential effects of induced mood on the recall of positive, negative, and neutral words. *British Journal of Clinical Psychology, 22,* 163–172.

Teasdale, J. D., & Taylor, R. (1981). Induced mood and accessibility of memories: An effect of mood state or of induction procedure? *British Journal of Clinical Psychology, 20,* 39–48.

te Linde, J. (1983). Pictures and words in semantic decisions. In J. C. Yuille (Ed.), *Imagery, memory, and cognition.* Hillsdale, N.J.: Erlbaum.

Terrace, H. S. (1971). By-products of discrimination learning. In G. H. Bower & J. Spence (Eds.), *The psychology of learning and motivation* (Vol. 5). New York: Academic Press.

Terrace, H. S., Gibbon, J., Farrell, L., & Baldock, M. D. (1975). Temporal factors influencing the acquisition and maintenance of an autoshaped keypeck. *Animal Learning and Behavior, 3,* 53–62.

Testa, T. J. (1974). Causal relationships and the acquisition of avoidance responses. *Psychological Review, 81,* 491–505.

Testa, T. J. (1975). Effects of similarity of location and temporal intensity pattern of conditioned and unconditioned stimuli on the acquisition of conditioned suppression in rats. *Journal of Experimental Psychology: Animal Behavior Processes, 104,* 114–121.

Thomas, D. R., Mariner, R. W., & Sherry, G. (1969). Role of pre-experimental experience in the development of stimulus control. *Journal of Experimental Psychology, 79,* 375–376.

Thompson, C. P., & Cowan, T. (1986). Flashbulb memories: A nicer interpretation of a Neisser recollection. *Cognition, 22,* 199–200.

Thompson, P. (1980). Margaret Thatcher: A new illusion. *Perception, 9,* 483–484.

Thompson, R. F., & Spencer, W. A. (1966). Habituation: A model phenomenon for the study of neuronal substrates of behavior. *Psychological Review, 73,* 16–43.

Thorndike, E. L. (1898). Animal intelligence: An experimental study of the associative processes in animals. *Psychological Monographs, 2* (Whole No. 8).

Thorndike, E. L. (1911). *Animal intelligence: Experimental studies.* New York: Macmillan.

Thorndyke, P. W. (1976). The role of inferences in discourse comprehension. *Journal of Verbal Learning and Verbal Behavior, 15,* 437–446.

Thorndyke, P. W., & Bower, G. H. (1974). Storage and retrieval processes in sentence memory. *Cognitive Psychology, 5,* 515–543.

Till, R. E., & Jenkins, J. J. (1973). The effects of cued orienting tasks on the free recall of words. *Journal of Verbal Learning and Verbal Behavior, 12,* 489–498.

Till, R. E., & Walsh, D. A. (1980). Encoding and retrieval factors in adult memory for implicational sentences. *Journal of Verbal Learning and Verbal Behavior,* *19,* 1–16.

Timberlake, W. (1980). A molar equilibrium theory of learned performance. In G. H. Bower (Ed.), *The psychology of learning and motivation* (Vol. 14). New York: Academic Press.

Timberlake, W., Gawley, D. J., & Lucas, G. A (1987). Time horizons in rats foraging for food in temporally separated patches. *Journal of Experimental Psychology: Animal Behavior Processes, 13,* 302–309.

Timberlake, W., & Peden, B. F. (1987). On the distinction between open and closed economies. *Journal of the Experimental Analysis of Behavior, 48,* 35–60.

Tomie, A. (1976). Interference with autoshaping by prior context conditioning. *Journal of Experimental Psychology: Animal Behavior Processes, 2,* 323–334.

Tranberg, D. K., & Rilling, M. (1980). Delay-interval illumination changes interfere with pigeon short-term memory. *Journal of the Experimental Analysis of Behavior, 33,* 39–50.

Tulving, E. (1962). Subjective organization in free recall of "unrelated" words. *Psychological Review, 69,* 344–354.

Tulving, E. (1972). Episodic and semantic memory. In E. Tulving & W. Donaldson (Eds.), *Organization of memory,* pp. 381–403. New York: Academic Press.

Tulving, E. (1983). *Elements of episodic memory.* Oxford: Oxford University Press.

Tulving, E. (1985). How many memory systems are there? *American Psychologist, 40,* 385–398.

Tulving, E. (1986). What kind of a hypothesis is the distinction between episodic and semantic memory? *Journal of Experimental Psychology: Learning, Memory, and Cognition, 12,* 307–311.

Tulving, E. (1989). Remembering and knowing the past. *American Scientist, 77,* 361–367.

Tulving, E., & Arbuckle, T. Y. (1963). Sources of intratrial interference in immediate recall of paired associates. *Journal of Verbal Learning and Verbal Behavior, 1,* 321–334.

Tulving, E., & Osler, S. (1968). Effectiveness of retrieval cues in memory for words. *Journal of Experimental Psychology, 77,* 593–601.

Tulving, E., & Psotka, J. (1971). Retroactive inhibition in free recall: Inaccessibility of information available in the memory store. *Journal of Experimental Psychology, 87,* 1–8.

Tulving, E., & Thomson, D. (1973). Encoding specificity and retrieval processes in episodic memory. *Psychological Review, 80,* 352–373.

Tversky, A., & Kahneman, D. (1973). Availability: A heuristic for judging frequency and probability. *Cognitive Psychology, 5,* 207–232.

Tversky, A., & Kahneman, D. (1974). Judgments under uncertainty: Heuristics and biases. *Science, 185,* 1124–1131.

Tversky, B. (1973). Encoding processes in recognition and recall. *Cognitive Psychology, 5,* 275–287.

Tversky, B., & Tuchin, M. (1989). A reconciliation of the evidence on eyewitness testimony: Comments on McCloskey and Zaragoza (1985). *Journal of Experimental Psychology: General, 118,* 86–91.

Tweney, R. D., Doherty, M. E., & Mynatt, C. R. (1981). *On scientific thinking.* New York: Columbia University Press.

Underwood, B. J. (1957). Interference and forgetting. *Psychological Review, 64,* 49–60.

Underwood, B. J., & Ekstrand, B. R. (1966). An analysis of some shortcomings in the interference theory of forgetting. *Psychological Review, 73,* 540–549.

Underwood, B. J., & Postman, L. (1960). Extraexperimental sources of interference in forgetting. *Psychological Review, 67,* 73–95.

Urcuioli, P. J. (1977). Transfer of oddity-from-sample performance in pigeons. *Journal of the Experimental Analysis of Behavior, 27,* 195–202.

Urcuioli, P. J., & Nevin, J. A. (1975). Transfer of hue matching in pigeons. *Journal of the Experimental Analysis of Behavior, 24,* 149–155.

Vallar, G., & Baddeley, A. D. (1982). Short-term forgetting and the articulatory loop. *Quarterly Journal of Experimental Psychology, 34,* 53–60.

Vaughan, W., & Greene, S. L. (1984). Pigeon visual memory capacity. *Journal of Experimental Psychology: Animal Behavior Processes, 10,* 256–272.

Visintainer, M. A., Volpicelli, J. R., & Seligman, M. E. P. (1982). Tumor rejection in rats after inescapable or escapable shock. *Science, 216,* 437–439.

Vogel, R., & Annau, Z. (1973). An operant discrimination task allowing variability of response patterning. *Journal of the Experimental Analysis of Behavior, 20,* 1–6.

Wagenaar, W. A. (1986). My memory: A study of autobiographical memory over six years. *Cognitive Psychology, 18,* 225–252.

Wagner, A. R. (1976). Priming in STM: An information processing mechanism for self-generated or retrieval-generated depression in performance. In T. J. Tighe & R. N. Leaton (Eds.), *Habituation: Perspectives from child development and animal behavior.* Hillsdale, N.J.: Erlbaum.

Wagner, A. R. (1978). Expectancies and the priming of STM. In S. H. Hulse, H. Fowler, & W. K. Honig (Eds.), *Cognitive processes in animal behavior.* Hillsdale, N.J.: Erlbaum.

Wagner, A. R. (1979). Habituation and memory. In A. Dickenson & R. A. Boakes (Eds.), *Mechanisms of learning and motivation.* Hillsdale, N.J.: Erlbaum.

Wagner, A. R. (1981). SOP: A model of automatic memory processing in animal behavior. In N. E. Spear & R. R. Miller (Eds.), *Information processing in animals: Memory mechanisms.* Hillsdale, N.J.: Erlbaum.

Wagner, A. R., & Larew, M. B. (1985). Opponent processes and Pavlovian inhibition. In R. R. Miller & N. E. Spear (Eds.), *Information processing in animals: Conditioned inhibition.* Hillsdale, N.J.: Erlbaum.

Wagner, A. R., Logan, F. A., Haberlandt, K., & Price, T. (1968). Stimulus selection in animal discrimination learning. *Journal of Experimental Psychology, 76,* 171–180.

Wagner, A. R., & Rescorla, R. A. (1972). Inhibition in Pavlovian conditioning: Application of a theory. In R. A. Boakes & M. S. Halliday (Eds.), *Inhibition and learning.* New York: Academic Press.

Waldfogel, S. (1948). The frequency and affective character of childhood memories. *Psychological Monographs, 62* (Whole No. 291).

Walley, R. E., & Weiden, T. D. (1973). Lateral inhibition and cognitive masking: A neuropsychological theory in attention. *Psychological Review, 80,* 284–302.

Walley, R. E., & Weiden, T. D. (1974). Giving flesh to a "straw man": A reply to Feeney, Pittman and Wagner. *Psychological Review, 81,* 540–542.

Ward, W. C., & Jenkins, H. M. (1965). The display of information and the judgment of contingency. *Canadian Journal of Psychology, 19,* 231–241.

Warrington, E. K., & Weiskrantz, L. (1978). Further analysis of the prior learning effect in amnesic patients. *Neuropsychologia, 16,* 169–176.

Wason, P. C. (1966). Reasoning. In B. Foss (Ed.), *New horizons in psychology.* Middlesex, England: Penguin.

Wasserman, E. A. (1981). Response evocation in autoshaping: Contributions of cognitive and comparative-evolutionary analyses to an understanding of directed action. In C. M. Locurto, H. S. Terrace, & J. Gibbon (Eds.), *Autoshaping and conditioning theory.* New York: Academic Press.

Watkins, M. J. (1977). The intricacy of memory span. *Memory and Cognition, 5,* 529–534.

Watkins, M. J., & Tulving, E. (1975). Episodic memory: When recognition fails. *Journal of Experimental Psychology: General, 104,* 5–29.

Watkins, M. J., & Watkins, O. C. (1974). Processing of recency items for free recall. *Journal of Experimental Psychology, 102,* 488–493.

Watson, J. S. (1967). Memory and "contingency analysis" in infant learning. *Merrill-Palmer Quarterly, 13,* 55–76.

Watson, J. S. (1971). Cognitive–perceptual development in infancy: Setting for the seventies. *Merrill-Palmer Quarterly, 12,* 139–152.

Waugh, N. C., & Norman, D. A. (1965). Primary memory. *Psychological Review, 72,* 89–104.

Weingartner, H., Adefris, W., Eich, J. E., & Murphy, D. L. (1976). Encoding-imagery specificity in alcohol state-dependent learning. *Journal of Experimental Psychology: Human Learning and Memory, 2,* 83–87.

Weisberg, R. W. (1969). Sentence processing assessed through intrasentence word associations. *Journal of Experimental Psychology, 82,* 332–338.

Weiss, J. M. (1970). Somatic effects of predictable and unpredictable shock. *Psychosomatic Medicine, 32,* 397–408.

Weiss, J. M. (1977). Ulcers. In J. D. Maser & M. E. P. Seligman (Eds.), *Psychopathology: Experimental models.* San Francisco: W. H. Freeman.

Wells, G. L., & Harvey, J. H. (1977). Do people use consensus information in making causal attributions? *Journal of Personality and Social Psychology, 35,* 279–293.

Wetzler, S. (1985). Mood state-dependent retrieval: A failure to replicate. *Psychological Reports, 56,* 759–765.

Wetzler, S. E., & Sweeney, J. A. (1986). Childhood amnesia: An empirical demonstration. In D. C. Rubin (Ed.), *Autobiographical memory.* Cambridge: Cambridge University Press.

Wexler, K. (1978). A review of John R. Anderson's language, memory, and thought. *Cognition, 6,* 327–351.

White, S. H., & Pillemer, D. B. (1979). Childhood amnesia and the development of a socially accessible memory system. In J. F. Kihlstrom & F. J. Evans (Eds.), *Functional disorders of memory.* Hillsdale, N.J.: Erlbaum.

Whitlow, J. W., Jr., & Wagner, A. R. (1984). Memory and habituation. In H. V. S. Peeke & L. Petrinovich (Eds.), *Habituation, sensitization and behavior.* New York: Academic Press.

Whorf, B. L. (1956). *Language, thought, and reality.* Cambridge: Technology Press.

Winograd, E., & Killinger, W. A., Jr. (1983). Relating age at encoding in early childhood to adult recall: Development of flashbulb memories. *Journal of Experimental Psychology: General, 112,* 413–422.

Winston, P. H. (1984). *Artificial intelligence,* 2nd ed. Reading, Mass.: Addison-Wesley.

Wiseman, S., & Neisser, U. (1974). Perceptual organization as a determinant of visual recognition memory. *American Journal of Psychology, 87,* 675–681.

Wittgenstein, L. (1953). *Philosophical investigations.* New York: Macmillan.

Wolfe, J. B. (1936). Effectiveness of token-rewards for chimpanzees. *Comparative Psychology Monographs, 12* (Whole No. 60).

Wollen, K. A., Weber, A., & Lowry, D. (1972). Bizarreness versus interaction of mental images as determinants of learning. *Cognitive Psychology, 3,* 518–523.

Wood, G. (1978). The knew-it-all-along effect. *Journal of Experimental Psychology: Human Performance and Perception, 4,* 345–353.

Woodhead, M. M., Baddeley, A. D., & Simmonds, D. C. V. (1979). On training people to recognise faces. *Ergonomics, 22,* 333–343.

Woodruff, G., Premack, D., & Kennel, K. (1978). Conservation of liquid and solid quantity by the chimpanzee. *Science, 202,* 991–994.

Woodward, A. E., Bjork, R. A., & Jongeward, R. H., Jr. (1973). Recall and recognition as a function of primary rehearsal. *Journal of Verbal Learning and Verbal Behavior, 12,* 608–617.

Wyckoff, L. B. (1952). The role of observing responses in discrimination learning: Part 1. *Psychological Review, 59,* 431–442.

Yates, F. A. (1966). *The art of memory.* London: Routledge and Kegan Paul.

Yin, R. (1969). Looking at upside-down faces. *Journal of Experimental Psychology, 81,* 141–145.

Yuille, J. C. (1983). *Imagery, memory, and cognition.* Hillsdale, N.J.: Erlbaum.

Zajonc, R. B. (1980). Feeling and thinking. *American Psychologist, 35,* 151–175.

Zajonc, R. B. (1984). On the primacy of affect. *American Psychologist, 39,* 117–123.

Zamble, E., Haddad, G. M., Mitchell, J. B., & Cutmore, T. R. H. (1985). Pavlovian conditioning of sexual arousal: First- and second-order effects. *Journal of Experimental Psychology: Animal Behavior Processes, 11,* 598–610.

Zangwill, O. L. (1972). Remembering revisited. *Quarterly Journal of Experimental Psychology, 24,* 123–138.

Zaragoza, M. S., & Koshmider, J. W. (1989). Misled subjects may know more than their performance implies. *Journal of Experimental Psychology: Learning, Memory, and Cognition, 15,* 246–255.

Zaragoza, M. S., & McCloskey, M. (1989). Misleading postevent information and the memory impairment hypothesis: Comment on Belli and reply to Tversky and Tuchin. *Journal of Experimental Psychology: General, 118,* 92–99.

Zechmeister, E. B., & McKillip, J. (1972). Recall of place on the page. *Journal of Educational Psychology, 63,* 446–453.

Zeiler, M. D. (1963). The ratio theory of intermediate size discrimination. *Psychological Review, 70,* 516–533.

Zener, K. (1937). The significance of behavior accompanying conditioned salivary secretion for theories of the conditioned response. *American Journal of Psychology, 50,* 384–403.

Zentall, T. R., & Hogan, D. E. (1974). Abstract concept learning in the pigeon. *Journal of Experimental Psychology, 102,* 393–398.

Zentall, T. R., & Hogan, D. E. (1976). Pigeons can learn identity or difference or both. *Science, 191,* 408–409.

Zentall, T. R., & Hogan, D. E. (1978). Same/different concept learning in the pigeon: The effect of negative instances and prior adaptation to the transfer stimuli. *Journal of the Experimental Analysis of Behavior, 30,* 177–186.

Zimler, J., & Keenan, J. M. (1983). Imagery in the congenitally blind: How visual are visual images? *Journal of Experimental Psychology: Learning, Memory, and Cognition, 9,* 269–282.

Zukier, H. (1982). The dilution effect: The role of the correlation and the dispersion of predictor variables in the use of nondiagnostic information. *Journal of Personality and Social Psychology, 43,* 1163–1174.

Credits

FIGURES

FIGURE 2–3 Schneiderman, N., Fuentes, I., & Gormezano, I. *Science,* 1962, 136, 650–652. Copyright 1962 by the American Association for the Advancement of Science.

FIGURE 2–7 Solomon, R.L. *American Psychologist,* 1980, 35, 691–712. Copyright 1980 by the American Psychological Association. Adapted by permission of the author.

FIGURE 2–11 Rescorla, R.A. *Journal of Experimental Psychology: Animal Behavior Processes,* 1979, 5, 79–95. Copyright 1979 by the American Psychological Association. Adapted by permission of the author.

FIGURE 2–14 Garcia, J., & Koelling, R.A. *Psychonomic Science,* 1966, 4, 123–124. Figure 1. Reprinted by permission of the Psychonomic Society, Inc.

FIGURE 4–3 Azzi, R., Fix, D.S.R., Keller, F.S., & Roche e Silva, M.I. *Journal of the Experimental Analysis of Behavior,* 1964, 7, 159–162. Figure 2. Copyright 1964 by the Society for the Experimental Analysis of Behavior, Inc.

FIGURE 4–7 Egger, M.D., & Miller, N.E. *Journal of Experimental Psychology,* 1962, 64, 97–104. Adapted by permission.

FIGURE 4–8 *Token Reinforcement.* Courtesy of Yerkes Regional Primate Research Center, Emory University.

FIGURES 6–5 and 6–9 Jenkins, H.M., & Harrison, R.H. *Journal of Experimental Psychology,* 1960, 59, 246–253. Adapted by permission of the authors. Copyright 1965 by the American Psychological Association.

FIGURE 6–6 Terrace, H.S. *The Psychology of Learning and Motivation,* Vol. 5, edited by G. H. Bower & J. Spence, 1971, 195–265. Figure 17, p. 241. Copyright 1971. Adapted by permission of Academic Press.

FIGURE 6–8 Newman, F.L., & Baron, M.R. *Journal of Comparative and Physiological Psychology,* 1965, 60, 59–63. Adapted by permission of the authors. Copyright 1965 by the American Psychological Association.

FIGURE 6–15 Hanson, H.M. *Journal of Comparative and Physiological Psychology,* 1961, 54, 181–185. Copyright 1961 by the American Psychological Association. Adapted by permission of the author.

FIGURE 6–19 *Discrimination of Natural Objects by Pigeons.* From Herrnstein, Loveland, & Cable, 1976. Photographs by Richard Herrnstein, copyright 1976.

FIGURES 6–21 and 6–22 Grant, D.S. *Learning and Motivation,* 1976, 7, 580–590. Adapted by permission.

FIGURE 6–24 Olton, D.S., & Samuelson, R.J. *Journal of Experimental Psychology: Animal Behavior Processes,* 1976, 2, 96–116. Reprinted by permission.

FIGURE 7–3 Glanzer, M., & Cunitz, A. *Journal of Verbal Learning and Verbal Behavior,* 1966, 5, 351–360. Adapted by permission of Academic Press.

FIGURE 7–4 Baddeley, A.D., & Hitch, G.J. In S. Dornic (ed.), *Attention and Performance VI,* pp. 646–667. Hillsdale, New Jersey: Erlbaum, 1977. Copyright 1977 Lawrence Erlbaum Associates, Inc. Adapted by permission.

FIGURE 7–5 Glanzer, M., & Cunitz, A. *Journal of Verbal Learning and Verbal Behavior,* 1966, 5, 351–360. Adapted by permission of Academic Press.

FIGURE 7–6 Rundus, D. *Journal of Experimental Psychology,* 1971, 89, 63–77. Copyright 1971 by the American Psychological Association. Adapted by permission.

FIGURE 7–7 Roediger, H.L., III, & Crowder, R.G. *Bulletin of the Psychonomic Society,* 1976, 8, 275–278. Reprinted by permission of the Psychonomic Society.

FIGURE 7–8 Craik, F., & Watkins, M. *Journal of Verbal Learning and Verbal Behavior,* 1973, 12, 599–607. Adapted by permission of Academic Press.

FIGURE 7–9 Watkins, M.J., & Watkins, O.C. *Journal of Experimental Psychology,* 1974, 102, 488–493. Copyright 1974 by the American Psychological Association. Adapted by permission.

FIGURE 7–10 Craik, F.I.M., & Tulving, E. *Journal of Experimental Psychology: General,* 1975, 104, 269–294. Copyright 1975 by the American Psychological Association. Adapted by permission.

FIGURE 8–1 Tversky, B. *Cognitive Psychology,* 1973, 5, 275–287. Adapted by permission of Academic Press.

FIGURE 8–4 Bower, G.H. *American Psychologist,* 1981, 36, 129–148. Copyright 1981 by the American Psychological Association. Adapted by permission.

FIGURE 8–5 Mandler, G. *American Scientist,* 1981, 69, 211–217. Adapted by permission of George Mandler.

FIGURE 8–6 Jacoby, L.L. *Journal of Experimental Psychology: Learning, Memory, and Cognition,* 1983, 9, 21–38. Copyright 1983 by the American Psychological Association. Adapted by permission.

FIGURE 9–1 Selfridge, O. In *Proceedings of the Western Joint Computer Conference.* Los Angeles: IRE (now IEEE), 1955. © 1955 IRE.

FIGURE 9–2 Wiseman, S., & Neisser, U. *American Journal of Psychology,* 1974, 87, 675–681. Copyright 1974 by the American Psychological Association. Adapted by permission.

FIGURE 9–3 Brewer, W.F., & Treyens, J.C. *Cognitive Psychology,* 1981, 13, 207–230. Reprinted by permission of Academic Press.

FIGURE 9–4 © 1988 by Sidney Harris, *American Scientist* magazine.

FIGURE 10–1 Drawing by Kaufman. © 1977 *The New Yorker* magazine, Inc.

FIGURE 10–2 Green, J. *Favorite Dogs Coloring Book.* New York: Dover Publications, Inc., 1983. Adapted by permission of Dover Publications.

FIGURE 10–3 Labov, W. In C.-J.N. Bailey & R.W. Shuy (eds.), *New Ways of Analyzing Variations in English.* Washington, D.C.: Georgetown University Press, 1973. Adapted by permission of Georgetown University Press.

FIGURE 10–4 Anderson, John R. *Cognitive Psychology and Its Implications.* San Francisco: W.H. Freeman and Company, 1980. Copyright © 1980 by W.H. Freeman and Company. Adapted by permission.

FIGURE 10–5 Anderson, John R. *Cognitive Psychology and Its Implications.* San Francisco: W.H. Freeman and Company, 1980. Copyright © 1980 by W.H. Freeman and Company. Adapted by permission.

FIGURE 11–4 Collins, A.M. & Quillian, M.R. *Journal of Verbal Learning and Verbal Behavior,* 1969, 8, 240–247. Adapted by permission of Academic Press.

FIGURE 11–5 Collins, A.M., & Quillian, M.R. *Journal of Verbal Learning and Verbal Behavior,* 1969, 8, 240–247. Adapted by permission of Academic Press.

FIGURE 11–8 Anderson, John R. *Cognitive Psychology and Its Implications.* San Francisco: W.H. Freeman and Company, 1980. Copyright © 1980 by W.H. Freeman and Company. Adapted by permission.

FIGURE 11–10 Anderson, John R. *Cognitive Psychology and Its Implications.* San Francisco: W.H.

Freeman and Company, 1980. Copyright © 1980 by W.H. Freeman and Company. Adapted by permission.

FIGURE 11–11 Anderson, John R. *Cognitive Psychology and Its Implications.* San Francisco: W.H. Freeman and Company, 1980. Copyright © 1980 by W.H. Freeman and Company. Adapted by permission.

FIGURE 12–1 Kosslyn, S.M. *Ghosts in the Mind's Machine* New York: W. W. Norton & Company, 1983. Reprinted by permission of W. W. Norton.

FIGURE 12–2 Kosslyn, S.M. *Ghosts in the Mind's Machine* New York: W. W. Norton & Company, 1983. Adapted by permission of W. W. Norton.

FIGURE 12–3 Shepard, R.N., & Metzler, J. *Science,* 1971, 171, 701–703. Copyright 1971 by the American Association for the Advancement of Science.

FIGURE 12–4 Segal, S.J., & Fusella, V. *Journal of Experimental Psychology,* 1970, 83, 458–474. Copyright 1970 by the American Psychological Association. Adapted by permission.

FIGURE 12–9 Wollen, K.A., Weber, A., & Lowry, D. *Cognitive Psychology,* 1972, 3, 518–523. Reprinted by permission of Academic Press.

FIGURE 12–10 Paivio, A., & Begg, I. *Psychology of Language,* p. 116. Englewood Cliffs, New Jersey: Prentice Hall, 1981. © 1981 and reprinted by permission of Prentice Hall.

FIGURE 12–12 te Linde, J. In J. C. Yuille (ed.), *Imagery, Memory, and Cognition.* Hillsdale, New Jersey: Lawrence Erlbaum Associates, 1983. Copyright 1983 Lawrence Erlbaum Associates, Inc. Adapted by permission.

FIGURE 12–13 Paivio, A. *Memory and Cognition,* 1975, 3, 635–647. Adapted by permission of the Psychonomic Society, Inc.

FIGURE 12–14 Yin, R. *Journal of Experimental Psychology,* 1969, 81, 141–145. Copyright 1969 by the American Psychological Association. Adapted by permission.

FIGURE 12–15 Thompson, P. Margaret Thatcher: A new illusion. *Perception,* 1980, 9, 483–484. Reprinted by permission of Pion, London.

FIGURE 12–16 Diamond, R., & Carey, S. *Journal of Experimental Psychology: General,* 1986, 115, 107–117. Copyright 1986 by the American Psychological Association. Adapted by permission.

FIGURE 13–3 Baddeley, A.D., & Hitch, G.J. In S. Dornic (ed.), *Attention and Performance VI,* pp. 646–667. Hillsdale, New Jersey: Lawrence Erlbaum Associates, 1977. Copyright 1977 Lawrence Erlbaum Associates, Inc. Adapted by permission.

FIGURE 13–4 Melton, A.W., & Irwin, J.M. *American Journal of Psychology,* 1940, 53, 173–203. Reprinted by permission of the University of Illinois Press, 1971.

FIGURE 13–5 Tulving, E., & Psotka, J. *Journal of Experimental Psychology,* 1971, 87, 1–8. Copyright 1971 by the American Psychological Association. Adapted by permission.

FIGURE 13–6 Erdelyi, M.H., & Kleinbard, J. *Journal of Experimental Psychology: Human Learning and Memory,* 1978, 4, 275–289. Copyright 1978 by the American Psychological Association. Adapted by permission.

FIGURE 13–7 Kleinsmith, L., & Kaplan, S. *Journal of Experimental Psychology,* 1963, 65, 190–193. Copyright 1963 by the American Psychological Association. Adapted by permission.

FIGURE 13–9 Bahrick, H.P., Bahrick, P.O., & Wittlinger, R.P. *Journal of Experimental Psychology: General,* 1975, 104, 54–75. Copyright 1975 by the American Psychological Association. Adapted by permission.

FIGURE 13–10 Linton, M. In M. Gruneberg, P. Morris, & R. Syms (eds.), *Practical Aspects of Memory.* London: Academic Press, 1978. Adapted by permission of Academic Press.

FIGURE 14–1 Jennings, D.L., Amabile, T.M., & Ross, L. In D. Kahneman, P. Slovic, & A. Tversky (eds.), *Judgments under Uncertainty: Heuristics and Biases.* Cambridge: Cambridge University Press, 1982.

FIGURE 14–2 Jennings, D.L., Amabile, T.M., & Ross, L. In D. Kahneman, P. Slovic, & A. Tversky (eds.), *Judgments under Uncertainty: Heuristics and Biases.* Cambridge: Cambridge University Press, 1982.

FIGURE 14–4 Wason, P., & Johnson-Laird, P.N. *Psychology of Reasoning.* Cambridge, Mass.: Harvard University Press, 1972.

FIGURE 14–5 Cheng, P.W., & Holyoak, K.J. *Cognitive Psychology,* 1985, 17, 391–416. Adapted by permission of Academic Press.

FIGURE 14–6 Cheng, P.W., & Holyoak, K.J. *Cognitive Psychology,* 1985, 17, 391–416. Adapted by permission of Academic Press.

TABLES

Table 8–1 Fisher, R.P., & Craik, F.I.M. *Journal of Experimental Psychology: Human Learning and Memory*, 1977, 3, 701–711. Copyright 1977 by the American Psychological Association. Adapted by permission.

Table 8–2 Eich, J., Weingartner, H., Stillman, R., & Gillin, J. *Journal of Verbal Learning and Verbal Behavior*, 1975, 14, 408–417. Adapted by permission of Academic Press.

Table 8–3 Godden, D.R., & Baddeley, A.D. *British Journal of Psychology*, 1975, 66, 325–332.

Table 8–4 Jacoby, L.L., & Dallas, M. *Journal of Experimental Psychology General*, 1981, 3, 306–340. Copyright 1981 by the American Psychological Association. Adapted by permission.

Table 8–5 Blaxton, T.A. *Journal of Experimental Psychology: Learning, Memory, and Cognition*, 1989, 15, 657–688. Copyright 1989 by the American Psychological Association. Adapted by permission.

Table 8–6 Blaxton, T.A. *Journal of Experimental Psychology: Learning, Memory, and Cognition*, 1989, 15, 657–688. Copyright 1989 by the American Psychological Association. Adapted by permission.

Table 9–1 Keenan, J., MacWhinney, B., & Mayhew, D. *Journal of Verbal Learning and Verbal Behavior*, 1977, 16, 549–560. Adapted by permission of Academic Press.

Table 9–2 Owens, J., Bower, G.H., & Black, J.B. *Memory and Cognition*, 1979, 7, 185–191. Adapted by permission of the Psychonomic Society, Inc.

Table 10–1 Malt, B., & Smith, E. *Journal of Verbal Learning and Verbal Behavior*, 1984, 23, 250–269. Adapted by permission of Academic Press.

Table 10–2 Armstrong, S., Gleitman, L., & Gleitman, H. *Cognition*, 1983, 13, 263–308. Adapted by permission of Elsevier Science Publishers.

Table 10–3 Medin, D.L., Altom, M.W., Edelson, S.M., & Freko, D. *Journal of Experimental Psychology: Learning, Memory, and Cognition*, 1982, 8, 37–50. Copyright 1982 by the American Psychological Association. Adapted by permission.

Table 11–1 Meyer, D.E., & Schvaneveldt, R.W. *Journal of Experimental Psychology*, 1971, 90, 227–234. Copyright 1971 by the American Psychological Association. Adapted by permission.

Table 11–2 Anderson, J.R. *Journal of Verbal Learning and Verbal Behavior*, 1974, 13, 149–162. Adapted by permission of Academic Press.

Table 14–1 Slovic, P., Fischhoff, B., & Lichtenstein, S. In D. Kahneman, P. Slovic, & A. Tversky (eds.), *Judgment under Uncertainty: Heuristics and Biases*. Cambridge: Cambridge University Press, 1982.

Table 14–2 Eddy, D.M. In D. Kahneman, P. Slovic, & A. Tversky (eds.), *Judgment under Uncertainty: Heuristics and Biases*. Cambridge: Cambridge University Press, 1982.

EXCERPTS

Excerpt from Bartlett, 1932, Chapter 9—Bartlett, F. C. *Remembering: A Study in Experimental and Social Psychology*. Cambridge: Cambridge University Press, 1932. Reprinted by permission of Cambridge University Press.

Excerpt from Borges, Chapter 13—Borges, Jorge Luis. *Labyrinths*. Copyright © 1963, 1964 by New Directions Publishing Corporation. Reprinted by permission of New Directions Publishing Corporation.

Excerpts from Bransford & Johnson, 1972, Chapter 9—Bransford, J. D., & Johnson, M. K. *Journal of Verbal Learning and Verbal Behavior*, 1972, 11, 717–726. Reprinted by permission of Academic Press.

Excerpts from Bransford & Johnson, 1973, Chapter 9—Bransford, J. D., & Johnson, M. K. In W. G. Chase (ed.), *Visual Information Processing*. New York: Academic Press, 1973. Reprinted by permission of Academic Press.

Excerpt from Erdelyi, 1985, Chapter 13—Erdelyi, Matthew Hugh. *Psychoanalysis: Freud's Cognitive Psychology*. San Francisco: W.H. Freeman and Company, 1985. Copyright © 1985 by Matthew Hugh Erdelyi. Reprinted by permission of W.H. Freeman and Company.

Name Index

Subject Index

exemplars
  classifying via, 394
  data supporting, 387–88
  definition of, 385
  explaining typicality data with model of, 386–87
  overview of, 405, 388–91
experience, a priori categories of, 17
explicit learning, 311
explicit memory
  in amnesiacs, 319–21
  created by concept-driven processing, 312–13
  explanation of, 305, 316, 323
  performance in, 312, 332
external inhibition, disinhibition and, 78–79
extinction, 46
  of avoidance, 147, 148, 150, 151
  as condition producing inhibition, 79–81
  operant conditioning and, 123, 501, 534
  reinforcement and, 154, 172, 501, 506–7
extradimensional shift, 216–18
eyeblink conditioning, 47–48
eyewitness accounts, 359
  effect of misleading questions on, 349–50
  role of emotion in, 519–20
eyewitness identification, of photographs, 308–10, 349

face recognition
  explanation of, 484–85, 488, 492
  eyewitness identification and, 308–10, 349
  study of, 485–87
fading-trace theory, 242
familiarity
  implicit memory and, 208–310
  remembering source of, 340
  remembering source vs. only, 298–303
family resemblances, 368–69
fan, degree of. See degree of fan
fear
  anxiety vs., 95–96
  avoidance and, 144–48, 150–51
  conditioned, 47–48, 94, 96–97, 149
FI scallop, 174
FI schedules. See fixed-interval schedules

fixed-interval (FI) schedules, 170, 172–74, 199
fixed-ratio (FR) schedules, 171–74, 188–90, 193, 199
flashbulb memories
  errors in, 519, 523
  explanation of, 518–20, 535
  quantity of peripheral data retained by, 522
flooding, to produce extinction, 148
foraging, 184–85
forced-choice procedure, 507
forgetting
  advantages of, 496–98
  decay theory of, 498–503, 534
  definition of, 496
  directed, 243
  existance of process of, 495–96
  interference theory and, 500, 503–11, 524, 534
  and loss of past, 532–33
  methods of viewing, 529–32
  repression theory and, 511–17
  temporary, 530
four-card problem, 569–70, 572–74, 577
frame, 469
free-operant avoidance, 142
free recall, 260, 314, 327–28
frequency, of encounter, 539
FR schedules. See fixed-ratio schedules
fuzzy boundary, 371, 404

gambler's fallacy, 548, 549, 576
generalization
  as condition producing inhibition, 81–84
  explanation of, 201–2, 246–47
  impact of absence of forgetting on, 497
  procedures for studying, 203–5
  process of, 219–28
  of responding, 219
generalization gradients, 204–8, 211
generalization tests, 206, 209
  after discrimination training, 213, 218, 227
  Spence theory and, 224, 226
generalized conditioned reinforcer, 159
generic knowledge
  role of, 497
  schema theory and, 397, 398
  source of, 401–5